GATEWAY TO THE GREAT BOOKS

GATEWAY
TO THE
GREAT BOOKS

Gateway
to the
Great Books

ROBERT M. HUTCHINS, MORTIMER J. ADLER
Editors in Chief

CLIFTON FADIMAN
Associate Editor

6

MAN AND

SOCIETY

Encyclopædia Britannica, Inc.

WILLIAM BENTON
Publisher

Chicago, London, Toronto, Geneva, Sydney, Tokyo, Manila

Contents
of Volume 6

John Stuart Mill

1806–1873

First son of the Scottish philosopher James Mill, John Stuart Mill [1] was born in London, May 20, 1806. The elder Mill, prompted by the schemes of Bentham and Helvétius, took his son's education in hand (see below). At three, young Mill was put to learning Greek. By the time he was thirteen, he had done more than enough work to earn a university degree.

After a year in France, where he branched out into chemistry, botany, advanced mathematics, and the French language, he read law and studied Condillac, Helvétius, and Dumont's treatise on Bentham. This led to writing for the newspapers and to the founding of the Utilitarian Society, dedicated to "the greatest good of the greatest number."

When young Mill was seventeen, his father got him a job with the India House, where he himself worked. From 1836, the year his father died, to 1856, J. S. Mill administered the company's relations with the native Indian states. His real career—as philosopher, political economist, logician, ethical theorist, and promoter of ideas—went on outside office hours.

He became the leader of social reform. His name appeared in every review. Wherever social neglect or abuse could be found, Mill attacked at once. His group played a strong hand in the English reform bills all through the century. His energy was prodigious. In one decade, the 1840's, among other books, Mill published his *Principles of Political Economy* and *System of Logic*, both two-volume works.

In 1851 he married Mrs. Harriet Taylor, his friend for twenty

---

[1] John Stuart Mill's *On Liberty, Representative Government,* and *Utilitarianism* are in *Great Books of the Western World,* Vol. 43.

years. She died some seven years later. *On the Subjection of Women* expressed their common view. Mill retired to a villa near Avignon, France, where she was buried. Except for one term in Parliament, he spent most of his later years there. During that period he wrote the famous *On Liberty, Considerations on Representative Government*, and the *Autobiography*, published after his death. He died in Avignon, May 8, 1873.

O ur ME," Carlyle wrote, "the only reality." His friend Mill would not have agreed with him. Mill's *Autobiography* is only in small part the story of a man. It stands largely as the history of a "continued mental progress," of the branching and flowering of ideas, and of what fruit they bore in the world.

The first three chapters of the *Autobiography* are reprinted here. In these chapters Mill looks back on his education. Not his childhood. He had no childhood in the ordinary sense—or at least he tells us of none. Augustine's *Confessions* is much occupied with his mother; Mill does not even mention his. He had no school, no playmates—or even play. The younger children in the family were his pupils. In the forefront of the book looms the gigantic presence of his father. Young Mill lived solely in his light, as eldest son, pupil, apprentice, and disciple. They worked at the same table, took the same walks together, and discussed the same ideas. But their relationship was moral and intellectual, not affectionate.

By the time he was eight, young Mill had learned arithmetic and read, in the Greek, Aesop's *Fables*, Herodotus, Xenophon's *Anabasis*, six dialogues of Plato, and other works. "But my father," he writes, "in all his teaching, demanded of me not only the utmost that I could do, but much that I could by no possibility have done." At

---

Notes from the artist: "An angular portrait of Mill resting above three figures representing his background and his work. At left is his father, James Mill, the sole tutor and teacher of Mill's youth. At center is Jeremy Bentham, an important source of the doctrine of Utilitarianism. At right is a cartoon reflecting Mill's interest in suffrage for women, a position he probably took at the behest of his wife, whom he adored. The quotation is from On Liberty."

John Stuart Mill

We can never be sure that the opinion we are endeavouring to stifle is a false opinion; and if we were sure, stifling it would be an evil still.

the same time he was reading and reporting on dozens of histories: Hume, Gibbon, Plutarch, even the *Annual Register*, a year-by-year chronicle of events, founded by Edmund Burke. Then he took up Latin, Euclid, and algebra, and at twelve began a rigorous term of scholastic logic, plus Aristotle.[2]

Small wonder, then, that at the age of twenty Mill had a nervous crisis. This was not so much what we should call a breakdown as a breaking away—from the domination of his father, of the intellect itself. He discovered that he liked poetry, the poetry of Wordsworth in particular. The whole life of feeling opened to him. He became what he had never been trained to be: a whole man. His education might well have produced a neurotic, a monster, or a mere "intellectual machine set to grind certain tunes." Instead, by some miracle of recovered balance, it helped to produce one of the most brilliant men of his generation.

---

[2] The writings of many of the authors mentioned above are to be found either in *Great Books of the Western World* or in this set of books.

Childhood and Youth
from *Autobiography*

It seems proper that I should prefix to the following biographical sketch, some mention of the reasons which have made me think it desirable that I should leave behind me such a memorial of so uneventful a life as mine. I do not for a moment imagine that any part of what I have to relate can be interesting to the public as a narrative, or as being connected with myself. But I have thought that in an age in which education and its improvement are the subject of more, if not of profounder, study than at any former period of English history, it may be useful that there should be some record of an education which was unusual and remarkable, and which, whatever else it may have done, has proved how much more than is commonly supposed may be taught, and well taught, in those early years which, in the common modes of what is called instruction, are little better than wasted. It has also seemed to me that in an age of transition in opinions, there may be somewhat both of interest and of benefit in noting the successive phases of any mind which was always pressing forward, equally ready to learn and to unlearn either from its own thoughts or from those of others. But a motive which weighs more with me than either of these, is a desire to make acknowledgment of the debts which my intellectual and moral development owes to other persons; some of them of recognized eminence, others less known than they deserve to be, and the one to whom most of all is due, one whom the world had no opportunity of knowing. The reader whom these things do not interest has only himself to blame if he reads farther, and I do not desire any other indulgence from him than that of bearing in mind, that for him these pages were not written.

I was born in London, on the 20th of May, 1806, and was the eldest son of James Mill, the author of *The History of British India*. My father, the son of a petty tradesman and (I believe) small farmer, at North-

5

water Bridge, in the county of Angus, was, when a boy, recommended by his abilities to the notice of Sir John Stuart, of Fettercairn, one of the Barons of the Exchequer in Scotland, and was, in consequence, sent to the University of Edinburgh at the expense of a fund established by Lady Jane Stuart (the wife of Sir John Stuart) and some other ladies for educating young men for the Scottish church. He there went through the usual course of study, and was licensed as a preacher, but never followed the profession; having satisfied himself that he could not believe the doctrines of that or any other church. For a few years he was a private tutor in various families in Scotland, among others that of the Marquis of Tweeddale; but ended by taking up his residence in London, and devoting himself to authorship. Nor had he any other means of support until 1819, when he obtained an appointment in the India House.

In this period of my father's life there are two things which it is impossible not to be struck with: one of them unfortunately a very common circumstance, the other a most uncommon one. The first is, that in his position, with no resource but the precarious one of writing in periodicals, he married and had a large family; conduct than which nothing could be more opposed, both as a matter of good sense and of duty, to the opinions which, at least at a later period of life, he strenuously upheld. The other circumstance is the extraordinary energy which was required to lead the life he led, with the disadvantages under which he laboured from the first, and with those which he brought upon himself by his marriage. It would have been no small thing, had he done no more than to support himself and his family during so many years by writing, without ever being in debt, or in any pecuniary difficulty; holding, as he did, opinions, both in politics and in religion, which were more odious to all persons of influence, and to the common run of prosperous Englishmen in that generation than either before or since; and being not only a man whom nothing would have induced to write against his convictions, but one who invariably threw into everything he wrote, as much of his convictions as he thought the circumstances would in any way permit: being, it must also be said, one who never did anything negligently; never undertook any task, literary or other, on which he did not conscientiously bestow all the labour necessary for performing it adequately. But he, with these burdens on him, planned, commenced, and completed the *History of India;* and this in the course of about ten years, a shorter time than has been occupied (even by writers who had no other employment) in the production of almost any other historical work of equal bulk, and of anything approaching to the same amount of reading and research.

And to this is to be added that, during the whole period, a considerable part of almost every day was employed in the instruction of his children: in the case of one of whom, myself, he exerted an amount of labour, care, and perseverance rarely, if ever, employed for a similar purpose, in endeavouring to give, according to his own conception, the highest order of intellectual education.

A man who, in his own practice, so vigorously acted up to the principle of losing no time, was likely to adhere to the same rule in the instruction of his pupil. I have no remembrance of the time when I began to learn Greek. I have been told that it was when I was three years old. My earliest recollection on the subject is that of committing to memory what my father termed vocables, being lists of common Greek words, with their signification in English, which he wrote out for me on cards. Of grammar, until some years later, I learnt no more than the inflections of the nouns and verbs, but, after a course of vocables, proceeded at once to translation; and I faintly remember going through Aesop's *Fables,* the first Greek book which I read. The *Anabasis,* which I remember better, was the second. I learnt no Latin until my eighth year. At that time I had read, under my father's tuition, a number of Greek prose authors, among whom I remember the whole of Herodotus, and of Xenophon's *Cyropaedia* and *Memorials of Socrates;* some of the lives of the philosophers by Diogenes Laertius; part of Lucian, and Isocrates' *ad Demonicum* and *ad Nicoclem.* I also read, in 1813, the first six dialogues (in the common arrangement) of Plato, from the *Euthyphro* to the *Theaetetus* inclusive: which last dialogue, I venture to think, would have been better omitted, as it was totally impossible I should understand it. But my father, in all his teaching, demanded of me not only the utmost that I could do, but much that I could by no possibility have done. What he was himself willing to undergo for the sake of my instruction may be judged from the fact that I went through the whole process of preparing my Greek lessons in the same room and at the same table at which he was writing: and as in those days Greek and English lexicons were not, and I could make no more use of a Greek and Latin lexicon than could be made without having yet begun to learn Latin, I was forced to have recourse to him for the meaning of every word which I did not know. This incessant interruption, he, one of the most impatient of men, submitted to, and wrote under that interruption several volumes of his History and all else that he had to write during those years.

The only thing besides Greek that I learnt as a lesson in this part of my childhood was arithmetic: this also my father taught me: it was the task of the evenings, and I well remember its disagreeableness. But the lessons were only a part of the daily instruction I received. Much of it consisted in the books I read by myself, and my father's discourses to me, chiefly during our walks. From 1810 to the end of 1813 we were living in Newington Green, then an almost rustic neighbourhood. My father's health required considerable and constant exercise, and he walked habitually before breakfast, generally in the green lanes towards Hornsey. In these walks I always accompanied him, and with my earliest recollections of green fields and wild flowers is mingled that of the account I gave him daily of what I had read the day before. To the best of my remembrance, this was a voluntary rather than a prescribed exercise. I made notes on slips of paper while reading, and from these, in the morning walks, I told the story to him; for the books were chiefly histories, of which I read in this manner a great number: Robertson's histories, Hume, Gibbon; but my greatest delight, then and for long afterwards, was Watson's Philip the Second and Third. The heroic defence of the Knights of Malta against the Turks, and of the revolted provinces of the Netherlands against Spain, excited in me an intense and lasting interest. Next to Watson, my favourite historical reading was Hooke's History of Rome. Of Greece I had seen at that time no regular history, except school abridgments and the last two or three volumes of a translation of Rollin's *Ancient History*, beginning with Philip of Macedon. But I read with great delight Langhorne's translation of Plutarch. In English history, beyond the time at which Hume leaves off, I remember reading Burnet's *History of His Own Time*, though I cared little for anything in it except the wars and battles; and the historical part of the *Annual Register*, from the beginning to about 1788, when the volumes my father borrowed for me from Mr. Bentham left off. I felt a lively interest in Frederic of Prussia during his difficulties, and in Paoli, the Corsican patriot; but when I came to the American war, I took my part, like a child as I was (until set right by my father) on the wrong side, because it was called the English side. In these frequent talks about the books I read, he used, as opportunity offered, to give me explanations and ideas respecting civilization, government, morality, mental cultivation, which he required me afterwards to restate to him in my own words. He also made me read, and give him a verbal account of, many books which would not have interested me sufficiently to induce me to read them of myself: among others, Millar's *Historical View of the English Government*, a book of great merit for its time, and which he highly valued; Mosheim's *Ecclesiastical History*, McCrie's *Life of John Knox*, and even Sewel's and Rutty's histories of the Quakers. He was fond of putting into my hands books which exhibited men of energy and resource in unusual circumstances, struggling against difficulties and overcoming them: of such works I remember Beaver's *African Memoranda,* and Collins's account of the first settlement of New South Wales. Two books which I never wearied of reading were Anson's *Voyage,* so delightful to most young persons, and a Collection (Hawkesworth's, I believe) of Voyages round the World, in four volumes, beginning with Drake and ending with Cook and Bougainville. Of children's books, any more than of playthings, I had scarcely any, except an occasional gift from a relation or acquaintance: among those I had, *Robinson Crusoe* was pre-eminent, and continued to delight me through all my boyhood. It was no part however of my father's system to exclude books of amusement, though he allowed them very sparingly. Of such books he possessed at that time next to none, but he borrowed several for me; those which I remember are the *Arabian Nights,* Cazotte's Arabian Tales, *Don Quixote,* Miss Edgeworth's *Popular Tales,* and a book of some reputation in its day, Brooke's *Fool of Quality.*

In my eighth year I commenced learning Latin, in conjunction with a younger sister, to whom I taught it as I went on, and who afterwards repeated the lessons to my father: and from this time, other sisters and brothers being successively added as pupils, a considerable part of my day's work consisted of this preparatory teaching. It was a part which I greatly disliked; the more so, as I was held responsible for the lessons of my pupils, in almost as full a sense as for my own: I however derived from this discipline the great advantage of learning more thoroughly and retaining more lastingly the things which I was set to teach: perhaps, too, the practice it afforded in explaining difficulties to others may even at that age have been useful. In other respects, the experience of my boyhood is not favourable to the plan of teaching children by means of one another. The teaching, I am sure, is very inefficient as teaching, and I well knew that the relation between teacher and taught is not a good moral discipline to either. I went in this manner through the Latin grammar, and a considerable part of Cornelius Nepos and Caesar's *Commentaries,* but afterwards added to the superintendence of these lessons, much longer ones of my own.

In the same year in which I began Latin, I made my first commencement in the Greek poets with the *Iliad.* After I had made some progress in this, my father put Pope's translation into my hands. It was the first English verse I had cared to read, and it became one of the books in which for many years I most delighted: I think I must have read it from

twenty to thirty times through. I should not have thought it worth-while
to mention a taste apparently so natural to boyhood, if I had not, as I
think, observed that the keen enjoyment of this brilliant specimen of
narrative and versification is not so universal with boys, as I should have
expected both *a priori* and from my individual experience. Soon after
this time I commenced Euclid, and somewhat later, algebra, still under
my father's tuition.

From my eighth to my twelfth year the Latin books which I remember
reading were, the *Bucolics* of Virgil, and the first six books of the *Aeneid;*
all Horace except the *Epodes;* the *Fables* of Phaedrus; the first five books
of Livy (to which from my love of the subject I voluntarily added, in
my hours of leisure, the remainder of the first decade); all Sallust; a considerable part of Ovid's *Metamorphoses;* some plays of Terence; two or
three books of Lucretius; several of the Orations of Cicero, and of his
writings on oratory; also his letters to Atticus, my father taking the trouble to translate to me from the French the historical explanations in Mon-
gault's notes. In Greek I read the *Iliad* and *Odyssey* through; one or two
plays of Sophocles, Euripides, and Aristophanes, though by these I
profited little; all Thucydides; the *Hellenics* of Xenophon; a great part of
Demosthenes, Aeschines, and Lysias; Theocritus; Anacreon; part of the
Anthology; a little of Dionysius; several books of Polybius; and lastly
Aristotle's *Rhetoric,* which, as the first expressly scientific treatise on any
moral or psychological subject which I had read, and containing many of
the best observations of the ancients on human nature and life, my father
made me study with peculiar care, and throw the matter of it into syn-
optic tables. During the same years I learnt elementary geometry and algebra thoroughly, the differential calculus and other portions of the
higher mathematics far from thoroughly: for my father, not having kept
up this part of his early acquired knowledge, could not spare time to
qualify himself for removing my difficulties, and left me to deal with
them, with little other aid than that of books; while I was continually
incurring his displeasure by my inability to solve difficult problems for
which he did not see that I had not the necessary previous knowledge.

As to my private reading, I can only speak of what I remember. History continued to be my strongest predilection, and most of all ancient
history. Mitford's *Greece* I read continually; my father had put me on my
guard against the Tory prejudices of this writer, and his perversions of
facts for the whitewashing of despots, and blackening of popular institutions. These points he discoursed on, exemplifying them from the Greek
orators and historians, with such effect that in reading Mitford my sym-

pathies were always on the contrary side to those of the author, and I could, to some extent, have argued the point against him: yet this did not diminish the ever new pleasure with which I read the book. Roman history, both in my old favourite, Hooke, and in Ferguson, continued to delight me. A book which, in spite of what is called the dryness of its style, I took great pleasure in, was the *Ancient Universal History,* through the incessant reading of which I had my head full of historical details concerning the obscurest ancient people, while about modern history, except detached passages, such as the Dutch war of independence, I knew and cared comparatively little. A voluntary exercise, to which throughout my boyhood I was much addicted, was what I called writing histories. I successively composed a Roman history, picked out of Hooke; an abridgment of the *Ancient Universal History;* a History of Holland, from my favourite Watson and from an anonymous compilation; and in my eleventh and twelfth year I occupied myself with writing what I flattered myself was something serious. This was no less than a history of the Roman Government, compiled (with the assistance of Hooke) from Livy and Dionysius: of which I wrote as much as would have made an octavo volume, extending to the epoch of the Licinian Laws. It was, in fact, an account of the struggles between the patricians and plebeians, which now engrossed all the interest in my mind which I had previously felt in the mere wars and conquests of the Romans. I discussed all the constitutional points as they arose: though quite ignorant of Niebuhr's researches, I, by such lights as my father had given me, vindicated the Agrarian Laws on the evidence of Livy, and upheld to the best of my ability the Roman democratic party. A few years later, in my contempt of my childish efforts, I destroyed all these papers, not then anticipating that I could ever feel any curiosity about my first attempts at writing and reasoning. My father encouraged me in this useful amusement, though, as I think judiciously, he never asked to see what I wrote; so that I did not feel that in writing it I was accountable to any one, nor had the chilling sensation of being under a critical eye.

But though these exercises in history were never a compulsory lesson, there was another kind of composition which was so, namely, writing verses, and it was one of the most disagreeable of my tasks. Greek and Latin verses I did not write, nor learnt the prosody of those languages. My father, thinking this not worth the time it required, contented himself with making me read aloud to him, and correcting false quantities. I never composed at all in Greek, even in prose, and but little in Latin. Not that my father could be indifferent to the value of this practice, in giving

a thorough knowledge of those languages, but because there really was
not time for it. The verses I was required to write were English. When I
first read Pope's Homer, I ambitiously attempted to compose something
of the same kind, and achieved as much as one book of a continuation of
the *Iliad*. There, probably, the spontaneous promptings of my poetical
ambition would have stopped; but the exercise, begun from choice, was
continued by command. Conformably to my father's usual practice of explaining to me, as far as possible, the reasons for what he required me to
do, he gave me, for this, as I well remember, two reasons highly characteristic of him: one was, that some things could be expressed better and
more forcibly in verse than in prose: this, he said, was a real advantage.
The other was, that people in general attached more value to verse than it
deserved, and the power of writing it, was, on this account, worth acquiring. He generally left me to choose my own subjects, which, as far as
I remember, were mostly addresses to some mythological personage
or allegorical abstractions; but he made me translate into English verse
many of Horace's shorter poems: I also remember his giving me Thomson's "Winter" to read, and afterwards making me attempt (without
book) to write something myself on the same subject. The verses I wrote
were, of course, the merest rubbish, nor did I ever attain any facility of
versification, but the practice may have been useful in making it easier
for me, at a later period, to acquire readiness of expression.[1] I had read,
up to this time, very little English poetry; Shakespeare my father had put
into my hands, chiefly for the sake of the historical plays, from which,
however, I went on to the others. My father never was a great admirer of
Shakespeare, the English idolatry of whom he used to attack with some
severity. He cared little for any English poetry except Milton (for whom
he had the highest admiration), Goldsmith, Burns, and Gray's "Bard,"
which he preferred to his *Elegy*: perhaps I may add Cowper and Beattie.
He had some value for Spenser, and I remember his reading to me (unlike his usual practice of making me read to him), the first book of the
Fairie Queene; but I took little pleasure in it. The poetry of the present
century he saw scarcely any merit in, and I hardly became acquainted
with any of it till I was grown up to manhood, except the metrical romances of Walter Scott, which I read at his recommendation and was
intensely delighted with; as I always was with animated narrative. Dry-

---

1. In a subsequent stage of boyhood, when these exercises had ceased to be compulsory, like most youthful writers I wrote tragedies; under the inspiration not so much
of Shakespeare as of Joanna Baillie, whose *Constantine Paleologus* in particular
appeared to me one of the most glorious of human compositions. I still think it
one of the best dramas of the last two centuries.

den's *Poems* were among my father's books, and many of these he made me read, but I never cared for any of them except "Alexander's Feast," which, as well as many of the songs in Walter Scott, I used to sing internally, to a music of my own: to some of the latter, indeed, I went so far as to compose airs, which I still remember. Cowper's short poems I read with some pleasure, but never got far into the longer ones; and nothing in the two volumes interested me like the prose account of his three hares. In my thirteenth year I met with Campbell's *Poems*, among which "Lochiel," "Hohenlinden," the "Exile of Erin," and some others, gave me sensations I had never before experienced from poetry. Here, too, I made nothing of the longer poems, except the striking opening of *Gertrude of Wyoming*, which long kept its place in my feelings as the perfection of pathos.

During this part of my childhood, one of my greatest amusements was experimental science; in the theoretical, however, not the practical sense of the word; not trying experiments—a kind of discipline which I have often regretted not having had—nor even seeing, but merely reading about them. I never remember being so wrapt up in any book, as I was in Joyce's *Scientific Dialogues;* and I was rather recalcitrant to my father's criticisms of the bad reasoning respecting the first principles of physics, which abounds in the early part of that work. I devoured treatises on chemistry, especially that of my father's early friend and schoolfellow, Dr. Thomson, for years before I attended a lecture or saw an experiment.

From about the age of twelve, I entered into another and more advanced stage in my course of instruction; in which the main object was no longer the aids and appliances of thought, but the thoughts themselves. This commenced with logic, in which I began at once with the *Organon*, and read it to the *Analytics* inclusive, but profited little by the *Posterior Analytics*, which belongs to a branch of speculation I was not yet ripe for. Contemporaneously with the *Organon*, my father made me read the whole or parts of several of the Latin treatises on the scholastic logic; giving each day to him, in our walks, a minute account of what I had read, and answering his numerous and searching questions. After this, I went in a similar manner through the *Computatio sive Logica* of Hobbes, a work of a much higher order of thought than the books of the school logicians, and which he estimated very highly; in my own opinion beyond its merits, great as these are. It was his invariable practice, whatever studies he exacted from me, to make me as far as possible understand and feel the utility of them: and this he deemed peculiarly fitting in the case of the syllogistic logic, the usefulness of which had been impugned by so many writers of authority. I well remember how, and in what particular walk, in the neighbourhood of Bagshot Heath (where we were on a visit to his old friend Mr. Wallace, then one of the mathematical professors at Sandhurst) he first attempted by questions to make me think on the subject, and frame some conception of what constituted the utility of the syllogistic logic, and when I had failed in this, to make me understand it by explanations. The explanations did not make the matter at all clear to me at the time; but they were not therefore useless; they remained as a nucleus for my observations and reflections to crystallize upon; the import of his general remarks being interpreted to me, by the particular instances which came under my notice afterwards. My own consciousness and experience ultimately led me to appreciate quite as highly as he did, the value of an early practical familiarity with the school logic. I know nothing, in my education, to which I think myself more indebted for whatever capacity of thinking I have attained. The first intellectual operation in which I arrived at any proficiency was dissecting a bad argument, and finding in what part the fallacy lay: and though whatever capacity of this sort I attained was due to the fact that it was an intellectual exercise in which I was most perseveringly drilled by my father, yet it is also true that the school logic, and the mental habits acquired in studying it, were among the principal instruments of this drilling. I am persuaded that nothing, in modern education, tends so much, when properly used, to form exact thinkers, who attach a precise meaning to words and propositions, and are not imposed on by vague, loose, or ambiguous terms. The boasted influence of mathematical studies is nothing to it; for in mathematical processes, none of the real difficulties of correct ratiocination occur. It is also a study peculiarly adapted to an early stage in the education of philosophical students, since it does not presuppose the slow process of acquiring, by experience and reflection, valuable thoughts of their own. They may become capable of disentangling the intricacies of confused and self-contradictory thought, before their own thinking faculties are much advanced; a power which, for want of some such discipline, many otherwise able men altogether lack; and when they have to answer opponents, only endeavour, by such arguments as they can command, to support the opposite conclusion, scarcely even attempting to confute the reasonings of their antagonists; and, therefore, at the utmost, leaving the question, as far as it depends on argument, a balanced one.

During this time, the Latin and Greek books which I continued to read with my father were chiefly such as were worth studying, not for the language merely, but also for the thoughts. This included much of the orators, and especially Demosthenes, some of whose principal orations I read several times over, and wrote out, by way of exercise, a full analysis of them. My father's comments on these orations when I read them to him were very instructive to me. He not only drew my attention to the insight they afforded into Athenian institutions, and the principles of legislation and government which they often illustrated, but pointed out the skill and art of the orator—how everything important to his purpose was said at the exact moment when he had brought the minds of his audience into the state most fitted to receive it; how he made steal into their minds, gradually and by insinuation, thoughts which if expressed in a more direct manner would have aroused their opposition. Most of these reflections were beyond my capacity of full comprehension at the time; but they left seed behind, which germinated in due season. At this time I also read the whole of Tacitus, Juvenal, and Quintilian. The latter, owing to his obscure style and to the scholastic details of which many parts of his treatise are made up, is little read, and seldom sufficiently appreciated. His book is a kind of encyclopaedia of the thoughts of the ancients on the whole field of education and culture; and I have retained through life many valuable ideas which I can distinctly trace to my reading of him, even at that early age. It was at this period that I read, for the first time, some of the most important dialogues of Plato, in particular the *Gorgias*, the *Protagoras*, and the *Republic*. There is no author to whom my father thought himself more indebted for his own mental culture, than Plato, or whom he more frequently recommended to young students. I can bear similar testimony in regard to myself. The Socratic method, of which the Platonic dialogues are the chief example, is unsurpassed as a discipline for correcting the errors, and clearing up the confusions incident to the *intellectus sibi permissus*, the understanding which has made up all its bundles of associations under the guidance of popular phraseology. The close, searching *elenchus* by which the man of vague generalities is constrained either to express his meaning to himself in definite terms, or to confess that he does not know what he is talking about; the perpetual testing of all general statements by particular instances; the siege in form which is laid to the meaning of large abstract terms, by fixing upon some still larger class-name which includes that and more, and dividing down to the thing sought—marking out its limits and definition by a series of accurately drawn distinctions between it and each of the cognate objects which are successively parted off from it—all this, as an education for precise thinking, is inestimable, and all this, even at that age, took such hold of me that it became part of my own mind. I have felt ever since that the title of Platonist belongs by far better right to those who have been nourished in, and have endeavoured to practise Plato's mode of investigation, than to those who are distinguished only by the adoption of certain dogmatical conclusions, drawn mostly from the least intelligible of his works, and which the character of his mind and writings makes it uncertain whether he himself regarded as anything more than poetic fancies, or philosophic conjectures.

In going through Plato and Demosthenes, since I could now read these authors, as far as the language was concerned, with perfect ease, I was not required to construe them sentence by sentence, but to read them aloud to my father, answering questions when asked: but the particular attention which he paid to elocution (in which his own excellence was remarkable) made this reading aloud to him a most painful task. Of all things which he required me to do, there was none which I did so constantly ill, or in which he so perpetually lost his temper with me. He had thought much on the principles of the art of reading, especially the most neglected part of it, the inflections of the voice, or *modulation* as writers on elocution call it (in contrast with *articulation* on the one side, and *expression* on the other), and had reduced it to rules, grounded on the logical analysis of a sentence. These rules he strongly impressed upon me, and took me severely to task for every violation of them: but I even then remarked (though I did not venture to make the remark to him) that though he reproached me when I read a sentence ill, and *told* me how I ought to have read it, he never, by reading it himself, *showed* me how it ought to be read. A defect running through his otherwise admirable modes of instruction, as it did through all his modes of thought, was that of trusting too much to the intelligibleness of the abstract, when not embodied in the concrete. It was at a much later period of my youth, when practising elocution by myself, or with companions of my own age, that I for the first time understood the object of his rules, and saw the psychological grounds of them. At that time I and others followed out the subject into its ramifications and could have composed a very useful treatise, grounded on my father's principles. He himself left those principles and rules unwritten. I regret that when my mind was full of the subject, from systematic practice, I did not put them, and our improvements of them, into a formal shape.

A book which contributed largely to my education, in the best sense of the term, was my father's *History of India*. It was published in the beginning of 1818. During the year previous, while it was passing through the press, I used to read the proof sheets to him; or rather, I read the manuscript to him while he corrected the proofs. The number of new ideas which I received from this remarkable book, and the impulse and stimulus as well as guidance given to my thoughts by its criticisms and disquisitions on society and civilization in the Hindu part, on institutions and the acts of governments in the English part, made my early familiarity with it eminently useful to my subsequent progress. And though I can perceive deficiencies in it now as compared with a perfect standard, I still think it, if not the most, one of the most instructive histories ever written, and one of the books from which most benefit may be derived by a mind in the course of making up its opinions.

The Preface, among the most characteristic of my father's writings, as well as the richest in materials of thought, gives a picture which may be entirely depended on, of the sentiments and expectations with which he wrote the History. Saturated as the book is with the opinions and modes of judgment of a democratic radicalism then regarded as extreme; and treating with a severity, at that time most unusual, the English Constitution, the English law, and all parties and classes who possessed any considerable influence in the country; he may have expected reputation, but certainly not advancement in life, from its publication; nor could he have supposed that it would raise up anything but enemies for him in powerful quarters: least of all could he have expected favour from the East India Company, to whose commercial privileges he was unqualifiedly hostile, and on the acts of whose government he had made so many severe comments: though, in various parts of his book, he bore a testimony in their favour, which he felt to be their just due, namely, that no government had on the whole given so much proof, to the extent of its lights, of good intention towards its subjects; and that if the acts of any other government had the light of publicity as completely let in upon them, they would, in all probability, still less bear scrutiny.

On learning, however, in the spring of 1819, about a year after the publication of the History, that the East India Directors desired to strengthen the part of their home establishment which was employed in carrying on the correspondence with India, my father declared himself a candidate for that employment, and, to the credit of the Directors, successfully. He was appointed one of the assistants of the Examiner of India Correspondence; officers whose duty it was to prepare drafts of despatches to India, for consideration by the Directors, in the principal departments of administration. In this office, and in that of Examiner, which he subsequently attained, the influence which his talents, his reputation, and his decision of character gave him, with superiors who really desired the good government of India, enabled him to a great extent to throw into his drafts of despatches, and to carry through the ordeal of the Court of Directors and Board of Control, without having their force much weakened, his real opinions on Indian subjects. In his History he had set forth, for the first time, many of the true principles of Indian administration: and his despatches, following his History, did more than had ever been done before to promote the improvement of India, and teach Indian officials to understand their business. If a selection of them were published, they would, I am convinced, place his character as a practical statesman fully on a level with his eminence as a speculative writer.

This new employment of his time caused no relaxation in his attention to my education. It was in this same year, 1819, that he took me through a complete course of political economy. His loved and intimate friend, Ricardo, had shortly before published the book which formed so great an epoch in political economy; a book which never would have been published or written, but for the entreaty and strong encouragement of my father; for Ricardo, the most modest of men, though firmly convinced of the truth of his doctrines, deemed himself so little capable of doing them justice in exposition and expression, that he shrank from the idea of publicity. The same friendly encouragement induced Ricardo, a year or two later, to become a member of the House of Commons; where, during the few remaining years of his life, unhappily cut short in the full vigour of his intellect, he rendered so much service to his and my father's opinions both on political economy and on other subjects.

Though Ricardo's great work was already in print, no didactic treatise embodying its doctrines, in a manner fit for learners, had yet appeared. My father, therefore, commenced instructing me in the science by a sort of lectures, which he delivered to me in our walks. He expounded each day a portion of the subject, and I gave him next day a written account of it, which he made me rewrite over and over again until it was clear, precise, and tolerably complete. In this manner I went through the whole extent of the science; and the written outline of it which resulted from my daily *compte rendu*, served him afterwards as notes from which to write his *Elements of Political Economy*. After this I read Ricardo, giving an account daily of what I read, and discussing, in the best manner I could, the collateral points which offered themselves in our progress.

On Money, as the most intricate part of the subject, he made me read in the same manner Ricardo's admirable pamphlets, written during what was called the Bullion controversy; to these succeeded Adam Smith; and in this reading it was one of my father's main objects to make me apply to Smith's more superficial view of political economy, the superior lights of Ricardo, and detect what was fallacious in Smith's arguments, or erroneous in any of his conclusions. Such a mode of instruction was excellently calculated to form a thinker; but it required to be worked by a thinker as close and vigorous as my father. The path was a thorny one, even to him, and I am sure it was so to me, notwithstanding the strong interest I took in the subject. He was often, and much beyond reason, provoked by my failures in cases where success could not have been expected; but in the main his method was right, and it succeeded. I do not believe that any scientific teaching ever was more thorough, or better fitted for training the faculties, than the mode in which logic and political economy were taught to me by my father. Striving, even in an exaggerated degree, to call forth the activity of my faculties, by making me find out everything for myself, he gave his explanations not before, but after, I had felt the full force of the difficulties; and not only gave me an accurate knowledge of these two great subjects, as far as they were then understood, but made me a thinker on both. I thought for myself almost from the first, and occasionally thought differently from him, though for a long time only on minor points, and making his opinion the ultimate standard. At a later period I even occasionally convinced him, and altered his opinion on some points of detail: which I state to his honour, not my own. It at once exemplifies his perfect candour, and the real worth of his method of teaching.

At this point concluded what can properly be called my lessons: when I was about fourteen I left England for more than a year; and after my return, though my studies went on under my father's general direction, he was no longer my schoolmaster. I shall therefore pause here, and turn back to matters of a more general nature connected with the part of my life and education included in the preceding reminiscences.

In the course of instruction which I have partially retraced, the point most superficially apparent is the great effort to give during the years of childhood an amount of knowledge in what are considered the higher branches of education, which is seldom acquired (if acquired at all) until the age of manhood. The result of the experiment shows the ease with which this may be done, and places in a strong light the wretched waste of so many precious years as are spent in acquiring the modicum of Latin and Greek commonly taught to schoolboys; a waste, which has led so many educational reformers to entertain the ill-judged proposal of discarding these languages altogether from general education. If I had been by nature extremely quick of apprehension, or had possessed a very accurate and retentive memory, or were of a remarkably active and energetic character, the trial would not be conclusive; but in all these natural gifts I am rather below than above par; what I could do, could assuredly be done by any boy or girl of average capacity and healthy physical constitution: and if I have accomplished anything, I owe it, among other fortunate circumstances, to the fact that through the early training bestowed on me by my father, I started, I may fairly say, with an advantage of a quarter of a century over my contemporaries.

There was one cardinal point in this training, of which I have already given some indication, and which, more than anything else, was the cause of whatever good it effected. Most boys or youths who have had much knowledge drilled into them, have their mental capacities not strengthened, but overlaid by it. They are crammed with mere facts, and with the opinions or phrases of other people, and these are accepted as a substitute for the power to form opinions of their own: and thus the sons of eminent fathers, who have spared no pains in their education, so often grow up mere parroters of what they have learnt, incapable of using their minds except in the furrows traced for them. Mine, however, was not an education of cram. My father never permitted anything which I learnt to degenerate into a mere exercise of memory. He strove to make the understanding not only go along with every step of the teaching, but, if possible, precede it. Anything which could be found out by thinking I never was told, until I had exhausted my efforts to find it out for myself. As far as I can trust my remembrance, I acquitted myself very lamely in this department; my recollection of such matters is almost wholly of failures, hardly ever of success. It is true the failures were often in things in which success in so early a stage of my progress was almost impossible. I remember at some time in my thirteenth year, on my happening to use the word idea, he asked me what an idea was; and expressed some displeasure at my ineffectual efforts to define the word: I recollect also his indignation at my using the common expression that something was true in theory but required correction in practice; and how, after making me vainly strive to define the word theory, he explained its meaning, and showed the fallacy of the vulgar form of speech which I had used; leaving me fully persuaded that in being unable to give a correct definition of Theory, and in speaking of it as something which might be at variance with practice, I had shown unparalleled ignorance. In this he seems, and perhaps was, very unreasonable; but I think, only in being angry at my failure. A pupil from whom nothing is ever demanded which he cannot do, never does all he can.

One of the evils most liable to attend on any sort of early proficiency, and which often fatally blights its promise, my father most anxiously guarded against. This was self-conceit. He kept me, with extreme vigilance, out of the way of hearing myself praised, or of being led to make self-flattering comparisons between myself and others. From his own intercourse with me I could derive none but a very humble opinion of myself; and the standard of comparison he always held up to me was not what other people did, but what a man could and ought to do. He completely succeeded in preserving me from the sort of influences he so much dreaded. I was not at all aware that my attainments were anything unusual at my age. If I accidentally had my attention drawn to the fact that some other boy knew less than myself—which happened less often than might be imagined—I concluded, not that I knew much, but that he, for some reason or other, knew little, or that his knowledge was of a different kind from mine. My state of mind was not humility, but neither was it arrogance. I never thought of saying to myself, I am, or I can do, so and so. I neither estimated myself highly nor lowly: I did not estimate myself at all. If I thought anything about myself, it was that I was rather backward in my studies, since I always found myself so, in comparison with what my father expected from me. I assert this with confidence, though it was not the impression of various persons who saw me in my childhood. They, as I have since found, thought me greatly and disagreeably self-conceited; probably because I was disputatious, and did not scruple to give direct contradictions to things which I heard said. I suppose I acquired this bad habit from having been encouraged in an unusual degree to talk on matters beyond my age, and with grown persons, while I never had inculcated in me the usual respect for them. My father did not correct this ill-breeding and impertinence, probably from not being aware of it, for I was always too much in awe of him to be otherwise than extremely subdued and quiet in his presence. Yet with all this I had no notion of any superiority in myself; and well was it for me that I had not. I remember the very place in Hyde Park where, in my fourteenth year, on the eve of leaving my father's house for a long absence, he told me that I should find, as I got acquainted with new people, that I had been taught many things which youths of my age did not commonly know; and that many persons would be disposed to talk to me of this, and to compliment me upon it. What other things he said on this topic I remember very imperfectly; but he wound up by saying that whatever I knew more than others could not be ascribed to any merit in me, but to the very unusual advantage which had fallen to my lot, of having a father who was able to teach me, and willing to give the necessary trouble and time; that it was no matter of praise to me, if I knew more than those who had not had a similar advantage, but the deepest disgrace to me if I did not. I have a distinct remembrance that the suggestion thus for the first time made to me, that I knew more than other youths who were considered well educated, was to me a piece of information, to which, as to all other things which my father told me, I gave implicit credence, but which did not at all impress me as a personal matter. I felt no disposition to glorify myself upon the circumstance that there were other persons who did not know what I knew; nor had I ever flattered myself that my acquirements, whatever they might be, were any merit of mine: but, now when my attention was called to the subject, I felt that what my father had said respecting my peculiar advantages was exactly the truth and common sense of the matter, and it fixed my opinion and feeling from that time forward.

It is evident that this, among many other of the purposes of my father's scheme of education, could not have been accomplished if he had not carefully kept me from having any great amount of intercourse with other boys. He was earnestly bent upon my escaping not only the ordinary corrupting influence which boys exercise over boys, but the contagion of vulgar modes of thought and feeling; and for this he was willing that I should pay the price of inferiority in the accomplishments which schoolboys in all countries chiefly cultivate. The deficiencies in my education were principally in the things which boys learn from being turned out to shift for themselves, and from being brought together in large numbers. From temperance and much walking, I grew up healthy and hardy, though not muscular; but I could do no feats of skill or physical strength, and knew none of the ordinary bodily exercises. It was not that play, or time for it, was refused me. Though no holidays were allowed, lest the habit of work should be broken, and a taste for idleness acquired, I had ample leisure in every day to amuse myself; but as I had no boy companions, and the animal need of physical activity was satisfied by walking, my amusements, which were mostly solitary, were in general of a quiet, if not a bookish turn, and gave little stimulus to any other kind even of mental activity than that which was already called forth by my studies: I consequently remained long, and in a less degree have always remained, inexpert in anything requiring manual dexterity; my mind as well as my hands did its work very lamely when it was applied, or ought to have been applied, to the practical details which, as they are the chief interest of life to the majority of men, are also the things in which whatever mental capacity they have chiefly shows itself: I was constantly meriting reproof by inattention, inobservance, and general slackness of mind in matters of daily life. My father was the extreme opposite in these particulars: his senses and mental faculties were always on the alert; he carried decision and energy of character in his whole manner and into every action of life: and this, as much as his talents, contributed to the strong impression which he always made upon those with whom he came into personal contact. But the children of energetic parents frequently grow up unenergetic, because they lean on their parents, and the parents are energetic for them. The education which my father gave me was in itself much more fitted for training me to *know* than to *do*. Not that he was unaware of my deficiencies; both as a boy and as a youth I was incessantly smarting under his severe admonitions on the subject. There was anything but insensibility or tolerance on his part towards such shortcomings: but, while he saved me from the demoralizing effects of school life, he made no effort to provide me with any sufficient substitute for its practicalizing influences. Whatever qualities he himself, probably, had acquired without difficulty or special training, he seems to have supposed that I ought to acquire as easily. He had not, I think, bestowed the same amount of thought and attention on this, as on most other branches of education; and here, as well as in some other points of my tuition, he seems to have expected effects without causes.

MORAL INFLUENCES IN EARLY YOUTH. MY FATHER'S CHARACTER AND OPINIONS

In my education, as in that of everyone, the moral influences, which are so much more important than all others, are also the most complicated, and the most difficult to specify with any approach to completeness. Without attempting the hopeless task of detailing the circumstances by which, in this respect, my early character may have been shaped, I shall confine myself to a few leading points, which form an indispensable part of any true account of my education.

I was brought up from the first without any religious belief, in the ordinary acceptation of the term. My father, educated in the creed of Scotch presbyterianism, had by his own studies and reflections been early led to reject not only the belief in revelation, but the foundations of what is commonly called Natural Religion. I have heard him say that the turning-point of his mind on the subject was reading Butler's *Analogy*. That work, of which he always continued to speak with respect, kept him, as he said, for some considerable time, a believer in the divine authority of Christianity; by proving to him, that whatever are the difficulties in believing that the Old and New Testaments proceed from, or record the acts of, a perfectly wise and good being, the same and still greater difficulties stand in the way of the belief, that a being of such a character can have been the Maker of the universe. He considered Butler's argument as conclusive against the only opponents for whom it was intended. Those who admit an omnipotent as well as perfectly just and benevolent maker and ruler of such a world as this can say little against Christianity but what can, with at least equal force, be retorted against themselves. Finding, therefore, no halting place in Deism, he remained in a state of perplexity, until, doubtless after many struggles, he yielded to the conviction that concerning the origin of things nothing whatever can be known. This is the only correct statement of his opinion; for dogmatic atheism he looked upon as absurd; as most of those whom the world has considered atheists have always done. These particulars are important, because they show that my father's rejection of all that is called religious belief was not, as many might suppose, primarily a matter of logic and evidence: the grounds of it were moral, still more than intellectual. He found it impossible to believe that a world so full of evil was the work of an Author combining infinite power with perfect goodness and righteousness. His intellect spurned the subtleties by which men attempt to blind themselves to this open contradiction. The Sabaean, or Manichaean theory of a Good and Evil Principle, struggling against each other for the government of the universe, he would not have equally condemned; and I have heard him express surprise, that no one revived it in our time. He would have regarded it as a mere hypothesis; but he would have ascribed to it no depraving influence. As it was, his aversion to religion, in the sense usually attached to the term, was of the same kind with that of Lucretius: he regarded it with the feelings due not to a mere mental delusion, but to a great moral evil. He looked upon it as the greatest enemy of morality: first, by setting up factitious excellencies—belief in creeds, devotional feelings, and ceremonies not connected with the good of human kind—and causing these to be accepted as substitutes for genuine virtues: but above all, by radically vitiating the standard of morals; making it consist in doing the will of a being, on whom it lavishes indeed all the phrases of adulation, but whom in sober truth it depicts as eminently hateful. I have a hundred times heard him say, that all ages and nations have represented their gods as wicked, in a constantly increasing progression, that mankind have gone on adding trait after trait till they reached the most perfect conception of wickedness which the human mind can devise, and have called this God, and prostrated themselves before it. This *ne plus ultra* of wickedness he considered to be embodied in what is commonly presented to mankind as the creed of Christianity. Think (he used to say) of a being who would make a Hell—who would create the human race with the infallible fore-knowledge, and therefore with the intention, that the great majority of them were to be consigned to horrible and everlasting torment. The time, I believe, is drawing near when this dreadful conception of an object of worship will be no longer identified with Christianity; and when all persons with any sense of moral good and evil will look upon it with the same indignation with which my father regarded it. My father was as well aware as anyone that Christians do not, in general, undergo the demoralizing consequences which seem inherent in such a creed, in the manner or to the extent which might have been expected from it. The same slovenliness of thought, and subjection of the reason to fears, wishes, and affections which enable them to accept a theory involving a contradiction in terms, prevents them from perceiving the logical consequences of the theory. Such is the facility with which mankind believe at one and the same time things inconsistent with one another, and so few are those who draw from what they receive as truths, any consequences but those recommended to them by their feelings, that multitudes have held the undoubting belief in an Omnipotent Author of Hell, and have nevertheless identified that being with the best conception they were able to form of perfect goodness. Their worship was not paid to the demon which such a being as they imagined would really be, but to their own idea of excellence. The evil is, that such a belief keeps the ideal wretchedly low; and opposes the most obstinate resistance to all thought which has a tendency to raise it higher. Believers shrink from every train of ideas which would lead the mind to a clear conception and an elevated standard of excellence, because they feel (even when they do not distinctly see) that such a standard would conflict with many of the dispensations of nature, and with much of what they are accustomed to consider as the Christian creed. And thus morality continues a matter of blind tradition, with no consistent principle, nor even any consistent feeling, to guide it.

It would have been wholly inconsistent with my father's ideas of duty to allow me to acquire impressions contrary to his convictions and feelings respecting religion: and he impressed upon me from the first that the manner in which the world came into existence was a subject on which nothing was known: that the question, "Who made me?" cannot be answered, because we have no experience or authentic information from which to answer it; and that any answer only throws the difficulty a step further back, since the question immediately presents itself, Who made God? He, at the same time, took care that I should be acquainted with what had been thought by mankind on these impenetrable problems. I have mentioned at how early an age he made me a reader of ecclesiastical history; and he taught me to take the strongest interest in the Reformation, as the great and decisive contest against priestly tyranny for liberty of thought.

I am thus one of the very few examples, in this country, of one who has not thrown off religious belief but never had it: I grew up in a negative state with regard to it. I looked upon the modern exactly as I did upon the ancient religion, as something which in no way concerned me. It did not seem to me more strange that English people should believe what I did not, than that the men I read of in Herodotus should have done so. History had made the variety of opinions among mankind a fact familiar to me, and this was but a prolongation of that fact. This point in my early education had, however, incidentally one bad consequence deserving notice. In giving me an opinion contrary to that of the world, my father thought it necessary to give it as one which could not prudently be avowed to the world. This lesson of keeping my thoughts to myself, at that early age, was attended with some moral disadvantages; though my limited intercourse with strangers, especially such as were likely to speak to me on religion, prevented me from being placed in the alternative of avowal or hypocrisy. I remember two occasions in my boyhood, on which I felt myself in this alternative, and in both cases I avowed my disbelief and defended it. My opponents were boys, considerably older than myself: one of them I certainly staggered at the time, but the subject was never renewed between us: the other who was surprised, and somewhat shocked, did his best to convince me for some time, without effect.

The great advance in liberty of discussion, which is one of the most important differences between the present time and that of my childhood, has greatly altered the moralities of this question; and I think that few men of my father's intellect and public spirit, holding with such intensity of moral conviction as he did, unpopular opinions on religion, or on any other of the great subjects of thought, would now either practise or inculcate the withholding of them from the world, unless in the cases, becoming fewer every day, in which frankness on these subjects would either risk the loss of means of subsistence, or would amount to exclusion from some sphere of usefulness peculiarly suitable to the capacities of the individual. On religion in particular the time appears to me to have come when it is the duty of all who being qualified in point of knowledge, have on mature consideration satisfied themselves that the current opinions are not only false but hurtful, to make their dissent known; at least, if they are among those whose station or reputation, gives their opinion a chance of being attended to. Such an avowal would put an end, at once and for ever, to the vulgar prejudice that what is called, very improperly, unbelief is connected with any bad qualities either of mind or heart. The world would be astonished if it knew how great a proportion of its brightest ornaments—of those most distinguished even in popular estimation for wisdom and virtue—are complete sceptics in religion; many of them refraining from avowal, less from personal considerations, than from a conscientious, though now in my opinion a most mistaken apprehension, lest by speaking out what would tend to weaken existing beliefs, and by consequence (as they suppose) existing restraints, they should do harm instead of good.

Of unbelievers (so called) as well as of believers, there are many species, including almost every variety of moral type. But the best among them, as no one who has had opportunities of really knowing them will hesitate to affirm (believers rarely have that opportunity), are more genuinely religious, in the best sense of the word religion, than those who exclusively arrogate to themselves the title. The liberality of the age, or in other words the weakening of the obstinate prejudice which makes men unable to see what is before their eyes because it is contrary to their expectations, has caused it to be very commonly admitted that a Deist may be truly religious: but if religion stands for any graces of character and not for mere dogma, the assertion may equally be made of many whose belief is far short of Deism. Though they may think the proof incomplete that the universe is a work of design, and though they assuredly disbelieve that it can have an Author and Governor who is absolute in power as well as perfect in goodness, they have that which constitutes the principal worth of all religions whatever, an ideal conception of a Perfect Being, to which they habitually refer as the guide of their conscience; and this ideal of Good is usually far nearer to perfection than the objective Deity of those who think themselves obliged to find absolute goodness in the author of a world so crowded with suffering and so deformed by injustice as ours.

My father's moral convictions, wholly dissevered from religion, were very much of the character of those of the Greek philosophers; and were delivered with the force and decision which characterized all that came from him. Even at the very early age at which I read with him the *Memorabilia* of Xenophon, I imbibed from that work and from his comments a deep respect for the character of Socrates, who stood in my mind as a model of ideal excellence: and I well remember how my father at that time impressed upon me the lesson of the "Choice of Hercules." At a somewhat later period the lofty moral standard exhibited in the writings of Plato operated upon me with great force. My father's moral inculcations were at all times mainly those of the *Socratici viri;* justice, temperance (to which he gave a very extended application), veracity, perseverance, readiness to encounter pain and especially labour; regard for the public good; estimation of persons according to their merits, and of things according to their intrinsic usefulness; a life of exertion in contradiction to one of self-indulgent sloth. These and other moralities he conveyed in brief sentences, uttered as occasion arose, of grave exhortation, or stern reprobation and contempt.

But though direct moral teaching does much, indirect does more; and the effect my father produced on my character did not depend solely on what he said or did with that direct object, but also, and still more, on what manner of man he was.

In his views of life he partook of the character of the Stoic, the Epicurean, and the Cynic, not in the modern but the ancient sense of the word. In his personal qualities the Stoic predominated. His standard of morals was Epicurean, inasmuch as it was utilitarian, taking as the exclusive test of right and wrong, the tendency of actions to produce pleasure or pain. But he had (and this was the Cynic element) scarcely any belief in pleasure; at least in his later years, of which alone, on this point, I can speak confidently. He was not insensible to pleasures; but he deemed very few of them worth the price which, at least in the present state of society, must be paid for them. The greater number of miscarriages in life, he considered to be attributable to the overvaluing of pleasures. Accordingly, temperance, in the large sense intended by the Greek philosophers—stopping short at the point of moderation in all indulgences—was with him, as with them, almost the central point of educational precept. His inculcations of this virtue fill a large place in my childish remembrances. He thought human life a poor thing at best, after the freshness of youth and of unsatisfied curiosity had gone by. This was a topic on which he did not often speak, especially, it may be supposed, in the presence of young persons: but when he did, it was with an air of settled and profound conviction. He would sometimes say that if life were made what it might be, by good government and good education, it would be worth having: but he never spoke with anything like enthusiasm even of that possibility. He never varied in rating intellectual enjoyments above all others, even in value as pleasures, independently of their ulterior benefits. The pleasures of the benevolent affections he placed high in the scale; and used to say that he had never known a happy old man, except those who were able to live over again in the pleasures of the young. For passionate emotions of all sorts, and for everything which has been said or written in exaltation of them, he professed the greatest contempt. He regarded them as a form of madness. "The intense" was with him a by-word of scornful disapprobation. He regarded as an aberration of the moral standard of modern times, compared with that of the ancients, the great stress laid upon feeling. Feelings, as such, he considered to be no proper subjects of praise or blame. Right and wrong, good and bad, he regarded as qualities solely of conduct—of acts and omissions; there being no feeling which may not lead, and does not frequently lead, either to good or to bad actions: conscience itself, the very desire to act right, often leading people to act wrong. Consistently carrying out the doctrine that the object of praise and blame should be the discouragement of wrong conduct and the encouragement of right, he refused to let his praise or blame be influenced by the motive of the agent. He blamed as severely what he thought a bad action, when the motive was a feeling of duty, as if the agents had been consciously evil-doers. He would not have accepted as a plea in mitigation for inquisitors, that they sincerely believed burning heretics to be an obligation of conscience. But though he did not allow honesty of purpose to soften his disapprobation of actions, it had its full effect on his estimation of characters. No one prized conscientiousness and rectitude of intention more highly, or was more incapable of valuing any person in whom he did not feel assurance of it. But he disliked people quite as much for any other deficiency, provided he thought it equally likely to make them act ill. He disliked, for instance, a fanatic in any bad cause, as much or more than one who adopted the same cause from self-interest, because he thought him even more likely to be practically mischievous. And thus, his aversion to many intellectual errors, or what he regarded as such, partook, in a certain sense, of the character of a moral feeling. All this is merely saying that he, in a degree once common, but now very unusual, threw his feelings into his opinions; which truly it is difficult to understand how any one who possesses much of both can fail to do. None but those who do not care about opinions will confound it with intolerance. Those who, having opinions which they hold to be immensely im-

portant, and their contraries to be prodigiously hurtful, have any deep regard for the general good, will necessarily dislike, as a class and in the
abstract, those who think wrong what they think right, and right what
they think wrong: though they need not therefore be, nor was my father,
insensible to good qualities in an opponent, nor governed in their estimation of individuals by one general presumption, instead of by the whole
of their character. I grant that an earnest person, being no more infallible
than other men, is liable to dislike people on account of opinions which
do not merit dislike; but if he neither himself does them any ill office, nor
connives at its being done by others, he is not intolerant: and the forbearance which flows from a conscientious sense of the importance to mankind of the equal freedom of all opinions is the only tolerance which is
commendable, or, to the highest moral order of minds, possible.

It will be admitted that a man of the opinions and the character above
described was likely to leave a strong moral impression on any mind principally formed by him, and that his moral teaching was not likely to err
on the side of laxity or indulgence. The element which was chiefly deficient in his moral relation to his children was that of tenderness. I do not
believe that this deficiency lay in his own nature. I believe him to have
had much more feeling than he habitually showed, and much greater capacities of feeling than were ever developed. He resembled most Englishmen in being ashamed of the signs of feeling, and by the absence of demonstration starving the feelings themselves. If we consider further that he
was in the trying position of sole teacher, and add to this that his temper
was constitutionally irritable, it is impossible not to feel true pity for a father who did, and strove to do, so much for his children, who would have
so valued their affection, yet who must have been constantly feeling that
fear of him was drying it up at its source. This was no longer the case later
in life, and with his younger children. They loved him tenderly: and if I
cannot say so much of myself, I was always loyally devoted to him. As regards my own education, I hesitate to pronounce whether I was more a
loser or gainer by his severity. It was not such as to prevent me from having a happy childhood. And I do not believe that boys can be induced to
apply themselves with vigour, and what is so much more difficult, perseverance, to dry and irksome studies, by the sole force of persuasion and
soft words. Much must be done, and much must be learnt, by children,
for which rigid discipline and known liability to punishment are indispensable as means. It is, no doubt, a very laudable effort, in modern
teaching, to render as much as possible of what the young are required to
learn easy and interesting to them. But when this principle is pushed to

the length of not requiring them to learn anything *but* what has been made easy and interesting, one of the chief objects of education is sacrificed. I rejoice in the decline of the old brutal and tyrannical system of teaching, which, however, did succeed in enforcing habits of application; but the new, as it seems to me, is training up a race of men who will be incapable of doing anything which is disagreeable to them. I do not, then, believe that fear, as an element in education, can be dispensed with; but I am sure that it ought not to be the main element; and when it predominates so much as to preclude love and confidence on the part of the child to those who should be the unreservedly trusted advisers of after-years, and perhaps to seal up the fountains of frank and spontaneous communicativeness in the child's nature, it is an evil for which a large abatement must be made from the benefits, moral and intellectual, which may flow from any other part of the education.

During this first period of my life, the habitual frequenters of my father's house were limited to a very few persons, most of them little known to the world, but whom personal worth, and more or less of congeniality with at least his political opinions (not so frequently to be met with then as since) inclined him to cultivate; and his conversations with them I listened to with interest and instruction. My being an habitual inmate of my father's study made me acquainted with the dearest of his friends, David Ricardo, who by his benevolent countenance, and kindliness of manner, was very attractive to young persons, and who, after I became a student of political economy, invited me to his house and to walk with him in order to converse on the subject. I was a more frequent visitor (from about 1817 or 1818) to Mr. Hume, who, born in the same part of Scotland as my father, and having been, I rather think, a younger schoolfellow or college companion of his, had on returning from India renewed their youthful acquaintance, and who coming like many others greatly under the influence of my father's intellect and energy of character, was induced partly by that influence to go into Parliament, and there adopt the line of conduct which has given him an honourable place in the history of his country. Of Mr. Bentham I saw much more, owing to the close intimacy which existed between him and my father. I do not know how soon after my father's first arrival in England they became acquainted. But my father was the earliest Englishman of any great mark who thoroughly understood, and in the main adopted, Bentham's general views of ethics, government and law: and this was a natural foundation for sympathy between them, and made them familiar companions in a period of Bentham's life during which he admitted much fewer visitors than was the case subsequently.

At this time Mr. Bentham passed some part of every year at Barrow Green House, in a beautiful part of the Surrey hills, a few miles from Godstone, and there I each summer accompanied my father in a long visit. In 1813, Mr. Bentham, my father, and I made an excursion, which included Oxford, Bath and Bristol, Exeter, Plymouth, and Portsmouth. In this journey I saw many things which were instructive to me, and acquired my first taste for natural scenery, in the elementary form of fondness for a "view." In the succeeding winter we moved into a house very near Mr. Bentham's, which my father rented from him, in Queen Square, Westminster. From 1814 to 1817 Mr. Bentham lived during half of each year at Ford Abbey, in Somersetshire (or rather in a part of Devonshire surrounded by Somersetshire), which intervals I had the advantage of passing at that place. This sojourn was, I think, an important circumstance in my education. Nothing contributes more to nourish elevation of sentiments in a people than the large and free character of their habitations. The middle-age architecture, the baronial hall, and the spacious and lofty rooms of this fine old place, so unlike the mean and cramped externals of English middle class life, gave the sentiment of a large and freer existence, and were to me a sort of poetic cultivation, aided also by the character of the grounds in which the Abbey stood; which were riant and secluded, umbrageous, and full of the sound of falling waters.

I owed another of the fortunate circumstances in my education, a year's residence in France, to Mr. Bentham's brother, General Sir Samuel Bentham. I had seen Sir Samuel Bentham and his family at their house near Gosport in the course of the tour already mentioned (he being then Superintendent of the Dockyard at Portsmouth), and during a stay of a few days which they made at Ford Abbey shortly after the peace, before going to live on the Continent. In 1820 they invited me for a six months' visit to them in the South of France, which their kindness ultimately prolonged to nearly a twelvemonth. Sir Samuel Bentham, though of a character of mind different from that of his illustrous brother, was a man of very considerable attainments and general powers, with a decided genius for mechanical art. His wife, a daughter of the celebrated chemist, Dr. Fordyce, was a woman of strong will and decided character, much general knowledge, and great practical good sense of the Edgeworth kind: she was the ruling spirit of the household, as she deserved, and was well qualified, to be. Their family consisted of one son (the eminent botanist) and three daughters, the youngest about two years my senior. I am indebted to them for much and various instruction, and for an almost parental interest in my welfare. When I first joined them, in May 1820, they occupied the Château of Pompignan (still belonging to a descendant of Voltaire's enemy) on the heights overlooking the plain of the Garonne between Montauban and Toulouse. I accompanied them in an excursion to the Pyrenees, including a stay of some duration at Bagnères de Bigorre, a journey to Pau, Bayonne, and Bagnères de Luchon, and an ascent of the Pic du Midi de Bigorre.

This first introduction to the highest order of mountain scenery made the deepest impression on me, and gave a colour to my tastes through life. In October we proceeded by the beautiful mountain route of Castres and St. Pons, from Toulouse to Montpellier, in which last neighbourhood Sir Samuel had just bought the estate of Restinclière, near the foot of the singular mountain of St. Loup. During this residence in France I acquired a familiar knowledge of the French language, and acquaintance with the ordinary French literature; I took lessons in various bodily exercises, in none of which however I made any proficiency; and at Montpellier I attended the excellent winter courses of lectures at the Faculté des Sciences, those of M. Anglada on chemistry, of M. Provençal on zoology, and of a very accomplished representative of the eighteenth century metaphysics, M. Gergonne, on logic, under the name of Philosophy of the Sciences. I also went through a course of the higher mathematics under the private tuition of M. Lenthéric, a professor at the Lycée of Montpellier. But the greatest, perhaps, of the many advantages which I owed to this episode in my education was that of having breathed for a whole year the free and genial atmosphere of Continental life. This advantage was not the less real though I could not then estimate, nor even consciously feel it. Having so little experience of English life, and the few people I knew being mostly such as had public objects, of a large and personally disinterested kind, at heart, I was ignorant of the low moral tone of what, in England, is called society; the habit of, not indeed professing, but taking for granted in every mode of implication, that conduct is of course always directed towards low and petty objects; the absence of high feelings which manifests itself by sneering depreciation of all demonstrations of them, and by general abstinence (except among a few of the stricter religionists) from professing any high principles of action at all, except in those preordained cases in which such profession is put on as part of the costume and formalities of the occasion. I could not then know or estimate the difference between this manner of existence, and that of a people like the French, whose faults, if equally real, are at all events different; among whom sentiments, which by comparison at least may be called elevated, are the current coin of human intercourse, both in books and in private life; and though often evaporating in profession, are yet kept alive in the nation at large by constant exercise, and stimulated by sympathy, so as to form a living and active part of the existence of great numbers of persons, and to be recognized and understood by all. Neither could I then appreciate the general culture of the understanding, which results from the habitual exercise of the feelings, and is thus carried down into the most uneducated classes of several countries on the Continent, in a degree not equalled in England among the so-called educated, except where an unusual tenderness of conscience leads to a habitual exercise of the intellect on questions of right and wrong. I did not know the way in which, among the ordinary English, the absence of interest in things of an unselfish kind, except occasionally in a special thing here and there, and the habit of not speaking to others, nor much even to themselves, about the things in which they do feel interest, causes both their feelings and their intellectual faculties to remain undeveloped, or to develop themselves only in some single and very limited direction; reducing them, considered as spiritual beings, to a kind of negative existence. All these things I did not perceive till long afterwards; but I even then felt, though without stating it clearly to myself, the contrast between the frank sociability and amiability of French personal intercourse, and the English mode of existence in which everybody acts as if everybody else (with few, or no exceptions) was either an enemy or a bore. In France, it is true, the bad as well as the good points, both of individual and of national character, come more to the surface, and break out more fearlessly in ordinary intercourse, than in England: but the general habit of the people is to show, as well as to expect, friendly feeling in every one towards every other, wherever there is not some positive cause for the opposite. In England it is only of the best-bred people, in the upper or upper middle ranks, that anything like this can be said.

In my way through Paris, both going and returning, I passed some time in the house of M. Say, the eminent political economist, who was a friend and correspondent of my father, having become acquainted with him on a visit to England a year or two after the peace. He was a man of the later period of the French Revolution, a fine specimen of the best kind of French Republican, one of those who had never bent the knee to Bonaparte though courted by him to do so; a truly upright, brave, and enlightened man. He lived a quiet and studious life, made happy by warm affections, public and private. He was acquainted with many of the chiefs of the Liberal party, and I saw various noteworthy persons while staying at his house; among whom I have pleasure in the recollection of having once seen Saint-Simon, not yet the founder either of a philosophy or a religion, and considered only as a clever *original*. The chief fruit which I carried away from the society I saw was a strong and permanent interest in Continental Liberalism, of which I ever afterwards kept myself *au courant*, as much as of English politics: a thing not at all usual in those days with Englishmen, and which had a very salutary influence on my development, keeping me free from the error always prevalent in England, and from which even my father with all his superiority to prejudice was not exempt, of judging universal questions by a merely English standard. After passing a few weeks at Caen with an old friend of my father's, I returned to England in July 1821; and my education resumed its ordinary course.

LAST STAGE OF EDUCATION AND FIRST OF SELF-EDUCATION

For the first year or two after my visit to France, I continued my old studies, with the addition of some new ones. When I returned, my father was just finishing for the press his "Elements of Political Economy," and he made me perform an exercise on the manuscript, which Mr. Bentham practised on all his own writings, making what he called, "marginal contents"; a short abstract of every paragraph, to enable the writer more easily to judge of, and improve, the order of the ideas, and the general character of the exposition. Soon after, my father put into my hands Condillac's *Traité des Sensations*, and the logical and metaphysical volumes of his *Cours d'Études;* the first (notwithstanding the superficial resemblance between Condillac's psychological system and my father's) quite as much for a warning as for an example. I am not sure whether it was in this winter or the next that I first read a history of the French Revolution. I learnt with astonishment that the principles of democracy, then apparently in so insignificant and hopeless a minority everywhere in Europe, had borne all before them in France thirty years earlier, and had been the creed of the nation. As may be supposed from this, I had previously a very vague idea of that great commotion. I knew only that the French had thrown off the absolute monarchy of Louis XIV and XV, had put the King and Queen to death, guillotined many persons, one of whom was Lavoisier, and had ultimately fallen under the despotism of Bonaparte. From this time, as was natural, the subject took an immense hold of my feelings. It allied itself with all my juvenile aspirations to the character of a democratic champion. What had happened so lately seemed as if it might easily happen again: and the most transcendant glory I was capable of conceiving was that of figuring, successful or unsuccessful, as a Girondist in an English Convention.

During the winter of 1821-2, Mr. John Austin, with whom at the time of my visit to France my father had but lately become acquainted, kindly allowed me to read Roman law with him. My father, notwithstanding his abhorrence of the chaos of barbarism called English Law, had turned his thoughts towards the bar as on the whole less ineligible for me than any other profession: and these readings with Mr. Austin, who had made Bentham's best ideas his own, and added much to them from other sources and from his own mind, were not only a valuable introduction to legal studies, but an important portion of general education. With Mr. Austin I read Heineccius on the Institutes, his *Roman Antiquities,* and part of his exposition of the Pandects; to which was added a considerable portion of Blackstone. It was at the commencement of these studies that my father, as a needful accompaniment to them, put into my hands Bentham's principal speculations, as interpreted to the Continent, and indeed to all the world, by Dumont, in the *Traité de Législation.* The reading of this book was an epoch in my life, one of the turning points in my mental history.

My previous education had been, in a certain sense, already a course of Benthamism. The Benthamic standard of "the greatest happiness" was that which I had always been taught to apply; I was even familiar with an abstract discussion of it, forming an episode in an unpublished dialogue on "Government," written by my father on the Platonic model. Yet in the first pages of Bentham it burst upon me with all the force of novelty. What thus impressed me was the chapter in which Bentham passed judgment on the common modes of reasoning in morals and legislation, deduced from phrases like "law of nature," "right reason," "the moral sense," "natural rectitude," and the like, and characterized them as dogmatism in disguise, imposing its sentiments upon others under cover of sounding expressions which convey no reason for the sentiment, but set up the sentiment as its own reason. It had not struck me before that Bentham's principle put an end to all this. The feeling rushed upon me, that all previous moralists were superseded, and that here indeed was the commencement of a new era in thought. This impression was strengthened by the manner in which Bentham put into scientific form the application of the happiness principle to the morality of actions, by analysing the various classes and orders of their consequences. But what struck me at the time most of all, was the Classification of Offences, which is much more clear, compact and imposing in Dumont's *rédaction* than in the original work of Bentham from which it was taken. Logic and the dialectics of Plato, which had formed so large a part of my previous training, had given me a strong relish for accurate classification. This taste had been strengthened and enlightened by the study of botany, on the principles of what is called the Natural Method, which I had taken up with great zeal, though only as an amusement, during my stay in France; and when I found scientific classification applied to the great and complex subject of Punishable Acts, under the guidance of the ethical principle of Pleasurable and Painful Consequences, followed out in the method of detail introduced into these subjects by Bentham, I felt taken up to an eminence from which I could survey a vast mental domain, and see stretching out into the distance intellectual results beyond all computation. As I proceeded further, there seemed to be added to this intellectual clearness, the most inspiring prospects of practical improvements in human affairs. To Bentham's general view of the construction of a body of law I was not altogether a stranger, having read with attention that admirable compendium, my father's article "Jurisprudence": but I had read it with little profit and scarcely any interest, no doubt from its extremely general and abstract character, and also because it concerned the form more than the substance of the *corpus juris,* the logic rather than the ethics of law. But Bentham's subject was Legislation, of which Jurisprudence is only the formal part: and at every page he seemed to open a clearer and broader conception of what human opinions and institutions ought to be, how they might be made what they ought to be, and how far removed from it they now are. When I laid down the last volume of the *Traité,* I had become a different being. The "principle of utility" understood as Bentham understood it, and applied in the manner in which he applied it through these three volumes, fell exactly into its place as the keystone which held together the detached and fragmentary component parts of my knowledge and beliefs. It gave unity to my conceptions of things. I now had opinions; a creed, a doctrine, a philosophy; in one among the best senses of the word, a religion; the inculcation and diffusion of which could be made the principal outward purpose of a life. And I had a grand conception laid before me of changes to be effected in the condition of mankind through that doctrine. The *Traité de Législation* wound up with what was to me a most impressive picture of human life as it would be made by such opinions and such laws as were recommended in the treatise. The anticipations of practicable improvement were studiously moderate, deprecating and discountenancing as reveries of vague enthusiasm many things which will one day seem so natural to human beings, that injustice will probably be done to those who once thought them chimerical. But, in my state of mind, this appearance of superiority to illusion added to the effect which Bentham's doctrines produced on me, by heightening the impression of mental power, and the vista of improvement which he did open was sufficiently large and brilliant to light up my life, as well as to give a definite shape to my aspirations.

After this I read, from time to time, the most important of the other works of Bentham which had then seen the light, either as written by himself or as edited by Dumont. This was my private reading: while, under my father's direction, my studies were carried into the higher branches of analytic psychology. I now read Locke's *Essay*, and wrote out an account of it, consisting of a complete abstract of every chapter, with such remarks as occurred to me: which was read by, or (I think) to, my father, and discussed throughout. I performed the same process with Helvétius' *De l'Esprit*, which I read of my own choice. This preparation of abstracts, subject to my father's censorship, was of great service to me, by compelling precision in conceiving and expressing psychological doctrines, whether accepted as truths or only regarded as the opinion of others. After Helvétius, my father made me study what he deemed the really master-production in the philosophy of mind, Hartley's *Observations on Man*. This book, though it did not, like the *Traité de Législation*, give a new colour to my existence, made a very similar impression on me in regard to its immediate subject. Hartley's explanation, incomplete as in many points it is, of the more complex mental phenomena by the law of association, commended itself to me at once as a real analysis, and made me feel by contrast the insufficiency of the merely verbal generalizations of Condillac, and even of the instructive gropings and feelings about for psychological explanations of Locke. It was at this very time that my father commenced writing his *Analysis of the Mind*, which carried Hartley's mode of explaining the mental phenomena to so much greater length and depth. He could only command the concentration of thought necessary for this work during the complete leisure of his holiday of a month or six weeks annually: and he commenced it in the summer of 1822, in the first holiday he passed at Dorking; in which neighbourhood, from that time to the end of his life, with the exception of two years, he lived, as far as his official duties permitted, for six months of every year. He worked at the *Analysis* during several successive vacations, up to the year 1829 when it was published, and allowed me to read the manuscript, portion by portion, as it advanced. The other principal English writers on mental philosophy I read as I felt inclined, particularly Berkeley, Hume's *Essays,* Reid, Dugald Stewart and Brown on *Cause and Effect.* Brown's *Lectures* I did not read until two or three years later, nor at that time had my father himself read them.

Among the works read in the course of this year, which contributed materially to my development, I ought to mention a book (written on the foundation of some of Bentham's manuscripts and published under the pseudonym of Philip Beauchamp) entitled *Analysis of the Influence of Natural Religion on the Temporal Happiness of Mankind.* This was an examination not of the truth, but of the usefulness of religious belief, in the most general sense, apart from the peculiarities of any special Revelation; which, of all the parts of the discussion concerning religion, is the most important in this age, in which real belief in any religious doctrine is feeble and precarious, but the opinion of its necessity for moral and social purposes almost universal; and when those who reject revelation very generally take refuge in an optimistic Deism, a worship of the order of Nature and the supposed course of Providence at least as full of contradictions, and perverting to the moral sentiments, as any of the forms of Christianity, if only it is as completely realized. Yet, very little, with any claim to a philosophical character, has been written by sceptics against the usefulness of this form of belief. The volume bearing the name of Philip Beauchamp had this for its special object. Having been shown to my father in manuscript, it was put into my hands by him, and I made a marginal analysis of it as I had done of the *Elements of Political Economy.* Next to the *Traité de Législation,* it was one of the books which by the searching character of its analysis produced the greatest effect upon me. On reading it lately after an interval of many years, I find it to have some of the defects as well as the merits of the Benthamic modes of thought, and to contain, as I now think, many weak arguments, but with a great overbalance of sound ones, and much good material for a more completely philosophic and conclusive treatment of the subject.

I have now, I believe, mentioned all the books which had any considerable effect on my early mental development. From this point I began to carry on my intellectual cultivation by writing still more than by reading. In the summer of 1822 I wrote my first argumentative essay. I remember very little about it, except that it was an attack on what I regarded as the aristocratic prejudice, that the rich were, or were likely to be, superior in moral qualities to the poor. My performance was entirely argumentative, without any of the declamation which the subject would admit of, and might be expected to suggest to a young writer. In that department however I was, and remained, very inapt. Dry argument was the only thing I could manage, or willingly attempted; though passively I was very susceptible to the effect of all composition, whether in the form of poetry or oratory, which appealed to the feelings on any basis of reason. My father, who knew nothing of this essay until it was finished, was well satisfied, and as I learnt from others, even pleased with it; but, perhaps from a desire to promote the exercise of other mental faculties than the purely logical, he advised me to make my next exercise in composition one of the oratorical kind: on which suggestion, availing myself of my familiarity with Greek history and ideas and with the Athenian orators, I wrote two speeches, one an accusation, the other a defence of Pericles, on a supposed impeachment for not marching out to fight the Lacedaemonians on their invasion of Attica. After this I continued to write papers on subjects often very much beyond my capacity, but with great benefit both from the exercise itself, and from the discussions which it led to with my father.

I had now also begun to converse, on general subjects, with the instructed men with whom I came in contact: and the opportunities of such contact naturally became more numerous. The two friends of my father from whom I derived most, and with whom I most associated, were Mr. Grote and Mr. John Austin. The acquaintance of both with my father was recent, but had ripened rapidly into intimacy. Mr. Grote was introduced to my father by Mr. Ricardo, I think in 1819 (being then about twenty-five years old), and sought assiduously his society and conversation. Already a highly instructed man, he was yet, by the side of my father, a tyro on the great subjects of human opinion; but he rapidly seized on my father's best ideas; and in the department of political opinion he made himself known as early as 1820, by a pamphlet in defence of Radical Reform, in reply to a celebrated article by Sir James Mackintosh, then lately published in the *Edinburgh Review*. Mr. Grote's father, the banker, was, I believe, a thorough Tory, and his mother intensely Evangelical; so that for his liberal opinions he was in no way indebted to home influences. But, unlike most persons who have the prospect of being rich by inheritance, he had, though actively engaged in the business of banking, devoted a great portion of time to philosophic studies; and his intimacy with my father did much to decide the character of the next stage in his mental progress. Him I often visited, and my conversations with him on political, moral, and philosophical subjects gave me, in addition to much valuable instruction, all the pleasure and benefit of sympathetic communion with a man of the high intellectual and moral eminence which his life and writings have since manifested to the world.

Mr. Austin, who was four or five years older than Mr. Grote, was the eldest son of a retired miller in Suffolk, who had made money by contracts during the war, and who must have been a man of remarkable qualities, as I infer from the fact that all his sons were of more than common ability and all eminently gentlemen. The one with whom we are now concerned, and whose writings on jurisprudence have made him celebrated, was for some time in the army, and served in Sicily under Lord William Bentinck. After the peace he sold his commission and studied for the bar, to which he had been called for some time before my father knew him. He was not, like Mr. Grote, to any extent a pupil of my father, but he had attained, by reading and thought, a considerable number of the same opinions, modified by his own very decided individuality of character. He was a man of great intellectual powers which in conversation appeared at their very best; from the vigour and richness of expression with which, under the excitement of discussion, he was accustomed to maintain some view or other of most general subjects; and from an appearance of not only strong, but deliberate and collected will; mixed with a certain bitterness, partly derived from temperament, and partly from the general cast of his feelings and reflections. The dissatisfaction with life and the world, felt more or less in the present state of society and intellect by every discerning and highly conscientious mind, gave in his case a rather melancholy tinge to the character, very natural to those whose passive moral susceptibilities are more than proportioned to their active energies. For it must be said, that the strength of will of which his manner seemed to give such strong assurance expended itself principally in manner. With great zeal for human improvement, a strong sense of duty, and capacities and acquirements the extent of which is proved by the writings he has left, he hardly ever completed any intellectual task of magnitude. He had so high a standard of what ought to be done, so exaggerated a sense of deficiencies in his own performances, and was so unable to content himself with the amount of elaboration sufficient for the occasion and the purpose, that he not only spoilt much of his work for ordinary use by overlabouring it, but spent so much time and exertion in superfluous study and thought, that when his task ought to have been completed, he had generally worked himself into an illness without having half finished what he undertook. From this mental infirmity (of which he is not the sole example among the accomplished and able men whom I have known), combined with liability to frequent attacks of disabling though not dangerous ill-health, he accomplished, through life, little in comparison with what he seemed capable of; but what he did produce is held in the very highest estimation by the most competent judges; and, like Coleridge, he might plead as a set-off that he had been to many persons, through his conversation, a source not only of much instruction but of great elevation of character. On me his influence was most salutary. It was moral in the best sense. He took a sincere and kind interest in me, far beyond what could have been expected towards a mere youth from a man of his age, standing, and what seemed austerity of character. There was in his conversation and demeanour a tone of highmindedness which did not show itself so much, if the quality existed as much, in any of the other persons with whom at that time I associated. My intercourse with him was the more beneficial, owing to his being of a different mental type from all other intellectual men whom I frequented, and he from the first set himself decidedly against the prejudices and narrownesses which are almost sure to be found in a young man formed by a particular mode of thought or a particular social circle.

His younger brother, Charles Austin, of whom at this time and for the next year or two I saw much, had also a great effect on me, though of a very different description. He was but a few years older than myself, and had then just left the University, where he had shone with great éclat as a man of intellect and a brilliant orator and converser. The effect he produced on his Cambridge contemporaries deserves to be accounted an historical event; for to it may in part be traced the tendency towards Liberalism in general, and the Benthamic and politico-economic form of it in particular, which showed itself in a portion of the more active-minded young men of the higher classes from this time to 1830. The Union Debating Society, at that time at the height of its reputation, was an arena where what were then thought extreme opinions, in politics and philosophy, were weekly asserted, face to face with their opposites, before audiences consisting of the élite of the Cambridge youth: and though many persons afterwards of more or less note (of whom Lord Macaulay is the most celebrated), gained their first oratorical laurels in those debates, the really influential mind among these intellectual gladiators was Charles Austin. He continued, after leaving the University, to be, by his conversation and personal ascendancy, a leader among the same class of young men who had been his associates there; and he attached me among others to his car. Through him I became acquainted with Macaulay, Hyde and Charles Villiers, Strutt (now Lord Belper), Romilly (now Lord Romilly and Master of the Rolls), and various others who subsequently figured in literature or politics, and among whom I heard discussions on many topics, as yet to a certain degree new to me. The influence of Charles Austin over me differed from that of the persons I have hitherto mentioned, in being not the influence of a man over a boy, but that of an elder contemporary. It was through him that I first felt myself, not a pupil under teachers, but a man among men. He was the first person of intellect whom I met on a ground of equality, though as yet much his inferior on that common ground. He was a man who never failed to impress greatly those with whom he came in contact, even when their opinions were the very reverse of his. The impression he gave was that of boundless strength, together with talents which, combined with such apparent force of will and character, seemed capable of dominating the world. Those who knew him, whether friendly to him or not, always anticipated that he would play a conspicuous part in public life. It is seldom that men produce so great an immediate effect by speech, unless they, in some degree, lay themselves out for it; and he did this in no ordinary degree. He loved to strike, and even to startle. He knew that decision is the greatest element of effect, and he uttered his opinions with all the decision he could throw into them, never so well pleased as when he astonished any one by their audacity. Very unlike his brother, who made war against the narrower interpretations and applications of the principles they both professed, he, on the contrary, presented the Benthamic doctrines in the most startling form of which they were susceptible, exaggerating everything in them which tended to consequences offensive to any one's preconceived feelings. All which, he defended with such verve and vivacity, and carried off by a manner so agreeable as well as forcible, that he always either came off victor, or divided the honours of the field. It is my belief that much of the notion popularly entertained of the tenets and sentiments of what are called Benthamites or Utilitarians had its origin in paradoxes thrown out by Charles Austin. It must be said, however, that his example was followed, *haud passibus aequis* [without restraint], by younger proselytes, and that to *outrer* whatever was by anybody considered offensive in the doctrines and maxims of Benthamism became at one time the badge of a small coterie of youths. All of these who had anything in them, myself among others, quickly outgrew this boyish vanity; and those who had not, became tired of differing from other people, and gave up both the good and the bad part of the heterodox opinions they had for some time professed.

It was in the winter of 1822-3 that I formed the plan of a little society, to be composed of young men agreeing in fundamental principles—acknowledging Utility as their standard in ethics and politics, and a certain number of the principal corollaries drawn from it in the philosophy I had accepted—and meeting once a fortnight to read essays and discuss questions conformably to the premises thus agreed on. The fact would hardly be worth mentioning, but for the circumstance that the name I gave to the society I had planned was the Utilitarian Society. It was the first time that any one had taken the title of Utilitarian; and the term made its way into the language from this humble source. I did not invent the word, but found it in one of Galt's novels, the *Annals of the Parish,* in which the Scotch clergyman, of whom the book is a supposed autobiography, is represented as warning his parishioners not to leave the Gospel and become utilitarians. With a boy's fondness for a name and a banner I seized on the word, and for some years called myself and others by it as a sectarian appellation; and it came to be occasionally used by some others holding the opinions which it was intended to designate. As those opinions attracted more notice, the term was repeated by strangers and opponents, and got into rather common use just about the time when those who had originally assumed it, laid down that along with other sectarian characteristics. The Society so called consisted at first of no more than three members, one of whom, being Mr. Bentham's amanuensis, obtained for us permission to hold our meetings in his house. The number never, I think, reached ten, and the society was broken up in 1826. It had thus an existence of about three years and a half. The chief effect of it as regards myself, over and above the benefit of practice in oral discussion, was that of bringing me in contact with several young men at that time less advanced than myself, among whom, as they professed the same opinions, I was for some time a sort of leader, and had considerable influence on their mental progress. Any young man of education who fell in my way, and whose opinions were not incompatible with those of the Society, I endeavoured to press into its service; and some others I probably should never have known, had they not joined it. Those of the members who became my intimate companions—no one of whom was in any sense of the word a disciple, but all of them independent thinkers on their own basis—were William Eyton Tooke, son of the eminent political economist, a young man of singular worth both moral and intellectual, lost to the world by an early death; his friend William Ellis, an original thinker in the field of political economy, now honourably known by his apostolic exertions for the improvement of education; George Graham, afterwards an official assignee of the Bankruptcy Court, a thinker of originality and power on almost all abstract subjects; and (from the time when he came first to England to study for the bar in 1824 or 1825) a man who has made considerably more noise in the world than any of these, John Arthur Roebuck.

In May 1823, my professional occupation and status for the next thirty-five years of my life were decided by my father's obtaining for me an appointment from the East India Company, in the office of the Examiner of India Correspondence, immediately under himself. I was appointed in the usual manner, at the bottom of the list of clerks, to rise, at least in the first instance, by seniority; but with the understanding that I should be employed from the beginning in preparing drafts of despatches, and be thus trained up as a successor to those who then filled the higher departments of the office. My drafts of course required, for some time, much revision from my immediate superiors, but I soon became well acquainted with the business, and by my father's instructions and the general growth of my own powers, I was in a few years qualified to be, and practically was, the chief conductor of the correspondence with India in one of the leading departments, that of the Native States. This continued to be my official duty until I was appointed Examiner, only two years before the time when the abolition of the East India Company as a political body determined my retirement. I do not know any one of the occupations by which a subsistence can now be gained, more suitable than such as this to any one who, not being in independent circumstances, desires to devote a part of the twenty-four hours to private intellectual pursuits. Writing for the press cannot be recommended as a permanent resource to any one qualified to accomplish anything in the higher departments of literature or thought: not only on account of the uncertainty of this means of livelihood, especially if the writer has a conscience, and will not consent to serve any opinions except his own, but also because the writings by which one can live are not the writings which themselves live, and are never those in which the writer does his best. Books destined to form future thinkers take too much time to write, and when written come, in general, too slowly into notice and repute, to be relied on for subsistence. Those who have to support themselves by their pen must depend on literary drudgery, or at best on writings addressed to the multitude; and can employ in the pursuits of their own choice only such time as they can spare from those of necessity; which is generally less than the leisure allowed by office occupations, while the effect on the mind is far more enervating and fatiguing. For my own part I have, through life, found office duties an actual rest from the other mental occupations which I have carried on simultaneously with them. They were sufficiently intellectual not to be a distasteful drudgery, without being such as to cause any strain upon the mental powers of a person used to abstract thought, or to the labour of careful literary composition. The drawbacks, for every mode of life has its drawbacks, were not, however, unfelt by me. I cared little for the loss of the chances of riches and honours held out by some of the professions, particularly the bar, which had been, as I have already said, the profession thought of for me. But I was not indifferent to exclusion from Parliament, and public life: and I felt very sensibly the more immediate unpleasantness of confinement to London; the holiday allowed by India-house practice not exceeding a month in the year, while my taste was strong for a country life, and my sojourn in France had left behind it an ardent desire of travelling. But though these tastes could not be freely indulged, they were at no time entirely sacrificed. I passed most Sundays, throughout the year, in the country, taking long rural walks on that day even when residing in London. The month's holiday was, for a few years, passed at my father's house in the country: afterwards a part or the whole was spent in tours, chiefly pedestrian, with some one or more of the young men who were my chosen companions; and, at a later period, in longer journeys or excursions, alone or with other friends. France, Belgium, and Rhenish Germany were within easy reach of the annual holiday: and two longer absences, one of three, the other of six months, under medical advice, added Switzerland, the Tyrol, and Italy to my list. Fortunately, also, both these journeys occurred rather early, so as to give the benefit and charm of the remembrance to a large portion of life.

I am disposed to agree with what has been surmised by others, that the opportunity which my official position gave me of learning by personal observation the necessary conditions of the practical conduct of public affairs has been of considerable value to me as a theoretical reformer of the opinions and institutions of my time. Not, indeed, that public business transacted on paper, to take effect on the other side of the globe, was of itself calculated to give much practical knowledge of life. But the occupation accustomed me to see and hear the difficulties of every course, and the means of obviating them, stated and discussed deliberately with a view to execution; it gave me opportunities of perceiving when public measures, and other political facts, did not produce the effects which had been expected of them, and from what causes; above all, it was valuable to me by making me, in this portion of my activity, merely one wheel in a machine, the whole of which had to work together. As a speculative writer, I should have had no one to consult but myself, and should have encountered in my speculations none of the obstacles which would have started up whenever they came to be applied to practice. But as a secretary conducting political correspondence, I could not issue an order or express an opinion, without satisfying various persons very unlike myself that the thing was fit to be done. I was thus in a good position for finding out by practice the mode of putting a thought which gives it easiest admittance into minds not prepared for it by habit; while I became practically conversant with the difficulties of moving bodies of men, the necessities of compromise, the art of sacrificing the non-essential to preserve the essential. I learnt how to obtain the best I could, when I could not obtain everything; instead of being indignant or dispirited because I could not have entirely my own way, to be pleased and encouraged when I could have the smallest part of it; and when even that could not be, to bear with complete equanimity the being overruled altogether. I have found, through life, these acquisitions to be of the greatest possible importance for personal happiness, and they are also a very necessary condition for enabling any one, either as theorist or as practical man, to effect the greatest amount of good compatible with his opportunities.

The foregoing consists of Chapters I–III of John Stuart Mill's AUTOBIOGRAPHY.

Mark Twain [1]

1835–1910

In 1883, when Mark Twain was already a famous author, he could look back with longing on his career as a river-boat pilot. "I loved the profession far better than any I have followed since," he wrote. What had been the great appeal? In *Life on the Mississippi* he explains.

The sleepy town of Hannibal, Missouri, was galvanized each day by the arrival of the packet boat. All was turmoil and excitement, and Mark Twain and other small boys raced to the dock, as to a circus. For them the desire to be a steamboat pilot was as fond a dream as being an airplane pilot or an astronaut is for boys today. Such dreams are achieved only by determination and courage.

Mark Twain's apprenticeship under his pilot chief was grueling, and he tells us that if he had known what was required he "should not have had the courage to begin." He was taught to recognize the changing shape of the river, the deadly shoals appearing overnight, the feel of the boat, and the face of the water. His memory had to be quick, his judgment alert, and he had to have the courage and confidence to rely on them. "Every trivial detail of twelve hundred miles of river" had to be known "with absolute exactness."

At the wheel on one occasion he was ordered to "shave those steamships as close as you'd peel an apple." It was certainly hair raising, for he knew that one little error could be fatal. Ship, cargo, and all hands and passengers, if there were any, would be swallowed up by the treacherous river. Yet Twain took "a measureless pride" in the profession, once he had learned it. The river-boat pilot, he said, is the most independent being on earth—more so than a king,

---

[1] For a biography of Mark Twain, see Vol. 2, pp. 342–344, in this set.

who is, after all, a servant of parliament. Once the ship is under way, the pilot's word is law, and not even a king would dare to contradict him.

Today we can read stories of aviation written by such flyers as Saint-Exupery and Charles Lindbergh. Our newspapers and magazines give us minute accounts of the astronauts' flights. Thousands of boys are stirred by the daring skill and absolute command of these modern heroes, as they were in Mark Twain's day by the lonely courage of the pilot.

Life on the Mississippi is unique as the saga of the nineteenth-century pilot on the majestic old river, and it is notable for its humorous realism. Rudyard Kipling had Mark Twain's humor in mind when he said, "Cervantes was a relation of his." As you read, you might keep a lookout for this alleged similarity.

Learning the River

from *Life on the Mississippi*

THE RIVER AND ITS HISTORY

The Mississippi is well worth reading about. It is not a commonplace river, but on the contrary is in all ways remarkable. Considering the Missouri its main branch, it is the longest river in the world—four thousand three hundred miles. It seems safe to say that it is also the crookedest river in the world, since in one part of its journey it uses up one thousand three hundred miles to cover the same ground that the crow would fly over in six hundred and seventy-five. It discharges three times as much water as the St. Lawrence, twenty-five times as much as the Rhine, and three hundred and thirty-eight times as much as the Thames. No other river has so vast a drainage basin; it draws its water supply from twenty-eight states and territories; from Delaware on the Atlantic seaboard, and from all the country between that and Idaho on the Pacific slope—a spread of forty-five degrees of longitude. The Mississippi receives and carries to the Gulf water from fifty-four subordinate rivers that are navigable by steamboats, and from some hundreds that are navigable by flats and keels. The area of its drainage basin is as great as the combined areas of England, Wales, Scotland, Ireland, France, Spain, Portugal, Germany, Austria, Italy, and Turkey; and almost all this wide region is fertile; the Mississippi valley, proper, is exceptionally so.

It is a remarkable river in this: that instead of widening toward its mouth, it grows narrower; grows narrower and deeper. From the junction of the Ohio to a point halfway down to the sea, the width averages a mile in high water; thence to the sea the width steadily diminishes, until, at the "Passes," above the mouth, it is but little over half a mile. At the junction of the Ohio the Mississippi's depth is eighty-seven feet; the depth increases gradually, reaching one hundred and twenty-nine just above the mouth.

The difference in rise and fall is also remarkable—not in the upper, but in the lower river. The rise is tolerably uniform down to Natchez (three hundred and sixty miles above the mouth)—about fifty feet. But at Bayou La Fourche the river rises only twenty-four feet; at New Orleans only fifteen, and just above the mouth only two and one-half.

An article in the New Orleans *Times-Democrat*, based upon reports of able engineers, states that the river annually empties four hundred and six million tons of mud into the Gulf of Mexico—which brings to mind Captain Marryat's rude name for the Mississippi—"the Great Sewer." This mud, solidified, would make a mass a mile square and two hundred and forty-one feet high.

The mud deposit gradually extends the land—but only gradually; it has extended it not quite a third of a mile in the two hundred years which have elapsed since the river took its place in history.

The belief of the scientific people is that the mouth used to be at Baton Rouge, where the hills cease, and that the two hundred miles of land between there and the Gulf was built by the river. This gives us the age of that piece of country, without any trouble at all—one hundred and twenty thousand years. Yet it is much the youthfulest batch of country that lies around there anywhere.

The Mississippi is remarkable in still another way—its disposition to make prodigious jumps by cutting through narrow necks of land, and thus straightening and shortening itself. More than once it has shortened itself thirty miles at a single jump!

These cutoffs have had curious effects: they have thrown several river towns out into the rural districts, and built up sand bars and forests in front of them. The town of Delta used to be three miles below Vicksburg; a recent cutoff has radically changed the position, and Delta is now *two miles above* Vicksburg.

Both of these river towns have been retired to the country by that cutoff. A cutoff plays havoc with boundary lines and jurisdictions: for instance, a man is living in the state of Mississippi today, a cutoff occurs tonight, and tomorrow the man finds himself and his land over on the other side of the river, within the boundaries and subject to the laws of the state of Louisiana! Such a thing, happening in the upper river in the old times, could have transferred a slave from Missouri to Illinois and made a free man of him.

The Mississippi does not alter its locality by cutoffs alone; it is always changing its habitat *bodily*—is always moving bodily *sidewise*. At Hard Times, Louisiana, the river is two miles west of the region it used to occupy. As a result, the original site of that settlement is not now in Louisiana at all, but on the other side of the river, in the state of Mississippi. *Nearly the whole of that one thousand three hundred miles of old Mississippi River which La Salle floated down in his canoes, two hundred years ago, is good solid dry ground now.* The river lies to the right of it, in places, and to the left of it in other places.

Although the Mississippi's mud builds land but slowly, down at the mouth, where the Gulf's billows interfere with its work, it builds fast enough in better-protected regions higher up: for instance, Prophet's Island contained one thousand five hundred acres of land thirty years ago; since then the river has added seven hundred acres to it.

THE BOY'S AMBITION

When I was a boy, there was but one permanent ambition among my comrades in our village [1] on the west bank of the Mississippi River. That was, to be a steamboatman. We had transient ambitions of other sorts, but they were only transient. When a circus came and went, it left us all burning to become clowns; the first Negro minstrel show that ever came to our section left us all suffering to try that kind of life; now and then we had a hope that, if we lived and were good, God would permit us to be pirates. These ambitions faded out, each in its turn; but the ambition to be a steamboatman always remained.

Once a day a cheap, gaudy packet arrived upward from St. Louis, and another downward from Keokuk. Before these events, the day was glorious with expectancy; after them, the day was a dead and empty thing. Not only the boys, but the whole village, felt this. After all these years I can picture that old time to myself now, just as it was then: the white town drowsing in the sunshine of a summer's morning; the streets empty, or pretty nearly so; one or two clerks sitting in front of the Water Street stores, with their splint-bottomed chairs tilted back against the walls, chins on breasts, hats slouched over their faces, asleep—with shingle-shavings enough around to show what broke them down; a sow and a litter of pigs loafing along the sidewalk, doing a good business in watermelon rinds and seeds; two or three lonely little freight piles scattered about the "levee"; a pile of "skids" on the slope of the stone-paved wharf, and the fragrant town drunkard asleep in the shadow of them; two or three wood flats at the head of the wharf, but nobody to listen to the

---

1. Hannibal, Missouri.

peaceful lapping of the wavelets against them; the great Mississippi, the majestic, the magnificent Mississippi, rolling its mile-wide tide along, shining in the sun; the dense forest away on the other side; the "point" above the town, and the "point" below, bounding the river glimpse and turning it into a sort of sea, and withal a very still and brilliant and lonely one. Presently a film of dark smoke appears above one of those remote "points"; instantly a Negro drayman, famous for his quick eye and prodigious voice, lifts up the cry, "S-t-e-a-m-boat a-comin'!" and the scene changes! The town drunkard stirs, the clerks wake up, a furious clatter of drays follows, every house and store pours out a human contribution, and all in a twinkling the dead town is alive and moving. Drays, carts, men, boys, all go hurrying from many quarters to a common center, the wharf. Assembled there, the people fasten their eyes upon the coming boat as upon a wonder they are seeing for the first time. And the boat *is* rather a handsome sight, too. She is long and sharp and trim and pretty; she has two tall, fancy-topped chimneys, with a gilded device of some kind swung between them; a fanciful pilothouse, all glass and "gingerbread," perched on top of the "texas" deck behind them; the paddle boxes are gorgeous with a picture or with gilded rays above the boat's name; the boiler deck, the hurricane deck, and the texas deck are fenced and ornamented with clean white railings; there is a flag gallantly flying from the jack staff; the furnace doors are open and the fires glaring bravely; the upper decks are black with passengers; the captain stands by the big bell, calm, imposing, the envy of all; great volumes of the blackest smoke are rolling and tumbling out of the chimneys—a husbanded grandeur created with a bit of pitch pine just before arriving at a town; the crew are grouped on the forecastle; the broad stage is run far out over the port bow, and an envied deck hand stands picturesquely on the end of it with a coil of rope in his hand; the pent steam is screaming through the gauge cocks; the captain lifts his hand, a bell rings, the wheels stop; then they turn back, churning the water to foam, and the steamer is at rest. Then such a scramble as there is to get aboard, and to get ashore, and to take in freight and to discharge freight, all at one and the same time; and such a yelling and cursing as the mates facilitate it all with! Ten minutes later the steamer is under way again, with no flag on the jack staff and no black smoke issuing from the chimneys. After ten more minutes the town is dead again, and the town drunkard asleep by the skids once more.

My father was a justice of the peace, and I supposed he possessed the power of life and death over all men, and could hang anybody that offended him. This was distinction enough for me as a general thing; but the desire to be a steamboatman kept intruding, nevertheless. I first wanted to be a cabin boy, so that I could come out with a white apron on and shake a tablecloth over the side, where all my old comrades could see me: later I thought I would rather be the deck hand who stood on the end of the stage plank with the coil of rope in his hand, because he was particularly conspicuous. But these were only daydreams—they were too heavenly to be contemplated as real possibilities. By and by one of our boys went away. He was not heard of for a long time. At last he turned up as apprentice engineer or "striker" on a steamboat. This thing shook the bottom out of all my Sunday-school teachings. That boy had been notoriously worldly, and I just the reverse; yet he was exalted to this eminence, and I left in obscurity and misery. There was nothing generous about this fellow in his greatness. He would always manage to have a rusty bolt to scrub while his boat tarried at our town, and he would sit on the inside guard and scrub it, where we all could see him and envy him and loathe him. And whenever his boat was laid up he would come home and swell around the town in his blackest and greasiest clothes, so that nobody could help remembering that he was a steamboatman; and he used all sorts of steamboat technicalities in his talk, as if he were so used to them that he forgot common people could not understand them. He would speak of the "labboard" side of a horse in an easy, natural way that would make one wish he was dead. And he was always talking about "St. Looy" like an old citizen; he would refer casually to occasions when he was "coming down Fourth Street," or when he was "passing by the Planter's House," or when there was a fire and he took a turn on the brakes of "the old Big Missouri"; and then he would go on and lie about how many towns the size of ours were burned down there that day. Two or three of the boys had long been persons of consideration among us because they had been to St. Louis once and had a vague general knowledge of its wonders, but the day of their glory was over now. They lapsed into a humble silence, and learned to disappear when the ruthless "cub"-engineer approached. This fellow had money, too, and hair oil. Also an ignorant silver watch and a showy brass watch chain. He wore a leather belt and used no suspenders. If ever a youth was cordially admired and hated by his comrades, this one was. No girl could withstand his charms. He "cut out" every boy in the village. When his boat blew up at last, it diffused a tranquil contentment among us such as we had not known for months. But when he came home the next week, alive, renowned, and appeared in church all battered up and bandaged, a shining hero, stared at and wondered over by everybody, it seemed to us that the partiality of Providence for an undeserving reptile had reached a point where it was open to criticism.

This creature's career could produce but one result, and it speedily followed. Boy after boy managed to get on the river. The minister's son became an engineer. The doctor's and the postmaster's sons became "mud clerks"; the wholesale liquor dealer's son became a barkeeper on a boat; four sons of the chief merchant, and two sons of the county judge, became pilots. Pilot was the grandest position of all. The pilot, even in those days of trivial wages, had a princely salary—from a hundred and fifty to two hundred and fifty dollars a month, and no board to pay. Two months of his wages would pay a preacher's salary for a year. Now some of us were left disconsolate. We could not get on the river—at least our parents would not let us.

So, by and by, I ran away. I said I would never come home again till I was a pilot and could come in glory. But somehow I could not manage it. I went meekly aboard a few of the boats that lay packed together like sardines at the long St. Louis wharf, and humbly inquired for the pilots, but got only a cold shoulder and short words from mates and clerks. I had to make the best of this sort of treatment for the time being, but I had comforting daydreams of a future when I should be a great and honored pilot, with plenty of money, and could kill some of these mates and clerks and pay for them.

A CUB-PILOT'S EXPERIENCE

What with lying on the rocks four days at Louisville, and some other delays, the poor old *Paul Jones* fooled away about two weeks in making the voyage from Cincinnati to New Orleans. This gave me a chance to get acquainted with one of the pilots, and he taught me how to steer the boat, and thus made the fascination of river life more potent than ever for me.

It also gave me a chance to get acquainted with a youth who had taken deck passage—more's the pity; for he easily borrowed six dollars of me on a promise to return to the boat and pay it back to me the day after we should arrive. But he probably died or forgot, for he never came. It was doubtless the former, since he had said his parents were wealthy, and he only traveled deck passage because it was cooler.[2]

---

2. "Deck" passage—*i. e.*, steerage passage.

I soon discovered two things. One was that a vessel would not be likely to sail for the mouth of the Amazon under ten or twelve years; and the other was that the nine or ten dollars still left in my pocket would not suffice for so impossible an exploration as I had planned, even if I could afford to wait for a ship. Therefore it followed that I must contrive a new career. The *Paul Jones* was now bound for St. Louis. I planned a siege against my pilot, and at the end of three hard days he surrendered. He agreed to teach me the Mississippi River from New Orleans to St. Louis for five hundred dollars, payable out of the first wages I should receive after graduating. I entered upon the small enterprise of "learning" twelve or thirteen hundred miles of the great Mississippi River with the easy confidence of my time of life. If I had really known what I was about to require of my faculties, I should not have had the courage to begin. I supposed that all a pilot had to do was to keep his boat in the river, and I did not consider that that could be much of a trick, since it was so wide.

The boat backed out from New Orleans at four in the afternoon, and it was "our watch" until eight. Mr. Bixby, my chief, "straightened her up," plowed her along past the sterns of the other boats that lay at the Levee, and then said, "Here, take her; shave those steamships as close as you'd peel an apple." I took the wheel, and my heartbeat fluttered up into the hundreds; for it seemed to me that we were about to scrape the side off every ship in the line, we were so close. I held my breath and began to claw the boat away from the danger; and I had my own opinion of the pilot who had known no better than to get us into such peril, but I was too wise to express it. In half a minute I had a wide margin of safety intervening between the *Paul Jones* and the ships; and within ten seconds more I was set aside in disgrace, and Mr. Bixby was going into danger again and flaying me alive with abuse of my cowardice. I was stung, but I was obliged to admire the easy confidence with which my chief loafed from side to side of his wheel, and trimmed the ships so closely that disaster seemed ceaselessly imminent. When he had cooled a little he told me that the easy water was close ashore and the current outside, and therefore we must hug the bank, upstream, to get the benefit of the former, and stay well out, downstream, to take advantage of the latter. In my own mind I resolved to be a downstream pilot and leave the upstreaming to people dead to prudence.

Now and then Mr. Bixby called my attention to certain things. Said he, "This is Six-Mile Point." I assented. It was pleasant enough information, but I could not see the bearing of it. I was not conscious that it was a matter of any interest to me. Another time he said, "This is Nine-Mile Point." Later he said, "This is Twelve-Mile Point." They were all about level with the water's edge; they all looked about alike to me; they were monotonously unpicturesque. I hoped Mr. Bixby would change the subject. But no; he would crowd up around a point, hugging the shore with affection, and then say: "The slack water ends here, abreast this bunch of China trees; now we cross over." So he crossed over. He gave me the wheel once or twice, but I had no luck. I either came near chipping off the edge of a sugar plantation, or I yawed too far from shore, and so dropped back into disgrace again and got abused.

The watch was ended at last, and we took supper and went to bed. At midnight the glare of a lantern shone in my eyes, and the night watchman said:

"Come, turn out!"

And then he left. I could not understand this extraordinary procedure; so I presently gave up trying to, and dozed off to sleep. Pretty soon the watchman was back again, and this time he was gruff. I was annoyed. I said:

"What do you want to come bothering around here in the middle of the night for? Now, as like as not, I'll not get to sleep again tonight."

The watchman said:

"Well, if this ain't good, I'm blessed."

The "off-watch" was just turning in, and I heard some brutal laughter from them, and such remarks as "Hello, watchman! ain't the new cub turned out yet? He's delicate, likely. Give him some sugar in a rag, and send for the chambermaid to sing 'Rock-a-by Baby' to him?"

About this time Mr. Bixby appeared on the scene. Something like a minute later I was climbing the pilothouse steps with some of my clothes on and the rest in my arms. Mr. Bixby was close behind, commenting. Here was something fresh—this thing of getting up in the middle of the night to go to work. It was a detail in piloting that had never occurred to me at all. I knew that boats ran all night, but somehow I had never happened to reflect that somebody had to get up out of a warm bed to run them. I began to fear that piloting was not quite so romantic as I had imagined it was; there was something very real and worklike about this new phase of it.

It was a rather dingy night, although a fair number of stars were out. The big mate was at the wheel, and he had the old tub pointed at a star and was holding her straight up the middle of the river. The shores on either hand were not much more than half a mile apart, but they seemed wonderfully far away and ever so vague and indistinct. The mate said:

"We've got to land at Jones's plantation, sir."

The vengeful spirit in me exulted. I said to myself, "I wish you joy of your job, Mr. Bixby; you'll have a good time finding Mr. Jones's plantation such a night as this; and I hope you never *will* find it as long as you live."

Mr. Bixby said to the mate:

"Upper end of the plantation, or the lower?"

"Upper."

"I can't do it. The stumps there are out of water at this stage. It's no great distance to the lower, and you'll have to get along with that."

"All right, sir. If Jones don't like it, he'll have to lump it, I reckon."

And then the mate left. My exultation began to cool and my wonder to come up. Here was a man who not only proposed to find this plantation on such a night, but to find either end of it you preferred. I dreadfully wanted to ask a question, but I was carrying about as many short answers as my cargo room would admit of, so I held my peace. All I desired to ask Mr. Bixby was the simple question whether he was ass enough to really imagine he was going to find that plantation on a night when all plantations were exactly alike and all of the same color. But I held in. I used to have fine inspirations of prudence in those days.

Mr. Bixby made for the shore and soon was scraping it, just the same as if it had been daylight. And not only that, but singing:

Father in heaven, the day is declining, etc.

It seemed to me that I had put my life in the keeping of a peculiarly reckless outcast. Presently he turned on me and said:

"What's the name of the first point above New Orleans?"

I was gratified to be able to answer promptly, and I did. I said I didn't know.

"Don't *know?*"

This manner jolted me. I was down at the foot again, in a moment. But I had to say just what I had said before.

"Well, you're a smart one!" said Mr. Bixby. "What's the name of the *next* point?"

Once more I didn't know.

"Well, this beats anything. Tell me the name of *any* point or place I told you."

I studied awhile and decided that I couldn't.

"Look here! What do you start out from, above Twelve-Mile Point, to cross over?"

"I—I—don't know."

"You—you—don't know?" mimicking my drawling manner of speech. "What *do* you know?"

"I—I—nothing, for certain."

"By the great Caesar's ghost, I believe you! You're the stupidest dunderhead I ever saw or ever heard of, so help me Moses! The idea of *you* being a pilot—*you!* Why, you don't know enough to pilot a cow down a lane."

Oh, but his wrath was up! He was a nervous man, and he shuffled from one side of his wheel to the other as if the floor was hot. He would boil awhile to himself, and then overflow and scald me again.

"Look here! What do you suppose I told you the names of those points for?"

I tremblingly considered a moment, and then the devil of temptation provoked me to say:

"Well, to—to—be entertaining, I thought."

This was a red rag to the bull. He raged and stormed so (he was crossing the river at the time) that I judged it made him blind, because he ran over the steering oar of a trading scow. Of course the traders sent up a volley of red-hot profanity. Never was a man so grateful as Mr. Bixby was; because he was brimful, and here were subjects who could *talk back.* He threw open a window, thrust his head out, and such an irruption followed as I never had heard before. The fainter and farther away the scowmen's curses drifted, the higher Mr. Bixby lifted his voice and the weightier his adjectives grew. When he closed the window he was empty. You could have drawn a seine through his system and not caught curses enough to disturb your mother with. Presently he said to me in the gentlest way:

"My boy, you must get a little memorandum book; and every time I tell you a thing, put it down right away. There's only one way to be a pilot, and that is to get this entire river by heart. You have to know it just like A B C."

That was a dismal revelation to me; for my memory was never loaded with anything but blank cartridges. However, I did not feel discouraged long. I judged that it was best to make some allowances, for doubtless Mr. Bixby was "stretching." Presently he pulled a rope and struck a few strokes on the big bell. The stars were all gone now, and the night was as black as ink. I could hear the wheels churn along the bank, and I was not entirely certain that I could see the shore. The voice of the invisible watchman called up from the hurricane deck:

"What's this, sir?"

"Jones's plantation."

I said to myself, "I wish I might venture to offer a small bet that it isn't." But I did not chirp. I only waited to see. Mr. Bixby handled the engine bells, and in due time the boat's nose came to the land, a torch glowed from the forecastle, a man skipped ashore, a darky's voice on the bank said: "Gimme de k'yarpetbag, Mass' Jones," and the next moment we were standing up the river again, all serene. I reflected deeply awhile, and then said—but not aloud—"Well, the finding of that plantation was the luckiest accident that ever happened; but it couldn't happen again in a hundred years." And I fully believed it *was* an accident, too.

By the time we had gone seven or eight hundred miles up the river, I had learned to be a tolerably plucky upstream steersman, in daylight; and before we reached St. Louis I had made a trifle of progress in night work, but only a trifle. I had a notebook that fairly bristled with the names of towns, "points," bars, islands, bends, reaches, etc.; but the information was to be found only in the notebook—none of it was in my head. It made my heart ache to think I had only got half of the river set down; for as our watch was four hours off and four hours on, day and night, there was a long four-hour gap in my book for every time I had slept since the voyage began.

My chief was presently hired to go on a big New Orleans boat, and I packed my satchel and went with him. She was a grand affair. When I stood in her pilothouse I was so far above the water that I seemed perched on a mountain; and her decks stretched so far away, fore and aft, below me, that I wondered how I could ever have considered the little *Paul Jones* a large craft. There were other differences, too. The *Paul Jones's* pilothouse was a cheap, dingy, battered rattletrap, cramped for room; but here was a sumptuous glass temple; room enough to have a dance in; showy red and gold window curtains; an imposing sofa; leather cushions and a back to the high bench where visiting pilots sit, to spin yarns and "look at the river"; bright, fanciful "cuspidors," instead of a broad wooden box filled with sawdust; nice new oilcloth on the floor; a hospitable big stove for winter; a wheel as high as my head, costly with inlaid work; a wire tiller rope; bright brass knobs for the bells; and a tidy, white-aproned, black "texas-tender," to bring up tarts and ices and coffee during midwatch, day and night. Now this was "something like"; and so I began to take heart once more to believe that piloting was a romantic sort

of occupation after all. The moment we were under way I began to
prowl about the great steamer and fill myself with joy. She was as clean
and as dainty as a drawing room; when I looked down her long, gilded
saloon, it was like gazing through a splendid tunnel; she had an oil picture, by some gifted sign painter, on every stateroom door; she glittered
with no end of prism-fringed chandeliers; the clerk's office was elegant,
the bar was marvelous, and the barkeeper had been barbered and up-
holstered at incredible cost. The boiler deck (*i. e.*, the second story of the
boat, so to speak) was as spacious as a church, it seemed to me; so
with the forecastle; and there was no pitiful handful of deck hands, firemen, and roustabouts down there, but a whole battalion of men. The fires
were fiercely glaring from a long row of furnaces, and over them were
eight huge boilers! This was unutterable pomp. The mighty engines—
but enough of this. I had never felt so fine before. And when I found
that the regiment of natty servants respectfully "sir'd" me, my satisfaction
was complete.

A DARING DEED

When I returned to the pilothouse St. Louis was gone, and I was lost.
Here was a piece of river which was all down in my book, but I could
make neither head nor tail of it; you understand, it was turned around. I
had seen it when coming upstream, but I had never faced about to see
how it looked when it was behind me. My heart broke again, for it was
plain that I had got to learn this troublesome river *both* ways.

The pilothouse was full of pilots, going down to "look at the river."
What is called the "upper river" (the two hundred miles between St.
Louis and Cairo, where the Ohio comes in) was low; and the Mississippi
changes its channel so constantly that the pilots used to always find it
necessary to run down to Cairo to take a fresh look, when their boats
were to lie in port a week; that is, when the water was at a low stage.
A deal of this "looking at the river" was done by poor fellows who seldom
had a berth, and whose only hope of getting one lay in their being always freshly posted and therefore ready to drop into the shoes of some
reputable pilot, for a single trip, on account of such pilot's sudden illness,
or some other necessity. And a good many of them constantly ran up and
down inspecting the river, not because they ever really hoped to get a
berth, but because (they being guests of the boat) it was cheaper to
"look at the river" than stay ashore and pay board. In time these fellows
grew dainty in their tastes, and only infested boats that had an estab-

lished reputation for setting good tables. All visiting pilots were useful, for they were always ready and willing, winter or summer, night or day, to go out in the yawl and help buoy the channel or assist the boat's pilots in any way they could. They were likewise welcomed because all pilots are tireless talkers, when gathered together, and as they talk only about the river they are always understood and are always interesting. Your true pilot cares nothing about anything on earth but the river, and his pride in his occupation surpasses the pride of kings.

We had a fine company of these river inspectors along this trip. There were eight or ten, and there was abundance of room for them in our great pilothouse. Two or three of them wore polished silk hats, elaborate shirt fronts, diamond breastpins, kid gloves, and patent-leather boots. They were choice in their English, and bore themselves with a dignity proper to men of solid means and prodigious reputation as pilots. The others were more or less loosely clad, and wore upon their heads tall felt cones that were suggestive of the days of the Commonwealth.

I was a cipher in this august company, and felt subdued, not to say torpid. I was not even of sufficient consequence to assist at the wheel when it was necessary to put the tiller hard down in a hurry; the guest that stood nearest did that when occasion required—and this was pretty much all the time, because of the crookedness of the channel and the scant water. I stood in a corner; and the talk I listened to took the hope all out of me. One visitor said to another:

"Jim, how did you run Plum Point, coming up?"

"It was in the night, there, and I ran it the way one of the boys on the *Diana* told me; started out about fifty yards above the woodpile on the false point, and held on the cabin under Plum Point till I raised the reef—quarter less twain—then straightened up for the middle bar till I got well abreast the old one-limbed cottonwood in the bend, then got my stern on the cottonwood, and head on the low place above the point, and came through a-booming—nine and a half."

"Pretty square crossing, an't it?"

"Yes, but the upper bar's working down fast."

Another pilot spoke up and said:

"I had better water than that, and ran it lower down; started out from the false point—mark twain—raised the second reef abreast the big snag in the bend, and had quarter less twain."

One of the gorgeous ones remarked:

"I don't want to find fault with your leadsmen, but that's a good deal of water for Plum Point, it seems to me."

There was an approving nod all around as this quiet snub dropped on the boaster and "settled" him. And so they went on talk-talk-talking. Meantime, the thing that was running in my mind was, "Now, if my ears hear aright, I have not only to get the names of all the towns and islands and bends, and so on, by heart, but I must even get up a warm personal acquaintanceship with every old snag and one-limbed cotton-wood and obscure woodpile that ornaments the banks of this river for twelve hundred miles; and more than that, I must actually know where these things are in the dark, unless these guests are gifted with eyes that can pierce through two miles of solid blackness. I wish the piloting business was in Jericho and I had never thought of it."

At dusk Mr. Bixby tapped the big bell three times (the signal to land), and the captain emerged from his drawing room in the forward end of the "texas," and looked up inquiringly. Mr. Bixby said:

"We will lay up here all night, captain."

"Very well, sir."

That was all. The boat came to shore and was tied up for the night. It seemed to me a fine thing that the pilot could do as he pleased, without asking so grand a captain's permission. I took my supper and went imme-diately to bed, discouraged by my day's observations and experiences. My late voyage's notebooking was but a confusion of meaningless names. It had tangled me all up in a knot every time I had looked at it in the daytime. I now hoped for respite in sleep; but no, it reveled all through my head till sunrise again, a frantic and tireless nightmare.

Next morning I felt pretty rusty and low-spirited. We went booming along, taking a good many chances, for we were anxious to "get out of the river" (as getting out to Cairo was called) before night should over-take us. But Mr. Bixby's partner, the other pilot, presently grounded the boat, and we lost so much time getting her off that it was plain the dark-ness would overtake us a good long way above the mouth. This was a great misfortune, especially to certain of our visiting pilots, whose boats would have to wait for their return, no matter how long that might be. It sobered the pilothouse talk a good deal. Coming upstream, pilots did not mind low water or any kind of darkness; nothing stopped them but fog. But downstream work was different; a boat was too nearly helpless, with a stiff current pushing behind her; so it was not customary to run downstream at night in low water.

There seemed to be one small hope, however: if we could get through the intricate and dangerous Hat Island crossing before night, we could venture the rest, for we would have plainer sailing and better water. But it would be insanity to attempt Hat Island at night. So there was a deal of looking at watches all the rest of the day, and a constant ciphering upon the speed we were making. Hat Island was the eternal subject; sometimes hope was high and sometimes we were delayed in a bad crossing, and down it went again. For hours all hands lay under the burden of this suppressed excitement; it was even communicated to me, and I got to feeling so solicitous about Hat Island, and under such an awful pressure of responsibility, that I wished I might have five minutes on shore to draw a good, full, relieving breath, and start over again. We were standing no regular watches. Each of our pilots ran such portions of the river as he had run when coming upstream, because of his greater familiarity with it; but both remained in the pilothouse constantly.

An hour before sunset Mr. Bixby took the wheel, and Mr. W. stepped aside. For the next thirty minutes every man held his watch in his hand and was restless, silent, and uneasy. At last somebody said, with a doomful sigh:

"Well, yonder's Hat Island—and we can't make it."

All the watches closed with a snap, everybody sighed and muttered something about its being "too bad, too bad—ah, if we could *only* have got here half an hour sooner!" and the place was thick with the atmosphere of disappointment. Some started to go out, but loitered, hearing no bell-tap to land. The sun dipped behind the horizon, the boat went on. Inquiring looks passed from one guest to another; and one who had his hand on the doorknob and had turned it, waited, then presently took away his hand and let the knob turn back again. We bore steadily down the bend. More looks were exchanged, and nods of surprised admiration—but no words. Insensibly the men drew together behind Mr. Bixby, as the sky darkened and one or two dim stars came out. The dead silence and sense of waiting became oppressive. Mr. Bixby pulled the cord, and two deep, mellow notes from the big bell floated off on the night. Then a pause, and one more note was struck. The watchman's voice followed, from the hurricane deck:

"Labboard lead, there! Stabboard lead!"

The cries of the leadsmen began to rise out of the distance, and were gruffly repeated by the word-passers on the hurricane deck.

"M-a-r-k three! M-a-r-k three! Quarter-less-three! Half twain! Quarter twain! M-a-r-k twain! Quarter-less—"

Mr. Bixby pulled two bell ropes, and was answered by faint jinglings far below in the engine room, and our speed slackened. The steam began to whistle through the gauge cocks. The cries of the leadsmen went on—and it is a weird sound, always, in the night. Every pilot in the lot was watching now, with fixed eyes, and talking under his breath. Nobody was calm and easy but Mr. Bixby. He would put his wheel down and stand on a spoke, and as the steamer swung into her (to me) utterly invisible marks—for we seemed to be in the midst of a wide and gloomy sea—he would meet and fasten her there. Out of the murmur of half-audible talk, one caught a coherent sentence now and then—such as:

"There; she's over the first reef all right!"

After a pause, another subdued voice:

"Her stern's coming down just *exactly* right, by *George!*"

"Now she's in the marks; over she goes!"

Somebody else muttered:

"Oh, it was done beautiful—*beautiful!*"

Now the engines were stopped altogether, and we drifted with the current. Not that I could see the boat drift, for I could not, the stars being all gone by this time. This drifting was the dismalest work; it held one's heart still. Presently I discovered a blacker gloom than that which surrounded us. It was the head of the island. We were closing right down upon it. We entered its deeper shadow, and so imminent seemed the peril that I was likely to suffocate; and I had the strongest impulse to do *something*, anything, to save the vessel. But still Mr. Bixby stood by his wheel, silent, intent as a cat, and all the pilots stood shoulder to shoulder at his back.

"She'll not make it!" somebody whispered.

The water grew shoaler and shoaler, by the leadsman's cries, till it was down to:

"Eight-and-a-half! E-i-g-h-t feet! E-i-g-h-t feet! Seven-and—"

Mr. Bixby said warningly through his speaking tube to the engineer:

"Stand by, now!"

"Ay, ay, sir!"

"Seven-and-a-half! Seven feet! *Six*-and—"

We touched bottom! Instantly Mr. Bixby set a lot of bells ringing, shouted through the tube, "*Now,* let her have it—every ounce you've got!" then to his partner, "Put her hard down! snatch her! snatch her!" The boat rasped and ground her way through the sand, hung upon the apex of disaster a single tremendous instant, and then over she went! And such a shout as went up at Mr. Bixby's back never loosened the roof of a pilothouse before.

There was no more trouble after that. Mr. Bixby was a hero that night; and it was some little time, too, before his exploit ceased to be talked about by rivermen.

Fully to realize the marvelous precision required in laying the great steamer in her marks in that murky waste of water, one should know that not only must she pick her intricate way through snags and blind reefs, and then shave the head of the island so closely as to brush the overhanging foliage with her stern, but at one place she must pass almost within arm's reach of a sunken and invisible wreck that would snatch the hull timbers from under her if she should strike it, and destroy a quarter of a million dollars' worth of steamboat and cargo in five minutes, and maybe a hundred and fifty human lives into the bargain.

The last remark I heard that night was a compliment to Mr. Bixby, uttered in soliloquy and with unction by one of our guests. He said:

"By the Shadow of Death, but he's a lightning pilot!"

PERPLEXING LESSONS

At the end of what seemed a tedious while, I had managed to pack my head full of islands, towns, bars, "points," and bends; and a curiously inanimate mass of lumber it was, too. However, inasmuch as I could shut my eyes and reel off a good long string of these names without leaving out more than ten miles of river in every fifty, I began to feel that I could take a boat down to New Orleans if I could make her skip those little gaps. But of course my complacency could hardly get start enough to lift my nose a trifle into the air, before Mr. Bixby would think of something to fetch it down again. One day he turned on me suddenly with this settler:

"What is the shape of Walnut Bend?"

He might as well have asked me my grandmother's opinion of protoplasm. I reflected respectfully, and then said I didn't know it had any particular shape. My gunpowdery chief went off with a bang, of course, and then went on loading and firing until he was out of adjectives.

I had learned long ago that he only carried just so many rounds of ammunition, and was sure to subside into a very placable and even remorseful old smoothbore as soon as they were all gone. That word "old" is merely affectionate; he was not more than thirty-four. I waited. By and by he said:

"My boy, you've got to know the *shape* of the river perfectly. It is all there is left to steer by on a very dark night. Everything else is blotted out and gone. But mind you, it hasn't the same shape in the night that it has in the daytime."

"How on earth am I ever going to learn it, then?"

"How do you follow a hall at home in the dark? Because you know the shape of it. You can't see it."

"Do you mean to say that I've got to know all the million trifling variations of shape in the banks of this interminable river as well as I know the shape of the front hall at home?"

"On my honor, you've got to know them *better* than any man ever did know the shapes of the halls in his own house."

"I wish I was dead!"

"Now, I don't want to discourage you, but—"

"Well, pile it on me; I might as well have it now as another time."

"You see, this has got to be learned; there isn't any getting around it. A clear starlight night throws such heavy shadows that, if you didn't know the shape of a shore perfectly, you would claw away from every bunch of timber, because you would take the black shadow of it for a solid cape; and you see you would be getting scared to death every fifteen minutes by the watch. You would be fifty yards from shore all the time when you ought to be within fifty feet of it. You can't see a snag in one of those shadows, but you know exactly where it is, and the shape of the river tells you when you are coming to it. Then there's your pitch-dark night; the river is a very different shape on a pitch-dark night from what it is on a starlight night. All shores seem to be straight lines, then, and mighty dim ones, too; and you'd *run* them for straight lines, only you know better. You boldly drive your boat right into what seems to be a solid, straight wall (you knowing very well that in reality there is a curve there), and that wall falls back and makes way for you. Then there's your gray mist. You take a night when there's one of these grisly, drizzly, gray mists, and then there isn't *any* particular shape to a shore. A gray mist would tangle the head of the oldest man that ever lived. Well, then, different kinds of *moonlight* change the shape of the river in different ways. You see—"

"Oh, don't say any more, please! Have I got to learn the shape of the river according to all these five hundred thousand different ways? If I tried to carry all that cargo in my head it would make me stoop-shouldered."

"*No!* you only learn *the* shape of the river; and you learn it with such absolute certainty that you can always steer by the shape that's *in your head*, and never mind the one that's before your eyes."

"Very well, I'll try it; but, after I have learned it, can I depend on it? Will it keep the same form and not go fooling around?"

Before Mr. Bixby could answer, Mr. W. came in to take the watch, and he said:

"Bixby, you'll have to look out for President's Island, and all that country clear away up above the Old Hen and Chickens. The banks are caving and the shape of the shores changing like everything. Why, you wouldn't know the point above 40. You can go up inside [3] the old sycamore snag, now."

So that question was answered. Here were leagues of shore changing shape. My spirits were down in the mud again. Two things seemed pretty apparent to me. One was that in order to be a pilot a man had got to learn more than any one man ought to be allowed to know; and the other was that he must learn it all over again in a different way every twenty-four hours.

That night we had the watch until twelve. Now it was an ancient river custom for the two pilots to chat a bit when the watch changed. While the relieving pilot put on his gloves and lit his cigar, his partner, the retiring pilot, would say something like this:

"I judge the upper bar is making down a little at Hale's Point; had quarter twain with the lower lead and mark twain [4] with the other."

"Yes, I thought it was making down a little, last trip. Meet any boats?"

"Met one abreast the head of 21, but she was away over hugging the bar, and I couldn't make her out entirely. I took her for the *Sunny South* —hadn't any skylights forward of the chimneys."

And so on. And as the relieving pilot took the wheel his partner [5] would mention that we were in such-and-such a bend, and say we were abreast of such-and-such a man's woodyard or plantation. This was courtesy; I supposed it was *necessity*. But Mr. W. came on watch full twelve minutes late on this particular night—a tremendous breach of etiquette; in fact, it is the unpardonable sin among pilots. So Mr. Bixby gave him no greeting whatever, but simply surrendered the wheel and marched out of the pilothouse without a word. I was appalled; it was a villainous night for blackness, we were in a particularly wide and blind part of the river, where there was no shape or substance to anything, and it seemed incredible that Mr. Bixby should have left that poor fellow to kill the boat,

---

3. It may not be necessary, but still it can do no harm to explain that "inside" means between the snag and the shore.—M. T.
4. Two fathoms. Quarter twain is 2¼ fathoms, 13½ feet. Mark three is three fathoms.
5. "Partner" is technical for "the other pilot."

trying to find out where he was. But I resolved that I would stand by him anyway. He should find that he was not wholly friendless. So I stood around, and waited to be asked where we were. But Mr. W. plunged on serenely through the solid firmament of black cats that stood for an atmosphere, and never opened his mouth. "Here is a proud devil!" thought I; "here is a limb of Satan that would rather send us all to destruction than put himself under obligations to me, because I am not yet one of the salt of the earth and privileged to snub captains and lord it over everything dead and alive in a steamboat." I presently climbed up on the bench; I did not think it was safe to go to sleep while this lunatic was on watch.

However, I must have gone to sleep in the course of time, because the next thing I was aware of was the fact that day was breaking, Mr. W. gone, and Mr. Bixby at the wheel again. So it was four o'clock and all well—but me; I felt like a skinful of dry bones, and all of them trying to ache at once.

Mr. Bixby asked me what I had stayed up there for. I confessed that it was to do Mr. W. a benevolence—tell him where he was. It took five minutes for the entire preposterousness of the thing to filter into Mr. Bixby's system, and then I judge it filled him nearly up to the chin; because he paid me a compliment—and not much of a one either. He said:

"Well, taking you by and large, you do seem to be more different kinds of an ass than any creature I ever saw before. What did you suppose he wanted to know for?"

I said I thought it might be a convenience to him.

"Convenience! D—— nation! Didn't I tell you that a man's got to know the river in the night the same as he'd know his own front hall?"

"Well, I can follow the front hall in the dark if I know it *is* the front hall; but suppose you set me down in the middle of it in the dark and not tell me which hall it is; how am *I* to know?"

"Well, you've *got* to, on the river!"

"All right. Then I'm glad I never said anything to Mr. W."

"I should say so! Why, he'd have slammed you through the window and utterly ruined a hundred dollars' worth of window sash and stuff."

I was glad this damage had been saved, for it would have made me unpopular with the owners. They always hated anybody who had the name of being careless and injuring things.

I went to work now to learn the shape of the river; and of all the eluding and ungraspable objects that ever I tried to get mind or hands on, that was the chief. I would fasten my eyes upon a sharp, wooded point that projected far into the river some miles ahead of me, and go to laboriously photographing its shape upon my brain; and just as I was beginning to succeed to my satisfaction, we would draw up toward it and the exasperating thing would begin to melt away and fold back into the bank! If there had been a conspicuous dead tree standing upon the very point of the cape, I would find that tree inconspicuously merged into the general forest, and occupying the middle of a straight shore, when I got abreast of it! No prominent hill would stick to its shape long enough for me to make up my mind what its form really was, but it was as dissolving and changeful as if it had been a mountain of butter in the hottest corner of the tropics. Nothing ever had the same shape when I was coming downstream that it had borne when I went up. I mentioned these little difficulties to Mr. Bixby. He said:

"That's the very main virtue of the thing. If the shapes didn't change every three seconds they wouldn't be of any use. Take this place where we are now, for instance. As long as that hill over yonder is only one hill, I can boom right along the way I'm going; but the moment it splits at the top and forms a V, I know I've got to scratch to starboard in a hurry, or I'll bang this boat's brains out against a rock; and·then the moment one of the prongs of the V swings behind the other, I've got to waltz to larboard again, or I'll have a misunderstanding with a snag that would snatch the keelson out of this steamboat as neatly as if it were a sliver in your hand. If that hill didn't change its shape on bad nights there would be an awful steamboat graveyard around here inside of a year."

It was plain that I had got to learn the shape of the river in all the different ways that could be thought of—upside down, wrong end first, inside out, fore-and-aft, and "thortships"—and then know what to do on gray nights when it hadn't any shape at all. So I set about it. In the course of time I began to get the best of this knotty lesson, and my self-complacency moved to the front once more. Mr. Bixby was all fixed, and ready to start it to the rear again. He opened on me after this fashion:

"How much water did we have in the middle crossing at Hole-in-the-Wall, trip before last?"

I considered this an outrage. I said:

"Every trip, down and up, the leadsmen are singing through that tangled place for three-quarters of an hour on a stretch. How do you reckon I can remember such a mess as that?"

"My boy, you've got to remember it. You've got to remember the exact

spot and the exact marks the boat lay in when we had the shoalest water, in every one of the five hundred shoal places between St. Louis and
New Orleans; and you mustn't get the shoal soundings and marks of one
trip mixed up with the shoal soundings and marks of another, either, for
they're not often twice alike. You must keep them separate."

When I came to myself again, I said.

"When I get so that I can do that, I'll be able to raise the dead, and
then I won't have to pilot a steamboat to make a living. I want to retire
from this business. I want a slush bucket and a brush; I'm only fit for a
roustabout. I haven't got brains enough to be a pilot; and if I had I
wouldn't have strength enough to carry them around, unless I went on
crutches."

"Now drop that! When I say I'll learn [6] a man the river, I mean it.
And you can depend on it, I'll learn him or kill him."

CONTINUED PERPLEXITIES

There was no use in arguing with a person like this. I promptly put
such a strain on my memory that by and by even the shoal water and
the countless crossing marks began to stay with me. But the result was
just the same. I never could more than get one knotty thing learned before another presented itself. Now I had often seen pilots gazing at the
water and pretending to read it as if it were a book; but it was a book
that told me nothing. A time came at last, however, when Mr. Bixby
seemed to think me far enough advanced to bear a lesson on water-
reading. So he began:

"Do you see that long, slanting line on the face of the water? Now,
that's a reef. Moreover, it's a bluff reef. There is a solid sand bar under
it that is nearly as straight up and down as the side of a house. There is
plenty of water close up to it, but mighty little on top of it. If you were
to hit it you would knock the boat's brains out. Do you see where the
line fringes out at the upper end and begins to fade away?"

"Yes, sir."

"Well, that is a low place; that is the head of the reef. You can climb
over there, and not hurt anything. Cross over, now, and follow along close
under the reef—easy water there—not much current."

I followed the reef along till I approached the fringed end. Then Mr.
Bixby said:

"Now get ready. Wait till I give the word. She won't want to mount

6. "Teach" is not in the river vocabulary.

the reef; a boat hates shoal water. Stand by—wait—*wait*—keep her well in hand. *Now* cramp her down! Snatch her! snatch her!"

He seized the other side of the wheel and helped to spin it around until it was hard down, and then we held it so. The boat resisted, and refused to answer for a while, and next she came surging to starboard, mounted the reef, and sent a long, angry ridge of water foaming away from her bows.

"Now watch her; watch her like a cat, or she'll get away from you. When she fights strong and the tiller slips a little, in a jerky, greasy sort of way, let up on her a trifle; it is the way she tells you' at night that the water is too shoal; but keep edging her up, little by little, toward the point. You are well up on the bar now; there is a bar under every point, because the water that comes down around it forms an eddy and allows the sediment to sink. Do you see those fine lines on the face of the water that branch out like the ribs of a fan? Well, those are little reefs; you want to just miss the ends of them, but run them pretty close. Now look out—look out! Don't you crowd that slick, greasy-looking place; there ain't nine feet there; she won't stand it. She begins to smell it; look sharp, I tell you! Oh, blazes, there you go! Stop the starboard wheel! Quick! Ship up to back! Set her back!"

The engine bells jingled and the engines answered promptly, shooting white columns of steam far aloft out of the 'scapepipes, but it was too late. The boat had "smelt" the bar in good earnest; the foamy ridges that radiated from her bows suddenly disappeared, a great swell came rolling forward, and swept ahead of her, she careened far over to larboard, and went tearing away toward the shore as if she were about scared to death. We were a good mile from where we ought to have been when we finally got the upper hand of her again.

During the afternoon watch the next day, Mr. Bixby asked me if I knew how to run the next few miles. I said:

"Go inside the first snag above the point, outside the next one, start out from the lower end of Higgins's woodyard, make a square crossing, and—"

"That's all right. I'll be back before you close up on the next point."

But he wasn't. He was still below when I rounded it and entered upon a piece of the river which I had some misgivings about. I did not know that he was hiding behind a chimney to see how I would perform. I went gaily along, getting prouder and prouder, for he had never left the boat in my sole charge such a length of time before. I even got to "setting" her and letting the wheel go entirely, while I vaingloriously turned my back and inspected the stern marks and hummed a tune, a sort of easy indifference which I had prodigiously admired in Bixby and other great pilots. Once I inspected rather long, and when I faced to the front again my heart flew into my mouth so suddenly that if I hadn't clapped my teeth together I should have lost it. One of those frightful bluff reefs was stretching its deadly length right across our bows! My head was gone in a moment; I did not know which end I stood on; I gasped and could not get my breath; I spun the wheel down with such rapidity that it wove itself together like a spider's web; the boat answered and turned square away from the reef, but the reef followed her! I fled, but still it followed, still it kept—right across my bows! I never looked to see where I was going, I only fled. The awful crash was imminent. Why didn't that villain come? If I committed the crime of ringing a bell I might get thrown overboard. But better that than kill the boat. So in blind desperation, I started such a rattling "shivaree" down below as never had astounded an engineer in this world before, I fancy. Amidst the frenzy of the bells the engines began to back and fill in a curious way, and my reason forsook its throne—we were about to crash into the woods on the other side of the river. Just then Mr. Bixby stepped calmly into view on the hurricane deck. My soul went out to him in gratitude. My distress vanished; I would have felt safe on the brink of Niagara with Mr. Bixby on the hurricane deck. He blandly and sweetly took his toothpick out of his mouth between his fingers, as if it were a cigar—we were just in the act of climbing an overhanging big tree, and the passengers were scudding astern like rats—and lifted up these commands to me ever so gently:

"Stop the starboard! Stop the larboard! Set her back on both!"

The boat hesitated, halted, pressed her nose among the boughs a critical instant, then reluctantly began to back away.

"Stop the larboard! Come ahead on it! Stop the starboard! Come ahead on it! Point her for the bar!"

I sailed away as serenely as a summer's morning. Mr. Bixby came in and said, with mock simplicity:

"When you have a hail, my boy, you ought to tap the big bell three times before you land, so that the engineers can get ready"

I blushed under the sarcasm, and said I hadn't had any hail.

"Ah! Then it was for wood, I suppose. The officer of the watch will tell you when he wants to wood up."

I went on consuming, and said I wasn't after wood.

"Indeed? Why? what could you want over here in the bend, then? Did you ever know of a boat following a bend upstream at this stage of the river?"

"No, sir—and *I* wasn't trying to follow it. I was getting away from a bluff reef."

"No, it wasn't a bluff reef; there isn't one within three miles of where you were."

"But I saw it. It was as bluff as that one yonder."

"Just about. Run over it!"

"Do you give it as an order?"

"Yes. Run over it!"

"If I don't, I wish I may die."

"All right; I am taking the responsibility."

I was just as anxious to kill the boat, now, as I had been to save it before. I impressed my orders upon my memory, to be used at the inquest, and made a straight break for the reef. As it disappeared under our bows I held my breath; but we slid over it like oil.

"Now, don't you see the difference? It wasn't anything but a *wind* reef. The wind does that."

"So I see. But it is exactly like a bluff reef. How am I ever going to tell them apart?"

"I can't tell you. It is an instinct. By and by you will just naturally *know* one from the other, but you never will be able to explain why or how you know them apart."

It turned out to be true. The face of the water, in time, became a wonderful book—a book that was a dead language to the uneducated passenger, but which told its mind to me without reserve, delivering its most cherished secrets as if it uttered them with a voice. And it was not a book to be read once and thrown aside, for it had a new story to tell every day. Throughout the long twelve hundred miles there was never a page that was void of interest, never one that you could leave unread without loss, never one that you would want to skip, thinking you could find higher enjoyment in some other thing. There never was so wonderful a book written by man; never one whose interest was so absorbing, so unflagging, so sparklingly renewed with every reperusal. The passenger who could not read it was charmed with a peculiar sort of faint dimple on its surface (on the rare occasions when he did not overlook it altogether); but to the pilot that was an *italicized* passage; indeed, it was more than

that, it was a legend of the largest capitals, with a string of shouting exclamation points at the end of it, for it meant that a wreck or a rock was
buried there that could tear the life out of the strongest vessel that ever
floated. It is the faintest and simplest expression the water ever makes,
and the most hideous to a pilot's eye. In truth, the passenger who could
not read this book saw nothing but all manner of pretty pictures in it,
painted by the sun and shaded by the clouds, whereas to the trained eye
these were not pictures at all, but the grimmest and most dead-earnest of
reading matter.

Now when I had mastered the language of this water, and had come
to know every trifling feature that bordered the great river as familiarly
as I knew the letters of the alphabet, I had made a valuable acquisition.
But I had lost something, too. I had lost something which could never be
restored to me while I lived. All the grace, the beauty, the poetry, had
gone out of the majestic river! I still kept in mind a certain wonderful
sunset which I witnessed when steamboating was new to me. A broad
expanse of the river was turned to blood; in the middle distance the red
hue brightened into gold, through which a solitary log came floating,
black and conspicuous; in one place a long, slanting mark lay sparkling
upon the water; in another the surface was broken by boiling, tumbling
rings, that were as many-tinted as an opal; where the ruddy flush
was faintest, was a smooth spot that was covered with graceful circles
and radiating lines, ever so delicately traced; the shore on our left was
densely wooded, and the somber shadow that fell from this forest was
broken in one place by a long, ruffled trail that shone like silver; and
high above the forest wall a clean-stemmed dead tree waved a single
leafy bough that glowed like a flame in the unobstructed splendor that
was flowing from the sun. There were graceful curves, reflected images,
woody heights, soft distances; and over the whole scene, far and near,
the dissolving lights drifted steadily, enriching it every passing moment
with new marvels of coloring.

I stood like one bewitched. I drank it in, in a speechless rapture. The
world was new to me, and I had never seen anything like this at home.
But as I have said, a day came when I began to cease from noting the
glories and the charms which the moon and the sun and the twilight
wrought upon the river's face; another day came when I ceased altogether to note them. Then, if that sunset scene had been repeated, I
should have looked upon it without rapture, and should have com-
mented upon it, inwardly, after this fashion: "This sun means that we are

going to have wind tomorrow; that floating log means that the river is rising, small thanks to it; that slanting mark on the water refers to a bluff reef which is going to kill somebody's steamboat one of these nights if it keeps on stretching out like that; those tumbling 'boils' show a dissolving bar and a changing channel there; the lines and circles in the slick water over yonder are a warning that that troublesome place is shoaling up dangerously; that silver streak in the shadow of the forest is the 'break' from a new snag, and he has located himself in the very best place he could have found to fish for steamboats; that tall dead tree, with a single living branch, is not going to last long, and then how is a body ever going to get through this blind place at night without the friendly old landmark?"

No, the romance and beauty were all gone from the river. All the value any feature of it had for me now was the amount of usefulness it could furnish toward compassing the safe piloting of a steamboat. Since those days, I have pitied doctors from my heart. What does the lovely flush in a beauty's cheek mean to a doctor but a "break" that ripples above some deadly disease? Are not all her visible charms sown thick with what are to him the signs and symbols of hidden decay? Does he ever see her beauty at all, or doesn't he simply view her professionally, and comment upon her unwholesome condition all to himself? And doesn't he sometimes wonder whether he has gained most or lost most by learning his trade?

COMPLETING MY EDUCATION

Whoever has done me the courtesy to read my chapters which have preceded this may possibly wonder that I deal so minutely with piloting as a science. It was the prime purpose of those chapters; and I am not quite done yet. I wish to show, in the most patient and painstaking way, what a wonderful science it is. Ship channels are buoyed and lighted, and therefore it is a comparatively easy undertaking to learn to run them; clear-water rivers with gravel bottoms change their channels very gradually, and therefore one needs to learn them but once; but piloting becomes another matter when you apply it to vast streams like the Mississippi and the Missouri, whose alluvial banks cave and change constantly, whose snags are always hunting up new quarters, whose sand bars are never at rest, whose channels are forever dodging and shirking, and whose obstructions must be confronted in all nights and all weathers without the aid of a single lighthouse or a single buoy; for there is neither light nor buoy to be found anywhere in all this three or four thousand miles of villainous river.[7] I feel justified in enlarging upon this great science for the reason that I feel sure no one has ever yet written a paragraph about it who had piloted a steamboat himself, and so had a practical knowledge of the subject. If the theme was hackneyed, I should be obliged to deal gently with the reader; but since it is wholly new, I have felt at liberty to take up a considerable degree of room with it.

When I had learned the name and position of every visible feature of the river; when I had so mastered its shape that I could shut my eyes and trace it from St. Louis to New Orleans; when I had learned to read the face of the water as one would cull the news from the morning paper; and finally, when I had trained my dull memory to treasure up an endless array of soundings and crossing marks, and keep fast hold on them, I judged that my education was complete; so I got to tilting my cap to the side of my head, and wearing a toothpick in my mouth at the wheel. Mr. Bixby had his eye on these airs. One day he said:

"What is the height of that bank yonder, at Burgess's?"

"How can I tell, sir? It is three-quarters of a mile away."

"Very poor eye—very poor. Take the glass."

I took the glass and presently said:

"I can't tell. I suppose that the bank is about a foot and a half high."

"Foot and a half? That's a six-foot bank. How high was the bank along here last trip?"

"I don't know; I never noticed."

"You didn't? Well, you must always do it hereafter."

"Why?"

"Because you'll have to know a good many things that it tells you. For one thing, it tells you the stage of the river—tells you whether there's more water or less in the river along here than there was last trip."

"The leads tell me that." I rather thought I had the advantage of him there.

"Yes, but suppose the leads lie? The bank would tell you so, and then you would stir those leadsmen up a bit. There was a ten-foot bank here last trip, and there is only a six-foot bank here now. What does that signify?"

"That the river is four feet higher than it was last trip."

"Very good. Is the river rising or falling?"

7. True at the time referred to; not true now (1882).

"Rising."

"No, it ain't."

"I guess I am right, sir. Yonder is some driftwood floating down the stream."

"A rise *starts* the driftwood, but then it keeps on floating awhile after the river is done rising. Now the bank will tell you about this. Wait till you come to a place where it shelves a little. Now here: do you see this narrow belt of fine sediment? That was deposited while the water was higher. You see the driftwood begins to strand, too. The bank helps in other ways. Do you see that stump on the false point?"

"Ay, ay, sir."

"Well, the water is just up to the roots of it. You must make a note of that."

"Why?"

"Because that means that there's seven feet in the chute of 103."

"But 103 is a long way up the river yet."

"That's where the benefit of the bank comes in. There is water enough in 103 *now*, yet there may not be by the time we get there, but the bank will keep us posted all along. You don't run close chutes on a falling river, upstream, and there are precious few of them that you are allowed to run at all downstream. There's a law of the United States against it. The river may be rising by the time we get to 103, and in that case we'll run it. We are drawing—how much?"

"Six feet aft—six and a half forward."

"Well, you do seem to know something."

"But what I particularly want to know is, if I have got to keep up an everlasting measuring of the banks of this river, twelve hundred miles, month in and month out?"

"Of course!"

My emotions were too deep for words for a while. Presently I said:

"And how about these chutes? Are there many of them?"

"I should say so! I fancy we sha'n't run any of the river this trip as you've ever seen it run before—so to speak. If the river begins to rise again, we'll go up behind bars that you've always seen standing out of the river, high and dry, like a roof of a house; we'll cut across low places that you've never noticed at all, right through the middle of bars that cover three hundred acres of river; we'll creep through cracks where you've always thought was solid land; we'll dart through the woods and leave twenty-five miles of river off to one side; we'll see the hindside of every island between New Orleans and Cairo."

"Then I've got to go to work and learn just as much more river as I already know."

"Just about twice as much more, as near as you can come at it."

"Well, one lives to find out. I think I was a fool when I went into this business."

"Yes, that is true. And you are yet. But you'll not be when you've learned it."

"Ah, I never can learn it."

"I will see that you *do*."

By and by I ventured again:

"Have I got to learn all this thing just as I know the rest of the river—shapes and all—and so I can run it at night?"

"Yes. And you've got to have good fair marks from one end of the river to the other, that will help the bank tell you when there is water enough in each of these countless places—like that stump, you know. When the river first begins to rise, you can run half a dozen of the deepest of them; when it rises a foot more you can run another dozen; the next foot will add a couple of dozen, and so on: so you see you have to know your banks and marks to a dead moral certainty, and never get them mixed; for when you start through one of those cracks, there's no backing out again, as there is in the big river; you've got to go through, or stay there six months if you get caught on a falling river. There are about fifty of these cracks which you can't run at all except when the river is brimful and over the banks."

"This new lesson is a cheerful prospect."

"Cheerful enough. And mind what I've just told you; when you start into one of those places you've got to go through. They are too narrow to turn around in, too crooked to back out of, and the shoal water is always *up at the head;* never elsewhere. And the head of them is always likely to be filling up, little by little, so that the marks you reckon their depth by, this season, may not answer for next."

"Learn a new set, then, every year?"

"Exactly. Cramp her up to the bar! What are you standing up through the middle of the river for?"

The next few months showed me strange things. On the same day that we held the conversation above narrated we met a great rise coming down the river. The whole vast face of the stream was black with drifting dead logs, broken boughs, and great trees that had caved in and been washed away. It required the nicest steering to pick one's way through this rushing raft, even in the daytime, when crossing from point to point; and at night the difficulty was mightily increased; every now and then a huge log, lying deep in the water, would suddenly appear right under our bows, coming head-on; no use to try to avoid it then; we could only stop the engines, and one wheel would walk over that log from one end to the other, keeping up a thundering racket and careening the boat in a way that was very uncomfortable to passengers. Now and then we would hit one of these sunken logs a rattling bang, dead in the center, with a full head of steam, and it would stun the boat as if she had hit a continent. Sometimes this log would lodge and stay right across our nose, and back the Mississippi up before it; we would have to do a little crawfishing, then, to get away from the obstruction. We often hit *white* logs in the dark, for we could not see them until we were right on them, but a black log is a pretty distinct object at night. A white snag is an ugly customer when the daylight is gone.

Of course, on the great rise, down came a swarm of prodigious timber rafts from the headwaters of the Mississippi, coal barges from Pittsburgh, little trading scows from everywhere, and broadhorns from "Posey County," Indiana, freighted with "fruit and furniture"—the usual term for describing it, though in plain English the freight thus aggrandized was hoop-poles and pumpkins. Pilots bore a mortal hatred to these craft, and it was returned with usury. The law required all such helpless traders to keep a light burning, but it was a law that was often broken. All of a sudden, on a murky night, a light would hop up, right under our bows, almost, and an agonized voice, with the backwoods "whang" to it, would wail out:

"Whar'n the —— you goin' to! Cain't you see nothin', you dash-dashed aig-suckin', sheep-stealin', one-eyed son of a stuffed monkey!"

Then for an instant, as he whistled by, the red glare from our furnaces would reveal the scow and the form of the gesticulating orator, as if under a lightning flash, and in that instant our firemen and deck hands would send and receive a tempest of missiles and profanity, one of our wheels would walk off with the crashing fragments of a steering oar, and down the dead blackness would shut again. And that flatboatman would be sure to go into New Orleans and sue our boat, swearing stoutly that he had a light burning all the time, when in truth his gang had the lantern down below to sing and lie and drink and gamble by, and no watch on deck. Once at night, in one of those forest-bordered crevices (behind an island) which steamboatmen intensely describe with the phrase "as dark as the inside of a cow," we should have eaten up a Posey County family,

fruit, furniture, and all, but that they happened to be fiddling down below and we just caught the sound of the music in time to sheer off,
doing no serious damage, unfortunately, but coming so near it that we
had good hopes for a moment. These people brought up their lantern,
then, of course; and as we backed and filled to get away, the precious
family stood in the light of it—both sexes and various ages—and cursed
us till everything turned blue. Once a coal-boatman sent a bullet through
our pilothouse where we borrowed a steering oar of him in a very narrow
place.

THE RIVER RISES

During this big rise these small-fry craft were an intolerable nuisance.
We were running chute after chute—a new world to me and if there was
a particularly cramped place in a chute, we would be pretty sure to meet
a broadhorn there; and if he failed to be there, we would find him in a
still worse locality, namely, the head of the chute, on the shoal water.
And then there would be no end of profane cordialities exchanged.

Sometimes, in the big river, when we would be feeling our way cautiously along through a fog, the deep hush would suddenly be broken by
yells and a clamor of tin pans, and all in an instant a log raft would
appear vaguely through the webby veil, close upon us; and then we did
not wait to swap knives, but snatched our engine bells out by the roots
and piled on all the steam we had, to scramble out of the way! One
doesn't hit a rock or a solid log raft with a steamboat when he can get
excused.

You will hardly believe it, but many steamboat clerks always carried a
large assortment of religious tracts with them in those old departed
steamboating days. Indeed they did! Twenty times a day we would be
cramping up around a bar, while a string of these small-fry rascals were
drifting down into the head of the bend away above and beyond us a
couple of miles. Now a skiff would dart away from one of them, and
come fighting its laborious way across the desert of water. It would
"ease all" in the shadow of our forecastle, and the panting oarsmen would
shout, "Gimme a pa-a-per!" as the skiff drifted swiftly astern. The clerk
would throw over a file of New Orleans journals. If these were picked
up *without comment*, you might notice that now a dozen other skiffs had
been drifting down upon us without saying anything. You understand,
they had been waiting to see how No. 1 was going to fare. No. 1 making

no comment, all the rest would bend to their oars and come on now; and as fast as they came the clerk would heave over neat bundles of religious tracts, tied to shingles. The amount of hard swearing which twelve packages of religious literature will command when impartially divided up among twelve raftsmen's crews, who have pulled a heavy skiff two miles on a hot day to get them, is simply incredible.

As I have said, the big rise brought a new world under my vision. By the time the river was over its banks we had forsaken our old paths and were hourly climbing over bars that had stood ten feet out of water before; we were shaving stumpy shores, like that at the foot of Madrid Bend, which I had always seen avoided before; we were clattering through chutes like that of 82, where the opening at the foot was an unbroken wall of timber till our nose was almost at the very spot. Some of these chutes were utter solitudes. The dense, untouched forest overhung both banks of the crooked little crack, and one could believe that human creatures had never intruded there before. The swinging grapevines, the grassy nooks and vistas glimpsed as we swept by, the flowering creepers waving their red blossoms from the tops of dead trunks, and all the spendthrift richness of the forest foliage, were wasted and thrown away there. The chutes were lovely places to steer in; they were deep, except at the head; the current was gentle; under the "points" the water was absolutely dead, and the invisible banks so bluff that where the tender willow thickets projected you could bury your boat's broadside in them as you tore along, and then you seemed fairly to fly.

Behind other islands we found wretched little farms, and wretcheder little log cabins; there were crazy rail fences sticking a foot or two above the water, with one or two jean-clad, chills-racked, yellow-faced male miserables roosting on the top rail, elbows on knees, jaws in hands, grinding tobacco and discharging the result at floating chips through crevices left by lost teeth; while the rest of the family and the few farm animals were huddled together in an empty wood flat riding at her moorings close at hand. In this flatboat the family would have to cook and eat and sleep for a lesser or greater number of days (or possibly weeks), until the river should fall two or three feet and let them get back to their log cabins and their chills again—chills being a merciful provision of an all-wise Providence to enable them to take exercise without exertion. And this sort of watery camping out was a thing which these people were rather liable to be treated to a couple of times a year: by the December rise out of the Ohio, and the June rise out of the Mississippi. And yet these were kindly dispensations, for they at least enabled the poor things to rise from the dead now and then, and look upon life when a steamboat went by. They appreciated the blessing, too, for they spread their mouths and eyes wide open and made the most of these occasions. Now what *could* these banished creatures find to do to keep from dying of the blues during the low-water season!

Once, in one of these lovely island chutes, we found our course completely bridged by a great fallen tree. This will serve to show how narrow some of the chutes were. The passengers had an hour's recreation in a virgin wilderness, while the boat hands chopped the bridge away; for there was no such thing as turning back, you comprehend.

From Cairo to Baton Rouge, when the river is over its banks, you have no particular trouble in the night; for the thousand-mile wall of dense forest that guards the two banks all the way is only gapped with a farm or woodyard opening at intervals, and so you can't "get out of the river" much easier than you could get out of a fenced lane; but from Baton Rouge to New Orleans it is a different matter. The river is more than a mile wide, and very deep—as much as two hundred feet, in places. Both banks, for a good deal over a hundred miles, are shorn of their timber and bordered by continuous sugar plantations, with only here and there a scattering sapling or a row of ornamental China trees. The timber is shorn off clear to the rear of the plantations, from two to four miles. When the first frost threatens to come, the planters snatch off their crops in a hurry. When they have finished grinding the cane, they form the refuse of the stalks (which they call *bagasse*) into great piles and set fire to them, though in other sugar countries the bagasse is used for fuel in the furnaces of the sugar mills. Now the piles of damp bagasse burn slowly, and smoke like Satan's own kitchen.

An embankment ten or fifteen feet high guards both banks of the Mississippi all the way down that lower end of the river, and this embankment is set back from the edge of the shore from ten to perhaps a hundred feet, according to circumstances; say thirty or forty feet, as a general thing. Fill that whole region with an impenetrable gloom of smoke from a hundred miles of burning bagasse piles, when the river is over the banks, and turn a steamboat loose along there at midnight and see how she will feel. And see how you will feel, too! You find yourself away out in the midst of a vague, dim sea that is shoreless, that fades out and loses itself in the murky distances; for you cannot discern the thin rib of embankment, and you are always imagining you see a straggling tree when you don't. The plantations themselves are transformed by the smoke, and look like a part of the sea. All through your watch you are tortured with the exquisite misery of uncertainty. You hope you are keeping in the river, but you do not know. All that you are sure about is that you are likely to be within six feet of the bank *and* destruction, when you think you are a good half mile from shore. And you are sure, also, that if you chance suddenly to fetch up against the embankment and topple your chimneys overboard, you will have the small comfort of knowing that it is about what you were expecting to do. One of the great Vicksburg packets darted out into a sugar plantation one night, at such a time, and had to stay there a week. But there was no novelty about it; it had often been done before.

I thought I had finished this chapter, but I wish to add a curious thing, while it is in my mind. It is only relevant in that it is connected with piloting. There used to be an excellent pilot on the river, a Mr. X, who was a somnambulist. It was said that if his mind was troubled about a bad piece of river, he was pretty sure to get up and walk in his sleep and do strange things. He was once fellow pilot for a trip or two with George Ealer, on a great New Orleans passenger packet. During a considerable part of the first trip George was uneasy, but got over it by and by, as X seemed content to stay in his bed when asleep. Late one night the boat was approaching Helena, Ark.; the water was low, and the crossing above the town in a very blind and tangled condition. X had seen the crossing since Ealer had, and as the night was particularly drizzly, sullen, and dark, Ealer was considering whether he had not better have X called to assist in running the place, when the door opened and X walked in. Now, on very dark nights, light is a deadly enemy to piloting; you are aware that if you stand in a lighted room, on such a night, you cannot see things in the street to any purpose; but if you put out the lights and stand in the gloom you can make out objects in the street pretty well. So, on very dark nights, pilots do not smoke; they allow no fire in the pilothouse stove, if there is a crack which can allow the least ray to escape; they order the furnaces to be curtained with huge tarpaulins and the skylights to be closely blinded. Then no light whatever issues from the boat. The undefinable shape that now entered the pilothouse had Mr. X's voice. This said:

"Let me take her, George; I've seen this place since you have, and it is so crooked that I reckon I can run it myself easier than I could tell you how to do it."

"It is kind of you, and I swear *I* am willing. I haven't got another drop of perspiration left in me. I have been spinning around and around the wheel like a squirrel. It is so dark I can't tell which way she is swinging till she is coming around like a whirligig."

So Ealer took a seat on the bench, panting and breathless. The black phantom assumed the wheel without saying anything, steadied the waltzing steamer with a turn or two, and then stood at ease, coaxing her a little to this side and then to that, as gently and as sweetly as if the time had been noonday. When Ealer observed this marvel of steering, he wished he had not confessed! He stared, and wondered, and finally said:

"Well, I thought I knew how to steer a steamboat, but that was another mistake of mine."

X said nothing, but went serenely on with his work. He rang for the leads; he rang to slow down the steam; he worked the boat carefully and neatly into invisible marks, then stood at the center of the wheel and peered blandly out into the blackness, fore and aft, to verify his position; as the leads shoaled more and more, he stopped the engines entirely, and the dead silence and suspense of "drifting" followed; when the shoalest water was struck, he cracked on the steam, carried her handsomely over, and then began to work her warily into the next system of shoal marks; the same patient, heedful use of leads and engines followed, the boat slipped through without touching bottom, and entered upon the third and last intricacy of the crossing; imperceptibly she moved through the gloom, crept by inches into her marks, drifted tediously till the shoalest water was cried, and then, under a tremendous head of steam, went swinging over the reef and away into deep water and safety!

Ealer let his long-pent breath pour in a great relieving sigh, and said:

"That's the sweetest piece of piloting that was ever done on the Mississippi River! I wouldn't believe it could be done, if I hadn't seen it."

There was no reply, and he added:

"Just hold her five minutes longer, partner, and let me run down and get a cup of coffee."

A minute later Ealer was biting into a pie, down in the "texas," and comforting himself with coffee. Just then the night watchman happened in, and was about to happen out again, when he noticed Ealer and exclaimed:

"Who is at the wheel, sir?"

"X."

"Dart for the pilothouse, quicker than lightning!"

The next moment both men were flying up the pilothouse companionway, three steps at a jump! Nobody there! The great steamer was whistling down the middle of the river at her own sweet will! The watchman shot out of the place again; Ealer seized the wheel, set an engine back with power, and held his breath while the boat reluctantly swung away from a "towhead," which she was about to knock into the middle of the Gulf of Mexico!

By and by the watchman came back and said:

"Didn't that lunatic tell you he was asleep, when he first came up here?"

"No."

"Well, he was. I found him walking along on top of the railings, just as unconcerned as another man would walk a pavement; and I put him to bed; now just this minute there he was again, away astern, going through that sort of tightrope deviltry the same as before."

"Well, I think I'll stay by next time he has one of those fits. But I hope he'll have them often. You just ought to have seen him take this boat through Helena crossing. *I* never saw anything so gaudy before. And if he can do such a gold-leaf, kid-glove, diamond-breastpin piloting when he is sound asleep, what *couldn't* he do if he was dead!"

SOUNDING

When the river is very low, and one's steamboat is "drawing all the water" there is in the channel—or a few inches more, as was often the case in the old times—one must be painfully circumspect in his piloting. We used to have to "sound" a number of particularly bad places almost every trip when the river was at a very low stage.

Sounding is done in this way: The boat ties up at the shore, just above the shoal crossing; the pilot not on watch takes his "cub" or steersman and a picked crew of men (sometimes an officer also), and goes out in the yawl—provided the boat has not that rare and sumptuous luxury, a regularly devised "sounding-boat"—and proceeds to hunt for the best water, the pilot on duty watching his movements through a spyglass, meantime, and in some instances assisting by signals of the boat's whistle, signifying "try higher up" or "try lower down"; for the surface of the water, like an oil painting, is more expressive and intelligible when inspected from a little distance than very close at hand. The whistle signals are seldom necessary, however; never, perhaps, except when the wind confuses the significant ripples upon the water's surface. When the yawl has reached the shoal place, the speed is slackened, the pilot begins to sound the depth with a pole ten or twelve feet long, and the steersman at the tiller

obeys the order to "hold her up to starboard"; so "let her fall off to larboard"; [8] or "steady—steady as you go."

When the measurements indicate that the yawl is approaching the
shoalest part of the reef, the command is given to "Ease all!" Then the
men stop rowing and the yawl drifts with the current. The next order is,
"Stand by with the buoy!" The moment the shallowest point is reached,
the pilot delivers the order, "Let go the buoy!" and over she goes. If the
pilot is not satisfied, he sounds the place again; if he finds the water
higher up or lower down, he removes the buoy to that place. Being
finally satisfied, he gives the order, and all the men stand their oars
straight up in the air, in line; a blast from the boat's whistle indicates that
the signal has been seen; then the men "give away" on their oars and
lay the yawl alongside the buoy; the steamer comes creeping carefully
down, is pointed straight at the buoy, husbands her power for the coming
struggle, and presently, at the critical moment, turns on all her steam and
goes grinding and wallowing over the buoy and the sand; and gains the
deep water beyond. Or maybe she doesn't; maybe she "strikes and
swings." Then she has to while away several hours (or days) sparring
herself off.

Sometimes a buoy is not laid at all, but the yawl goes ahead, hunting
the best water, and the steamer follows along in its wake. Often there is a
deal of fun and excitement about sounding, especially if it is a glorious
summer day, or a blustering night. But in winter the cold and the peril
take most of the fun out of it.

A buoy is nothing but a board four or five feet long, with one end
turned up; it is a reversed schoolhouse bench, with one of the supports
left and the other removed. It is anchored on the shoalest part of the
reef by a rope with a heavy stone made fast to the end of it. But for the
resistance of the turned-up end of the reversed bench, the current would
pull the buoy under water. At night, a paper lantern with a candle in it is
fastened on top of the buoy, and this can be seen a mile or more, a little
glimmering spark in the waste of blackness.

Nothing delights a cub so much as an opportunity to go out sounding.
There is such an air of adventure about it; often there is danger; it is so
gaudy and man-of-warlike to sit up in the stern sheets and steer a swift
yawl; there is something fine about the exultant spring of the boat when
an experienced old sailor crew throw their souls into the oars; it is
lovely to see the white foam stream away from the bows; there is music

8. The term "larboard" is never used at sea, now, to signify the left hand; but was always used on the river in my time.

in the rush of the water; it is deliciously exhilarating, in summer, to go speeding over the breezy expanses of the river when the world of wavelets is dancing in the sun. It is such grandeur, too, to the cub, to get a chance to give an order; for often the pilot will simply say, "Let her go about!" and leave the rest to the cub, who instantly cries, in his sternest tone of command, "Ease starboard! Strong on the larboard! Starboard, give way! With a will, men!" The cub enjoys sounding for the further reason that the eyes of the passengers are watching all the yawl's movements with absorbing interest, if the time be daylight; and if it be night, he knows that those same wondering eyes are fastened upon the yawl's lantern as it glides out into the gloom and dims away in the remote distance.

One trip a pretty girl of sixteen spent her time in our pilothouse with her uncle and aunt, every day and all day long. I fell in love with her. So did Mr. Thornburg's cub, Tom G. Tom and I had been bosom friends until this time; but now a coolness began to arise. I told the girl a good many of my river adventures, and made myself out a good deal of a hero; Tom tried to make himself appear to be a hero, too, and succeeded to some extent, but then he always had a way of embroidering. However, virtue is its own reward, so I was a barely perceptible trifle ahead in the contest. About this time something happened which promised handsomely for me: the pilots decided to sound the crossing at the head of 21. This would occur about nine or ten o'clock at night, when the passengers would be still up; it would be Mr. Thornburg's watch, therefore my chief would have to do the sounding. We had a perfect love of a sounding boat—long, trim, graceful, and as fleet as a greyhound; her thwarts were cushioned; she carried twelve oarsmen; one of the mates was always sent in her to transmit orders to her crew, for ours was a steamer where no end of "style" was put on.

We tied up at the shore above 21, and got ready. It was a foul night, and the river was so wide there that a landsman's uneducated eyes could discern no opposite shore through such a gloom. The passengers were alert and interested; everything was satisfactory. As I hurried through the engine room, picturesquely gotten up in storm toggery, I met Tom, and could not forbear delivering myself of a mean speech:

"Ain't you glad *you* don't have to go out sounding?"

Tom was passing on, but he quickly turned, and said:

"Now just for that, you can go and get the sounding pole yourself. I was going after it, but I'd see you in Halifax, now, before I'd do it."

"Who wants you to get it? I don't. It's in the sounding boat."

"It ain't, either. It's been new-painted; and it's been up on the ladies' cabin guards two days, drying."

I flew back, and shortly arrived among the crowd of watching and wondering ladies just in time to hear the command:

"Give way, men!"

I looked over, and there was the gallant sounding boat booming away, the unprincipled Tom presiding at the tiller, and my chief sitting by him with the sounding pole which I had been sent on a fool's errand to fetch. Then that young girl said to me:

"Oh, how awful to have to go out in that little boat on such a night! Do you think there is any danger?"

I would rather have been stabbed. I went off, full of venom, to help in the pilothouse. By and by the boat's lantern disappeared, and after an interval a wee spark glimmered upon the face of the water a mile away. Mr. Thornburg blew the whistle in acknowledgment, backed the steamer out, and made for it. We flew along for a while, then slackened steam and went cautiously gliding toward the spark. Presently Mr. Thornburg exclaimed:

"Hello, the buoy lantern's out!"

He stopped the engines. A moment or two later he said:

"Why, there it is again!"

So he came ahead on the engines once more, and rang for the leads. Gradually the water shoaled up, and then began to deepen again! Mr. Thornburg muttered:

"Well, I don't understand this. I believe that buoy has drifted off the reef. Seems to be a little too far to the left. No matter, it is safest to run over it, anyhow."

So, in that solid world of darkness we went creeping down on the light. Just as our bows were in the act of plowing over it, Mr. Thornburg seized the bell ropes, rang a startling peal, and exclaimed:

"My soul, it's the sounding boat!"

A sudden chorus of wild alarms burst out far below—a pause—and then a sound of grinding and crashing followed. Mr. Thornburg exclaimed:

"There! The paddle wheel has ground the sounding boat to lucifer matches! Run! See who is killed!"

I was on the main deck in the twinkling of an eye. My chief and the third mate and nearly all the men were safe. They had discovered their danger when it was too late to pull out of the way; then, when the great guards overshadowed them a moment later, they were prepared and knew what to do; at my chief's order they sprang at the right instant, seized the guard, and were hauled aboard. The next moment the sounding yawl swept aft to the wheel and was struck and splintered to atoms. Two of the men and the cub Tom were missing—a fact which spread like wildfire over the boat. The passengers came flocking to the forward gangway, ladies and all, anxious-eyed, white-faced, and talked in awed voices of the dreadful thing. And often and again I heard them say, "Poor fellows! poor boy, poor boy!"

By this time the boat's yawl was manned and away, to search for the missing. Now a faint call was heard, off to the left. The yawl had disappeared in the other direction. Half the people rushed to one side to encourage the swimmer with their shouts; the other half rushed the other way to shriek to the yawl to turn about. By the callings the swimmer was approaching, but some said the sound showed failing strength. The crowd massed themselves against the boiler-deck railings, leaning over and staring into the gloom; and every faint and fainter cry wrung from them such words as "Ah, poor fellow, poor fellow! is there *no* way to save him?"

But still the cries held out, and drew nearer, and presently the voice said pluckily:

"I can make it! Stand by with a rope!"

What a rousing cheer they gave him! The chief mate took his stand in the glare of a torch basket, a coil of rope in his hand, and his men grouped about him. The next moment the swimmer's face appeared in the circle of light, and in another one the owner of it was hauled aboard, limp and drenched, while cheer on cheer went up. It was that devil Tom.

The yawl crew searched everywhere, but found no sign of the two men. They probably failed to catch the guard, tumbled back, and were struck by the wheel and killed. Tom had never jumped for the guard at all, but had plunged headfirst into the river and dived under the wheel. It was nothing; I could have done it easy enough, and I said so; but everybody went on just the same, making a wonderful to-do over that ass, as if he had done something great. That girl couldn't seem to have enough of that pitiful "hero" the rest of the trip; but little I cared; I loathed her, anyway.

The way we came to mistake the sounding boat's lantern for the buoy light was this: My chief said that after laying the buoy he fell away and watched it till it seemed to be secure; then he took up a position a few hundred yards below it and a little to one side of the steamer's course, headed the sounding boat upstream, and waited. Having to wait some time, he and the officer got to talking; he looked up when he judged that the steamer was about on the reef; saw that the buoy was gone, but supposed that the steamer had already run over it; he went on with his talk; he noticed that the steamer was getting very close down to him, but that was the correct thing; it was her business to shave him closely, for convenience in taking him aboard; he was expecting her to sheer off, until the last moment; then it flashed upon him that she was trying to run him down, mistaking his lantern for the buoy light; so he sang out, "Stand by to spring for the guard, men!" and the next instant the jump was made.

A PILOT'S NEEDS

But I am wandering from what I was intending to do; that is, make plainer than perhaps appears in the previous chapters some of the peculiar requirements of the science of piloting. First of all, there is one faculty which a pilot must incessantly cultivate until he has brought it to absolute perfection. Nothing short of perfection will do. That faculty is memory. He cannot stop with merely thinking a thing is so and so; he must *know* it; for this is eminently one of the "exact" sciences. With what scorn a pilot was looked upon, in the old times, if he ever ventured to deal in that feeble phrase "I think," instead of the vigorous one, "I know!" One cannot easily realize what a tremendous thing it is to know every trivial detail of twelve hundred miles of river and know it with absolute exactness. If you will take the longest street in New York, and travel up and down it, conning its features patiently until you know every house and window and lamppost and big and little sign by heart, and know them so accurately that you can instantly name the one you are abreast of when you are set down at random in that street in the middle of an inky black night, you will then have a tolerable notion of the amount and the exactness of a pilot's knowledge who carries the Mississippi River in his head. And then, if you will go on until you know every street crossing, the character, size, and position of the crossing stones, and the varying depth of mud in each of these numberless places, you will have some idea of what the pilot must know in order to keep a Mississippi steamer out of trouble. Next, if you will take half of the signs in that long street, and *change their places* once a month, and still manage to know their new positions accurately on dark nights, and keep up with these repeated changes without making any mistakes, you will understand what is required of a pilot's peerless memory by the fickle Mississippi.

I think a pilot's memory is about the most wonderful thing in the world. To know the Old and New Testaments by heart, and be able to recite them glibly, forward or backward, or begin at random anywhere in the book and recite both ways and never trip or make a mistake, is no extravagant mass of knowledge, and no marvelous facility, compared to a pilot's massed knowledge of the Mississippi and his marvelous facility in the handling of it. I make this comparison deliberately, and believe I am not expanding the truth when I do it. Many will think my figure too strong, but pilots will not.

And how easily and comfortably the pilot's memory does its work; how placidly effortless is its way; how *unconsciously* it lays up its vast stores, hour by hour, day by day, and never loses or mislays a single valuable package of them all! Take an instance. Let a leadsman cry, "Half twain! half twain! half twain! half twain! half twain!" until it becomes as monotonous as the ticking of a clock; let conversation be going on all the time, and the pilot be doing his share of the talking, and no longer consciously listening to the leadsman; and in the midst of this endless string of half twains let a single "quarter twain!" be interjected, without emphasis, and then the half-twain cry go on again, just as before; two or three weeks later that pilot can describe with precision the boat's position in the river when that quarter twain was uttered, and give you such a lot of head marks, stern marks, and side marks to guide you, that you ought to be able to take the boat there and put her in that same spot again yourself! The cry of "quarter twain" did not really take his mind from his talk, but his trained faculties instantly photographed the bearings, noted the change of depth, and laid up the important details for future reference without requiring any assistance from *him* in the matter. If you were walking and talking with a friend, and another friend at your side kept up a monotonous repetition of the vowel sound A, for a couple of blocks, and then in the midst interjected an R, thus, A, A, A, A, A, R, A, A, A, etc., and gave the R no emphasis, you would not be able to state, two or three weeks afterward, that the R had been put in, nor be able to tell what objects you were passing at the moment it was done. But you could if your memory had been patiently and laboriously trained to do that sort of thing mechanically.

Give a man a tolerably fair memory to start with, and piloting will develop it into a very colossus of capability. But *only in the matters it is daily drilled in.* A time would come when the man's faculties could not help noticing landmarks and soundings, and his memory could not help holding on to them with the grip of a vise; but if you asked that same man at noon what he had had for breakfast, it would be ten chances to one that he could not tell you. Astonishing things can be done with the human memory if you will devote it faithfully to one particular line of business.

At the time that wages soared so high on the Missouri River, my chief, Mr. Bixby, went up there and learned more than a thousand miles of that stream with an ease and rapidity that were astonishing. When he had seen each division *once* in the daytime and *once* at night, his education was so nearly complete that he took out a "daylight" license; a few trips later he took out a full license, and went to piloting day and night—and he ranked A1, too.

Mr. Bixby placed me as steersman for a while under a pilot whose feats of memory were a constant marvel to me. However, his memory was born in him, I think, not built. For instance, somebody would mention a name. Instantly Mr. Brown would break in:

"Oh, I knew *him*. Sallow-faced, redheaded fellow, with a little scar on the side of his throat, like a splinter under the flesh. He was only in the Southern trade six months. That was thirteen years ago. I made a trip with him. There was five feet in the upper river then; the *Henry Blake* grounded at the foot of Tower Island drawing four and a half; the *George Elliott* unshipped her rudder on the wreck of the *Sunflower*—"

"Why, the *Sunflower* didn't sink until—"

"*I* know when she sunk; it was three years before that, on the 2d of December; Asa Hardy was captain of her, and his brother John was first clerk; and it was his first trip in her, too; Tom Jones told me these things a week afterward in New Orleans; he was first mate of the *Sunflower*. Captain Hardy stuck a nail in his foot the 6th of July of the next year, and died of the lockjaw on the 15th. His brother John died two years after—3rd of March—erysipelas. I never saw either of the Hardys— they were Alleghany River men—but people who knew them told me all these things. And they said Captain Hardy wore yarn socks winter and summer just the same, and his first wife's name was Jane Shook— she was from New England—and his second one died in a lunatic asylum. It was in the blood. She was from Lexington, Kentucky. Name was Horton before she was married."

And so on, by the hour, the man's tongue would go. He could *not* forget anything. It was simply impossible. The most trivial details remained as distinct and luminous in his head, after they had lain there for years, as the most memorable events. His was not simply a pilot's memory; its grasp was universal. If he were talking about a trifling letter he had received seven years before, he was pretty sure to deliver you the entire screed from memory. And then, without observing that he was departing from the true line of his talk, he was more than likely to hurl in a long-drawn parenthetical biography of the writer of that letter; and you were lucky indeed if he did not take up that writer's relatives, one by one, and give you their biographies, too.

Such a memory as that is a great misfortune. To it, all occurrences are of the same size. Its possessor cannot distinguish an interesting circumstance from an uninteresting one. As a talker, he is bound to clog his narrative with tiresome details and make himself an insufferable bore. Moreover, he cannot stick to his subject. He picks up every little grain of memory he discerns in his way, and so is led aside. Mr. Brown would start out with the honest intention of telling you a vastly funny anecdote about a dog. He would be "so full of laugh" that he could hardly begin; then his memory would start with the dog's breed and personal appearance; drift into a history of his owner; of his owner's family, with descriptions of weddings and burials that had occurred in it, together with recitals of congratulatory verses and obituary poetry provoked by the same; then this memory would recollect that one of these events occurred during the celebrated "hard winter" of such-and-such a year, and a minute description of that winter would follow, along with the names of people who were frozen to death, and statistics showing the high figures which pork and hay went up to. Pork and hay would suggest corn and fodder; corn and fodder would suggest cows and horses; cows and horses would suggest the circus and certain celebrated bareback riders; the transition from the circus to the menagerie was easy and natural; from the elephant to equatorial Africa was but a step; then of course the heathen savages would suggest religion; and at the end of three or four hours' tedious jaw, the watch would change, and Brown would go out of the pilothouse muttering extracts from sermons he had heard years before about the efficacy of prayer as a means of grace. And the original first mention would be all you had learned about that dog, after all this waiting and hungering.

A pilot must have a memory; but there are two higher qualities which he must also have. He must have good and quick judgment and decision, and a cool, calm courage that no peril can shake. Give a man the merest trifle of pluck to start with, and by the time he has become a pilot he cannot be unmanned by any danger a steamboat can get into; but one cannot quite say the same for judgment. Judgment is a matter of brains, and a man must *start* with a good stock of that article or he will never succeed as a pilot.

The growth of courage in the pilothouse is steady all the time, but it does not reach a high and satisfactory condition until some time after the young pilot has been "standing his own watch" alone and under the staggering weight of all the responsibilities connected with the position. When the apprentice has become pretty thoroughly acquainted with the river, he goes clattering along so fearlessly with his steamboat, night or day, that he presently begins to imagine that it is *his* courage that animates him; but the first time the pilot steps out and leaves him to his own devices he finds out it was the other man's. He discovers that the article has been left out of his own cargo altogether. The whole river is bristling with exigencies in a moment; he is not prepared for them; he does not know how to meet them; all his knowledge forsakes him; and within fifteen minutes he is as white as a sheet and scared almost to death. Therefore pilots wisely train these cubs by various strategic tricks to look danger in the face a little more calmly. A favorite way of theirs is to play a friendly swindle upon the candidate.

Mr. Bixby served me in this fashion once, and for years afterward I used to blush, even in my sleep, when I thought of it. I had become a good steersman; so good, indeed, that I had all the work to do on our watch, night and day. Mr. Bixby seldom made a suggestion to me; all he ever did was to take the wheel on particularly bad nights or in particularly bad crossings, land the boat when she needed to be landed, play gentleman of leisure nine-tenths of the watch, and collect the wages. The lower river was about bankfull, and if anybody had questioned my ability to run any crossing between Cairo and New Orleans without help or instruction, I should have felt irreparably hurt. The idea of being afraid of any crossing in the lot, in the *daytime*, was a thing too preposterous for contemplation. Well, one matchless summer's day I was bowling down the bend above Island 66, brimful of self-conceit and carrying my nose as high as a giraffe's, when Mr. Bixby said:

"I am going below awhile. I suppose you know the next crossing?"

This was almost an affront. It was about the plainest and simplest crossing in the whole river. One couldn't come to any harm, whether he ran it right or not; and as for depth, there never had been any bottom there. I knew all this, perfectly well.

"Know how to *run* it? Why, I can run it with my eyes shut."

"How much water is there in it?"

"Well, that is an odd question. I couldn't get bottom there with a church steeple."

"You think so, do you?"

The very tone of the question shook my confidence. That was what Mr. Bixby was expecting. He left, without saying anything more. I began to imagine all sorts of things. Mr. Bixby, unknown to me, of course, sent somebody down to the forecastle with some mysterious instructions to the leadsmen, another messenger was sent to whisper among the officers, and then Mr. Bixby went into hiding behind a smokestack where he could observe results. Presently the captain stepped out on the hurricane deck; next the chief mate appeared; then a clerk. Every moment or two a straggler was added to my audience; and before I got to the head of the island I had fifteen or twenty people assembled down there under my nose. I began to wonder what the trouble was. As I started across, the captain glanced aloft at me and said, with a sham uneasiness in his voice:

"Where is Mr. Bixby?"

"Gone below, sir."

But that did the business for me. My imagination began to construct dangers out of nothing, and they multiplied faster than I could keep the run of them. All at once I imagined I saw shoal water ahead! The wave of coward agony that surged through me then came near dislocating every joint in me. All my confidence in that crossing vanished. I seized the bell rope; dropped it, ashamed; seized it again; dropped it once more; clutched it tremblingly once again, and pulled it so feebly that I could hardly hear the stroke myself. Captain and mate sang out instantly, and both together:

"Starboard lead there! and quick about it!"

This was another shock. I began to climb the wheel like a squirrel; but I would hardly get the boat started to port before I would see new dangers on that side, and away I would spin to the other; only to find perils accumulating to starboard, and be crazy to get to port again. Then came the leadsman's sepulchral cry:

"D-e-e-p four!"

Deep four in a bottomless crossing! The terror of it took my breath away.

"M-a-r-k three! M-a-r-k three! Quarter-less-three! Half twain!"

This was frightful! I seized the bell ropes and stopped the engines.

"Quarter twain! Quarter twain! *Mark* twain!"

I was helpless. I did not know what in the world to do. I was quaking from head to foot, and I could have hung my hat on my eyes, they stuck out so far.

"Quarter-*less*-twain! Nine-and-a-*half!*"

We were *drawing* nine! My hands were in a nerveless flutter. I could not ring a bell intelligibly with them. I flew to the speaking tube and shouted to the engineer:

"Oh, Ben, if you love me, *back* her! Quick, Ben! Oh, back the immortal *soul* out of her!"

I heard the door close gently. I looked around, and there stood Mr. Bixby, smiling a bland, sweet smile. Then the audience on the hurricane deck sent up a thundergust of humiliating laughter. I saw it all, now, and I felt meaner than the meanest man in human history. I laid it in the lead, set the boat in her marks, came ahead on the engines, and said:

"It was a fine trick to play on an orphan, *wasn't* it? I suppose I'll never hear the last of how I was ass enough to heave the lead at the head of 66."

"Well, no, you won't, maybe. In fact I hope you won't; for I want you to learn something by that experience. Didn't you *know* there was no bottom in that crossing?"

"Yes, sir, I did."

"Very well, then. You shouldn't have allowed me or anybody else to shake your confidence in that knowledge. Try to remember that. And another thing: when you get into a dangerous place, don't turn coward. That isn't going to help matters any."

It was a good enough lesson, but pretty hardly learned. Yet about the hardest part of it was that for months I so often had to hear a phrase which I had conceived a particular distaste for. It was, "Oh, Ben, if you love me, back her!"

RANK AND DIGNITY OF PILOTING

In my preceding chapters I have tried, by going into the minutiae of the science of piloting, to carry the reader step by step to a comprehension of what the science consists of; and at the same time I have tried to show him that it is a very curious and wonderful science, too, and very worthy of his attention. If I have seemed to love my subject, it is no surprising thing, for I loved the profession far better than any I have followed since, and I took a measureless pride in it. The reason is plain: a pilot, in those days, was the only unfettered and entirely independent human being that lived in the earth. Kings are but the hampered servants of parliament and the people; parliaments sit in chains forged by their constituency; the editor of a newspaper cannot be independent, but must work with one hand tied behind him by party and patrons, and be content to utter only half or two-thirds of his mind; no clergyman is a free man and may speak the whole truth, regardless of his parish's opinions; writers of all kinds are manacled servants of the public. We write frankly and fearlessly, but then we "modify" before we print. In truth, every man and woman and child has a master, and worries and frets in servitude; but, in the day I write of, the Mississippi pilot had *none*. The captain could stand upon the hurricane deck, in the pomp of a very brief authority, and give him five or six orders while the vessel backed into the stream, and then that skipper's reign was over. The moment that the boat was under way in the river, she was under the sole and unquestioned control of the pilot. He could do with her exactly as he pleased, run her when and whither he chose, and tie her up to the bank whenever his judgment said that that course was best. His movements were entirely free; he consulted no one, he received commands from nobody, he promptly resented even the merest suggestions. Indeed, the law of the United States forbade him to listen to commands or suggestions, rightly considering that the pilot necessarily knew better how to handle the boat than anybody could tell him. So here was the novelty of a king without a keeper, an absolute monarch who was absolute in sober truth and not by a fiction of words. I have seen a boy of eighteen taking a great steamer serenely into what seemed almost certain destruction, and the aged captain standing mutely by, filled with apprehension but powerless to interfere. His interference, in that particular instance, might have been an excellent thing, but to permit it would have been to establish a most pernicious precedent. It will easily be guessed, considering the pilot's boundless authority, that he was a great personage in the old steamboating days. He was treated with marked courtesy by the captain and with marked deference by all the officers and servants; and this deferential spirit was quickly communicated to the passengers, too. I think pilots were about the only people I ever knew who failed to show, in some degree, embarrassment in the presence of traveling foreign princes. But then, people in one's own grade of life are not usually embarrassing objects.

The foregoing consists of Chapters 1, 4, and 6 through 14 of Mark Twain's LIFE ON THE MISSISSIPPI.

La Bruyère

1645–1696

The French critic and essayist Jean de la Bruyère was born in Paris in 1645, the son of a commoner who was a government official. He studied at the University of Orléans and passed the bar examination, but he never practiced law. In 1673 he bought a post in the Revenue Department at Caen that conferred prestige and an income. He sold the post fourteen years later and returned to Paris.

A few years earlier, La Bruyère had been introduced to the Condé household by the influential historian and theologian Bishop Bossuet. The Prince de Condé was one of the great nobles of France, and La Bruyère was engaged to tutor Condé's grandson, Louis, duc de Bourbon. He also taught the young man's child wife, Mlle de Nantes, a daughter of Louis XIV.

At the age of forty, soon after entering the Condé household, La Bruyère published the first edition of his great work, the *Characters*. The work consisted of short portrait sketches, some of them translated from the Greek of Theophrastus, some original with La Bruyère.

Many of the portraits, though they were given classical names, depicted courtiers and literary figures of the time. La Bruyère made many enemies, but the friendship of Bossuet and the influence of Condé were sufficient protection. La Bruyère continued to bring out new editions of his book, each containing more biting and satirical characters than the last. The books were read avidly, if indignantly, and a series of "keys" were circulated in manuscript purporting to identify the persons he described.

Because so many powerful literary figures were offended by his work, La Bruyère was turned down by the French Academy on three different occasions. Finally, in 1693, his friends pushed through his election. His speech of admission, thoroughly unrepentant, was criticized as sharply as his books. This speech, a few letters to Condé, a disputed posthumous treatise, and the successive editions of the *Characters* are all that survive of what was probably a considerable body of writings. La Bruyère died suddenly on May 10, 1696.

His classical model, Theophrastus (371/370—288/287 B.C.), the Greek philosopher and scientist, was a friend and student of both Plato and Aristotle, and the latter's successor as director of the Lyceum at Athens. He produced two extant works of botany and a collection of ethical *Characters*—brief, witty delineations of moral types. The publication of the *Characters* in 1592, in a Latin version by Casaubon, immediately created a vogue. Scores of authors, both in England and France, began to produce books of characters. Some imitated the moral, philosophical tone of Theophrastus, but others were sharp and satirical. Many writers saw in the Theophrastian characters an ideal way to express their criticisms of society—and of their enemies.

No one, perhaps, was a more successful writer of characters than La Bruyère, whose work had the advantage of appearing after nearly a century of experiment with the form. He learned from his predecessors, particularly what should be avoided in a character, and added to this knowledge an extremely ready wit, a precise faculty of observation, and the capacity to write what is called classical French style better than any other French writer, it is said, with the single exception of Racine.

La Bruyère was a conservative man. In "the battle of the books," he took the side of the ancients, holding that their books excelled those of the moderns. He respected royalty and would not tolerate revolutionary or even critical ideas in politics or religion. As a tutor in the household of a great prince, however, he could observe at firsthand the corruption of high society and court life. The pretensions of hypocritical courtiers, of would-be intellectuals, sanctimonious churchmen, and the newly rich all lay before him.

La Bruyère was too intelligent and independent to tolerate the vice, wastefulness, and stupidity that he saw all around him. But he satirized individuals rather than the traditions and institutions. He showed his sympathy with the poor by ridiculing the people who exploited them, but he did not attack the institutions which kept them impoverished. He exposed the monumental selfishness of the high official Champagne, who wallowed in luxuries while depriving the poor of bread; but he said nothing against the venal system of government in which Champagne held office.

It is perhaps this shortcoming in La Bruyère which has kept him from being ranked with such great essayists and social critics as Montaigne and Voltaire. He did not examine into causes, as they did, but only exposed their symptoms on the surface of life. On the other hand, La Bruyère has much of Montaigne's urbane wit, and there are flashes of bitter truth in his *Characters* that would do credit to Voltaire. He reminds us often of a great artist who requires only half a dozen lines to draw a portrait. In swiftness and skill, his characterizations have never been surpassed.

Characters

ARSÈNE

Arsène contemplates mankind from the summit of his mind and, seen from that eminence, men frighten him, so to speak, by their littleness. Praised and exalted to the skies by certain people who have arranged to admire each other reciprocally, he believes he possesses not only the good qualities he really has but all a man can have, which he will never have; thus occupied and filled with his sublime thoughts he barely gives himself time to deliver a few oracular statements; uplifted above human judgments by his character, he leaves to common minds the merit of an orderly, coherent life, and is himself responsible for his irregularities only to the circle of friends who regard them in a spirit of idolatry. They alone are competent to judge, can think and write; they alone ought to be writers. There is no other literary work, however well received in the world, however universally enjoyed by men of taste, which he—I will not say approves—but even condescends to read. He cannot be reformed by this portrait, for he will not read it.

CLÉANTE

Cléante is a gentleman; he chose a wife who is the most agreeable and reasonable woman in the world. Both are the delight and pleasure of the society they frequent; it would be impossible to find more probity and politeness anywhere else. To-morrow they leave each other and their deed of separation is drawn up at the notary's. Indeed, there are some merits which are not made to go together, there are certain incompatible virtues.

CHAMPAGNE

Champagne, at the moment he leaves a long dinner which inflates his belly, in the agreeable fumes of Avenay and Sillery wines, signs an order someone presents to him by which a whole province will be deprived of bread, unless it is countermanded. He is excusable; how can anyone in the first hour of digestion understand that people somewhere else may die of hunger?

GITON

Giton has a fresh complexion, a full face and bulging cheeks, a fixed and assured gaze, broad shoulders, a projecting stomach, a firm and deliberate tread. He speaks with confidence; he makes those who converse with him repeat what they have said and he only moderately enjoys what is said. He unfolds an ample handkerchief and blows his nose noisily; he spits to a great distance and sneezes very loudly. He sleeps by day, he sleeps by night; he snores in company. At table and in walking he occupies more room than anyone else. He takes the centre and walks with his equals; he stops and they stop; he walks on and they walk on; all regulate themselves by him. He interrupts and corrects those who are talking; he is not interrupted, he is listened to as long as he likes to talk; his opinion is accepted, the rumours he spreads are believed. If he sits down you will see him settle into an arm-chair, cross his legs, frown, pull his hat over his eyes and see no one, or lift it up again and show his brow from pride and audacity. He is cheerful, a hearty laugher, impatient, presumptuous, quick to anger, irreligious, politic, mysterious about current affairs; he believes he has talents and wit.

He is rich.

PHÉDON

Phédon has hollow eyes, a bilious complexion, a dry body and a thin face; he sleeps little and his slumber is very light; he is abstracted, dreamy and with all his wit seems stupid; he forgets to say what he knows or to speak of events which are known to him; and if he does so sometimes he comes out badly, he thinks he is a nuisance to those he speaks to, he relates things briefly but frigidly; he is not listened to, he does not stir laughter. He applauds, he smiles at what others say to him, he is of their opinion; he runs, he flies to render them little services. He is complaisant, flattering, eager, he is mysterious about his own affairs, sometimes a liar; he is superstitious, scrupulous, timid. He walks gently and lightly, he seems afraid to touch the ground; he walks with lowered eyes and dares not raise them to the passers-by. He is never among those who form a circle for discussion; he places himself behind the person who is speaking, furtively gathers what he says and goes away if he is looked at. He occupies no space, claims no place; he walks with hunched shoulders, his hat pulled over his eyes so as not to be seen; he shrinks and hides himself in his cloak; there are no streets or galleries so overcrowded and filled with people but that he finds a means of traversing them easily, of slipping through them without being noticed. If he is asked to sit down, he places himself just on the edge of the chair; he speaks in a low tone in conversation and articulates badly; yet with his friends he is open about public affairs, bitter against the age, very little disposed in favour of the ministers of state and the government. He never opens his mouth except to reply; he coughs and blows his nose behind his hat; he spits almost on himself, and he waits until he is alone to sneeze, or if it happens to him it is unperceived by the company present: he costs nobody a salute or a compliment.

He is poor.

DÉMOPHILE

Démophile, at my right, laments and exclaims: "All is lost, the country is done for, at least it is on the road to destruction. How can so strong, so general a coalition be resisted? What means are there, I do not say to overcome, but even to resist so many powerful enemies? There is no precedent for it in the monarchy. A hero, an Achilles, would succumb to it. Grievous faults have been committed (he goes on), I know what I am saying, it is my occupation, I have seen war and history has taught me a great deal." Then he speaks with admiration of Olivier Le Daim and Jacques Coeur: "There were men!" says he, "There were ministers!" He relates the worst and most unlucky news which could be invented; sometimes a party of our troops have been lured into an ambush and cut to pieces; sometimes certain troops besieged in a castle have surrendered unconditionally and have all been slaughtered: if you say the rumour is false and has not been confirmed, he does not listen, he adds that such a general has been killed; and although it is true that the general has only been slightly wounded and you assure him of the fact, he deplores his death, pities his widow, his children, the state; he pities himself: "He has lost a good friend and a powerful protector." He says that the German cavalry is invincible and grows pale at the very name of the Emperor's cuirassiers. "If such a place is attacked," he continues, "the siege will be raised. Either we shall remain on the defensive without risking battle;

or, if we fight, we shall lose, and if we lose it, there is the enemy at the frontier." And as Démophile gives the enemy wings, here he is in the heart of the kingdom: already he hears the tocsin sounding from the belfries and the call to arms; he thinks of his property and his estates; where will he place his money, his furniture, his family? Where will he fly to? Switzerland or Venice?

The foregoing consists
of a selection of sketches
from La Bruyère's CHARACTERS.

Thomas Carlyle

1795–1881

Thomas Carlyle, the prophet of heroes and hero worship, was born of humble parents in Ecclefechan, Scotland, in 1795. His father, a stonemason and small farmer, strained the family resources to provide his talented son with an education. The family bonds of the Carlyles were to remain strong through thick and thin—mostly thin —and Thomas later gave much financial assistance to his brothers.

At the age of fourteen, Thomas walked ninety miles to the University of Edinburgh, where he enrolled to study the ministry. Things turned out differently. He was attracted to mathematics and even more to literature, became a teacher for a spell, and then, in 1818, a hack writer for Edinburgh publications. It was about this time that he fell in love with the writings and the personality of Goethe, and read voraciously in German authors of the time, who were little known in England. In 1823–24, he published a life of the poet Schiller and a translation of Goethe's *Wilhelm Meister's Apprenticeship*. He was fast becoming, with Coleridge, the interpreter of German thinkers in England. He was himself profoundly influenced by the philosophy of Kant and Fichte. He thenceforth looked for the reality and divinity of men, especially heroes, behind the appearances. Clothes do not make the man, he wrote in his *Sartor Resartus;* they conceal the spiritual self. Neither is the world to be

*Notes from the artist: "The quiet mood of Carlyle reading
in his garden is interrupted by the dynamic figure
of Oliver Cromwell, and that of the symbol of 'Liberty'
in the French Revolution. These are two examples of the 'strong-man'
concept, which so attracted Carlyle. The quotation is from his book
on this subject, On Heroes, Hero-Worship, and the Heroic in History."*

In books lies the soul of the whole Past Time; the articulate audible voice of the Past, when the body and material substance of it has altogether vanished like a dream.

T. Carlyle

judged by its sordid strivings for pleasure and economic gains—its mere outer garment.

In 1826 Carlyle had married the brilliant Jane Baillie Welsh, and soon after settled down with her on a lonely farm at Craigenputtock, where he lived inexpensively and wrote for periodicals. There Ralph Waldo Emerson paid him a visit, and the two men remained close friends for life. In 1834 John Stuart Mill persuaded Carlyle to come to London, where materials for his work in progress, *The French Revolution*, would be available. When the first volume was completed, he gave it to Mill to read, but a foolish servant girl used it to make a fire. Carlyle was undaunted. "It will be good for the character," he reflected; and he wrote the whole volume over again. The finished work, published in 1837, was immensely popular and established Carlyle's fame on firm ground.

Carlyle's theme is the divinely inspired hero-king. He is no ordinary hereditary monarch; without him the nation falters and disintegrates. He is the "Ablest Man . . . the truest hearted, justest, the Noblest Man." The Anglo-Saxon word for king is *Könning*, which means Able-man. He is the man who is able to direct the scattered forces of the nation, torn by jealousies and special interests, to an ideal goal.

The first problem is to find this man. Although there are many counterfeit heroes, Carlyle warns us against skepticism and faultfinding. It is better that the leader make mistakes than that there should be no leader at all. A second problem which crops up is whether leaders or laws are the best safeguard of our liberties and welfare. Sometimes the fate of a country seems to depend on a single man, a Washington or a Lincoln. Yet we see to it that laws are passed to which all heroes and would-be heroes must bow. There is no doubt how Carlyle would stand on this issue.

Of the two heroes whom Carlyle portrays in the essay which follows, Napoleon had a much better reputation than Cromwell. Carlyle reverses this judgment, and makes a stirring defense of the real Cromwell—so much misunderstood and maligned. Even his rigors and cruelties were virtues—marks of an indomitable will to do what had to be done. Napoleon was also an "Able-man." Yet in the end he betrayed his cause for a throne, whereas Cromwell remained true to the Revolution, and could not be tempted.

What are the moving forces of history? is the question that has been raised. It cannot be avoided if we are to understand the things that are going on today, and what the future is likely to bring. In the nineteenth century several theories were advanced. For Hegel world history was a battleground of ideas and spiritual forces; for Marx it was a battleground of classes, technologies, and economic forces. Hegel saw history progressing toward something like the Prussian monarchy, whereas for Marx the goal is the classless society.

Carlyle's interpretation was altogether different. The decisive and constructive forces in history are its great men and heroes. Every era and every crisis of history has its superlative men, who are able to take the helm and to convert chaos and destruction into something meaningful and worthy. But they must be given a chance. They must be recognized for what they are. When doubt, distrust, and envy stifle the natural inclination to revere and obey true leaders, stagnation and degeneracy follow. This was what had happened in his own time, Carlyle thought. Petty men, calculation, meanness dominated the national scene.

The very opposite view was put forward by Tolstoy a few years later. In his novel *War and Peace*, he argues that the leaders supposed to have shaped history were actually its pawns—and heartless egoists at that. He shows us Napoleon on the battlefield and Napoleon grunting in his bathtub. In neither role is he exceptional or admirable.

Such clashes of opposing judgments help us to find the truth for ourselves.

The Hero
as King

We come now to the last form of Heroism, that which we call Kingship. The Commander over men, he to whose will our wills are to be subordinated, and loyally surrender themselves, and find their welfare in doing so, may be reckoned the most important of Great Men. He is practically the summary for us of all the various figures of Heroism; Priest, Teacher, whatsoever of earthly or of spiritual dignity we can fancy to reside in a man, embodies itself here, to command over us, to furnish us with constant practical teaching, to tell us for the day and hour what we are to do. He is called *Rex*, Regulator, *Roi;* our own name is still better: King, *Könning*, which means *Can*-ning, Able-man.

Numerous considerations, pointing towards deep, questionable, and indeed unfathomable regions, present themselves here: on the most of which we must resolutely for the present forbear to speak at all. As Burke said that perhaps fair trial by jury was the soul of government, and that all legislation, administration, parliamentary debating, and the rest of it, went on, in "order to bring twelve impartial men into a jury-box"; so, by much stronger reason, may I say here that the finding of your Ableman and getting him invested with the symbols of ability, with dignity, worship (worth-ship), royalty, kinghood, or whatever we call it, so that he may actually have room to guide according to his faculty of doing it, is the business, well or ill accomplished, of all social procedure whatsoever in this world! Hustings speeches, parliamentary motions, Reform Bills, French Revolutions, all mean at heart this; or else nothing. Find in any country the Ablest Man that exists there; raise him to the supreme place, and loyally reverence him: you have a perfect government for that country; no ballot-box, parliamentary eloquence, voting, constitution-building, or other machinery whatsoever can improve it a whit. It is in the perfect state: an ideal country. The Ablest Man; he means also the truest hearted, justest, the Noblest Man: what he tells us to do must be precisely the wisest, fittest that we could anywhere or anyhow learn: the thing which it will in all ways behove us, with right loyal thankfulness, and nothing doubting, to do! Our doing and life were then, so far as government could regulate it, well regulated; that were the ideal of constitutions.

Alas, we know very well that Ideals can never be completely embodied in practice. Ideals must ever lie a very great way off; and we will right thankfully content ourselves with any not intolerable approximation thereto! Let no man, as Schiller says, too querulously "measure by a scale of perfection the meagre product of reality" in this poor world of ours. We will esteem him no wise man; we will esteem him a sickly, discontented, foolish man. And yet, on the other hand, it is never to be forgotten that Ideals do exist; that if they be not approximated to at all, the whole matter goes to wreck! Infallibly. No bricklayer builds a wall perfectly perpendicular; mathematically this is not possible; a certain degree of perpendicularity suffices him; and he, like a good bricklayer, who must have done with his job, leaves it so. And yet if he sway too much from the perpendicular; above all, if he throw plummet and level quite away from him, and pile brick on brick heedless, just as it comes to hand! Such bricklayer, I think, is in a bad way. He has forgotten himself: but the Law of Gravitation does not forget to act on him; he and his wall rush down into confused welter of ruin!

This is the history of all rebellions, French Revolutions, social explosions in ancient or modern times. You have put the too Unable man at the head of affairs! The too ignoble, unvaliant, fatuous man. You have forgotten that there is any rule, or natural necessity whatever, of putting the Able Man there. Brick must lie on brick as it may and can. Unable Simulacrum of Ability, quack, in a word, must adjust himself with quack, in all manner of administration of human things—which accordingly lie unadministered, fermenting into unmeasured masses of failure, of indigent misery: in the outward, and in the inward or spiritual, miserable millions stretch out the hand for their due supply, and it is not there. The law of gravitation acts; Nature's laws do none of them forget to act. The miserable millions burst forth into Sansculottism, or some other sort of madness; bricks and bricklayers lie as a fatal chaos!

Much sorry stuff, written some hundred years ago or more, about the Divine right of Kings, moulders unread now in the Public Libraries of this country. Far be it from us to disturb the calm process by which it is disappearing harmlessly from the earth, in those repositories! At the same time, not to let the immense rubbish go without leaving us, as it ought, some soul of it behind—I will say that it did mean something; something true, which it is important for us and all men to keep in mind. To assert that in whatever man you chose to lay hold of (by this or the other plan of clutching at him); and clapped a round piece of metal on the head of, and called King—there straightway came to reside a divine virtue, so that he became a kind of God, and a Divinity inspired him with faculty and right to rule over you to all lengths: this—what can we do with this but leave it to rot silently in the Public Libraries? But I will say withal, and that is what these Divine-right men meant, that in Kings, and in all human authorities, and relations that men god-created can form among each other, there is verily either a Divine Right or else a Diabolic Wrong: one or the other of these two! For it is false altogether what the last Sceptical Century taught us, that this world is a steam engine. There is a God in this world; and a God's-sanction, or else the violation of such, does look out from all ruling and obedience, from all moral acts of men. There is no act more moral between men than that of rule and obedience. Woe to him that claims obedience when it is not due; woe to him that refuses it when it is! God's law is in that, I say, however the Parchment laws may run: there is a Divine Right or else a Diabolic Wrong at the heart of every claim that one man makes upon another.

It can do none of us harm to reflect on this: in all the relations of life it will concern us; in Loyalty and Royalty, the highest of these. I esteem the modern error, that all goes by self-interest and the checking and balancing of greedy knaveries, and that, in short, there is nothing divine whatever in the association of men, a still more despicable error, natural as it is to an unbelieving century, than that of a divine right in people called Kings. I say, find me the true *Könning*, King, or Able-man, and he has a divine right over me. That we knew in some tolerable measure how to find him, and that all men were ready to acknowledge his divine right when found: this is precisely the healing which a sick world is everywhere, in these ages, seeking after! The true King, as guide of the practical, has ever something of the Pontiff in him—guide of the spiritual, from which all practice has its rise. This too is a true saying, That the King is head of the Church. But we will leave the Polemic stuff of a dead century to lie quiet on its bookshelves.

Certainly it is a fearful business, that of having your Ableman to seek, and not knowing in what manner to proceed about it! That is the world's sad predicament in these times of ours. They are times of Revolution, and have long been. The bricklayer with his bricks, no longer heedful of plummet or the law of gravitation, have toppled, tumbled, and it all welters as we see! But the beginning of it was not the French Revolution; that is rather the end, we can hope. It were truer to say, the beginning was three centuries farther back: in the Reformation of Luther. That the thing which still called itself Christian Church had become a Falsehood, and brazenly went about pretending to pardon men's sins for metallic coined money, and to do much else which in the everlasting truth of Nature it did not now do: here lay the vital malady. The inward being wrong, all outward went ever more and more wrong. Belief died away; all was Doubt, Disbelief. The builder cast away his plummet; said to himself, "What is gravitation? Brick lies on brick there!" Alas, does it not still sound strange to many of us, the assertion that there is a God's truth in the business of god-created men; that all is not a kind of grimace, an "expediency," diplomacy, one knows not what!

From that first necessary assertion of Luther's, "You, self-styled *Papa*, you are no Father in God at all; you are—a Chimera, whom I know not how to name in polite language!"—from that onward to the shout which rose round Camille Desmoulins in the Palais Royal, *"Aux armes!"* when the people had burst up against all manner of Chimeras—I find a natural historical sequence. That shout too, so frightful, half-infernal, was a great matter. Once more the voice of awakened nations; starting confusedly, as out of nightmare, as out of death-sleep, into some dim feeling that Life was real; that God's world was not an expediency and diplomacy! Infernal; yes, since they would not have it otherwise. Infernal, since not celestial or terrestrial! Hollowness, insincerity has to cease; sincerity of some sort has to begin. Cost what it may, reigns of terror, horrors of French Revolution or what else, we have to return to truth. Here is a Truth, as I said: a Truth clad in hell-fire, since they would not but have it so!

A common theory among considerable parties of men in England and elsewhere used to be that the French Nation had, in those days, as it were gone mad; that the French Revolution was a general act of insanity, a temporary conversion of France and large sections of the world into a kind of Bedlam. The event had risen and raged; but was a madness and nonentity, gone now happily into the region of Dreams and the Picturesque! To such comfortable philosophers, the Three Days of July 1830 must have been a surprising phenomenon. Here is the French Nation risen again, in musketry and death-struggle, out shooting and being shot, to make that same mad French Revolution good! The sons and grandsons of those men, it would seem, persist in the enterprise: they do not disown it; they will have it made good; will have themselves shot, if it be not made good! To philosophers who had made up their life-system on that "madness" quietus, no phenomenon could be more alarming. Poor Niebuhr, they say, the Prussian professor and historian, fell broken-hearted in consequence; sickened, if we can believe it, and died of the Three Days! It was surely not a very heroic death: little better than Racine's, dying because Louis XIV looked sternly on him once. The world had stood some considerable shocks, in its time; might have been expected to survive the Three Days too, and be found turning on its axis after even them! The Three Days told all mortals that the old French Revolution, mad as it might look, was not a transitory ebullition of Bedlam, but a genuine product of this Earth where we all live; that it was verily a fact, and that the world in general would do well everywhere to regard it as such.

Truly, without the French Revolution, one would not know what to make of an age like this at all. We will hail the French Revolution, as shipwrecked mariners might the sternest rock, in a world otherwise all of baseless sea and waves. A true Apocalypse, though a terrible one, to this false withered artificial time; testifying once more that Nature is preternatural; if not divine, then diabolic; that Semblance is not reality; that it has to become reality, or the world will take fire under it—burn it into what it is, namely Nothing! Plausibility has ended; empty Routine has ended; much has ended. This, as with a Trump of Doom, has been proclaimed to all men. They are the wisest who will learn it soonest. Long confused generations before it be learned; peace impossible till it be! The earnest man, surrounded, as ever, with a world of inconsistencies, can await patiently, patiently strive to do his work, in the midst of that. Sentence of Death is written down in Heaven against all that; sentence of Death is now proclaimed on the Earth against it: this he with his eyes may see. And surely, I should say, considering the other side of the matter, what enormous difficulties lie there, and how fast, fearfully fast, in all countries, the inexorable demand for solution of them is pressing on— he may easily find other work to do than labouring in the Sansculottic province at this time of day!

To me, in these circumstances, that of "Hero worship" becomes a fact inexpressibly precious—the most solacing fact one sees in the world at present. There is an everlasting hope in it for the management of the world. Had all traditions, arrangements, creeds, societies that men ever instituted sunk away, this would remain. The certainty of heroes being sent us; our faculty, our necessity, to reverence heroes when sent: it shines like a polestar through smoke-clouds, dust-clouds, and all manner of downrushing and conflagration.

Hero worship would have sounded very strange to those workers and fighters in the French Revolution. Not reverence for Great Men; not any hope or belief, or even wish, that Great Men could again appear in the world! Nature, turned into a "Machine," was as if effete now; could not any longer produce Great Men: I can tell her, she may give up the trade altogether, then; we cannot do without Great Men! But neither have I any quarrel with that of "Liberty and Equality"; with the faith that, wise great men being impossible, a level immensity of foolish small men would suffice. It was a natural faith then and there. "Liberty and Equality; no Authority needed any longer. Hero worship, reverence for such Authorities, has proved false, is itself a falsehood; no more of it! We have had such forgeries, we will now trust nothing. So many base plated coins passing in the market, the belief has now become common that no gold any longer exists—and even that we can do very well without gold!" I find this, among other things, in that universal cry of Liberty and Equality; and find it very natural, as matters then stood.

And yet surely it is but the transition from false to true. Considered as the whole truth, it is false altogether—the product of entire sceptical blindness, as yet only struggling to see. Hero worship exists forever, and everywhere: not Loyalty alone; it extends from divine adoration down to the lowest practical regions of life. "Bending before men," if it is not to be a mere empty grimace, better dispensed with than practised, is Hero worship—a recognition that there does dwell in that presence of our brother something divine; that every created man, as Novalis said, is a "revelation in the Flesh." They were Poets too that devised all those graceful courtesies which make life noble! Courtesy is not a falsehood or grimace; it need not be such. And Loyalty, religious Worship itself, are still possible; nay still inevitable.

May we not say, moreover, while so many of our late heroes have worked rather as revolutionary men, that nevertheless every Great Man, every genuine man, is by the nature of him a son of order, not of disorder? It is a tragical position for a true man to work in revolutions. He seems an anarchist; and indeed a painful element of anarchy does encumber him at every step—him to whose whole soul anarchy is hostile, hateful. His mission is order; every man's is. He is here to make what was disorderly, chaotic, into a thing ruled, regular. He is the missionary of order. Is not all work of man in this world a making of order? The carpenter finds rough trees: shapes them, constrains them into square fitness, into purpose and use. We arc all born enemies of disorder: it is tragical for us all to be concerned in image-breaking and down-pulling; for the Great Man, more a man than we, it is doubly tragical.

Thus too all human things, maddest French Sansculottisms, do and must work towards order. I say, there is not a man in them, raging in the thickest of the madness, but is impelled withal, at all moments, towards order. His very life means that; disorder is dissolution, death. No chaos but it seeks a centre to revolve round. While man is man, some Cromwell or Napoleon is the necessary finish of a Sansculottism. Curious: in those days when Hero worship was the most incredible thing to every one, how it does come out nevertheless, and assert itself practically, in a way which all have to credit. Divine right, take it on the great scale, is found to mean divine might withal! While old false formulas are getting trampled everywhere into destruction, new genuine substances unexpectedly unfold themselves indestructible. In rebellious ages, when Kingship itself seems dead and abolished, Cromwell, Napoleon step forth again as Kings. The history of these men is what we have now to look at, as our last phasis of Heroism. The old ages are brought back to us; the manner in which Kings were made, and Kingship itself first took rise, is again exhibited in the history of these two.

We have had many civil wars in England; wars of Red and White Roses, wars of Simon de Montfort; wars enough which are not very memorable. But that war of the Puritans has a significance which belongs to no one of the others. Trusting to your candour, which will suggest on the other side what I have not room to say, I will call it a section once more of that great universal war which alone makes up the true history of the world—the war of belief against unbelief! The struggle of men intent on the real essence of things, against men intent on the semblances and forms of things. The Puritans, to many, seem mere savage iconoclasts, fierce destroyers of forms; but it were more just to call them haters of untrue forms. I hope we know how to respect Laud and his King as well as them. Poor Laud seems to me to have been weak and ill-starred, not dishonest—an unfortunate pedant rather than anything worse. His "dreams" and superstitions, at which they laugh so, have an affectionate, lovable kind of character. He is like a college tutor, whose whole world is forms, college rules; whose notion is that these are the life and safety of the world. He is placed suddenly, with that unalterable luckless notion of his, at the head not of a college but of a nation, to regulate the most complex deep-reaching interests of men. He thinks they ought to go by the old decent regulations; nay that their salvation will lie in extending and improving these. Like a weak man, he drives with spasmodic vehemence towards his purpose; cramps himself to it, heeding no voice of prudence, no cry of pity: He will have his college rules obeyed by his collegians; that first; and till that, nothing. He is an ill-starred pedant, as I said. He would have it the world was a college of that kind, and the world *was not* that. Alas, was not his doom stern enough? Whatever wrongs he did, were they not all frightfully avenged on him?

It is meritorious to insist on forms; Religion and all else naturally clothes itself in forms. Everywhere the formed world is the only habitable one. The naked formlessness of Puritanism is not the thing I praise in the Puritans; it is the thing I pity—praising only the spirit which had rendered that inevitable! All substances clothe themselves in forms: but there are suitable true forms, and then there are untrue unsuitable. As the briefest definition, one might say, forms which *grow* round a substance, if we rightly understand that, will correspond to the real nature and purport of it, will be true, good; forms which are consciously *put* round a substance, bad. I invite you to reflect on this. It distinguishes true from false in ceremonial form, earnest solemnity from empty pageant, in all human things.

There must be a veracity, a natural spontaneity in forms. In the commonest meeting of men, a person making what we call "set speeches," is not he an offence? In the mere drawing-room, whatsoever courtesies you see to be grimaces, prompted by no spontaneous reality within, are a thing you wish to get away from. But suppose now it were some matter of vital concernment, some transcendent matter (as Divine Worship is), about which your whole soul, struck dumb with its excess of feeling, knew not how to *form* itself into utterance at all, and preferred formless silence to any utterance there possible—what should we say of a man coming forward to represent or utter it for you in the way of upholsterer-mummery? Such a man—let him depart swiftly, if he love himself! You have lost your only son; are mute, struck down, without even tears: an importunate man importunately offers to celebrate funeral games for him in the manner of the Greeks! Such mummery is not only not to be accepted—it is hateful, unendurable. It is what the old prophets called "idolatry," worshipping of hollow shows; what all earnest men do and will reject. We can partly understand what those poor Puritans meant. Laud dedicating that St. Catherine Creed's Church, in the manner we have it described, with his multiplied ceremonial bowings, gesticulations, exclamations: surely it is rather the rigorous formal pedant, intent on his "college rules," than the earnest prophet, intent on the essence of the matter!

Puritanism found such forms insupportable; trampled on such forms; we have to excuse it for saying, No form at all rather than such! It stood preaching in its bare pulpit, with nothing but the Bible in its hand. Nay, a man preaching from his earnest soul into the earnest souls of men: is not this virtually the essence of all Churches whatsoever? The nakedest, savagest reality, I say, is preferable to any semblance, however dignified. Besides, it will clothe itself with due semblance by and by, if it be real. No fear of that; actually no fear at all. Given the living man, there will be found clothes for him; he will find himself clothes. But the suit of clothes pretending that *it* is both clothes and man! We cannot "fight the French" by three hundred thousand red uniforms; there must be *men* in the inside of them! Semblance, I assert, must actually *not* divorce itself from Reality. If Semblance do, why then there must be men found to rebel against Semblance, for it has become a lie! These two antagonisms at war here, in the case of Laud and the Puritans, are as old nearly as the world. They went to fierce battle over England in that age; and fought out their confused controversy to a certain length, with many results for all of us.

In the age which directly followed that of the Puritans, their cause or themselves were little likely to have justice done them. Charles II and his Rochesters were not the kind of men you would set to judge what the worth or meaning of such men might have been. That there could be any faith or truth in the life of a man was what these poor Rochesters, and the age they ushered in, had forgotten. Puritanism was hung on gibbets, like the bones of the leading Puritans. Its work nevertheless went on accomplishing itself. All true work of a man, hang the author of it on what gibbet you like, must and will accomplish itself. We have our *habeas corpus*, our free representation of the people; acknowledgment, wide as the world, that all men are, or else must, shall, and will become, what we call free men; men with their life grounded on reality and justice, not on tradition, which has become unjust and a chimera! This in part and much besides this was the work of the Puritans.

And indeed, as these things became gradually manifest, the character of the Puritans began to clear itself. Their memories were, one after another, taken down from the gibbet; nay a certain portion of them are now, in these days, as good as canonized. Eliot, Hampden, Pym, nay Ludlow, Hutchinson, Vane himself, are admitted to be a kind of Heroes; political Conscript Fathers, to whom in no small degree we owe what makes us a free England: it would not be safe for anybody to designate these men as wicked now. Few Puritans of note but find their apologists somewhere, and have a certain reverence paid them by earnest men. One Puritan, I think, and almost he alone, our poor Cromwell, seems to hang yet on the gibbet, and find no hearty apologist anywhere. Him neither saint nor sinner will acquit of great wickedness. A man of ability, infinite talent, courage, and so forth: but he betrayed the cause. Selfish ambition, dishonesty, duplicity; a fierce, coarse, hypocritical *Tartuffe;* turning all that noble struggle for constitutional liberty into a sorry farce played for his own benefit: this and worse is the character they give of Cromwell. And then there come contrasts with Washington and others; above all, with these noble Pyms and Hampdens, whose noble work he stole for himself, and ruined into a futility and deformity.

This view of Cromwell seems to me the not unnatural product of a century like the eighteenth. As we said of the valet, so of the sceptic: He does not know a Hero when he sees him! The valet expected purple mantles, gilt sceptres, body-guards and flourishes of trumpets: the sceptic of the eighteenth century looks for regulated respectable formulas, principles, or what else he may call them; a style of speech and conduct which has got to seem "respectable," which can plead for itself in a handsome articulate manner, and gain the suffrages of an enlightened sceptical eighteenth century! It is, at bottom, the same thing that both the valet and he expect: the garnitures of some acknowledged royalty, which then they will acknowledge! The King coming to them in the rugged unformulistic state shall be no King.

For my own share, far be it from me to say or insinuate a word of disparagement against such characters as Hampden, Eliot, Pym, whom I believe to have been right worthy and useful men. I have read diligently what books and documents about them I could come at—with the honestest wish to admire, to love and worship them like Heroes; but I am sorry to say, if the real truth must be told, with very indifferent success! At bottom, I found that it would not do. They are very noble men, these; step along in their stately way, with their measured euphemisms, philosophies, parliamentary eloquences, ship-moneys, *Monarchies of Man:* a most constitutional, unblamable, dignified set of men. But the heart remains cold before them; the fancy alone endeavours to get up some worship of them. What man's heart does, in reality, break forth into any fire of brotherly love for these men? They are become dreadfully dull men! One breaks down often enough in the constitutional eloquence of the admirable Pym, with his "seventhly and lastly." You find that it may be the admirablest thing in the world, but that it is heavy—heavy as lead, barren as brick-clay; that, in a word, for you there is little or nothing now surviving there! One leaves all these nobilities standing in their niches of honour: the rugged outcast Cromwell, he is the man of them all in whom one still finds human stuff. The great savage Baresark: he could write no euphemistic *Monarchy of Man;* did not speak, did not work with glib regularity; had no straight story to tell for himself anywhere. But he stood bare, not cased in euphemistic coat of mail; he grappled like a giant, face to face, heart to heart, with the naked truth of things! That, after all, is the sort of man for one. I plead guilty to valuing such a man beyond all other sorts of men. Smooth-shaven Respectabilities not a few one finds, that are not good for much. Small thanks to a man for keeping his hands clean, who would not touch the work but with gloves on!

Neither, on the whole, does this constitutional tolerance of the eighteenth century for the other happier Puritans seem to be a very great matter. One might say it is but a piece of Formulism and Scepticism, like the rest. They tell us it was a sorrowful thing to consider that the foundation of our English Liberties should have been laid by "superstition." These Puritans came forward with Calvinistic incredible Creeds, Anti-Laudisms, Westminster Confessions; demanding, chiefly of all, that they should have liberty to worship in their own way. Liberty to tax themselves: that was the thing they should have demanded! It was superstition, fanaticism, disgraceful ignorance of constitutional philosophy to insist on the other thing! Liberty to tax oneself? Not to pay out money from your pocket except on reason shown? No century, I think, but a rather barren one would have fixed on that as the first right of man! I should say, on the contrary, a just man will generally have better cause than money in what shape soever, before deciding to revolt against his government. Ours is a most confused world, in which a good man will be thankful to see any kind of government maintain itself in a not insupportable manner; and here in England, to this hour, if he is not ready to pay a great many taxes which he can see very small reason in, it will not go well with him, I think! He must try some other climate than this. Taxgatherer? Money? He will say: "Take my money, since you can, and it is so desirable to you; take it, and take yourself away with it; and leave me alone to my work here. *I* am still here; can still work, after all the money you have taken from me!" But if they come to him, and say, "Acknowledge a lie; pretend to say you are worshipping God, when you are not doing it: believe not the thing that *you* find true, but the thing that I find, or pretend to find true!" He will answer: "No; by God's help, no! You may take my purse; but I cannot have my moral Self annihilated. The purse is any highwayman's who might meet me with a loaded pistol: but the Self is mine and God my maker's; it is not yours; and I will resist you to the death, and revolt against you, and, on the whole, front all manner of extremities, accusations and confusions, in defence of that!"

Really, it seems to me the one reason which could justify revolting, this of the Puritans. It has been the soul of all just revolts among men. Not hunger alone produced even the French Revolution: no, but the feeling of the insupportable all-pervading falsehood which had now embodied itself in hunger, in universal material scarcity and nonentity, and thereby become indisputably false in the eyes of all! We will leave the eighteenth century with its "liberty to tax itself." We will not astonish ourselves that the meaning of such men as the Puritans remained dim to it. To men who believe in no reality at all, how shall a real human soul, the intensest of all realities, as it were the Voice of this world's Maker still speaking to us, be intelligible? What it cannot reduce into constitutional doctrines relative to "taxing," or other the like material interest, gross, palpable to the sense, such a century will needs reject as an amorphous heap of rubbish. Hampdens, Pyms, and ship-money will be the theme of much constitutional eloquence, striving to be fervid— which will glitter, if not as fire does, then as ice does: and the irreducible Cromwell will remain a chaotic mass of "madness," "hypocrisy," and much else.

From of old, I will confess, this theory of Cromwell's falsity has been incredible to me. Nay I cannot believe the like of any Great Man whatever. Multitudes of Great Men figure in history as false, selfish men; but if we will consider it, they are but figures for us, unintelligible shadows; we do not see into them as men that could have existed at all. A superficial unbelieving generation only, with no eye but for the surfaces and semblances of things, could form such notions of Great Men. Can a great soul be possible without a conscience in it, the essence of all real souls, great or small? No, we cannot figure Cromwell as a falsity and fatuity; the longer I study him and his career, I believe this the less. Why should we? There is no evidence of it. Is it not strange that, after all the mountains of calumny this man has been subject to, after being represented as the very prince of liars, who never, or hardly ever, spoke truth, but always some cunning counterfeit of truth, there should not yet have been one falsehood brought clearly home to him? A prince of liars, and no lie spoken by him. Not one that I could yet get sight of. It is like Pococke asking Grotius, Where is your proof of Mohammed's Pigeon? No proof! Let us leave all these calumnious chimeras, as chimeras ought to be left. They are not portraits of the man; they are distracted phantasms of him, the joint product of hatred and darkness.

Looking at the man's life with our own eyes, it seems to me, a very different hypothesis suggests itself. What little we know of his earlier obscure years, distorted as it has come down to us, does it not all betoken an earnest, affectionate, sincere kind of man? His nervous melancholic temperament indicates rather a seriousness *too* deep for him. Of those stories of "Spectres"; of the white Spectre in broad daylight, predicting that he should be King of England, we are not bound to believe much; probably no more than of the other black Spectre, or Devil in person, to whom the officer saw him sell himself before Worcester Fight! But the mournful, over-sensitive, hypochondriac humour of Oliver, in his young years, is otherwise indisputably known. The Huntingdon Physician told Sir Philip Warwick himself, he had often been sent for at midnight; Mr. Cromwell was full of hypochondria, thought himself near dying, and "had fancies about the Town-cross." These things are significant. Such an excitable deep-feeling nature, in that rugged stubborn strength of his, is not the symptom of falsehood; it is the symptom and promise of quite other than falsehood!

The young Oliver is sent to study law; falls, or is said to have fallen, for a little period, into some of the dissipations of youth; but if so, speedily repents, abandons all this: not much above twenty, he is married, settled as an altogether grave and quiet man. "He pays-back what money he had won at gambling," says the story; he does not think any gain of that kind could be really his. It is very interesting, very natural, this "conversion," as they well name it; this awakening of a great true soul from the worldly slough, to see into the awful truth of things; to see that time and its shows all rested on eternity, and this poor Earth of ours was the threshold either of Heaven or of Hell! Oliver's life at St. Ives or Ely, as a sober industrious farmer, is it not altogether as that of a true and devout man? He has renounced the world and its ways; its prizes are not the thing that can enrich him. He tills the earth; he reads his Bible; daily assembles his servants round him to worship God. He comforts persecuted ministers, is fond of preachers; nay can himself preach—exhorts his neighbours to be wise, to redeem the time. In all this what "hypocrisy," "ambition," "cant," or other falsity? The man's hopes, I do believe, were fixed on the other

Higher World; his aim to get well thither, by walking well through his humble course in this world. He courts no notice: what could notice here do for him? "Ever in his great Taskmaster's eye."

It is striking, too, how he comes out once into public view; he, since no other is willing to come: in resistance to a public grievance. I mean, in that matter of the Bedford Fens. No one else will go to law with authority; therefore he will. That matter once settled, he returns back into obscurity, to his Bible and his plough. Gain influence? His influence is the most legitimate; derived from personal knowledge of him, as a just, religious, reasonable and determined man. In this way he has lived till past forty; old age is now in view of him, and the earnest portal of death and eternity; it was at this point that he suddenly became "ambitious"! I do not interpret his parliamentary mission in that way!

His successes in parliament, his successes through the war, are honest successes of a brave man who has more resolution in the heart of him, more light in the head of him than other men. His prayers to God; his spoken thanks to the God of Victory, who had preserved him safe, and carried him forward so far, through the furious clash of a world all set in conflict, through desperate looking envelopments at Dunbar; through the death-hail of so many battles; mercy after mercy; to the "crowning mercy" of Worcester Fight: all this is good and genuine for a deep-hearted Calvinistic Cromwell. Only to vain unbelieving Cavaliers, worshipping not God but their own "lovelocks," frivolities and formalities, living quite apart from contemplations of God, living without God in the world, need it seem hypocritical.

Nor will his participation in the King's death involve him in condemnation with us. It is a stern business killing of a King! But if you once go to war with him, it lies there; this and all else lies there. Once at war, you have made wager of battle with him: it is he to die, or else you. Reconciliation is problematic; may be possible, or, far more likely, is impossible. It is now pretty generally admitted that the parliament, having vanquished Charles I, had no way of making any tenable arrangement with him. The large Presbyterian party, apprehensive now of the Independents, were most anxious to do so; anxious indeed as for their own existence; but it could not be. The unhappy Charles, in those final Hampton Court negotiations, shows himself as a man fatally incapable of being dealt with. A man who, once for all, could not and would not understand: whose thought did not in any measure represent to him the real fact of the matter; nay worse, whose *word* did not at all represent his thought. We may say this of him without cruelty, with deep pity rather: but it is true and undeniable. Forsaken there of all but the name of Kingship, he still, finding himself treated with outward respect as a King, fancied that he might play off party against party, and smuggle himself into his old power by deceiving both. Alas, they both discovered that he was deceiving them. A man whose word will not inform you at all what he means or will do is not a man you can bargain with. You must get out of that man's way, or put him out of yours! The Presbyterians, in their despair, were still for believing Charles, though found false, unbelievable again and again. Not so Cromwell: "For all our fighting," says he, "we are to have a little bit of paper?" No!

In fact, everywhere we have to note the decisive practical eye of this man; how he drives toward the practical and practicable; has a genuine insight into what *is* fact. Such an intellect, I maintain, does not belong to a false man: the false man sees false shows, plausibilities, expediences: the true man is needed to discern even practical truth. Cromwell's advice about the parliament's Army, early in the contest, how they were to dismiss their city tapsters, flimsy riotous persons, and choose substantial yeomen, whose heart was in the work, to be soldiers for them: this is advice by a man who *saw*. Fact answers, if you see into fact. Cromwell's Ironsides were the embodiment of this insight of his; men fearing God; and without any other fear. No more conclusively genuine set of fighters ever trod the soil of England, or of any other land.

Neither will we blame greatly that word of Cromwell's to them; which was so blamed: "If the King should meet me in battle, I would kill the King." Why not? These words were spoken to men who stood as before a Higher than Kings. They had set more than their own lives on the cast. The parliament may call it, in official language, a fighting "*for* the King"; but we, for our share, cannot understand that. To us it is no dilettante work, no sleek officiality; it is sheer rough death and earnest. They have brought it to the calling forth of war; horrid internecine fight, man grappling with man in fire-eyed rage—the infernal element in man called forth, to try it by that! *Do* that therefore; since that is the thing to be done. The successes of Cromwell seem to me a very natural thing! Since he was not shot in battle, they were an inevitable thing. That such a man, with the eye to see, with the heart to dare, should advance, from post to post, from victory to victory, till the Huntingdon Farmer became, by whatever name you might call him, the acknowledged Strongest Man in England, virtually the King of England, requires no magic to explain it!

Truly it is a sad thing for a people, as for a man, to fall into scepticism, into dilettantism, insincerity; not to know a sincerity when they see it. For this world, and for all worlds, what curse is so fatal? The heart lying dead, the eye cannot see. What intellect remains is merely the vulpine intellect. That a true King be sent them is of small use; they do not know him when sent. They say scornfully, Is this your King? The Hero wastes his heroic faculty in bootless contradiction from the unworthy; and can accomplish little. For himself he does accomplish a heroic life, which is much, which is all; but for the world he accomplishes comparatively nothing. The wild rude sincerity, direct from Nature, is not glib in answering from the witness-box; in your small-debt *piepowder* court, he is scouted as a counterfeit. The vulpine intellect "detects" him. For being a man worth any thousand men, the response, your Knox, your Cromwell gets, is an argument for two centuries, whether he was a man at all. God's greatest gift to this Earth is sneeringly flung away. The miraculous talisman is a paltry plated coin, not fit to pass in the shops as a common guinea.

Lamentable this! I say, this must be remedied. Till this be remedied in some measure, there is nothing remedied. "Detect quacks"? Yes do, for Heaven's sake; but know withal the men that are to be trusted! Till we know that, what is all our knowledge; how shall we even so much as "detect"? For the vulpine sharpness, which considers itself to be knowledge, and "detects" in that fashion, is far mistaken. Dupes indeed are many: but, of all dupes, there is none so fatally situated as he who lives in undue terror of being duped. The world does exist; the world has truth in it or it would not exist! First recognize what is true, we shall then discern what is false; and properly never till then.

"Know the men that are to be trusted": alas, this is yet, in these days, very far from us. The sincere alone can recognize sincerity. Not a Hero only is needed, but a world fit for him; a world not of valets—the Hero comes almost in vain to it otherwise! Yes, it is far from us: but it must come; thank God, it is visibly coming. Till it do come, what have we? Ballot-boxes, suffrages, French Revolutions: if we are as valets, and do not know the Hero when we see him, what good are all these? A heroic Cromwell comes; and for a hundred and fifty years he cannot have a vote from us. Why, the insincere, unbelieving world is the natural property of the quack, and of the father of quacks and quackeries! Misery, confusion, unveracity are alone possible there. By ballot-boxes we alter the figure of our quack; but the substance of him continues. The valet world has to be governed by the sham hero, by the King merely dressed in King gear. It is his; he is its! In brief, one of two things: We shall either learn to know a Hero, a true governor and captain, somewhat better when we see him; or else go on to be forever governed by the unheroic; had we ballot-boxes clattering at every street-corner, there were no remedy in these.

Poor Cromwell, great Cromwell! The inarticulate prophet; prophet who could not speak. Rude, confused, struggling to utter himself, with his savage depth, with his wild sincerity; and he looked so strange, among the elegant euphemisms, dainty little Falklands, didactic Chillingworths, diplomatic Clarendons! Consider him. An outer hull of chaotic confusion, visions of the Devil, nervous dreams, almost semi-madness; and yet such a clear determinate man's energy working in the heart of that. A kind of chaotic man. The ray as of pure starlight and fire, working in such an element of boundless hypochondria, unformed black of darkness! And yet withal this hypochondria, what was it but the very greatness of the man? The depth and tenderness of his wild affections: the quantity of sympathy he had with things—the quantity of insight he would yet get into the heart of things, the mastery he would yet get over things: this was his hypochondria. The man's misery, as man's misery always does, came of his greatness. Samuel Johnson too is that kind of man. Sorrow-stricken, half-distracted; the wide element of mournful black enveloping him—wide as the world. It is the character of a prophetic man; a man with his whole soul *seeing*, and struggling to see.

On this ground, too, I explain to myself Cromwell's reputed confusion of speech. To himself the internal meaning was sun-clear; but the material with which he was to clothe it in utterance was not there. He had lived silent; a great unnamed sea of thought round him all his days; and in his way of life little call to attempt naming or uttering that. With his sharp power of vision, resolute power of action, I doubt not he could have learned to write books withal, and speak fluently enough: he did harder things than writing of books. This kind of man is precisely he who is fit for doing manfully all things you will set him on doing. Intellect is not speaking and logicizing; it is seeing and ascertaining. Virtue, *Vir-tus*, manhood, *hero*-hood, is not fair-spoken immaculate regularity; it is first of all what the Germans well name it, *Tugend* (*Taugend*, *dow*-ing or *Dough*-tiness), Courage and the Faculty to *do*. This basis of the matter Cromwell had in him.

One understands moreover how, though he could not speak in parliament, he might preach, rhapsodic preaching; above all, how he might be great in extempore prayer. These are the free outpouring utterances of what is in the heart: method is not required in them; warmth, depth, sincerity are all that is required. Cromwell's habit of prayer is a notable feature of him. All his great enterprises were commenced with prayer.

In dark inextricable-looking difficulties, his officers and he used to assemble, and pray alternately, for hours, for days, till some definite resolution rose among them, some "door of hope," as they would name it, disclosed itself. Consider that. In tears, in fervent prayers, and cries to the great God, to have pity on them, to make His light shine before them. They, armed Soldiers of Christ, as they felt themselves to be; a little band of Christian Brothers, who had drawn the sword against a great black devouring world not Christian, but Mammonish, Devilish—they cried to God in their straits, in their extreme need, not to forsake the Cause that was His. The light which now rose upon them—how could a human soul, by any means at all, get better light? Was not the purpose so formed like to be precisely the best, wisest, the one to be followed without hesitation any more? To them it was as the shining of Heaven's own splendour in the waste-howling darkness; the Pillar of Fire by night that was to guide them on their desolate perilous way. Was it not such? Can a man's soul, to this hour, get guidance by any other method than intrinsically by that same—devout prostration of the earnest struggling soul before the Highest, the Giver of all Light; be such prayer a spoken, articulate, or be it a voiceless, inarticulate one? There is no other method. "Hypocrisy"? One begins to be weary of all that. They who call it so have no right to speak on such matters. They never formed a purpose, what one can call a purpose. They went about balancing expediences, plausibilities; gathering votes, advices; they never were alone with the truth of a thing at all. Cromwell's prayers were likely to be "eloquent," and much more than that. His was the heart of a man who *could* pray.

But indeed his actual speeches, I apprehend, were not nearly so ineloquent, incondite, as they look. We find he was, what all speakers aim to be, an impressive speaker, even in parliament; one who, from the first, had weight. With that rude passionate voice of his, he was always understood to mean something, and men wished to know what. He disregarded eloquence, nay despised and disliked it; spoke always without premeditation of the words he was to use. The reporters, too, in those days seem to have been singularly candid; and to have given the printer precisely what they found on their own notepaper. And withal, what a strange proof is it of Cromwell's being the premeditative ever-calculating hypocrite, acting a play before the world, That to the last he took no more charge of his speeches! How came he not to study his words a little, before flinging them out to the public? If the words were true words, they could be left to shift for themselves.

But with regard to Cromwell's "lying," we will make one remark. This, I suppose, or something like this, to have been the nature of it. All parties found themselves deceived in him; each party understood him to be meaning this, heard him even say so, and behold he turns out to have been meaning that! He was, cry they, the chief of liars. But now, intrinsically, is not all this the inevitable fortune, not of a false man in such times, but simply of a superior man? Such a man must have reticences in him. If he walk wearing his heart upon his sleeve for daws to peck at, his journey will not extend far! There is no use for any man's taking up his abode in a house built of glass. A man always is to be himself the judge how much of his mind he will show to other men; even to those he would have work along with him. There are impertinent inquiries made: your rule is to leave the inquirer *un*informed on that matter; not, if you can help it, *mis*informed; but precisely as dark as he was! This, could one hit the right phrase of response, is what the wise and faithful man would aim to answer in such a case.

Cromwell, no doubt of it, spoke often in the dialect of small subaltern parties; uttered to them a part of his mind. Each little party thought him all its own. Hence their rage, one and all, to find him not of their party, but of his own party! Was it his blame? At all seasons of his history he must have felt, among such people, how, if he explained to them the deeper insight he had, they must either have shuddered aghast at it, or believing it, their own little compact hypothesis must have gone wholly to wreck. They could not have worked in his province any more; nay perhaps they could not now have worked in their own province. It is the inevitable position of a great man among small men. Small men, most active, useful, are to be seen everywhere, whose whole activity depends on some conviction which to you is palpably a limited one, imperfect, what we call an error. But would it be a kindness always, is it a duty always or often, to disturb them in that? Many a man, doing loud work in the world, stands only on some thin traditionality, conventionality; to him indubitable, to you incredible: break that beneath him, he sinks to endless depths! "I might have my hand full of truth," said Fontenelle, "and open only my little finger."

And if this be the fact even in matters of doctrine, how much more in all departments of practice! He that cannot withal keep his mind to himself cannot practise any considerable thing whatever. And we call it "dissimulation," all this? What would you think of calling the general of an army a dissembler because he did not tell every corporal and private soldier, who pleased to put the question, what his thoughts were about everything? Cromwell, I should rather say, managed all this in a manner we must admire for its perfection. An endless vortex of such questioning "corporals" rolled confusedly round him through his whole course whom he did answer. It must have been as a great true-seeing man that he managed this too. Not one proved falsehood, as I said; not one! Of what man that ever wound himself through such a coil of things will you say so much?

But in fact there are two errors, widely prevalent, which pervert to the very basis our judgments formed about such men as Cromwell; about their "ambition," "falsity," and suchlike. The first is what I might call substituting the goal of their career for the course and starting point of it. The vulgar historian of a Cromwell fancies that he had determined on being Protector of England at the time when he was ploughing the marsh lands of Cambridgeshire. His career lay all mapped out: a program of the whole drama which he then step by step dramatically unfolded, with all manner of cunning, deceptive dramaturgy, as he went on—the hollow, scheming ὑποκριτής [hypokrites] or play-actor that he was! This is a radical perversion; all but universal in such cases. And think for an instant how different the fact is! How much does one of us foresee of his own life? Short way ahead of us it is all dim; an unwound skein of possibilities, of apprehensions, attemptabilities, vague-looming hopes. This Cromwell had not his life lying all in that fashion of program, which he needed then, with that unfathomable cunning of his, only to enact dramatically, scene after scene! Not so. We see it so; but to him it was in no measure so. What absurdities would fall away of themselves, were this one undeniable fact kept honestly in view by history! Historians indeed will tell you that they do keep it in view; but look whether such is practically the fact! Vulgar history, as in this Cromwell's case, omits it altogether; even the best kinds of history only remember it now and then. To remember it duly with rigorous perfection, as in the fact it stood, requires indeed a rare faculty; rare, nay impossible. A very Shakespeare for faculty; or more than Shakespeare; who could enact a brother man's biography, see with the brother man's eyes at all points of his course what things he saw; in short, know his course and him, as few "historians" are like to do. Half or more of all the thick-plied perversions which distort our image of Cromwell will disappear if we honestly so much as try to represent them so; in sequence, as they were; not in the lump, as they are thrown down before us.

But a second error, which I think the generality commit, refers to this same "ambition" itself. We exaggerate the ambition of Great Men; we mistake what the nature of it is. Great Men are not ambitious in that sense; he is a small poor man that is ambitious so. Examine the man who lives in misery because he does not shine above other men; who goes about producing himself, pruriently anxious about his gifts and claims; struggling to force everybody, as it were begging everybody for God's sake to acknowledge him a great man, and set him over the heads of men! Such a creature is among the wretchedest sights seen under this sun. A great man? A poor, morbid, prurient, empty man; fitter for the ward of a hospital than for a throne among men. I advise you to keep out of his way. He cannot walk on quiet paths; unless you will look at him, wonder at him, write paragraphs about him, he cannot live. It is the emptiness of the man, not his greatness. Because there is nothing in himself, he hungers and thirsts that you would find something in him. In good truth, I believe no great man, not so much as a genuine man who had health and real substance in him of whatever magnitude, was ever much tormented in this way.

Your Cromwell, what good could it do him to be "noticed" by noisy crowds of people? God his Maker already noticed him. He, Cromwell, was already there; no notice would make him other than he already was. Till his hair was grown grey; and Life from the downhill slope was all seen to be limited, not infinite but finite, and all a measurable matter how it went—he had been content to plough the ground, and read his Bible. He in his old days could not support it any longer, without selling himself to falsehood that he might ride in gilt carriages to Whitehall, and have clerks with bundles of papers haunting him, "Decide this, decide that," which in utmost sorrow of heart no man can perfectly decide! What could gilt carriages do for this man? From of old, was there not in his life a weight of meaning, a terror and a splendour as of Heaven itself? His existence there as man set him beyond the need of gilding. Death, Judgment and Eternity: these already lay as the background of whatsoever he thought or did. All his life lay begirt as in a sea of nameless thoughts, which no speech of a mortal could name. God's word, as the Puritan prophets of that time had read it: this was great, and all else was little to him. To call such a man "ambitious," to figure him as the prurient windbag described above, seems to me the poorest solecism. Such a man will say: "Keep your gilt carriages and huzzaing mobs, keep your red-tape clerks, your influentialities, your important businesses. Leave me alone, leave me alone; there is too much of life in me already!" Old Samuel Johnson, the greatest soul in England in his day, was not ambitious. "Corsica Boswell" flaunted at public shows with printed ribbons round his hat; but the great old Samuel stayed at home. The world-wide soul wrap-up in its thoughts, in its sorrows; what could paradings, and ribbons in the hat, do for it?

Ah yes, I will say again: The great silent men! Looking round on the noisy inanity of the world, words with little meaning, actions with little worth, one loves to reflect on the great Empire of Silence. The noble silent men, scattered here and there, each in his department; silently thinking, silently working; whom no morning newspaper makes mention of! They are the salt of the Earth. A country that has none or few of these is in a bad way. Like a forest which had no roots, which had all turned into leaves and boughs; which must soon wither and be no forest. Woe for us if we had nothing but what we can show, or speak. Silence, the great Empire of Silence: higher than the stars; deeper than the Kingdoms of Death! It alone is great; all else is small. I hope we English will long maintain our *grand talent pour le silence.* Let others that cannot do without standing on barrel-heads, to spout, and be seen of all the marketplace, cultivate speech exclusively—become a most green forest without roots! Solomon says, there is a time to speak; but also a time to keep silence. Of some great silent Samuel, not urged to writing, as old Samuel Johnson says he was, by want of money, and nothing other, one might ask, "Why do not you too get up and speak; promulgate your system, found your sect?" "Truly," he will answer, "I am continent of my thought hitherto; happily I have yet had the ability to keep it in me, no compulsion strong enough to speak it. My "system" is not for promulgation first of all; it is for serving myself to live by. That is the great purpose of it to me. And then the "honour"? Alas, yes; but as Cato said of the statue: "So many statues in that Forum of yours, may it not be better if they ask, Where is Cato's statue?"

But, now, by way of counterpoise to this of silence, let me say that there are two kinds of ambition; one wholly blamable, the other laudable and inevitable. Nature has provided that the great silent Samuel shall not be silent too long. The selfish wish to shine over others, let it be accounted altogether poor and miserable. "Seekest thou great things, seek them not": this is most true. And yet, I say, there is an irrepressible tendency in every man to develop himself according to the magnitude which Nature has made him of; to speak out, to act out, what Nature has laid in him. This is proper, fit, inevitable; nay it is a duty, and even the summary of duties for a man. The meaning of life here on earth might be defined as consisting in this: To unfold your self, to work what thing you have the faculty for. It is a necessity for the human being, the first law of our existence. Coleridge beautifully remarks that the infant learns to speak by this necessity it feels. We will say therefore: To decide about ambition, whether it is bad or not, you have two things to take into view. Not the coveting of the place alone, but the fitness of the man for the place withal: that is the question. Perhaps the place was his; perhaps he had a natural right, and even obligation, to seek the place! Mirabeau's ambition to be Prime Minister, how shall we blame it, if he were "the only man in France that could have done any good there"? Hopefuler perhaps had he not so clearly felt how much good he could do! But a poor Necker, who could do no good, and had even felt that he could do none, yet sitting broken-hearted because they had flung him out, and he was now quit of it, well might Gibbon mourn over him. Nature, I say, has provided amply that the silent great man shall strive to speak withal; *too* amply, rather!

Fancy, for example, you had revealed to the brave old Samuel Johnson, in his shrouded-up existence, that it was possible for him to do priceless divine work for his country and the whole world. That the perfect Heavenly Law might be made law on this earth; that the prayer he prayed daily, "Thy kingdom come," was at length to be fulfilled! If you had convinced his judgment of this; that it was possible, practicable; that he the mournful silent Samuel was called to take a part in it! Would not the whole soul of the man have flamed up into a divine clearness, into noble utterance and determination to act; casting all sorrows and misgivings under his feet, counting all affliction and contradiction small—the whole dark element of his existence blazing into articulate radiance of light and lightning? It were a true ambition this! And think now how it actually was with Cromwell. From of old, the sufferings of God's Church, true zealous preachers of the truth flung into dungeons, whipped, set on pillories, their ears cropped off, God's Gospel-cause trodden under foot of the unworthy: all this had lain heavy on his soul. Long years he had looked upon it, in silence, in prayer; seeing no remedy on Earth; trusting well that a remedy in Heaven's goodness would come—that such a course was false, unjust, and could not last forever. And now behold the dawn of it; after twelve years silent waiting, all England stirs itself; there is to be once more a parliament, the Right will get a voice for itself: inexpressible well-grounded hope has come again into the Earth. Was not such a parliament worth being a member of? Cromwell threw down his ploughs and hastened thither.

He spoke there—rugged bursts of earnestness, of a self-seen truth, where we get a glimpse of them. He worked there; he fought and strove, like a strong true giant of a man, through cannon tumult and all else—

on and on, till the Cause triumphed, its once so formidable enemies all
swept from before it, and the dawn of hope had become clear light of
victory and certainty. That *he* stood there as the strongest soul of England, the undisputed Hero of all England—what of this? It was possible
that the law of Christ's Gospel could now establish itself in the world!
The Theocracy which John Knox in his pulpit might dream of as a "devout
imagination," this practical man, experienced in the whole chaos of most
rough practice, dared to consider as capable of being realized. Those
that were highest in Christ's Church, the devoutest wisest men, were to
rule the land: in some considerable degree, it might be so and should be
so. Was it not true, God's truth? And if true, was it not then the very
thing to do? The strongest practical intellect in England dared to answer,
Yes! This I call a noble true purpose; is it not, in its own dialect, the
noblest that could enter into the heart of statesman or man? For a Knox
to take it up was something; but for a Cromwell, with his great sound
sense and experience of what our world was—history, I think, shows it
only this once in such a degree. I account it the culminating point of
Protestantism; the most heroic phasis that "Faith in the Bible" was appointed to exhibit here below. Fancy it: that it were made manifest to
one of us, how we could make the Right supremely victorious over
Wrong, and all that we had longed and prayed for, as the highest good
to England and all lands, an attainable fact!

Well, I must say, the vulpine intellect, with its knowingness, its alert-
ness and expertness in "detecting hypocrites," seems to me a rather sorry
business. We have had one such statesman in England; one may, that I
can get sight of, who never had in the heart of him any such purpose at all.
One man, in the course of fifteen hundred years; and this was his welcome. He had adherents by the hundred or the ten; opponents by the
million. Had England rallied all round him—why, then, England might
have been a Christian land! As it is, vulpine knowingness sits yet at its
hopeless problem, "Given a world of Knaves, to educe an Honesty from
their united action"; how cumbrous a problem, you may see in Chancery
Law-Courts, and some other places! Till at length, by Heaven's just
anger, but also by Heaven's great grace, the matter begins to stagnate;
and this problem is becoming to all men a palpably hopeless one.

But with regard to Cromwell and his purposes: Hume and a multitude following him come upon me here with an admission that Cromwell
was sincere at first; a sincere "Fanatic" at first, but gradually became a
"Hypocrite" as things opened round him. This of the Fanatic-Hypocrite

is Hume's theory of it; extensively applied since—to Mohammed and many others. Think of it seriously, you will find something in it—not much, not at all, very far from all. Sincere hero hearts do not sink in this miserable manner. The Sun flings forth impurities, gets balefully incrusted with spots; but it does not quench itself, and become no Sun at all, but a mass of Darkness! I will venture to say that such never befell a great, deep Cromwell; I think, never. Nature's own lion-hearted son! Antaeus-like, his strength is got by touching the Earth, his mother; lift him up from the Earth, lift him up into hypocrisy, inanity, his strength is gone. We will not assert that Cromwell was an immaculate man; that he fell into no faults, no insincerities among the rest. He was no dilettante professor of "perfections," "immaculate conducts." He was a rugged Orson, rending his rough way through actual true work—doubtless with many a fall therein. Insincerities, faults, very many faults daily and hourly: it was too well known to him; known to God and him! The Sun was dimmed many a time; but the Sun had not himself grown a Dimness. Cromwell's last words, as he lay waiting for death, are those of a Christian heroic man. Broken prayers to God, that He would judge him and this cause, He since man could not, in justice yet in pity. They are most touching words. He breathed out his wild great soul, its toils and sins all ended now, into the presence of his Maker, in this manner.

I, for one, will not call the man a Hypocrite! Hypocrite, mummer, the life of him a mere theatricality; empty barren quack, hungry for the shouts of mobs? The man had made obscurity do very well for him till his head was grey; and now he was, there as he stood recognized unblamed, the virtual King of England. Cannot a man do without King's coaches and cloaks? Is it such a blessedness to have clerks forever pestering you with bundles of papers in red-tape? A simple Diocletian prefers planting of cabbages; a George Washington, no very immeasurable man, does the like. One would say, it is what any genuine man could do; and would do. The instant his real work were out in the matter of Kingship—away with it!

Let us remark, meanwhile, how indispensable everywhere a King is, in all movements of men. It is strikingly shown, in this very War, what becomes of men when they cannot find a Chief Man, and their enemies can. The Scotch nation was all but unanimous in Puritanism, zealous and of one mind about it, as in this English end of the Island was far from being the case. But there was no great Cromwell among them; poor tremulous, hesitating, diplomatic Argyles and suchlike; none of them had a heart true enough for the truth, or durst commit himself to the truth.

They had no leader; and the scattered Cavalier party in that country had one: Montrose, the noblest of all the Cavaliers; an accomplished, gallant-hearted, splendid man; what one may call the Hero-Cavalier. Well, look at it; on the one hand subjects without a King; on the other a King without subjects! The subjects without King can do nothing; the subjectless King can do something. This Montrose, with a handful of Irish or Highland savages, few of them so much as guns in their hands, dashes at the drilled Puritan armies like a wild whirlwind; sweeps them, time after time, some five times over, from the field before him. He was at one period, for a short while, master of all Scotland. One man; but he was a man: a million zealous men, but without the one; they against him were powerless! Perhaps of all the persons in that Puritan struggle, from first to last, the single indispensable one was verily Cromwell. To see and dare, and decide; to be a fixed pillar in the welter of uncertainty; a King among them, whether they called him so or not.

Precisely here, however, lies the rub for Cromwell. His other proceedings have all found advocates, and stand generally justified; but this dismissal of the Rump Parliament and assumption of the Protectorship is what no one can pardon him. He had fairly grown to be King in England; Chief Man of the victorious party in England: but it seems he could not do without the King's cloak, and sold himself to perdition in order to get it. Let us see a little how this was.

England, Scotland, Ireland, all lying now subdued at the feet of the Puritan Parliament, the practical question arose, What was to be done with it? How will you govern these nations, which Providence in a wondrous way has given up to your disposal? Clearly those hundred surviving members of the Long Parliament, who sit there as supreme authority, cannot continue for ever to sit. What is to be done? It was a question which theoretical constitution-builders may find easy to answer; but to Cromwell, looking there into the real practical facts of it, there could be none more complicated. He asked of the Parliament, What it was they would decide upon? It was for the Parliament to say. Yet the Soldiers too, however contrary to formula, they who had purchased this victory with their blood, it seemed to them that they also should have something to say in it! We will not "For all our fighting have nothing but a little piece of paper." We understand that the Law of God's Gospel, to which He through us has given the victory, shall establish itself, or try to establish itself, in this land!

For three years, Cromwell says, this question had been sounded in the ears of the Parliament. They could make no answer; nothing but talk, talk. Perhaps it lies in the nature of parliamentary bodies; perhaps no Parliament could in such case make any answer but even that of talk, talk! Nevertheless the question must and shall be answered. You sixty men there, becoming fast odious, even despicable, to the whole nation, whom the nation already calls Rump Parliament, you cannot continue to sit there: who or what then is to follow? "Free Parliament," right of Election, constitutional formulas of one sort or the other—the thing is a hungry fact coming on us, which we must answer or be devoured by it! And who are you that prate of constitutional formulas, rights of parliament? You have had to kill your King, to make Pride's Purges, to expel and banish by the law of the stronger whosoever would not let your cause prosper: there are but fifty or three-score of you left there, debating in these days. Tell us what we shall do; not in the way of formula, but of practicable fact!

How they did finally answer remains obscure to this day. The diligent Godwin himself admits that he cannot make it out. The likeliest is that this poor parliament still would not and indeed could not dissolve and disperse; that when it came to the point of actually dispersing, they again, for the tenth or twentieth time, adjourned it—and Cromwell's patience failed him. But we will take the favourablest hypothesis ever started for the Parliament; the favourablest, though I believe it is not the true one, but too favourable.

According to this version: At the uttermost crisis, when Cromwell and his officers were met on the one hand, and the fifty or sixty Rump Members on the other, it was suddenly told Cromwell that the Rump in its despair *was* answering in a very singular way; that in their splenetic envious despair, to keep out the army at least, these men were hurrying through the House a kind of Reform Bill—Parliament to be chosen by the whole of England; equable electoral division into districts; free suffrage, and the rest of it! A very questionable, or indeed for them an unquestionable thing. Reform Bill, free suffrage of Englishmen? Why, the Royalists themselves, silenced indeed but not exterminated, perhaps outnumber us; the great numerical majority of England was always indifferent to our cause, merely looked at it and submitted to it. It is in weight and force, not by counting of heads, that we are the majority! And now with your formulas and Reform Bills, the whole matter, sorely won by our swords, shall again launch itself to sea; become a mere hope, and likelihood, small even as a likelihood? And it is not a likelihood; it is a certainty, which we have won, by God's strength and our own right hands, and do now hold here. Cromwell walked down to these refractory members; interrupted them in that rapid speed of their Reform Bill; ordered them to begone, and talk there no more. Can we not forgive him? Can we not understand him? John Milton, who looked on it all near at hand, could applaud him. The Reality had swept the formulas away before it. I fancy most men who were realities in England might see into the necessity of that.

The strong daring man, therefore, has set all manner of Formulas and logical superficialities against him; has dared appeal to the genuine fact of this England, Whether it will support him or not? It is curious to see how he struggles to govern in some constitutional way; find some Parliament to support him; but cannot. His first parliament, the one they call Barebones's Parliament, is, so to speak, a Convocation of the Notables. From all quarters of England the leading Ministers and chief Puritan officials nominate the men most distinguished by religious reputation, influence and attachment to the true cause: these are assembled to shape out a plan. They sanctioned what was past; shaped as they could what was to come. They were scornfully called Barebones's Parliament, the man's name, it seems, was not Barebones, but Barbone—a good enough man. Nor was it a jest, their work; it was a most serious reality—a trial on the part of these Puritan notables how far the law of Christ could become the law of this England. There were men of sense among them, men of some quality; men of deep piety I suppose the most of them were. They failed, it seems, and broke down, endeavouring to reform the Court of Chancery! They dissolved themselves, as incompetent; delivered up their power again into the hands of the Lord-General Cromwell, to do with it what he liked and could.

What will he do with it? The Lord-General Cromwell, "Commander-in-Chief of all the Forces raised and to be raised"; he hereby sees himself, at this unexampled juncture, as it were the one available Authority left in England, nothing between England and utter Anarchy but him alone. Such is the undeniable fact of his position and England's, there and then. What will he do with it? After deliberation, he decides that he will accept it; will formally, with public solemnity, say and vow before God and men, "Yes, the fact is so, and I will do the best I can with it!" Protectorship, Instrument of Government—these are the external forms of the thing; worked out and sanctioned as they could in the circumstances be, by the judges, by the leading official people, "Council of Officers and Persons of Interest in the Nation"; and as for the thing itself, undeniably enough, at the pass matters had now come to, there *was* no alternative but anarchy or that. Puritan England might accept it or not; but Puritan

England was, in real truth, saved from suicide thereby! I believe the Puritan people did, in an inarticulate, grumbling, yet on the whole grateful and real way, accept this anomalous act of Oliver's; at least, he and they together made it good, and always better to the last. But in their parliamentary articulate way, they had their difficulties, and never knew fully what to say to it!

Oliver's second parliament, properly his *first* regular parliament, chosen by the rule laid down in the Instrument of Government, did assemble, and worked; but got, before long, into bottomless questions as to the Protector's right, as to "usurpation," and so forth; and had at the earliest legal day to be dismissed. Cromwell's concluding speech to these men is a remarkable one. So likewise to his third parliament, in similar rebuke for their pedantries and obstinacies. Most rude, chaotic, all these speeches are; but most earnest-looking. You would say, it was a sincere helpless man; not used to speak the great inorganic thought of him, but to act it rather! A helplessness of utterance, in such bursting fulness of meaning. He talks much about "births of Providence." All these changes, so many victories and events, were not forethoughts, and theatrical contrivances of men, of me or of men; it is blind blasphemers that will persist in calling them so! He insists with a heavy sulphurous wrathful emphasis on this. As he well might. As if a Cromwell in that dark, huge game he had been playing, the world wholly thrown into chaos round him, had foreseen it all, and played it all off like a precontrived puppet-show by wood and wire! These things were foreseen by no man, he says; no man could tell what a day would bring forth: they were "births of Providence," God's finger guided us on, and we came at last to clear height of victory, God's Cause triumphant in these nations; and you as a parliament could assemble together, and say in what manner all this could be organized, reduced into rational feasibility among the affairs of men. You were to help with your wise counsel in doing that. "You have had such an opportunity as no parliament in England ever had." Christ's Law, the Right and True, was to be in some measure made the law of this land. In place of that, you have got into your idle pedantries, constitutionalities, bottomless cavillings and questionings about written laws for my coming here; and would send the whole matter into chaos again, because I have no notary's parchment, but only God's voice from the battle whirlwind, for being President among you! That opportunity is gone; and we know not when it will return. You have had your constitutional Logic; and Mammon's Law, not Christ's Law, rules yet in this land. "God be judge between you and me!" These are his final words to them: Take you your constitution formulas in your hand; and I my informal struggles, purposes, realities and acts; and "God be judge between you and me!"

We said above what shapeless, involved chaotic things the printed speeches of Cromwell are. Wilfully ambiguous, unintelligible, say the most: a hypocrite shrouding himself in confused Jesuitic jargon! To me they do not seem so. I will say rather, they afforded the first glimpses I could ever get into the reality of this Cromwell, nay into the possibility of him. Try to believe that he means something, search lovingly what that may be: you will find a real *speech* lying imprisoned in these broken rude tortuous utterances; a meaning in the great heart of this inarticulate man! You will, for the first time, begin to see that he was a man; not an enigmatic chimera, unintelligible to you, incredible to you. The histories and biographies written of this Cromwell, written in shallow sceptical generations that could not know or conceive of a deep believing man, are far more obscure than Cromwell's speeches. You look through them only into the infinite vague of Black and the Inane. "Heats and Jealousies," says Lord Clarendon himself: "heats and jealousies," mere crabbed whims, theories and crochets; these induced slow, sober, quiet Englishmen to lay down their ploughs and work; and fly into red fury of confused war against the best-conditioned of Kings! Try if you can find that true Scepticism writing about belief may have great gifts; but it is really *ultra vires* there. It is blindness laying down the laws of optics.

Cromwell's third Parliament split on the same rock as his second. Ever the constitutional Formula: How came *you* there? Show us some notary parchment! Blind pedants: "Why, surely the same power which makes you a Parliament, that, and something more, made me a Protector!" If my Protectorship is nothing, what in the name of wonder is your Parliamenteership, a reflex and creation of that?

Parliaments having failed, there remained nothing but the way of despotism. Military dictators, each with his district, to coerce the Royalists and other gainsayers, to govern them, if not by act of parliament, then by the sword. Formula shall not carry it, while the reality is here! I will go on, protecting oppressed Protestants abroad, appointing just judges, wise managers, at home, cherishing true Gospel ministers; doing the best I can to make England a Christian England, greater than old Rome, the Queen of Protestant Christianity; I, since you will not help me; I while God leaves me life! Why did he not give it up; retire into obscurity again, since the law would not acknowledge him? cry several. That is where they mistake. For him there was no giving of it up! Prime Ministers have governed countries, Pitt, Pombal, Choiseul; and their word was a law

while it held: but this Prime Minister was one that could not get resigned. Let him once resign, Charles Stuart and the Cavaliers waited to
kill him; to kill the Cause and him. Once embarked, there is no retreat,
no return. This Prime Minister could retire nowhither except into his
tomb.

One is sorry for Cromwell in his old days. His complaint is incessant of
the heavy burden Providence has laid on him. Heavy; which he must bear
till death. Old Colonel Hutchinson, as his wife relates it, Hutchinson, his
old battle-mate, coming to see him on some indispensable business, much
against his will—Cromwell "follows him to the door," in a most fraternal,
domestic, conciliatory style; begs that he would be reconciled to him, his
old brother in arms; says how much it grieves him to be misunderstood,
deserted by true fellow-soldiers, dear to him from of old: the rigorous
Hutchinson, cased in his republican formula, sullenly goes his way. And
the man's head now white; his strong arm growing weary with its long
work! I think always too of his poor mother, now very old, living in that
palace of his; a right brave woman: as indeed they lived all an honest
God-fearing Household there: if she heard a shot go off, she thought it
was her son killed. He had to come to her at least once a day that she
might see with her own eyes that he was yet living. The poor old mother!
What had this man gained; what had he gained? He had a life of sore
strife and toil, to his last day. Fame, ambition, place in history? His dead
body was hung in chains; his "place in history"—place in history forsooth!
—has been a place of ignominy, accusation, blackness and disgrace; and
here, this day, who knows if it is not rash in me to be among the first that
ever ventured to pronounce him not a knave and a liar, but a genuinely
honest man! Peace to him. Did he not, in spite of all, accomplish much
for us? We walk smoothly over his great rough heroic life; step over his
body sunk in the ditch there. We need not spurn it, as we step on it! Let
the Hero rest. It was not to men's judgment that he appealed; nor have
men judged him very well.

Precisely a century and a year after this of Puritanism had got itself
hushed up into decent composure, and its results made smooth in 1688,
there broke out a far deeper explosion, much more difficult to hush up,
known to all mortals, and like to be long known, by the name of French
Revolution. It is properly the third and final act of Protestantism; the explosive confused return of mankind to reality and fact, now that they
were perishing of semblance and sham. We call our English Puritanism
the second act: "Well then, the Bible is true; let us go by the Bible!" "In
Church," said Luther; "In Church and State," said Cromwell, "let us go
by what actually is God's Truth." Men have to return to reality; they

cannot live on semblance. The French Revolution, or third act, we may well call the final one; for lower than that savage Sansculottism men cannot go. They stand there on the nakedest haggard fact, undeniable in all seasons and circumstances; and may and must begin again confidently to build up from that. The French explosion, like the English one, got its King—who had no notary parchment to show for himself. We have still to glance for a moment at Napoleon, our second modern King.

Napoleon does by no means seem to me so great a man as Cromwell. His enormous victories which reached over all Europe, while Cromwell abode mainly in our little England, are but as the high stilts on which the man is seen standing; the stature of the man is not altered thereby. I find in him no such sincerity as in Cromwell; only a far inferior sort. No silent walking, through long years, with the Awful Unnamable of this Universe; "walking with God," as he called it; and faith and strength in that alone: latent thought and valour, content to lie latent, then burst out as in blaze of Heaven's lightning! Napoleon lived in an age when God was no longer believed; the meaning of all silence, latency was thought to be nonentity: he had to begin not out of the Puritan Bible, but out of poor sceptical *Encyclopédies*. This was the length the man carried it. Meritorious to get so far. His compact, prompt, everyway articulate character is in itself perhaps small, compared with our great chaotic inarticulate Cromwell's. Instead of "dumb Prophet struggling to speak," we have a portentous mixture of the Quack withal! Hume's notion of the Fanatic-Hypocrite, with such truth as it has, will apply much better to Napoleon than it did to Cromwell, to Mohammed or the like—where indeed taken strictly it has hardly any truth at all. An element of blamable ambition shows itself, from the first, in this man; gets the victory over him at last, and involves him and his work in ruin.

"False as a bulletin" became a proverb in Napoleon's time. He makes what excuse he could for it: that it was necessary to mislead the enemy, to keep up his own men's courage, and so forth. On the whole, there are no excuses. A man in no case has liberty to tell lies. It had been, in the long run, better for Napoleon too if he had not told any. In fact, if a man have any purpose reaching beyond the hour and day, meant to be found extant next day, what good can it ever be to promulgate lies? The lies are found out; ruinous penalty is exacted for them. No man will believe the liar next time even when he speaks truth, when it is of the last importance that he be believed. The old cry of wolf! A Lie is *no*-thing; you cannot of nothing make something; you make *nothing* at last, and lose your labour into the bargain.

Yet Napoleon had a sincerity; we are to distinguish between what is superficial and what is fundamental in insincerity. Across these outer manoeuverings and quackeries of his, which were many and most blamable, let us discern withal that the man had a certain instinctive ineradicable feeling for reality; and did base himself upon fact, so long as he had any basis. He has an instinct of Nature better than his culture was. His *savants,* Bourrienne tells us, in that voyage to Egypt were one evening busily occupied arguing that there could be no God. They had proved it, to their satisfaction, by all manner of logic. Napoleon looking up into the stars, answers, "Very ingenious, Messieurs: but who made all that?" The atheistic logic runs off from him like water; the great fact stares him in the face: "Who made all that?" So too in practice: he, as every man that can be great, or have victory in this world, sees, through all entanglements, the practical heart of the matter; drives straight towards that. When the steward of his Tuileries Palace was exhibiting the new upholstery, with praises, and demonstration how glorious it was, and how cheap withal, Napoleon, making little answer, asked for a pair of scissors, clipped one of the gold tassels from a window-curtain, put it in his pocket, and walked on. Some days afterwards, he produced it at the right moment, to the horror of his upholstery functionary; it was not gold but tinsel! In Saint Helena, it is notable how he still, to his last days, insists on the practical, the real. "Why talk and complain; above all, why quarrel with one another? There is no result in it; it comes to nothing that one can do. Say nothing, if one can do nothing!" He speaks often so, to his poor discontented followers; he is like a piece of silent strength in the middle of their morbid querulousness there.

And accordingly was there not what we can call a faith in him, genuine so far as it went? That this new enormous democracy asserting itself here in the French Revolution is an insuppressible fact, which the whole world, with its old forces and institutions cannot put down; this was a true insight of his, and took his conscience and enthusiasm along with it—a faith. And did he not interpret the dim purport of it well? *"La carrière ouverte aux talens,* The implements to him who can handle them": this actually is the truth, and even the whole truth; it includes whatever the French Revolution, or any Revolution, could mean. Napoleon, in his first period, was a true democrat. And yet by the nature of him, fostered too by his military trade, he knew that democracy, if it were a true thing at all, could not be an anarchy: the man had a heart-hatred for anarchy. On that twentieth of June (1792), Bourrienne and he sat in a coffee-house as the mob rolled by: Napoleon expresses the deepest contempt for persons in authority that they do not restrain this rabble. On the tenth of

August he wonders why there is no man to command these poor Swiss; they would conquer if there were. Such a faith in democracy, yet hatred of Anarchy, it is that carries Napoleon through all his great work. Through his brilliant Italian Campaigns, onwards to the Peace of Leoben, one would say, his inspiration is: "Triumph to the French Revolution; assertion of it against these Austrian Simulacra that pretend to call it a Simulacrum!" Withal, however, he feels, and has a right to feel, how necessary a strong authority is; how the Revolution cannot prosper or last without such. To bridle in that great devouring, self-devouring French Revolution; to tame it, so that its intrinsic purpose can be made good, that it may become organic, and be able to live among other organisms and formed things, not as a wasting destruction alone: is not this still what he partly aimed at, as the true purport of his life; nay what he actually managed to do? Through Wagrams, Austerlitzes; triumph after triumph—he triumphed so far. There was an eye to see in this man, a soul to dare and do. He rose naturally to be the King. All men saw that he *was* such. The common soldiers used to say on the march: "These babbling *avocats*, up at Paris; all talk and no work! What wonder it runs all wrong? We shall have to go and put our *Petit Caporal* there!" They went, and put him there; they and France at large. Chief-consulship, Emperorship, victory over Europe; till the poor Lieutenant of *La Fère*, not unnaturally, might seem to himself the greatest of all men that had been in the world for some ages.

But at this point, I think, the fatal charlatan element got the upper hand. He apostatized from his old faith in facts: took to believing in semblances; strove to connect himself with Austrian dynasties, Popedoms, with the old false feudalities which he once saw clearly to be false; considered that he would found "his dynasty" and so forth; that the enormous French Revolution meant only that! The man was "given-up to strong delusion, that he should believe a lie"; a fearful but most sure thing. He did not know true from false now when he looked at them—the fearfulest penalty a man pays for yielding to untruth of heart. Self and false ambition had now become his god: self-deception once yielded to, all other deceptions follow naturally more and more. What a paltry patchwork of theatrical paper mantles, tinsel and mummery had this man wrapped his own great reality in, thinking to make it more real thereby! His hollow Pope's-Concordat, pretending to be a re-establishment of Catholicism, felt by himself to be the method of extirpating it, *la vaccine de la religion:* his ceremonial coronations, consecrations by the old Italian chimera in Notre Dame—"wanting nothing to complete the pomp of it," as Augereau said, "nothing but the half-million of men who had died to put an end to all that"! Cromwell's inauguration was by the sword and Bible; what we must call a genuinely true one. Sword and Bible were borne before him, without any chimera: were not these the real emblems of Puritanism; its true decoration and insignia? It had used them both in a very real manner, and pretended to stand by them now! But this poor Napoleon mistook: he believed too much in the dupeability of men; saw no fact deeper in men than hunger and this! He was mistaken. Like a man that should build upon cloud; his house and he fall down in confused wreck, and depart out of the world.

Alas, in all of us this charlatan element exists; and might be developed, were the temptation strong enough. "Lead us not into temptation"! But it is fatal, I say, that it be developed. The thing into which it enters as a cognisable ingredient is doomed to be altogether transitory, and, however huge it may look, is in itself small. Napoleon's working, accordingly, what was it with all the noise it made? A flash as of gunpowder widespread; a blazing up as of dry heath. For an hour the whole Universe seems wrapped in smoke and flame; but only for an hour. It goes out: the Universe with its old mountains and streams, its stars above and kind soil beneath is still there.

The Duke of Weimar told his friends always, To be of courage; this Napoleonism was unjust, a falsehood, and could not last. It is true doctrine. The heavier this Napoleon trampled on the world, holding it tyrannously down, the fiercer would the world's recoil against him be, one day. Injustice pays itself with frightful compound interest. I am not sure but he had better have lost his best park of artillery, or had his best regiment drowned in the sea, than shot that poor German bookseller, Palm! It was a palpable tyrannous murderous injustice, which no man, let him paint an inch thick, could make out to be other. It burnt deep into the hearts of men, it and the like of it; suppressed fire flashed in the eyes of men, as they thought of it—waiting their day! Which day came: Germany rose round him. What Napoleon did will in the long-run amount to what he did justly; what Nature with her laws will sanction. To what of reality was in him; to that and nothing more. The rest was all smoke and waste. *La carrière ouverte aux talens:* that great true message, which has yet to articulate and fulfil itself everywhere, he left in a most inarticulate state. He was a great *ébauche*, a rude draught never completed; as indeed what great man is other? Left in *too* rude a state, alas!

His notions of the world, as he expresses them there at Saint Helena, are almost tragical to consider. He seems to feel the most unaffected surprise that it has all gone so; that he is flung out on the rock here, and the world is still moving on its axis. France is great, and all great; and at bottom, he is France. England itself, he says, is by nature only an appendage of France; "another Isle of Oleron to France." So it was by nature, by Napoleon-nature; and yet look how in fact—here am I! He cannot understand it: inconceivable that the reality has not corresponded to his program of it; that France was not all great, that he was not France. "Strong delusion," that he should believe the thing to be which *is* not! The compact, clear-seeing, decisive Italian nature of him, strong, genuine, which he once had, has enveloped itself, half-dissolved itself, in a turbid atmosphere of French fanfaronade. The world was not disposed to be trodden down underfoot; to be bound into masses, and built together, as he liked, for a pedestal to France and him: the world had quite other purposes in view! Napoleon's astonishment is extreme. But alas, what help now? He had gone that way of his; and Nature also had gone her way. Having once parted with reality, he tumbles helpless in vacuity; no rescue for him. He had to sink there, mournfully as man seldom did; and break his great heart, and die—this poor Napoleon: a great implement too soon wasted, till it was useless: our last Great Man!

The foregoing consists of Lecture VI
in Carlyle's
ON HEROES, HERO-WORSHIP, AND THE HEROIC IN HISTORY.

Ralph Waldo Emerson

1803–1882

Descended from a line of Massachusetts clergymen, Ralph Waldo Emerson was born in Boston, May 25, 1803. His father, a Unitarian minister, died when he was a small boy. All but penniless, Emerson finished Harvard with honors at eighteen, taught and preached his way through divinity school, and in 1829 was ordained minister of the Second Church in Boston. A little later he married Ellen Tucker. When she died in 1831, he was already known as a preacher second only to the famous William Ellery Channing.

This was his point of crisis. He left the ministry and set up shop as lay preacher to America and the world. He wanted new ideas, new men, a new age. In England he visited Wordsworth and Coleridge, and became a lifelong friend of Carlyle. Settled in Concord and married again, he lived by lecturing and published an anonymous first book, *Nature*, in 1836. In it most of his chief ideas were laid out for use. His 1837 Harvard address, "The American Scholar," announced his broad program.

This was regarded as "the latest form of infidelity." He was a rebel, and attracted others. The Transcendentalist movement, derived in part from Coleridge, Carlyle, and the German philosophers, began to be talked about. By 1849, when he had published *Representative Men* and the first and second series of *Essays*, Emerson

---

Notes from the artist: "The standing figure of Emerson is set in a fantasy of figures and objects significant in his life and work. Below the quotation from the essay Self-Reliance *is Thoreau, who put into practice the principles of Transcendentalism. At lower left is a Phi Beta Kappa key, recalling 'The American Scholar' address. Next to the key is Louisa May Alcott, another admirer of Emerson. Other symbols suggest the New England countryside and Emerson's early manifesto* Nature."

To believe your own thought, to believe that what is true for you in your private heart is true for all men, that is genius.

R. Waldo Emerson

ΦBK

was known in Europe and already accepted as a great figure in his own country. His reputation was still building when he died, after years of fading health, on April 27, 1882. What now seems to us his best work survives in a few of the poems, his vigorous and solid *English Traits*, several studies of character, and the *Journals*.

Emerson's essay on Henry David Thoreau was written after his friend's death. It is a shrewd and vivid picture, made with fresh colors, and touched here and there with humor. Beyond that, we may find a little comedy of provincial character in it.

They had both grown up in poor families (Emerson's mother was left with six children, and Thoreau's mother kept a boardinghouse). They were both Massachusetts men and Concord men (one of Emerson's ancestors had helped found the town and Thoreau was born there). They were both educated at Harvard (Emerson tells us how highhandedly Thoreau treated his old college), both poets and writer-philosophers.

"The other world is all my art; my pencils will draw no other," said Thoreau, echoing Plato's vision of the ideal. It was perhaps the one basic idea that he shared with Emerson. Beyond that, in their views of the world and universe, they were more often than not widely apart. Each came from one of the sharply marked classes in early New England: Emerson from the ruling professional class and Thoreau from the laboring and farming class. Emerson made a living at lecturing, where Thoreau failed. Surveying and pencil making earned Thoreau what little money he needed. Emerson felt that it was enough to expound his ideas; Thoreau believed that his must be acted out. He could build a boat; it was all Emerson could do to row one. Emerson meant to take the world for his province; Thoreau made his province the world. Like Whitman, Emerson said *yes* to his time; Thoreau, like Melville, said *no*.

How then could they understand each other? There lies the comedy. It is remarkable how much Emerson did understand. He gives us a clear and affectionate view of Thoreau as the "born protestant," a man who could be a hedgehog to his neighbors. But how much of this *was* downright oddity of character, and how much a deliberate acting out of his ideas? He refused to pay taxes to what he considered an unjust government and went to jail for it. (A friend paid the fine without letting him know.) *Was* this defiant individualism, or was it a truly social act? Did it come out of a sense, higher than most men could boast, of what citizen and government should demand of each other?

Emerson does not mention how he tried to take care of the younger man. He "provided the acres" for Thoreau's experiment at Walden. But he was doubtful. These were the years in which all America seemed to be moving westward. Thoreau, who might have been one of the leaders, was wasted as "the captain of a huckleberry party." Was it true? Was he, in fact, a potential Audubon and Kit Carson, with a larger grasp than either? Did he need a glimpse of Lake Chad, or even Grand Lake in Colorado, to give him the relative scale of his Walden Pond? Or was he right in believing that if he could live deeply with his own countryside, get his own bass tree and muskrat and dragonfly down on the page, that would be enough for any man's lifetime? Emerson gives us the means to ask these questions. He does not answer them.

Thoreau

Henry David Thoreau was the last male descendant of a French ancestor who came to this country from the Isle of Guernsey. His character exhibited occasional traits drawn from this blood, in singular combination with a very strong Saxon genius.

He was born in Concord, Massachusetts, on the 12th of July, 1817. He was graduated at Harvard College in 1837, but without any literary distinction. An iconoclast in literature, he seldom thanked colleges for their service to him, holding them in small esteem, while yet his debt to them was important. After leaving the university he joined his brother in teaching a private school, which he soon renounced. His father was a manufacturer of lead pencils, and Henry applied himself for a time to this craft, believing he could make a better pencil than was then in use. After completing his experiments, he exhibited his work to chemists and artists in Boston, and having obtained their certificates to its excellence and to its equality with the best London manufacture, he returned home contented. His friends congratulated him that he had now opened his way to fortune. But he replied that he should never make another pencil. "Why should I? I would not do again what I have done once." He resumed his endless walks and miscellaneous studies, making every day some new acquaintance with Nature, though as yet never speaking of zoology or botany, since, though very studious of natural facts, he was incurious of technical and textual science.

At this time, a strong, healthy youth fresh from college, while all his companions were choosing their profession or eager to begin some lucrative employment, it was inevitable that his thoughts should be exercised on the same question, and it required rare decision to refuse all the accustomed paths and keep his solitary freedom at the cost of disappointing the natural expectations of his family and friends: all the more difficult that he had a perfect probity, was exact in securing his own independence, and in holding every man to the like duty. But Thoreau never faltered. He was a born protestant. He declined to give up his large ambition of knowledge and action for any narrow craft or profession, aiming at a much more comprehensive calling, the art of living well. If he slighted and defied the opinions of others, it was only that he was more intent to reconcile his practice with his own belief. Never idle or self-indulgent, he preferred, when he wanted money, earning it by some piece of manual labor agreeable to him, as building a boat or a fence, planting, grafting, surveying or other short work, to any long engagements. With his hardy habits and few wants, his skill in woodcraft, and his powerful arithmetic, he was very competent to live in any part of the world. It would cost him less time to supply his wants than another. He was therefore secure of his leisure.

A natural skill for mensuration, growing out of his mathematical knowledge and his habit of ascertaining the measures and distances of objects which interested him, the size of trees, the depth and extent of ponds and rivers, the height of mountains and the air-line distance of his favorite summits—this, and his intimate knowledge of the territory about Concord, made him drift into the profession of land surveyor. It had the advantage for him that it led him continually into new and secluded grounds, and helped his studies of Nature. His accuracy and skill in this work were readily appreciated, and he found all the employment he wanted.

He could easily solve the problems of the surveyor, but he was daily beset with graver questions, which he manfully confronted. He interrogated every custom, and wished to settle all his practice on an ideal foundation. He was a protestant à outrance, and few lives contain so many renunciations. He was bred to no profession; he never married; he lived alone; he never went to church; he never voted; he refused to pay a tax to the state; he ate no flesh, he drank no wine, he never knew the use of tobacco; and, though a naturalist, he used neither trap nor gun. He chose, wisely no doubt for himself, to be the bachelor of thought and Nature. He had no talent for wealth, and knew how to be poor without the least hint of squalor or inelegance. Perhaps he fell into his way of living without forecasting it much, but approved it with later wisdom. "I am often reminded," he wrote in his journal, "that if I had bestowed on me the wealth of Croesus, my aims must be still the same, and my means essentially the same." He had no temptations to fight against— no appetites, no passions, no taste for elegant trifles. A fine house, dress, the manners and talk of highly cultivated people were all thrown away on him. He much preferred a good Indian, and considered these refinements as impediments to conversation, wishing to meet his companion on the simplest terms. He declined invitations to dinner parties, because there each was in everyone's way, and he could not meet the individuals to any purpose. "They make their pride," he said, "in making their dinner cost much; I make my pride in making my dinner cost little." When asked at table what dish he preferred, he answered, "The nearest." He did not like the taste of wine, and never had a vice in his life. He said—"I have a faint recollection of pleasure derived from smoking dried lily stems, before I was a man. I had commonly a supply of these. I have never smoked anything more noxious."

He chose to be rich by making his wants few, and supplying them himself. In his travels, he used the railroad only to get over so much country as was unimportant to the present purpose, walking hundreds of miles, avoiding taverns, buying a lodging in farmers' and fishermen's houses, as cheaper and more agreeable to him, and because there he could better find the men and the information he wanted.

There was somewhat military in his nature, not to be subdued, always manly and able, but rarely tender, as if he did not feel himself except in opposition. He wanted a fallacy to expose, a blunder to pillory, I may say required a little sense of victory, a roll of the drum, to call his powers into full exercise. It cost him nothing to say No; indeed he found it much easier than to say Yes. It seemed as if his first instinct on hearing a proposition was to controvert it, so impatient was he of the limitations of our daily thought. This habit, of course, is a little chilling to the social affections; and though the companion would in the end acquit him of any malice or untruth, yet it mars conversation. Hence, no equal companion stood in affectionate relations with one so pure and guileless. "I love Henry," said one of his friends, "but I cannot like him; and as for taking his arm, I should as soon think of taking the arm of an elm tree."

Yet, hermit and stoic as he was, he was really fond of sympathy, and threw himself heartily and childlike into the company of young people whom he loved, and whom he delighted to entertain, as he only could, with the varied and endless anecdotes of his experiences by field and river: and he was always ready to lead a huckleberry party or a search for chestnuts or grapes. Talking, one day, of a public discourse, Henry remarked that whatever succeeded with the audience was bad. I said, "Who would not like to write something which all can read, like Robinson Crusoe? and who does not see with regret that his page is not solid with a right materialistic treatment, which delights everybody?" Henry objected, of course, and vaunted the better lectures which reached only a few persons. But at supper a young girl, understanding that he was to lecture at the Lyceum, sharply asked him, "Whether his lecture would be a nice, interesting story, such as she wished to hear, or whether it was one of those old philosophical things that she did not care about." Henry turned to her, and bethought himself, and, I saw, was trying to believe that he had matter that might fit her and her brother, who were to sit up and go to the lecture, if it was a good one for them.

He was a speaker and actor of the truth, born such, and was ever running into dramatic situations from this cause. In any circumstance it interested all bystanders to know what part Henry would take, and what he would say; and he did not disappoint expectation, but used an original judgment on each emergency. In 1845 he built himself a small framed house on the shores of Walden Pond, and lived there two years alone, a life of labor and study. This action was quite native and fit for him. No one who knew him would tax him with affectation. He was more unlike his neighbors in his thought than in his action. As soon as he had exhausted the advantages of that solitude, he abandoned it. In 1847, not approving some uses to which the public expenditure was applied, he refused to pay his town tax, and was put in jail. A friend paid the tax for him, and he was released. The like annoyance was threatened the next year. But as his friends paid the tax, notwithstanding his protest, I believe he ceased to resist. No opposition or ridicule had any weight with him. He coldly and fully stated his opinion without affecting to believe that it was the opinion of the company. It was of no consequence if every one present held the opposite opinion. On one occasion he went to the university library to procure some books. The librarian refused to lend them. Mr. Thoreau repaired to the President, who stated to him the rules and usages, which permitted the loan of books to resident graduates, to clergymen who were alumni, and to some others resident within a circle of ten miles' radius from the college. Mr. Thoreau explained to the President that the railroad had destroyed the old scale of distances—that the library was useless, yes, and President and college useless, on the terms of his rules—that the one benefit he owed to the college was its library—that, at this moment, not only his want of books was imperative, but he wanted a large number of books, and assured him that he, Thoreau, and not the librarian, was the proper custodian of these. In short, the President found the petitioner so formidable, and the rules getting to look so ridiculous, that he ended by giving him a privilege which in his hands proved unlimited thereafter.

No truer American existed than Thoreau. His preference of his country and condition was genuine, and his aversation from English and European manners and tastes almost reached contempt. He listened impatiently to news or bon mots gleaned from London circles; and though he tried to be civil, these anecdotes fatigued him. The men were all imitating each other, and on a small mold. Why can they not live as far apart as possible, and each be a man by himself? What he sought was the most energetic nature; and he wished to go to Oregon, not to London. "In every part of Great Britain," he wrote in his diary, "are discovered traces of the Romans, their funereal urns, their camps, their roads, their dwellings. But New England, at least, is not based on any Roman ruins. We have not to lay the foundations of our houses on the ashes of a former civilization."

But idealist as he was, standing for abolition of slavery, abolition of tariffs, almost for abolition of government, it is needless to say he found himself not only unrepresented in actual politics, but almost equally opposed to every class of reformers. Yet he paid the tribute of his uniform respect to the Anti-Slavery party. One man, whose personal acquaintance he had formed, he honored with exceptional regard. Before the first friendly word had been spoken for Captain John Brown, he sent notices to most houses in Concord that he would speak in a public hall on the condition and character of John Brown, on Sunday evening, and invited all people to come. The Republican Committee, the Abolitionist Committee, sent him word that it was premature and not advisable. He replied:"I did not send to you for advice, but to announce that I am to speak." The hall was filled at an early hour by people of all parties, and his earnest eulogy of the hero was heard by all respectfully, by many with a sympathy that surprised themselves.

It was said of Plotinus that he was ashamed of his body, and 'tis very likely he had good reason for it—that his body was a bad servant, and he had not skill in dealing with the material world, as happens often to men of abstract intellect. But Mr. Thoreau was equipped with a most adapted and serviceable body. He was of short stature, firmly built, of light complexion, with strong, serious blue eyes, and a grave aspect— his face covered in the late years with a becoming beard. His senses were acute, his frame well-knit and hardy, his hands strong and skillful in the use of tools. And there was a wonderful fitness of body and mind. He could pace sixteen rods more accurately than another man could measure them with rod and chain. He could find his path in the woods at night, he said, better by his feet than his eyes. He could estimate the measure of a tree very well by his eye; he could estimate the weight of a calf or a pig, like a dealer. From a box containing a bushel or more of loose pencils, he could take up with his hands fast enough just a dozen pencils at every grasp. He was a good swimmer, runner, skater, boatman, and would probably outwalk most countrymen in a day's journey. And the relation of body to mind was still finer than we have indicated. He said he wanted every stride his legs made. The length of his walk uniformly made the length of his writing. If shut up in the house he did not write at all.

He had a strong common sense, like that which Rose Flammock, the weaver's daughter in Scott's romance, commends in her father, as resembling a yardstick, which, while it measures dowlas and diaper, can equally well measure tapestry and cloth of gold. He had always a new resource. When I was planting forest trees, and had procured half a peck of acorns, he said that only a small portion of them would be sound, and proceeded to examine them and select the sound ones. But finding this took time, he said, "I think if you put them all into water the good ones will sink"; which experiment we tried with success. He could plan a garden or a house or a barn; would have been competent to lead a "Pacific Exploring Expedition"; could give judicious counsel in the gravest private or public affairs.

He lived for the day, not cumbered and mortified by his memory. If he brought you yesterday a new proposition, he would bring you today another not less revolutionary. A very industrious man, and setting, like all highly organized men, a high value on his time, he seemed the only man of leisure in town, always ready for any excursion that promised well or for conversation prolonged into late hours. His trenchant sense was never stopped by his rules of daily prudence, but was always up to the new occasion. He liked and used the simplest food, yet, when someone urged a vegetable diet, Thoreau thought all diets a very small matter, saying that "the man who shoots the buffalo lives better than the man who boards at the Graham House." He said, "You can sleep near the railroad and never be disturbed: Nature knows very well what sounds are worth attending to, and has made up her mind not to hear the railroad whistle. But things respect the devout mind, and a mental ecstasy was never interrupted." He noted what repeatedly befell him, that, after receiving from a distance a rare plant, he would presently find the same in his own haunts. And those pieces of luck which happen only to good players happened to him. One day, walking with a stranger, who inquired where Indian arrowheads could be found, he replied, "Everywhere," and, stooping forward, picked one on the instant from the ground. At Mount Washington, in Tuckerman's Ravine, Thoreau had a bad fall and sprained his foot. As he was in the act of getting up from his fall, he saw for the first time the leaves of the *Arnica mollis.*

His robust common sense, armed with stout hands, keen perceptions and strong will, cannot yet account for the superiority which shone in his simple and hidden life. I must add the cardinal fact, that there was an excellent wisdom in him, proper to a rare class of men, which showed him the material world as a means and symbol. This discovery, which sometimes yields to poets a certain casual and interrupted light, serving for the ornament of their writing, was in him an unsleeping insight; and whatever faults or obstructions of temperament might cloud it, he was not disobedient to the heavenly vision. In his youth, he said, one day, "The other world is all my art; my pencils will draw no other; my jackknife will cut nothing else; I do not use it as a means." This was the muse and genius that ruled his opinions, conversation, studies, work and course of life. This made him a searching judge of men. At first glance he measured his companion and, though insensible to some fine traits of culture, could very well report his weight and caliber. And this made the impression of genius which his conversation sometimes gave.

He understood the matter in hand at a glance, and saw the limitations and poverty of those he talked with, so that nothing seemed concealed from such terrible eyes. I have repeatedly known young men of sensibility converted in a moment to the belief that this was the man they were in search of, the man of men, who could tell them all they should do. His own dealing with them was never affectionate, but superior, didactic, scorning their petty ways—very slowly conceding, or not conceding at all, the promise of his society at their houses, or even at his own. "Would he not walk with them?" "He did not know. There was nothing so important to him as his walk; he had no walks to throw away on company." Visits were offered him from respectful parties, but he declined them. Admiring friends offered to carry him at their own cost to the Yellowstone River—to the West Indies—to South America. But though nothing could be more grave or considered than his refusals, they remind one, in quite new relations, of that fop Brummel's reply to the gentleman who offered him his carriage in a shower, "But where will *you* ride, then?"—and what accusing silences, and what searching and irresistible speeches, battering down all defenses, his companions can remember!

Mr. Thoreau dedicated his genius with such entire love to the fields, hills and waters of his native town that he made them known and interesting to all reading Americans, and to people over the sea. The river on whose banks he was born and died he knew from its springs to its confluence with the Merrimack. He had made summer and winter observations on it for many years, and at every hour of the day and night. The result of the recent survey of the water commissioners appointed by the State of Massachusetts he had reached by his private experiments several years earlier. Every fact which occurs in the bed, on the banks or in the air over it; the fishes, and their spawning and nests, their manners, their food; the shad flies which fill the air on a certain evening once a year, and which are snapped at by the fishes so ravenously that many of these die of repletion; the conical heaps of small stones on the river shallows; the huge nests of small fishes, one of which will sometimes overfill a cart; the birds which frequent the stream, heron, duck, sheldrake, loon, osprey; the snake, muskrat, otter, woodchuck and fox, on the banks; the turtle, frog, hyla and cricket, which make the banks vocal— were all known to him, and, as it were, townsmen and fellow creatures; so that he felt an absurdity or violence in any narrative of one of these by itself apart, and still more of its dimensions on an inch rule, or in the exhibition of its skeleton, or the specimen of a squirrel or a bird in brandy. He liked to speak of the manners of the river, as itself a lawful creature, yet with exactness, and always to an observed fact. As he knew the river, so the ponds in this region.

One of the weapons he used, more important to him than microscope, or alcohol receiver to other investigators, was a whim which grew on him by indulgence, yet appeared in gravest statement, namely, of extolling his own town and neighborhood as the most favored center for natural observation. He remarked that the flora of Massachusetts embraced almost all the important plants of America—most of the oaks, most of the willows, the best pines, the ash, the maple, the beech, the nuts. He returned Kane's Arctic Voyage to a friend of whom he had borrowed it, with the remark that "Most of the phenomena noted might be observed in Concord." He seemed a little envious of the Pole, for the coincident sunrise and sunset, or five minutes' day after six months: a splendid fact, which Annursnuc had never afforded him. He found red snow in one of his walks, and told me that he expected to find yet the *Victoria regia* in Concord. He was the attorney of the indigenous plants, and owned to a preference of the weeds to the imported plants, as of the Indian to the civilized man, and noticed, with pleasure, that the willow bean poles of his neighbor had grown more than his beans. "See these weeds," he said, "which have been hoed at by a million farmers all spring and summer, and yet have prevailed, and just now come out triumphant over all lanes, pastures, fields and gardens, such is their vigor. We have insulted them with low names, too—as Pigweed, Wormwood, Chickweed, Shad-blossom." He says, "They have brave names, too— Ambrosia, Stellaria, Amelanchier, Amaranth, etc."

I think his fancy for referring everything to the meridian of Concord did not grow out of any ignorance or depreciation of other longitudes or latitudes, but was rather a playful expression of his conviction of the indifferency of all places, and that the best place for each is where he stands. He expressed it once in this wise: "I think nothing is to be hoped from you, if this bit of mold under your feet is not sweeter to you to eat than any other in this world, or in any world."

The other weapon with which he conquered all obstacles in science was patience. He knew how to sit immovable, a part of the rock he rested on, until the bird, the reptile, the fish, which had retired from him, should come back and resume its habits, nay, moved by curiosity, should come to him and watch him.

It was a pleasure and a privilege to walk with him. He knew the country like a fox or a bird, and passed through it as freely by paths of his own. He knew every track in the snow or on the ground, and what creature had taken this path before him. One must submit abjectly to such a guide, and the reward was great. Under his arm he carried an old music book to press plants; in his pocket, his diary and pencil, a spyglass for birds, microscope, jackknife and twine. He wore a straw hat, stout shoes, strong gray trousers, to brave scrub oaks and smilax, and to climb a tree for a hawk's or a squirrel's nest. He waded into the pool for the water plants, and his strong legs were no insignificant part of his armor. On the day I speak of he looked for the Menyanthes, detected it across the wide pool, and, on examination of the florets, decided that it had been in flower five days. He drew out of his breast pocket his diary, and read the names of all the plants that should bloom on this day, whereof he kept account as a banker when his notes fall due. The Cypripedium not due till tomorrow. He thought that, if waked up from a trance, in this swamp, he could tell by the plants what time of the year it was within two days. The redstart was flying about, and presently the fine grosbeaks, whose brilliant scarlet "makes the rash gazer wipe his eye," and whose fine clear note Thoreau compared to that of a tanager which has got rid of its hoarseness. Presently he heard a note which he called that of the night warbler, a bird he had never identified, had been in search of twelve years, which always, when he saw it, was in the act of diving down into a tree or bush, and which it was vain to seek:

the only bird which sings indifferently by night and by day. I told him he must beware of finding and booking it, lest life should have nothing more to show him. He said, "What you seek in vain for, half your life, one day you come full upon, all the family at dinner. You seek it like a dream, and as soon as you find it you become its prey."

His interest in the flower or the bird lay very deep in his mind, was connected with Nature—and the meaning of Nature was never attempted to be defined by him. He would not offer a memoir of his observations to the Natural History Society. "Why should I? To detach the description from its connections in my mind would make it no longer true or valuable to me: and they do not wish what belongs to it." His power of observation seemed to indicate additional senses. He saw as with microscope, heard as with ear trumpet, and his memory was a photographic register of all he saw and heard. And yet none knew better than he that it is not the fact that imports, but the impression or effect of the fact on your mind. Every fact lay in glory in his mind, a type of the order and beauty of the whole.

His determination on Natural History was organic. He confessed that he sometimes felt like a hound or a panther, and, if born among Indians, would have been a fell hunter. But, restrained by his Massachusetts culture, he played out the game in this mild form of botany and ichthyology. His intimacy with animals suggested what Thomas Fuller records of Butler the apiologist, that "either he had told the bees things or the bees had told him." Snakes coiled round his legs; the fishes swam into his hand, and he took them out of the water; he pulled the woodchuck out of its hole by the tail, and took the foxes under his protection from the hunters. Our naturalist had perfect magnanimity; he had no secrets: he would carry you to the heron's haunt, or even to his most prized botanical swamp—possibly knowing that you could never find it again, yet willing to take his risks.

No college ever offered him a diploma, or a professor's chair; no academy made him its corresponding secretary, its discoverer or even its member. Perhaps these learned bodies feared the satire of his presence. Yet so much knowledge of Nature's secret and genius few others possessed; none in a more large and religious synthesis. For not a particle of respect had he to the opinions of any man or body of men, but homage solely to the truth itself; and as he discovered everywhere among doctors some leaning of courtesy, it discredited them. He grew to be revered and admired by his townsmen, who had at first known him only as an oddity. The farmers who employed him as a surveyor soon discovered his rare accuracy and skill, his knowledge of their lands, of trees, of birds, of Indian remains and the like, which enabled him to tell every farmer more than he knew before of his own farm, so that he began to feel a little as if Mr. Thoreau had better rights in his land than he. They felt, too, the superiority of character which addressed all men with a native authority.

Indian relics abound in Concord—arrowheads, stone chisels, pestles and fragments of pottery; and on the riverbank, large heaps of clamshells and ashes mark spots which the savages frequented. These, and every circumstance touching the Indian, were important in his eyes. His visits to Maine were chiefly for love of the Indian. He had the satisfaction of seeing the manufacture of the bark canoe, as well as of trying his hand in its management on the rapids. He was inquisitive about the making of the stone arrowhead, and in his last days charged a youth setting out for the Rocky Mountains to find an Indian who could tell him that: "It was well worth a visit to California to learn it." Occasionally, a small party of Penobscot Indians would visit Concord, and pitch their tents for a few weeks in summer on the riverbank. He failed not to make acquaintance with the best of them, though he well knew that asking questions of Indians is like catechizing beavers and rabbits. In his last visit to Maine he had great satisfaction from Joseph Polis, an intelligent Indian of Oldtown, who was his guide for some weeks.

He was equally interested in every natural fact. The depth of his perception found likeness of law throughout Nature, and I know not any genius who so swiftly inferred universal law from the single fact. He was no pedant of a department. His eye was open to beauty, and his ear to music. He found these, not in rare conditions, but wheresoever he went. He thought the best of music was in single strains, and he found poetic suggestion in the humming of the telegraph wire.

His poetry might be bad or good; he no doubt wanted a lyric facility and technical skill, but he had the source of poetry in his spiritual perception. He was a good reader and critic, and his judgment on poetry was to the ground of it. He could not be deceived as to the presence or absence of the poetic element in any composition, and his thirst for this made him negligent and perhaps scornful of superficial graces. He would pass by many delicate rhythms, but he would have detected every live stanza or line in a volume and knew very well where to find an equal poetic charm in prose. He was so enamored of the spiritual beauty that he held all actual written poems in very light esteem in the comparison. He admired Aeschylus and Pindar; but when someone was commending them, he said that Aeschylus and the Greeks, in describing Apollo and Orpheus, had given no song, or no good one. "They ought not to have moved trees, but to have chanted to the gods such a hymn as would have sung all their old ideas out of their heads, and new ones in." His own verses are often rude and defective. The gold does not yet run pure, is drossy and crude. The thyme and marjoram are not yet honey. But if he want lyric fineness and technical merits, if he have not the poetic temperament, he never lacks the causal thought, showing that his genius was better than his talent. He knew the worth of the Imagination for the uplifting and consolation of human life, and liked to throw every thought into a symbol. The fact you tell is of no value, but only the impression. For this reason his presence was poetic, always piqued the curiosity to know more deeply the secrets of his mind. He had many reserves, an unwillingness to exhibit to profane eyes what was still sacred in his own, and knew well how to throw a poetic veil over his experience. All readers of Walden will remember his mythical record of his disappointments: "I long ago lost a hound, a bay horse and a turtledove, and am still on their trail. Many are the travelers I have spoken concerning them, describing their tracks, and what calls they answered to. I have met one or two who have heard the hound, and the tramp of the horse, and even seen the dove disappear behind a cloud, and they seemed as anxious to recover them as if they had lost them themselves."

His riddles were worth the reading, and I confide that if at any time I do not understand the expression, it is yet just. Such was the wealth of his truth that it was not worth his while to use words in vain. His poem entitled "Sympathy" reveals the tenderness under that triple steel of stoicism, and the intellectual subtility it could animate. His classic poem on "Smoke" suggests Simonides, but is better than any poem of Simonides. His biography is in his verses. His habitual thought makes all his poetry a hymn to the Cause of causes, the Spirit which vivifies and controls his own:

> I hearing get, who had but ears,
> And sight, who had but eyes before;
> I moments live, who lived but years,
> And truth discern, who knew but learning's lore.

And still more in these religious lines:

> Now chiefly is my natal hour,
> And only now my prime of life;
> I will not doubt the love untold,

Which not my worth nor want have bought,
Which wooed me young, and woos me old,
And to this evening hath me brought.

While he used in his writings a certain petulance of remark in reference to churches or churchmen, he was a person of a rare, tender and absolute religion, a person incapable of any profanation, by act or by thought. Of course, the same isolation which belonged to his original thinking and living detached him from the social religious forms. This is neither to be censured nor regretted. Aristotle long ago explained it, when he said, "One who surpasses his fellow citizens in virtue is no longer a part of the city. Their law is not for him, since he is a law to himself."

Thoreau was sincerity itself, and might fortify the convictions of prophets in the ethical laws by his holy living. It was an affirmative experience which refused to be set aside. A truth-speaker he, capable of the most deep and strict conversation; a physician to the wounds of any soul; a friend, knowing not only the secret of friendship, but almost worshipped by those few persons who resorted to him as their confessor and prophet, and knew the deep value of his mind and great heart. He thought that without religion or devotion of some kind nothing great was ever accomplished: and he thought that the bigoted sectarian had better bear this in mind.

His virtues, of course, sometimes ran into extremes. It was easy to trace to the inexorable demand on all for exact truth that austerity which made this willing hermit more solitary even than he wished. Himself of a perfect probity, he required not less of others. He had a disgust at crime, and no worldly success would cover it. He detected paltering as readily in dignified and prosperous persons as in beggars, and with equal scorn. Such dangerous frankness was in his dealing that his admirers called him "that terrible Thoreau," as if he spoke when silent, and was still present when he had departed. I think the severity of his ideal interfered to deprive him of a healthy sufficiency of human society.

The habit of a realist to find things the reverse of their appearance inclined him to put every statement in a paradox. A certain habit of antagonism defaced his earlier writings—a trick of rhetoric not quite outgrown in his later, of substituting for the obvious word and thought its diametrical opposite. He praised wild mountains and winter forests for their domestic air, in snow and ice he would find sultriness, and commended the wilderness for resembling Rome and Paris. "It was so dry, that you might call it wet."

The tendency to magnify the moment, to read all the laws of Nature in the one object or one combination under your eye, is of course comic to those who do not share the philosopher's perception of identity. To him there was no such thing as size. The pond was a small ocean; the Atlantic, a large Walden Pond. He referred every minute fact to cosmical laws. Though he meant to be just, he seemed haunted by a certain chronic assumption that the science of the day pretended completeness, and he had just found out that the savants had neglected to discriminate a particular botanical variety, had failed to describe the seeds or count the sepals. "That is to say," we replied, "the blockheads were not born in Concord; but who said they were? It was their unspeakable misfortune to be born in London, or Paris, or Rome; but, poor fellows, they did what they could, considering that they never saw Bateman's Pond, or Nine-Acre Corner, or Becky Stow's Swamp; besides, what were you sent into the world for, but to add this observation?"

Had his genius been only contemplative, he had been fitted to his life, but with his energy and practical ability he seemed born for great enterprise and for command; and I so much regret the loss of his rare powers of action that I cannot help counting it a fault in him that he had no ambition. Wanting this, instead of engineering for all America, he was the captain of a huckleberry party. Pounding beans is good to the end of pounding empires one of these days; but if, at the end of years, it is still only beans!

But these foibles, real or apparent, were fast vanishing in the incessant growth of a spirit so robust and wise, and which effaced its defeats with new triumphs. His study of Nature was a perpetual ornament to him, and inspired his friends with curiosity to see the world through his eyes, and to hear his adventures. They possessed every kind of interest.

He had many elegancies of his own, while he scoffed at conventional elegance. Thus, he could not bear to hear the sound of his own steps, the grit of gravel; and therefore never willingly walked in the road, but in the grass, on mountains and in woods. His senses were acute, and he remarked that by night every dwelling house gives out bad air, like a slaughterhouse. He liked the pure fragrance of melilot. He honored certain plants with special regard, and, over all, the pond lily—then, the gentian, and the *Mikania scandens,* and "life-everlasting," and a bass tree which he visited every year when it bloomed, in the middle of July. He thought the scent a more oracular inquisition than the sight— more oracular and trustworthy. The scent, of course, reveals what is concealed from the other senses. By it he detected earthiness. He delighted in echoes, and said they were almost the only kind of kindred voices that he heard. He loved Nature so well, was so happy in her solitude, that he became very jealous of cities and the sad work which their refinements and artifices made with man and his dwelling. The axe was always destroying his forest. "Thank God," he said, "they cannot cut down the clouds!" "All kinds of figures are drawn on the blue ground with this fibrous white paint."

I subjoin a few sentences taken from his unpublished manuscripts, not only as records of his thought and feeling, but for their power of description and literary excellence:

Some circumstantial evidence is very strong, as when you find a trout in the milk.

The chub is a soft fish, and tastes like boiled brown paper salted.

The youth gets together his materials to build a bridge to the moon, or, perchance, a palace or temple on the earth, and, at length the middle-aged man concludes to build a woodshed with them.

The locust z-ing.

Devil's-needles zigzagging along the Nut-Meadow brook.

Sugar is not so sweet to the palate as sound to the healthy ear.

I put on some hemlock boughs, and the rich salt crackling of their leaves was like mustard to the ear, the crackling of uncountable regiments. Dead trees love the fire.

The bluebird carries the sky on his back.

The tanager flies through the green foliage as if it would ignite the leaves.

If I wish for a horsehair for my compass sight I must go to the stable; but the hairbird, with her sharp eyes, goes to the road.

Immortal water, alive even to the superficies.

Fire is the most tolerable third party.

Nature made ferns for pure leaves, to show what she could do in that line.

No tree has so fair a bole and so handsome an instep as the beech.

How did these beautiful rainbow tints get into the shell of the fresh-water clam, buried in the mud at the bottom of our dark river?

Hard are the times when the infant's shoes are second foot.

We are strictly confined to our men to whom we give liberty.

Nothing is so much to be feared as fear. Atheism may comparatively be popular with God himself.

Of what significance the things you can forget? A little thought is sexton to all the world.

How can we expect a harvest of thought who have not had a seed-time of character?

Only he can be trusted with gifts who can present a face of bronze to expectations.

I ask to be melted. You can only ask of the metals that they be tender to the fire that melts them. To nought else can they be tender.

There is a flower known to botanists, one of the same genus with our summer plant called "Life-Everlasting," a *Gnaphalium* like that, which grows on the most inaccessible cliffs of the Tyrolese mountains, where the chamois dare hardly venture, and which the hunter, tempted by its beauty, and by his love (for it is immensely valued by the Swiss maidens), climbs the cliffs to gather, and is sometimes found dead at the foot, with the flower in his hand. It is called by botanists the *Gnaphalium leontopodium*, but by the Swiss *Edelweisse*, which signifies *Noble Purity*. Thoreau seemed to me living in the hope to gather this plant, which belonged to him of right. The scale on which his studies proceeded was so large as to require longevity, and we were the less prepared for his sudden disappearance. The country knows not yet, or in the least part, how great a son it has lost. It seems an injury that he should leave in the midst his broken task which none else can finish, a kind of indignity to so noble a soul that he should depart out of Nature before yet he has been really shown to his peers for what he is. But he, at least, is content. His soul was made for the noblest society; he had in a short life exhausted the capabilities of this world; wherever there is knowledge, wherever there is virtue, wherever there is beauty, he will find a home.

Nathaniel Hawthorne[1]

1804–1864

Hawthorne's sketch of Lincoln is one of the most famous face-to-face impressions of the President ever written. It described Lincoln as he appeared in 1862, a year after he took office. At this time he was not generally popular nor even well known. He had been elected to the presidency in what Hawthorne called a "jumble of human vicissitudes." He had won the Republican nomination in 1860, though Seward had been expected to be named, and he had won the presidential election because the vote was split among four candidates.

After a year in office, the war, which Lincoln had reluctantly declared against his countrymen, had gone steadily against the North. Lincoln had not yet been able to unify the command of the armed forces, nor find good generals. But he had suspended constitutional rights, established conscription, and levied huge sums to carry on the war. Such things, though unavoidable, did not tend to make Lincoln popular.

What Hawthorne would say about Lincoln, however, depended not only on the existing situation but upon Hawthorne's appraisal—his vision and faith. How would the fastidious scholar and novelist, representing the oldest and proudest cultural tradition of New England, size up the ungainly backwoods lawyer who had been catapulted into the highest office in the land? Lincoln was "the homeliest man I ever saw," Hawthorne wrote. "The whole physiognomy is as coarse a one as you would meet anywhere. . . ." His manners were uncouth, his clothes a little disreputable, and his innumerable yarns and anecdotes smacked of "frontier freedom." He was clearly lack-

---

[1] For a biography of Hawthorne, see Vol. 3, pp. 124–126, in this set.

ing in refinement and "bookish cultivation." On the other hand, he possessed a natural dignity, kindness, subtlety, and an unpretentious wisdom. And, in short, Hawthorne would as soon have "Uncle Abe for a ruler" as any man in the country. Even his backwoods faults were piquant and exciting.

Hawthorne could not have known, at this time, that some of Lincoln's speeches would be rated as the best in the English language. He missed many points of his greatness. Yet his estimate of the President was as glowing and affirmative as that of Walt Whitman,[2] who wrote after Lincoln's death. One thing that Hawthorne loved in Lincoln was his basic humility and humanity. What he disliked most in human beings, as his novels and tales show, was pride and pretense.

A year after writing the sketch of Lincoln, Hawthorne insisted on standing by his friend, Franklin Pierce, then regarded as a traitor to the North. He knew he would lose friends and money by it but nevertheless insisted. Yet he does not want to be regarded as a hero or martyr. "I always measure out my heroism very accurately according to the exigencies of the occasion," he wrote, "and should be the last man in the world to throw away a bit of it needlessly."

It was a similar ironic humor, and dislike of pretense, that Hawthorne saw in Lincoln.

---

[2] See *Death of Abraham Lincoln*, Vol. 6, pp. 174–183, in this set.

Sketch
of Abraham Lincoln

Of course, there was one other personage, in the class of statesmen, whom I should have been truly mortified to leave Washington without seeing; since (temporarily, at least, and by force of circumstances) he was the man of men. But a private grief had built up a barrier about him, impeding the customary free intercourse of Americans with their chief magistrate; so that I might have come away without a glimpse of his very remarkable physiognomy, save for a semiofficial opportunity of which I was glad to take advantage. The fact is, we were invited to annex ourselves, as supernumeraries, to a deputation that was about to wait upon the President, from a Massachusetts whip factory, with a present of a splendid whip.

Our immediate party consisted only of four or five (including Major Ben Perley Poore, with his notebook and pencil), but we were joined by several other persons, who seemed to have been lounging about the precincts of the White House, under the spacious porch, or within the hall, and who swarmed in with us to take the chances of a presentation. Nine o'clock had been appointed as the time for receiving the deputation, and we were punctual to the moment; but not so the President, who sent us word that he was eating his breakfast, and would come as soon as he could. His appetite, we were glad to think, must have been a pretty fair one; for we waited about half an hour in one of the antechambers, and then were ushered into a reception room, in one corner of which sat the secretaries of War and of the Treasury, expecting, like ourselves, the termination of the Presidential breakfast. During this interval there were several new additions to our group, one or two of whom were in a working garb, so that we formed a very miscellaneous collection of people, mostly unknown to each other, and without any common sponsor, but all with an equal right to look our head servant in the face.

By and by there was a little stir on the staircase and in the passageway,[1] [and in lounged a tall, loose-jointed figure, as of an exaggerated Yankee port and demeanor, whom (as being about the homeliest man I ever saw, yet by no means repulsive or disagreeable) it was impossible not to recognize as Uncle Abe.

Unquestionably, Western man though he be, and Kentuckian by birth, President Lincoln is the essential representative of all Yankees, and the veritable specimen, physically, of what the world seems determined to regard as our characteristic qualities. It is the strangest and yet the fittest thing in the jumble of human vicissitudes that he, out of so many millions, unlooked for, unselected by any intelligible process that could be based upon his genuine qualities, unknown to those who chose him, and un-suspected of what endowments may adapt him for his tremendous re-sponsibility, should have found the way open for him to fling his lank personality into the chair of state—where, I presume, it was his first impulse to throw his legs on the council table, and tell the Cabinet min-isters a story. There is no describing his lengthy awkwardness, nor the un-couthness of his movement; and yet it seemed as if I had been in the habit of seeing him daily, and had shaken hands with him a thousand times in some village street; so true was he to the aspect of the pattern American, though with a certain extravagance which, possibly, I exag-gerated still further by the delighted eagerness with which I took it in. If put to guess his calling and livelihood, I should have taken him for a country schoolmaster as soon as anything else. He was dressed in a rusty black frock coat and pantaloons, unbrushed, and worn so faithfully that the suit had adapted itself to the curves and angularities of his figure, and had grown to be an outer skin of the man. He had shabby slippers on his feet. His hair was black, still unmixed with gray, stiff, somewhat bushy, and had apparently been acquainted with neither brush nor comb that morning, after the disarrangement of the pillow; and as to a nightcap, Uncle Abe probably knows nothing of such effeminacies. His complexion is dark and sallow, betokening, I fear, an insalubrious atmosphere around

1. We are compelled to omit two or three pages, in which the author describes the interview, and gives his idea of the personal appearance and deportment of the President. The sketch appears to have been written in a benign spirit, and perhaps conveys a not inaccurate impression of its august subject; but it lacks *reverence*, and it pains us to see a gentleman of ripe age, and who has spent years under the corrective influence of foreign institutions, falling into the characteristic and most ominous fault of Young America. [This footnote, the apparent addition of a genteel editor, was actually written by Hawthorne himself for a version of the *Sketch* in which part of his portrait of Lincoln was omitted (*Atlantic Monthly*, July, 1862). The suppressed passage was subsequently printed in the *Atlantic* and in this text is set off by brackets (Ed.).]

the White House; he has thick black eyebrows and an impending brow; his nose is large, and the lines about his mouth are very strongly defined.

The whole physiognomy is as coarse a one as you would meet anywhere in the length and breadth of the States; but, withal, it is redeemed, illuminated, softened, and brightened by a kindly though serious look out of his eyes, and an expression of homely sagacity, that seems weighted with rich results of village experience. A great deal of native sense; no bookish cultivation, no refinement; honest at heart, and thoroughly so, and yet, in some sort, sly—at least, endowed with a sort of tact and wisdom that are akin to craft, and would impel him, I think, to take an antagonist in flank, rather than to make a bull-run at him right in front. But, on the whole, I like this sallow, queer, sagacious visage, with the homely human sympathies that warmed it; and, for my small share in the matter, would as lief have Uncle Abe for a ruler as any man whom it would have been practicable to put in his place.

Immediately on his entrance the President accosted our member of Congress, who had us in charge, and, with a comical twist of his face, made some jocular remark about the length of his breakfast. He then greeted us all round, not waiting for an introduction, but shaking and squeezing everybody's hand with the utmost cordiality, whether the individual's name was announced to him or not. His manner towards us was wholly without pretense, but yet had a kind of natural dignity, quite sufficient to keep the forwardest of us from clapping him on the shoulder and asking him for a story. A mutual acquaintance being established, our leader took the whip out of its case, and began to read the address of presentation. The whip was an exceedingly long one, its handle wrought in ivory (by some artist in the Massachusetts State Prison, I believe), and ornamented with a medallion of the President, and other equally beautiful devices; and along its whole length there was a succession of golden bands and ferrules. The address was shorter than the whip, but equally well made, consisting chiefly of an explanatory description of these artistic designs, and closing with a hint that the gift was a suggestive and emblematic one, and that the President would recognize the use to which such an instrument should be put.

This suggestion gave Uncle Abe rather a delicate task in his reply, because, slight as the matter seemed, it apparently called for some declaration, or intimation, or faint foreshadowing of policy in reference to the conduct of the war, and the final treatment of the Rebels. But the President's Yankee aptness and not-to-be-caughtness stood him in good stead, and he jerked or wiggled himself out of the dilemma with an uncouth dexterity that was entirely in character; although, without his gesticulation of eye and mouth—and especially the flourish of the whip, with which he imagined himself touching up a pair of fat horses—I doubt whether his words would be worth recording, even if I could remember them. The gist of the reply was, that he accepted the whip as an emblem of peace, not punishment; and, this great affair over, we retired out of the presence in high good humor, only regretting that we could not have seen the President sit down and fold up his legs (which is said to be a most extraordinary spectacle), or have heard him tell one of those delectable stories for which he is so celebrated. A good many of them are afloat upon the common talk of Washington, and are certainly the aptest, pithiest, and funniest little things imaginable; though, to be sure, they smack of the frontier freedom, and would not always bear repetition in a drawing room, or on the immaculate page of the *Atlantic*].

Good Heavens! what liberties have I been taking with one of the potentates of the earth, and the man on whose conduct more important consequences depend than on that of any other historical personage of the century! But with whom is an American citizen entitled to take a liberty, if not with his own chief magistrate? However, lest the above allusions to President Lincoln's little peculiarities (already well known to the country and to the world) should be misinterpreted, I deem it proper to say a word or two in regard to him, of unfeigned respect and measurable confidence. He is evidently a man of keen faculties, and, what is still more to the purpose, of powerful character. As to his integrity, the people have that intuition of it which is never deceived. Before he actually entered upon his great office, and for a considerable time afterwards, there is no reason to suppose that he adequately estimated the gigantic task about to be imposed on him, or, at least, had any distinct idea how it was to be managed; and I presume there may have been more than one veteran politician who proposed to himself to take the power out of President Lincoln's hands into his own, leaving our honest friend only the public responsibility for the good or ill success of the career. The extremely imperfect development of his statesmanly qualities, at that period, may have justified such designs. But the President is teachable by events, and has now spent a year in a very arduous course of education; he has a flexible mind, capable of much expansion, and convertible towards far loftier studies and activities than those of his early life; and if he came to Washington a backwoods humorist, he has already transformed himself into as good a statesman (to speak moderately) as his prime minister.

Walt Whitman[1]

1819–1892

This lecture on Lincoln was first given fifteen years after the assassination of the sixteenth President. The popularity of Abraham Lincoln had risen to the highest pinnacle. What words could Whit- could Whitman find in any way worthy of such a man? Would not any praise or tribute, so close to the unbelievable tragedy, sound paltry and insincere?

In Whitman's case there was a special difficulty. He had no use for histories which see the meaning of events "in single eminent persons," and was impatient with Carlyle's *Cromwell* and with hero worship in general. Speaking of the Civil War heroes, including Lincoln, he warned against giving undue weight to personalities. It is easy to exaggerate the role of saviors and "exceptional men." The real heroes of the Civil War in Whitman's poetry were the rank and file soldiers and the embattled people. His *Leaves of Grass* began with:

> One's-self I sing, a simple separate person,
> Yet utter the word Democratic, the word En-Masse.

Whitman was no hero-worshiper; he was the apostle of the average man, or of every man.

> The sum of all known reverence I add up to you, whoever you are.

How then can Whitman give the greatest hero in American history his due?

There is no use trying to anticipate too closely what your reaction to this speech will be, but one or two general impressions may help

---

[1] For a biography of Whitman, see Vol. 5, pp. 243–245 in this set.

you to form yours. We are given only one close-up picture of Lincoln; it is imposing but also touching. We see him in 1861, just before he took office—a tall, ungainly figure, stretching his long limbs with composure as he faced the curious gaze of thirty or forty thousand men, unknown to him, and stared back with equal curiosity. They wanted to see the man who had been placed in command, and would take on his shoulders the vast impending conflict. And when they had seen him, they went quietly away.

The story of the murder of the President is told with moving and vivid simplicity—as if by an eyewitness. We also see the tragedy in the perspective of other great martyrs. The course of history had been altered when Socrates was given the hemlock and when Caesar was cut down in the Senate House. The death of Lincoln had already left its mark on America, consecrating and strengthening the Union so dearly paid for in blood and sacrifice.

Yet throughout Whitman's speech we hear little of Lincoln's wisdom, courage, magnanimity, shrewdness, humor, and humanity. His great personal gifts and achievements are scarcely mentioned, never praised. Whitman's theme seems rather to be the national struggle for the preservation of the Union, a struggle enmeshing the lives of the soldiers in the battlefield, and all the men and women who worked and suffered through the long years at home. The tribute to Lincoln thus tends to become a tribute to the people whom he led to victory. They are the heroes, collectively, and Lincoln is one with them; when they suffer he suffers and their achievement is his achievement.

Whitman called himself the poet of democracy. Do you think that in his democratic outlook Lincoln loses something of greatness and appeal? Is there perhaps a gain in realism and conviction?

Death of Abraham Lincoln

How often since that dark and dripping Saturday—that chilly April day, now fifteen years bygone—my heart has entertained the dream, the wish, to give of Abraham Lincoln's death its own special thought and memorial. Yet now the sought-for opportunity offers, I find my notes incompetent (why, for truly profound themes, is statement so idle? why does the right phrase never offer?) and the fit tribute I dreamed of waits unprepared as ever. My talk here indeed is less because of itself or anything in it, and nearly altogether because I feel a desire, apart from any talk, to specify the day, the martyrdom. It is for this, my friends, I have called you together. Oft as the rolling years bring back this hour, let it again, however briefly, be dwelt upon. For my own part, I hope and desire, till my own dying day, whenever the 14th or 15th of April comes, to annually gather a few friends and hold its tragic reminiscence. No narrow or sectional reminiscence. It belongs to these states in their entirety—not the North only, but the South—perhaps belongs most tenderly and devoutly to the South, of all; for there, really, this man's birth-stock. There and thence his antecedent stamp. Why should I not say that thence his manliest traits—his universality—his canny, easy ways and words upon the surface—his inflexible determination and courage at heart? Have you never realized it, my friends, that Lincoln, though grafted on the West, is essentially, in personnel and character, a Southern contribution?

And though by no means proposing to resume the secession war to-night, I would briefly remind you of the public conditions preceding that contest. For twenty years, and especially during the four or five before the war actually began, the aspect of affairs in the United States, though without the flash of military excitement, presents more than the survey of a battle, or any extended campaign, or series, even of Nature's convulsions. The hot passions of the South—the strange mixture at the North

174

of inertia, incredulity, and conscious power—the incendiarism of the abolitionists—the rascality and *grip* of the politicians, unparalleled in any land, any age. To these I must not omit adding the honesty of the essential bulk of the people everywhere—yet with all the seething fury and contradiction of their natures more aroused than the Atlantic's waves in wildest equinox. In politics, what can be more ominous (though generally unappreciated then), what more significant than the Presidentiads of Fillmore and Buchanan? proving conclusively that the weakness and wickedness of elected rulers are just as likely to afflict us here, as in the countries of the Old World, under their monarchies, emperors, and aristocracies. In that Old World were everywhere heard underground rumblings that died out, only to again surely return. While in America the volcano, though civic yet, continued to grow more and more convulsive—more and more stormy and threatening.

In the height of all this excitement and chaos, hovering on the edge at first, and then merged in its very midst, and destined to play a leading part, appears a strange and awkward figure. I shall not easily forget the first time I ever saw Abraham Lincoln. It must have been about the 18th or 19th of February, 1861. It was rather a pleasant afternoon, in New York City, as he arrived there from the West, to remain a few hours, and then pass on to Washington, to prepare for his inauguration. I saw him in Broadway, near the site of the present post office. He came down, I think from Canal Street, to stop at the Astor House. The broad spaces, sidewalks, and street in the neighborhood, and for some distance, were crowded with solid masses of people, many thousands. The omnibuses and other vehicles had all been turned off, leaving an unusual hush in that busy part of the city. Presently two or three shabby hack barouches made their way with some difficulty through the crowd, and drew up at the Astor House entrance. A tall figure stepped out of the center of these barouches, paused leisurely on the sidewalk, looked up at the granite walls and looming architecture of the grand old hotel—then, after a relieving stretch of arms and legs, turned round for over a minute to slowly and good-humoredly scan the appearance of the vast and silent crowds. There were no speeches—no compliments—no welcome—as far as I could hear, not a word said. Still much anxiety was concealed in that quiet. Cautious persons had feared some marked insult or indignity to the President-elect, for he possessed no personal popularity at all in New York City, and very little political. But it was evidently tacitly agreed that if the few political supporters of Mr. Lincoln present would entirely abstain from any demonstration on their side, the immense majority, who were anything but supporters, would abstain on their side also. The result was a sulky, unbroken silence, such as certainly never before characterized so great a New York crowd.

Almost in the same neighborhood I distinctly remembered seeing La Fayette on his visit to America in 1825. I had also personally seen and heard, various years afterward, how Andrew Jackson, Clay, Webster, Hungarian Kossuth, Filibuster Walker, the Prince of Wales on his visit, and other celebres, native and foreign, had been welcomed there—all that indescribable human roar and magnetism, unlike any other sound in the universe—the glad exulting thundershouts of countless unloosed throats of men! But on this occasion, not a voice—not a sound. From the top of an omnibus (driven up one side, close by, and blocked by the curbstone and the crowds), I had, I say, a capital view of it all, and especially of Mr. Lincoln, his look and gait—his perfect composure and coolness—his unusual and uncouth height, his dress of complete black, stovepipe hat pushed back on the head, dark-brown complexion, seamed and wrinkled yet canny-looking face, black, bushy head of hair, disproportionately long neck, and his hands held behind as he stood observing the people. He looked with curiosity upon that immense sea of faces, and the sea of faces returned the look with similar curiosity. In both there was a dash of comedy, almost farce, such as Shakespeare puts in his blackest tragedies. The crowd that hemmed around consisted I should think of thirty to forty thousand men, not a single one his personal friend—while I have no doubt (so frenzied were the ferments of the time) many an assassin's knife and pistol lurked in hip or breast pocket there, ready, soon as break and riot came.

But no break or riot came. The tall figure gave another relieving stretch or two of arms and legs; then with moderate pace, and accompanied by a few unknown-looking persons, ascended the portico steps of the Astor House, disappeared through its broad entrance—and the dumb show ended.

I saw Abraham Lincoln often the four years following that date. He changed rapidly and much during his presidency—but this scene, and him in it, are indelibly stamped upon my recollection. As I sat on the top of my omnibus and had a good view of him, the thought, dim and inchoate then, has since come out clear enough, that four sorts of genius, four mighty and primal hands, will be needed to the complete limning of this man's future portrait—the eyes and brains and finger touch of Plutarch and Aeschylus and Michelangelo, assisted by Rabelais.

And now—(Mr. Lincoln passing on from this scene to Washington, where he was inaugurated, amid armed cavalry, and sharpshooters at every point—the first instance of the kind in our history—and I hope it will be the last)—now the rapid succession of well-known events (too well known—I believe, these days, we almost hate to hear them mentioned)—the national flag fired on at Sumter—the uprising of the North, in paroxysms of astonishment and rage—the chaos of divided councils—the call for troops—the first Bull Run—the stunning cast-down, shock, and dismay of the North—and so in full flood the secession war. Four years of lurid, bleeding, murky, murderous war. Who paint those years, with all their scenes?—the hard-fought engagements—the defeats, plans, failures—the gloomy hours, days, when our nationality seemed hung in pall of doubt, perhaps death—the Mephistophelean sneers of foreign lands and attachés—the dreaded Scylla of European interference, and the Charybdis of the tremendously dangerous latent strata of secession sympathizers throughout the free States (far more numerous than is supposed)—the long marches in summer—the hot sweat, and many a sunstroke, as on the rush to Gettysburg in '63—the night battles in the woods, as under Hooker at Chancellorsville—the camps in winter—the military prisons—the hospitals—(alas! alas! the hospitals).

The secession war? Nay, let me call it the Union war. Though whatever called, it is even yet too near us—too vast and too closely overshadowing—its branches unformed yet (but certain) shooting too far into the future—and the most indicative and mightiest of them yet ungrown. A great literature will yet arise out of the era of those four years, those scenes—era compressing centuries of native passion, first-class pictures, tempests of life and death—an inexhaustible mine for the histories, drama, romance, and even philosophy of peoples to come—indeed the vertebre of poetry and art (of personal character too) for all future America—far more grand, in my opinion, to the hands capable of it, than Homer's siege of Troy, or the French wars to Shakespeare.

But I must leave these speculations, and come to the theme I have assigned and limited myself to. Of the actual murder of President Lincoln, though so much has been written, probably the facts are yet very indefinite in most persons' minds. I read from my memoranda, written at the time, and revised frequently and finally since.

The day, April 14, 1865, seems to have been a pleasant one throughout the whole land—the moral atmosphere pleasant too—the long storm, so dark, so fratricidal, full of blood and doubt and gloom, over and ended at last by the sunrise of such an absolute national victory, and utter breakdown of secessionism—we almost doubted our own senses! Lee had capitulated beneath the apple tree of Appomattox. The other armies, the flanges of the revolt, swiftly followed. And could it really be, then? Out of all the affairs of this world of woe and failure and disorder, was there really come the confirmed, unerring sign of plan, like a shaft of pure light—of rightful rule—of God? So the day, as I say, was propitious. Early herbage, early flowers were out. (I remember where I was stopping at the time, the season being advanced, there were many lilacs in full bloom. By one of those caprices that enter and give tinge to events without being at all a part of them, I find myself always reminded of the great tragedy of that day by the sight and odor of these blossoms. It never fails.)

But I must not dwell on accessories. The deed hastens. The popular afternoon paper of Washington, the little *Evening Star*, had spattered all over its third page, divided among the advertisements in a sensational manner, in a hundred different places, *The President and his Lady will be at the Theatre this evening. . . .* (Lincoln was fond of the theatre. I have myself seen him there several times. I remember thinking how funny it was that he, in some respects the leading actor in the stormiest drama known to real history's stage through centuries, should sit there and be so completely interested and absorbed in those human jackstraws, moving about with their silly little gestures, foreign spirit, and flatulent text.)

On this occasion the theatre was crowded, many ladies in rich and gay costumes, officers in their uniforms, many well-known citizens, young folks, the usual clusters of gaslights, the usual magnetism of so many people, cheerful, with perfumes, music of violins and flutes (and over all, and saturating all, that vast, vague wonder, *Victory*, the nation's victory, the triumph of the Union, filling the air, the thought, the sense, with exhilaration more than all music and perfumes).

The President came betimes, and, with his wife, witnessed the play from the large stage boxes of the second tier, two thrown into one, and profusely draped with the national flag. The acts and scenes of the piece —one of those singularly written compositions which have at least the merit of giving entire relief to an audience engaged in mental action or business excitements and cares during the day, as it makes not the slightest call on either the moral, emotional, aesthetic, or spiritual nature —a piece (*Our American Cousin*) in which, among other characters, so called, a Yankee, certainly such a one as was never seen, or the least like it ever seen, in North America, is introduced in England, with a varied fol-de-rol of talk, plot, scenery, and such phantasmagoria as goes to make up a modern popular drama—had progressed through perhaps a couple of its acts, when in the midst of this comedy, or nonesuch, or whatever it is to be called, and to offset it, or finish it out, as if in Nature's and the great Muse's mockery of those poor mimes, came interpolated that scene, not really or exactly to be described at all (for on the many hundreds who were there it seems to this hour to have left a passing blur, a dream, a blotch)—and yet partially to be described as I now proceed to give it. There is a scene in the play representing a modern parlor, in which two unprecedented English ladies are informed by the impossible Yankee that he is not a man of fortune, and therefore undesirable for marriage-catching purposes; after which, the comments being finished, the dramatic trio make exit, leaving the stage clear for a moment. At this period came the murder of Abraham Lincoln. Great as all its manifold train, circling round it, and stretching into the future for many a century, in the politics, history, art, etc., of the New World, in point of fact the main thing, the actual murder, transpired with the quiet and simplicity of any commonest occurrence—the bursting of a bud or pod in the growth of vegetation, for instance. Through the general hum following the stage pause, with the change of positions, came the muffled sound of a pistol shot, which not one-hundredth part of the audience heard at the time—and yet a moment's hush—somehow, surely, a vague startled thrill—and then, through the ornamented, draperied, starred and striped space-way of the President's box, a sudden figure, a man, raises himself with hands and feet, stands a moment on the railing, leaps below to the stage (a distance of perhaps fourteen or fifteen feet), falls out of position, catching his boot heel in the copious drapery (the American flag), falls on one knee, quickly recovers himself, rises as if nothing had happened (he really sprains his ankle, but unfelt then)—and so the figure, Booth, the murderer, dressed in plain black broadcloth, bareheaded, with full, glossy, raven hair, and his eyes like some mad animal's flashing with light and resolution, yet with a certain strange calmness, holds aloft in one hand a large knife—walks along not much back from the footlights—turns fully toward the audience his face of statuesque beauty, lit by those basilisk eyes, flashing with desperation, perhaps insanity—launches out in a firm and steady voice the words *Sic semper tyrannis*—and then walks with neither slow nor very rapid pace diagonally across to the back of the stage, and disappears. (Had not all this terrible scene—making the mimic ones preposterous—had it not all been rehearsed, in blank, by Booth, beforehand?)

A moment's hush—a scream—the cry of *murder*—Mrs. Lincoln leaning out of the box, with ashy cheeks and lips, with involuntary cry, pointing to the retreating figure, *He has killed the President.* And still a moment's strange, incredulous suspense—and then the deluge!—then that mixture of horror, noises, uncertainty—(the sound, somewhere back, of a horse's hoofs clattering with speed)—the people burst through chairs and railings, and break them up—there is inextricable confusion and terror—women faint—quite feeble persons fall, and are trampled on—many cries of agony are heard—the broad stage suddenly fills to suffocation with a dense and motley crowd, like some horrible carnival—the audience rush generally upon it, at least the strong men do—the actors and actresses are all there in their play-costumes and painted faces, with mortal fright showing through the rouge—the screams and calls, confused talk—redoubled, trebled—two or three manage to pass up water from the stage to the President's box—others try to clamber up—etc., etc.

In the midst of all this, the soldiers of the President's guard, with others, suddenly drawn to the scene, burst in—(some two hundred altogether)—they storm the house, through all the tiers, especially the upper ones, inflamed with fury, literally charging the audience with fixed bayonets, muskets and pistols, shouting *Clear out! clear out! you sons of* ——. . . . Such the wild scene, or a suggestion of it rather, inside the playhouse that night.

Outside, too, in the atmosphere of shock and craze, crowds of people, filled with frenzy, ready to seize any outlet for it, come near committing murder several times on innocent individuals. One such case was especially exciting. The infuriated crowd, through some chance, got started against one man, either for words he uttered, or perhaps without any cause at all, and were proceeding at once to actually hang him on a neighboring lamppost, when he was rescued by a few heroic policemen, who placed him in their midst, and fought their way slowly and amid great peril toward the station house. It was a fitting episode of the whole affair. The crowd rushing and eddying to and fro—the night, the yells, the pale faces, many frightened people trying in vain to extricate themselves—the attacked man, not yet freed from the jaws of death, looking like a corpse—the silent, resolute, half-dozen policemen, with no weapons but their little clubs, yet stern and steady through all those eddying swarms—made a fitting side-scene to the grand tragedy of the murder. They gained the station house with the protected man, whom they placed in security for the night, and discharged him in the morning.

And in the midst of that pandemonium, infuriated soldiers, the audience and the crowd, the stage, and all its actors and actresses, its paintpots, spangles, and gaslights—the life blood from those veins, the best and sweetest of the land, drips slowly down, and death's ooze already begins its little bubbles on the lips.

Thus the visible incidents and surroundings of Abraham Lincoln's murder, as they really occurred. Thus ended the attempted secession of these States; thus the four years' war. But the main things come subtly and invisibly afterward, perhaps long afterward—neither military, political, nor (great as those are) historical. I say, certain secondary and indirect results, out of the tragedy of this death, are, in my opinion, greatest. Not the event of the murder itself. Not that Mr. Lincoln strings the principal points and personages of the period, like beads, upon the single string of his career. Not that his idiosyncrasy, in its sudden appearance and disappearance, stamps this Republic with a stamp more marked and enduring than any yet given by any one man—(more even than Washington's)—but, joined with these, the immeasurable value and meaning of that whole tragedy lies, to me, in senses finally dearest to a nation (and here all our own)—the imaginative and artistic senses—the literary and dramatic ones. Not in any common or low meaning of those terms, but a meaning precious to the race, and to every age. A long and varied series of contradictory events arrives at last at its highest poetic, single, central, pictorial denouement. The whole involved, baffling, multiform whirl of the secession period comes to a head, and is gathered in one brief flash of lightning-illumination—one simple, fierce deed. Its sharp culmination, and as it were solution, of so many bloody and angry problems illustrates those climax-moments on the stage of universal Time, where the historic Muse at one entrance and the tragic Muse at the other, suddenly ringing down the curtain, close an immense act in the long drama of creative thought, and give it radiation, tableau, stranger than fiction. Fit radiation—fit close! How the imagination—how the student loves these things! America, too, is to have them. For not in all great deaths, nor far or near—not Caesar in the Roman senate-house, or Napoleon passing away in the wild night storm at St. Helena—not Paleologus, falling, desperately fighting, piled over dozens deep with Grecian corpses—not calm old Socrates, drinking the hemlock—outvies that terminus of the secession war, in one man's life, here in our midst, in our own time—that seal of the emancipation of three million slaves—that parturition and delivery of our at last really free Republic, born again, henceforth to commence its career of genuine homogeneous Union, compact, consistent with itself.

Nor will ever future American patriots and Unionists, indifferently over the whole land, or North or South, find a better moral to their lesson. The final use of the greatest men of a nation is, after all, not with reference to their deeds in themselves, or their direct bearing on their times or lands. The final use of a heroic-eminent life—especially of a heroic-eminent death—is its indirect filtering into the nation and the race, and to give, often at many removes, but unerringly, age after age, color and fiber to the personalism of the youth and maturity of that age, and of mankind. Then there is a cement to the whole people, subtler, more underlying, than any thing in written constitution, or courts or armies—namely, the cement of a death identified thoroughly with that people, at its head, and for its sake. Strange (is it not?) that battles, martyrs, agonies, blood, even assassination, should so condense—perhaps only really, lastingly condense —a nationality.

I repeat it—the grand deaths of the race—the dramatic deaths of every nationality—are its most important inheritance value—in some respects beyond its literature and art—(as the hero is beyond his finest portrait, and the battle itself beyond its choicest song or epic). Is not here indeed the point underlying all tragedy? the famous pieces of the Grecian masters—and all masters? Why, if the old Greeks had had this man, what trilogies of plays—what epics—would have been made out of him! How the rhapsodes would have recited him! How quickly that quaint tall form would have entered into the region where men vitalize gods, and gods divinify men! But Lincoln, his times, his death—great as any, any age— belong altogether to our own, and our autochthonic. (Sometimes indeed I think our American days, our own stage—the actors we know and have shaken hands, or talked with—more fateful than any thing in Aeschylus —more heroic than the fighters around Troy—afford kings of men for our democracy prouder than Agamemnon—models of character cute and hardy as Ulysses—deaths more pitiful than Priam's.)

When, centuries hence (as it must, in my opinion, be centuries hence before the life of these States, or of democracy, can be really written and illustrated), the leading historians and dramatists seek for some personage, some special event, incisive enough to mark with deepest cut, and mnemonize, this turbulent nineteenth century of ours (not only these states, but all over the political and social world)—something, perhaps, to close that gorgeous procession of European feudalism, with all its pomp and caste prejudices (of whose long train we in America are yet so inextricably the heirs)—something to identify with terrible identification, by far the greatest revolutionary step in the history of the United

States (perhaps the greatest of the world, our century)—the absolute extirpation and erasure of slavery from the States—those historians will seek in vain for any point to serve more thoroughly their purpose, than Abraham Lincoln's death.

Dear to the Muse—thrice dear to nationality—to the whole human race —precious to this Union—precious to democracy—unspeakably and forever precious—their first great Martyr Chief.

Virginia Woolf[1]

1882–1941

The *Art of Biography* is not a manual for biographers, any more than Lucian's *The Way to Write History* is a manual for historians. Both raise more questions than they answer. This is particularly true of Mrs. Woolf's essay, which, despite its title, is concerned to ask whether biography can be considered an art at all. But if it is not an art, Virginia Woolf wonders, is it then a science? Or if not that, a craft?

Great English biographies did not appear, she says, until the later eighteenth century—long after there were great poets, novelists, and other literary artists. She seems to consider only three biographers as of the highest class: Johnson, for his *Lives of the English Poets;* Boswell, for his *Life of Johnson;* and John Gibson Lockhart, for his *Life of Sir Walter Scott.*

Why are great biographies so rare? The answer, says Mrs. Woolf, lies in the limitations of the genre itself. The biographer is caught in a kind of trap. If he decides to be bound by such facts about his subject as he can discover from written records and from his subject's friends and relations, he soon discovers that there are gaps in the story that must either be left unfilled or be filled by his own intuitions and knowledge of general human nature. On the other hand, if he decides to "create," in an artistic sense, a unified, meaningful character out of his subject, he will find that this character is in some cases, at least, contradicted by the facts. It is the biographer's misfortune, she suggests, that something is known about everybody, but not everything about anybody. The biographer is thus limited in his use of facts, and frustrated in the use of his imagination.

---

[1] For a biography of Virginia Woolf, see Vol. 5, pp. 1–3, in this set.

In addition to this, Virginia Woolf points out, popular opinion about great men is bound to change. The reader of Macaulay's essay on Machiavelli or Carlyle's on Cromwell will not fail to see that different generations have different views of the same men. The biographer "must go ahead of the rest of us. . . . His sense of truth must be alive and on tiptoe." But since this is so, she is saying, biography cannot be called a science.

There remains the question whether biography can be called an art. Even such superb biographies as Boswell's *Johnson* cannot, Virginia Woolf says, be compared with Shakespeare's characterization of Falstaff, for example, or Dickens' portrait of Mr. Micawber. The poet or novelist is free. Biography, on the other hand, is too restricted by facts to be a creative art.

Is this not an exaggeration? Was Shakespeare free in creating Falstaff? In combining his traits he had to preserve plausibility, and make him fit in with the other characters of *Henry IV*. And once he had created this lovable rascal, he was bound to see that he continued to act in character. The poet is not entirely free, then, nor the biographer completely bound by facts. Are there not gaps in any life which must be creatively supplied by the biographer? These are questions that are likely to occur to you. But Mrs. Woolf is persuasive. She is also disarming when she admits that, though biography is not an art, the biographer "does more to stimulate the imagination than any poet or novelist save the very greatest."

The Art
of Biography

The art of biography, we say—but at once we go on to ask, Is biography an art? The question is foolish perhaps, and ungenerous certainly, considering the keen pleasure that biographers have given us. But the question asks itself so often that there must be something behind it. There it is, whenever a new biography is opened, casting its shadow on the page; and there would seem to be something deadly in that shadow, for after all, of the multitude of lives that are written, how few survive!

But the reason for this high death rate, the biographer might argue, is that biography, compared with the arts of poetry and fiction, is a young art. Interest in ourselves and in other people's selves is a late development of the human mind. Not until the eighteenth century in England did that curiosity express itself in writing the lives of private people. Only in the nineteenth century was biography fully grown and hugely prolific. If it is true that there have been only three great biographers—Johnson, Boswell, and Lockhart—the reason, he argues, is that the time was short; and his plea, that the art of biography has had but little time to establish itself and develop itself, is certainly borne out by the textbooks. Tempting as it is to explore the reason—why, that is, the self that writes a book of prose came into being so many centuries after the self that writes a poem, why Chaucer preceded Henry James—it is better to leave that insoluble question unasked, and so pass to his next reason for the lack of masterpieces. It is that the art of biography is the most restricted of all the arts. He has his proof ready to hand. Here it is in the preface in which Smith, who has written the life of Jones, takes this opportunity of thanking old friends who have lent letters, and "last but not least" Mrs. Jones, the widow, for that help "without which," as he puts it, "this biography could not have been written." Now the novelist, he points out, simply says in his foreword, "Every character in this book is fictitious." The novelist is free; the biographer is tied.

There, perhaps, we come within hailing distance of that very difficult, again perhaps insoluble, question: What do we mean by calling a book a work of art? At any rate, here is a distinction between biography and fiction—a proof that they differ in the very stuff of which they are made. One is made with the help of friends, of facts; the other is created without any restrictions save those that the artist, for reasons that seem good to him, chooses to obey. That is a distinction; and there is good reason to think that in the past biographers have found it not only a distinction but a very cruel distinction.

The widow and the friends were hard taskmasters. Suppose, for example, that the man of genius was immoral, ill-tempered, and threw the boots at the maid's head. The widow would say, "Still I loved him—he was the father of my children; and the public, who love his books, must on no account be disillusioned. Cover up; omit." The biographer obeyed. And thus the majority of Victorian biographies are like the wax figures now preserved in Westminster Abbey, that were carried in funeral processions through the street—effigies that have only a smooth superficial likeness to the body in the coffin.

Then, towards the end of the nineteenth century, there was a change. Again for reasons not easy to discover, widows became broader-minded, the public keener-sighted; the effigy no longer carried conviction or satisfied curiosity. The biographer certainly won a measure of freedom. At least he could hint that there were scars and furrows on the dead man's face. Froude's Carlyle is by no means a wax mask painted rosy red. And following Froude there was Sir Edmund Gosse, who dared to say that his own father was a fallible human being. And following Edmund Gosse in the early years of the present century came Lytton Strachey.

The figure of Lytton Strachey is so important a figure in the history of biography that it compels a pause. For his three famous books, *Eminent Victorians, Queen Victoria,* and *Elizabeth and Essex,* are of a stature to show both what biography can do and what biography cannot do. Thus they suggest many possible answers to the question whether biography is an art, and if not, why it fails.

Lytton Strachey came to birth as an author at a lucky moment. In 1918, when he made his first attempt, biography, with its new liberties, was a form that offered great attractions. To a writer like himself, who had wished to write poetry or plays but was doubtful of his creative power, biography seemed to offer a promising alternative. For at last it was possible to tell the truth about the dead; and the Victorian age was rich in re-

markable figures many of whom had been grossly deformed by the effigies
that had been plastered over them. To recreate them, to show them as
they really were, was a task that called for gifts analogous to the poet's
or the novelist's, yet did not ask for that inventive power in which he
found himself lacking.

It was well worth trying. And the anger and the interest that his short
studies of Eminent Victorians aroused showed that he was able to make
Manning, Florence Nightingale, Gordon, and the rest live as they had
not lived since they were actually in the flesh. Once more they were the
centre of a buzz of discussion. Did Gordon really drink, or was that an invention? Had Florence Nightingale received the Order of Merit in her
bedroom or in her sitting-room? He stirred the public, even though a
European war was raging, to an astonishing interest in such minute matters. Anger and laughter mixed; and editions multiplied.

But these were short studies with something of the over-emphasis and
the foreshortening of caricatures. In the lives of the two great Queens,
Elizabeth and Victoria, he attempted a far more ambitious task. Biography had never had a fairer chance of showing what it could do. For it
was now being put to the test by a writer who was capable of making use
of all the liberties that biography had won: he was fearless; he had
proved his brilliance; and he had learned his job. The result throws great
light upon the nature of biography. For who can doubt that after reading
the two books again, one after the other, that the *Victoria* is a triumphant
success, and that the *Elizabeth* by comparison is a failure? But it seems
too, as we compare them, that it was not Lytton Strachey who failed; it
was the art of biography. In the *Victoria* he treated biography as a craft;
he submitted to its limitations. In the *Elizabeth* he treated biography as
an art; he flouted its limitations.

But we must go on to ask how we have come to this conclusion and
what reasons support it. In the first place it is clear that the two Queens
present very different problems to their biographer. About Queen Victoria everything was known. Everything she did, almost everything she
thought, was a matter of common knowledge. No one has ever been
more closely verified and exactly authenticated than Queen Victoria.
The biographer could not invent her, because at every moment some
document was at hand to check his invention. And, in writing of Victoria, Lytton Strachey submitted to the conditions. He used to the full
the biographer's power of selection and relation, but he kept strictly
within the world of fact. Every statement was verified; every fact was
authenticated. And the result is a life which, very possibly, will do for the

old Queen what Boswell did for the old dictionary maker. In time to come Lytton Strachey's Queen Victoria will be Queen Victoria, just as Boswell's Johnson is now Dr. Johnson. The other versions will fade and disappear. It was a prodigious feat, and no doubt, having accomplished it, the author was anxious to press further. There was Queen Victoria, solid, real, palpable. But undoubtedly she was limited. Could not biography produce something of the intensity of poetry, something of the excitement of drama, and yet keep also the peculiar virtue that belongs to fact—its suggestive reality, its own, proper creativeness?

Queen Elizabeth seemed to lend herself perfectly to the experiment. Very little was known about her. The society in which she lived was so remote that the habits, the motives, and even the actions of the people of that age were full of strangeness and obscurity. "By what art are we to worm our way into those strange spirits? those even stranger bodies? The more clearly we perceive it, the more remote that singular universe becomes," Lytton Strachey remarked on one of the first pages. Yet there was evidently a "tragic history" lying dormant, half-revealed, half-concealed, in the story of the Queen and Essex. Everything seemed to lend itself to the making of a book that combined the advantages of both worlds, that gave the artist freedom to invent, but helped his invention with the support of facts—a book that was not only a biography but also a work of art.

Nevertheless, the combination proved unworkable; fact and fiction refused to mix. Elizabeth never became real in the sense that Queen Victoria had been real, yet she never became fictitious in the sense that Cleopatra or Falstaff is fictitious. The reason would seem to be that very little was known—he was urged to invent; yet something was known—his invention was checked. The Queen thus moves in an ambiguous world, between fact and fiction, neither embodied nor disembodied. There is a sense of vacancy and effort, of a tragedy that has no crisis, of characters that meet but do not clash.

If this diagnosis is true we are forced to say that the trouble lies with biography itself. It imposes conditions, and those conditions are that it must be based upon fact. And by fact in biography we mean facts that can be verified by other people besides the artist. If he invents facts as an artist invents them—facts that no one else can verify—and tries to combine them with facts of the other sort, they destroy each other.

Lytton Strachey himself seems in the *Queen Victoria* to have realized the necessity of this condition, and to have yielded to it instinctively. "The first forty-two years of the Queen's life," he wrote, "are illuminated by a great and varied quantity of authentic information. With Albert's death a veil descends." And when with Albert's death the veil descended and authentic information failed, he knew that the biographer must follow suit. "We must be content with a brief and summary relation," he wrote and the last years are briefly disposed of. But the whole of Elizabeth's life was lived behind a far thicker veil than the last years of Victoria. And yet, ignoring his own admission, he went on to write, not a brief and summary relation, but a whole book about those strange spirits and even stranger bodies of whom authentic information was lacking. On his own showing, the attempt was doomed to failure.

It seems, then, that when the biographer complained that he was tied by friends, letters, and documents he was laying his finger upon a necessary element in biography; and that it is also a necessary limitation. For the invented character lives in a free world where the facts are verified by one person only—the artist himself. Their authenticity lies in the truth of his own vision. The world created by that vision is rarer, intenser, and more wholly of a piece than the world that is largely made of authentic information supplied by other people. And because of this difference the two kinds of fact will not mix; if they touch they destroy each other. No one, the conclusion seems to be, can make the best of both worlds; you must choose, and you must abide by your choice.

But though the failure of *Elizabeth and Essex* leads to this conclusion, that failure, because it was the result of a daring experiment carried out with magnificent skill, leads the way to further discoveries. Had he lived, Lytton Strachey would no doubt himself have explored the vein that he had opened. As it is, he has shown us the way in which others may advance. The biographer is bound by facts—that is so; but, if it is so, he has the right to all the facts that are available. If Jones threw boots at the maid's head, had a mistress in Islington, or was found drunk in a ditch after a night's debauch, he must be free to say so—so far at least as the law of libel and human sentiment allow.

But these facts are not like the facts of science—once they are discovered, always the same. They are subject to changes of opinion; opinions change as the times change. What was thought a sin is now known, by the light of facts won for us by the psychologists, to be perhaps a misfortune; perhaps a curiosity; perhaps neither one nor the other, but a trifling foible of no great importance one way or the other. The accent on sex has changed within living memory. This leads to the destruction of a great deal of dead matter still obscuring the true features of the human face. Many of the old chapter headings—life at college, marriage, career—are shown to be very arbitrary and artificial distinctions. The real current of the hero's existence took, very likely, a different course.

Thus the biographer must go ahead of the rest of us, like the miner's canary, testing the atmosphere, detecting falsity, unreality, and the presence of obsolete conventions. His sense of truth must be alive and on tiptoe. Then again, since we live in an age when a thousand cameras are pointed, by newspapers, letters, and diaries, at every character from every angle, he must be prepared to admit contradictory versions of the same face. Biography will enlarge its scope by hanging up looking glasses at odd corners. And yet from all this diversity it will bring out, not a riot of confusion, but a richer unity. And again, since so much is known that used to be unknown, the question now inevitably asks itself, whether the lives of great men only should be recorded. Is not anyone who has lived a life, and left a record of that life, worthy of biography—the failures as well as the successes, the humble as well as the illustrious? And what is greatness? And what smallness? He must revise our standards of merit and set up new heroes for our admiration.

Biography thus is only at the beginning of its career; it has a long and active life before it, we may be sure—a life full of difficulty, danger, and hard work. Nevertheless, we can also be sure that it is a different life from the life of poetry and fiction—a life lived at a lower degree of tension. And for that reason its creations are not destined for the immortality which the artist now and then achieves for his creations.

There would seem to be certain proof of that already. Even Dr. Johnson as created by Boswell will not live as long as Falstaff as created by Shakespeare. Micawber and Miss Bates we may be certain will survive Lockhart's Sir Walter Scott and Lytton Strachey's Queen Victoria. For they are made of more enduring matter. The artist's imagination at its most intense fires out what is perishable in fact; he builds with what is durable; but the biographer must accept the perishable, build with it, imbed it in the very fabric of his work. Much will perish; little will live. And thus we come to the conclusion, that he is a craftsman, not an artist; and his work is not a work of art, but something betwixt and between.

Yet on that lower level the work of the biographer is invaluable; we cannot thank him sufficiently for what he does for us. For we are incapable of living wholly in the intense world of the imagination. The imagination is a faculty that soon tires and needs rest and refreshment.

But for a tired imagination the proper food is not inferior poetry or minor fiction—indeed they blunt and debauch it—but sober fact, that "authentic information" from which, as Lytton Strachey has shown us, good biography is made. When and where did the real man live; how did he look; did he wear laced boots or elastic-sided; who were his aunts, and his friends; how did he blow his nose; whom did he love, and how; and when he came to die did he die in his bed like a Christian, or . . .

By telling us the true facts, by sifting the little from the big, and shaping the whole so that we perceive the outline, the biographer does more to stimulate the imagination than any poet or novelist save the very greatest. For few poets and novelists are capable of that high degree of tension which gives us reality. But almost any biographer, if he respects facts, can give us much more than another fact to add to our collection. He can give us the creative fact; the fertile fact; the fact that suggests and engenders. Of this, too, there is certain proof. For how often, when a biography is read and tossed aside, some scene remains bright, some figure lives on in the depths of the mind, and causes us, when we read a poem or a novel, to feel a start of recognition, as if we remembered something that we had known before.

Xenophon

c. 430–355 B.C.

Xenophon, the Greek historian and essayist, was born in Athens about 430 B.C., of an aristocratic family. He made the acquaintance of the philosopher Socrates, who at the time was instructing the youth of Athens through his brilliant conversations. He may have taken part in the war with Sparta, which ended, in 404, with the downfall of the Athenian empire. In 401 he was asked, along with other Greeks, to join the expedition of the younger Cyrus against the latter's brother Artaxerxes, who, according to Cyrus, had usurped the Persian throne. Xenophon appears to have accepted the invitation with alacrity, partly, no doubt, because the venture held promise of riches and honor, but also because it gave him an opportunity to escape from the uncongenial atmosphere of democratic Athens. His book, the *Anabasis* (or "Upcountry March"), is a description of the events that occurred on this expedition.

After the main body of the Greeks returned home, Xenophon remained in Asia and served with troops fighting the Persians. He captured a wealthy Persian near Pergamum and the ransom he obtained gave him an income for life.

In Greece once more, Xenophon, rather than return to Athens, went into the service of Agesilous, king of Sparta. He fought in a battle against his fellow citizens and was banished by them. The Spartans gave him a home in Elis, where he lived for a time in retirement, hunting, enjoying country life, and writing his memoirs and histories. When Athens and Sparta later became allies, Xenophon's banishment was repealed. He did not return to Athens, however, but spent his last years at Corinth.

The *Anabasis* is Xenophon's most famous book, but he also wrote the *Cyropaedia*, an account of the youth and training of Cyrus, the

Hellenica, a continuation of Thucydides' history to 362, the *Memorabilia*, a portrait and defense of Socrates, and numerous other works on country life, hunting, military training, and politics.

The Persian expedition that Xenophon describes in the *Anabasis* started from Sardis in 401. Ten thousand Greeks marched inland to Cunaxa, where a great battle was fought in which Cyrus was killed. The Greeks then attempted to negotiate a safe return with the Persian satrap, Tissaphernes, but their officers were treacherously murdered and they were left leaderless, deep in enemy country, without knowledge of the terrain and almost totally without money or supplies. Faced with disaster, the Greeks maintained strict discipline and elected new officers, one of whom was Xenophon. It was he, more than any other leader in that long retreat, who invented the stratagems and maintained the morale of the troops.

The selection reprinted here covers the most dramatic part of the journey. It had been decided to march up the valley of the Tigris River and to make for the shores of the Euxine (Black) Sea, where there were several Greek colonies. Part of the way led through the wilds of Kurdistan, where the ten thousand had to defend themselves against almost constant raids by savage tribesmen; and part of the way led through the forbidding and desolate highlands of Armenia and Georgia. The Greeks were a sea-faring, island people, and this march over a thousand miles of rough country was bitter and hard. Many times, Xenophon says, they wanted to give up, but he inspired them to take heart, and they went on. Finally they reached Trebizond. Xenophon, at the center of the line, could hear the vanguard shouting something. He gathered together some cavalry and "rode forward to give support, and, quite soon, they heard the soldiers shouting 'The sea! The sea!' and passing the word down the column. Then certainly they all began to run . . . and when they had all got to the top, the soldiers, with tears in their eyes, embraced each other and their generals and captains."

This scene is one of the most famous in all literature. It bears comparison with Prescott's [1] account of Cortés' first view of the valley of Mexico and the story, in the Bible, of Moses and his people

---

[1] See Vol. 6, pp. 231–243, in this set.

looking down on the land of Canaan. Indeed, for these Greeks the sea was the Promised Land.

The selection from the *Memorabilia* portrays Socrates at the zenith and close of his career. For Xenophon, Socrates is the perfect man, the embodiment of the highest humanity and morality. Justice, courage, self-restraint, piety, patriotism were combined in him with affability and kindness, and with a rare ability to impart these qualities to others. It is easy to see that Xenophon is defending Socrates against the charges that had been brought against him at his trial and after. He is saying, in effect: How could such a man have been guilty of "atheism," of "corrupting the youth," and of "making the worse appear the better cause"?

Plato is also concerned to defend the good name of Socrates. In his dialogues, especially the *Phaedo, Crito,* and *Apology,*[2] he also describes Socrates as a model of virtue. In other respects, however, Plato's portrait is strikingly different from Xenophon's. Socrates becomes highly complex and subtle, full of charm, ironic humor and paradox—close to common sense, but also to mysticism. His eloquence is said to have paralyzed and bewitched his listeners. Those reputed to be wise ended by bowing to his wisdom, the enchanting youth were themselves enchanted, and the revelers were drunk under the table by the imperturbable Socrates, who continued meanwhile his customary philosophical discourse.

A similar contrast is seen in the accounts given of Socrates' moral teachings. For Plato they are subtle proposals backed by ingenious arguments. For Xenophon they are simply common sense rules of morality and piety.

Which of these contrasting reports of Socrates and his teachings is nearer the truth? Most authorities favor Plato's version. But could not both accounts be valid in a sense? Plato, the greatest pupil of Socrates, would have the closest view and understanding. But Xenophon's impression was that of a soldier and popular historian, and was intelligible to everyone. It was very effective in clearing Socrates' name of the false charges that had led to his execution.

---

[2] See *Great Books of the Western World,* Vol. 7.

The March to the Sea
from *The Persian Expedition*

THE ENTRY INTO KURDISTAN

At about the last watch, with enough of the night remaining for them to be able to cross the plain under cover of darkness, they got up when the signal was given and marched toward the mountain, which they reached at dawn. Chirisophus then took the lead with his own troops and also all the light troops; Xenophon brought up the rear with the hoplites of the rear-guard, but with no light troops at all, as there seemed to be no danger of any attack being made on them from the rear while they were on the ascent.

Chirisophus reached the summit before any of the enemy realized what was happening. He then went steadily forward, and as the various contingents of the army crossed the pass they followed him into the villages which lay in the folds and recesses of the mountains. The Carduchi immediately abandoned their houses and fled into the mountains with their women and children. Plenty of food remained for the Greeks to take, and there were a lot of brazen utensils in the furniture of the houses too. The Greeks did not take any of these, or pursue the people. They wished to behave leniently on the chance that the Carduchi, since they were enemies of the King, might be willing for them to go through their country peaceably. Food, however, was a matter of necessity, and they took whatever they came across. The Carduchi paid no attention when they called out to them, and indeed gave no signs at all of friendly feeling.

It was already dark when the last of the Greeks had come down from the summit to the villages, since, owing to the narrowness of the road, the ascent and descent had taken up the whole day. At this point some of the Carduchi got together in a body and made an attack on the last of the Greeks. They killed some and wounded others with stones and arrows, though they were not in great numbers, as the Greek army had come upon them unexpectedly. Indeed, if more of them had got together on this occasion, a large part of the army might possibly have been wiped out.

So for that night they encamped as they were in the villages, and the Carduchi lit a number of beacons on the mountains all round them as signals to each other. At dawn it was decided at a meeting of the Greek generals and captains to take on the march only the strongest and most essential of the baggage animals, and to leave the rest behind; also to let go all the slaves in the army that had been captured recently. This was because the great numbers of baggage animals and slaves slowed up the march, and there were numbers of men who were in charge of these and so were out of action; and with so many people on the march, they had to provide and transport double the necessary quantity of supplies. After having made this decision, they gave orders by herald that it was to be carried into effect.

When they had had breakfast and started on their way, the generals stationed themselves in a narrow part of the road and took away from the soldiers any of the proscribed articles which they found had not been left behind. The men did as they were told, though there were some cases of people getting away with things, cases when a soldier was in love with a particularly good-looking boy or woman. For that day, then, they went ahead, having a certain amount of fighting to do and resting from time to time.

On the next day there was a great storm, but they had to go forward as there were not sufficient supplies. Chirisophus was leading the march and Xenophon was with the rear-guard. The enemy made violent attacks and in the narrow passes came to close range with their bows and slings with the result that they had to travel slowly, as they were constantly chasing the enemy off and then returning again. Xenophon had often to order a halt when the enemy launched his violent attacks; and on these occasions Chirisophus, when the word was passed forward, halted his men too; but on one occasion he did not stop, but led on fast, passing back the word to follow him. It was obvious that something was the matter, but there was no time to go forward and see what was the cause of this haste. The result was that for the rear-guard the march almost turned into a full retreat. Here a gallant Spartan soldier, called Leonymus, was killed by an arrow which went into the side of his body through the shield and the jerkin, and Basias the Arcadian was also killed, shot clean through the head.

When they reached the place where they were to camp, Xenophon went just as he was to Chirisophus and blamed him for not waiting, the result of which had been that the soldiers had had to fight at the same time as they were retreating. "And now," he said, "two most gallant fellows have been killed, and we could not recover their bodies or bury them."

Chirisophus replied: "Look at the mountains. See how impassable they are in every direction. This one road, which you see, is a steep one, and you can see that there are men on it, a great crowd, who have occupied the pass and are on guard there. That is why I was in a hurry and so did not wait for you. I thought there was a chance of being able to get there first, before the pass was seized. The guides we have say that there is no other road."

Xenophon said: "I have got two men. When the enemy were giving us trouble, we set an ambush—which also gave us a chance of getting our breath back—and we killed some of them, and made up our minds to take a few alive just for this very reason, to have the services of guides who know the country."

At once they brought the two men and questioned them separately, to see if they knew of any other road apart from the obvious one. One of the two, although he was threatened in every kind of way, said that he did not know of any other road. Since he said nothing that was of any help he was killed, with the other man looking on. The survivor then said that the reason why the other man had denied knowledge of another road was that he happened to have a daughter who had been married to somebody in that direction. He declared that he would lead them by a road that was a possible one for animals as well as men. He was then asked whether there was any part of the road which was difficult to get past, and he replied that there was one height which it would be impossible to pass, unless it was occupied in advance. It was then decided to call a meeting of the captains, peltasts and hoplites as well, to give them an account of the situation, and ask who was willing to do a good job and come forward as a volunteer for the expedition. The hoplites who came forward were Aristonymus the Methydrian and Agasias the Stymphalian, and Callimachus of Parrhasia put forward a separate claim for himself, saying that he was willing to go, if he could take with him volunteers from the whole army. "Personally," he said, "I am sure that a lot of the young men will follow if I am their leader." Then they asked if any of the officers of the light-armed troops would volunteer to join with the others. Aristeas of Chios came forward, a man who, on many occasions of this sort, was worth a lot to the army.

FIGHTING IN THE MOUNTAINS

It was now afternoon, and they told the volunteers to have their food and then start. They bound the guide and handed him over to them, and made arrangements that, if they took the height, they should guard the position for the night and give a trumpet signal at dawn: those on the height should then make an attack on the Carduchi holding the regular way out of the valley, while the rest of them should proceed as quickly as they could and join up with them.

After agreeing on this plan, the volunteers set out, a force of about two thousand. There was a lot of rain at the time. Xenophon, with the rear-guard, led on towards the regular exit from the valley, in order that the enemy might give their attention to this part of the road and that the party which was making a detour might, as far as possible, escape detection. However, when the rear-guard got to a watercourse which they had to cross to make their way up to the higher ground, the natives at this point rolled down boulders big enough to fill a wagon, some bigger, some smaller, which came crashing down against the rocks and ricocheted off, so that it was absolutely impossible even to get near the pass. Some of the captains, finding things impossible in one direction, tried somewhere else, and continued their efforts until it became dark. Then, when they thought that their retreat would be unobserved, they went back for supper. Those of them who had been in the rear-guard had not had any breakfast either. The enemy, however, went on rolling down stones all through the night, as was evident from the noise.

Meanwhile the men who had taken the guide went round in a detour and came upon the guards sitting round their campfire. They killed some of them and drove the others downhill, and then stayed there under the impression that they were occupying the height. This, however, was not the case. Above them there was a small hill, past which ran the narrow road where the guard had been stationed. Nevertheless there was a way from this position to where the enemy was stationed on the regular road.

They passed the night where they were, and, at the first sign of dawn, formed up and marched in silence against the enemy. As there was a mist they got close up to them without being noticed. Then, as soon as they came into sight of each other, the trumpet sounded, and they raised their war-cry and charged down on the men, who did not wait for them, but abandoned the road and fled. Only a few were killed, as they were quick on their feet.

Meanwhile Chirisophus' men, on hearing the trumpet, immediately attacked uphill along the regular road; and some of the generals advanced along little-used paths, just where they happened to find themselves, climbing up as best they could and pulling each other up with their spears. These were the first ones to join up with the party that had previously occupied the position.

Xenophon, with half the rear-guard, went by the same way as those who had the guide, as it was the easiest going for the baggage animals. He had placed the other half of his men in the rear of the animals. As they went forward they came to a ridge commanding the road and found it occupied by the enemy. They had either to dislodge them or else be cut off from the rest of the Greeks. They themselves might have gone by the same road as the others, but this was the only possible route for the baggage animals. Then they shouted out words of encouragement to each other and made an assault on the ridge with the companies in column. They did not attack from every direction but left the enemy a way of escape, if he wanted to run away. So long as they were climbing up, each man by the best route he could find, the natives shot arrows at them and hurled down stones; but they made no attack when it came to close quarters, and, in the end, abandoned the position and fled.

The Greeks had no sooner got past this hill when they saw in front of them another hill, also occupied by the enemy. They decided to make an assault on this hill too, but Xenophon realized that, if they left the hill which they had just taken unguarded, the enemy might reoccupy it and make an attack on the baggage animals as they were going past. (The baggage train extended a long way, as it was going along a narrow road.) He therefore left on the hill the captains Cephisodorus, the son of Cephisophon, an Athenian, and Archagoras, an exile from Argos, while he himself advanced with the rest upon the second hill and took it too by the same methods as before.

There was still a third hill left to deal with, and much the steepest of the three. It was the one that overlooked the guard who had been surprised at their fire during the night by the volunteers. However, when the Greeks got close to it, the natives gave up this hill without putting up a fight, a thing which surprised everyone and made them think that they had abandoned the hill through fear of being cut off and surrounded. Actually they had seen from the top what had happened further down the road and had all gone off to attack the rear-guard.

Xenophon climbed to the summit with the youngest of his men, and ordered the rest to lead on slowly, so that the companies in the rear could join up with them, and he told them to halt under arms on level ground when they had gone a little way along the road. At this point Archagoras of Argos came running with the news that his men had been driven off the hill and that Cephisodorus and Amphicrates had been killed together with all the rest who had not managed to jump down from the rock and reach the rear-guard. After achieving this success, the natives appeared on a ridge opposite the third hill. Xenophon spoke to them through an interpreter. He suggested a truce and asked them to hand over the dead. They replied that they would give back the bodies on condition that the Greeks did not burn their houses, and Xenophon agreed to this. However, while this conversation was going on and the rest of the army was going forward, all the natives in the district had rushed up: and when the Greeks began to come down from the hill and make their way towards the rest where they were standing by their arms, then, in great numbers and with terrific shouting, the enemy launched an attack. On reaching the summit of the hill from which Xenophon was descending, they began to roll down rocks. They broke one man's leg, and the man who was carrying Xenophon's shield ran away, taking the shield with him. Eurylochus of Lusia, however, a hoplite, ran up and held his shield in front of both of them during the retreat. The rest rejoined their comrades who were already in battle order.

The whole Greek army was now together again. They camped where they were and found a number of comfortable houses and plenty of food. There was a lot of wine, so much so that the people stored it in cellars which were plastered over the top. Xenophon and Chirisophus came to an arrangement with the enemy by which they got back the dead bodies and gave up their guide. For the dead they did, to the best of their ability, everything that is usually done at the burial of brave men. On the next day they set out without a guide, and the enemy fought back at them, and tried to stop their march by occupying any narrow passes there might be ahead of them. Whenever they got in the way of the vanguard, Xenophon led his men up into the mountains from the rear and made the road-block in front of the vanguard ineffectual by trying to get on to higher ground than those who were manning it; and whenever they made an attack on the rear-guard, Chirisophus rendered this attempt to block the march ineffectual by altering direction and trying to get on to higher ground than those who were attempting it. So they were continually coming to each other's help and giving each other the most valuable support. There were times, too, when the natives gave a lot of trouble to the parties who had climbed up to higher ground, when they were on their way down again. The natives were quick on their feet, and so could get away even when they did not start running until we were right on top of them. Their only arms were bows and slings, and as bowmen they were very good. The bows they had were between four and five feet long and their arrows were of more than three feet. When they shot they put out the left foot and rested the bottom of the bow against it as they drew back the string. Their arrows went through shields and breastplates. When the Greeks got hold of any, they fitted them with straps and used them as javelins. In this type of country the Cretans were extremely useful. Stratocles, a Cretan himself, was their commander.

THE CROSSING INTO ARMENIA

They camped for this day in the villages overlooking the plain of the river Centrites, which is about two hundred feet across, and forms the boundary between Armenia and the country of the Carduchi. The Greeks rested here and were glad to see the plain. The river was more than half a mile distant from the Carduchian mountains. They felt very pleased, then, as they camped here, with plenty of provisions, and often talked over the hardships they had been through; for they had been fighting continually through all the seven days during which they had been going through the country of the Carduchi, and had suffered more than they had suffered in all their engagements with the King and with Tissaphernes. Consequently the thought that they had escaped from all this made them sleep well.

At dawn, however, they saw that on the other side of the river there were cavalry, ready for action, and prepared to prevent them crossing over: on the high ground above the cavalry were infantry formations to stop them getting into Armenia. These were Armenian, Mardian and Chaldaean mercenaries in the service of Orontas and Artouchas. The Chaldaeans were said to be a free nation and good fighting men. They were armed with long wicker shields and spears. The high ground, on which the infantry was formed up, was three or four hundred feet away from the river. The only visible road led uphill and looked as though it had been specially built.

It was at this point that the Greeks attempted to cross; but, on making the attempt, they found that the water rose above their breasts, and the river-bed was uneven, covered with large slippery boulders. It was impossible for them to hold their arms in the water and, if they tried, the river swept them off their feet, while, if one held one's arms above one's head, one was left with no defence against the arrows and other missiles. They therefore withdrew and camped where they were on the bank of the river. They then saw that great numbers of the Carduchi had got together under arms and were occupying the position on the mountain where they had been themselves on the previous night. At this point the Greeks certainly felt very downhearted: they saw how difficult the river was to cross, and they saw also the troops ready to stop them crossing, and now the Carduchi waiting to set upon them from the rear if they attempted it. So for that day and the following night they stayed where they were, not knowing what to do.

Xenophon had a dream. He dreamed that he was bound in fetters, but the fetters fell off of their own accord, so that he was free and recovered the complete use of his limbs. Just before dawn he went to Chirisophus and told him that he felt confident that things would be all right, and he related his dream. Chirisophus was delighted, and at the first sign of dawn all the generals assembled and offered a sacrifice. The appearance of the victims was favourable from the very first. Then the generals and captains left the sacrifice and passed round the word to the troops to have their breakfast.

While Xenophon was having breakfast two young men came running up to him. Everyone knew that it was permissible to come to him whether he was in the middle of breakfast or supper, or to wake him from his sleep and talk to him, if they had anything to say which had a bearing on the fighting. These young men now told him that they had been collecting kindling for their fire, and had then seen on the other side of the river, on the rocks that went right down to the water, an old man and a woman and some girls storing away what looked like bundles of clothing in a hollow rock. On seeing this, they had come to the conclusion that this was a safe place to get across, as the ground there was inaccessible to the enemy's cavalry. So they had undressed and taken their daggers and gone across naked, expecting that they would have to swim. However, they went ahead and got to the other side without the water ever reaching up to the crutch. Once on the other side they made off with the clothing and came back again.

Xenophon at once poured a libation and gave directions for the young men to join in it and pray to the gods who had sent the dream and re-

vealed the ford, that they should bring what remained to a happy fulfilment. As soon as he had made the libation he took the young men to
Chirisophus and they told their story to him. Chirisophus, after hearing
it, also made a libation, and, when the libations were over, they gave instructions for the soldiers to pack their belongings, while they themselves
called a meeting of the generals and discussed the question of how to
make the crossing as efficient as possible, and how they could defeat the
enemy in front and at the same time suffer no losses from those in the
rear. They decided that Chirisophus should go first with half the army,
while the other half stayed behind with Xenophon, and that the baggage animals and the general crowd should go across between the
two.

When things were in order, they set off, and the two young men led the
way, keeping the river on their left. The way to the ford was a distance
of less than half a mile and, as they marched, the enemy's cavalry formations on the other bank kept pace with them. On reaching the bank of the
river where the ford was, they grounded arms, and then Chirisophus himself first put a ceremonial wreath on his head, threw aside his cloak and
took up his arms, telling the rest to follow his example. He ordered the
captains to lead their companies across in columns, some on the left and
others on the right of him. The soothsayers then cut the throats of the
animals over the river, and meanwhile the enemy were shooting arrows
and slinging. However, they were still out of range. The appearance of
the victims was pronounced favourable, and then all the soldiers sang
the paean and raised the battle-cry, and all the women joined in the
cry; for a number of the soldiers had their mistresses with them in the
army.

Chirisophus and his men then went into the river. Xenophon, with
those of the rear-guard who were quickest on their feet, ran back at
full speed to the ford opposite the road into the Armenian mountains.
He was trying to give the impression that he intended to make a crossing
there and so cut off the cavalry on the river-bank. When the enemy saw
that Chirisophus' men were getting across the river easily and that
Xenophon's men were running back on their tracks, they became frightened of being cut off and fled at full speed in the direction, apparently,
of the river crossing further up. However, on reaching the road, they
turned uphill into the mountains. Lycius, who was in command of the
cavalry formation, and Aeschines, who was in command of the formation
of peltasts that accompanied Chirisophus, gave pursuit as soon as they
saw the enemy in full retreat, and the soldiers shouted out to each other

not to stay behind but to go on after them into the mountains. However, when Chirisophus had got across he did not pursue the cavalry, but immediately went up on to the high ground that went down to the river to attack the enemy who were up there. They, seeing their own cavalry in flight and hoplites moving up to attack them, abandoned the heights overlooking the river.

When Xenophon saw that things were going well on the other side, he made his way back as quickly as he could to that part of the army which had crossed, for there were also the Carduchi to think of, and they were evidently coming down into the plain with the intention of making an attack on the rear. Chirisophus was now holding the high ground, and Lycius, who with a few men had made an attempt at a pursuit, had captured some of their baggage animals, which they had abandoned, and some fine clothing and some drinking cups as well. The Greek baggage train and the general crowd was actually engaged in crossing. Xenophon then brought his men round and halted them in battle order, facing the Carduchi. He ordered the captains to split up their companies into sections of twenty-five men and bring each section round into line on the left: the captains and the section commanders were then to advance towards the Carduchi while those in the rear were to halt facing the river.

As soon as the Carduchi saw that the troops in the rear of the general crowd were thinning out and that there appeared now to be only a few of them, they began to come on faster, chanting their songs as they came. Chirisophus, however, when his own position was secure, sent Xenophon the peltasts and slingers and archers, and told them to do what they were ordered. Xenophon saw them coming across, and sent a messenger to tell them not to cross, but to stay on the further bank: when his own men started to cross over, they were to go into the river on each side of them as though they intended to cross to the other side, the javelin throwers with their weapons at the ready, and the archers with arrows fitted to their bowstrings; but they were not to go far into the river. The orders he gave to his own men were that, when they were within range of the enemy slingers and could hear the stones rattling on the shields, they were to sing the paean and charge: when the enemy ran away and the trumpeter sounded the attack from the river, the men in the rear were to wheel right and go first, and then they were all to run to the river and get across as fast as they could, each at the point opposite his own position, so as not to get in each other's way: the best man would be the one who got to the other side first.

The Carduchi saw that there were now not many left in the baggage train; for a number even of those who had been detailed to remain behind had gone over to see what was happening either to the animals or to their kit or to their mistresses. Consequently the Carduchi came on with confidence and began to sling stones and shoot arrows. The Greeks then sang the paean and advanced on them at the double. The natives could not stand up to them, since, though they were armed well enough for quick attacks and retreats in the mountains, when it came to standing up to close fighting they were insufficiently armed. At this point the trumpeter sounded the attack, and the enemy ran away all the faster, while the Greeks turned about and escaped across the river as quickly as they could. Some of the enemy saw what they were doing and ran back again to the river where they wounded a few men with their arrows; but the majority of them were obviously still running away even when the Greeks had got to the other side. The relieving party, in their desire to show off their courage, had gone into the water further than they should, and came back across the river after Xenophon's party. A few of these men too were wounded.

THEY SACK THE CAMP OF TIRIBAZUS

After crossing the river they formed up in order about midday and marched at least fifteen miles through Armenia, over country that was entirely flat, with gently sloping hills. Because of the wars between the Armenians and the Carduchi there were no villages near the river; but the one which they reached at the end of their march was a big one, containing a palace belonging to the satrap; most of the houses were built like fortresses and there were plenty of provisions. Then a two days' march of thirty miles took them past the sources of the river Tigris, and from here a three days' march of forty-five miles brought them to the Teleboas, a beautiful river, but not a large one. There were a number of villages near the river, and all this part is called Western Armenia. Its governor was Tiribazus who was a personal friend of the King, and when he was present no one else had the right to assist the King in mounting his horse. He now rode up to the Greeks with a cavalry escort and sent forward an interpreter to say that he would like to speak with their commanders. The generals thought it best to hear what he had to say and, going forward till they were within hearing distance, asked him what he wanted. He replied that he would like to come to terms by which he would undertake to do the Greeks no harm and they would undertake not to burn the houses, though they could take any supplies which they needed. The generals agreed to this and made a treaty on these terms.

After this came a three days' march of forty-five miles over level ground. Tiribazus with his force kept pace with them, with about a mile between the armies. In the course of the march they came to a palace with a number of villages, full of all kinds of supplies, in the vicinity. There was a heavy fall of snow in the night, while they were in camp here, and at dawn it was decided that troops with their officers should take up quarters separately in the villages. There were no enemies in sight, and it seemed a safe thing to do because of the quantity of snow that had fallen. In these quarters they had all kinds of good food—meat, corn, old wines with a delicious bouquet, raisins, and all sorts of vegetables. However, some of the soldiers who had wandered off some way from the camp reported that at night they had clearly seen a number of camp-fires. The generals then decided that it was not safe for the troops to be in separate quarters, and that the whole army should be brought together again. Consequently they camped all together; and it looked also as though the weather was clearing up. However, while they were spending the night here, there was a tremendous fall of snow, so much of it that it covered over both the arms and the men lying on the ground. The baggage animals too were embedded in the snow. The soldiers felt very reluctant to get to their feet, as, when they were lying down, the snow which fell on them and did not slip off kept them warm. But when Xenophon was tough enough to get up and, without putting his clothes on, to start splitting logs, someone else soon got up too and took over the job of splitting the wood from him. Then others also got up and lit fires and rubbed themselves down with ointment. A lot of ointment was found in this place and they used it instead of olive oil. It was made of hog's lard, sesame, bitter almonds and turpentine. A perfumed oil, too, made from the same ingredients, was found here.

After the snowstorm it was decided to take up separate quarters again under cover, and the soldiers went back with a lot of shouting and jubilation to the houses and the stores of food. The ones who, when they had left the houses, had acted like hooligans and burned them down, now had to pay for it by having uncomfortable quarters. The generals gave a detachment of men to Democrates of Temenus, and sent him out from here by night to the mountains where those who had been out of camp had said they had seen the fires. They chose him because he had already on previous occasions won the reputation for bringing in accurate information on subjects like this. When he said something was there, it was there; and when he said it wasn't, it wasn't. He now went out to the mountains and said that he had not seen any fires, but he returned with a prisoner who was armed with a Persian bow and quiver and a battle-ax like those which the Amazons carry. This prisoner was questioned as to where he came from, and said that he was a Persian and was going from Tiribazus' army to get provisions. They then asked him what was the size of the army and what was the purpose for which it had been mobilized. He replied that Tiribazus had under him his own force together with mercenary troops from the Chalybes and Taochi: his plan was to attack the Greeks, as they crossed the mountain, in a narrow pass through which went their only possible road.

When they heard this the generals decided to bring the army together again. They left a guard, with Sophaenetus the Stymphalian in command of those who stayed behind, and immediately set out, with the man who had been captured to show them the way. After they had crossed the mountains, the peltasts went forward, and, coming in sight of the enemy's camp, raised a shout and charged down on it without waiting for the hoplites. When the natives heard the noise, they did not stand their ground, but took to flight. In spite of this, some of them were killed and about twenty horses were captured, as was Tiribazus' own tent which contained some couches with silver legs and some drinking vessels; also some men who said that they were his bakers and cup-bearers.

As soon as the generals of the hoplites found out what had occurred, they decided to return to their camp as quickly as possible, in case an attack might be made on those who had been left behind. So they sounded the trumpet to call the men back, set off and got back to their camp on the same day.

MARCHING THROUGH THE SNOW

Next day they decided that they ought to get away as fast as they could, before the native army could reassemble and occupy the pass. They packed their belongings at once and, taking a number of guides with them, set off through deep snow. On the same day they passed the height where Tiribazus had intended to attack them, and then pitched camp. From here a three days' march of forty-five miles through desert country brought them to the river Euphrates, which they crossed without getting wet beyond the navel. The source of the river was said to be not far from here.

Next came a three days' march of forty-five miles over level ground and through deep snow. The third day's march was a hard one, with a north wind blowing into their faces, cutting into absolutely everything like a knife and freezing people stiff. One of the soothsayers then proposed making a sacrifice to the wind and his suggestion was carried out. It was agreed by all that there was then a distinct falling off in the violence of the wind. The snow was six feet deep and many of the animals and the slaves perished in it, as did about thirty of the soldiers. They kept their fires going all night, as there was plenty of wood in the place where they camped, though those who came up late got no wood. The ones who had arrived before and had lit the fires would not let the latecomers approach their fire unless they gave them a share of their corn or any other foodstuff they had. So each shared with the other party what he had. When the fires were made, great pits were formed reaching down to the ground as the snow melted. This gave one a chance of measuring the depth of the snow.

The whole of the next day's march from here was through the snow, and a number of the soldiers suffered from bulimia. Xenophon, who, as he commanded the rear-guard, came upon men who had collapsed, did not know what the disease was. However, someone who had had experience of it told him that it was a clear case of bulimia, and that if they had something to eat they would be able to stand up. So he went through the baggage train and distributed to the sufferers any edibles that he could find there, and also sent round those who were able to run with more supplies to them. As soon as they had had something to eat they stood up and went on marching.

On this march Chirisophus came to a village about nightfall, and found by the well some women and girls, who had come out of the village in front of the fortification to get water. They asked the Greeks who they were, and the interpreter replied in Persian and said they were on their way from the King to the satrap. The women answered that he was not there, and said that he was about three miles away. Since it was late, they went inside the fortification with the water-carriers to see the headman of the village. So Chirisophus and as many of the troops as could camped there, but as for the rest of the soldiers, those who were unable to finish the march spent the night without food and without fires, and some died in the course of it. Some of the enemy too had formed themselves into bands and seized upon any baggage animals that could not make the journey, fighting among themselves for the animals. Soldiers who had lost the use of their eyes through snow-blindness or whose toes had dropped off from frost-bite were left behind.

It was a relief to the eyes against snow-blindness if one held something black in front of the eyes while marching; and it was a help to the feet if one kept on the move and never stopped still, and took off one's shoes at night. If one slept with one's shoes on, the straps sank into the flesh and the soles of the shoes froze to the feet. This was the more likely to happen since, when their old shoes were worn out, they had made themselves shoes of undressed leather from the skins of oxen that had just been flayed. Some soldiers who were suffering from these kinds of complaints were left behind. They had seen a piece of ground that looked black because the snow had gone from it, and they imagined that the snow there had melted—as it actually had done—this being the effect of a fountain which was sending up vapour in a wooded hollow near by. The soldiers turned aside here, sat down, and refused to go any further.

As soon as Xenophon, who was with the rear-guard, heard of this, he begged them, using every argument he could think of, not to get left behind. He told them that there were large numbers of the enemy, formed into bands, who were coming up in the rear, and in the end he got angry. They told him to kill them on the spot, for they could not possibly go on. Under the circumstances the best thing to do seemed to be to scare, if possible, the enemy who were coming up and so prevent them from falling upon the soldiers in their exhausted condition. By this time it was already dark, and the enemy were making a lot of noise as they advanced, quarrelling over the plunder which they had. Then the rear-guard, since they had the use of their limbs, jumped up and charged the enemy at the double, while the sick men shouted as hard as they could and clashed their shields against their spears. The enemy were panic-stricken and threw themselves down through the snow into the wooded hollows, and not a sound was heard from them afterwards. Xenophon and his troops told the sick men that a detachment would come to help them on the next day, and he then proceeded with the march. However, before they had gone half a mile they came across some more soldiers resting by the road in the snow, all covered up, with no guard posted. Xenophon's men roused them up, but they said that the troops in front were not going forward. Xenophon then went past them and sent on the most able-bodied of the peltasts to find out what was holding them up. They reported back that the whole army was resting in this way; so Xenophon's men posted what guards they could, and also spent the night there, without a fire and without supper. When it was near daybreak Xenophon sent the youngest of his men back to the sick with instructions to make them get up and force them to march on. At this point Chirisophus sent a detachment from his troops in the village to see what was happening to the troops in the rear. Xenophon's men were glad to see them and handed over the sick to them to escort to the camp. They then went on themselves and, before they had marched two miles, got to the village where Chirisophus was camping. Now that they had joined forces again, it seemed safe for the troops to take up their quarters in the villages. Chirisophus stayed where he was, and the other officers drew lots for the villages which were in sight, and each went with his men to the one he got.

On this occasion Polycrates, an Athenian captain, asked leave to go on independently and, taking with him the men who were quickest on their feet, ran to the village which had been allotted to Xenophon and surprised all the villagers, with their head-man, inside the walls, together with seventeen colts which were kept there for tribute to the King, and the head-man's daughter, who had only been married nine days ago. Her husband had gone out to hunt hares and was not captured in the village.

The houses here were built underground; the entrances were like wells, but they broadened out lower down. There were tunnels dug in the ground for the animals, while the men went down by ladder. Inside the houses there were goats, sheep, cows and poultry with their young. All these animals were fed on food that was kept inside the houses. There was also wheat, barley, beans and barley-wine in great bowls. The actual grains of barley floated on top of the bowls, level with the brim, and in the bowls there were reeds of various sizes and without joints in them. When one was thirsty, one was meant to take a reed and suck the wine into one's mouth. It was a very strong wine, unless one mixed it with water, and, when one got used to it, it was a very pleasant drink.

Xenophon invited the chief of the village to have supper with him, and told him to be of good heart, as he was not going to be deprived of his children, and that, if he showed himself capable of doing the army a good turn until they reached another tribe, they would restock his house with provisions when they went away. He promised to co-operate and, to show his good intentions, told them of where some wine was buried. So for that night all the soldiers were quartered in the villages and slept there with all sorts of food around them, setting a guard over the head-man of the village and keeping a watchful eye on his children too.

On the next day Xenophon visited Chirisophus and took the head-man with him. Whenever he went past a village he turned into it to see those who were quartered there. Everywhere he found them feasting and merrymaking, and they would invariably refuse to let him go before they had given him something for breakfast. In every single case they would have on the same table lamb, kid, pork, veal and chicken, and a number of loaves, both wheat and barley. When anyone wanted, as a gesture of friendship, to drink to a friend's health, he would drag him to a huge bowl, over which he would have to lean, sucking up the drink like an ox. They invited the head-man too to take what he liked, but he refused their invitations, only, if he caught sight of any of his relatives, he would take them along with him.

When they came to Chirisophus, they found his men also feasting, with wreaths of hay round their heads, and with Armenian boys in native dress waiting on them. They showed the boys what to do by signs, as though they were deaf mutes. After greeting each other, Chirisophus and Xenophon together interrogated the head-man through the interpreter who spoke Persian, and asked him what country this was. He replied that it was Armenia. Then they asked him for whom the horses were being kept, and he said that they were a tribute paid to the King. The next country, he said, was the land of the Chalybes, and he told them the way there.

Xenophon then went away and took the head-man back to his own people. He gave him back the horse (rather an old one) which he had taken, and told him to fatten it up and sacrifice it. This was because he had heard that it was sacred to the sun and he was afraid that it might die, as the journey had done it no good. He took some of the colts himself, and gave one colt to each of the generals and captains. The horses in this part of the world were smaller than the Persian horses, but much more finely bred. The head-man told the Greeks to tie small bags round the feet of the horses and baggage animals whenever they made them go through snow, as, without these bags, they sank in up to their bellies.

THEY CAPTURE A PASS BY A MANOEUVRE

When the eighth day came, Xenophon handed over the head-man of the village to Chirisophus for a guide. He left behind all his family for him in the village, except for his son, who was just growing up. He gave the young man to Plisthenes of Amphipolis to look after, with the idea that, if the father was a reliable guide, he could take back his son too when he left them. They brought all the provisions they could into the head-man's house, and then packed their belongings and set out.

The head-man was not put under any restraint and led them on through the snow. When they had already marched for three days Chirisophus got angry with him for not having brought them to any villages. The man said that there were none in this part of the country. Chirisophus then struck him, but did not have him bound. As a result of this he ran away and escaped in the night, leaving his son behind. This affair—ill-treating the guide and then not taking adequate precautions —was the only occasion on the march when Chirisophus and Xenophon fell out. Plisthenes was devoted to the young man, took him home with him, and found him a most trusty companion.

They then marched for seven days, doing fifteen miles a day, to the river Phasis, which was a hundred feet across. Next came a two days' march of thirty miles. At the pass which led down into the plain there were Chalybes, Taochi and Phasians to bar their way, and, when Chirisophus saw that the enemy was holding the pass, he came to a halt, keeping about three miles away from them, so as not to approach them while marching in column. He sent orders to the other officers to bring up their companies on his flank, so that the army should be in line. When the rear-guard had got into position he called a meeting of the generals and captains, and spoke as follows: "As you see, the enemy are holding the pass over the mountain. Now is the time to decide what is the best method of dealing with them. What I suggest is that we give orders to the troops to have a meal, and meanwhile decide whether it is best to cross the mountain to-day or to-morrow."

"I think, on the other hand," said Cleanor, "that we should get ready for battle and make an attack, as soon as we have finished our meal. My reason is that, if we let this day go by, the enemy who are now watching us will gain confidence and, if they do, others will probably join them in greater numbers."

Xenophon spoke next, and said: "This is my view. If we have to fight a battle, what we must see to is how we may fight with the greatest efficiency. But if we want to get across the mountain with the minimum of inconvenience, then, I think, what we must consider is how to ensure that our casualties in dead and wounded are as light as possible. The mountain, so far as we can see, extends for more than six miles, but except just for the part on our road, there is no evidence anywhere of men on guard against us. It would be a much better plan, then, for us to try to steal a bit of the undefended mountain from them when they are not looking, and to capture it from them, if we can, by taking the initiative, than to fight an action against a strong position and against troops who are waiting ready for us. It is much easier to march uphill without fighting than to march on the level when one has enemies on all sides; and one can see what is in front of one's feet better by night, when one is not fighting, than by day, if one is; and rough ground is easier for the feet, if one is not fighting as one marches, than level ground is, when there are weapons flying round one's head. I do not think that it is impossible for us to steal this ground from them. We can go by night, so as to be out of their observation; and we can keep far enough away from them to give them no chance of hearing us. And I would suggest that, if we make a feint at attacking here, we should find the rest of the mountain even less defended, as the enemy would be likely to stay here in a greater concentration. But I am not the person who ought to be talking about stealing. I gather that you Spartans, Chirisophus—I mean the real officer class—study how to steal from your earliest boyhood, and think that so far from it being a disgrace it is an actual distinction to steal anything that is not forbidden by law. And, so that you may become expert thieves and try to get away with what you steal, it is laid down by law that you get a beating if you are caught stealing. Here then is an excellent opportunity for you to give an exhibition of the way in which you were brought up, and to preserve us from blows, by seeing to it that we are not caught stealing our bit of mountain."

"Well," said Chirisophus, "what I have gathered about you Athenians is that you are remarkably good at stealing public funds, even though it is a very risky business for whoever does so; and your best men are the greatest experts at it, that is if it is your best men who are considered the right people to be in the government. So here is a chance for you too to give an exhibition of the way in which you were brought up."

"Then," said Xenophon, "I am prepared, as soon as we have had our meal, to take the rear-guard and go to seize the position in the mountains. I have got guides already, as my light troops ambushed and made prisoners of a few of the natives who have been following behind to pick up what they could. I have also been informed by them that the mountains are not impassable: they provide pasture for goats and cattle. If, therefore, we once get hold of a part of the range, there will be a possible route for our baggage animals as well. I do not expect either that the enemy will stand their ground when they see that we are holding the heights and on a level with them, as they show no willingness at the moment to come down on to a level with us."

"But why," said Chirisophus, "should you go and leave vacant the command of the rear-guard? It would be better to send others, that is if some good soldiers do not come forward as volunteers."

Then Aristonymus of Methydria, a commander of hoplites, and Aristeas of Chios, and Nicomachus of Oeta, commanders of light infantry, came forward, and it was agreed that they would light a number of fires as soon as they had seized the heights. When this was settled they had their meal, and afterwards Chirisophus led the army forward about a mile in the direction of the enemy, so as to give the impression that it was at this point that he intended to attack.

When they had had supper and it became dark, the troops detailed for the job set off and seized the mountain height, while the others rested where they were. As soon as the enemy realized that the heights had been occupied, they were on the look out and kept a number of fires burning through the night. At daybreak Chirisophus offered sacrifices and then advanced on the road, while the troops who had seized the mountain ridge made an attack along the heights. Most of the enemy stood their ground at the pass, but part of them went to engage the troops on the heights. However, before the main bodies came to close quarters, the troops on the heights were in action and the Greeks were winning and driving the enemy back. At the same moment in the plain the Greek peltasts advanced at the double against the enemy's battle line, and Chirisophus with the hoplites followed at a quick march behind. However, when the enemy guarding the road saw that their troops higher up were being defeated, they took to flight. Not many of them were killed, but a very great number of shields were captured. The Greeks cut these shields up with their swords and so made them useless. When they reached the summit, they offered sacrifices and set up a trophy. Then they descended into the plain and came among villages full of plenty of good food.

THE GREEKS CATCH SIGHT OF THE SEA

Next came a five days' march of ninety miles into the country of the Taochi, and here provisions began to run short. The Taochi lived behind strong fortifications inside which they had all their provisions stored up. The Greeks arrived at one of these fortifications, which had no city or dwellings attached to it, but into which men and women and a lot of cattle had got together, and Chirisophus, as soon as he reached the place, launched an attack on it. When the first body of attackers became tired, another body of troops relieved them, and then another, since it was impossible to surround the place with the whole lot together, as there was precipitous ground all round it. On the arrival of Xenophon with the rear-guard, both hoplites and peltasts, Chirisophus exclaimed: "You have come where you are needed. This position must be taken. If we fail to do so, there are no supplies for the army."

They then discussed the situation together, and, when Xenophon asked what it was that was stopping them from getting inside, Chirisophus said: "This approach, which you see, is the only one there is. But when one tries to get in by that way, they roll down boulders from that rock which overhangs the position. Whoever gets caught by one, ends up like this." And he pointed out some men who had had their legs and ribs broken.

"But," said Xenophon, "when they have used up their boulders, what is there to stop us getting inside? In front of us we see only these few men, and of these only two or three who are armed. And, as you can see yourself, the piece of ground where we are bound to be exposed to the stones, as we go over it, is about a hundred and fifty feet in length. Of this distance, about a hundred feet is covered with large pine trees spaced at intervals. If the men take shelter against their trunks, what damage could come to them either from the rolling stones or the stones flying through the air? All that is left is fifty feet, over which we must run when the stones cease coming at us."

"But," said Chirisophus, "as soon as we begin to advance towards the wooded part, great numbers of stones are hurled down at us."

"That," said Xenophon, "is just what we want. They will use up their stones all the quicker. Let us advance, then, to the point from which we shall not have far to run forward if we are to do so, and from which we can easily retreat if we want to."

Then Chirisophus and Xenophon went forward, accompanied by one of the captains, Callimachus of Parrhasia, since on that day he held the position of chief officer among the captains of the rear-guard. The other captains stayed behind in safety. Afterwards about seventy men reached the shelter of the trees, not in a body, but one by one, each man looking after himself as well as he could. Agasias of Stymphalus and Aristonymus of Methydria (also captains of the rear-guard) with some others were standing by outside the trees, as it was not safe for more than one company to stand among them.

Callimachus had a good scheme. He kept running forward two or three paces from the tree under which he was sheltering, and, when the stones came down on him, he nimbly drew back again. Each time he ran forward more than ten wagon-loads of stones were used. Agasias saw that the whole army was watching what Callimachus was doing, and feared that he would not be the first man to get into the fortification; so, without calling in the help of Aristonymus, who was next to him, or of Eurylochus of Lusia, though both of them were friends of his, he went ahead by himself and got beyond everyone. When Callimachus saw that he was going past him he seized hold of him by his shield. Meantime Aristonymus of Methydria ran past them, and after him Eurylochus of Lusia. All of these men were keen rivals of each other in doing brave things, and so, struggling amongst themselves, they took the place. For, once they were inside, no more stones were thrown down from above.

Then it was certainly a terrible sight. The women threw their children down from the rocks and then threw themselves after them, and the men did the same. While this was going on Aeneas of Stymphalus, a captain, saw one of them, who was wearing a fine garment, running to throw himself down, and he caught hold of him in order to stop him; but the man dragged him with him and they both went hurtling down over the rocks and were killed. Consequently very few prisoners were taken, but there were great numbers of oxen and asses and sheep.

Then came a seven days' march of a hundred and fifty miles through the country of the Chalybes. These were the most warlike of all the tribes on their way, and they fought with the Greeks at close quarters. They had body-armour of linen, reaching down to the groin, and instead of skirts to their armour they wore thick twisted cords. They also wore greaves and helmets, and carried on their belts a knife of about the size of the Spartan dagger. With these knives they cut the throats of those whom they managed to overpower, and then would cut off their heads and carry them as they marched, singing and dancing whenever their enemies were likely to see them. They also carried a spear with one point, about twenty feet long. They used to stay inside their settlements, and then, when the Greeks had gone past, they would follow behind and were always ready for a fight. They had their houses in fortified positions, and had brought all their provisions inside the fortifications. Consequently the Greeks could take nothing from them, but lived on the supplies which they had seized from the Taochi.

The Greeks arrived next at the river Harpasus which was four hundred feet across. Then they marched through the territory of the Scytheni, a four days' march of sixty miles over level ground until they came to some villages, where they stayed for three days and renewed their stocks of provisions. Then a four days' march of sixty miles brought them to a large, prosperous and inhabited city, which was called Gymnias. The governor of the country sent the Greeks a guide from this city, with the idea that he should lead them through country which was at war with his own people. When the guide arrived, he said that in five days he would lead them to a place from which they could see the sea; and he said he was ready to be put to death if he failed to do so. So he led the way, and, when they had crossed the border into his enemies' country, he urged them to burn and lay waste the land, thus making it clear that it was for this purpose that he had come to them, and not because of any goodwill to the Greeks.

They came to the mountain on the fifth day, the name of the mountain being Thekes. When the men in front reached the summit and caught sight of the sea there was great shouting. Xenophon and the rear-guard heard it and thought that there were some more enemies attacking in the front, since there were natives of the country they had ravaged following them up behind, and the rear-guard had killed some of them and made prisoners of others in an ambush, and captured about twenty raw ox-hide shields, with the hair on. However, when the shouting got louder and drew nearer, and those who were constantly going forward started running towards the men in front who kept on shouting, and the more there were of them the more shouting there was, it looked then as though this was something of considerable importance. So Xenophon mounted his horse and, taking Lycius and the cavalry with him, rode forward to give support, and, quite soon, they heard the soldiers shouting out "The sea! The sea!" and passing the word down the column. Then certainly they all began to run, the rear-guard and all, and drove on the baggage animals and the horses at full speed; and when they had all got to the top, the soldiers, with tears in their eyes, embraced each other and their generals and captains. In a moment, at somebody or other's suggestion, they collected stones and made a great pile of them. On top they put a lot of raw ox-hides and staves and the shields which they had captured. The guide himself cut the shields into pieces and urged the others to do so too. Afterwards the Greeks sent the guide back and gave him as presents from the common store a horse, and a silver cup and a Persian robe and ten darics. What he particularly wanted was the rings which the soldiers had and he got a number of these from them. He pointed out to them a village where they could camp, and showed them the road by which they had to go to the country of the Macrones. It was then evening and he went away, traveling by night.

THEY ARRIVE AT TRAPEZUS

Then the Greeks did a three days' march of thirty miles through the country of the Macrones. On the first day they came to the river which forms the boundary between the territories of the Macrones and the Scytheni. On their right there was a defensive position which looked a very awkward one, and on the left there was another river, into which flowed the river that formed the boundary and which they had to cross. The banks of this river were covered with trees which, though not large, were growing thickly together. The Greeks cut the trees down when they came up to them, being anxious to get away from the place as quickly as they could. The Macrones, armed with shields and spears, and wearing hair tunics, were drawn up in battle order facing the crossing-place. They kept shouting to each other and hurling stones which fell harmlessly into the river as they failed to reach the other side.

At this point one of the peltasts came up to Xenophon. He said that he had been a slave in Athens and that he knew the language of these people. "Indeed," he went on, "I think that this is my own country. If there is no objection, I should like to speak to them."

"There is no objection at all," Xenophon said. "Speak to them and find out first of all who they are."

He asked them this, and they replied that they were Macrones.

"Now ask them," said Xenophon, "why they are drawn up to oppose us and why they want to be our enemies."

Their reply to this was: "Because it is you who are invading our country."

The generals then told the man to say, "We are not coming with any hostile intentions. We have been making war on the King, and now we are going back to Greece and want to get to the sea."

The Macrones asked whether the Greeks would give pledges that they meant what they said, and they replied that they would like both to give and to receive pledges. The Macrones then gave the Greeks a native spear, and the Greeks gave them a Greek one, as they said that these were the usual pledges. Both sides called on the gods to witness the agreement.

After exchanging pledges, the Macrones immediately helped the Greeks to cut down the trees and made a path for them in order to help them across. They mixed freely with the Greeks and provided them, as well as they could, with opportunities for buying food, and led them through their country for three days, until they brought them to the Colchian frontier. There were mountains here, which, though high, were not steep, and the Colchians were drawn up in battle order on the mountains. At first the Greeks formed up opposite them in line, with the intention of advancing on the mountain in that formation; but in the end the generals decided to meet and discuss what would be the best method of making the attack. Xenophon then expressed the opinion that it would be better to break up their present formation and to advance in columns. "The line," he said, "will lose its cohesion directly, since we shall find some parts of the mountain easy going and other parts difficult. It will immediately make the men lose heart, if after being drawn up in line they see the line broken. Then, if we advance in a line many ranks deep, the enemy will have men on both our flanks, and can use them however they like. On the other hand, if we go forward in a line which is only a few ranks deep, there would be nothing surprising in our line being broken through, with masses of missiles and men all falling on us together. And if this takes place at any single point, the whole line will suffer for it. No, I propose that we should form up with the companies in column, spaced out so as to cover the ground in such a way that the companies on our extreme flanks are beyond the two wings of the enemy. By adopting this plan we shall outflank the enemy's line, and, as we are advancing in columns, our bravest men will be the first to engage the enemy, and each officer will lead his company by the easiest route. As for the gaps between the columns, it will not be easy for the enemy to infiltrate, when there are companies both on his right and left; and it will not be easy to break through a company that is advancing in column. If any company is in difficulties, the nearest one will give support; and if at any point any one company can reach the summit, you can be sure that not a man among the enemy will stand his ground any longer."

This plan was agreed upon, and they formed the companies into columns. Xenophon rode along from the right wing to the left and said to the soldiers: "My friends, these people whom you see are the last obstacle which stops us from being where we have so long struggled to be. We ought, if we could, to eat them up alive."

When everyone was in position and they had formed the companies, there were about eighty companies of hoplites, each company with roughly the strength of a hundred. They formed up the peltasts and the archers in three divisions, one beyond the left flank, one beyond the right, and one in the centre, each division being about six hundred strong. The order was then passed along for the soldiers to make their vows and to sing the paean. When this was done, they moved forward. Chirisophus and Xenophon, with the peltasts attached to them, were advancing outside the flanks of the enemy's line, and, when the enemy observed this, they ran to meet them, some to the right, some to the left, and lost cohesion, leaving a great gap in the centre of their line. The peltasts in the Arcadian division, commanded by Aeschines the Acarnanian, thinking that the enemy were running away, raised their battle-cry and advanced at the double. They were the first to get to the top of the mountain, and the Arcadian hoplites, commanded by Cleanor of Orchomenus, came after them. As soon as they charged, the enemy failed to stand their ground and ran away in a disorganized flight.

The Greeks ascended the mountain and camped in a number of villages which were well stocked with food. There was nothing remarkable about them, except that there were great numbers of beehives in these parts, and all the soldiers who ate the honey went off their heads and suffered from vomiting and diarrhoea and were unable to stand upright. Those who had only eaten a little behaved as though they were drunk, and those who had eaten a lot were like mad people. Some actually died. So there were numbers of them lying on the ground, as though after a defeat, and there was a general state of despondency. However, they were all alive on the next day, and came to themselves at about the same hour as they had eaten the honey the day before. On the third and fourth days they were able to get up, and felt just as if they had been taking medicine.

A two days' march of twenty-one miles from here brought them to the sea at Trapezus, an inhabited Greek city on the Euxine, a colony of Sinope in Colchian territory. They stayed here, camping in the Colchian villages, for about thirty days, and, using these villages as their base, they ravaged the Colchian country. The people of Trapezus provided the Greeks with facilities for buying food, and gave them presents of oxen and barley and wine. They also negotiated with them on behalf of the Colchians in the neighbourhood, particularly those who lived in the plain, and from them too there arrived presents of oxen.

Then the Greeks prepared to offer the sacrifice which they had vowed. Enough cattle had come in for them to be able to sacrifice to Zeus the Saviour and to Heracles, for safe guidance, and to make the offerings which they had vowed to the other gods. They also held athletic sports on the mountain where they were camping. They elected as organizer and president of the sports the Spartan Dracontius, who had been an exile from his home since boyhood because he had accidentally killed another boy with a dagger.

When the sacrifice was finished, they gave the hides to Dracontius and told him to lead the way to the place where he had set out the course. He then pointed to the ground where they were actually standing, and said: "This hill is an excellent place for running, wherever one likes."

"But how," they asked, "will people be able to wrestle on ground that is so hard and rough?" To which he replied: "All the worse for the man who gets thrown." Boys, mostly from among the prisoners, competed in the short-distance race, and more than sixty Cretans ran in the race over a long distance. There were also wrestling and boxing events, and all-in wrestling. It was a very fine performance, as there were many entrants for the events, and, with their comrades as spectators, the rivalry was keen. There was also a horse race in which they had to gallop down a steep bit of ground, turn round in the sea, and ride back to the altar. On the way down most of them had a thorough shaking, and on the way up, when the ground got very steep, the horses could scarcely get along at walking pace. So there was a lot of noise and laughter and people shouting out encouragements.

The foregoing is Book IX
of Xenophon's ANABASIS *or* THE PERSIAN EXPEDITION
translated by Rex Warner.

The Character of Socrates
from *Memorabilia*

I think that I have said enough to show that Socrates stated his own opinion plainly to those who consorted with him. I will now show that he also took pains to make them independent in doing the work that they were fitted for. For I never knew a man who was so careful to discover what each of his companions knew. Whatever it befits a gentleman to know he taught most zealously, so far as his own knowledge extended; if he was not entirely familiar with a subject, he took them to those who knew. He also taught them how far a well-educated man should make himself familiar with any given subject.

For instance, he said that the study of geometry should be pursued until the student was competent to measure a parcel of land accurately in case he wanted to take over, convey or divide it, or to compute the yield; and this knowledge was so easy to acquire, that anyone who gave his mind to mensuration knew the size of the piece and carried away a knowledge of the principles of land measurement. He was against carrying the study of geometry so far as to include the more complicated figures, on the ground that he could not see the use of them. Not that he was himself unfamiliar with them, but he said that they were enough to occupy a lifetime, to the complete exclusion of many other useful studies.

Similarly he recommended them to make themselves familiar with astronomy, but only so far as to be able to find the time of night, month and year, in order to use reliable evidence when planning a journey by land or sea, or setting the watch, and in all other affairs that are done in the night or month or year, by distinguishing the times and seasons aforesaid. This knowledge, again, was easily to be had from night hunters and pilots and others who made it their business to know such things. But he strongly deprecated studying astronomy so far as to include the knowledge of bodies revolving in different courses, and of planets and comets, and wearing oneself out with the calculation of their distance from the earth, their periods of revolution and the causes of these. Of such researches, again he said that he could not see what useful purpose they served. He had indeed attended lectures on these subjects too; but these again, he said, were enough to occupy a lifetime to the complete exclusion of many useful studies.

In general, with regard to the phenomena of the heavens, he deprecated curiosity to learn how the deity contrives them: he held that their secrets could not be discovered by man, and believed that any attempt to search out what the gods had not chosen to reveal must be displeasing to them. He said that he who meddles with these matters runs the risk of losing his sanity as completely as Anaxagoras, who took an insane pride in his explanation of the divine machinery.

For that sage, in declaring the sun to be fire, ignored the facts that men can look at fire without inconvenience, but cannot gaze steadily at the sun; that their skin is blackened by the sun's rays, but not by fire. Further, he ignored the fact that sunlight is essential to the health of all vegetation, whereas if anything is heated by fire it withers. Again, when he pronounced the sun to be a red-hot stone, he ignored the fact that a stone in fire neither glows nor can resist it long, whereas the sun shines with unequalled brilliance forever.

He also recommended the study of arithmetic. But in this case as in the others he recommended avoidance of vain application; and invariably, whether theories or ascertained facts formed the subject of his conversation, he limited it to what was useful.

He also strongly urged his companions to take care of their health. "You should find out all you can," he said, "from those who know. Everyone should watch himself throughout his life, and notice what sort of meat and drink and what form of exercise suit his constitution, and how he should regulate them in order to enjoy good health. For by such attention to yourselves you can discover better than any doctor what suits your constitution."

When anyone was in need of help that human wisdom was unable to give he advised him to resort to divination; for he who knew the means whereby the gods give guidance to men concerning their affairs never lacked divine counsel.

As for his claim that he was forewarned by "the deity" what he ought to do and what not to do, some may think that it must have been a delusion because he was condemned to death. But they should remember two facts. First, he had already reached such an age that, had he not died then, death must have come to him soon after. Secondly, he escaped the most irksome stage of life and the inevitable diminution of mental powers, and instead won glory by the moral strength revealed in the wonderful honesty and frankness and probity of his defence, and in the equanimity and manliness with which he bore the sentence of death.

In fact it is admitted that there is no record of death more nobly borne. For he was forced to live for thirty days after the verdict was given, because it was the month of the Delia, and the law did not allow any public execution to take place until the sacred embassy had returned from Delos. During this interval, as all his intimate acquaintances could see, he continued to live exactly as before; and, in truth, before that time he had been admired above all men for his cheerfulness and serenity. How, then, could man die more nobly? Or what death could be nobler than the death most nobly faced? What death more blessed than the noblest? Or what dearer to the gods than the most blessed?

I will repeat what Hermogenes, son of Hipponicus, told me about him. "When Meletus had actually formulated his indictment," he said, "Socrates talked freely in my presence, but made no reference to the case. I told him that he ought to be thinking about his defence. His first remark was, 'Don't you think that I have been preparing for it all my life?' And when I asked him how, he said that he had been constantly occupied in the consideration of right and wrong, and in doing what was right and avoiding what was wrong, which he regarded as the best preparation for a defence. Then I said, 'Don't you see, Socrates, that the juries in our courts are apt to be misled by argument, so that they often put the innocent to death, and acquit the guilty?' 'Ah, yes, Hermogenes,' he answered, 'but when I did try to think out my defence to the jury, the deity at once resisted.' 'Strange words,' said I; and he, 'Do you think it strange if it seems better to God that I should die now? Don't you see that to this day I never would acknowledge that any man had lived a better or a pleasanter life than I? For they live best, I think, who strive best to become as good as possible: and the pleasantest life is theirs who are conscious that they are growing in goodness. And to this day that has been my experience; and mixing with others and closely comparing myself with them, I have held without ceasing to this opinion of myself. And not I only, but my friends cease not to feel thus towards me, not because of their love for me (for why does not love make others feel thus towards their friends?), but because they think that they too would rise highest in goodness by being with me. But if I am to live on, haply I may be forced to pay the old man's forfeit—to become sand-blind and deaf and dull of wit, slower to learn, quicker to forget, outstripped now by those who were behind me. Nay, but even were I unconscious of the change, life would be a burden to me; and if I knew, misery and bitterness would surely be my lot.

"'But now, if I am to die unjustly, they who unjustly kill me will bear the shame of it. For if to do injustice is shameful, whatever is unjustly done must surely bring shame. But to me what shame is it that others fail to decide and act justly concerning me? I see that posterity judges differently of the dead according as they did or suffered injustice. I know that men will remember me too, and, if I die now, not as they will remember those who took my life. For I know that they will ever testify of me that I wronged no man at any time, nor corrupted any man, but strove ever to make my companions better.'"

This was the tenor of his conversation with Hermogenes and with the others. All who knew what manner of man Socrates was and who seek after virtue continue to this day to miss him beyond all others, as the chief of helpers in the quest of virtue. For myself, I have described him as he was: so religious that he did nothing without counsel from the gods; so just that he did no injury, however small, to any man, but conferred the greatest benefits on all who dealt with him; so self-controlled that he never chose the pleasanter rather than the better course; so wise that he was unerring in his judgment of the better and the worse, and needed no counsellor, but relied on himself for his knowledge of them; masterly in expounding and defining such things; no less masterly in putting others to the test, and convincing them of error and exhorting them to follow virtue and gentleness. To me then he seemed to be all that a truly good and happy man must be. But if there is any doubter, let him set the character of other men beside these things; then let him judge.

---

*The foregoing consists of Chapters VII–VIII
taken from Book IV
of Xenophon's* MEMORABILIA.

William H. Prescott

1796–1859

William Hickling Prescott was born of a well-to-do New England family in Salem, Massachusetts, on May 4, 1796. His grandfather, Colonel William Prescott, had commanded the Colonial troops in the Battle of Bunker Hill. His father was a well-known lawyer.

While Prescott was at Harvard College, he was the victim of an accident that affected his entire later life. At the Commons dining hall, a fellow student threw a crust of bread across the table. It struck Prescott and blinded him in one eye. In spite of this he managed to complete his college education and was graduated with honors in 1814. He attempted after that to enter his father's law office, but doctors both at home and abroad felt that he must preserve the dimming vision in his remaining eye.

Prescott therefore withdrew from the law office and embarked on a literary career. He worked in a darkened study while assistants read aloud to him from source materials. He took notes with the help of a machine known as a noctograph, a frame with guide wires strung across it, which enabled him to write without running lines together. The assistant then read his notes back to him and Prescott committed them to memory. With the material firmly in his mind, he was able to shape and organize it during his everyday activities of walking or driving.

His first book, a *History of the Reign of Ferdinand and Isabella,* established his fame as a historian. With this background in Spanish history, Prescott turned next to *The Conquest of Mexico.* This was followed by the *History of the Conquest of Peru,* both books being translated into many languages. Prescott was working on an ambitious history of Philip II of Spain when he suffered a stroke in

1858. He continued working until January 28, 1859, when he died of another stroke.

Because of his infirmity, Prescott developed a memory for details as remarkable as Macaulay's. In this vivid chapter from *The Conquest of Mexico*, one can almost believe that Prescott was there when the Spanish soldiers under Hernando Cortés descended the mountains into the Valley of Mexico. The scene they beheld was so beautiful that Prescott writes: "In the warm glow of their feelings, they cried out 'It is the promised land!'" It was the island city of Tenochtitlán, or Mexico City, set in the midst of glimmering lakes. So explicit is Prescott's description that it is hard to realize that it was never seen by Prescott. Within a generation after Cortés conquered Mexico, this city was wrecked, its gardens destroyed, and the retreating waters had left desolate swamps behind. Prescott's account is based entirely on eyewitness records of the conquest, but it is as glowing as if he had been there himself.

The beauty, art, and wealth of the great Inca capital, which make the conquistadors themselves uneasily aware that they face more than ignorant savages, were to be ruthlessly destroyed or shipped to Spain. The tragic loss is felt throughout Prescott's book. In an early chapter he says: "The difficulty that meets us in the outset is, to find a justification of the right of conquest at all." On the other hand, he concedes that the Spaniards' zeal to convert the heathen Indians may have been as strong a motive as their personal greed and ambition.

Prescott shows us that the Aztec Empire was in its death throes. Montezuma, the product of generations of Aztec warrior kings, awaits Cortés in a paralysis of fear. Knowing the Spaniard can be merciless, he is yet incapable of a resolute defense. The Emperor prays now for his aged and feeble citizens and wonders how to protect them. He is lord of a domain which stretches from the

---

Notes from the artist: "Prescott is shown wearing an Aztec ceremonial bird costume. The surrounding illustrations depict Indian interpretations of Cortés' battles with the Aztecs."

prescott

Atlantic to the Pacific. Outlying cities pay unwilling tribute to his capital; young men and women are sent as human sacrifices to his gods. It is fatal for an empire to overextend itself, Gibbon said. Is this what the Aztecs have done? The cities which were conquered by Montezuma's ancestors are restless under his tyranny. But the gods Montezuma worships demand greater and greater sacrifices, which means more and more conquest.

Like the Romans, too, Montezuma and his noblemen have been softened by their own luxurious civilization. Only one prince wants to fight the Spaniards; the others want to treat with them, to bribe them to go away. Perhaps the Aztec Empire is declining, perhaps the warrior princes have lost faith in their own religion. They may have viewed Cortés and his men as another species of god. Certainly the horses and guns, which had never been seen before, evoked awe and consternation.

Somehow a handful of Spaniards had been able to overthrow a rich and numerous nation, and to bring an end to a whole civilization. The Spaniards were favored by a more advanced military art. They also knew exactly what they wanted, and were single and united in their purpose under Cortés, whereas the Indians were sadly divided. Was this perhaps the decisive factor? Could the Spaniards have succeeded against a united country? We can also ask ourselves whether the British could have conquered India without substantial aid from the Indians themselves? As we read history, we naturally form hypotheses. What is yours?

The Land of Montezuma
from *The Conquest of Mexico*

1519

Everything being now restored to quiet in Cholula, the allied army of Spaniards and Tlascalans set forward in high spirits, and resumed the march on Mexico. The road lay through the beautiful savannas and luxuriant plantations that spread out for several leagues in every direction. On the march, they were met occasionally by embassies from the neighboring places, anxious to claim the protection of the white men, and to propitiate them by gifts, especially of gold, for which their appetite was generally known throughout the country.

Some of these places were allies of the Tlascalans, and all showed much discontent with the oppressive rule of Montezuma. The natives cautioned the Spaniards against putting themselves in his power by entering his capital; and they stated, as evidence of his hostile disposition, that he had caused the direct road to it to be blocked up, that the strangers might be compelled to choose another, which, from its narrow passes and strong positions, would enable him to take them at great disadvantage.

The information was not lost on Cortés, who kept a strict eye on the movements of the Mexican envoys, and redoubled his own precautions against surprise. Cheerful and active, he was ever where his presence was needed, sometimes in the van, at others in the rear, encouraging the weak, stimulating the sluggish, and striving to kindle in the breasts of others the same courageous spirit which glowed in his own. At night he never omitted to go the rounds, to see that every man was at his post. On one occasion, his vigilance had well-nigh proved fatal to him. He approached so near a sentinel that the man, unable to distinguish his person in the dark, leveled his crossbow at him, when fortunately an exclamation of the general, who gave the watchword of the night, arrested a movement which might else have brought the campaign to a close, and given a respite for some time longer to the empire of Montezuma.

The army came at length to the place mentioned by the friendly Indians, where the road forked, and one arm of it was found, as they had foretold, obstructed with large trunks of trees, and huge stones which had been strewn across it. Cortés inquired the meaning of this from the Mexican ambassadors. They said it was done by the emperor's orders, to prevent their taking a route which, after some distance, they would find nearly impracticable for the cavalry. They acknowledged, however, that it was the most direct road; and Cortés declaring that this was enough to decide him in favor of it, as the Spaniards made no account of obstacles, commanded the rubbish to be cleared away. Some of the timber might still be seen by the roadside, as Bernal Díaz tells us, many years after. The event left little doubt in the general's mind of the meditated treachery of the Mexicans. But he was too polite to betray his suspicions.

They were now leaving the pleasant champaign country, as the road wound up the bold sierra which separates the great plateaus of Mexico and Puebla. The air, as they ascended, became keen and piercing; and the blasts, sweeping down the frozen sides of the mountains, made the soldiers shiver in their thick harness of cotton, and benumbed the limbs of both men and horses.

They were passing between two of the highest mountains on the North American continent; Popocatépetl, "the hill that smokes," and Iztaccihuatl [Ixtacihuatl], or "white woman," a name suggested, doubtless, by the bright robe of snow spread over its broad and broken surface. A puerile supersitition of the Indians regarded these celebrated mountains as gods, and Iztaccihuatl as the wife of her more formidable neighbor. A tradition of a higher character described the northern volcano as the abode of the departed spirits of wicked rulers, whose fiery agonies, in their prison house, caused the fearful bellowings and convulsions in times of eruption. It was the classic fable of antiquity. These superstitious legends had invested the mountain with a mysterious horror that made the natives shrink from attempting its ascent, which, indeed, was from natural causes a work of incredible difficulty.

The great *volcan*, as Popocatépetl was called, rose to the enormous height of 17,852 feet above the level of the sea; more than 2,000 feet above the "monarch of mountains"—the highest elevation in Europe.[1]

---

1. By "the highest elevation in Europe" Prescott means Mont Blanc, in the French Alps. It is 15,771 feet high. Modern geographers, however, include the Caucasus among European mountains. Thus Mt. Elbrus, at 18,481 feet, is now said to be the highest point in Europe.

The height of Popocatépetl has been established as 17,887 feet. The highest point in Mexico is Citlaltepetl, at 18,701 feet [Ed.].

During the present century, it has rarely given evidence of its volcanic origin, and "the hill that smokes" has almost forfeited its claim to the appellation. But at the time of the Conquest it was frequently in a state of activity, and raged with uncommon fury while the Spaniards were at Tlascala; an evil omen, it was thought, for the natives of Anahuac. Its head, gathered into a regular cone by the deposit of successive eruptions, wore the usual form of volcanic mountains, when not disturbed by the falling in of the crater. Soaring towards the skies, with its silver sheet of everlasting snow, it was seen far and wide over the broad plains of Mexico and Puebla, the first object which the morning sun greeted in his rising, the last where his evening rays were seen to linger, shedding a glorious effulgence over its head, that contrasted strikingly with the ruinous waste of sand and lava immediately below, and the deep fringe of funereal pines that shrouded its base.

The mysterious terrors which hung over the spot, and the wild love of adventure, made some of the Spanish cavaliers desirous to attempt the ascent, which the natives declared no man could accomplish and live. Cortés encouraged them in the enterprise, willing to show the Indians that no achievement was above the dauntless daring of his followers. One of his captains, accordingly, Diego Ordaz, with nine Spaniards, and several Tlascalans, encouraged by their example, undertook the ascent. It was attended with more difficulty than had been anticipated.

The lower region was clothed with a dense forest, so thickly matted that in some places it was scarcely possible to penetrate it. It grew thinner, however, as they advanced, dwindling, by degrees, into a straggling, stunted vegetation, till, at the height of somewhat more than thirteen thousand feet, it faded away altogether. The Indians who had held on thus far, intimidated by the strange subterranean sounds of the volcano, even then in a state of combustion, now left them. The track opened on a black surface of glazed volcanic sand and of lava, the broken fragments of which, arrested in its boiling progress in a thousand fantastic forms, opposed continual impediments to their advance. Amidst these, one huge rock, the *Pico del Fraile*, a conspicuous object from below, rose to the perpendicular height of a hundred and fifty feet, compelling them to take a wide circuit. They soon came to the limits of perpetual snow, where new difficulties presented themselves, as the treacherous ice gave an imperfect footing, and a false step might precipitate them into the frozen chasms that yawned around. To increase their distress, respiration in these aerial regions became so difficult that every effort was attended with sharp pains in the head and limbs. Still they pressed on, till, drawing nearer the crater, such volumes of smoke, sparks and cinders were belched forth from its burning entrails, and driven down the sides of the mountain, as nearly suffocated and blinded them. It was too much even for their hardy frames to endure, and, however reluctantly, they were compelled to abandon the attempt on the eve of its completion. They brought back some huge icicles—a curious sight in these tropical regions —as a trophy of their achievement, which, however imperfect, was sufficient to strike the minds of the natives with wonder by showing that with the Spaniards the most appalling and mysterious perils were only as pastimes. The undertaking was eminently characteristic of the bold spirit of the cavalier of that day, who, not content with the dangers that lay in his path, seems to court them from the mere Quixotic love of adventure. A report of the affair was transmitted to the emperor Charles V, and the family of Ordaz was allowed to commemorate the exploit by assuming a burning mountain on their escutcheon.

The general was not satisfied with the result. Two years after, he sent up another party, under Francisco Montaño, a cavalier of determined resolution. The object was to obtain sulphur to assist in making gunpowder for the army. The mountain was quiet at this time, and the expedition was attended with better success. The Spaniards, five in number, climbed to the very edge of the crater, which presented an irregular ellipse at its mouth, more than a league in circumference. Its depth might be from eight hundred to a thousand feet. A lurid flame burned gloomily at the bottom, sending up a sulphurous steam, which, cooling as it rose, was precipitated on the sides of the cavity. The party cast lots, and it fell on Montaño himself to descend in a basket into this hideous abyss, into which he was lowered by his companions to the depth of four hundred feet! This was repeated several times, till the adventurous cavalier had collected a sufficient quantity of sulphur for the wants of the army. This doughty enterprise excited general admiration at the time. Cortés concludes his report of it to the emperor with the judicious reflection that it would be less inconvenient, on the whole, to import their powder from Spain.

But it is time to return from our digression, which may, perhaps, be excused as illustrating, in a remarkable manner, the chimerical spirit of enterprise—not inferior to that in his own romances of chivalry—which glowed in the breast of the Spanish cavalier in the sixteenth century.

The army held on its march through the intricate gorges of the sierra. The route was nearly the same as that pursued at the present day by the courier from the capital to Puebla, by the way of Mecameca. It was not that usually taken by travelers from Veracruz, who follow the more circuitous road round the northern base of Iztaccihuatl as less fatiguing than the other, though inferior in picturesque scenery and romantic points of view. The icy winds that now swept down the sides of the mountains brought with them a tempest of arrowy sleet and snow, from which the Christians suffered even more than the Tlascalans, reared from infancy among the wild solitudes of their own native hills. As night came on, their sufferings would have been intolerable, but they luckily found a shelter in the commodious stone buildings which the Mexican government had placed at stated intervals along the roads for the accommodation of the traveler and their own couriers. It little dreamed it was providing a protection for its enemies.

The troops, refreshed by a night's rest, succeeded, early on the following day, in gaining the crest of the sierra of Ahualco, which stretches like a curtain between the two great mountains on the north and south. Their progress was now comparatively easy, and they marched forward with a buoyant step, as they felt they were treading the soil of Montezuma.

They had not advanced far, when, turning an angle of the sierra, they suddenly came on a view which more than compensated the toils of the preceding day. It was that of the Valley of Mexico, or Tenochtitlán, as more commonly called by the natives, which, with its picturesque assemblage of water, woodland, and cultivated plains, its shining cities and shadowy hills, was spread out like some gay and gorgeous panorama before them. In the highly rarefied atmosphere of these upper regions, even remote objects have a brilliancy of coloring and a distinctness of outline which seem to annihilate distance.[2] Stretching far away at their feet, were seen noble forests of oak, sycamore, and cedar, and beyond, yellow fields of maize and the towering maguey, intermingled with orchards and blooming gardens; for flowers, in such demand for their religious festivals, were even more abundant in this populous valley than in other parts of Anahuac. In the center of the great basin were beheld the lakes, occupying then a much larger portion of its surface than at present, their borders thickly studded with towns and hamlets, and, in the midst—like some Indian empress with her corona of pearls—the fair city of Mexico, with her white towers and pyramidal temples, reposing, as it were, on the bosom of the waters—the far-famed "Venice of the Aztecs." High over all rose the royal hill of Chapultepec, the residence of the Mexican monarchs, crowned with the same grove of gigantic cypresses which at this day fling their broad shadows over the land. In the distance beyond the

---

2. The lake of Tezcuco, on which the capital of Mexico stood, is nearly 7,500 feet above sea level. The modern Mexico City is at an altitude of 7,349 feet [Ed.].

blue waters of the lake, and nearly screened by intervening foliage, was seen a shining speck, the rival capital of Tezcuco, and, still further on, the dark belt of porphyry, girdling the valley around, like a rich setting which Nature had devised for the fairest of her jewels.

Such was the beautiful vision which broke on the eyes of the conquerors. And even now, when so sad a change has come over the scene; when the stately forests have been laid low, and the soil, unsheltered from the fierce radiance of a tropical sun, is in many places abandoned to sterility; when the waters have retired, leaving a broad and ghastly margin white with the incrustation of salts, while the cities and hamlets on their borders have moldered into ruins;—even now that desolation broods over the landscape; so indestructible are the lines of beauty which Nature has traced on its features that no traveler, however cold, can gaze on them with any other emotions than those of astonishment and rapture.

What, then, must have been the emotions of the Spaniards when, after working their toilsome way into the upper air, the cloudy tabernacle parted before their eyes, and they beheld these fair scenes in all their pristine magnificence and beauty! It was like the spectacle which greeted the eyes of Moses from the summit of Pisgah, and, in the warm glow of their feelings, they cried out, "It is the promised land!"

But these feelings of admiration were soon followed by others of a very different complexion as they saw in all this the evidences of a civilization and power far superior to anything they had yet encountered. The more timid, disheartened by the prospect, shrunk from a contest so unequal, and demanded, as they had done on some former occasions, to be led back again to Veracruz. Such was not the effect produced on the sanguine spirit of the general. His avarice was sharpened by the display of the dazzling spoil at his feet; and, if he felt a natural anxiety at the formidable odds, his confidence was renewed as he gazed on the lines of his veterans, whose weather-beaten visages and battered armor told of battles won and difficulties surmounted, while his bold barbarians, with appetites whetted by the view of their enemies' country, seemed like eagles on the mountains, ready to pounce upon their prey. By argument, entreaty, and menace, he endeavored to restore the faltering courage of the soldiers, urging them not to think of retreat, now that they had reached the goal for which they had panted and the golden gates were opened to receive them. In these efforts, he was well seconded by the brave cavaliers, who held honor as dear to them as fortune, until the dullest spirits caught somewhat of the enthusiasm of their leaders, and the general had the satisfaction to see his hesitating columns, with their usual buoyant step, once more on their march down the slopes of the sierra.

With every step of their progress, the woods became thinner; patches of cultivated land more frequent; and hamlets were seen in the green and sheltered nooks, the inhabitants of which, coming out to meet them, gave the troops a kind reception. Everywhere they heard complaints of Montezuma, especially of the unfeeling manner in which he carried off their young men to recruit his armies, and their maidens for his harem. These symptoms of discontent were noticed with satisfaction by Cortés, who saw that Montezuma's "mountain-throne," as it was called, was, indeed, seated on a volcano, with the elements of combustion so active within that it seemed as if any hour might witness an explosion. He encouraged the disaffected natives to rely on his protection, as he had come to redress their wrongs. He took advantage, moreover, of their favorable dispositions to scatter among them such gleams of spiritual light as time and the preaching of Father Olmedo could afford.

He advanced by easy stages, somewhat retarded by the crowd of curious inhabitants gathered on the highways to see the strangers, and halting at every spot of interest or importance. On the road, he was met by another embassy from the capital. It consisted of several Aztec lords, freighted, as usual, with a rich largess of gold, and robes of delicate furs and feathers. The message of the emperor was couched in the same deprecatory terms as before. He even condescended to bribe the return of the Spaniards, by promising, in that event, four loads[3] of gold to the general, and one to each of the captains, with a yearly tribute to their sovereign. So effectually had the lofty and naturally courageous spirit of the barbarian monarch been subdued by the influence of superstition!

But the man, whom the hostile array of armies could not daunt, was not to be turned from his purpose by a woman's prayers. He received the embassy with his usual courtesy, declaring, as before, that he could not answer it to his own sovereign if he were now to return without visiting the emperor in his capital. It would be much easier to arrange matters by a personal interview than by distant negotiation. The Spaniards came in the spirit of peace. Montezuma would so find it, but, should their presence prove burdensome to him, it would be easy for them to relieve him of it.

The Aztec monarch, meanwhile, was a prey to the most dismal apprehensions. It was intended that the embassy above noticed should reach

---

3. A load was about 50 pounds, or 800 ounces of gold—worth, at the present rate of $35.00 to an ounce, about $28,000 [Ed.].

the Spaniards before they crossed the mountains. When he learned that this was accomplished, and that the dread strangers were on their march across the valley, the very threshold of his capital, the last spark of hope died away in his bosom. Like one who suddenly finds himself on the brink of some dark and yawning gulf, he was too much bewildered to be able to rally his thoughts, or even to comprehend his situation. He was the victim of an absolute destiny, against which no foresight or precautions could have availed. It was as if the strange beings, who had thus invaded his shores, had dropped from some distant planet, so different were they from all he had ever seen, in appearance and manners; so superior—though a mere handful, in numbers—to the banded nations of Anahuac in strength and science, and all the fearful accompaniments of war! They were now in the valley. The huge mountain screen, which nature had so kindly drawn around it, for its defense, had been overleaped. The golden visions of security and repose, in which he had so long indulged, the lordly sway descended from his ancestors, his broad imperial domain, were all to pass away. It seemed like some terrible dream—from which he was now, alas! to awake to a still more terrible reality.

In a paroxysm of despair, he shut himself up in his palace, refused food, and sought relief in prayer and in sacrifice. But the oracles were dumb. He then adopted the more sensible expedient of calling a council of his principal and oldest nobles. Here was the same division of opinion which had before prevailed. Cacama, the young king of Tezcuco, his nephew, counseled him to receive the Spaniards courteously, as ambassadors, so styled by themselves, of a foreign prince. Cuitlahua, Montezuma's more warlike brother, urged him to muster his forces on the instant, and drive back the invaders from his capital, or die in its defense. But the monarch found it difficult to rally his spirits for this final struggle. With downcast eye and dejected mien, he exclaimed, "Of what avail is resistance, when the gods have declared themselves against us! Yet I mourn most for the old and infirm, the women and children, too feeble to fight or to fly. For myself and the brave men around me, we must bare our breasts to the storm, and meet it as we may!" Such are the sorrowful and sympathetic tones in which the Aztec emperor is said to have uttered the bitterness of his grief. He would have acted a more glorious part had he put his capital in a posture of defense, and prepared, like the last of the Palaeologi, to bury himself under its ruins.

He straightway prepared to send a last embassy to the Spaniards, with his nephew, the lord of Tezcuco, at its head, to welcome them to Mexico.

The Christian army, meanwhile, had advanced as far as Amaquemecan, a well-built town of several thousand inhabitants. They were kindly received by the cacique, lodged in large, commodious, stone buildings, and at their departure presented, among other things, with gold to the amount of three thousand *castellanos*. Having halted there a couple of days, they descended among flourishing plantations of maize and of maguey, the latter of which might be called the Aztec vineyards, towards the lake of Chalco. Their first resting place was Ajotzinco, a town of considerable size, with a great part of it then standing on piles in the water. It was the first specimen which the Spaniards had seen of this maritime architecture. The canals which intersected the city, instead of streets, presented an animated scene, from the number of barks which glided up and down freighted with provisions and other articles for the inhabitants. The Spaniards were particularly struck with the style and commodious structure of the houses, built chiefly of stone, and with the general aspect of wealth and even elegance which prevailed there.

Though received with the greatest show of hospitality, Cortés found some occasion for distrust in the eagerness manifested by the people to see and approach the Spaniards. Not content with gazing at them in the roads, some even made their way stealthily into their quarters, and fifteen or twenty unhappy Indians were shot down by the sentinels as spies. Yet there appears, as well as we can judge, at this distance of time, to have been no real ground for such suspicion. The undisguised jealousy of the Court, and the cautions he had received from his allies, while they very properly put the general on his guard, seem to have given an unnatural acuteness, at least in the present instance, to his perceptions of danger.

Early on the following morning, as the army was preparing to leave the place, a courier came, requesting the general to postpone his departure till after the arrival of the king of Tezcuco, who was advancing to meet him. It was not long before he appeared, borne in a palanquin or litter, richly decorated with plates of gold and precious stones, having pillars curiously wrought, supporting a canopy of green plumes, a favorite color with the Aztec princes. He was accompanied by a numerous suite of nobles and inferior attendants. As he came into the presence of Cortés, the lord of Tezcuco descended from his palanquin, and the obsequious officers swept the ground before him as he advanced. He appeared to be a young man of about twenty-five years of age, with a comely presence, erect and stately in his deportment. He made the Mexican saluta-

tion usually addressed to persons of high rank, touching the earth with
his right hand, and raising it to his head. Cortés embraced him as he rose,
when the young prince informed him that he came as the representative
of Montezuma to bid the Spaniards welcome to his capital. He then presented the general with three pearls of uncommon size and luster. Cortés,
in return, threw over Cacama's neck a chain of cut glass, which, where
glass was as rare as diamonds, might be admitted to have a value as real
as the latter. After this interchange of courtesies, and the most friendly
and respectful assurances on the part of Cortés, the Indian prince withdrew, leaving the Spaniards strongly impressed with the superiority of
his state and bearing over anything they had hitherto seen in the
country.

Resuming its march, the army kept along the southern borders of the
lake of Chalco, overshadowed, at that time, by noble woods, and by orchards glowing with autumnal fruits, of unknown names, but rich and
tempting hues. More frequently it passed through cultivated fields waving with the yellow harvest, and irrigated by canals introduced from the
neighboring lake, the whole showing a careful and economical husbandry,
essential to the maintenance of a crowded population.

Leaving the mainland, the Spaniards came on the great dike or causeway which stretches some four or five miles in length, and divides Lake
Chalco from Xochicalco on the west. It was a lance in breadth in the narrowest part, and in some places wide enough for eight horsemen to ride
abreast. It was a solid structure of stone and lime, running directly
through the lake, and struck the Spaniards as one of the most remarkable
works which they had seen in the country.

As they passed along, they beheld the gay spectacle of multitudes of
Indians darting up and down in their light pirogues, eager to catch a
glimpse of the strangers, or bearing the products of the country to the
neighboring cities. They were amazed, also, by the sight of the *chinampas,*
or floating gardens—those wandering islands of verdure, to which we
shall have occasion to return hereafter—teeming with flowers and vegetables, and moving like rafts over the waters. All round the margin, and
occasionally far in the lake, they beheld little towns and villages, which,
half-concealed by the foliage, and gathered in white clusters round the
shore, looked in the distance like companies of wild swans riding quietly
on the waves. A scene so new and wonderful filled their rude hearts with
amazement. It seemed like enchantment; and they could find nothing to
compare it with but the magical pictures in the *Amadis de Gaula.* Few

pictures, indeed, in that or any other legend of chivalry, could surpass the realities of their own experience. The life of the adventurer in the New World was romance put into action. What wonder, then, if the Spaniard of that day, feeding his imagination with dreams of enchantment at home, and with its realities abroad, should have displayed a Quixotic enthusiasm—a romantic exaltation of character, not to be comprehended by the colder spirits of other lands!

Midway across the lake the army halted at the town of Cuitlahuac, a place of moderate size, but distinguished by the beauty of the buildings, —the most beautiful, according to Cortés, that he had yet seen in the country. After taking some refreshment at this place, they continued their march along the dike. Though broader in this northern section, the troops found themselves much embarrassed by the throng of Indians, who, not content with gazing on them from the boats, climbed up the causeway, and lined the sides of the road. The general, afraid that his ranks might be disordered, and that too great familiarity might diminish a salutary awe in the natives, was obliged to resort not merely to command, but menace, to clear a passage. He now found, as he advanced, a considerable change in the feelings shown towards the government. He heard only of the pomp and magnificence, nothing of the oppressions, of Montezuma. Contrary to the usual fact, it seemed that the respect for the Court was greatest in its immediate neighborhood.

From the causeway, the army descended on that narrow point of land which divides the waters of the Chalco from the Tezcucan lake, but which in those days was overflowed for many a mile now laid bare. Traversing this peninsula, they entered the royal residence of Iztapalapan, a place containing twelve or fifteen thousand houses, according to Cortés. It was governed by Cuitlahua, the emperor's brother, who, to do greater honor to the general, had invited the lords of some neighboring cities, of the royal house of Mexico, like himself, to be present at the interview. This was conducted with much ceremony, and, after the usual present of gold and delicate stuffs, a collation was served to the Spaniards in one of the great halls of the palace. The excellence of the architecture here, also, excited the admiration of the general, who does not hesitate, in the glow of his enthusiasm, to pronounce some of the buildings equal to the best in Spain. They were of stone, and the spacious apartments had roofs of odorous cedarwood, while the walls were tapestried with fine cottons stained with brilliant colors.

But the pride of Iztapalapan, on which its lord had freely lavished his care and his revenues, was its celebrated gardens. They covered an immense tract of land, were laid out in regular squares, and the paths intersecting them were bordered with trellises, supporting creepers and aromatic shrubs that loaded the air with their perfumes. The gardens were stocked with fruit trees imported from distant places, and with the gaudy family of flowers which belong to the Mexican flora, scientifically arranged, and growing luxuriant in the equable temperature of the table-land. The natural dryness of the atmosphere was counteracted by means of aqueducts and canals that carried water into all parts of the grounds.

In one quarter was an aviary, filled with numerous kinds of birds, remarkable in this region both for brilliancy of plumage and of song. The gardens were intersected by a canal communicating with the lake of Tezcuco, and of sufficient size for barges to enter from the latter. But the most elaborate piece of work was a huge reservoir of stone, filled to a considerable height with water well supplied with different sorts of fish. This basin was sixteen hundred paces in circumference, and was surrounded by a walk, made also of stone, wide enough for four persons to go abreast. The sides were curiously sculptured, and a flight of steps led to the water below, which fed the aqueducts above noticed, or, collected into fountains, diffused a perpetual moisture.

Such are the accounts transmitted of these celebrated gardens, at a period when similar horticultural establishments were unknown in Europe; and we might well doubt their existence in this semi-civilized land were it not a matter of such notoriety at the time, and so explicitly attested by the invaders. But a generation had scarcely passed after the Conquest before a sad change came over these scenes so beautiful. The town itself was deserted, and the shore of the lake was strewn with the wreck of buildings which once were its ornament and its glory. The gardens shared the fate of the city. The retreating waters withdrew the means of nourishment, converting the flourishing plains into a foul and unsightly morass, the haunt of loathsome reptiles; and the waterfowl built her nest in what had once been the palaces of princes!

In the city of Iztapalapan, Cortés took up his quarters for the night. We may imagine what a crowd of ideas must have pressed on the mind of the Conqueror, as, surrounded by these evidences of civilization, he prepared with his handful of followers to enter the capital of a monarch, who, as he had abundant reason to know, regarded him with distrust and aversion. This capital was now but a few miles distant, distinctly visible from Iztapalapan. And as its long lines of glittering edifices, struck by the rays of the evening sun, trembled on the dark-blue waters of the lake, it looked like a thing of fairy creation, rather than the work of mortal hands. Into this city of enchantment Cortés prepared to make his entry on the following morning.

The foregoing is Chapter VIII
from Prescott's
THE CONQUEST OF MEXICO.

Haniel Long

1888–1956

The *Power Within Us* may be characterized as an adventure story, as history, as anthropology, as religion; and it will stand up under the scrutiny of all these disciplines. But its place as a classic is assured first of all by its beauty. It is a piece of prose that had to be written by a poet. It was.

Haniel Long was an American of our own day; he died in 1956, a respected critic, historian, and "minor" poet, unaware that in *The Power Within Us* he had produced a little book which should make, and continually magnify, his reputation. The son of a missionary, he was born in Rangoon, and brought up in Pittsburgh. After Exeter and Harvard, he did newspaper work and college teaching until 1929, when he moved with his family to Santa Fe, New Mexico.

There he remained, his heart committed to the American Southwest and to the Indians whose land it had been. Among them, and among their friends throughout the country, he was well known, both as a man of great feeling and also as a painstaking writer.

This masterpiece of feeling and writing is no longer than a long short story. As a story alone it is spellbinding in the heroic mold of *Robinson Crusoe*. A "civilized" man is shipwrecked and finds himself confronted with his naked condition, unarmed except by reason and faith. Lost to the sophisticated world in which he was reared, he encounters the true savage and, through this encounter, comes to know his own kind and himself.

Thus far, high adventure and wonderment. The Spaniard Nuñez Cabeza de Vaca crosses the United States—centuries before there was a United States—from Florida to the Pacific on foot. His eight-year odyssey (1528–36) ends in Spanish Mexico where, after having long since given up all idea of seeing country or countrymen again, he is "rescued" by those gallants on horseback in whom he sees, to his horror, the man he once was. *The Power Within Us* is a report of his experience to his "Christian" master, the King of Spain.

But this is not fiction; it is truth. And Cabeza was no dreamy sailor boy of fiction equipped like an eagle scout with marvelous powers of improvisation and dexterity; he was a Spanish conquistador, a gentleman of that "irresistible" European culture bred to the mastery of armor and guns, of ships and horses, and of men. He was one of the officers of an imperial expedition of 578 glittering adventurers who believed that "on the pages of history we would share the glory of Cortés and his murderous band. . . ."

Wrecked on a coast they had intended to despoil, left to the mercy of natives they had thought to enslave, the 578 soon became 400, and then 40, and then four. There the story begins, the story of the human spirit stripped of all its fine disguises of power, pride, and pomp.

Through the whole tradition of the great books, beginning with the Greeks and the "barbarians," the meaning of civilization is pondered and the meeting of civilized and uncivilized man recited. And as often as not the civilized man comes off second best, not merely in conquest but even in history's long view of what is and is not civilized. Are the arts of civilization a net gain or a net loss? A loss, says Jean Jacques Rousseau, the French philosopher, who calls mankind back to the woods to enjoy the unadorned existence of the "noble savage."

Cabeza de Vaca's savages were not noble—nor were they ignoble. They were credulous, and their credulity awakened in the elegant Spaniard a nobility of soul which the life he had known had never aroused. Out of that surprised nobility—where else?—came power. In absolute helplessness, and in it alone, he found the strength to save others and thus himself, and to know himself, and to know what it is to be a man. *The Power Within Us*—a half hour or so of exciting reading—is a religious experience never to be forgotten.

The *Naufragios* ("Shipwrecks") of Cabeza de Vaca was published in Spain in the middle of the 16th century and went through many forms before Haniel Long took hold of the historical materials and put them in their present version. To the actual documentation of the terrible expedition Mr. Long added, from his knowledge of the country, the people, and of man himself, the true triumph of the conquistador—a man's conquest of himself in his search for the power to bear suffering.

The Power
within Us

Along in late November, 1528, a handful of Spaniards, survivors of an ill-starred expedition to Florida, were washed ashore in the Gulf of Mexico, some think near the present site of Galveston. One of these men was Nuñez Cabeza de Vaca, thirty-eight years old, the lieutenant of the expedition, an adaptable man with some secret of growth in him. Despite the privations he had endured, this Nuñez led two other Spaniards and a Moor on a journey across the entire continent, barefoot and naked, which occupied them eight years.

After he reached Mexico City, Nuñez wrote a letter to his King, relating what had befallen him. It begins as the usual story of a European adventurer who leaves home to exploit people. But Nuñez little by little finds out that people are his brothers and sisters, and feels genuine concern for them. Stories require the right audience, and he seems afraid that His Majesty might not be interested in what he has to say, for it is the story of a disaster in Spanish colonial history and in the King's personal finances. In the world of the individual, nonetheless, it is a story of triumph, however lackadaisical the manner of its telling.

My account of Nuñez is not the account he sent the King, apart of course from the actual facts. But I believe it to be the account he wished to send the King. I preserve the core of his narrative, as translated by Fanny Bandelier, and I try to show what, quite plainly, was happening to the spirit of the man. That is, I allow him to speak as though unafraid of his King and his times. I wish him to address us four hundred years later, in this world of ours where human relation is still the difficult problem, and exploitation the cancer.

Nuñez found the limitless within the narrowly limited. He helped when he had no means of helping, and gave when he had nothing to give. So, what is interesting is that at a certain point he ceases to be a historical personage and becomes a symbol. If he were alive today, he would be free to bring into the open the inwardness of his adventure. Thus he would greatly concern the present western world and our entire human world, for we are his proper audience.

In his emergency Nuñez slides out of theories and prejudices which unfit one to live on. Possibly the capacity to survive depends upon courage of spirit to accept one's fate. Possibly also, danger can be a real benefit to the physical man. Nuñez was remarkably flexible; he had what seems unlimited courage, unlimited strength. To him life itself was not different from hardship and danger, life was these things, and they are what make life good. His plight was hopeless, but he set in motion a train of thought and action which saved him. My attention wanders from the perfunctory narrative to the thing he refrains from confiding to the royal ear. That thing is a mystical feeling about the increase of life in a man from effort and from taking thought of his fellows. The weather-beaten explorer of the 16th century, lost in a thorny land among copper-colored savages and facing a blank future, discovered religion to be a reality of which he had never dreamed. His effort, his feeling for others, take novel paths; but underneath, quite apparently, lies an ageless and universal experience.

Cabeza de Vaca's Relation
of His Journey from Florida to the Pacific
1528–1536

Your Majesty, I am that Nuñez Cabeza de Vaca who lately sent you a Relation of his shipwrecks and mischances during the eight years he was absent from your dominions. In painful doubt whether my words were clear enough, I write again. My meanings being new to your Majesty and at a hasty glance unconcerned with your prestige, you might consider my narrative a poor occasion for exercising your serene power of understanding. The fault would then lie in me, not in what I have to say. Be my forgiving reader, your Majesty. Grant me your grace.

I was at the Battle of Ravenna in 1512. Between dawn and sunset that day perished a thousand score. Young as I was, Ravenna taught me something of how easy to tear asunder and destroy a man is, body and spirit. In the days that followed, in my desolation first confronted with slaughter, I saw a far-off light, heard a far-off strain of music. Such words serve as well as any: what can describe a happening in the shadows of the soul?

Again that far-off flicker of music came to me in the disorders at Seville in 1521, when I fought under the Duke of Medina-Sidonia.

Seven years passed without that flash of inward fire and I forgot about it. Seville was then a marvelous, disturbing world. I saw the heretics burning in the arms of the iron prophets. I saw Columbus as an old man, Magellan as a young man. The sailors came ashore with parrots and gold ingots and Indian girls.

Then I too sailed across the seas, Lord Treasurer of the expedition of Pámfilo Narvaez.

All that day when we were in sight of Tenerife I thought of my grandfather, the conqueror of the Grand Canary. In my childhood I was surrounded by the natives of that island, the Guanches, whom he brought home as slaves. I listened to their vague and melancholy singing, learned to be at ease with inarticulate people.

For the money to conquer the Grand Canary, perhaps your Majesty will remember, Pedro de Vera Mendoza had pawned to the Moor his two sons, my father and my uncle.

As I told your Majesty in my account of that journey, never had expedition more calamities than ours. Some of our ships foundered from hurricanes in the harbors of Cuba. The others we left behind deliberately in the lagoons of Florida.

Our greatest misfortune, aside from our greed and ignorance, lay in our commander, Pámfilo Narvaez himself. Pámfilo believed himself born under a lucky star, though nothing justified such a belief. Before Hernán Cortés he could have marched to Tenochtitlan. But he did not. When Cortés and his soldiers were richly quartered in the palaces of Montezuma, he could have replaced him in command. For that purpose was he dispatched from Havana by Velásquez. But Cortés came flying on horseback all the way to Veracruz, and talked Pámfilo's soldiers away from under his very nose. Pámfilo was not without a magnetism. But he was cocksure, a braggart, and what was worse, uncertain of the line between dream and reality. He forgot that Cortés burned his ships only after studying the jeweled emissaries of Montezuma, and becoming sure of the value of the quarry. Pámfilo had nothing to be sure of. And yet he pictured himself another Cortés, he pictured another Tenochtitlan concealed in the fronds of Florida. Having pictured these things he was as certain that they existed as of the vein in his neck.

Your Majesty is at liberty to picture *us* under this aging, adipose, credulous commander. Across that steaming land we marched with our armor glittering and our horses covered with gaudy trappings, 578 of us, towards utter ruin. Believing that on the page of history we would share the glory of Cortés and his murderous band . . .

Pámfilo would summon the copper-colored natives and tell them with gestures that he was searching for a city of the size and value of Tenochtitlan. The Indians had never heard of Tenochtitlan nor of Montezuma. But they had heard of a big town and pointed northward exclaiming, "Apaláchee!"

We marched and we marched, and had fevers and fevers. Yes, your Majesty is at liberty to picture us.

Apaláchee was no Tenochtitlan . . . We found it. It was in an immense swamp, a large impoverished settlement of thatched huts, a place of unbearable squalor.

There was nothing for it but seek the sea again and sail back to Cuba. Our arms and armor made us feel like dolts, and we wished we had pierced the jungle carrying carpenter's tools. For now, without ax, adz, or hammer, we had to build ourselves boats.

This is the tale of what men can and cannot do when they must do something or die. We built nine open boats. During the weeks it required, some of us went with scant food, and those whose palates allowed it devoured the horses.

Our 580 men had become 400 when at last we set sail and left behind us the Indian marksmen and the snakes, neither of which in Florida err when they strike.

Day after day tide and wind washed us out to sea and then washed us in to land, along a dazzling and uncertain coast. From thirst, and from the exposure to the frightful sun, our 400 became 40.

Who knows what was lost in these boats? Another Magellan, another Camões, another Cervantes, another St. John of the Cross . . .

No one has so sympathetic an imagination as your Majesty. You will understand what I am not telling you; that I saw men jump overboard, mad from thirst and sun. That I saw them swell and die slowly in delirium, heard their words and songs pour out the pitiful contents of their minds. That I saw men gnaw at corpses. And that these were Spanish gentlemen.

It is curious to have so graphic a lesson in what life may become. We had been a proud band, relying on our united strength, our armor, and our horses. Slowly our strength disunited, until nothing that we had in common remained to help any of us.

As I say, it is curious when one has nobody and nothing to rely upon outside of oneself.

Yet again that music, that fitful run and flash of brightness I first heard on the battlefield of Ravenna. Your Majesty is renowned as a patron of music; here was a music it is possible you may never have heard.

Somewhere on that coast a handful of us crawled ashore, and were fed and tended by kindly Indians till we regathered nervous vitality for the hopeless voyage to Cuba. We stripped and launched the boat, first putting our clothes aboard her. But a great comber capsized the rotten heavy hulk, imprisoning and drowning three of us. The others emerged mother-naked on the beach, shivering in the November wind of that overcast afternoon.

The Indians came back and found us as naked as they were, and our barge gone, and in tears. They sat down beside us and cried, too. I cried all the harder, to think people so miserable had pity for us. I have informed your Majesty of their tears and mine. These simple Indians were the first relenting of nature to us in months and months. That evening, for fear we might die on the way, the Indians made fires at intervals along the path to their village, warming us at each fire. That night and many nights after we slept beside them on the oyster shells which floor their huts, wrapped in hides against the cold winds from the sea.

While we were subjects of your Majesty, we had everything life offers, and now we had nothing. To understand what it means to have nothing one must have nothing. No clothing against the weather might appear the worst. But for us poor skeletons who survived it, it was not.

The worst lay in parting little by little with the thoughts that clothe the soul of a European, and most of all of the idea that a man attains strength through dirk and dagger, and serving in your Majesty's guard. We had to surrender such fantasies till our inward nakedness was the nakedness of an unborn babe, starting life anew in a womb of sensations which in themselves can mysteriously nourish. Several years went by before I could relax in that living plexus for which even now I have no name; but only when at last I relaxed, could I see the possibilities of a life in which to be deprived of Europe was not to be deprived of too much.

Tempests came, we could pull no more roots from the sea channels, the canebrake yielded no more fish. People died in the flimsy lodges. News came that five Spaniards further down the coast, men from another barge, had eaten one another up till but one remained. This deed startled the innocence of our Indians. They debated whether to kill us, to be rid of us. Instead, they made us their beasts of burden.

In April the Indians went down to the sea taking us with them; for a whole month we ate the blackberries of the sand dunes. The Indians danced incessantly. They asked us to cure their sick. When we said we did not know how to cure, they withheld our food from us. We began to watch the procedure of their medicine men. It seemed to us both irreligious and uninstructed. Besides, we found the notion of healing Indians somewhat repellent, as your Majesty will understand. But we had to heal them or die. So we prayed for strength. We prayed on bended knees and in an agony of hunger. Then over each ailing Indian we made the sign of the Cross, and recited the Ave Maria and a Pater Noster. To our amazement the ailing said they were well. And not only they but the whole tribe went without food so that we might have it. Yet so great was the lack of food for us all, it seemed impossible that life could last.

Truly, it was to our amazement that the ailing said they were well. Being Europeans, we thought we had given away to doctors and priests our ability to heal. But here it was, still in our possession, even if we had only Indians to exercise it upon. It was ours after all, we were more than we had thought we were.

I am putting my words together for whatever intelligence there may be in the world. There is no other reality among men than this intelligence; Sire, it is greatly to your glory that you can incarnate it.

To be more than I thought I was—a sensation utterly new to me . . .

Starvation, nakedness, slavery: sensations utterly new to me, also . . . The last of my fellow Spaniards on the island dies . . . Nothing to eat after the sea roots sprouted but the blackberries of the sand dunes. Nothing to protect me from the attack of the terrible frost, or the terrible sun. No one who knew my language . . . And it endured for months, for years maybe . . . Everyone I saw as starved as I was. The human body emaciated, the lean cheek, the burning eye—the ribs showing, each rib distinct—the taut skin, the weak loins, the shrunken haunch and pap. In the whole world there can be no poverty like the poverty of these people. I could not stand it. I ran away . . .

At this time, as I remember it, I began to think of Indians as fellow human beings. If I introduce this idea it is to prepare your Majesty for other ideas which came to me later, in consequence.

These were days when I reassorted the pictures of my childhood, as a child turns his kaleidoscope. I saw the Guanche slaves anew, and as though I were one of them. I saw my grandfather through the eyes of his slaves. I remembered, now without laughing, how he had tricked the Guanches into slavery. He pretended to enlist them to sail from the Grand Canary to conquer Tenerife, and when he had them below decks he battened down the hatches and set sail for Cádiz . . .

My grandfather's brutality earned him the public denunciation of Bishop Juan de Frías. This too I remembered.

In this wilderness I became a trader, and went to and fro on the coast and a little inland. I went inland with sea shells and cockles, and a certain shell used to cut beans, which the natives value. I came out with hides, and red ocher for the face and hair, flint for arrow points, and tassels of deer hide. I came to be well known among the tribes, and found out the lay of the land.

One day I heard someone calling me by name, "Alvar Nuñez, Alvar Nuñez!" It was Alonso del Castillo, one of the captains of the expedition. He said that Pámfilo's barge had drifted ashore among unfriendly Indians, and left of its occupants were only himself and Captain Andrés Dorantes, and Dorantes' blackamoor, Estevanico. We hid ourselves in a thicket and laid our plans.

That summer, when the coast tribes came together for the summer orgies, we four made good our escape westward.

Thus our 580 had become 400, our 400, forty, and our forty, four.

Certain natives came to Castillo. From ribs to cleft they were having spasms, and they begged him to cure them. He prayed, and required us anxiously to pray with him. When he had done praying he made the sign of the Cross over the Indians, and their spasms left off. We knelt down to give thanks for this new amazement.

Through this region there are no trails, and I lost my way. I found a burning tree to spend that very cold night beside. In the morning I loaded myself with dry wood, and took two burning sticks. Thus with fuel and fire, I went on for five days, seeing nobody, but having the sun with me by day and Mazzaroth and Arcturus by night. These five days I felt a numbness of those organs which keep one aware of the misery of existence. When curing sick Indians, I have struggled to shut out the thought of Andrés and Alonso (for we are self-conscious, knowing one another's sins); and in the effort of praying I have felt as though something in me had broken, to give me the power of healing. But alone in this wilderness no tissue of the body hindered the mysterious power.

Nothing of me, your Majesty, existed then outside of that music I first heard at Ravenna.

The sixth day I found my companions, who had concluded that a snake must have bitten me. I told them we ought not to be self-conscious with one another. That power we had felt flowing in us and through us could not, in the nature of things, be acutely conscious of us as individuals. It must come rather as wind comes to the trees of a forest, or as the ocean continues to murmur in the sea shell it has thrown ashore.

A gulf deeper than ocean yawns between the old world and the new; and what by now I was accustomed to would startle a burgher of Madrid or of Salamanca.

At Seville in my youth, as I have said, I saw the heretics burning in the arms of the iron prophets. This picture was with me often. Perhaps, like me, those heretics had had to pick up their notions of the Invisible as they went through life, and without the assistance of book or priest. What I myself was learning came from many blinding days in an open boat, while men died beside me crying for their mothers; and from living among these simple Indians, who insisted on our curing them of their ills. And so my notions of the Invisible may differ from what the books say. I mention it in passing, your Majesty.

When he assailed my grandfather openly in his cathedral, calling him coward and fiend, did Juan de Frías follow a lesson he had learned by rote? That good bishop had a heart and mind to which life itself could speak, and speak forcibly.

Indians came bringing five persons shriveled and paralyzed and very ill. Each of the five offered Castillo silently his bows and arrows. Castillo prayed, we with him; in the morning the five were cured . . .

Indians came from many places. But Castillo was always afraid his sins would interfere with his working miracles. The Indians turned to me. I told Castillo it was no moment for indulging the idea of being sinful, and then I followed the Indians to their ranch. The dying man was dead; Dorantes and I found him with eyes upturned, and no pulse. I removed the mat that covered him and prayed. At last the something in me like a membrane broke, and I was confident the old man would rise up again. As he did. During the night the natives came to tell us he had talked, eaten and walked about. They gave us many presents, and we left them the happiest people on earth, for they had given away their very best.

Your Majesty may by now have had enough of our cures and curing, exertions outside of Holy Church, and for the sole benefit of miserable Indians. Yet so profound is your courtesy, I know, that you will let me reveal all that is within my heart. We found ourselves so pressed that Dorantes and the Moor, who had little taste for it, had to become medicine men, too. Boys and girls, men and women, old men and women, human bodies deformed, starved, wasted by affliction (only rarely one sound and firm) . . . Their eyes followed us every moment. I do not forget those eyes . . . Your Majesty, since I addressed you first, you have become more mysterious to me and more majestic, and this increases my sense of freedom in speaking to you. To the understanding of such days and events this additional narrative becomes necessary, like a real figure to walk beside a ghost. Those eyes . . . they thrust me out of myself, into a world where nothing, if done for another, seems impossible.

Months went by as in a dream. The nerve of vision no longer rendered plausible that European world of which we had been a part. That world grew fantastic, and fantastic our countrymen there. We ourselves were only too real. From lack of clothing we had big sores and deep skin fissures on our backs and shoulders, and it hurt us to carry the hides we slept in. And it hurt us to find firewood among the cactus. My thighs and arms bled so much I stood it only by remembering—and yet whom or what did I remember? Was it a Person—was it a quality of life—was it an emotion? Was it even a remembering, was it not perhaps a listening?

Often for a time it rained gently at dusk, soothing our thighs and arms. In one such dusk we encountered squinting women in an opening. They were afraid to run away from the three pale figures and the shadowy blackamoor, for they took us to be gods floating about in the mist and rain. They led us to a village of fifty huts. Here we cured, and cured . . .

Our journey westward was but a long series of encounters. Your Majesty, encounters have become my meditation. The moment one accosts a stranger or is accosted by him is above all in this life the moment of drama. The eyes of Indians who crossed my trail have searched me to the very depths to estimate my *power*. It is true the world over. It is true of a Spaniard meeting another on the road between Toledo and Salamanca. Whoever we meet watches us intently at the quick strange moment of meeting, to see whether we are disposed to be friendly.

Seeing our bodies, seeing my own, and Alonso's, and Andrés', and the black Moor's, sometimes I think how once I was different, and we all were. What would Doña Alonza Maldonado and her husband Dr. Castillo of Salamanca think if they could see their little boy Alonso today, striding here ahead of me, lashed by starvation, scorched and baked by the sun, his hair and beard unkempt, small about the flanks, his body shriveled like a mummy?

In youth the human body drew me and was the object of my secret and natural dreams. But body after body has taken away from me that sensual phosphorescence which my youth delighted in. Within me is no disturbing interplay now, but only the steady currents of adaptation and of sympathy.

Your Majesty's piercing mind glides pliantly through what is interstitial and hidden. But upon me it was dawning only slowly that I had it in my discretion to grant life and health to others . . . Imagine me then perturbed; you are aware of what my training had been as one of your Majesty's soldiers.

Dark clouds rise to the south. To the west a great rainbow spreads its double arc. Alonso strides sturdily towards it. After him comes the Arab Negro from Azamor, whose black limbs endure every privation and still shine with superfluous sweat. For this blackamoor am I specially grateful. His reflections on our suffering do not reduce him to apathy. No adverse heats and chills deprive his loins of their strength. He is a sight to see, carrying a copper rattle in his hand, and on his shoulder a green and orange parrot.

There was the afternoon we crossed a big river, more than waist deep, as wide as the Guadalquivir at Seville, and with a swift current. I speak of it again because I loved it.

There was the village where each Indian wished to be the first to touch us, and we were squeezed almost to death in the sweating crowd . . .

. . . the village so solicitous to be blessed that Alonso fainted of exhaustion . . .

. . . the village where a new custom began: the Indians who came with us took from the villagers all their bows, arrows, shoes and beads. From that time on, those who accompanied us took tribute of those to whom they brought us. It made us uneasy, but the victims reassured us. They said they were too glad to see us to feel the loss of their property —and besides, they could make good their losses at the next village, who were very rich Indians . . .

. . . the plain where first we saw mountains, very low, like white sheep lying down . . .

. . . the village where they were so pertinacious about touching us all over that in three hours we could not get through with them . . .

. . . the village where many had one eye clouded, and others were totally blind from the same cause: which amazed us . . .

To clarify the same occurrences, words can be arranged differently, as no one knows better than your Majesty. It was a drunkenness, this feeling

I began to have of power to render life and happiness to others. Yet I was concerned about it. The concern was the important thing—not the wondering about the nature of the power, how widespread it might be, how deep, whether Andrés or Alonso or Estevanico had it in equal measure with me. What occupied me was whether I myself knew how to use it, whether I could master it, whether indeed it was for me to master— perhaps being a self-directing power that came through me. But after one accustoms oneself to the idea, it is good to be able to give out health and joy whether one man have it, or whether we all have it. Had this thought occurred to your Majesty? Never before had it occurred to me.

I said to Andrés, "If we reach Spain I shall petition His Majesty to return me to this land, with a troop of soldiers. And I shall teach the world how to conquer by gentleness, not by slaughter." "Why then a troop of soldiers?" asked Dorantes, smiling. "Soldiers look for Indian girls and gold." "Perhaps I could teach them otherwise." "They would kill you, or tie you to a tree and leave you. What a dunce you are, Alvar Nuñez!"

"And what will *you* do if we reach Spain again?" I asked Andrés. "It will be enough to reach Mexico," he answered. "I may look about for a rich widow, and spend the rest of my life as a rancher." "I could not care for such a life," I said. "To each his adventure," replied Andrés.

It occurred to me that Andrés might be afraid of the great power at this period within us. I inquired of him. "Yes, I am afraid—who would not be?" he answered, earnestly.

Another day, after he had been silent a long time, Andrés said to us: "If I could always heal these people and help them, I might be willing to stay among them. I don't know. But our present relation to them is caused by our novelty, our transiency, and the surprise at our good works. That state of things would wear off. Besides, it is not miracles these people need. They need everything fate has stripped us of in bringing us among them naked and on equal terms. Yet not quite equal. We can remember childhood and youth in a land where people live in stone houses, till the same fields year after year, build barns to store the harvests in. The towns are related to one another and support the mutual good. Each nobleman and alcalde is an avenue leading to the king; and king, alcalde, thief, and villager all bow to the will of God through Holy Church."

I take my time thinking these words over. They are true and yet I cannot assent to them. Then I answer Andrés: "When these Indians call upon

us to have mercy and heal them, is the power they feel in us derived
from stone houses, barns and tilled fields—from alcalde or nobleman, or
from Holy Church, for that matter? Let the truth be said, Andrés: All that
we learned across the water we have had to throw away. Only what we
learned as babes in our mothers' arms has stayed with us to help others."
"And what did we learn in our mothers' arms, good dunce?" asked Andrés, putting his arm round my shoulder.

. . . a mountain seven leagues long, the stones of which were iron
slags . . .

. . . a night when the moon was round, and in its light a multitude of
dwellings beside an unexpected and charming river . . .

. . . a man who some years since had been shot through the left side
of the back with an arrow. He told me the wound make him feel sick all
the while. I observed that the head of the arrow lay in the cartilage. I
prayed for an hour, and then grasped the very sharp thin stone which
served me as a knife, and cut open the breast. Feeling for the arrowhead, I thrust my hand into the palpitating tissue of the body. Your Majesty, that we human beings should be made of limp wet meat appeared
to me as strange as that we should be also air and spirit; and in that hour
nausea and a quick curiosity mingled with my pity. . . .

This cure was a misfortune to us; it gained us fame in every direction.
We soon had with us three or four thousand persons. It went past human
endurance to breathe on and make the sign of the Cross over every morsel they ate. In these parts mountain deer, quail, birds, rabbits abounded,
and what they killed the Indians set before us. They would not touch it
and would have died of hunger had we not yielded the blessing they
asked for. Besides, they asked our permission for various things they felt
like doing, and it soon wore us out. Even doing good, it appears, can
lead to ennui, even the sight of the happiness one causes can satiate. And
yet your Majesty will rejoice that heaven vouchsafed us a weariness such
as this, perhaps never before experienced by a European.

Tribe after tribe, language after language . . . nobody's memory could
recall them all. Always they robbed one another, but those who lost and
those who gained were equally content.

Estevanico, the good black, the good link between the aloofness of
white men and the warm spermatic life of the Indians. Men, women
and children joked and played with him. What matter what he did, he

was not wearied of it. What matter what he did, the mystery failed not to act through him to heal and restore.

. . . fifty leagues through a land of desert, with nothing to eat and little to drink. Through villages where the women dressed in white deerskin and people lived in real houses . . . people the best formed we had seen, the liveliest and most capable, and those who best understood us . . .

. . . moonlight in another adobe village, and we four alternately standing or lying down in the center of the plaza, and the Indians running to us from all the houses with gifts, touching us and running back to their houses for more gifts, running to us again and touching us—a living glistening cobweb of runners in the moon—keeping up for hours this naked flash to and fro from center to periphery, periphery to center.

Your Majesty, such were the scenes in which I found myself treating all human beings alike. I screw up my courage to confess it. Perhaps it is the secret thing which life has it in itself to become—a long, long march on the road, meeting people, thrown into relations with them, having to meet demands often terrible and without the aid of mysterious power impossible: demands of healing and understanding, and constantly the exorcism of fear.

With a reasonable man and a timorous man and a carnal man as my companions and even part of me. And who is any of us that without starvation he can go through the kingdoms of starvation?

And seventeen successive days of starvation.

And a sunset, on a plain between very high mountains, with a people who for four months of the year eat only powdered straw . . .

And more starvation . . .

And permanent houses once more, where maize is harvested, and where they gave us brightly decorated blankets. For a hundred leagues good houses and harvested crops, the women better treated than anywhere else. They wear shoes, and blouses open in front and tied with deer string. At sunrise these people lift their clasped hands to the horizon and pass them over their bodies. At sunset they repeat the gesture. As I watched them at these devotions, I recalled a youngster from Cádiz, one of those who died of thirst beside me in the open boat. That boy drank in the beauty of Florida, watched palm and headland along the coast even in his final delirium. I was sorry he had not lived on to see these natives laving their golden figures in the gold of dawn.

At last we found a sign of our countrymen—what through months and years we had been praying for. On the neck of an Indian a little silver buckle from a sword belt, with a horseshoe nail sewed inside it. . . . We questioned him. He said that men with beards like ours had come from heaven to that river; that they had horses, lances, and swords, and had lanced two Indians.

The country grew more and more doleful. The natives had fled to the mountains, leaving their fields. The land was fertile and full of streams, but the people were wan. They told us our countrymen had burned all the villages, taking with them half the men and all the women and children . . .

Then a day when Indians said that on the night before they had watched the Christians from behind some trees. They saw them take along many persons in chains.

Our countrymen, these slave catchers, were startled when they saw us approaching. Yet almost with their first words they began to recite their troubles. For many days they had been unable to find Indians to capture. They did not know what to do, and were on the point of starvation. The idea of enslaving our Indians occurred to them in due course, and they were vexed at us for preventing it. They had their interpreter make a fine speech. He told our Indians that we were as a matter of fact Christians too, but had gone astray for a long while, and were people of no luck and little heart. But the Christians on horseback were real Christians, and the lords of the land to be obeyed and served. Our Indians considered this point of view. They answered that the real Christians apparently lied, that we could not possibly be Christians. For we appeared out of sunrise, they out of sunset; we cured the sick, while they killed even the healthy; we went naked and barefoot, while they wore clothes, and rode horseback and stuck people with lances; we asked for nothing and gave away all we were given, while they never gave anybody anything and had no other aim than to steal.

Your Majesty will remember my indignation in my first narrative that Christians should be so wicked, especially such as had the advantages of being your subjects. I did not at the time understand the true source of my indignation. I do now, and I will explain it. In facing these marauders

I was compelled to face the Spanish gentleman I myself had been eight years before. It was not easy to think of it. Andrés and Alonso agreed that it was not easy. What, your Majesty, is so melancholy as to confront one's former unthinking and unfeeling self?

It was many days before I could endure the touch of clothing, many a night before I could sleep in a bed.

Shoes were the worst. In the Spanish settlements I dared not go barefoot, for provincials are the most easily shocked of Spaniards. I had not valued enough the pressure of earth on my naked feet while permitted that refreshment.

At first I did not notice other ways in which our ancient civilization was affecting me. Yet soon I observed a certain reluctance in me to do good to others. I would say to myself, "Need I exert what is left of me, I who have undergone tortures in an open boat and every privation and humiliation among the Indians, when there are strong healthy men about me, fresh from Holy Church and from school, who know their Christian duty?" We Europeans all talk this way to ourselves. It has become second nature to us. Each nobleman and alcalde and villager is an avenue that leads us to this way of talking; we can admit it privately, your Majesty, can we not? If a man need a cloak, we do not give it to him if we have our wits about us; nor are we to be caught stretching out our finger in aid of a miserable woman. Someone else will do it, we say. Our communal life dries up our milk: we are barren as the fields of Castile. We regard our native land as a power which acts of itself, and relieves us each of exertion. While with them I thought only about doing the Indians good. But back among my fellow countrymen, I had to be on my guard not to do them positive harm. If one lives where all suffer and starve, one acts on one's own impulse to help. But where plenty abounds, we surrender our generosity, believing that our country replaces us each and several. This is not so, and indeed a delusion. On the contrary the power or maintaining life in others lives within each of us, and from each of us does it recede when unused. It is a concentrated power. If you are not acquainted with it, your Majesty can have no inkling of what it is like, what it portends, or the ways in which it slips from one. In the name of God, your Majesty,

FAREWELL.

Pliny the Younger

c. 61–c. 113

Pliny the Younger (Gaius Plinius Caecilius Secundus) was born in
A.D. 61 or 62 in Novum Comum, now the Como region of Italy. He
was a member of a distinguished Roman family. His mother was
Plinia, sister of Pliny the Elder; the latter adopted the boy in his will,
thus making him his heir. Pliny the Younger inherited all the possessions of his famous and affluent uncle, including his valuable library,
and including also his name.

The young man was educated in rhetoric under the celebrated
Quintilian and had also as his guardian L. Verginius Rufus, who
three times declined to become emperor. Thus, when at eighteen
Pliny began his career as an advocate, he did so under the most
favorable auspices. He held various and important public offices. He
was a tribune of the plebs, or representative of the people in the
Senate, a commissioner of the military treasury; and in the year 100,
he was appointed a consul by the emperor Trajan. Tacitus and possibly Plutarch were also honored in this way by Trajan.

In 111, Pliny was made Governor of Bithynia. There it is supposed
that he remained until his death, which probably occurred in 113.
His extant works consist of a panegyric on Trajan, delivered at the
time of Pliny's elevation to the consulship, and ten volumes of published letters. The tenth of these comprises correspondence with
Trajan on administrative matters in Bithynia. Several of the letters
are of particular interest, for they contain some of the first descriptions of early Christian ritual and practice.

The younger Pliny was a friend of the historian Tacitus, and many
of his published letters were addressed to him. There is no date on

the two letters to Tacitus that are reprinted below. The events which they relate occurred in A.D. 79, when Pliny was eighteen, but the letters were not published until nearly thirty years had passed. It is thus not known when they were written. Nevertheless, they sound as if they were written while Pliny's memory was fresh. It is possible that they were rewritten long after the event from first drafts or notes. In any event, Tacitus had asked Pliny to describe the circumstances of the death of his famous uncle, and the letters do so. The fact that this death occurred as a result of the eruption of Vesuvius gives us an eyewitness account of that famous and terrible disaster.

The first letter has a solemn tone, as if the author knew that it would be preserved for the record. The eruption of Vesuvius which destroyed Pompeii and Herculaneum appears in it only as the rather remote background that gives emphasis to the stoic nobility of the elder Pliny's death. The latter was an important public official as well as a celebrated writer, and his nephew treats him here accordingly.

In the second letter, however, Pliny the Younger's youthfulness emerges. Imitating his uncle's stoicism, he reads Livy under a shower of ashes; and, refusing to flee, strikes what appear to be self-consciously noble attitudes. Nevertheless, he frankly admits his fear. The Stoics and Epicureans held that the world would end in fire. The young Pliny confesses that he believed that the final day had come.

Both of Pliny's letters are self-conscious and a little self-complacent, too. He has been criticized for this; he never wrote with the freedom and naturalness of, for example, Cicero. He always seemed to have one eye on posterity; and, even in the second letter, his protests that his personal experiences are of no importance have a hollow ring. Nevertheless, the qualities emerge that have made Pliny readable throughout the ages, and that may have helped his letters to survive.

There are touches of vainglory that may make us laugh, but at the same time the letters are so modern that we can almost conceive of Pliny as a young college friend writing about a modern disaster. We have read of the last days of Pompeii in our history books, and some may have visited its excavated ruins. But nothing makes that historic tragedy more real than this clear and vivid account of it by a boy, still shaken by fright.

The Eruption of Vesuvius
from *Letters*

TO TACITUS

Your request that I would send you an account of my uncle's death, in order to transmit a more exact relation of it to posterity, deserves my acknowledgments; for, if this accident shall be celebrated by your pen, the glory of it, I am well assured, will be rendered for ever illustrious. And notwithstanding he perished by a misfortune, which, as it involved at the same time a most beautiful country in ruins, and destroyed so many populous cities, seems to promise him an everlasting remembrance; notwithstanding he has himself composed many and lasting works; yet I am persuaded the mentioning of him in your immortal writings will greatly contribute to render his name immortal. Happy I esteem those to be to whom by provision of the gods has been granted the ability either to do such actions as are worthy of being related or to relate them in a manner worthy of being read; but peculiarly happy are they who are blessed with both these uncommon talents: in the number of which my uncle, as his own writings and your history will evidently prove, may justly be ranked. It is with extreme willingness, therefore, that I execute your commands; and should indeed have claimed the task if you had not enjoined it. He was at that time with the fleet under his command at Misenum.[1] On the 24th of August, about one in the afternoon, my mother desired him to observe a cloud which appeared of a very unusual size and shape. He had just taken a turn in the sun,[2] and,

---

1. In the Bay of Naples.
2. The Romans used to lie or walk naked in the sun after anointing their bodies with oil, which was esteemed as greatly contributing to health, and therefore daily practiced by them. This custom, however, of anointing themselves is inveighed against by the satirists as in the number of their luxurious indulgences; but since we find the elder Pliny here, and the amiable Spurinna in a former letter, practicing

after bathing himself in cold water, and making a light luncheon, gone back to his books: he immediately arose and went out upon a rising ground from whence he might get a better sight of this very uncommon appearance. A cloud, from which mountain was uncertain at this distance (but it was found afterwards to come from Mount Vesuvius), was ascending, the appearance of which I cannot give you a more exact description of than by likening it to that of a pine tree, for it shot up to a great height in the form of a very tall trunk, which spread itself out at the top into a sort of branches; occasioned, I imagine, either by a sudden gust of air that impelled it, the force of which decreased as it advanced upwards, or the cloud itself, being pressed back again by its own weight, expanded in the manner I have mentioned; it appeared sometimes bright and sometimes dark and spotted, according as it was either more or less impregnated with earth and cinders. This phenomenon seemed to a man of such learning and research as my uncle extraordinary and worth further looking into. He ordered a light vessel to be got ready, and gave me leave, if I liked, to accompany him. I said I had rather go on with my work; and it so happened he had himself given me something to write out. As he was coming out of the house, he received a note from Rectina, the wife of Bassus, who was in the utmost alarm at the imminent danger which threatened her, for her villa lying at the foot of Mount Vesuvius, there was no way of escape but by sea; she earnestly entreated him therefore to come to her assistance. He accordingly changed his first intention, and what he had begun from a philosophical, he now carries out in a noble and generous spirit. He ordered the galleys to be put to sea, and went himself on board with an intention of assisting not only Rectina, but the several other towns which lay thickly strewn along that beautiful coast. Hastening then to the place from whence others fled with the utmost terror, he steered his course direct to the point of danger, and with so much calmness and presence of mind as to be able to make and dictate his observations upon the motion and all the phenomena of that dreadful scene. He was now so close to the mountain that the cinders, which grew thicker and hotter the nearer he approached, fell into the ships, together with pumice stones and black pieces of burning rock; they were in danger too not only of being aground by the sudden retreat of the sea but also from the vast fragments which rolled down from the mountain and obstructed all the shore. Here he stopped to consider

---

this method, we cannot suppose the thing itself was esteemed unmanly, but only when it was attended with some particular circumstances of an overrefined delicacy [Translator].

whether he should turn back again; to which the pilot advising him, "Fortune," said he, "favours the brave; steer to where Pomponianus is." Pomponianus was then at Stabiae,[3] separated by a bay, which the sea, after several insensible windings, forms with the shore. He had already sent his baggage on board; for though he was not at that time in actual danger, yet being within sight of it, and indeed extremely near, if it should in the least increase, he was determined to put to sea as soon as the wind, which was blowing dead inshore, should go down. It was favourable, however, for carrying my uncle to Pomponianus, whom he found in the greatest consternation; he embraced him tenderly, encouraging and urging him to keep up his spirits, and, the more effectually to soothe his fears by seeming unconcerned himself, ordered a bath to be got ready, and then, after having bathed, sat down to supper with great cheerfulness, or at least (what is just as heroic) with every appearance of it. Meanwhile broad flames shone out in several places from Mount Vesuvius, which the darkness of the night contributed to render still brighter and clearer. But my uncle, in order to soothe the apprehensions of his friend, assured him it was only the burning of the villages, which the country people had abandoned to the flames; after this he retired to rest, and it is most certain he was so little disquieted as to fall into a sound sleep, for his breathing, which, on account of his corpulence, was rather heavy and sonorous, was heard by the attendants outside. The court which led to his apartment being now almost filled with stones and ashes, if he had continued there any time longer, it would have been impossible for him to have made his way out. So he was awoke and got up, and went to Pomponianus and the rest of his company, who were feeling too anxious to think of going to bed. They consulted together whether it would be most prudent to trust to the houses, which now rocked from side to side with frequent and violent concussions as though shaken from their very foundations; or fly to the open fields, where the calcined stones and cinders, though light indeed, yet fell in large showers, and threatened destruction. In this choice of dangers they resolved for the fields: a resolution which, while the rest of the company were hurried into by their fears, my uncle embraced upon cool and deliberate consideration. They went out then, having pillows tied upon their heads with napkins; and this was their whole defence against the storm of stones that fell round them. It was now day everywhere else, but *there* a deeper darkness prevailed than in the thickest night, which, however,

---

3. Now called Castellammare, in the Bay of Naples [Translator].

was in some degree alleviated by torches and other lights of various kinds. They thought proper to go farther down upon the shore to see if they might safely put out to sea, but found the waves still running extremely high and boisterous. There my uncle, laying himself down upon a sail-cloth, which was spread for him, called twice for some cold water, which he drank, when immediately the flames, preceded by a strong whiff of sulphur, dispersed the rest of the party, and obliged him to rise. He raised himself up with the assistance of two of his servants, and instantly fell down dead; suffocated, as I conjecture, by some gross and noxious vapour, having always had a weak throat, which was often inflamed. As soon as it was light again, which was not till the third day after this melancholy accident, his body was found entire, and without any marks of violence upon it, in the dress in which he fell, and looking more like a man asleep than dead. During all this time my mother and I, who were at Misenum—but this has no connection with your history, and you did not desire any particulars besides those of my uncle's death; so I will end here, only adding that I have faithfully related to you what I was either an eye-witness of myself or received immediately after the accident happened, and before there was time to vary the truth. You will pick out of this narrative whatever is most important, for a letter is one thing, a history another; it is one thing writing to a friend, another thing writing to the public. Farewell.

TO CORNELIUS TACITUS

The letter which, in compliance with your request, I wrote to you concerning the death of my uncle has raised, it seems, your curiosity to know what terrors and dangers attended me while I continued at Misenum, for there, I think, my account broke off:

Though my shock'd soul recoils, my tongue shall tell.

My uncle having left us, I spent such time as was left on my studies (it was on their account indeed that I had stopped behind), till it was time for my bath. After which I went to supper, and then fell into a short and uneasy sleep. There had been noticed for many days before a trembling of the earth, which did not alarm us much, as this is quite an ordinary occurrence in Campania; but it was so particularly violent that night that it not only shook but actually overturned, as it would seem, everything about us. My mother rushed into my chamber, where she found me rising in order to awaken her. We sat down in the open court of the house, which occupied a small space between the buildings and the sea. As I was at that time but eighteen years of age, I know not whether I should call my behaviour, in this dangerous juncture, courage or folly; but I took up Livy, and amused myself with turning over that author, and even making extracts from him, as if I had been perfectly at my leisure. Just then, a friend of my uncle's, who had lately come to him from Spain, joined us, and observing me sitting by my mother with a book in my hand, reproved her for her calmness, and me at the same time for my careless security: nevertheless I went on with my author. Though it was now morning, the light was still exceedingly faint and doubtful; the buildings all around us tottered, and though we stood upon open ground, yet as the place was narrow and confined, there was no remaining without imminent danger: we therefore resolved to quit the town. A panic-striken crowd followed us, and (as to a mind distracted with terror every suggestion seems more prudent than its own) pressed on us in dense array to drive us forward as we came out. Being at a convenient distance from the houses, we stood still, in the midst of a most dangerous and dreadful scene. The chariots, which we had ordered to be drawn out, were so agitated backwards and forwards, though upon the most level ground, that we could not keep them steady, even by supporting them with large stones. The sea seemed to roll back upon itself, and to be driven from its banks by the convulsive motion of the earth; it is certain at least the shore was considerably enlarged, and several sea animals were left upon it. On the other side, a black and dreadful cloud, broken with rapid, zigzag flashes, revealed behind it variously shaped masses of flame: these last were like sheet-lightning, but much larger. Upon this our Spanish friend, whom I mentioned above, addressing himself to my mother and me with great energy and urgency: "If your brother," he said, "if your uncle be safe, he certainly wishes you may be so too; but if he perished, it was his desire, no doubt, that you might both survive him: why therefore do you delay your escape a moment?" We could never think of our own safety, we said, while we were uncertain of his. Upon this our friend left us, and withdrew from the danger with the utmost precipitation. Soon afterwards, the cloud began to descend, and cover the sea. It had already surrounded and concealed the island of Capreae and the promontory of Misenum. My mother now besought, urged, even commanded me to make my escape at any rate, which, as I was young, I might easily do; as for herself, she said, her age and corpulency rendered all attempts of that sort impossible; however, she would willingly meet death if she could have the satisfaction of seeing that she was not the occasion of mine. But I absolutely refused to leave her, and, taking her by the hand, compelled her to go with me. She complied with great reluctance, and not without many reproaches to herself for retarding my flight. The ashes now began to fall upon us, though in no great quantity. I looked back; a dense, dark mist seemed to be following us, spreading itself over the country like a cloud. "Let us turn out of the highroad," I said, "while we can still see, for fear that, should we fall in the road, we should be pressed to death in the dark by the crowds that are following us." We had scarcely sat down when night came upon us, not such as we have when the sky is cloudy, or when there is no moon, but that of a room when it is shut up, and all the lights put out. You might hear the shrieks of women, the screams of children, and the shouts of men; some calling for their children, others for their parents, others for their husbands, and seeking to recognize each other by the voices that replied; one lamenting his own fate, another that of his family; some wishing to die, from the very fear of dying; some lifting their hands to the gods; but the greater part convinced that there were now no gods at all, and that the final endless night of which we have heard had come upon the world.[4] Among these there were some who augmented the real terrors by others imaginary or wilfully invented. I remember some who declared that one part of Misenum had fallen, that another was on fire; it was false, but they found people to believe them. It now grew rather lighter, which we imagined to be rather the forerunner of an approaching burst of flames (as in truth it was) than the return of day; however, the fire fell at a distance from us: then again we were immersed in thick darkness, and a heavy shower of ashes rained upon us, which we were obliged every now and then to stand up to shake off, otherwise we should have been crushed and buried in the heap. I might boast that, during all this scene of horror, not a sigh, or expression of fear, escaped me: my support was grounded in that miserable, though mighty, consolation that all mankind were involved in the same calamity, and that I was perishing with the world itself. At last this dreadful darkness was dissipated by degrees, like a cloud or smoke; the real day returned, and even the sun shone out, though with a lurid light, as when an eclipse is coming on. Every object that presented itself to our eyes (which were extremely weakened) seemed changed, being covered deep with ashes as if with snow. We returned to Misenum, where we refreshed ourselves as well as we could, and passed

---

4. The Stoic and Epicurean philosophers held that the world was to be destroyed by fire, and all things fall again into original chaos; not excepting even the national gods themselves from the destruction of this general conflagration [Translator].

an anxious night between hope and fear; though, indeed, with a much larger share of the latter, for the earthquake still continued, while many frenzied persons ran up and down heightening their own and their friends' calamities by terrible predictions. However, my mother and I, notwithstanding the danger we had passed, and that which still threatened us, had no thoughts of leaving the place till we could receive some news of my uncle.

And now, you will read this narrative without any view of inserting it in your history, of which it is not in the least worthy; and, indeed, you must put it down to your own request if it should appear not worth even the trouble of a letter. Farewell.

The foregoing consists of Letters LXV and LXVI translated by William Melmoth.

Cornelius Tacitus

c. 55–c. 120

Tacitus (his given name may have been Publius or Gaius) was probably of noble Roman blood. Much of what little we can find out about him is in his own works and the letters of his friend, the Younger Pliny. "I know that your *Histories* will be immortal," said Pliny. They are.

Nine emperors, Nero among them, governed or misgoverned Rome in his lifetime. Three of these—Vespasian, Titus, Domitian—lifted Tacitus rank by rank in the public service. Fame touched him early, as an orator. He married the daughter of Julius Agricola. In A.D. 79 or 80, Agricola became the first general to put all Britain under Roman control. His name was loud in the city. Domitian feared him as a rival. Agricola died "in the prime of a vigorous manhood," probably poisoned.

Tacitus composed a burning memorial to his father-in-law (see below). Much earlier, he had published the *Dialogue on Orators*. Four years away from Rome may have given him the source for his *Germania*. This brings us our fullest early news of the Germans, as *Agricola* does of the Britons.

Under the insane terror of Domitian's last years, Tacitus was forced to look on at the imperial murder of friends and fellow officials. It marked his mind with blackness and shadowed his two major works. Of these, the *Histories* laid down events from A.D. 69 to 97; the *Annals* traced out the disorders of Rome from Tiberius to Nero's end in 68. These were written under the new "liberal" emperors, Nerva and Trajan.

In A.D. 97 Tacitus became a consul or chief magistrate. With his friend Pliny he convicted Marius Priscus, a notorious African governor accused of crimes against his subjects. An inscription found in the twentieth century names Tacitus as proconsul of Asia Minor about 112. After that we hear no more of him.

Suppose you were a member of the Supreme Soviet under Joseph Stalin, dictator of Russia between 1927 and 1953. Day after day, during the state trials of the 1930's, you watched the old Bolsheviks, men whom you had lived and worked with, stand up and confess treason against the state. You yourself were forced to praise the dictator. You approved the death sentence. And all the while you knew that these acts of treason were unbelievable. You knew these men. They could never have betrayed their party and their country. It was a lie. Stalin feared them. He had ordered their destruction; and the whole engine of the state, even the accused themselves, moved to give a color of justice to what was in fact persecution and madness.

Then Stalin was dead, and after a while it became possible to tell at least some part of the truth. How would you feel? That is how Tacitus must have felt when the emperor Domitian was finally murdered. And what would you do? We know what Tacitus did. He set out to write the life story of one of Domitian's victims, an honorable man well known to him, his father-in-law and his friend. He called it *The Life of Gnaeus Julius Agricola*. He meant to make Agricola's name stand for all those other men of principle destroyed by the tyrant. Moreover, since Agricola had been a great Roman general, Tacitus would be writing history, too. History, he said, could do nothing better than "to let no worthy action be uncommemorated," to condemn "evil words and deeds" in the eyes of later ages.

His book would become in some measure a hymn of praise to a good soldier. He would, in fact, make Agricola a kind of ideal West Pointer. He would tell how he went to school at soldiering under Suetonius Paulinus in Britain; how "he would learn from the skillful, and keep pace with the bravest, would attempt nothing for display, would avoid nothing from fear." He would mention Agricola's term as governor of Asia, where he had to deal with a swindling proconsul, and his service in Aquitania. Then he would bring him back to Britain and show his talent as a soldier rising gradually to its crest at the battle of Mons Graupius. He would describe how Agricola returned to Rome, his prudent behavior in the face of great popularity, and his mysterious death. Tacitus' geography might be shaky, and the speeches he gave to his characters were certainly made up; but he would be careful to set down only such matters as he believed to be fact, even as to the lack of evidence that Agricola had been poisoned.

Like his contemporary Plutarch, Tacitus was more a student of man than a historian; and in an age "so cruel, so hostile to all virtue," he was more moralist than either. What we have called the great ideas were well known to him. He lived by them. History? It was his trade. Tyranny? Who knew it better than Tacitus? War and peace? He could hardly tell one from another in his time. Plainly he belonged to an aristocracy, the Roman senatorial class. More often than not, this was also an oligarchy—a rule by the prosperous few. Like the best men of his class, he lived according to the principles of courage and honor. And virtue? He gave us proof of this in the great speech which ends his *Agricola*. Meant as praise of Agricola, it is also his own confession. See, he says, our shame. In the madness of Domitian, we were faced with a moral conflict we could not solve: a conflict between loyalty to the empire and loyalty to a class, to justice, to truth itself. We could not act, and because of this the best men in Rome died.

The Life
of Gnaeus Julius Agricola

To bequeath to posterity a record of the deeds and characters of distinguished men is an ancient practice which even the present age, careless as it is of its own sons, has not abandoned whenever some great and conspicuous excellence has conquered and risen superior to that failing, common to petty and to great states, blindness and hostility to goodness. But in days gone by, as there was a greater inclination and a more open path to the achievement of memorable actions, so the man of highest genius was led by the simple reward of a good conscience to hand on without partiality or self-seeking the remembrance of greatness. Many too thought that to write their own lives showed the confidence of integrity rather than presumption. Of Rutilius and Scaurus no one doubted the honesty or questioned the motives. So true is it that merit is best appreciated by the age in which it thrives most easily. But in these days, I, who have to record the life of one who has passed away, must crave an indulgence, which I should not have had to ask had I only to inveigh against an age so cruel, so hostile to all virtue.

We have read that the panegyrics pronounced by Arulenus Rusticus on Thrasea Paetus, and by Herennius Senecio on Helvidius Priscus, were made capital crimes, that not only their persons but their very books were objects of rage, and that the triumvirs were commissioned to burn in the forum those works of splendid genius. They fancied, forsooth, that in that fire the voice of the Roman people, the freedom of the Senate, and the conscience of the human race were perishing, while at the same time they banished the teachers of philosophy, and exiled every noble pursuit, that nothing good might anywhere confront them. Certainly we showed a magnificent example of patience; as a former age had witnessed the extreme of liberty, so we witnessed the extreme of servitude, when the informer robbed us of the interchange of speech and hearing. We should

274

have lost memory as well as voice, had it been as easy to forget as to keep silence.

Now at last our spirit is returning. And yet, though at the dawn of a most happy age Nerva Caesar blended things once irreconcilable, sovereignty and freedom, though Nerva Trajan is now daily augmenting the prosperity of the time, and though the public safety has not only our hopes and good wishes, but has also the certain pledge of their fulfillment, still, from the necessary condition of human frailty, the remedy works less quickly than the disease. As our bodies grow but slowly, perish in a moment, so it is easier to crush than to revive genius and its pursuits. Besides, the charm of indolence steals over us, and the idleness which at first we loathed we afterwards love. What if during those fifteen years, a large portion of human life, many were cut off by ordinary casualties, and the ablest fell victims to the Emperor's rage, if a few of us survive, I may almost say, not only others but our own selves, survive, though there have been taken from the midst of life those many years which brought the young in dumb silence to old age, and the old almost to the very verge and end of existence! Yet we shall not regret that we have told, though in language unskillful and unadorned, the story of past servitude, and borne our testimony to present happiness. Meanwhile this book, intended to do honor to Agricola, my father-in-law, will, as an expression of filial regard, be commended, or at least excused.

Gnaeus Julius Agricola was born at the ancient and famous colony of Forum Julii. Each of his grandfathers was an Imperial procurator, that is, of the highest equestrian rank. His father, Julius Graecinus, a member of the Senatorian order, and distinguished for his pursuit of eloquence and philosophy, earned for himself by these very merits the displeasure of Caius Caesar. He was ordered to impeach Marcus Silanus, and because he refused was put to death. His mother was Julia Procilla, a lady of singular virtue. Brought up by her side with fond affection, he passed his boyhood and youth in the cultivation of every worthy attainment. He was guarded from the enticements of the profligate not only by his own good and straightforward character, but also by having, when quite a child, for the scene and guide of his studies, Massilia, a place where refinement and provincial frugality were blended and happily combined. I remember that he used to tell us how in his early youth he would have imbibed a keener love of philosophy than became a Roman and a senator, had not his mother's good sense checked his excited and ardent spirit. It was the case of a lofty and aspiring soul craving with more eagerness than caution the beauty and splendor of great and glorious renown. But it was soon mellowed by reason and experience, and he retained from his learning that most difficult of lessons—moderation.

He served his military apprenticeship in Britain to the satisfaction of Suetonius Paulinus, a painstaking and judicious officer, who, to test his merits, selected him to share his tent. Without the recklessness with which young men often make the profession of arms a mere pastime, and without indolence, he never availed himself of his tribune's rank or his inexperience to procure enjoyment or to escape from duty. He sought to make himself acquainted with the province and known to the army; he would learn from the skillful, and keep pace with the bravest, would attempt nothing for display, would avoid nothing from fear, and would be at once careful and vigilant.

Never indeed had Britain been more excited, or in a more critical condition. Veteran soldiers had been massacred, colonies burnt, armies cut off. The struggle was then for safety; it was soon to be for victory. And though all this was conducted under the leadership and direction of another, though the final issue and the glory of having won back the province belonged to the general, yet skill, experience, and ambition were acquired by the young officer. His soul too was penetrated with the desire of warlike renown, a sentiment unwelcome to an age which put a sinister construction on eminent merit, and made glory as perilous as infamy.

From Britain he went to Rome, to go through the regular course of office, and there allied himself with Domitia Decidiana, a lady of illustrious birth. The marriage was one which gave a man ambitious of advancement distinction and support. They lived in singular harmony, through their mutual affection and preference of each other to self. However, the good wife deserves the greater praise, just as the bad incurs a heavier censure.

Appointed Quaestor, the ballot gave him Asia for his province, Salvius Titianus for his proconsul. Neither the one nor the other corrupted him, though the province was rich and an easy prey to the wrongdoer, while the proconsul, a man inclined to every species of greed, was ready by all manner of indulgence to purchase a mutual concealment of guilt.

A daughter was there added to his family to be his stay and comfort, for shortly after he lost the son that had before been born to him. The year between his quaestorship and tribunate, as well as the year of the tribunate itself, he passed in retirement and inaction, for he knew those times of Nero when indolence stood for wisdom. His praetorship was passed in the same consistent quietude, for the usual judicial functions did not fall to his lot. The games and the pageantry of his office he ordered according to the mean between strictness and profusion, avoiding extravagance, but not missing distinction. He was afterwards appointed by Galba to draw up an account of the temple offerings, and his searching scrutiny relieved the conscience of the state from the burden of all sacrileges but those committed by Nero.

The following year inflicted a terrible blow on his affections and his fortunes. Otho's fleet, while cruising idly about, cruelly ravaged Intemelii, a district of Liguria; his mother, who was living there on her own estate, was murdered. The estate itself and a large part of her patrimony were plundered. This was indeed the occasion of the crime. Agricola, who instantly set out to discharge the duties of affection, was overtaken by the tidings that Vespasian was aiming at the throne. He at once joined his party. Vespasian's early policy, and the government of Rome were directed by Mucianus, for Domitian was a mere youth, and from his father's elevation sought only the opportunities of indulgence.

Agricola, having been sent by Mucianus to conduct a levy of troops, and having done his work with integrity and energy, was appointed to command the 20th Legion, which had been slow to take the new oath of allegiance, and the retiring officer of which was reported to be acting disloyally. It was a trying and formidable charge for even officers of consular rank, and the late praetorian officer, perhaps from his own disposition, perhaps from that of the soldiers, was powerless to restrain them. Chosen thus at once to supersede and to punish, Agricola, with a singular moderation, wished it to be thought that he had found rather than made an obedient soldiery.

Britain was then under Vettius Bolanus, who governed more mildly than suited so turbulent a province. Agricola moderated his energy and restrained his ardor, that he might not grow too important, for he had learned to obey, and understood well how to combine expediency with honor. Soon afterwards Britain received for its governor a man of consular rank, Petilius Cerialis. Agricola's merits had now room for display. Cerialis let him share at first indeed only the toils and dangers, but before long the glory of war, often by way of trial putting him in command of part of the army, and sometimes, on the strength of the result, of larger forces. Never to enhance his own renown did Agricola boast of his exploits; he always referred his success, as though he were but an instrument, to his general and director. Thus by his valor in obeying orders and by his modesty of speech he escaped jealousy without losing distinction.

As he was returning from the command of the legion, Vespasian admitted him into the patrician order, and then gave him the province of Aquitania, a pre-eminently splendid appointment both from the importance of its duties and the prospect of the consulate to which the Emperor destined him. Many think the genius of the soldier wants subtlety, because military law, which is summary and blunt, and apt to appeal to the sword, finds no exercise for the refinements of the forum. Yet Agricola, from his natural good sense, though called to act among civilians, did his work with ease and correctness. And, besides, the times of business and relaxation were kept distinct. When his public and judicial duties required it, he was dignified, thoughtful, austere, and yet often merciful; when business was done with, he wore no longer the official character. He was altogether without harshness, pride, or the greed of gain. With a most rare felicity, his good nature did not weaken his authority, nor his strictness the attachment of his friends. To speak of uprightness and purity in such a man would be an insult to his virtues. Fame itself, of which even good men are often weakly fond, he did not seek by an ostentation of virtue or by artifice. He avoided rivalry with his colleagues, contention with his procurator, thinking such victories no honor and defeat disgrace. For somewhat less than three years he was kept in his governorship, and was then recalled with an immediate prospect of the consulate. A general belief went with him that the province of Britain was to be his, not because he had himself hinted it, but because he seemed worthy of it. Public opinion is not always mistaken; sometimes even it chooses the right man. He was consul, and I but a youth, when he betrothed to me his daughter, a maiden even then of noble promise. After his consulate he gave her to me in marriage, and was then at once appointed to the government of Britain, with the addition of the sacred office of the pontificate.

The geography and inhabitants of Britain, already described by many writers, I will speak of, not that my research and ability may be compared with theirs, but because the country was then for the first time thoroughly subdued. And so matters, which as being still not accurately known my predecessors embellished with their eloquence, shall now be related on the evidence of facts.

Britain, the largest of the islands which Roman geography includes, is so situated that it faces Germany on the east, Spain on the west; on the south it is even within sight of Gaul; its northern extremities, which have no shores opposite to them, are beaten by the waves of a vast open sea. The form of the entire country has been compared by Livy and Fabius Rusticus, the most graphic among ancient and modern historians, to an oblong shield or battle-ax. And this no doubt is its shape without Caledonia, so that it has become the popular description of the whole island. There is, however, a large and irregular tract of land which juts out from its furthest shores, tapering off in a wedgelike form. Round these coasts of remotest ocean the Roman fleet then for the first time sailed, ascertained that Britain is an island, and simultaneously discovered and conquered what are called the Orcades, islands hitherto unknown. Thule too was descried in the distance, which as yet had been hidden by the snows of winter. Those waters, they say, are sluggish, and yield with difficulty to the oar, and are not even raised by the wind as other seas. The reason, I suppose, is that lands and mountains, which are the cause and origin of storms, are here comparatively rare, and also that the vast depths of that unbroken expanse are more slowly set in motion. But to investigate the nature of the ocean and the tides is no part of the present work, and many writers have discussed the subject. I would simply add that nowhere has the sea a wider dominion, that it has many currents running in every direction, that it does not merely flow and ebb within the limits of the shore, but penetrates and winds far inland, and finds a home among hills and mountains as though in its own domain.

Who were the original inhabitants of Britain, whether they were indigenous or foreign, is, as usual among barbarians, little known. Their physical characteristics are various, and from these conclusions may be drawn. The red hair and large limbs of the inhabitants of Caledonia point clearly to a German origin. The dark complexion of the Silures, their usually curly hair, and the fact that Spain is the opposite shore to them, are an evidence that Iberians of a former date crossed over and occupied these parts. Those who are nearest to the Gauls are also like them, either from the permanent influence of original descent, or because in countries which run out so far to meet each other climate has produced similar physical qualities. But a general survey inclines me to believe that the Gauls established themselves in an island so near to them. Their religious belief may be traced in the strongly marked British superstition. The language differs but little; there is the same boldness in challenging danger, and, when it is near, the same timidity in shrinking from it. The Britons, however, exhibit more spirit, as being a people whom a long peace has not yet enervated. Indeed we have understood that even the Gauls were once renowned in war; but, after a while, sloth following on ease crept over them, and they lost their courage along with their freedom. This too has happened to the long-conquered tribes of Britain; the rest are still what the Gauls once were.

Their strength is in infantry. Some tribes fight also with the chariot. The higher in rank is the charioteer; the dependants fight. They were once ruled by kings, but are now divided under chieftains into factions and parties. Our greatest advantage in coping with tribes so powerful is that they do not act in concert. Seldom is it that two or three states meet together to ward off a common danger. Thus, while they fight singly, all are conquered.

Their sky is obscured by continual rain and cloud. Severity of cold is unknown. The days exceed in length those of our part of the world; the nights are bright, and in the extreme north so short that between sunlight and dawn you can perceive but a slight distinction. It is said that, if there are no clouds in the way, the splendor of the sun can be seen throughout the night, and that he does not rise and set, but only crosses the heavens. The truth is that the low shadow thrown from the flat extremities of the earth's surface does not raise the darkness to any height, and the night thus fails to reach the sky and stars.

With the exception of the olive and vine, and plants which usually grow in warmer climates, the soil will yield, and even abundantly, all ordinary produce. It ripens indeed slowly, but is of rapid growth, the cause in each case being the same, namely, the excessive moisture of the soil and of the atmosphere. Britain contains gold and silver and other metals, as the prize of conquest. The ocean, too, produces pearls, but of a dusky and bluish hue. Some think that those who collect them have not the requisite skill, as in the Red Sea the living and breathing pearl is torn from the rocks, while in Britain they are gathered just as they are thrown up. I could myself more readily believe that the natural properties of the pearls are in fault than our keenness for gain.

The Britons themselves bear cheerfully the conscription, the taxes, and the other burdens imposed on them by the Empire, if there be no oppression. Of this they are impatient; they are reduced to subjection, not as yet to slavery. The deified Julius, the very first Roman who entered Britain with an army, though by a successful engagement he struck terror into the inhabitants and gained possession of the coast, must be regarded as having indicated rather than transmitted the acquisition to future generations. Then came the civil wars, and the arms of our leaders were turned against their country, and even when there was peace, there was a long neglect of Britain. This Augustus spoke of as policy, Tiberius as an inherited maxim. That Caius Caesar meditated an invasion of Britain is perfectly clear, but his purposes, rapidly formed, were easily changed, and his vast attempts on Germany had failed. Claudius was the first to renew the attempt, and conveyed over into the island some legions and auxiliaries, choosing Vespasian to share with him the campaign, whose approaching elevation had this beginning. Several tribes were subdued and kings made prisoners, and destiny learned to know its favorite.

Aulus Plautius was the first governor of consular rank, and Ostorius Scapula the next. Both were famous soldiers, and by degrees the nearest portions of Britain were brought into the condition of a province, and a colony of veterans was also introduced. Some of the states were given to King Cogidumnus, who lived down to our day a most faithful ally. So was maintained the ancient and long-recognized practice of the Roman people, which seeks to secure among the instruments of dominion even kings themselves. Soon after, Didius Gallus consolidated the conquests of his predecessors, and advanced a very few positions into parts more remote, to gain the credit of having enlarged the sphere of government. Didius was succeeded by Veranius, who died within the year. Then Suetonius Paulinus enjoyed success for two years; he subdued several tribes and strengthened our military posts. Thus encouraged, he made an attempt on the island of Mona, as a place from which the rebels drew reinforcements; but in doing this he left his rear open to attack.

Relieved from apprehension by the legate's absence, the Britons dwelt much among themselves on the miseries of subjection, compared their wrongs, and exaggerated them in the discussion. "All we get by patience," they said, "is that heavier demands are exacted from us, as from men who will readily submit. A single king once ruled us; now two are set over us; a legate to tyrannize over our lives, a procurator to tyrannize over our property. Their quarrels and their harmony are alike ruinous to their subjects. The centurions of the one, the slaves of the other, combine violence with insult. Nothing is now safe from their avarice, nothing from their lust. In war it is the strong who plunders; now, it is for the most part by cowards and poltroons that our homes are rifled, our children torn from us, the conscription enforced, as though it were for our country alone that we could not die. For, after all, what a mere handful of soldiers has crossed over, if we Britons look at our own numbers. Germany did thus actually shake off the yoke, and yet its defense was a river, not the ocean. With us, fatherland, wives, parents, are the motives to war; with them, only greed and profligacy. They will surely fly, as did the now deified Julius, if once we emulate the valor of our sires. Let us not be panic-stricken at the result of one or two engagements. The miserable have more fury and greater resolution. Now even the gods are beginning to pity us, for they are keeping away the Roman general, and detaining his army far from us in another island. We have already taken the hardest step; we are deliberating. And indeed, in all such designs, to dare is less perilous than to be detected."

Rousing each other by this and like language, under the leadership of Boudicca, a woman of kingly descent (for they admit no distinction of sex in their royal successions), they all rose in arms. They fell upon our troops, which were scattered on garrison duty, stormed the forts, and burst into the colony itself, the headquarters, as they thought, of tyranny. In their rage and their triumph, they spared no variety of a barbarian's cruelty. Had not Paulinus on hearing of the outbreak in the province rendered prompt succor, Britain would have been lost. By one successful engagement, he brought it back to its former obedience, though many, troubled by the conscious guilt of rebellion and by particular dread of the legate, still clung to their arms. Excellent as he was in other respects, his policy to the conquered was arrogant, and exhibited the cruelty of one who was avenging private wrongs. Accordingly Petronius Turpilianus was sent out to initiate a milder rule. A stranger to the enemy's misdeeds and so more accessible to their penitence, he put an end to old troubles, and, attempting nothing more, handed the province over to Trebellius Maximus. Trebellius, who was somewhat indolent, and never ventured on a campaign, controlled the province by a certain courtesy in his administration. Even the barbarians now learned to excuse many attractive vices, and the occurrence of the civil war gave a good pretext for inaction. But we were sorely troubled with mutiny, as troops habituated to service grew demoralized by idleness. Trebellius, who had escaped the soldiers' fury by flying and hiding himself, governed henceforth on sufferance, a disgraced and humbled man. It was a kind of bargain; the soldiers had their license, the general had his life; and so the mutiny cost no bloodshed. Nor did Vettius Bolanus, during the continuance of the civil wars, trouble Britain with discipline. There was the same inaction with respect to the enemy, and similar unruliness in the camp, only Bolanus, an upright man, whom no misdeeds made odious, had secured affection in default of the power of control.

When however Vespasian had restored to unity Britain as well as the rest of the world, in the presence of great generals and renowned armies the enemy's hopes were crushed. They were at once panic-stricken by the attack of Petilius Cerialis on the state of the Brigantes, said to be the most prosperous in the entire province. There were many battles, some by no means bloodless, and his conquests, or at least his wars, embraced a large part of the territory of the Brigantes. Indeed he would have altogether thrown into the shade the activity and renown of any other successor; but Julius Frontinus was equal to the burden, a great man as far as greatness was then possible, who subdued by his arms the powerful and warlike tribe of the Silures, surmounting the difficulties of the country as well as the valor of the enemy.

Such was the state of Britain, and such were the vicissitudes of the war, which Agricola found on his crossing over about midsummer. Our soldiers made it a pretext for carelessness, as if all fighting was over, and the enemy were biding their time. The Ordovices, shortly before Agricola's arrival, had destroyed nearly the whole of a squadron of allied cavalry quartered in their territory. Such a beginning raised the hopes of the country, and all who wished for war approved the precedent, and anxiously watched the temper of the new governor. Meanwhile Agricola, though summer was past and the detachments were scattered throughout the province, though the soldiers' confident anticipation of inaction for that year would be a source of delay and difficulty in beginning a campaign, and most advisers thought it best simply to watch all weak points, resolved to face the peril. He collected a force of veterans and a small body of auxiliaries; then as the Ordovices would not venture to descend into the plain, he put himself in front of the ranks to inspire all with the same courage against a common danger, and led his troops up a hill. The tribe was all but exterminated.

Well aware that he must follow up the prestige of his arms, and that in proportion to his first success would be the terror of the other tribes, he formed the design of subjugating the island of Mona, from the occupation of which Paulinus had been recalled, as I have already related, by the rebellion of the entire province. But, as his plans were not matured, he had no fleet. The skill and resolution of the general accomplished the passage. With some picked men of the auxiliaries, disencumbered of all baggage, who knew the shallows and had that national experience in swimming which enables the Britons to take care not only of themselves but of their arms and horses, he delivered so unexpected an attack that the astonished enemy who were looking for a fleet, a naval armament, and an assault by sea, thought that to such assailants nothing could be formidable or invincible. And so, peace having been sued for and the island given up, Agricola became great and famous as one who, when entering on his province, a time which others spend in vain display and a round of ceremonies, chose rather toil and danger. Nor did he use his success for self-glorification, or apply the name of campaigns and victories to the repression of a conquered people. He did not even describe his achievements in a laureled letter. Yet by thus disguising his renown he really increased it, for men inferred the grandeur of his aspirations from his silence about services so great.

Next, with thorough insight into the feelings of his province, and taught also, by the experience of others, that little is gained by conquest if followed by oppression, he determined to root out the causes of war. Beginning first with himself and his dependants, he kept his household under restraint, a thing as hard to many as ruling a province. He transacted no public business through freedmen or slaves; no private leanings, no recommendations or entreaties of friends, moved him in the selection of centurions and soldiers, but it was ever the best man whom he thought most trustworthy. He knew everything, but did not always act on his knowledge. Trifling errors he treated with leniency, serious offenses with severity. Nor was it always punishment, but far oftener penitence, which satisfied him. He preferred to give office and power to men who would not transgress, rather than have to condemn a transgressor. He lightened the exaction of corn and tribute by an equal distribution of the burden, while he got rid of those contrivances for gain which were more intolerable than the tribute itself. Hitherto the people had been compelled to endure the farce of waiting by the closed granary and of purchasing corn unnecessarily and raising it to a fictitious price. Difficult byroads and distant places were fixed for them, so that states with a winter camp close to them had to carry corn to remote and inaccessible parts of the country, until what was within the reach of all became a source of profit to the few.

Agricola, by the repression of these abuses in his very first year of office, restored to peace its good name, when, from either the indifference or the harshness of his predecessors, it had come to be as much dreaded as war. When, however, summer came, assembling his forces, he continually showed himself in the ranks, praised good discipline, and kept the stragglers in order. He would himself choose the position of the camp, himself explore the estuaries and forests. Meanwhile he would allow the enemy no rest, laying waste his territory with sudden incursions, and, having sufficiently alarmed him, would then by forbearance display the allurements of peace. In consequence, many states, which up to that time had been independent, gave hostages, and laid aside their animosities; garrisons and forts were established among them with a skill and diligence with which no newly-acquired part of Britain had before been treated.

The following winter passed without disturbance, and was employed in salutary measures. For, to accustom to rest and repose through the charms of luxury a population scattered and barbarous and therefore inclined to war, Agricola gave private encouragement and public aid to the building of temples, courts of justice and dwelling houses, praising the energetic, and reproving the indolent. Thus an honorable rivalry took the place of compulsion. He likewise provided a liberal education for the sons of the chiefs, and showed such a preference for the natural powers of the Britons over the industry of the Gauls that they who lately disdained the tongue of Rome now coveted its eloquence. Hence, too, a liking sprang up for our style of dress, and the "toga" became fashionable. Step by step they were led to things which dispose to vice, the lounge, the bath, the elegant banquet. All this in their ignorance they called civilization, when it was but a part of their servitude.

The third year of his campaigns opened up new tribes, our ravages on the native population being carried as far as the Taus, an estuary so called. This struck such terror into the enemy that he did not dare to attack our army, harassed though it was by violent storms; and there was even time for the erection of forts. It was noted by experienced officers that no general had ever shown more judgment in choosing suitable positions, and that not a single fort established by Agricola was either stormed by the enemy or abandoned by capitulation or flight. Sorties were continually made; for these positions were secured from protracted siege by a year's supply. So winter brought with it no alarms, and each garrison could hold its own, as the baffled and despairing enemy, who had been accustomed often to repair his summer losses by winter successes, found himself repelled alike both in summer and winter.

Never did Agricola in a greedy spirit appropriate the achievements of others; the centurion and the prefect both found in him an impartial witness of their every action. Some persons used to say that he was too harsh in his reproofs, and that he was as severe to the bad as he was gentle to the good. But his displeasure left nothing behind it; reserve and silence in him were not to be dreaded. He thought it better to show anger than to cherish hatred.

The fourth summer he employed in securing what he had overrun. Had the valor of our armies and the renown of the Roman name permitted it, a limit to our conquests might have been found in Britain itself. Clota and Bodotria, estuaries which the tides of two opposite seas carry far back into the country, are separated by but a narrow strip of land.

This Agricola then began to defend with a line of forts, and, as all the country to the south was now occupied, the enemy were pushed into what might be called another island.

In the fifth year of the war Agricola, himself in the leading ship, crossed the Clota, and subdued in a series of victories tribes hitherto unknown. In that part of Britain which looks towards Ireland, he posted some troops, hoping for fresh conquests rather than fearing attack, inasmuch as Ireland, being between Britain and Spain and conveniently situated for the seas round Gaul, might have been the means of connecting with great mutual benefit the most powerful parts of the empire. Its extent is small when compared with Britain, but exceeds the islands of our seas. In soil and climate, in the disposition, temper, and habits of its population, it differs but little from Britain. We know most of its harbors and approaches, and that through the intercourse of commerce. One of the petty kings of the nation, driven out by internal faction, had been received by Agricola, who detained him under the semblance of friendship till he could make use of him. I have often heard him say that a single legion with a few auxiliaries could conquer and occupy Ireland, and that it would have a salutary effect on Britain for the Roman arms to be seen everywhere, and for freedom, so to speak, to be banished from its sight.

In the summer in which he entered on the sixth year of his office, his operations embraced the states beyond Bodotria, and, as he dreaded a general movement among the remoter tribes, as well as the perils which would beset an invading army, he explored the harbors with a fleet, which, at first employed by him as an integral part of his force, continued to accompany him. The spectacle of war thus pushed on at once by sea and land was imposing; while often infantry, cavalry, and marines, mingled in the same encampment and joyously sharing the same meals, would dwell on their own achievements and adventures, comparing, with a soldier's boastfulness, at one time the deep recesses of the forest and the mountain with the dangers of waves and storms, or, at another, battles by land with victories over the ocean. The Britons too, as we learned from the prisoners, were confounded by the sight of a fleet, as if, now that their inmost seas were penetrated, the conquered had their last refuge closed against them. The tribes inhabiting Caledonia flew to arms, and with great preparations, made greater by the rumors which always exaggerate the unknown, themselves advanced to attack our fortresses, and thus challenging a conflict, inspired us with alarm. To retreat south of the Bodotria, and to retire rather than to be driven out, was the advice of timid pretenders to prudence, when Agricola learned that the enemy's attack would be made with more than one army. Fearing that their superior numbers and their knowledge of the country might enable them to hem him in, he too distributed his forces into three divisions, and so advanced.

This becoming known to the enemy, they suddenly changed their plan, and with their whole force attacked by night the ninth Legion, as being the weakest, and cutting down the sentries, who were asleep or panic-stricken, they broke into the camp. And now the battle was raging within the camp itself, when Agricola, who had learned from his scouts the enemy's line of march and had kept close on his track, ordered the most active soldiers of his cavalry and infantry to attack the rear of the assailants, while the entire army were shortly to raise a shout. Soon his standards glittered in the light of daybreak. A double peril thus alarmed the Britons, while the courage of the Romans revived; and feeling sure of safety, they now fought for glory. In their turn they rushed to the attack, and there was a furious conflict within the narrow passages of the gates till the enemy were routed. Both armies did their utmost, the one for the honor of having given aid, the other for that of not having needed support. Had not the flying enemy been sheltered by morasses and forests, this victory would have ended the war.

Knowing this, and elated by their glory, our army exclaimed that nothing could resist their valor—that they must penetrate the recesses of Caledonia, and at length after an unbroken succession of battles, discover the furthest limits of Britain. Those who but now were cautious and prudent became after the event eager and boastful. It is the singularly unfair peculiarity of war that the credit of success is claimed by all, while a disaster is attributed to one alone. But the Britons thinking themselves baffled, not so much by our valor as by our general's skillful use of an opportunity, abated nothing of their arrogant demeanor, arming their youth, removing their wives and children to a place of safety, and assembling together to ratify, with sacred rites, a confederacy of all their states. Thus, with angry feelings on both sides, the combatants parted.

The same summer a Usipian cohort, which had been levied in Germany and transported into Britain, ventured on a great and memorable exploit. Having killed a centurion and some soldiers, who, to impart military discipline, had been incorporated with their ranks and were employed at once to instruct and command them, they embarked on board three swift galleys with pilots pressed into their service. Under the direction of one of them—for two of the three they suspected and consequently put to death—they sailed past the coast in the strangest way before any rumor about them was in circulation. After a while, dispersing in search of water and provisions, they encountered many of the Britons, who sought to defend their property. Often victorious, though now and then beaten, they were at last reduced to such an extremity of want as to be compelled to eat, at first, the feeblest of their number, and then victims selected by lot. Having sailed round Britain and lost their vessels from not knowing how to manage them, they were looked upon as pirates and were intercepted, first by the Suevi and then by the Frisii. Some who were sold as slaves in the way of trade, and were brought through the process of barter as far as our side of the Rhine, gained notoriety by the disclosure of this extraordinary adventure.

Early in the summer Agricola sustained a domestic affliction in the loss of a son born a year before, a calamity which he endured, neither with the ostentatious fortitude displayed by many brave men, nor, on the other hand, with womanish tears and grief. In his sorrow he found one source of relief in war. Having sent on a fleet, which by its ravages at various points might cause a vague and widespread alarm, he advanced with a lightly equipped force, including in its ranks some Britons of remarkable bravery, whose fidelity had been tried through years of peace, as far as the Grampian Mountains, which the enemy had already occupied. For the Britons, indeed, in no way cowed by the result of the late engagement, had made up their minds to be either avenged or enslaved, and convinced at length that a common danger must be averted by union, had, by embassies and treaties, summoned forth the whole strength of all their states. More than 30,000 armed men were now to be seen, and still there were pressing in all the youth of the country, with all whose old age was yet hale and vigorous, men renowned in war and bearing each decorations of his own. Meanwhile, among the many leaders, one superior to the rest in valor and in birth, Galgacus by name, is said to have thus harangued the multitude gathered around him and clamoring for battle:

"Whenever I consider the origin of this war and the necessities of our position, I have a sure confidence that this day, and this union of yours, will be the beginning of freedom to the whole of Britain. To all of us slavery is a thing unknown; there are no lands beyond us, and even the sea is not safe, menaced as we are by a Roman fleet. And thus in war and battle, in which the brave find glory, even the coward will find safety. Former contests, in which, with varying fortune, the Romans were resisted, still left in us a last hope of succor, inasmuch as being the most renowned nation of Britain, dwelling in the very heart of the country, and out of sight of the shores of the conquered, we could keep even our eyes unpolluted by the contagion of slavery. To us who dwell on the uttermost confines of the earth and of freedom, this remote sanctuary of Britain's glory has up to this time been a defense. Now, however, the furthest limits of Britain are thrown open, and the unknown always passes for the marvelous. But there are no tribes beyond us, nothing indeed but waves and rocks, and the yet more terrible Romans, from whose oppression escape is vainly sought by obedience and submission. Robbers of the world, having by their universal plunder exhausted the land, they rifle the deep. If the enemy be rich, they are rapacious; if he be poor, they lust for dominion; neither the east nor the west has been able to satisfy them. Alone among men they covet with equal eagerness poverty and riches. To robbery, slaughter, plunder, they give the lying name of empire; they make a solitude and call it peace.

"Nature has willed that every man's children and kindred should be his dearest objects. Yet these are torn from us by conscriptions to be slaves elsewhere. Our wives and our sisters, even though they may escape violation from the enemy, are dishonored under the names of friendship and hospitality. Our goods and fortunes they collect for their tribute, our harvests for their granaries. Our very hands and bodies, under the lash and in the midst of insult, are worn down by the toil of clearing forests and morasses. Creatures born to slavery are sold once for all, and are, moreover, fed by their masters; but Britain is daily purchasing, is daily feeding, her own enslaved people. And as in a household the last comer among the slaves is always the butt of his companions, so we in a world long used to slavery, as the newest and the most contemptible, are marked out for destruction. We have neither fruitful plains, nor mines, nor harbors, for the working of which we may be spared. Valor, too, and high spirit in subjects, are offensive to rulers; besides, remoteness and seclusion, while they give safety, provoke suspicion. Since then you cannot hope for quarter, take courage, I beseech you, whether it be safety or renown that you hold most precious. Under a woman's leadership the Brigantes were able to burn a colony, to storm a camp, and had not success ended in supineness, might have thrown off the yoke. Let us, then, a fresh and unconquered people, never likely to abuse our freedom, show forthwith at the very first onset what heroes Caledonia has in reserve.

"Do you suppose that the Romans will be as brave in war as they are licentious in peace? To our strifes and discords they owe their fame, and they turn the errors of an enemy to the renown of their own army, an army which, composed as it is of every variety of nations, is held together by success and will be broken up by disaster. These Gauls and Germans, and, I blush to say, these numerous Britons, who, though they lend their lives to support a stranger's rule, have been its enemies longer than its subjects, you cannot imagine to be bound by fidelity and affection. Fear and terror there certainly are, feeble bonds of attachment; remove them, and those who have ceased to fear will begin to hate. All the incentives to victory are on our side. The Romans have no wives to kindle their courage; no parents to taunt them with flight; many have either no country or one far away. Few in number, dismayed by their ignorance, looking around upon a sky, a sea, and forests which are all unfamiliar to them; hemmed in, as it were, and enmeshed, the Gods have delivered them into our hands. Be not frightened by idle display, by the glitter of gold and of silver, which can neither protect nor wound. In the very ranks of the enemy we shall find our own forces. Britons will acknowledge their own cause; Gauls will remember past freedom; the other Germans will abandon them, as but lately did the Usipii. Behind them there is nothing to dread. The forts are ungarrisoned; the colonies in the hands of aged men; what with disloyal subjects and oppressive rulers, the towns are ill-affected and rife with discord. On the one side you have a general and an army; on the other, tribute, the mines, and all the other penalties of an enslaved people. Whether you endure these forever, or instantly avenge them, this field is to decide. Think, therefore, as you advance to battle, at once of your ancestors and of your posterity."

They received his speech with enthusiasm, and as is usual among barbarians, with songs, shouts and discordant cries. And now was seen the assembling of troops and the gleam of arms, as the boldest warriors stepped to the front. As the line was forming, Agricola, who, though his troops were in high spirits and could scarcely be kept within the entrenchments, still thought it right to encourage them, spoke as follows—

"Comrades, this is the eighth year since, thanks to the greatness and good fortune of Rome and to your own loyalty and energy, you conquered Britain. In our many campaigns and battles, whether courage in meeting the foe, or toil and endurance in struggling, I may say, against nature herself, have been needed, I have ever been well satisfied with my soldiers, and you with your commander. And so you and I have passed beyond the limits reached by former armies or by former governors, and we now occupy the last confines of Britain, not merely in rumor and report, but with an actual encampment and armed force. Britain has been both discovered and subdued. Often on the march, when morasses, mountains, and rivers were wearing out your strength, did I hear our bravest men exclaim, 'When shall we have the enemy before us?—when shall we fight?' He is now here, driven from his lair, and your wishes and your valor have free scope, and everything favors the conqueror, everything is adverse to the vanquished. For as it is a great and glorious achievement, if we press on, to have accomplished so great a march, to have traversed forests and to have crossed estuaries, so, if we retire, our present most complete success will prove our greatest danger. We have not the same knowledge of the country or the same abundance of supplies, but we have arms in our hands, and in them we have everything. For myself I have long been convinced that neither for an army nor for a general is retreat safe. Better, too, is an honorable death than a life of shame, and safety and renown are for us to be found together. And it would be no inglorious end to perish on the extreme confines of earth and of nature.

"If unknown nations and an untried enemy confronted you, I should urge you on by the example of other armies. As it is, look back upon your former honors, question your own eyes. These are the men who last year under cover of darkness attacked a single legion, whom you routed by a shout. Of all the Britons these are the most confirmed runaways, and this is why they have survived so long. Just as when the huntsman penetrates the forest and the thicket, all the most courageous animals rush out upon him, while the timid and feeble are scared away by the very sound of his approach, so the bravest of the Britons have long since fallen; and the rest are a mere crowd of spiritless cowards. You have at last found them, not because they have stood their ground, but because they have been overtaken. Their desperate plight, and the extreme terror that paralyzes them, have riveted their line to this spot, that you might achieve in it a splendid and memorable victory. Put an end to campaigns; crown your fifty years' service with a glorious day; prove to your country that her armies could never have been fairly charged with protracting a war or with causing a rebellion."

While Agricola was yet speaking, the ardor of the soldiers was rising to its height, and the close of his speech was followed by a great outburst of enthusiasm. In a moment they flew to arms. He arrayed his eager and impetuous troops in such a manner that the auxiliary infantry, 8,000 in number, strengthened his center, while 3,000 cavalry were posted on his wings. The legions were drawn up in front of the intrenched camp; his victory would be vastly more glorious if won without the loss of Roman blood, and he would have a reserve in case of repulse. The enemy, to make a formidable display, had posted himself on high ground; his van was on the plain, while the rest of his army rose in an archlike form up the slope of a hill. The plain between resounded with the noise and with the rapid movements of chariots and cavalry. Agricola, fearing that from the enemy's superiority of force he would be simultaneously attacked in front and on the flanks, widened his ranks, and though his line was likely to be too extended, and several officers advised him to bring up the legions, yet, so sanguine was he, so resolute in meeting danger, he sent away his horse and took his stand on foot before the colors.

The action began with distant fighting. The Britons with equal steadiness and skill used their huge swords and small shields to avoid or to parry the missiles of our soldiers, while they themselves poured on us a dense shower of darts, till Agricola encouraged three Batavian and two Tungrian cohorts to bring matters to the decision of close fighting with swords. Such tactics were familiar to these veteran soldiers, but were embarrassing to an enemy armed with small bucklers and unwieldy weapons. The swords of the Britons are not pointed, and do not allow them to close with the foe, or to fight in the open field. No sooner did the Batavians begin to close with the enemy, to strike them with their shields, to disfigure their faces, and overthrowing the force on the plain to advance their line up the hill, than the other auxiliary cohorts joined with eager rivalry in cutting down all the nearest of the foe. Many were left behind half-dead, some even unwounded, in the hurry of victory. Meantime the enemy's cavalry had fled, and the charioteers had mingled in the engagement of the infantry. But although these at first spread panic, they were soon impeded by the close array of our ranks and by the inequalities of the ground. The battle had anything but the appearance of a cavalry action, for men and horses were carried along in confusion together, while chariots, destitute of guidance, and terrified horses without drivers dashed as panic urged them, sideways, or in direct collision against the ranks.

Those of the Britons who, having as yet taken no part in the engagement, occupied the hilltops, and who without fear for themselves sat idly disdaining the smallness of our numbers, had begun gradually to descend and to hem in the rear of the victorious army, when Agricola, who feared this very movement, opposed their advance with four squadrons of cavalry held in reserve by him for any sudden emergencies of battle. Their repulse and rout was as severe as their onset had been furious.

Thus the enemy's design recoiled on himself, and the cavalry which by the general's order had wheeled round from the van of the contending armies attacked his rear. Then, indeed, the open plain presented an awful and hideous spectacle. Our men pursued, wounded, made prisoners of the fugitives only to slaughter them when others fell in their way. And now the enemy, as prompted by their various dispositions, fled in whole battalions with arms in their hands before a few pursuers, while some, who were unarmed, actually rushed to the front and gave themselves up to death. Everywhere there lay scattered arms, corpses, and mangled limbs, and the earth reeked with blood. Even the conquered now and then felt a touch of fury and of courage. On approaching the woods, they rallied, and as they knew the ground, they were able to pounce on the foremost and least cautious of the pursuers. Had not Agricola, who was present everywhere, ordered a force of strong and lightly equipped cohorts, with some dismounted troopers for the denser parts of the forest, and a detachment of cavalry where it was not so thick, to scour the woods like a party of huntsmen, serious loss would have been sustained through the excessive confidence of our troops. When, however, the enemy saw that we again pursued them in firm and compact array, they fled no longer in masses as before, each looking for his comrade; but dispersing and avoiding one another, they sought the shelter of distant and pathless wilds. Night and weariness of bloodshed put an end to the pursuit. About 10,000 of the enemy were slain; on our side there fell 360 men, and among them Aulus Atticus, the commander of the cohort, whose youthful impetuosity and mettlesome steed had borne him into the midst of the enemy.

Elated by their victory and their booty, the conquerors passed a night of merriment. Meanwhile the Britons, wandering amidst the mingled wailings of men and women, were dragging off their wounded, calling to the unhurt, deserting their homes, and in their rage actually firing them, choosing places of concealment only instantly to abandon them. One moment they would take counsel together, the next, part company, while the sight of those who were dearest to them sometimes melted their hearts, but oftener roused their fury. It was an undoubted fact that some of them vented their rage on their wives and children, as if in pity for their lot. The following day showed more fully the extent of the calamity, for the silence of desolation reigned everywhere: the hills were forsaken, houses were smoking in the distance, and no one was seen by the scouts. These were dispatched in all directions; and it having been ascertained that the track of the flying enemy was uncertain, and that there was no attempt at rallying, it being also impossible, as summer was now over, to extend the war, Agricola led back his army into the territory of the Boresti. He received hostages from them, and then ordered the commander of the fleet to sail round Britain. A force for this purpose was given him, which great panic everywhere preceded. Agricola himself, leading his infantry and cavalry by slow marches, so as to overawe the newly-conquered tribes by the very tardiness of his progress, brought them into winter quarters, while the fleet with propitious breezes and great renown entered the harbor of Trutulium, to which it had returned after having coasted along the entire southern shore of the island.

Of this series of events, though not exaggerated in the dispatches of Agricola by any boastfulness of language, Domitian heard, as was his wont, with joy in his face but anxiety in his heart. He felt conscious that all men laughed at his late mock triumph over Germany, for which there had been purchased from traders people whose dress and hair might be made to resemble those of captives, whereas now a real and splendid victory, with the destruction of thousands of the enemy, was being celebrated with just applause. It was, he thought, a very alarming thing for him that the name of a subject should be raised above that of the Emperor; it was to no purpose that he had driven into obscurity the pursuit of forensic eloquence and the graceful accomplishments of civil life, if another were to forestall the distinctions of war. To other glories he could more easily shut his eyes, but the greatness of a good general was a truly imperial quality. Harassed by these anxieties, and absorbed in an incommunicable trouble, a sure prognostic of some cruel purpose, he decided that it was best for the present to suspend his hatred until the freshness of Agricola's renown and his popularity with the army should begin to pass away.

For Agricola was still the governor of Britain. Accordingly the Emperor ordered that the usual triumphal decorations, the honor of a laureled statue, and all that is commonly given in place of the triumphal procession, with the addition of many laudatory expressions, should be decreed in the senate, together with a hint to the effect that Agricola was to have the province of Syria, then vacant by the death of Atilius Rufus, a man of consular rank, and generally reserved for men of distinction. It was believed by many persons that one of the freedmen employed on confidential services was sent to Agricola, bearing a dispatch in which Syria was offered him, and with instructions to deliver it should he be in Britain; that this freedman in crossing the straits met Agricola, and without even saluting him made his way back to Domitian;

though I cannot say whether the story is true, or is only a fiction invented to suit the Emperor's character.

Meanwhile Agricola had handed over his province in peace and safety to his successor. And not to make his entrance into Rome conspicuous by the concourse of welcoming throngs, he avoided the attentions of his friends by entering the city at night, and at night too, according to orders, proceeded to the palace, where, having been received with a hurried embrace and without a word being spoken, he mingled in the crowd of courtiers. Anxious henceforth to temper the military renown, which annoys men of peace, with other merits, he studiously cultivated retirement and leisure, simple in dress, courteous in conversation, and never accompanied but by one or two friends, so that the many who commonly judge of great men by their external grandeur, after having seen and attentively surveyed him, asked the secret of a greatness which but few could explain.

During this time he was frequently accused before Domitian in his absence, and in his absence acquitted. The cause of his danger lay not in any crime, nor in any complaint of injury, but in a ruler who was the foe of virtue, in his own renown, and in that worst class of enemies—the men who praise. And then followed such days for the commonwealth as would not suffer Agricola to be forgotten; days when so many of our armies were lost in Moesia, Dacia, Germany, and Pannonia, through the rashness or cowardice of our generals, when so many of our officers were besieged and captured with so many of our auxiliaries, when it was no longer the boundaries of empire and the banks of rivers which were imperiled, but the winter quarters of our legions and the possession of our territories. And so when disaster followed upon disaster, and the entire year was marked by destruction and slaughter, the voice of the people called Agricola to the command; for they all contrasted his vigor, firmness, and experience in war, with the inertness and timidity of other generals. This talk, it is quite certain, assailed the ears of the Emperor himself, while affection and loyalty in the best of his freedmen, malice and envy in the worst, kindled the anger of a prince ever inclined to evil. And so at once, by his own excellences and by the faults of others, Agricola was hurried headlong to a perilous elevation.

The year had now arrived in which the proconsulate of Asia or Africa was to fall to him by lot, and, as Civica had been lately murdered, Agricola did not want a warning, or Domitian a precedent. Persons well acquainted with the Emperor's feelings came to ask Agricola, as if on their own account, whether he would go. First they hinted their purpose by praises of tranquillity and leisure; then offered their services in procuring acceptance for his excuses; and at last, throwing off all disguise, brought him by entreaties and threats to Domitian. The Emperor, armed beforehand with hypocrisy, and assuming a haughty demeanor, listened to his prayer that he might be excused, and having granted his request allowed himself to be formally thanked, nor blushed to grant so sinister a favor. But the salary usually granted to a proconsul, and which he had himself given to some governors, he did not bestow on Agricola, either because he was offended at its not having been asked, or was warned by his conscience that he might be thought to have purchased the refusal which he had commanded. It is, indeed, human nature to hate the man whom you have injured; yet the Emperor, notwithstanding his irascible temper and an implacability proportioned to his reserve, was softened by the moderation and prudence of Agricola, who neither by a perverse obstinacy nor an idle parade of freedom challenged fame or provoked his fate. Let it be known to those whose habit it is to admire the disregard of authority, that there may be great men even under bad emperors, and that obedience and submission, when joined to activity and vigor, may attain a glory which most men reach only by a perilous career, utterly useless to the state, and closed by an ostentatious death.

The end of his life, a deplorable calamity to us and a grief to his friends, was regarded with concern even by strangers and those who knew him not. The common people and this busy population continually inquired at his house, and talked of him in public places and in private gatherings. No man when he heard of Agricola's death could either be glad or at once forget it. Men's sympathy was increased by a prevalent rumor that he was destroyed by poison. For myself, I have nothing which I should venture to state for fact. Certainly during the whole of his illness the Emperor's chief freedmen and confidential physicians came more frequently than is usual with a court which pays its visits by means of messengers. This was, perhaps, solicitude, perhaps espionage. Certain it is, that on the last day the very agonies of his dying moments were reported by a succession of couriers, and no one believed that there would be such haste about tidings which would be heard with regret. Yet in his manner and countenance the Emperor displayed some signs of sorrow, for he could now forget his enmity, and it was easier to conceal his joy than his fear. It was well known that on reading the will, in which he was named coheir with Agricola's excellent wife and most dutiful daughter, he expressed delight, as if it had been a complimentary choice. So blinded and perverted was his mind by incessant flattery that he did not know that it was only a bad Emperor whom a good father would make his heir.

Agricola was born on the 13th of June, in the third consulate of Caius Caesar; he died on the 23rd of August, during the consulate of Collega and Priscus, being in the fifty-sixth year of his age. Should posterity wish to know something of his appearance, it was graceful rather than commanding. There was nothing formidable in his appearance; a gracious look predominated. One would easily believe him a good man, and willingly believe him to be great. As for himself, though taken from us in the prime of a vigorous manhood, yet, as far as glory is concerned, his life was of the longest. Those true blessings, indeed, which consist in virtue, he had fully attained; and on one who had reached the honors of a consulate and a triumph, what more had fortune to bestow? Immense wealth had no attractions for him, and wealth he had, even to splendor. As his daughter and his wife survived him, it may be thought that he was even fortunate—fortunate, in that while his honors had suffered no eclipse, while his fame was at its height, while his kindred and his friends still prospered, he escaped from the evil to come. For, though to survive until the dawn of this most happy age and to see a Trajan on the throne was what he would speculate upon in previsions and wishes confided to my ears, yet he had this mighty compensation for his premature death, that he was spared those later years during which Domitian, leaving now no interval or breathing space of time, but, as it were, with one continuous blow, drained the lifeblood of the Commonwealth.

Agricola did not see the senate house besieged, or the senate hemmed in by armed men, or so many of our consulars falling at one single massacre, or so many of Rome's noblest ladies exiles and fugitives. Carus Metius had as yet the distinction of but one victory, and the noisy counsels of Messalinus were not heard beyond the walls of Alba, and Massa Baebius was then answering for his life. It was not long before our hands dragged Helvidius to prison, before we gazed on the dying looks of Manricus and Rusticus, before we were steeped in Senecio's innocent blood. Even Nero turned his eyes away, and did not gaze upon the atrocities which he ordered; with Domitian it was the chief part of our miseries to see and to be seen, to know that our sighs were being recorded, to have, ever ready to note the pallid looks of so many faces, that savage countenance reddened with the hue with which he defied shame.

Thou wast indeed fortunate, Agricola, not only in the splendor of thy life, but in the opportune moment of thy death. Thou submittedst to thy fate, so they tell us who were present to hear thy last words, with courage and cheerfulness, seeming to be doing all thou couldst to give thine Emperor full acquittal. As for me and thy daughter, besides all the bitterness of a father's loss, it increases our sorrow that it was not permitted us to watch over thy failing health, to comfort thy weakness, to satisfy ourselves with those looks, those embraces. Assuredly we should have received some precepts, some utterances to fix in our inmost hearts. This is the bitterness of our sorrow, this the smart of our wound, that from the circumstance of so long an absence thou wast lost to us four years before. Doubtless, best of fathers, with that most loving wife at thy side, all the dues of affection were abundantly paid thee, yet with too few tears thou wast laid to thy rest, and in the light of thy last day there was something for which thine eyes longed in vain.

If there is any dwelling place for the spirits of the just; if, as the wise believe, noble souls do not perish with the body, rest thou in peace; and call us, thy family, from weak regrets and womanish laments to the contemplation of thy virtues, for which we must not weep nor beat the breast. Let us honor thee not so much with transitory praises as with our reverence, and, if our powers permit us, with our emulation. That will be true respect, that the true affection of thy nearest kin. This, too, is what I would enjoin on daughter and wife, to honor the memory of that father, that husband, by pondering in their hearts all his words and acts, by cherishing the features and lineaments of his character rather than those of his person. It is not that I would forbid the likenesses which are wrought in marble or in bronze; but as the faces of men, so all similitudes of the face are weak and perishable things, while the fashion of the soul is everlasting, such as may be expressed not in some foreign substance, or by the help of art, but in our own lives. Whatever we loved, whatever we admired in Agricola, survives, and will survive in the hearts of men, in the succession of the ages, in the fame that waits on noble deeds. Over many indeed, of those who have gone before, as over the inglorious and ignoble, the waves of oblivion will roll; Agricola, made known to posterity by history and tradition, will live forever.

François Guizot

1787–1874

Frrançois Pierre Guillaume Guizot is famous both as a historian and as a statesman. As a historian, he is the author of several important works on European history; as a statesman, he had a long and impressive political career, climaxed by his becoming chief minister of the government of France.

Guizot was born at Nîmes, France, in 1787. His father died on the scaffold in 1794, a victim of the Reign of Terror which followed the French Revolution. François and his mother fled to Geneva, where he remained until he was eighteen. In 1805 he went to Paris to study law. He soon abandoned the law to do literary and historical work, including an annotated translation of Gibbon's *Decline and Fall of the Roman Empire*.[1] His writings brought him considerable fame, and at the age of 25 he was appointed professor of modern history at the famous Sorbonne in Paris.

Guizot's political career began in 1814, when he became a member of the government formed under Louis XVIII, the restored monarch of France. Though he was a conservative and a monarchist, Guizot's political views were too liberal for the king, and he soon fell out of favor. In 1820 he left the government and returned to his lectures at the Sorbonne.

Guizot's political opinions were even less acceptable to Louis's successor, Charles X, and in 1822 he was forbidden to continue his lectures. During the next few years, he did his most important historical research and writing. His works of this period include: *History of Representative Government, History of the English Revolution, History of Civilization in Europe*, and *History of Civilization in*

---

[1] See *Great Books of the Western World*, Vols. 40 and 41.

France. In 1828, as the result of a change in government, he was permitted to resume his lectures. He was enthusiastically received upon his return to the podium, and the lectures he gave during the next two years were very popular. His lecture on "Civilization" was the first of this series.

Guizot returned to political life in 1830, when he was elected to the Chamber of Deputies. He was appointed to various ministry positions during the next decade, and in 1840 he was named Minister of Foreign Affairs. This made him head of the government. He held that position until his government fell in 1848. One of his chief political opponents during this period was Alexis de Tocqueville. The downfall of Guizot's government is usually attributed to his unwillingness to make any concessions of principle.

Guizot never again took part in French politics. After a brief exile in London, he returned to France to write his memoirs and a history of France for young people. He died in 1874 at the age of 86.

Civilization and civilized are words we come across frequently in reading and in conversation. We usually pass over them quickly because we feel certain that we know what they mean. But how well do we understand them? Do we know what standards are used to determine whether a nation or a people is civilized? Do we know what qualities must be present in a culture for it to be considered a civilization? Most of us do not. No doubt it would be impossible to arrive at definitions for these terms which would satisfy everyone, but we can find out how a great historian of culture defines them by reading Guizot's lecture on "Civilization."

Guizot maintains that the most essential element in a civilization is progress: "The idea of progress, of development, appears to me the fundamental idea contained in the word civilization." The progress should be both social and individual. By social progress Guizot means a constant advance toward "an increasing production of the means of giving strength and happiness to society" and "a more equitable distribution, among individuals, of the strength." The progress of the individual is marked by "the development of the individual, internal life, the development of man himself, of his faculties, his sentiments, his ideas." Though at times it may appear that progress takes place in one of these areas and not in the other, Guizot insists that this cannot happen. "All the great developments of the internal man," he writes, "have turned to the profit of society; all the great developments of the social state to the profit of individual man."

In recent years, when discussing nations and peoples, we have tried to avoid using such words as uncivilized and barbaric because they seem to suggest inferiority. Instead we use words like underdeveloped and emergent. In a similar fashion, we substitute advanced and industrialized for civilized. But these substituted words are almost as difficult to define as the words they replace. What are the characteristics of an underdeveloped nation? What is an advanced society? It is important that we find answers to questions like these, so that we will know in what direction we should attempt to lead the peoples of the emergent nations. Guizot's discussion of the concept of civilization will help us to answer them.

Civilization

from *History of Civilization in Europe* [1]

I have used the term European civilization, because it is evident that there is a European civilization; that a certain unity pervades the civilization of the various European states; that, notwithstanding infinite diversities of time, place and circumstance, this civilization takes its first rise in facts almost wholly similar, proceeds everywhere upon the same principles, and tends to produce well-nigh everywhere analogous results. There is, then, a European civilization, and it is to the subject of this aggregate civilization that I will request your attention.

Again, it is evident that this civilization cannot be traced back, that its history cannot be derived from the history of any single European state. If, on the one hand, it is manifestly characterized by brevity, on the other, its variety is no less prodigious; it has not developed itself with completeness in any one particular country. The features of its physiognomy are widespread; we must seek the elements of its history, now in France, now in England, now in Germany, now in Spain.

We of France occupy a favorable position for pursuing the study of European civilization. Flattery of individuals, even of our country, should be at all times avoided: it is without vanity, I think, we may say that France has been the center, the focus of European civilization. I do not pretend, it were monstrous to do so, that she has always, and in every direction, marched at the head of nations. At different epochs, Italy has taken the lead of her, in the arts; England, in political institutions; and there may be other respects under which, at particular periods, other European nations have manifested a superiority to her; but it is impossi-

1. Omitted here are the opening remarks in which Guizot announces to his lecture audience his intention to treat of the history of European civilization, its origin, its progress, its aim, and its character [Ed.].

ble to deny that whenever France has seen herself thus outstripped in the career of civilization, she has called up fresh vigor, has sprung forward with a new impulse, and has soon found herself abreast with, or in advance of, all the rest. And not only has this been the peculiar fortune of France, but we have seen that when the civilizing ideas and institutions which have taken their rise in other lands have sought to extend their sphere, to become fertile and general, to operate for the common benefit of European civilization, they have been necessitated to undergo, to a certain extent, a new preparation in France; and it has been from France, as from a second native country, that they have gone forth to the conquest of Europe. There is scarcely any great idea, any great principle of civilization which, prior to its diffusion, has not passed in this way through France.

And for this reason: there is in the French character something sociable, something sympathetic, something which makes its way with greater facility and effect than does the national genius of any other people; whether from our language, whether from the turn of our mind, of our manners, certain it is that our ideas are more popular than those of other people, present themselves more clearly and intelligibly to the masses and penetrate among them more readily; in a word, perspicuity, sociability, sympathy are the peculiar characteristics of France, of her civilization, and it is these qualities which rendered her eminently fit to march at the very head of European civilization.

In entering, therefore, upon the study of this great fact, it is no arbitrary or conventional choice to take France as the center of this study; we must needs do so if we would place ourselves, as it were, in the very heart of civilization, in the very heart of the fact we are about to consider.

I use the term *fact*, and I do so purposely; civilization is a fact like any other—a fact susceptible, like any other, of being studied, described, narrated.

For some time past, there has been much talk of the necessity of limiting history to the narration of facts: nothing can be more just; but we must always bear in mind that there are far more facts to narrate, and that the facts themselves are far more various in their nature than people are at first disposed to believe; there are material, visible facts, such as wars, battles, the official acts of governments; there are moral facts, none the less real that they do not appear on the surface; there are individual facts which have denominations of their own; there are general facts, without any particular designation, to which it is impossible to assign any precise date, which it is impossible to bring within strict limits, but which are yet no less facts than the rest, historical facts, facts which we cannot exclude from history without mutilating history.

The very portion of history which we are accustomed to call its philosophy, the relation of events to each other, the connection which unites them, their causes and their effects—these are all facts, these are all history, just as much as the narratives of battles, and of other material and visible events. Facts of this class it is doubtless more difficult to disentangle and explain; we are more liable to error in giving an account of them, and it is no easy thing to give them life and animation, to exhibit them in clear and vivid colors; but this difficulty in no degree changes their nature; they are none the less an essential element of history.

Civilization is one of these facts; general, hidden, complex fact; very difficult, I allow, to describe, to relate, but which none the less for that exists, which none the less for that has a right to be described and related. We may raise as to this fact a great number of questions; we may ask, it has been asked, whether it is a good or an evil? Some bitterly deplore it; others rejoice at it. We may ask whether it is a universal fact, whether there is a universal civilization of the human species, a destiny of humanity; whether the nations have handed down from age to age something which has never been lost, which must increase, form a larger and larger mass, and thus pass on to the end of time? For my own part, I am convinced that there is, in reality, a general destiny of humanity, a transmission of the aggregate of civilization; and, consequently, a universal history of civilization to be written. But without raising questions so great, so difficult to solve, if we restrict ourselves to a definite limit of time and space, if we confine ourselves to the history of a certain number of centuries, of a certain people, it is evident that within these bounds, civilization is a fact which can be described, related—which is history. I will at once add that this history is the greatest of all, that it includes all.

And, indeed, does it not seem to yourselves that the fact civilization is the fact *par excellence*—the general and definitive fact, in which all the others terminate, into which they all resolve themselves? Take all the facts which compose the history of a nation, and which we are accustomed to regard as the elements of its life; take its institutions, its commerce, its industry, its wars, all the details of its government: when we would consider these facts in their aggregate, in their connection, when we would estimate them, judge them, we ask in what they have contributed to the civilization of that nation, what part they have taken in it, what influence they have exercised over it. It is in this way that we not only form a complete idea of them but measure and appreciate their true value; they are, as it were, rivers, of which we ask what quantity of water it is they contribute to the ocean? For civilization is a sort of ocean, constituting the wealth of a people, and on whose bosom all the elements of the life of that people, all the powers supporting its existence, assemble and unite. This is so true that even facts, which from their nature are odious, pernicious, which weigh painfully upon nations, despotism, for example, and anarchy, if they have contributed in some way to civilization, if they have enabled it to make an onward stride, up to a certain point we pardon them, we overlook their wrongs, their evil nature; in a word, wherever we recognize civilization, whatever the facts which have created it, we are tempted to forget the price it has cost.

There are, moreover, facts which, properly speaking, we cannot call social; individual facts, which seem to interest the human soul rather than the public life: such are religious creeds and philosophical ideas, sciences, letters, arts. These facts appear to address themselves to man with a view to his moral perfection, his intellectual gratification; to have for their object his internal amelioration, his mental pleasure, rather than his social condition. But, here again, it is with reference to civilization that these very facts are often considered, and claim to be considered.

At all times, in all countries, religion has assumed the glory of having civilized the people; sciences, letters, arts, all the intellectual and moral pleasures, have claimed a share in this glory; and we have deemed it a praise and an honor to them when we have recognized this claim on their part. Thus, facts the most important and sublime in themselves, independently of all external result, and simply in their relations with the soul of man, increase in importance, rise in sublimity from their affinity with civilization. Such is the value of this general fact, that it gives value to everything it touches. And not only does it give value; there are even occasions when the facts of which we speak, religious creeds, philosophical ideas, letters, arts, are especially considered and judged of with reference to their influence upon civilization; an influence which becomes, up to a certain point and during a certain time, the conclusive measure of their merit, of their value.

What, then, I will ask, before undertaking its history, what, considered only in itself, what is this so grave, so vast, so precious fact, which seems the sum, the expression of the whole life of nations?

I shall take care here not to fall into pure philosophy; not to lay down some ratiocinative principle, and then deduce from it the nature of civilization as a result; there would be many chances of error in this method. And here again we have a fact to verify and describe.

For a long period, and in many countries, the word *civilization* has been in use; people have attached to the word ideas more or less clear, more or less comprehensive; but there it is in use, and those who use it attach some meaning or other to it. It is the general, human, popular meaning of this word that we must study. There is almost always in the usual acceptation of the most general terms more accuracy than in the definitions, apparently more strict, more precise, of science. It is common sense which gives to words their ordinary signification, and common sense is the characteristic of humanity. The ordinary signification of a word is formed by gradual progress and in the constant presence of facts; so that when a fact presents itself which seems to come within the meaning of a known term, it is received into it, as it were, naturally; the signification of the term extends itself, expands, and by degrees the various facts, the various ideas which from the nature of the things themselves men should include under this word, are included.

When the meaning of a word, on the other hand, is determined by science, this determination, the work of one individual, or of a small number of individuals, takes place under the influence of some particular fact which has struck upon the mind. Thus, scientific definitions are, in general, much more narrow, and, hence, much less accurate, much less true, at bottom, than the popular meanings of the terms. In studying as a fact the meaning of the word civilization, in investigating all the ideas which are comprised within it, according to the common sense of mankind, we shall make a much greater progress toward a knowledge of the fact itself than by attempting to give it ourselves a scientific definition, however more clear and precise the latter might appear at first.

I will commence this investigation by endeavoring to place before you some hypotheses: I will describe a certain number of states of society, and we will then inquire whether general instinct would recognize in them the condition of a people civilizing itself; whether we recognize in them the meaning which mankind attaches to the word civilization.

First, suppose a people whose external life is easy, is full of physical comfort; they pay few taxes, they are free from suffering; justice is well administered in their private relations—in a word, material existence is for them altogether happy and happily regulated. But at the same time, the intellectual and moral existence of this people is studiously kept in a state of torpor and inactivity; of, I will not say, oppression, for they do not understand the feeling, but of compression. We are not without instances of this state of things. There has been a great number of small aristocratic republics in which the people have been thus treated like flocks of sheep, well kept and materially happy, but without moral and intellectual activity. Is this civilization? Is this a people civilizing itself?

Another hypothesis: here is a people whose material existence is less easy, less comfortable, but still supportable. On the other hand, moral and intellectual wants have not been neglected, a certain amount of mental pasture has been served out to them; elevated, pure sentiments are cultivated in them; their religious and moral views have attained a certain degree of development; but great care is taken to stifle in them the principle of liberty; the intellectual and moral wants, as in the former case the material wants, are satisfied; each man has meted out to him his portion of truth; no one is permitted to seek it for himself. Immobility is the characteristic of moral life; it is the state into which have fallen most of the populations of Asia; wherever theocratic dominations keep humanity in check; it is the state of the Hindus, for example. I ask the same question here as before; is this a people civilizing itself?

I change altogether the nature of the hypothesis: here is a people among whom is a great display of individual liberties, but where disorder and inequality are excessive: it is the empire of force and of chance; every man, if he is not strong, is oppressed, suffers, perishes; violence is the predominant feature of the social state. No one is ignorant that Europe has passed through this state. Is this a civilized state? It may, doubtless, contain principles of civilization which will develop themselves by successive degrees; but the fact which dominates in such a society is, assuredly, not that which the common sense of mankind calls civilization.

I take a fourth and last hypothesis: the liberty of each individual is very great, inequality among them is rare, and at all events, very transient. Every man does very nearly just what he pleases, and differs little in power from his neighbor; but there are very few general interests, very few public ideas, very little society—in a word, the faculties and existence of individuals appear and then pass away, wholly apart and without acting upon each other, or leaving any trace behind them; the successive generations leave society at the same point at which they found it: this is the state of savage tribes; liberty and equality are there, but assuredly not civilization.

I might multiply these hypotheses, but I think we have before us enough to explain what is the popular and natural meaning of the word civilization.

It is clear that none of the states I have sketched corresponds, according to the natural good sense of mankind, to this term. Why? It appears to me that the first fact comprised in the word civilization (and this results from the different examples I have rapidly placed before you) is the fact of progress, of development; it presents at once the idea of a people marching onward, not to change its place, but to change its condition; of a people whose culture is conditioning itself, and ameliorating itself. The idea of progress, of development, appears to me the fundamental idea contained in the word civilization. What is this progress? What this development? Herein is the greatest difficulty of all.

The etymology of the word would seem to answer in a clear and satisfactory manner: it says that it is the perfecting of civil life, the development of society, properly so called, of the relations of men among themselves.

Such is, in fact, the first idea which presents itself to the understanding when the word civilization is pronounced; we at once figure forth to ourselves the extension, the greatest activity, the best organization of the social relations: on the one hand, an increasing production of the means of giving strength and happiness to society; on the other, a more equitable distribution, among individuals, of the strength.

Is this all? Have we here exhausted all the natural, ordinary meaning of the word civilization? Does the fact contain nothing more than this?

It is almost as if we asked: Is the human species after all a mere ant-hill, a society in which all that is required is order and physical happiness, in which the greater the amount of labor, and the more equitable the division of the fruits of labor, the more surely is the object attained, the progress accomplished?

Our instinct at once feels repugnant to so narrow a definition of human destiny. It feels at the first glance that the word civilization comprehends something more extensive, more complex, something superior to the simple perfection of the social relations, of social power and happiness.

Fact, public opinion, the generally received meaning of the term, are in accordance with this instinct.

Take Rome in the palmy days of the republic, after the Second Punic War, at the time of its greatest virtues, when it was marching to the empire of the world, when its social state was evidently in progress. Then take Rome under Augustus, at the epoch when her decline began, when, at all events, the progressive movement of society was arrested, when evil principles were on the eve of prevailing: yet there is no one who does not think and say that the Rome of Augustus was more civilized than the Rome of Fabricius or of Cincinnatus.

Let us transport ourselves beyond the Alps: let us take the France of the seventeenth and eighteenth centuries: it is evident that, in a social point of view, considering the actual amount and distribution of happiness among individuals, the France of the seventeenth and eighteenth centuries was inferior to some other countries of Europe, to Holland and to England, for example. I believe that in Holland and in England the social activity was greater, was increasing more rapidly, distributing its fruit more fully, than in France, yet ask general good sense, and it will say that the France of the seventeenth and eighteenth centuries was the most civilized country in Europe. Europe has not hesitated in her affirmative reply to the question: traces of this public opinion, as to France, are found in all the monuments of European literature.

We might point out many other states in which the prosperity is greater, is of more rapid growth, is better distributed among individuals than elsewhere, and in which, nevertheless, by the spontaneous instinct, the general good sense of men, the civilization is judged inferior to that of countries not so well portioned out in a purely social sense.

What does this mean; what advantages do these latter countries possess? What is it gives them, in the character of civilized countries, this privilege; what so largely compensates in the opinion of mankind for what they so lack in other respects?

A development other than that of social life has been gloriously manifested by them; the development of the individual, internal life, the development of man himself, of his faculties, his sentiments, his ideas. If society with them be less perfect than elsewhere, humanity stands forth in more grandeur and power. There remain, no doubt, many social conquests to be made; but immense intellectual and moral conquests are accomplished; worldly goods, social rights, are wanting to many men; but many great men live and shine in the eyes of the world. Letters, sciences, the arts, display all their splendor. Wherever mankind beholds these great signs, these signs glorified by human nature, wherever it sees created these treasures of sublime enjoyment, it there recognizes and names civilization.

Two facts, then, are comprehended in this great fact; it subsists on two conditions, and manifests itself by two symptoms: the development of social activity and that of individual activity; the progress of society and the progress of humanity. Wherever the external condition of man extends itself, vivifies, ameliorates itself; wherever the internal nature of man displays itself with luster, with grandeur; at these two signs, and often despite the profound imperfection of the social state, mankind with loud applause proclaims civilization.

Such, if I do not deceive myself, is the result of simple and purely common-sense examination of the general opinion of mankind. If we interrogate history, properly so called, if we examine what is the nature of the great crises of civilization, of those facts which, by universal consent, have propelled it onward, we shall constantly recognize one or other of the two elements I have just described. They are always crises of individual or social development, facts which have changed the internal man, his creed, his manners, or his external condition, his position in his relation with his fellows. Christianity, for example, not merely on its first appearance, but during the first stages of its existence, Christianity in no degree addressed itself to the social state; it announced aloud that it would not meddle with the social state; it ordered the slave to obey his master; it attacked none of the great evils, the great wrongs of the society of that period. Yet who will deny that Christianity was a great crisis of civilization? Why was it so? Because it changed the internal man, creeds, sentiments; because it regenerated the moral man, the intellectual man.

We have seen a crisis of another nature, a crisis which addressed itself, not to the internal man, but to his external condition; one which changed and regenerated society. This also was assuredly one of the decisive crises of civilization. Look through all history, you will find everywhere the same result; you will meet with no important fact instrumental in the development of civilization, which has not exercised one or other of the two sorts of influence I have spoken of.

Such, if I mistake not, is the natural and popular meaning of the term; you have here the fact, I will not say defined, but described, verified almost completely, or, at all events, in its general features. We have before us the two elements of civilization. Now comes the question, would one of these two suffice to constitute it; would the development of the social state, the development of the individual man, separately presented, be civilization? Would the human race recognize it as such, or have the two facts so intimate and necessary a relation between them, that if they are not simultaneously produced, they are notwithstanding inseparable, and sooner or later one brings on the other?

We might, as it appears to me, approach this question on three several sides. We might examine the nature itself of the two elements of civilization, and ask ourselves whether by that alone they are or are not closely united with, and necessary to, each other. We might inquire of history whether they had manifested themselves isolately, apart the one from the other, or whether they had invariably produced the one the other.

We may, lastly, consult upon this question the common opinion of mankind—common sense. I will address myself first to common sense.

When a great change is accomplished in the state of a country, when there is operated in it a large development of wealth and power, a revolution in the distribution of the social means, this new fact encounters adversaries, undergoes opposition: this is inevitable. What is the general cry of the adversaries of the change? They say that this progress of the social state does not ameliorate, does not regenerate in like manner, in a like degree, the moral, the internal state of man; that it is a false, delusive progress, the result of which is detrimental to morality, to man. The friends of social development energetically repel this attack; they maintain, on the contrary, that the progress of society necessarily involves and carries with it the progress of morality; that when the external life is better regulated, the internal life is refined and purified. Thus stands the question between the adversaries and partisans of the new state.

Reverse the hypothesis: suppose the moral development in progress: what do the laborers in this progress generally promise? What, in the origin of societies, have promised the religious rulers, the sages, the poets, who have labored to soften and to regulate men's manners? They have promised the amelioration of the social condition, the more equitable distribution of the social means. What, then, I ask you, is involved in these disputes, these promises? What do they mean? What do they imply?

They imply that in the spontaneous, instinctive conviction of mankind, the two elements of civilization, the social development and the moral development, are closely connected together; that at sight of the one, man at once looks forward to the other. It is to this natural instinctive conviction that those who are maintaining or combating one or other of the two developments address themselves, when they affirm or deny their union. It is well understood that if we can persuade mankind that the amelioration of the social state will be adverse to the internal progress of individuals, we shall have succeeded in decrying and enfeebling the revolution in operation throughout society. On the other hand, when we promise mankind the amelioration of society by means of the amelioration of the individual, it is well understood that the tendency is to place faith in these promises, and it is accordingly made use of with success. It is evidently, therefore, the instinctive belief of humanity that the movements of civilization are connected the one with the other, and reciprocally produce the one the other.

If we address ourselves to the history of the world, we shall receive the same answer. We shall find that all the great developments of the internal man have turned to the profit of society; all the great developments of the social state to the profit of individual man. We find the one or other of the two facts predominating, manifesting itself with striking effect, and impressing upon the movement in progress a distinctive character. It is, sometimes, only after a very long interval of time, after a thousand obstacles, a thousand transformations, that the second fact, developing itself, comes to complete the civilization which the first had commenced. But if you examine them closely, you will soon perceive the bond which unites them. The march of Providence is not restricted to narrow limits; it is not bound, and it does not trouble itself, to follow out today the consequences of the principle which it laid down yesterday. The consequences will come in due course, when the hour for them has arrived, perhaps not till hundreds of years have passed away; though its reasoning may appear to us slow, its logic is none the less true and sound. To Providence, time is as nothing; it strides through time as the gods of Homer through space: it makes but one step, and ages have vanished behind it. How many centuries, what infinite events passed away before the regeneration of the moral man by Christianity exercised upon the regeneration of the social state its great and legitimate influence? Yet who will deny that it any the less succeeded?

If from history we extend our inquiries to the nature itself of the two facts which constitute civilization, we are infallibly led to the same result. There is no one who has not experienced this in his own case. When a moral change is operated in man, when he acquires an idea, or a virtue, or a faculty, more than he had before—in a word, when he develops himself individually, what is the desire, what the want, which at the same moment takes possession of him? It is the desire, the want, to communicate the new sentiment to the world about him, to give realization to his thoughts externally. As soon as a man acquires anything, as soon as his being takes in his own conviction a new development, assumes an additional value, forthwith he attaches to this new development, this fresh value, the idea of possession; he feels himself impelled, compelled, by his instinct, by an inward voice, to extend to others the change, the amelioration, which has been accomplished in his own person. We owe the great reformers solely to this cause; the mighty men who have changed the face of the world, after having changed themselves, were urged onward, were guided on their course, by no other want than this. So much for the alteration which is operated in the internal man; now to the other. A revolution is accomplished in the state of society; it is better regulated, rights and property are more equitably distributed among its members—that is to say, the aspect of the world becomes purer and more beautiful, the action of government, the conduct of men in their mutual relations, more just, more benevolent. Do you suppose that this improved aspect of the world, this amelioration of external facts, does not react upon the interior of man, upon humanity? All that is said as to the authority of examples, of customs, of noble models, is founded upon this only: that an external fact, good, well regulated, leads sooner or later, more or less completely, to an internal fact of the same nature, the same merit; that a world better regulated, a world more just, renders man himself more just; that the inward is reformed by the outward, as the outward by the inward; that the two elements of civilization are closely connected the one with the other; that centuries, that obstacles of all sorts, may interpose between them; that it is possible they may have to undergo a thousand transformations in order to regain each other; but sooner or later they will rejoin each other: this is the law of their nature, the general fact of history, the instinctive faith of the human race.

I think I have thus not exhausted the subject, very far from it, but exhibited in a well-nigh complete, though cursory, manner, the fact of civilization; I think I have described it, settled its limits, and stated the principal, the fundamental questions to which it gives rise. I might stop here; but I cannot help touching upon a question which meets me at this point; one of those questions which are not historical questions, properly so called; which are questions, I will not call them hypothetical, but conjectural; questions of which man holds but one end, the other end being permanently beyond his reach; questions of which he cannot make the circuit, nor view on more than one side; and yet questions not the less real, not the less calling upon him for thought; for they present themselves before him, despite himself, at every moment.

Of those two developments of which we have spoken, and which constitute the fact of civilization, the development of society on the one hand and of humanity on the other, which is the end, which is the means? Is it to perfect his social condition, to ameliorate his existence on earth, that man develops himself, his faculties, sentiments, ideas, his whole being?—or rather, is not the amelioration of the social condition, the progress of society, society itself, the theater, the occasion, the *mobile,* of the development of the individual; in a word, is society made to serve the individual, or the individual to serve society? On the answer to this question inevitably depends that whether the destiny of man is purely social;

whether society drains up and exhausts the whole man; or whether he bears within him something intrinsic—something superior to his existence on earth.

A man whom I am proud to call my friend, a man who has passed though meetings like our own to assume the first place in assemblies less peaceable and more powerful, a man all whose words are engraven on the hearts of those who hear them, M. Royer-Collard, has solved this question according to his own conviction, at least, in his speech on the Sacrilege Bill. I find in that speech these two sentences: "Human societies are born, live and die, on the earth; it is there their destinies are accomplished. . . . But they contain not the whole man. After he has engaged himself to society, there remains to him the noblest part of himself, those high faculties by which he elevates himself to God, to a future life, to unknown felicity in an invisible world. . . . We, persons individual and indentical, veritable beings endowed with immortality, we have a different destiny from that of states."

I will add nothing to this; I will not undertake to treat the question itself; I content myself with stating it. It is met with at the history of civilization: when the history of civilization is completed, when there is nothing more to say as to our present existence, man inevitably asks himself whether all is exhausted, whether he has reached the end of all things. This then is the last, the highest of all those problems to which history of civilization can lead. It is sufficient for me to have indicated its position and its grandeur.

From all I have said it is evident that the history of civilization might be treated in two methods, drawn from two sources, considered under two different aspects. The historian might place himself in the heart of the human mind for a given period, a series of ages, or among the determinate people; he might study, describe, relate all the events, all the transformations, all the revolutions which had been accomplished in the internal man; and when he should arrive at the end he would have a history of civilization among the people, and in the period he had selected. He may proceed in another manner: instead of penetrating the internal man, he may take his stand—he may place himself in the midst of the world; instead of describing the vicissitudes of the ideas, the sentiments of the individual being, he may describe external facts, the events, the changes of the social state. These two portions, these two histories of civilization are closely connected with each other; they are the reflection, the image of each other. Yet, they may be separated; perhaps, indeed, they ought to be so, at least at the onset, in order that both the one and the other may be treated of in detail, and with perspicuity. For my part I do not propose to study with you the history of civilization in the interior of the human soul; it is the history of external events of the visible and social world that I shall occupy myself with. I had wished, indeed, to exhibit to you the whole fact of civilization, such as I can conceive it in all its complexity and extent, to set forth before you all the high questions which may arise from it. At present I restrict myself; mark out my field of inquiry within narrower limits; it is only the history of the social state that I purpose investigating.

We shall begin by seeking all the elements of European civilization in its cradle at the fall of the Roman Empire; we will study with attention society, such as it was, in the midst of those famous ruins. We will endeavor not to resuscitate but to place its elements side by side, and when we have done so, we will endeavor to make them move and follow them in their developments through the fifteen centuries which have elapsed since that epoch.

I believe that when we have got but a very little way into this study, we shall acquire the conviction that civilization is as yet very young; that the world has by no means as yet measured the whole of its career. Assuredly human thought is at this time very far from being all that it is capable of becoming; we are very far from comprehending the whole future of humanity: let each of us descend into his own mind, let him interrogate himself as to the utmost possible good he has formed a conception of and hopes for; let him then compare his idea with what actually exists in the world; he will be convinced that society and civilization are very young; that notwithstanding the length of the road they have come, they have incomparably further to go. This will lessen nothing of the pleasure that we shall take in the contemplation of our actual condition. As I endeavor to place before you the great crises in the history of civilization in Europe during the last fifteen centuries, you will see to what a degree, even up in our own days, the condition of man has been laborious, stormy, not only in the outward and social state, but inwardly in the life of the soul. During all those ages, the human mind has had to suffer as much as the human race; you will see that in modern times, for the first time, perhaps, the human mind has attained a state, as yet very imperfect, but still a state in which reigns some peace, some harmony. It is the same with society; it has evidently made immense progress, the human condition is easy and just, compared with what it was previously; we may almost when thinking of our ancestors apply to ourselves the verses of Lucretius:

Suave mari magno, turbantibus æquora ventis,
E terrâ magnum alterius spectare laborem.

['Tis pleasant, in a great storm, to contemplate, from a safe position on
shore, the perils of some ships tossed about by the furious winds and the
stormy ocean.]

We may say of ourselves, without too much pride, as Sthenelus in Homer:

Thank Heaven, we are infinitely better than those who went before us.

Let us be careful, however, not to give ourselves up too much to the
idea of our happiness and amelioration, or we may fall into two grave
dangers, pride and indolence; we may conceive an overconfidence in the
power and success of the human mind, in our own enlightenment, and, at
the same time, suffer ourselves to become enervated by the luxurious ease
of our condition. It appears to me that we are constantly fluctuating between a tendency to complain upon light grounds, on the one hand, and
to be content without reason, on the other. We have a susceptibility of
spirit, a craving, an unlimited ambition in the thought, in our desire, in
the movement of the imagination; but when it comes to the practical work
of life, when we are called upon to give ourselves any trouble, to make
any sacrifices, to use any efforts to attain the object, our arms fall down
listlessly by our sides, and we give the matter up in despair, with a facility equaled only by the impatience with which we had previously desired its attainment. We must beware how we allow ourselves to yield to
either of these defects. Let us accustom ourselves duly to estimate beforehand the extent of our force, our capacity, our knowledge; and let us
aim at nothing which we feel we cannot attain legitimately, justly,
regularly, and with unfailing regard to the principles upon which our
civilization itself rests. We seem at times tempted to adopt the principles which, as a general rule, we assail and hold up to scorn—the principles, the right of the strongest of barbarian Europe; the brute force, the
violence, the downright lying which were matters of course, of daily occurrence, four or five hundred years ago. But when we yield for a moment to this desire, we find in ourselves neither the perseverance nor the
savage energy of the men of that period, who, suffering greatly from their
condition, were naturally anxious, and incessantly essaying, to emancipate themselves from it. We, of the present day, are content with our condition; let us not expose it to danger by indulging in vague desires, the
time for realizing which has not come. Much has been given to us,
much will be required of us; we must render to posterity a strict account

of our conduct; the public, the government, all are now subjected to discussion, examination, responsibility. Let us attach ourselves firmly, faithfully, undeviatingly, to the principles of our civilization—justice, legality, publicity, liberty; and let us never forget that while we ourselves require, and with reason, that all things shall be open to our inspection and inquiry, we ourselves are under the eye of the world, and shall, in our turn, be discussed, be judged.

The foregoing is Lecture I
from Guizot's HISTORY OF CIVILIZATION IN EUROPE.

Henry Adams

1838–1918

Henry Adams was born in Boston in 1838, the grandson of the sixth President of the United States and the great-grandson of the second. Although a man of such ancestry was more or less expected to seek a career in politics, neither Henry's times nor his temperament permitted him to do so. The sort of scholar-statesman he might have been was inconceivable in the later nineteenth century—the Gilded Age—while the analytical turn of mind that had been a family trait emerged in him as a fatal habit of self-doubt. He became instead a historian, spending his life in the study of the social forces over which he could have no active control.

In this profession, Adams achieved by common consent the highest rank among his countrymen. His writings, celebrated for their style, convey the witty and ironic detachment with which he viewed every subject, most of all himself. They show as well the scientific and philosophical concerns of his unresting intelligence. As such they have always seemed more than ordinarily interesting. Yet Adams scorned his work, or pretended to, believing that it had made no difference in his day. Convinced that his life had been a failure, he said so at the end of his autobiography, *The Education of Henry Adams*, the one book by which he has become best known. He was

---

Notes from the artist: "The head of Adams, with a background suggesting his work Mont-Saint-Michel and Chartres. *At left is Mont-Saint-Michel atop its rock pinnacle; at right is a saint from the sculpture on the north porch of Chartres Cathedral."*

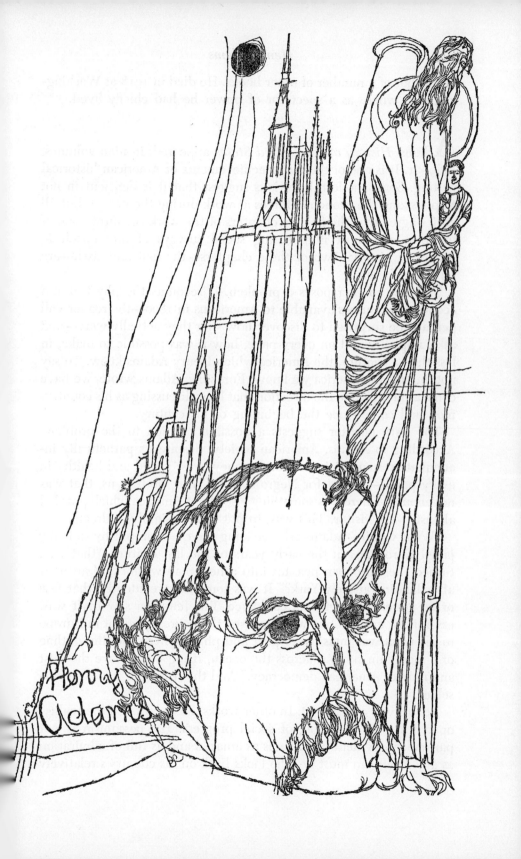

Henry Adams

the author of a number of other books. He died in 1918 at Washington, D.C., where as a spectator of power he had chiefly lived.

Adams' *History of the United States* appeared, in nine volumes, 1889–91. It is one of the major achievements of American historical writing. Some modern historians suggest that it is deficient in not emphasizing the economic forces at work during the period, but all critics agree that the first six chapters of the work constitute one of the best and most illuminating social surveys of any epoch in American history. Two of these chapters—the first and sixth—are reprinted here.

The first chapter poses a problem. It recounts the physical and economic resources available to Americans in 1800—the reader will perhaps be surprised to discover how slim they actually were—and asks, implicity and on every page, how it was possible to make, in less than a century, the America which Henry Adams knew. To say nothing of the America we know! For, since Adams wrote, we have come as far again in the direction that he is discussing as his countrymen had come since the beginning of his century.

The sixth chapter suggests a possible solution to the problem. According to Adams, American society, despite its pathetically inadequate resources in men and money, was "sound and healthy in every part"—"except for Negro slavery." But, he tells us, that was not enough. There was something else about America which puzzled almost every visitor. This was, to put it very simply, a dream.

"What was it," Adams asks, echoing the question put by so many jaded Europeans in the early years of the last century, "that . . . turned the European peasant into a new man within half an hour after landing at New York?" It was something, evidently, that few or no educated foreigners could see. But Jefferson saw it. It was, essentially, an "emotion which caused the poorest peasant in Europe to see what was invisible to poet and philosopher—the dim outline of a mountain summit across the ocean, rising high above the mist and mud of American democracy." And the results of it we see ourselves.

Adams was a pessimist. In other works, he questioned the reality, or at least the direction, of social progress. His pessimism is not particularly evident here. He is as amazed and as full of admiration as any American must be who looks back on his country's relatively short history. He feels that, despite our faults, despite our errors and mistakes, we have come a long way. Nevertheless, some trace of Adams' pessimism may be found in the last paragraph of the sixth chapter.

He asks a series of questions about the American dream, and about the American effort to achieve it. Could American society "produce," he wonders, "or was it compatible with, the differentiation of a higher variety of the human race?" He concludes that "nothing less than this was necessary for its complete success." He forces us to ask whether the American story is a success story after all. In spite of the distance we have come, have we come far enough? Have we done all that we could do? Or is the hardest victory still to be won?

The United States in 1800

from *History of the United States of America*

A PHYSICAL AND ECONOMICAL CONDITIONS

ccording to the census of 1800, the United States of America contained 5,308,483 persons. In the same year the British Islands contained upwards of fifteen millions; the French Republic, more than twenty-seven millions. Nearly one-fifth of the American people were Negro slaves; the true political population consisted of four and a half million free whites, or less than one million able-bodied males, on whose shoulders fell the burden of a continent. Even after two centuries of struggle the land was still untamed; forest covered every portion, except here and there a strip of cultivated soil; the minerals lay undisturbed in their rocky beds, and more than two-thirds of the people clung to the seaboard within fifty miles of tidewater, where alone the wants of civilized life could be supplied. The center of population rested within eighteen miles of Baltimore, north and east of Washington. Except in political arrangement, the interior was little more civilized than in 1750, and was not much easier to penetrate than when La Salle and Hennepin found their way to the Mississippi more than a century before.

A great exception broke this rule. Two wagon roads crossed the Allegheny Mountains in Pennsylvania,—one leading from Philadelphia to Pittsburgh; one from the Potomac to the Monongahela; while a third passed through Virginia southwestward to the Holston River and Knoxville in Tennessee, with a branch through the Cumberland Gap into Kentucky. By these roads and by trails less passable from North and South Carolina, or by waterways from the lakes, between four and five hundred thousand persons had invaded the country beyond the Alleghenies. At Pittsburgh and on the Monongahela existed a society, already old, numbering seventy or eighty thousand persons, while on the Ohio River the settlements had grown to an importance which threatened to force a difficult problem on the union of the older states. One hundred and eighty thousand whites, with forty thousand Negro slaves, made Kentucky the largest community west of the mountains; and about ninety thousand whites and fourteen thousand slaves were scattered over Tennessee. In the territory north of the Ohio less progress had been made. A New England colony existed at Marietta; some fifteen thousand people were gathered at Cincinnati; halfway between the two, a small town had grown up at Chillicothe, and other villages or straggling cabins were to be found elsewhere; but the whole Ohio territory contained only forty-five thousand inhabitants. The entire population, both free and slave, west of the mountains, reached not yet half a million; but already they were partly disposed to think themselves, and the old thirteen states were not altogether unwilling to consider them, the germ of an independent empire, which was to find its outlet, not through the Alleghenies to the seaboard, but by the Mississippi River to the Gulf.

Nowhere did eastern settlements touch the western. At least one hundred miles of mountainous country held the two regions everywhere apart. The shore of Lake Erie, where alone contact seemed easy, was still unsettled. The Indians had been pushed back to the Cuyahoga River, and a few cabins were built on the site of Cleveland; but in 1800, as in 1700, this intermediate region was only a portage where emigrants and merchandise were transferred from Lake Erie to the Muskingum and Ohio valleys. Even western New York remained a wilderness: Buffalo was not laid out; Indian titles were not extinguished; Rochester did not exist; and the county of Onondaga numbered a population of less than eight thousand. In 1799 Utica contained fifty houses, mostly small and temporary. Albany was still a Dutch city, with some five thousand inhabitants; and the tide of immigration flowed slowly through it into the valley of the Mohawk, while another stream from Pennsylvania, following the Susquehanna, spread toward the Genesee country.

The people of the old thirteen states, along the Atlantic seaboard, thus sent westward a wedge-shaped mass of nearly half a million persons, penetrating by the Tennessee, Cumberland, and Ohio rivers toward the western limit of the Union. The Indians offered sharp resistance to this invasion, exacting life for life, and yielding only as their warriors perished. By the close of the century the wedge of white settlements, with its apex at Nashville and its flanks covered by the Ohio and Tennessee rivers, nearly split the Indian country in halves. The northern half—consisting of the later States of Wisconsin, Michigan, Illinois, and Indiana, and one third of Ohio—contained Wyandottes and Shawanese, Miamis, Kickapoos, and other tribes, able to send some five thousand warriors to hunt or fight. In the southern half, powerful confederates of Creeks, Cherokees, Chickasaws, and Choctaws lived and hunted where the states of Mississippi, Alabama, and the western parts of Georgia, Tennessee, and Kentucky were to extend; and so weak was the state of Georgia, which claimed the southwestern territory for its own, that a well-concerted movement of Indians might without much difficulty have swept back its white population of one hundred thousand toward the ocean or across the Savannah River. The Indian power had been broken in halves, but each half was still terrible to the colonists on the edges of their vast domain, and was used as a political weapon by the governments whose territory bounded the Union on the north and south. The governors general of Canada intrigued with the northwestern Indians that they might hold in check any aggression from Washington; while the Spanish governors of West Florida and Louisiana maintained equally close relations with the Indian confederacies of the Georgia territory.

With the exception that half a million people had crossed the Alleghenies and were struggling with difficulties all their own, in an isolation like that of Jutes or Angles in the fifth century, America, so far as concerned physical problems, had changed little in fifty years. The old landmarks remained nearly where they stood before. The same bad roads and difficult rivers, connecting the same small towns, stretched into the same forests in 1800 as when the armies of Braddock and Amherst pierced the western and northern wilderness, except that these roads extended a few miles farther from the seacoast. Nature was rather man's master than his servant, and the five million Americans struggling with the untamed continent seemed hardly more competent to their task than the beavers and buffalo which had for countless generations made bridges and roads of their own.

Even by water, along the seaboard, communication was as slow and almost as irregular as in colonial times. The wars in Europe caused a sudden and great increase in American shipping employed in foreign commerce, without yet leading to general improvement in navigation. The ordinary seagoing vessel carried a freight of about two hundred and fifty tons; the largest merchant ships hardly reached four hundred tons; the largest frigate in the United States navy, the "line-of-battle ship in disguise," had a capacity of fifteen hundred and seventy-six tons. Elaborately rigged as ships or brigs, the small merchant craft required large crews and were slow sailers; but the voyage to Europe was comparatively more comfortable and more regular than the voyage from New York to Albany, or through Long Island Sound to Providence. No regular packet plied between New York and Albany. Passengers waited till a sloop was advertised to sail; they provided their own bedding and supplies; and within the nineteenth century Captain Elias Bunker won much fame by building the sloop "Experiment," of one hundred and ten tons, to start regularly on a fixed day for Albany, for the convenience of passengers only, supplying beds, wine, and provisions for the voyage of one hundred and fifty miles. A week on the North River or on the Sound was an experience not at all unknown to travelers.

While little improvement had been made in water travel, every increase of distance added to the difficulties of the westward journey. The settler who after buying wagon and horses hauled his family and goods across the mountains might buy or build a broad flat-bottomed ark, to float with him and his fortunes down the Ohio, in constant peril of upsetting or of being sunk; but only light boats with strong oars could mount the stream, or boats forced against the current by laboriously poling in shallow water. If he carried his tobacco and wheat down the Mississippi to the Spanish port of New Orleans, and sold it, he might return to his home in Kentucky or Ohio by a long and dangerous journey on horseback through the Indian country from Natchez to Nashville, or he might take ship to Philadelphia, if a ship were about to sail, and again cross the Alleghenies. Compared with river travel, the sea was commonly an easy and safe highway. Nearly all the rivers which penetrated the interior were unsure, liable to be made dangerous by freshets, and both dangerous and impassable by drought; yet such as they were, these streams made the main paths of traffic. Through the mountainous gorges of the Susquehanna the produce of western New York first found an outlet; the Cuyahoga and Muskingum were the first highway from the Lakes to the Ohio; the Ohio itself, with its great tributaries the Cumberland and the Tennessee, marked the lines of western migration; and every stream which could at high water float a boat was thought likely to become a path for commerce. As General Washington, not twenty years earlier, hoped that the brawling waters of the Cheat and Youghiogheny might become the channel of trade between Chesapeake Bay and Pittsburgh, so the Americans of 1800 were prepared to risk life and property on any streamlet that fell foaming down either flank of the Alleghenies. The experience of mankind proved trade to be dependent on water communications, and as yet Americans did not dream that the experience of mankind was useless to them.

If America was to be developed along the lines of water communication alone, by such means as were known to Europe, Nature had decided that the experiment of a single republican government must meet extreme difficulties. The valley of the Ohio had no more to do with that of the Hudson, the Susquehanna, the Potomac, the Roanoke, and the Santee than the valley of the Danube with that of the Rhône, the Po, or the Elbe. Close communication by land could alone hold the great geographical divisions together either in interest or in fear. The union of New England with New York and Pennsylvania was not an easy task even as a problem of geography, and with an ocean highway; but the union of New England with the Carolinas, and of the seacoast with the interior, promised to be a hopeless undertaking. Physical contact alone could make one country of these isolated empires, but to the patriotic American of 1800, struggling for the continued existence of an embryo nation, with machinery so inadequate, the idea of ever bringing the Mississippi River, either by land or water, into close contact with New England, must have seemed wild. By water, an Erie Canal was already foreseen; by land, centuries of labor could alone conquer those obstacles which Nature permitted to be overcome.

In the minds of practical men, the experience of Europe left few doubts on this point. After two thousand years of public labor and private savings, even despotic monarchs, who employed the resources of their subjects as they pleased, could in 1800 pass from one part of their European dominions to another little more quickly than they might have done in the age of the Antonines. A few short canals had been made, a few bridges had been built, an excellent post road extended from Madrid to St. Petersburg; but the heavy diligence that rumbled from Calais to Paris required three days for its journey of one hundred and fifty miles, and if travelers ventured on a trip to Marseilles they met with rough roads and hardships like those of the Middle Ages. Italy was in 1800 almost as remote from the north of Europe as when carriage roads were first built. Neither in time nor in thought was Florence or Rome much nearer to London in Wordsworth's youth than in the youth of Milton or Gray. Indeed, such changes as had occurred were partly for the worse, owing to the violence of revolutionary wars during the last ten years of the eighteenth century. Horace Walpole at his life's close saw about him a world which in many respects was less civilized than when as a boy he made the grand tour of Europe.

While so little had been done on the great highways of European travel, these highways were themselves luxuries which furnished no sure measure of progress. The post horses toiled as painfully as ever through the sand from Hamburg to Berlin, while the coach between York and London rolled along an excellent road at the rate of ten miles an hour; yet neither in England nor on the Continent was the post road a great channel of commerce. No matter how good the road, it could not compete with water, nor could heavy freights in great quantities be hauled long distances without extravagant cost. Water communication was as necessary for European commerce in 1800 as it had been for the Phoenicians and Egyptians; the Rhine, the Rhône, the Danube, the Elbe were still the true commercial highways, and except for government post roads, Europe was as dependent on these rivers in the eighteenth century as in the thirteenth. No certainty could be offered of more rapid progress in the coming century than in the past; the chief hope seemed to lie in the construction of canals.

While Europe had thus consumed centuries in improving paths of trade, until merchandise could be brought by canal a few score miles from the Rhône to the Loire and Seine, to the Garonne and the Rhine, and while all her wealth and energy had not yet united the Danube with other river systems, America was required to construct, without delay, at least three great roads and canals, each several hundred miles long, across mountain ranges, through a country not yet inhabited, to points where no great markets existed—and this under constant peril of losing her political union, which could not even by such connections be with certainty secured. After this should be accomplished, the Alleghenies must still remain between the eastern and western states, and at any known rate of travel Nashville could not be reached in less than a fortnight or three weeks from Philadelphia. Meanwhile the simpler problem of bringing New England nearer to Virginia and Georgia had not advanced even with the aid of a direct ocean highway. In becoming politically independent of England, the old thirteen provinces developed little more commercial intercourse with each other in proportion to their wealth and population than they had maintained in colonial days. The material ties that united them grew in strength no more rapidly than the ties which bound them to Europe. Each group of states lived a life apart.

Even the lightly equipped traveler found a short journey no slight effort. Between Boston and New York was a tolerable highway, along which, thrice a week, light stagecoaches carried passengers and the mail, in three days. From New York a stagecoach started every weekday for Philadelphia, consuming the greater part of two days in the journey; and the road between Paulus Hook, the modern Jersey City, and Hackensack was declared by the newspapers in 1802 to be as bad as any other part of the route between Maine and Georgia. South of Philadelphia the road was tolerable as far as Baltimore, but between Baltimore and the new city of Washington it meandered through forests; the driver chose the track which seemed least dangerous, and rejoiced if in wet seasons he reached Washington without miring or upsetting his wagon. In the northern states, four miles an hour was the average speed for any coach between Bangor and Baltimore. Beyond the Potomac the roads became steadily worse, until south of Petersburg even the mails were carried on horseback. Except for a stagecoach which plied between Charleston and Savannah, no public conveyance of any kind was mentioned in the three southernmost states.

The stagecoach was itself a rude conveyance, of a kind still familiar to experienced travelers. Twelve persons, crowded into one wagon, were jolted over rough roads, their bags and parcels, thrust inside, cramping their legs, while they were protected from the heat and dust of midsummer and the intense cold and driving snow of winter only by leather flaps buttoned to the roof and sides. In fine, dry weather this mode of travel was not unpleasant, when compared with the heavy vehicles of Europe and the hard English turnpikes; but when spring rains drew the frost from the ground the roads became nearly impassable, and in winter, when the rivers froze, a serious peril was added, for the Susquehanna or the North River at Paulus Hook must be crossed in an open boat—an affair of hours at best, sometimes leading to fatal accidents. Smaller annoyances of many kinds were habitual. The public, as a rule, grumbled less than might have been expected, but occasionally newspapers contained bitter complaints. An angry Philadelphian, probably a foreigner, wrote in 1796 that, "with a few exceptions, brutality, negligence, and filching are as naturally expected by people accustomed to traveling in America as a mouth, a nose, and two eyes are looked for in a man's face." This sweeping charge, probably unjust, and certainly supported by little public evidence, was chiefly founded on the experience of an alleged journey from New York:

> At Bordentown we went into a second boat where we met with very sorry accommodation. This was about four o'clock in the afternoon. We had about twenty miles down the Delaware to reach Philadelphia. The captain, who had a most provoking tongue, was a boy about eighteen years of age. He and a few companions despatched a dozen or eighteen

bottles of porter. We ran three different times against other vessels that were coming up the stream. The women and children lay all night on the bare boards of the cabin floor. . . . We reached Arch Street wharf about eight o'clock on the Wednesday morning, having been about sixteen hours on a voyage of twenty miles.

In the southern states the difficulties and perils of travel were so great as to form a barrier almost insuperable. Even Virginia was no exception to this rule. At each interval of a few miles the horseman found himself stopped by a river, liable to sudden freshets, and rarely bridged. Jefferson in his frequent journeys between Monticello and Washington was happy to reach the end of the hundred miles without some vexatious delay. "Of eight rivers between here and Washington," he wrote to his attorney general in 1801, "five have neither bridges nor boats."

Expense caused an equally serious obstacle to travel. The usual charge in the northern states was six cents a mile by stage. In the year 1796, according to Francis Baily, president of the Royal Astronomical Society, three or four stages ran daily from Baltimore to Philadelphia, the fare six dollars, with charges amounting to two dollars and a quarter a day at the inns on the road. Baily was three days in making the journey. From Philadelphia to New York he paid the same fare and charges, arriving in one day and a half. The entire journey of two hundred miles cost him twenty-one dollars. He remarked that traveling on the main lines of road in the settled country was about as expensive as in England, and when the roads were good, about as rapid. Congress allowed its members six dollars for every twenty miles traveled. The actual cost, including hotel expenses, could hardly have fallen below ten cents a mile.

Heavy traffic never used stage routes if it could find cheaper. Commerce between one state and another, or even between the seaboard and the interior of the same state, was scarcely possible on any large scale unless navigable water connected them. Except the great highway to Pittsburgh, no road served as a channel of commerce between different regions of the country. In this respect New England east of the Connecticut was as independent of New York as both were independent of Virginia, and as Virginia in her turn was independent of Georgia and South Carolina. The chief value of interstate communication by land rested in the postal system; but the post furnished another illustration of the difficulties which barred progress. In the year 1800 one general mail route extended from Portland in Maine to Louisville in Georgia, the time required for the trip being twenty days. Between New York and Petersburg in Virginia was a daily service, between New York and Boston, and also between Petersburg and Augusta, the mail was carried thrice a week. Branching from the main line at New York, a mail went to Canandaigua in ten days; from Philadelphia another branch line went to Lexington in sixteen days, to Nashville in twenty-two days. Thus more than twenty thousand miles of post road, with nine hundred post offices, proved the vastness of the country and the smallness of the result; for the gross receipts for postage in the year ending Oct. 1, 1801, were only $320,000.

Throughout the land the eighteenth century ruled supreme. Only within a few years had the New Englander begun to abandon his struggle with a barren soil, among granite hills, to learn the comforts of easier existence in the valleys of the Mohawk and Ohio; yet the New England man was thought the shrewdest and most enterprising of Americans. If the Puritans and the Dutch needed a century or more to reach the Mohawk, when would they reach the Mississippi? The distance from New York to the Mississippi was about one thousand miles; from Washington to the extreme southwestern military post, below Natchez, was about twelve hundred. Scarcely a portion of western Europe was three hundred miles distant from some sea, but a width of three hundred miles was hardly more than an outskirt of the United States. No civilized country had yet been required to deal with physical difficulties so serious, nor did experience warrant conviction that such difficulties could be overcome.

If the physical task which lay before the American people had advanced but a short way toward completion, little more change could be seen in the economical conditions of American life. The man who in the year 1800 ventured to hope for a new era in the coming century could lay his hand on no statistics that silenced doubt. The machinery of production showed no radical difference from that familiar to ages long past. The Saxon farmer of the eighth century enjoyed most of the comforts known to Saxon farmers of the eighteenth. The eorls and ceorls of Offa and Ecgbert could not read or write, and did not receive a weekly newspaper with such information as newspapers in that age could supply; yet neither their houses, their clothing, their food and drink, their agricultural tools and methods, their stock, nor their habits were so greatly altered or improved by time that they would have found much difficulty in accommodating their lives to that of their descendants in the eighteenth century. In this respect America was backward. Fifty or a hundred miles inland more than half the houses were log cabins, which might or might not enjoy the luxury of a glass window. Throughout the South and West houses showed little attempt at luxury; but even in New England the ordinary farmhouse was hardly so well built, so spacious, or so warm as that of a well-to-do contemporary of Charlemagne. The cloth which the farmer's family wore was still homespun. The hats were manufactured by the village hatter; the clothes were cut and made at home; the shirts, socks, and nearly every other article of dress were also homemade. Hence came a marked air of rusticity which distinguished country from town—awkward shapes of hat, coat, and trousers, which gave to the Yankee caricature those typical traits that soon disappeared almost as completely as coats of mail and steel headpieces. The plow was rude and clumsy; the sickle as old as Tubal-cain, and even the cradle not in general use; the flail was unchanged since the Aryan exodus; in Virginia, grain was still commonly trodden out by horses. Enterprising gentlemen-farmers introduced threshing machines and invented scientific plows; but these were novelties. Stock was as a rule not only unimproved, but ill cared for. The swine ran loose; the cattle were left to feed on what pasture they could find, and even in New England were not housed until the severest frosts, on the excuse that exposure hardened them. Near half a century afterward a competent judge asserted that the general treatment of cows in New England was fair matter of presentment by a grand jury. Except among the best farmers, drainage, manures, and rotation of crops were uncommon. The ordinary cultivator planted his corn as his father had planted it, sowing as much rye to the acre, using the same number of oxen to plow, and getting in his crops on the same day. He was even known to remove his barn on account of the manure accumulated round it, although the New England soil was never so rich as to warrant neglect to enrich it. The money for which he sold his wheat and chickens was of the Old World; he reckoned in shillings or pistareens, and rarely handled an American coin more valuable than a large copper cent.

At a time when the wealth and science of London and Paris could not supply an article so necessary as a common sulphur match, the backwardness of remote country districts could hardly be exaggerated. Yet remote districts were not the only sufferers. Of the whole United States New England claimed to be the most civilized province, yet New England was a region in which life had yet gained few charms of sense and few advantages over its rivals. Wilson, the ornithologist, a Pennsylvania Scotchman, a confirmed grumbler, but a shrewd judge, and the most thorough of American travelers, said in 1808: "My journey through almost the whole of New England has rather lowered the Yankees in my esteem. Except a few neat academies, I found their schoolhouses equally ruinous and deserted with ours; fields covered with stones; stone fences; scrubby oaks and pine trees; wretched orchards; scarcely one grainfield in twenty miles; the taverns along the road dirty, and filled with loungers brawling about lawsuits and politics; the people snappish and extortioners, lazy, and two hundred years behind the Pennsylvanians in agricultural improvements." The description was exaggerated, for Wilson forgot to speak of the districts where fields were not covered with stones, and where wheat could be grown to advantage. Twenty years earlier, Albert Gallatin, who knew Pennsylvania well, having reached Hartford on his way to Boston, wrote: "I have seen nothing in America equal to the establishments on the Connecticut River." Yet Wilson's account described the first general effect of districts in the New England states, where agriculture was backward and the country poor. The houses were thin wooden buildings, not well suited to the climate; the churches were unwarmed; the clothing was poor; sanitary laws were few, and a bathroom or a soil pipe was unknown. Consumption, typhoid, scarlet fever, diphtheria, and rheumatic fevers were common; habits of drinking were still a scourge in every family, and dyspepsia destroyed more victims than were consumed by drink. Population increased slowly, as though the conditions of life were more than usually hard. A century earlier, Massachusetts was supposed to contain sixty thousand inhabitants. Governor Hutchinson complained that while the other colonies quadrupled their numbers, Massachusetts failed to double its population in fifty years. In 1790 the state contained 378,000 people, not including the province of Maine; in 1800 the number rose to 423,000, which showed that a period of more rapid growth had begun, for the emigration into other states was also large.

A better measure of the difficulties with which New England struggled was given by the progress of Boston, which was supposed to have contained about eighteen thousand inhabitants as early as 1730, and twenty thousand in 1770. For several years after the Revolution it numbered less than twenty thousand, but in 1800 the census showed twenty-five thousand inhabitants. In appearance, Boston resembled an English market town, of a kind even then old-fashioned. The footways or sidewalks were paved, like the crooked and narrow streets, with round cobblestones, and were divided from the carriage way only by posts and a gutter. The streets were almost unlighted at night, a few oil lamps rendering the darkness more visible and the rough pavement rougher. Police hardly existed. The system of taxation was defective. The town was managed by selectmen, the elected instruments of town meetings whose jealousy of granting power was even greater than their objection to spending money, and whose hostility to city government was not to be overcome.

Although on all sides increase of ease and comfort was evident, and roads, canals, and new buildings, public and private, were already in course of construction on a scale before unknown, yet in spite of more than a century and a half of incessant industry, intelligent labor, and pinching economy Boston and New England were still poor. A few merchants enjoyed incomes derived from foreign trade, which allowed them to imitate in a quiet way the style of the English mercantile class; but the clergy and the lawyers, who stood at the head of society, lived with much economy. Many a country clergyman, eminent for piety and even for hospitality, brought up a family and laid aside some savings on a salary of five hundred dollars a year. President Dwight, who knew well the class to which he belonged, eulogizing the life of Abijah Weld, pastor of Attleborough, declared that on a salary of two hundred and twenty dollars a year Mr. Weld brought up eleven children, besides keeping a hospitable house and maintaining charity to the poor.

On the Exchange a few merchants had done most of the business of Boston since the peace of 1783, but a mail thrice a week to New York, and an occasional arrival from Europe or the departure of a ship to China, left ample leisure for correspondence and even for gossip. The habits of the commercial class had not been greatly affected by recent prosperity. Within ten or fifteen years before 1800 three banks had been created to supply the commercial needs of Boston. One of these was a branch Bank of the United States, which employed there whatever part of its capital it could profitably use; the two others were local banks, with capital of $1,600,000, toward which the state subscribed $400,000. Altogether the banking capital of Boston might amount to two millions and a half. A number of small banks, representing in all about two and a half millions more, were scattered through the smaller New England towns. The extraordinary prosperity caused by the French wars opened to Boston a new career. Wealth and population were doubling; the exports and imports of New England were surprisingly large, and the shipping was greater than that of New York and Pennsylvania combined; but Boston had already learned, and was to learn again, how fleeting were the riches that depended on foreign commerce, and conservative habits were not easily changed by a few years of accidental gain.

Of manufactures New England had many, but none on a large scale. The people could feed or clothe themselves only by household industry; their whale oil, salt fish, lumber, and rum were mostly sent abroad; but they freighted coasters with turners' articles, home-made linens and cloths, cheese, butter, shoes, nails, and what were called Yankee Notions of all sorts, which were sent to Norfolk and the Southern ports, and often peddled from the deck, as goods of every sort were peddled on the flatboats of the Ohio. Two or three small mills spun cotton with doubtful success; but England supplied ordinary manufactures more cheaply and better than Massachusetts could hope to do. A tri-weekly mail and a few coasting sloops provided for the business of New England with domestic ports. One packet sloop plied regularly to New York.

The state of New York was little in advance of Massachusetts and Maine. In 1800 for the first time New York gained the lead in population by the difference between 589,000 and 573,000. The valuation of New York for the direct tax in 1799 was $100,000,000; that of Massachusetts was $84,000,000. New York was still a frontier state, and although the city was European in its age and habits, travelers needed to go few miles from the Hudson in order to find a wilderness like that of Ohio and Tennessee. In most material respects the state was behind New England; outside the city was to be seen less wealth and less appearance of comfort. The first impression commonly received of any new country was from its inns, and on the whole few better tests of material condition then existed. President Dwight, though maintaining that the best old-fashioned inns of New England were in their way perfect, being in fact excellent private houses, could not wholly approve what he called the modern inns, even in Connecticut; but when he passed into New York he asserted that everything suffered an instant change for the worse. He explained that in Massachusetts the authorities were strict in refusing licenses to any but respectable and responsible persons, whereas in New York licenses were granted to anyone who would pay for them—which caused a multiplication of dramshops, bad accommodations, and a gathering of loafers and tipplers about every tavern porch, whose rude appearance, clownish manners, drunkenness, swearing, and obscenity confirmed the chief of Federalist clergymen in his belief that democracy had an evil influence on morals.

Far more movement was to be seen, and accumulation was more rapid than in colonial days; but little had yet been done for improvement, either by government or by individuals, beyond some provision for extending roads and clearing watercourses behind the advancing settlers. If Washington Irving was right, Rip Van Winkle, who woke from his long slumber about the year 1800, saw little that was new to him, except the head of President Washington where that of King George had once hung, and strange faces instead of familiar ones. Except in numbers, the city was relatively no farther advanced than the country. Between 1790 and

1800 its population rose from 33,000 to 60,000; and if Boston resembled an old-fashioned English market town, New York was like a foreign seaport, badly paved, undrained, and as foul as a town surrounded by the tides could be. Although the Manhattan Company was laying wooden pipes for a water supply, no sanitary regulations were enforced, and every few years—as in 1798 and 1803—yellow fever swept away crowds of victims, and drove the rest of the population, panic stricken, into the highlands. No day police existed; constables were still officers of the courts; the night police consisted of two captains, two deputies, and seventy-two men. The estimate for the city's expenses in 1800 amounted to $130,000. One marked advantage New York enjoyed over Boston, in the possession of a city government able to introduce reforms. Thus, although still medieval in regard to drainage and cleanliness, the town had taken advantage of recurring fires to rebuild some of the streets with brick sidewalks and curbstones. Travelers dwelt much on this improvement, which only New York and Philadelphia had yet adopted, and Europeans agreed that both had the air of true cities: that while Boston was the Bristol of America, New York was the Liverpool, and Philadelphia the London.

In respect to trade and capital, New York possessed growing advantages, supplying half New Jersey and Connecticut, a part of Massachusetts, and all the rapidly increasing settlements on the branches of the Hudson; but no great amount of wealth, no considerable industry or new creation of power was yet to be seen. Two banks, besides the branch Bank of the United States, supplied the business wants of the city, and employed about the same amount of capital in loans and discounts as was required for Boston. Besides these city institutions but two other banks existed in the state—at Hudson and at Albany.

The proportion of capital in private hands seemed to be no larger. The value of exports from New York in 1800 was but $14,000,000; the net revenue on imports for 1799 was $2,373,000, against $1,607,000 collected in Massachusetts. Such a foreign trade required little capital, yet these values represented a great proportion of all the exchanges. Domestic manufactures could not compete with foreign, and employed little bank credit. Speculation was slow, mostly confined to lands which required patience to exchange or sell. The most important undertakings were turnpikes, bridges such as Boston built across the Charles, or new blocks of houses; and a canal, such as Boston designed to the Merrimack, overstrained the resources of capital. The entire banking means of the United States in 1800 would not have answered the stockjobbing purposes of one great operator of Wall Street in 1875. The nominal capital of all the banks, including the Bank of the United States, fell short of $29,000,000. The limit of credit was quickly reached, for only the richest could borrow more than fifteen or twenty thousand dollars at a time, and the United States government itself was gravely embarrassed whenever obliged to raise money. In 1798 the secretary of the treasury could obtain five million dollars only by paying eight per cent interest for a term of years; and in 1814 the government was forced to stop payments for the want of twenty millions.

The precise value of American trade was uncertain, but in 1800 the gross exports and imports of the United States may have balanced at about seventy-five million dollars. The actual consumption of foreign merchandise amounted perhaps to the value of forty or fifty million dollars, paid in wheat, cotton, and other staples, and by the profits on the shipping employed in carrying West India produce to Europe. The amount of American capital involved in a trade of fifty millions, with credits of three, six, and nine months, must have been small, and the rates of profit large.

As a rule American capital was absorbed in shipping or agriculture, whence it could not be suddenly withdrawn. No stock exchange existed, and no broker exclusively engaged in stockjobbing, for there were few stocks. The national debt, of about eighty millions, was held abroad, or as a permanent investment at home. States and municipalities had not learned to borrow. Except for a few banks and insurance offices, turnpikes, bridges, canals, and land companies, neither bonds nor stocks were known. The city of New York was so small as to make extravagance difficult; the Battery was a fashionable walk, Broadway a country drive, and Wall Street an uptown residence. Great accumulations of wealth had hardly begun. The patroon was still the richest man in the state. John Jacob Astor was a fur merchant living where the Astor House afterward stood, and had not yet begun those purchases of real estate which secured his fortune. Cornelius Vanderbilt was a boy six years old, playing about his father's ferryboat at Staten Island. New York City itself was what it had been for a hundred years past—a local market.

As a national capital New York made no claim to consideration. If Bostonians for a moment forgot their town meetings, or if Virginians overcame their dislike for cities and pavements, they visited and admired, not New York, but Philadelphia. "Philadelphia," wrote the Duc de Liancourt, "is not only the finest city in the United States, but may be deemed one of the most beautiful cities in the world." In truth, it surpassed any of its size on either side of the Atlantic for most of the comforts and some of the elegancies of life. While Boston contained twenty-five thousand inhabitants and New York sixty thousand, the census of 1800 showed that Philadelphia was about the size of Liverpool—a city of seventy thousand people. The repeated ravages of yellow fever roused there a regard for sanitary precautions and cleanliness; the city, well paved and partly drained, was supplied with water in wooden pipes, and was the best-lighted town in America; its market was a model, and its jail was intended also for a model—although the first experiment proved unsuccessful, because the prisoners went mad or idiotic in solitary confinement. In and about the city flourished industries considerable for the time. The iron-works were already important; paper and gunpowder, pleasure carriages and many other manufactures were produced on a larger scale than elsewhere in the Union. Philadelphia held the seat of government until July, 1800, and continued to hold the Bank of the United States, with its capital of ten millions, besides private banking capital to the amount of five millions more. Public spirit was more active in Pennsylvania than in New York. More roads and canals were building; a new turnpike ran from Philadelphia to Lancaster, and the great highway to Pittsburgh was a more important artery of national life than was controlled by any other state. The exports of Pennsylvania amounted to $12,000,000, and the custom-house produced $1,350,000. The state contained six hundred thousand inhabitants—a population somewhat larger than that of New York.

Of all parts of the Union, Pennsylvania seemed to have made most use of her national advantages; but her progress was not more rapid than the natural increase of population and wealth demanded, while to deal with the needs of America, man's resources and his power over Nature must be increased in a ratio far more rapid than that which governed his numbers. Nevertheless, Pennsylvania was the most encouraging spectacle in the field of vision. Baltimore, which had suddenly sprung to a population and commerce greater than those of Boston, also offered strong hope of future improvement; but farther South the people showed fewer signs of change.

The city of Washington, rising in a solitude on the banks of the Potomac, was a symbol of American nationality in the southern states. The contrast between the immensity of the task and the paucity of means seemed to challenge suspicion that the nation itself was a magnificent scheme like the federal city, which could show only a few log cabins and Negro quarters where the plan provided for the traffic of London and the elegance of Versailles. When in the summer of 1800 the government was transferred to what was regarded by most persons as a fever-stricken morass, the half-finished White House stood in a naked field overlooking the Potomac, with two awkward department buildings near it, a single row of brick houses and a few isolated dwellings within sight, and nothing more; until across a swamp, a mile and a half away, the shapeless, unfinished Capitol was seen, two wings without a body, ambitious enough in design to make more grotesque the nature of its surroundings. The conception proved that the United States understood the vastness of their task, and were willing to stake something on their faith in it. Never did hermit or saint condemn himself to solitude more consciously than Congress and the Executive in removing the government from Philadelphia to Washington: the discontented men clustered together in eight or ten boardinghouses as near as possible to the Capitol, and there lived, like a convent of monks, with no other amusement or occupation than that of going from their lodgings to the chambers and back again. Even private wealth could do little to improve their situation, for there was nothing which wealth could buy; there were in Washington no shops or markets, skilled labor, commerce, or people. Public efforts and lavish use of public money could alone make the place tolerable; but Congress doled out funds for this national and personal object with so sparing a hand that their Capitol threatened to crumble in pieces and crush Senate and House under the ruins, long before the building was complete.

A government capable of sketching a magnificent plan, and willing to give only a halfhearted pledge for its fulfilment; a people eager to advertise a vast undertaking beyond their present powers, which when completed would become an object of jealousy and fear—this was the impression made upon the traveler who visited Washington in 1800, and mused among the unraised columns of the Capitol upon the destiny of the United States. As he traveled farther south his doubts were strengthened, for across the Potomac he could detect no sign of a new spirit. Manufactures had no existence. Alexandria owned a bank with half a million of capital, but no other was to be found between Washington and Charleston, except the branch Bank of the United States at Norfolk, nor any industry to which loans and discounts could safely be made. Virginia, the most populous and powerful of all the States, had a white population of 514,000, nearly equal to that of Pennsylvania and New York, besides about 350,000 slaves. Her energies had pierced the mountains and settled the western territory before the slow-moving northern people had torn themselves from the safer and more comfortable life by the seaboard; but the Virginia ideal was patriarchal, and an American continent on the Virginia type might reproduce the virtues of Cato, and perhaps the eloquence of Cicero, but was little likely to produce anything more practical in the way of modern progress. The Shenandoah Valley rivaled Pennsylvania and Connecticut in richness and skill of husbandry; but even agriculture, the favorite industry in Virginia, had suffered from the competition of Kentucky and Tennessee, and from the emigration which had drawn away fully one hundred thousand people. The land was no longer very productive. Even Jefferson, the most active-minded and sanguine of all Virginians—the inventor of the first scientific plow, the importer of the first threshing machine known in Virginia, the experimenter with a new drilling machine, the owner of one hundred and fifty slaves and ten thousand acres of land, whose Negroes were trained to carpentry, cabinetmaking, housebuilding, weaving, tailoring, shoemaking—claimed to get from his land no more than six or eight bushels of wheat to an acre, and had been forced to abandon the more profitable cultivation of tobacco. Except in a few favored districts like the Shenandoah Valley, land in Virginia did not average eight bushels of wheat to an acre. The cultivation of tobacco had been almost the sole object of landowners, and even where the lands were not exhausted, a bad system of agriculture and the force of habit prevented improvement.

The great planters lavished money in vain on experiments to improve their crops and their stock. They devoted themselves to the task with energy and knowledge; but they needed a diversity of interests and local markets, and except at Baltimore these were far from making their appearance. Neither the products, the markets, the relative amount of capital, nor the machinery of production had perceptibly changed. "The Virginians are not generally rich," said the Duc de Liancourt, "especially in net revenue. Thus one often finds a well-served table, covered with silver, in a room where for ten years half the window panes have been missing, and where they will be missed for ten years more. There are few houses in a passable state of repair, and of all parts of the establishment those best cared for are the stables." Wealth reckoned in slaves or land was plenty; but the best Virginians, from President Washington downward, were most outspoken in their warnings against the Virginia system both of slavery and agriculture.

The contrast between Virginia and Pennsylvania was the subject of incessant comment.

In Pennsylvania [said Robert Sutcliffe, an English Friend who published travels made in 1804–1806] we meet great numbers of wagons drawn by four or more fine fat horses, the carriages firm and well made, and covered with stout good linen, bleached almost white; and it is not uncommon to see ten or fifteen together travelling cheerfully along the road, the driver riding on one of his horses. Many of these come more than three hundred miles to Philadelphia from the Ohio, Pittsburg, and other places, and I have been told by a respectable Friend, a native of Philadelphia, that more than one thousand covered carriages frequently come to Philadelphia market. . . . The appearance of things in the Slave States is quite the reverse of this. We sometimes meet a ragged black boy or girl driving a team consisting of a lean cow and a mule; sometimes a lean bull or an ox and a mule; and I have seen a mule, a bull, and a cow each miserable in its appearance, composing one team, with a half-naked black slave or two riding or driving as occasion suited. The carriage or wagon, if it may be called such, appeared in as wretched a condition as the team and its driver. Sometimes a couple of horses, mules, or cows would be dragging a hogshead of tobacco, with a pivot or axle driven into each end of the hogshead, and something like a shaft attached, by which it was drawn or rolled along the road. I have seen two oxen and two slaves pretty fully employed in getting along a single hogshead; and some of these come from a great distance inland.

In the middle of these primitive sights, Sutcliffe was startled by a contrast such as Virginia could always show. Between Richmond and Fredericksburg—

In the afternoon, as our road lay through the woods, I was surprised to meet a family party travelling along in as elegant a coach as is usually met with in the neighborhood of London, and attended by several gayly dressed footmen.

The country south of Virginia seemed unpromising even to Virginians. In the year 1796 President Washington gave to Sir John Sinclair his opinion upon the relative value of American lands. He then thought the valley of Virginia the garden of America; but he would say nothing to induce others to settle in more southern regions.

The uplands of North and South Carolina and Georgia are not dissimilar in soil [he wrote] but as they approach the lower latitudes are less congenial to wheat, and are supposed to be proportionably more unhealthy. Towards the seaboard of all the Southern States, and farther south more so, the lands are low, sandy, and unhealthy; for which reason I shall say little concerning them, for as I should not choose to be an inhabitant of them myself, I ought not to say anything that would induce others to be so. . . . I understand that from thirty to forty dollars per acre may be denominated the medium price in the vicinity of the Susquehanna in the State of Pennsylvania, from twenty to thirty on the Potomac in what is called the Valley, . . . and less, as I have noticed before, as you proceed southerly.

Whatever was the cause, the state of North Carolina seemed to offer few temptations to immigrants or capital. Even in white population ranking fifth among the sixteen states, her 478,000 inhabitants were unknown to the world. The beautiful upper country attracted travelers neither for pleasure nor for gain, while the country along the seacoast was avoided except by hardy wanderers. The grumbling Wilson, who knew every nook and corner of the United States, and who found New England so dreary, painted this part of North Carolina in colors compared with which his sketch of New England was gay. "The taverns are the most desolate and beggarly imaginable; bare, bleak, and dirty walls, one or two old broken chairs and a bench form all the furniture. The white females seldom make their appearance. At supper you sit down to a meal the very sight of which is sufficient to deaden the most eager appetite, and you are surrounded by half-a-dozen dirty, half-naked blacks, male and female, whom any man of common scent might smell a quarter of a mile off. The house itself is raised upon props four or five feet, and the space below is left open for the hogs, with whose charming vocal performance the wearied traveler is serenaded the whole night long." The landscape pleased him no better—"immense solitary pine savannahs, through which the road winds among stagnant ponds; dark, sluggish creeks of the color of brandy, over which are thrown high wooden bridges without railings," crazy and rotten.

North Carolina was relatively among the poorest states. The exports and imports were of trifling value, less than one-tenth of those returned for Massachusetts, which were more than twice as great as those of North Carolina and Virginia together. That under these conditions America should receive any strong impulse from such a quarter seemed unlikely; yet perhaps for the moment more was to be expected from the Carolinas than from Virginia. Backward as these states in some respects were, they possessed one new element of wealth which promised more for them than anything Virginia could hope. The steam engines of Watt had been applied in England to spinning, weaving, and printing cotton; an immense demand had risen for that staple, and the cotton gin had been simultaneously invented. A sudden impetus was given to industry; land which had been worthless and estates which had become bankrupt acquired new value, and in 1800 every planter was growing cotton, buying Negroes, and breaking fresh soil. North Carolina felt the strong flood of prosperity, but South Carolina, and particularly the town of Charleston, had most to hope. The exports of South Carolina were nearly equal in value to those of Massachusetts or Pennsylvania; the imports were equally large. Charleston might reasonably expect to rival Boston, New York, Philadelphia, and Baltimore. In 1800 these cities still stood, as far as concerned their foreign trade, within some range of comparison; and between Boston, Baltimore, and Charleston, many plausible reasons could be given for thinking that the last might have the most brilliant future. The three towns stood abreast. If Charleston had but about eighteen thousand inhabitants, this was the number reported by Boston only ten years before, and was five thousand more than Baltimore then boasted. Neither Boston nor Baltimore saw about them a vaster region to supply, or so profitable a staple to export. A cotton crop of two hundred thousand pounds sent abroad in 1791 grew to twenty millions in 1801, and was to double again by 1803. An export of fifty thousand bales was enormous, yet was only the beginning. What use might not Charleston, the only considerable town in the entire South, make of this golden flood?

The town promised hopefully to prove equal to its task. Nowhere in the Union was intelligence, wealth, and education greater in proportion to numbers than in the little society of cotton and rice planters who ruled South Carolina; and they were in 1800 not behind—they hoped soon to outstrip—their rivals. If Boston was building a canal to the Merrimack, and Philadelphia one along the Schuylkill to the Susquehanna, Charleston had nearly completed another which brought the Santee River to its harbor, and was planning a road to Tennessee which should draw the whole interior within reach. Nashville was nearer to Charleston than to any other seaport of the Union, and Charleston lay nearest to the rich trade of the West Indies. Not even New York seemed more clearly marked for prosperity than this solitary southern city, which already possessed banking capital in abundance, intelligence, enterprise, the traditions of high culture and aristocratic ambition, all supported by slave labor, which could be indefinitely increased by the African slave trade.

If any portion of the United States might hope for a sudden and magnificent bloom, South Carolina seemed entitled to expect it. Rarely had such a situation, combined with such resources, failed to produce some wonderful result. Yet as Washington warned Sinclair, these advantages were counterbalanced by serious evils. The climate in summer was too relaxing. The sun was too hot. The seacoast was unhealthy, and at certain seasons even deadly to the whites. Finally, if history was a guide, no permanent success could be prophesied for a society like that of the low country in South Carolina, where some thirty thousand whites were surrounded by a dense mass of nearly one hundred thousand Negro slaves Even Georgia, then only partially settled, contained sixty thousand slaves and but one hundred thousand whites. The cotton states might still argue that if slavery, malaria, or summer heat barred civilization, all the civilization that was ever known must have been blighted in its infancy; but although the future of South Carolina might be brilliant, like that of other oligarchies in which only a few thousand freemen took part, such a development seemed to diverge far from the path likely to be followed by northern society, and bade fair to increase and complicate the social and economical difficulties with which Americans had to deal.

A probable valuation of the whole United States in 1800 was eighteen hundred million dollars, equal to $328 for each human being, including slaves; or $418 to each free white. This property was distributed with an approach to equality, except in a few of the southern states. In New York and Philadelphia a private fortune of one hundred thousand dollars was considered handsome, and three hundred thousand was great wealth. Inequalities were frequent; but they were chiefly those of a landed aristocracy. Equality was so far the rule that every white family of five persons might be supposed to own land, stock, or utensils, a house and furniture, worth about two thousand dollars; and as the only considerable industry was agriculture, their scale of life was easy to calculate—taxes amounting to little or nothing, and wages averaging about a dollar a day.

Not only were these slender resources, but they were also of a kind not easily converted to the ready uses required for rapid development. Among the numerous difficulties with which the Union was to struggle, and which were to form the interest of American history, the disproportion between the physical obstacles and the material means for overcoming them was one of the most striking.

AMERICAN IDEALS

Nearly every foreign traveler who visited the United States during these early years carried away an impression sober if not sad. A thousand miles of desolate and dreary forest, broken here and there by settlements; along the seacoast a few flourishing towns devoted to commerce; no arts, a provincial literature, a cancerous disease of Negro slavery, and differences of political theory fortified within geographical lines—what could be hoped for such a country except to repeat the story of violence and brutality which the world already knew by heart, until repetition for thousands of years had wearied and sickened mankind? Ages must probably pass before the interior could be thoroughly settled; even Jef-

ferson, usually a sanguine man, talked of a thousand years with acquiescence, and in his first Inaugural Address, at a time when the Mississippi River formed the western boundary, spoke of the country as having "room enough for our descendants to the hundredth and thousandth
generation." No prudent person dared to act on the certainty that when
settled, one government could comprehend the whole; and when the day
of separation should arrive, and America should have her Prussia,
Austria, and Italy, as she already had her England, France, and Spain,
what else could follow but a return to the old conditions of local jealousies, wars, and corruption which had made a slaughterhouse of Europe?

The mass of Americans were sanguine and self-confident, partly by
temperament, but partly also by reason of ignorance; for they knew little
of the difficulties which surrounded a complex society. The Duc de
Liancourt, like many critics, was struck by this trait. Among other instances, he met with one in the person of a Pennsylvania miller,
Thomas Lea, "a sound American patriot, persuading himself that nothing
good is done, and that no one has any brains, except in America; that
the wit, the imagination, the genius of Europe are already in decrepitude"; and the duke added: "This error is to be found in almost all Americans,—legislators, administrators, as well as millers, and is less innocent
there." In the year 1796 the House of Representatives debated whether
to insert in the Reply to the President's Speech a passing remark that the
nation was "the freest and most enlightened in the world," a nation as
yet in swaddling clothes, which had neither literature, arts, sciences, nor
history; nor even enough nationality to be sure that it was a nation. The
moment was peculiarly ill-chosen for such a claim, because Europe was
on the verge of an outburst of genius. Goethe and Schiller, Mozart and
Haydn, Kant and Fichte, Cavendish and Herschel were making way for
Walter Scott, Wordsworth, and Shelley, Heine and Balzac, Beethoven and
Hegel, Oersted and Cuvier, great physicists, biologists, geologists,
chemists, mathematicians, metaphysicians, and historians by the score.
Turner was painting his earliest landscapes, and Watt completing his
latest steam engine; Napoleon was taking command of the French
armies, and Nelson of the English fleets; investigators, reformers, scholars,
and philosophers swarmed, and the influence of enlightenment, even
amid universal war, was working with an energy such as the world had
never before conceived. The idea that Europe was in her decrepitude
proved only ignorance and want of enlightenment, if not of freedom, on
the part of Americans who could only excuse their error by pleading that
notwithstanding these objections, in matters which for the moment most

concerned themselves Europe was a full century behind America. If they were right in thinking that the next necessity of human progress was to lift the average man upon an intellectual and social level with the most favored, they stood at least three generations nearer than Europe to their common goal. The destinies of the United States were certainly staked, without reserve or escape, on the soundness of this doubtful and even improbable principle, ignoring or overthrowing the institutions of church, aristocracy, family, army, and political intervention, which long experience had shown to be needed for the safety of society. Europe might be right in thinking that without such safeguards society must come to an end; but even Europeans must concede that there was a chance, if no greater than one in a thousand, that America might, at least for a time, succeed. If this stake of temporal and eternal welfare stood on the winning card; if man actually should become more virtuous and enlightened, by mere process of growth, without church or paternal authority; if the average human being could accustom himself to reason with the logical processes of Descartes and Newton!—what then?

Then, no one could deny that the United States would win a stake such as defied mathematics. With all the advantages of science and capital, Europe must be slower than America to reach the common goal. American society might be both sober and sad, but except for Negro slavery it was sound and healthy in every part. Stripped for the hardest work, every muscle firm and elastic, every ounce of brain ready for use, and not a trace of superfluous flesh on his nervous and supple body, the American stood in the world a new order of man. From Maine to Florida, society was in this respect the same, and was so organized as to use its human forces with more economy than could be approached by any society of the world elsewhere. Not only were artificial barriers carefully removed, but every influence that could appeal to ordinary ambition was applied. No brain or appetite active enough to be conscious of stimulants could fail to answer the intense incentive. Few human beings, however sluggish, could long resist the temptation to acquire power; and the elements of power were to be had in America almost for the asking. Reversing the Old World system, the American stimulant increased in energy as it reached the lowest and most ignorant class, dragging and whirling them upward as in the blast of a furnace. The penniless and homeless Scotch or Irish immigrant was caught and consumed by it; for every stroke of the ax and the hoe made him a capitalist, and made gentlemen of his children. Wealth was the strongest agent for moving the mass of mankind; but political power was hardly less tempting to the more intelligent and better-educated swarms of American-born citizens, and the instinct of activity, once created, seemed heritable and permanent in the race.

Compared with this lithe young figure, Europe was actually in decrepitude. Mere class distinctions, the patois or dialect of the peasantry, the fixity of residence, the local costumes and habits marking a history that lost itself in the renewal of identical generations, raised from birth barriers which paralyzed half the population. Upon this mass of inert matter rested the Church and the State, holding down activity of thought. Endless wars withdrew many hundred thousand men from production, and changed them into agents of waste; huge debts, the evidence of past wars and bad government, created interests to support the system and fix its burdens on the laboring class; courts, with habits of extravagance that shamed common sense, helped to consume private economies. All this might have been borne; but behind this stood aristocracies, sucking their nourishment from industry, producing nothing themselves, employing little or no active capital or intelligent labor, but pressing on the energies and ambition of society with the weight of an incubus. Picturesque and entertaining as these social anomalies were, they were better fitted for the theatre or for a museum of historical costumes than for an active workshop preparing to compete with such machinery as America would soon command. From an economical point of view, they were as incongruous as would have been the appearance of a medieval knight in helmet and armor, with battle-ax and shield, to run the machinery of Arkwright's cotton mill; but besides their bad economy they also tended to prevent the rest of society from gaining a knowledge of its own capacities. In Europe, the conservative habit of mind was fortified behind power. During nearly a century Voltaire himself—the friend of kings, the wit and poet, historian and philosopher of his age—had carried on, in daily terror, in exile and excommunication, a protest against an intellectual despotism contemptible even to its own supporters. Hardly was Voltaire dead, when Priestley, as great a man if not so great a wit, trying to do for England what Voltaire tried to do for France, was mobbed by the people of Birmingham and driven to America. Where Voltaire and Priestley failed, common men could not struggle; the weight of society stifled their thought. In America the balance between conservative and liberal forces was close; but in Europe conservatism held the physical power of government. In Boston a young Buckminster might be checked for a time by his father's prayers or commands in entering that path that led toward freer thought; but youth beckoned him on, and every reward that society could offer was dangled before his eyes. In London or Paris,

Rome, Madrid, or Vienna, he must have sacrificed the worldly prospects of his life.

Granting that the American people were about to risk their future on a new experiment, they naturally wished to throw aside all burdens of which they could rid themselves. Believing that in the long run interest, not violence, would rule the world, and that the United States must depend for safety and success on the interests they could create, they were tempted to look upon war and preparations for war as the worst of blunders; for they were sure that every dollar capitalized in industry was a means of overthrowing their enemies more effective than a thousand dollars spent on frigates or standing armies. The success of the American system was, from this point of view, a question of economy. If they could relieve themselves from debts, taxes, armies, and government interference with industry, they must succeed in outstripping Europe in economy of production; and Americans were even then partly aware that if their machine were not so weakened by these economies as to break down in the working, it must of necessity break down every rival. If their theory was sound, when the day of competition should arrive, Europe might choose between American and Chinese institutions, but there would be no middle path; she might become a confederated democracy, or a wreck.

Whether these ideas were sound or weak, they seemed self-evident to those northern democrats who, like Albert Gallatin, were comparatively free from slave-owning theories, and understood the practical forces of society. If Gallatin wished to reduce the interference of government to a minimum, and cut down expenditures to nothing, he aimed not so much at saving money as at using it with the most certain effect. The revolution of 1800 was in his eyes chiefly political, because it was social; but as a revolution of society, he and his friends hoped to make it the most radical that had occurred since the downfall of the Roman Empire. Their ideas were not yet cleared by experience, and were confused by many contradictory prejudices, but wanted neither breadth nor shrewdness.

Many apparent inconsistencies grew from this undeveloped form of American thought, and gave rise to great confusion in the different estimates of American character that were made both at home and abroad.

That Americans should not be liked was natural; but that they should not be understood was more significant by far. After the downfall of the French Republic they had no right to expect a kind word from Europe, and during the next twenty years they rarely received one. The liberal movement of Europe was cowed, and no one dared express democratic sympathies until the Napoleonic tempest had passed. With this attitude Americans had no right to find fault, for Europe cared less to injure them than to protect herself. Nevertheless, observant readers could not but feel surprised that none of the numerous Europeans who then wrote or spoke about America seemed to study the subject seriously. The ordinary traveler was apt to be little more reflective than a bee or an ant, but some of these critics possessed powers far from ordinary; yet Talleyrand alone showed that had he but seen America a few years later than he did, he might have suggested some sufficient reason for apparent contradictions that perplexed him in the national character. The other travelers—great and small, from the Duc de Liancourt to Basil Hall, a long and suggestive list—were equally perplexed. They agreed in observing the contradictions, but all, including Talleyrand, saw only sordid motives. Talleyrand expressed extreme astonishment at the apathy of Americans in the face of religious sectarians; but he explained it by assuming that the American ardor of the moment was absorbed in money-making. The explanation was evidently insufficient, for the Americans were capable of feeling and showing excitement, even to their great pecuniary injury, as they frequently proved; but in the foreigner's range of observation, love of money was the most conspicuous and most common trait of American character. "There is, perhaps, no civilized country in the world," wrote Félix de Beaujour, soon after 1800, "where there is less generosity in the souls, and in the heads fewer of those illusions which make the charm or the consolation of life. Man here weighs everything, calculates everything, and sacrifices everything to his interest." An Englishman named Fearon, in 1818, expressed the same idea with more distinctness: "In going to America, I would say generally, the emigrant must expect to find, not an economical or cleanly people; not a social or generous people; not a people of enlarged ideas; not a people of liberal opinions, or toward whom you can express your thoughts free as air; not a people friendly to the advocates of liberty in Europe; not a people who understand liberty from investigation and principle; not a people who comprehend the meaning of words 'honor' and 'generosity.'" Such quotations might be multiplied almost without limit. Rapacity was the accepted explanation of American peculiarities; yet every traveler was troubled by inconsistencies that required explanations of a different kind. "It is not in order to hoard that the Americans are rapacious," observed Liancourt as early as 1796. The extravagance, or what economical Europeans thought extravagance, with which American women were allowed and encouraged to spend money, was as notorious in 1790 as a century later; the recklessness with which Americans often risked their money, and the liberality with which they used it, were marked even then, in comparison with the ordinary European habit. Europeans saw such contradictions, but made no attempt to reconcile them. No foreigner of that day—neither poet, painter, nor philosopher—could detect in American life anything higher than vulgarity; for it was something beyond the range of their experience, which education and culture had not framed a formula to express. Moore came to Washington, and found there no loftier inspiration than any Federalist rhymester of Dennie's school.

> Take Christians, Mohawks, democrats and all,
> From the rude wigwam to the Congress hall,—
> From man the savage, whether slaved or free,
> To man the civilized, less tame than he:
> 'T is one dull chaos, one unfertile strife
> Betwixt half-polished and half-barbarous life;
> Where every ill the ancient world can brew
> Is mixed with every grossness of the new;
> Where all corrupts, though little can entice,
> And nothing 's known of luxury but vice.

Moore's two small volumes of Epistles, printed in 1807, contained much more so-called poetry of the same tone—poetry more polished and less respectable than that of Barlow and Dwight; while, as though to prove that the Old World knew what grossness was, he embalmed in his lines the slanders which the Scotch libeler Callender invented against Jefferson:

> The weary statesman for repose hath fled
> From halls of council to his negro's shed;
> Where, blest, he woos some black Aspasia's grace,
> And dreams of freedom in his slave's embrace.

To leave no doubt of his meaning, he explained in a footnote that his allusion was to the President of the United States; and yet even Moore, trifler and butterfly as he was, must have seen, if he would, that between the morals of politics and society in America and those then prevailing in Europe, there was no room for comparison—there was room only for contrast.

Moore was but an echo of fashionable England in his day. He seldom affected moral sublimity; and had he in his wanderings met a race of embodied angels, he would have sung of them or to them in the slightly erotic notes which were so well received in the society he loved to frequent and flatter. His remarks upon American character betrayed more temper than truth; but even in this respect he expressed only the common feeling of Europeans, which was echoed by the Federalist society of the United States. Englishmen especially indulged in unbounded invective against the sordid character of American society, and in shaping their national policy on this contempt they carried their theory into practice with so much energy as to produce its own refutation. To their astonishment and anger, a day came when the Americans, in defiance of self-interest and in contradiction of all the qualities ascribed to them, insisted on declaring war; and readers of this narrative will be surprised at the cry of incredulity, not unmixed with terror, with which Englishmen started to their feet when they woke from their delusion on seeing what they had been taught to call the meteor flag of England, which had burned terrific at Copenhagen and Trafalgar, suddenly waver and fall on the bloody deck of the "Guerriere." Fearon and Beaujour, with a score of other contemporary critics, could see neither generosity, economy, honor, nor ideas of any kind in the American breast; yet the obstinate repetition of these denials itself betrayed a lurking fear of the social forces whose strength they were candid enough to record. What was it that, as they complained, turned the European peasant into a new man within half an hour after landing at New York? Englishmen were never at a loss to understand the poetry of more prosaic emotions. Neither they nor any of their kindred failed in later times to feel the "large excitement" of the country boy, whose "spirit leaped within him to be gone before him," when the lights of London first flared in the distance; yet none seemed ever to feel the larger excitement of the American immigrant. Among the Englishmen who criticized the United States was one greater than Moore —one who thought himself at home only in the stern beauty of a moral presence. Of all poets, living or dead, Wordsworth felt most keenly what he called the still, sad music of humanity; yet the highest conception he could create of America was not more poetical than that of any Cumberland beggar he might have met in his morning walk:

> Long-wished-for sight, the Western World appeared;
> And when the ship was moored, I leaped ashore
> Indignantly,—resolved to be a man,
> Who, having o'er the past no power, would live
> No longer in subjection to the past,
> With abject mind—from a tyrannic lord
> Inviting penance, fruitlessly endured.
> So, like a fugitive whose feet have cleared

Some boundary which his followers may not cross
In prosecution of their deadly chase,
Respiring, I looked round. How bright the sun,
The breeze how soft! Can anything produced
In the Old World compare, thought I, for power
And majesty, with this tremendous stream
Sprung from the desert? And behold a city
Fresh, youthful, and aspiring! . . .
                              Sooth to say,
On nearer view, a motley spectacle
Appeared, of high pretensions—unreproved
But by the obstreperous voice of higher still;
Big passions strutting on a petty stage,
Which a detached spectator may regard
Not unamused. But ridicule demands
Quick change of objects; and to laugh alone,
. . . in the very centre of the crowd
To keep the secret of a poignant scorn,
                              . . . is least fit
For the gross spirit of mankind.

Thus Wordsworth, although then at his prime, indulging in what sounded like a boast that he alone had felt the sense sublime of something interfused, whose dwelling is the light of setting suns, and the round ocean, and the living air, and the blue sky, and in the mind of man—even he, to whose moods the heavy and the weary weight of all this unintelligible world was lightened by his deeper sympathies with nature and the soul, could do no better, when he stood in the face of American democracy, than "keep the secret of a poignant scorn."

Possibly the view of Wordsworth and Moore, of Weld, Dennie, and Dickens was right. The American democrat possessed little art of expression, and did not watch his own emotions with a view of uttering them either in prose or verse; he never told more of himself than the world might have assumed without listening to him. Only with diffidence could history attribute to such a class of men a wider range of thought or feeling than they themselves cared to proclaim. Yet the difficulty of denying or even ignoring the wider range was still greater, for no one questioned the force or the scope of an emotion which caused the poorest peasant in Europe to see what was invisible to poet and philosopher—the dim outline of a mountain summit across the ocean, rising high above the mist and mud of American democracy. As though to call attention to some such difficulty, European and American critics, while affirming that

Americans were a race without illusions or enlarged ideas, declared in the same breath that Jefferson was a visionary whose theories would cause the heavens to fall upon them. Year after year, with endless iteration, in every accent of contempt, rage, and despair, they repeated this charge against Jefferson. Every foreigner and Federalist agreed that he was a man of illusions, dangerous to society and unbounded in power of evil; but if this view of his character was right, the same visionary qualities seemed also to be a national trait, for everyone admitted that Jefferson's opinions, in one form or another, were shared by a majority of the American people.

Illustrations might be carried much further, and might be drawn from every social class and from every period in national history. Of all presidents, Abraham Lincoln has been considered the most typical representative of American society, chiefly because his mind, with all its practical qualities, also inclined, in certain directions, to idealism. Lincoln was born in 1809, the moment when American character stood in lowest esteem. Ralph Waldo Emerson, a more distinct idealist, was born in 1803. William Ellery Channing, another idealist, was born in 1780. Men like John Fitch, Oliver Evans, Robert Fulton, Joel Barlow, John Stevens, and Eli Whitney were all classed among visionaries. The whole society of Quakers belonged in the same category. The records of the popular religious sects abounded in examples of idealism and illusion to such an extent that the masses seemed hardly to find comfort or hope in any authority, however old or well established. In religion as in politics, Americans seemed to require a system which gave play to their imagination and their hopes.

Some misunderstanding must always take place when the observer is at cross purposes with the society he describes. Wordsworth might have convinced himself by a moment's thought that no country could act on the imagination as America acted upon the instincts of the ignorant and poor, without some quality that deserved better treatment than poignant scorn; but perhaps this was only one among innumerable cases in which the unconscious poet breathed an atmosphere which the self-conscious poet could not penetrate. With equal reason he might have taken the opposite view—that the hard, practical, money-getting American democrat, who had neither generosity nor honor nor imagination, and who inhabited cold shades where fancy sickened and where genius died, was in truth living in a world of dream, and acting a drama more instinct with poetry than all the avatars of the East, walking in gardens of emerald and rubies, in ambition already ruling the world and guiding

Nature with a kinder and wiser hand than had ever yet been felt in human history. From this point his critics never approached him—they stopped at a stone's throw; and at the moment when they declared that the man's mind had no illusions, they added that he was a knave or a lunatic. Even on his practical and sordid side, the American might easily have been represented as a victim to illusion. If the Englishman had lived as the American speculator did—in the future—the hyperbole of enthusiasm would have seemed less monstrous. "Look at my wealth!" cried the American to his foreign visitor. "See these solid mountains of salt and iron, of lead, copper, silver, and gold! See these magnificent cities scattered broadcast to the Pacific! See my cornfields rustling and waving in the summer breeze from ocean to ocean, so far that the sun itself is not high enough to mark where the distant mountains bound my golden seas! Look at this continent of mine, fairest of created worlds, as she lies turning up to the sun's never failing caress her broad and exuberant breasts, overflowing with milk for her hundred million children! See how she glows with youth, health, and love!" Perhaps it was not altogether unnatural that the foreigner, on being asked to see what needed centuries to produce, should have looked about him with bewilderment and indignation. "Gold! cities! cornfields! continents! Nothing of the sort! I see nothing but tremendous wastes, where sickly men and women are dying of homesickness or are scalped by savages! mountain ranges a thousand miles long, with no means of getting to them, and nothing in them when you get there! swamps and forests choked with their own rotten ruins! nor hope of better for a thousand years! Your story is a fraud, and you are a liar and swindler!"

Met in this spirit, the American, half-perplexed and half-defiant, retaliated by calling his antagonist a fool, and by mimicking his heavy tricks of manner. For himself he cared little, but his dream was his whole existence. The men who denounced him admitted that they left him in his forest swamp quaking with fever, but clinging in the delirium of death to the illusions of his dazzled brain. No class of men could be required to support their convictions with a steadier faith, or pay more devotedly with their persons for the mistakes of their judgment. Whether imagination or greed led them to describe more than actually existed, they still saw no more than any inventor or discoverer must have seen in order to give him the energy of success. They said to the rich as to the poor, "Come and share our limitless riches! Come and help us bring to light these unimaginable stores of wealth and power!" The poor came, and from them were seldom heard complaints of deception or delusion.

Within a moment, by the mere contact of a moral atmosphere, they saw the gold and jewels, the summer cornfields and the glowing continent. The rich for a long time stood aloof—they were timid and narrow-minded; but this was not all—between them and the American democrat was a gulf.

The charge that Americans were too fond of money to win the confidence of Europeans was a curious inconsistency; yet this was a common belief. If the American deluded himself and led others to their death by baseless speculations; if he buried those he loved in a gloomy forest where they quaked and died while he persisted in seeing there a splendid, healthy, and well-built city—no one could deny that he sacrificed wife and child to his greed for gain, that the dollar was his god, and a sordid avarice his demon. Yet had this been the whole truth, no European capitalist would have hesitated to make money out of his grave; for, avarice against avarice, no more sordid or meaner type existed in America than could be shown on every 'change in Europe. With much more reason Americans might have suspected that in America Englishmen found everywhere a silent influence, which they found nowhere in Europe, and which had nothing to do with avarice or with the dollar, but, on the contrary, seemed likely at any moment to sacrifice the dollar in a cause and for an object so illusory that most Englishmen could not endure to hear it discussed. European travelers who passed through America noticed that everywhere, in the White House at Washington and in log cabins beyond the Alleghenies, except for a few Federalists, every American, from Jefferson and Gallatin down to the poorest squatter, seemed to nourish an idea that he was doing what he could to overthrow the tyranny which the past had fastened on the human mind. Nothing was easier than to laugh at the ludicrous expressions of this simple-minded conviction, or to cry out against its coarseness, or grow angry with its prejudices; to see its nobler side, to feel the beatings of a heart underneath the sordid surface of a gross humanity, was not so easy. Europeans seemed seldom or never conscious that the sentiment could possess a noble side, but found only matter for complaint in the remark that every American democrat believed himself to be working for the overthrow of tyranny, aristocracy, hereditary privilege, and priesthood, wherever they existed. Even where the American did not openly proclaim this conviction in words, he carried so dense an atmosphere of the sentiment with him in his daily life as to give respectable Europeans an uneasy sense of remoteness.

Of all historical problems, the nature of a national character is the most difficult and the most important. Readers will be troubled, at almost every chapter of the coming narrative,[1] by the want of some formula to explain what share the popular imagination bore in the system pursued by government. The acts of the American people during the administrations of Jefferson and Madison were judged at the time by no other test. According as bystanders believed American character to be hard, sordid, and free from illusion, they were severe and even harsh in judgment. This rule guided the governments of England and France. Federalists in the United States, knowing more of the circumstances, often attributed to the democratic instinct a visionary quality which they regarded as sentimentality, and charged with many bad consequences. If their view was correct, history could occupy itself to no better purpose than in ascertaining the nature and force of the quality which was charged with results so serious; but nothing was more elusive than the spirit of American democracy. Jefferson, the literary representative of the class, spoke chiefly for Virginians, and dreaded so greatly his own reputation as a visionary that he seldom or never uttered his whole thought. Gallatin and Madison were still more cautious. The press in no country could give shape to a mental condition so shadowy. The people themselves, although millions in number, could not have expressed their finer instincts had they tried, and might not have recognized them if expressed by others.

In the early days of colonization, every new settlement represented an idea and proclaimed a mission. Virginia was founded by a great, liberal movement aiming at the spread of English liberty and empire. The Pilgrims of Plymouth, the Puritans of Boston, the Quakers of Pennsylvania, all avowed a moral purpose, and began by making institutions that consciously reflected a moral idea. No such character belonged to the colonization of 1800. From Lake Erie to Florida, in long, unbroken line, pioneers were at work, cutting into the forests with the energy of so many beavers, and with no more express moral purpose than the beavers they drove away. The civilization they carried with them was rarely illumined by an idea; they sought room for no new truth, and aimed neither at creating, like the Puritans, a government of saints, nor, like the Quakers, one of love and peace; they left such experiments behind them, and wrestled only with the hardest problems of frontier life. No wonder that foreign observers, and even the educated, well-to-do Americans of the seacoast, could seldom see anything to admire in the ignorance and brutality of

---

1. Henry Adams is here referring to the later chapters of his *History of the United States* [Ed.].

frontiersmen, and should declare that virtue and wisdom no longer guided the United States! What they saw was not encouraging. To a new society, ignorant and semibarbarous, a mass of demagogues insisted on applying every stimulant that could inflame its worst appetites, while at the same instant taking away every influence that had hitherto helped to restrain its passions. Greed for wealth, lust for power, yearning for the blank void of savage freedom such as Indians and wolves delighted in— these were the fires that flamed under the caldron of American society, in which, as conservatives believed, the old, well-proven, conservative crust of religion, government, family, and even common respect for age, education, and experience was rapidly melting away, and was indeed already broken into fragments, swept about by the seething mass of scum ever rising in greater quantities to the surface.

Against this Federalist and conservative view of democratic tendencies, democrats protested in a thousand forms, but never in any mode of expression which satisfied them all, or explained their whole character. Probably Jefferson came nearest to the mark, for he represented the hopes of science as well as the prejudices of Virginia; but Jefferson's writings may be searched from beginning to end without revealing the whole measure of the man, far less of the movement. Here and there in his letters a suggestion was thrown out, as though by chance, revealing larger hopes—as in 1815, at a moment of despondency, he wrote: "I fear from the experience of the last twenty-five years that morals do not of necessity advance hand in hand with the sciences." In 1800, in the flush of triumph, he believed that his task in the world was to establish a democratic republic, with the sciences for an intellectual field, and physical and moral advancement keeping pace with their advance. Without an excessive introduction of more recent ideas, he might be imagined to define democratic progress, in the somewhat affected precision of his French philosophy: "Progress is either physical or intellectual. If we can bring it about that men are on the average an inch taller in the next generation than in this; if they are an inch larger round the chest; if their brain is an ounce or two heavier, and their life a year or two longer, —that is progress. If fifty years hence the average man shall invariably argue from two ascertained premises where he now jumps to a conclusion from a single supposed revelation,—that is progress! I expect it to be made here, under our democratic stimulants, on a great scale, until every man is potentially an athlete in body and an Aristotle in mind." To this doctrine the New Englander replied, "What will you do for moral progress?" Every possible answer to this question opened a chasm. No doubt

Jefferson held the faith that men would improve morally with their physical and intellectual growth; but he had no idea of any moral improvement other than that which came by nature. He could not tolerate a priesthood, a state church, or revealed religion. Conservatives, who could tolerate no society without such pillars of order, were, from their point of view, right in answering, "Give us rather the worst despotism of Europe—there our souls at least may have a chance of salvation!" To their minds vice and virtue were not relative, but fixed terms. The Church was a divine institution. How could a ship hope to reach port when the crew threw overboard sails, spars, and compass, unshipped their rudder, and all the long day thought only of eating and drinking? Nay, even should the new experiment succeed in a worldly sense, what was a man profited if he gained the whole world, and lost his own soul? The Lord God was a jealous God, and visited the sins of the parents upon the children; but what worse sin could be conceived than for a whole nation to join their chief in chanting the strange hymn with which Jefferson, a new false prophet, was deceiving and betraying his people: "It does me no injury for my neighbor to say there are twenty Gods or no God!"

On this ground conservatism took its stand, as it had hitherto done with success in every similar emergency in the world's history, and fixing its eyes on moral standards of its own, refused to deal with the subject as further open to argument. The two parties stood facing opposite ways, and could see no common ground of contact.

Yet even then one part of the American social system was proving itself to be rich in results. The average American was more intelligent than the average European, and was becoming every year still more active-minded as the new movement of society caught him up and swept him through a life of more varied experiences. On all sides the national mind responded to its stimulants. Deficient as the American was in the machinery of higher instruction; remote, poor; unable by any exertion to acquire the training, the capital, or even the elementary textbooks he needed for a fair development of his natural powers—his native energy and ambition already responded to the spur applied to them. Some of his triumphs were famous throughout the world; for Benjamin Franklin had raised high the reputation of American printers, and the actual President of the United States, who signed with Franklin the treaty of peace with Great Britain, was the son of a small farmer, and had himself kept a school in his youth. In both these cases social recognition followed success; but the later triumphs of the American mind were becoming more and more popular. John Fitch was not only one of the poorest but one of the least-educated Yankees who ever made a name; he could never spell with tolerable correctness, and his life ended as it began—in the lowest social obscurity. Eli Whitney was better educated than Fitch, but had neither wealth, social influence, nor patron to back his ingenuity. In the year 1800 Eli Terry, another Connecticut Yankee of the same class, took into his employ two young men to help him make wooden clocks, and this was the capital on which the greatest clock manufactory in the world began its operations. In 1797 Asa Whittemore, a Massachusetts Yankee, invented a machine to make cards for carding wool, which "operated as if it had a soul," and became the foundation for a hundred subsequent patents. In 1790 Jacob Perkins, of Newburyport, invented a machine capable of cutting and turning out two hundred thousand nails a day; and then invented a process for transferring engraving from a very small steel cylinder to copper, which revolutionized cotton printing. The British traveler Weld, passing through Wilmington, stopped, as Liancourt had done before him, to see the great flour mills on the Brandywine. "The improvements," he said, "which have been made in the machinery of the flour mills in America are very great. The chief of these consist in a new application of the screw, and the introduction of what are called elevators, the idea of which was evidently borrowed from the chain-pump." This was the invention of Oliver Evans, a native of Delaware, whose parents were in very humble life, but who was himself, in spite of every disadvantage, an inventive genius of the first order. Robert Fulton, who in 1800 was in Paris with Joel Barlow, sprang from the same source in Pennsylvania. John Stevens, a native of New York, belonged to a more favored class, but followed the same impulses. All these men were the outcome of typical American society, and all their inventions transmuted the democratic instinct into a practical and tangible shape. Who would undertake to say that there was a limit to the fecundity of this teeming source? Who that saw only the narrow, practical, money-getting nature of the devices could venture to assert that as they wrought their end and raised the standard of millions, they would not also raise the creative power of those millions to a higher plane? If the priests and barons who set their names to Magna Carta had been told that in a few centuries every swineherd and cobbler's apprentice would write and read with an ease such as few kings could then command, and reason with better logic than any university could then practice, the priest and baron would have been more incredulous than any man who was told in 1800 that within another five centuries the plowboy would go afield whistling a sonata of Beethoven, and figure out in quaternions the relation of his furrows. The American democrat knew so little of art that among his popular illusions he could not then nourish artistic ambition; but leaders like Jefferson, Gallatin, and Barlow might without extravagance count upon a coming time when the diffused ease and education should bring the masses into familiar contact with higher forms of human achievement, and their vast creative power, turned toward a nobler culture, might rise to the level of that democratic genius which found expression in the Parthenon; might revel in the delights of a new Buonarroti [Michelangelo] and a richer Titian; might create for five hundred million people the America of thought and art which alone could satisfy their omnivorous ambition.

Whether the illusions, so often affirmed and so often denied to the American people, took such forms or not, these were in effect the problems that lay before American society: Could it transmute its social power into the higher forms of thought? Could it provide for the moral and intellectual needs of mankind? Could it take permanent political shape? Could it give new life to religion and art? Could it create and maintain in the mass of mankind those habits of mind which had hitherto belonged to men of science alone? Could it physically develop the convolutions of the human brain? Could it produce, or was it compatible with, the differentiation of a higher variety of the human race? Nothing less than this was necessary for its complete success.

The foregoing consists of Chapters I and VI from Volume I of Henry Adams' HISTORY OF THE UNITED STATES OF AMERICA.

John Bagnell Bury

1861–1927

John Bagnell Bury, classicist and historian, was born at Monaghan, Ireland, in 1861, the son of an Anglican clergyman of more than ordinary learning. The boy was taught Greek and Latin at an early age. By the time he was ten he had exhausted the ingenuity of his tutor at Foyle College, Londonderry, who could find no question in Greek grammar too difficult for his pupil. Subsequently, Bury carried off all the prizes in classics at Trinity College, Dublin, from which he was graduated in 1882.

In 1885 he was made a fellow of the College, having achieved distinction as a philologist with two books on the *Odes* of Pindar. He had by then become interested in history, however, and in 1889 he published a work on the later Roman Empire that was received with high praise. In consequence of this, he was in 1895 appointed to a professorship in history. Thereafter he produced a steady stream of scholarly books, including an annotated edition of Gibbon in seven volumes (1896–1900), and a *History of Greece to the Death of Alexander the Great* (1900) which at once became a standard text.

As these works firmly established Bury's reputation, he was the logical choice for Regius Professor of Modern History at Cambridge when Lord Acton died; and, being appointed to that august chair in 1902, he occupied it until his death in 1927. Throughout his later

Notes from the artist: "The portrait of Bury is surrounded with Greek and Byzantine designs, reflecting his writings on early Mediterranean history. At the bottom is a small head of Gibbon, whose Decline and Fall was annotated by Bury in a seven-volume edition."

J. B. Bury

life he continued to publish works which ranged from the most detailed monographs to the widely read *History of Freedom of Thought* (1913) and *The Idea of Progress* (1920). In all, his bibliography amounted to no less than 369 items, while his erudition extended to perhaps a dozen languages, including Hebrew, Sanskrit, and Hungarian.

In this chapter of *The Ancient Greek Historians*, Bury appraises the work of the "Father of History," as Herodotus has been called. He was not the first historian, however, any more than Hippocrates, who is termed the "Father of Medicine," was the first physician. So much does not come out of nothing. We are amazed at the complexity of the medical tradition that lay behind Hippocrates; we are surprised also by the amount of historical literature that had accumulated in fifth-century Greece, which Herodotus could have absorbed before he set out on his most important journeys to Babylonia and Egypt. Other much older civilizations, such as the Indian, had little sense of history, or even of chronology.

In explaining the long geographical sections of *The History*,[1] Bury says that Herodotus was following the example set by Hecataeus and his "school," and points out that the geography of Egypt and Scythia had a "practical interest" for Athenians. The geography is not something imported from outside, as had been supposed, but is a calculated part of the story. So also are the numerous digressions. They add piquancy and charm, and rest the mind from a too continuous narrative. The invented dialogues also enliven *The History*, lending verisimilitude and fascination. Herodotus' aim, unlike the modern scientific historian's, was to capture the mind of the ordinary reader.

In his dialogues, digressions, and epic sweep, Herodotus followed the model of his greatest master—the poet Homer. The *Iliad*, as you will remember, abounds in digressions and resounding speeches, and it also recounts the war of Greeks and Ionians. Herodotus' epic theme, in *The History*, is not merely the military conflict of Greece and Persia, but also the clash of two very different civilizations—the liberty of "Hellenic constitutionalism" v. "oriental autocracy." Although he was born in Ionia, under the sway of Persia, Herodotus'

---

[1] For *The History of Herodotus* see *Great Books of the Western World*, Vol. 6.

sympathies are clearly with the Greeks, or rather, the Athenians. In this respect also, as Bury implies, he was not a scientific historian.

Yet in spite of his bias, which most of us probably share, Herodotus wrote "universal history," depicting life on both sides of the trenches, and thus giving us "a lesson in the unity of history"—"the common history of man." He (and his immediate predecessors) also made an important advance in de-mythologizing human history. In the *Iliad*, the gods are the principal actors or at least pull the strings, whereas in *The History* they are gently pushed aside and deflated by irony. Not entirely, to be sure, for portents and other supernatural influences are still accepted, not only as reports, but as facts. Yet Herodotus' skepticism, though mixed with naïve, often piquant, gullibility, was a signal advance in the writing of history.

Bury thinks Herodotus' maxims of historical criticism are all valid. The historian should "suspect superhuman and miraculous occurrences, which contradict ordinary experience." When there is a conflict of evidence, he *should* "keep an open mind," and observations of results and "first-hand oral information" *are* more trustworthy than "stories at second hand." Bury regrets only that Herodotus did not follow his own maxims more consistently. He calls attention to numbers of glaring errors of fact and interpretation in *The History*, some of which are enough in themselves "to stamp Herodotus as more of an epic poet than a historian."

This judgment, in spite of Bury's praise, is so severe that the generous reader may want to make some defense of Herodotus. Could we not say that the business of the historian is not only to report the facts correctly, but also to construct a plausible picture of the past—to make it live? This is Herodotus' special talent. His version of the Persian War will outlive better-documented accounts, partly because it captures the true color and momentum of the period.

Herodotus

Of the life of Herodotus, son of Lyxes, of Halicarnassus, we know hardly anything except what may be gleaned from his own statements. Born early in the fifth century, he left his birthplace before 454 B.C., banished by Lygdamis the tyrant, who put his cousin Panyassis, the epic poet, to death. He stayed apparently for some time in Samos, and then went to Athens, whence he proceeded to Italy as one of the first citizens of the new colony of Thurii (443 B.C.). He survived the first years of the Peloponnesian War (431–0 B.C.). Into this framework we have to fit his travels, which included the coasts of the Euxine, Babylon, Phoenicia, Egypt, and probably Cyrene. It is not necessary to discuss the disputed subject of the chronology of his journeys. I need only say that his most important journeys, those to Babylonia and Egypt, were probably undertaken in the later period of his life, while he was a citizen of Thurii. The years which elapsed between his banishment from his native city and his departure for his new home seem to have been spent in Greece, perhaps chiefly at Athens, and to have been devoted, as we shall see, to investigating and composing the story of the invasion of Xerxes. Though he may naturally have visited Athens again, on his way to or from the East, there is no evidence to entitle us to presume, as some have thought, that he deserted Thurii permanently and dwelled at Athens during the last years of his life.

The argument of his history is a narrative of the relations between the Greeks and the oriental powers from the accession of Croesus to the capture of Sestos in 478 B.C.—a "modern" history in the fullest sense of the term. The division into nine books is not due to the author himself, for in his day such divisions had not yet come into fashion. But the Alexandrine editor who was responsible for it was a man of extraordinary insight. His distribution perfectly exhibits the construction of the book and could not be improved by any change. But it can be rendered more

364

perspicuous by observing that each of the nine books is truly a sub-division and that the primary partition is a threefold one. The work falls naturally into three sections, each consisting of three parts. The first section, or triad of books, comprises the reigns of Cyrus and Cambyses, and the accession of Darius; the second deals with the reign of Darius; the third with that of Xerxes. The first is mainly concerned with Asia including Egypt; the second with Europe; the third with Hellas. The first displays the rise and the triumphs of the power of Persia; the last relates the defeat of Persia by Greece; while the middle triad represents a chequered picture, Persian failure in Scythia and at Marathon, Greek failure in Ionia. And each of the nine subdivisions has a leading theme which constitutes a minor unity. Cyrus is the theme of the first book, Egypt of the second, Scythia of the fourth, the Ionian rebellion of the fifth, Marathon of the sixth. The seventh describes the invasion of Xerxes up to his success at Thermopylae; the eighth relates the reversal of fortune at Salamis; the final triumphs of Greece at Plataea and Mycale occupy the ninth. In the third alone the unity is less marked; yet there is a central interest in the dynastic revolution which set Darius on the throne. Thus the unity of the whole composition sharply displays itself in three parts, of which each again is threefold. The simplicity with which this architectural symmetry has been managed, without any apparent violence, constraint, or formality, was an achievement of consummate craft. The writer's management of the digressions, for which he is notorious, is hardly less striking, exhibiting a rare skill in the choice of the best and perhaps the only fitting places to stow away loose material he wished to make use of.

But, perfect as is the architectural unity of the work of Herodotus, it would seem that the plan as it was finally carried out was not conceived when he commenced to write, and that the unity was achieved not in conformity to a design thought out from the beginning, but by a process of expansion due to an afterthought. There is a variety of internal evidence which points convincingly to the conclusion that the last three books were composed before the first six, and there are indications that he wrote this portion between 456 and 445 B.C., before he began his travels. The natural inference is that he originally contemplated no more than a history of the invasion of Xerxes; and that it was in the course of his travels that he conceived the idea of a larger work, of which the "Invasion of Xerxes" should form the finale. The idea doubtless shaped itself gradually; and the first six books were not composed in the order in which they stand. But the author has worked with such skill that only a searching analysis has detected the series of facts which demonstrate the priority of the last three books and make it clear that the Persian War was his original inspiration.

At whatever moment the idea of expanding his original history to its fuller compass presented itself, whether it was suggested by his journeys or prompted him to become a traveller, it was certainly connected closely with his travels, and the occurrence of long geographical excursus is one of the most striking features of the expansion.

So strongly marked indeed is the geographical element, so long are the geographical sections, in the work of Herodotus, that some critics have been led to think that considerable parts of it were originally intended to form part of a geography, and were afterwards incorporated in his history. There is nothing that compels us to adopt a hypothesis of this kind. Association with geography was a characteristic of the early historical literature of the Greeks, and these excursus in Herodotus attest the influence of the Hecataean school, and were natural in the work of a historian who was himself a traveller. And it is worth observing that when he was writing, both Egypt and Scythia, the subjects of his longest historico-geographical digressions, had a particular practical interest for the Athenians; and of the Greek public it was unquestionably the Athenians to whom the historian designed his work pre-eminently to appeal. I need only remind you of the Athenian adventure in Egypt in the middle of the fifth century and of the voyage of Pericles in the Euxine Sea. It has even been conjectured that this Periclean expedition (444 B.C.) was the occasion of the historian's visit to the Pontic regions. However this may be, it is not insignificant, in judging these digressions, that Egypt and Scythia possessed, at the time Herodotus wrote, an interest of a political kind, subordinate indeed to that of Persia, but distinctly actual.

It is also to be noted that the digressions in general had an artistic justification. They are an epic feature, deliberately designed; one of the epic notes of the work. Homer was the literary master of Herodotus; without imitating him in any obvious way, the first great master of prose studied and caught the secrets of his effects. By means of digressions he achieved epic variety. We cannot do better than read the observations of the accomplished literary critic Dionysius. "Herodotus knew that every narrative of great length wearies the ears of the hearer, if it dwell without a break on the same subject; but, if pauses are introduced at intervals, it affects the mind agreeably. And so he desired to lend variety to his work and imitated Homer. If we take up his book, we admire it to the last syllable, and always want more."

Besides diversifying his work with digressions and episodes, Herodotus adopted another epic feature, not less characteristic. Like Homer, the historian makes his characters speak. He introduces not only short and pointed conversations, but dialogues and orations of considerable length. For instance, Xerxes, Mardonius, and Artabanus make each a speech in council before it is decided to invade Greece. I may recall the conversations of Solon with Croesus, of Xerxes with Artabanus and with Demaratus; and the speech made by the Corinthian envoy when the Spartans were considering the policy of forcing Athens to restore the Peisistratids. If the historian were charged with abusing this artifice by introducing in the Corinthian envoy's speech a long episode from Corinthian history, which is really quite irrelevant, he could appeal to the discourses of Phoenix and Nestor in Homer; and this case illustrates the fact that in introducing speeches he was influenced by the Ionian epic and not by the Athenian drama. It is impossible to say whether any of the older prose writers had adopted this practice, which makes the scenes vivid and the work alive. The bits of Hecataeus we possess are too brief to judge; but I may note that in one case at least he put words into the mouth of an actor.

The Homeric qualities of Herodotus, which communicate to his history an epic flavour, accord with the object to produce a work which like Homer should fascinate the minds of men. It was his aim to hold his audience or readers entertained; to do for his own world in prose what Homer had done for the ancient world in numbers. We cannot tell how far any of his prose predecessors had sought to make their works attractive or entertaining, or whether the influence of epic poetry affected their method of presentation. But we may confidently say that Herodotus was the first who discerned in "modern" history the possibilities of a treatment which was epic, and not Hesiodic but Homeric, in spirit and style.

His theme, the struggle of Greece with the Orient, possessed for him a deeper meaning than the political result of the Persian War. It was the contact and collision of two different types of civilization, of peoples of two different characters and different political institutions. In the last division of his work, where the final struggle of Persia and Greece is related, this contrast between the slavery of the barbarian and the liberty of the Greek, between oriental autocracy and Hellenic constitutionalism, is ever present and is forcibly brought out. But the contrast of Hellenic with oriental culture pervades the whole work; it informs the unity of the external theme with the deeper unity of an inner meaning. It is the key-note of the history of Herodotus. The digressions and stories which delay the action, besides their intrinsic interest, and besides their epic use as pleasant pauses, have also the value of sounding that note, and of contributing distinctly, but without emphasis or iteration, towards impressing that contrast on the reader's mind. The interview, for example, of Croesus with Solon, the self-confident Eastern potentate with the thoughtful, self-controlled Greek, strikes this chord loudly; and most of the oriental and Hellenic stories are calculated to suggest the antithesis which finds its supreme expression, and is more elaborately wrought out, in the final collision of the Persian Wars.

In the execution of this conception the Herodotean work has assumed the character of a study in the history of civilization. Just as the Homeric poems present a large and living picture of the culture of ancient Greece, so the history of Herodotus gives us panoramic views in the Hellenic civilization of the sixth century, and describes the cultures of all the Eastern peoples who directly or indirectly come within range.

And if it is a study in the history of civilization, we may also say that it has certain features of a universal history. It is not universal either in space or in time. Not in time; it does not attempt to go back far in Greek history, and only touches upon the ancient period incidentally. Not in space, for it hardly touches upon the western Greeks at all, and does not include what Hecataeus would have supplied about the peoples of the western Mediterranean. But it has the higher quality of what we mean by universal history or *Weltgeschichte,* in focusing under one point of view, and fitting into a connected narrative, the histories of the various peoples who came into relations with one another, within a given range; so that they are drawn out of their isolation and recognized to have a meaning, greater or less, in the common history of man. Within that range, which is determined by his theme, Herodotus is irreproachably comprehensive; and his book, though he never formulates the idea, is a lesson in the unity of history.

Although Herodotus does not enter upon the history of the heroic period, he has frequently occasion to refer to mythical tradition, and here he shows himself distinctly a sceptic. Not that he was a rationalist in regard to theology generally, or had any clear and consistent philosophical view. He looked upon human life as under the control of superhuman powers, who in exercising their incalculable government were prompted by motives of envy and nemesis or righteous anger, who acted to some extent on principles of justice and retribution, and who might communicate knowledge to men by means of oracles, portents, or dreams. But any further converse of gods with men, any divine appearances alleged to have happened in recent times, Herodotus is not prepared to accept, though he is never dogmatic. His philosophy was not strong enough to deny that the gods had ever carried on the sort of intercourse with men that is described in the epics, or generated human progeny; for his ultimate line between the divine and the human was not fast. But it was a great comfort for common sense and everyday experience, to push the age in which such things could happen as far back as possible. Herodotus reveals unmistakably his incredulity about all the mythical wonders in which, according to tradition, ancestors of living people, some fifteen or twenty generations back, played bright or shady parts. He accepted the genealogies, but when he got to Perseus or Hercules, he did not regard them as sons of a god. Hercules is the son of Amphitryon, Helen is the daughter of Tyndareus. Sometimes he relates legends or tells tales involving superhuman agency, but he never takes any responsibility for them, and occasionally treats them with delicate irony. He mentions a legend of the Thessalians that the ravine through which the Peneus makes its way to the sea was wrought by Poseidon. "Their tale is plausible; and any one who thinks that Poseidon shakes the earth and that clefts produced by earthquakes are the works of that god would on seeing this mountain-ravine ascribe it to Poseidon. For it appeared to me to be the result of an earthquake." Gibbon might have taken lessons in the art of irony from Herodotus as well as from Pascal. Consider again the admirable caution with which he speaks of the divine snake said to live on the Athenian Acropolis. "The Athenians say that a great snake lives in the Sanctuary as guardian of the citadel; and they present a honey-cake every month as to a creature existing." This commits him to nothing.

But though disposed to accept only what experience led him to regard as possible, in any given case, Herodotus, as I have said, did not draw theoretically a hard and fast line between the human and the divine; and he did not reject as ridiculous the notion that at one time gods moved visibly on the earth and consorted with men. Why then did he reject the divine parentage of heroes like Hercules and Perseus? It is important to comprehend the reason for this scepticism which he derived from Hecataeus. I touched on this point in the first lecture. It was not due to the canons of Ionian science or to the influence of Ionian philosophy. It was due to the study of comparative mythology which had opened for Hecataeus a new perspective of the world's history. The Egyptian studies which Herodotus pursued in the footsteps of the Milesian traveller taught him that human history in that country went back for thousands of years before the age of the gods was reached. The Egyptians, for instance, had a god corresponding to Hercules, and they reckoned that 17,000 years had elapsed since he had appeared in Egypt. Hence the conclusion which Herodotus accepts that there was an ancient god Hercules, but that he must be sharply distinguished from the human son of Amphitryon, ancestor of the Heraclidae.[1] The Greek tradition that the age in which gods walked the earth was still current some eight or nine hundred years ago could not be true. For even apart from the suggestions of comparative mythology, it was inadmissible to suppose that while Egypt was in a prosaic age of mere men, Greece was trodden by deities and the scene of miracles; and the Egyptian tradition was vouched for by records. The argument demolished the received mythology of the heroic age so far as it was superhuman.

Herodotus deserves credit for having accepted the argument, to which contemporary writers like Pherecydes were deaf; and if he asks pardon from the gods and heroes for his boldness, this does not mean that he felt hesitation or reluctance; it was merely an insincere and graceful genuflection. He was doing what a Christian preacher sometimes does when having delivered an extremely heterodox sermon he winds up with a formal homage to orthodox dogma. Herodotus is extremely courteous, perhaps ironically courteous, to both parties. He says, as it were, to the gods and heroes, "Please, do not be angry with me—supposing you to exist. But at this time of day, you know, one must really draw the line somewhere." On the other hand he says to the infidels who disbelieve in oracular prophecy, "I know you will think me credulous. But still in this case the evidence is so remarkably clear that I do not see my way to resisting it." The mythological argument, however, of which I am speaking was not due to Herodotus himself. He may have put it in his own way, and added some points, but he owed it, as I have said, to Hecataeus. It has long been recognized that his description of Egypt is not an original work, put together exclusively from his own observations and inquiries, but largely reproduces the account which Hecataeus had given in his *Map of the World*. When Herodotus visited Egypt, he doubtless had the book of Hecataeus with him, and used it like a barrister's brief for cross-examining the temple-servants and guiding him in his investigations. He added corrections and new information, but the great Ionian supplied the groundwork. He does not say so; he does not acknowledge his debt to Hecataeus; for, as you know, the ancients had very different views from the moderns about literary obligations. It was not the fashion or etiquette

1. Similarly Pan son of Penelope, Dionysus son of Semele, are to be distinguished from the synonymous gods.

to name your authorities except for some special reason—for instance, to criticize them, or to display your own learning; and you were not considered a plagiarist if you plundered somebody else's work without mentioning his name. Hecataeus brought out the importance of the Nile by the striking phrase that Egypt was the gift of the river; Herodotus adopts the phrase as if it were his own. One of the most convincing tests by which suspected plagiarism can be established is the occurrence of the same mistakes. Now Herodotus reproduces the errors which Hecataeus had committed about the hippopotamus. But there are a whole series of points in which we can trace the contact between the two writers in regard to Egypt. As for the mythology, we are left in no doubt because Herodotus names Hecataeus in this connection. "When Hecataeus was in Thebes he told his pedigree to the priests and connected himself with a god in the sixteenth generation. And the priests did to him what they did to me, though *I* did not relate *my* pedigree. They took him into the hall of the temple and showed him wooden statues of the high priests. The high priesthood descends from father to son, and each high priest sets up his own statue in his lifetime. They counted 345 statues, and they set this genealogy against that of Hecataeus, but *they* did not derive their pedigree from a god or a hero."

The author's motive in naming his predecessor here is, obviously, to rally him for having "given himself away" by stating his own genealogy and divine ancestry to the priests. "*I* was not so incautious" is the implication. But we have no right to infer that Hecataeus had not already drawn the sceptical conclusions which Herodotus explains. The sceptical words with which Hecataeus introduced his *Genealogies* show that he was not deaf to the lessons in history which he learned in Egyptian temples. His very expression when he says that "the *logoi* of the Hellenes are absurd," not "the stories of the poets," suggests the contrast of non-Hellenes whose *logoi* he had compared. The distinction of what the Greeks say from what the Persians, Phoenicians, or Egyptians say often recurs in Herodotus, and is an echo, I believe, from Hecataeus. But we have another proof. Herodotus cites the Egyptian priests as dating the age of the gods in relation to the reign of Amasis [Ahmose]. As the visit of Hecataeus to Egypt would have fallen not long after the death of Amasis, the dating indicates that Herodotus was copying the statement of Hecataeus.

The note of scepticism, perhaps we may say the characteristic note of Ionian scepticism, is struck in the first paragraphs of the Herodotean work. It opens with the statement of a theory that the wars of the Greeks and Persians were the manifestation of a secular antagonism between Asia and Europe—what our English historian, Freeman, was fond of calling the Eternal Question. This at least is the abstract way we should formulate the tenor of the statement which I may abbreviate as follows: "The quarrel began thus: Phoenician traders carried off from Argos Io, the king's daughter. Subsequently Greek adventurers from Crete carried off the princess Europa from Tyre. The next aggression came from the Greek side, when the Argonauts ravished Medea from Colchis. The Asiatic reply to this outrage was the rape of Helen by Paris. The Trojan War, which followed, generated in Asia a feeling of hostility to the Greeks, and the Persian War was the ultimate issue of this feeling." But the theory was not originated by Herodotus. He disavows all responsibility. It was a theory of the Persians, he tells us, and he states it only to set it aside in his ironical way.

The whole passage reads as if it might be the condensation of a friendly discussion between a Greek and a Persian as to the responsibility for the Persian War. It was undeniable that the Persians and not the Greeks had been the aggressors; the conquest of Ionia by Cyrus had been the beginning. The Persian advocate could only remove the blame from Asia by going farther back. The summary I gave of the argument does not reproduce its flavour, and I will take the liberty of throwing it into the form of a dialogue.

Persian. The Greeks had no business in Asia. They belong to Europe, and they should have stayed there. Their expedition against Troy was the first trespass; it began their encroachments on a continent which belongs to Asiatic peoples of whom the Persians are the heirs.

Greek. Oh, but you are forgetting that on that occasion the Trojans were the offenders; Paris carried off Helen.

Persian. That was no sufficient reason; but even if it were, the act of Paris was only a reprisal for the Greek crimes of carrying off Medea and Europa. And the Asiatics were far too sensible to make a *causa belli* of such foolish elopements.

Greek. Well, if you go back so far, you must go back farther still. What about the rape of Io from Argos?

Persian. Well, yes, I admit it. That was a Phoenician business, and we Persians must allow that the Phoenicians began the mischief, though we hold you really responsible, through your folly in taking such an affair seriously. Only fools would make war on account of such escapades. Men of the world know that, if these women were carried off, they were not more reluctant than they should be.

Evidently we have here an invention of Ionian *esprit*. The nature of the argument, dealing as it does entirely with Greek legend, shows that the Persian was a fictitious disputant; and the attribution of the theory to a Persian is an effect of literary subtlety quite in the manner of Voltaire. Though Herodotus thought little of this speculation about ancient wrongs, he seems to have taken it as seriously meant. "Whatever we think about all this," he says, "I will begin with the first Eastern monarch who undoubtedly committed injustice against Greece, Croesus, who subdued Ionia without provocation." But it is highly significant that he should place in the portals of his work a speculation which set mythical tradition in a ridiculous light.

The passage I have discussed is one of several that evince those acute tendencies in the Hellenic mind which culminated in the movement of the Sophists. For instance, the story of the wife of Intaphernes. She chose to save her brother rather than her husband or children, on the ground that husband and children might be replaced but she could never have another brother. That is a clever Ionian subtlety; there is no reason to suppose that it was invented in the period of the Sophists. Or take the demonstration of the power of custom by Darius. He dismayed some Greeks by the question what they would take to eat their dead fathers, and then equally horrified some Indians of a tribe who ate dead parents, by asking them how much they would take to cremate theirs. The immense power of custom was an observation redolent of the age of the Wise Men; Pindar, whom Herodotus quotes, designated Custom as king of the world; and the idea afterwards became the basis of sophistic theories. The story quoted by Herodotus is a drastic Ionian illustration.

Again, the famous discussion of the comparative merits of democracy, aristocracy, and monarchy by the seven Persian conspirators who overthrew the false Smerdis belongs also to pre-sophistic speculation. It is obviously a fiction; for the discussion was appropriate in the Greek world, but was quite out of place in Persia. But it was not a fiction of Herodotus, for he states expressly (careful though he generally is not to commit himself) that these opinions were really uttered by the Persian noblemen, although some of the Greeks consider this incredible. The historian was taken in, just as he was taken in by the persiflage about the rapes of the fair women of legend. There can hardly be much doubt that some publicist threw his reflections on the comparative merits of constitutions into the shape of this historical deliberation. The distinction of three fundamental types of constitution is older than the period of the Sophists; it is recognized in an ode of Pindar not later than 473 B.C., and it was then probably a commonplace. We may suspect that we have to do with some publication of the first half of the fifth century.

Now there is one feature common to these passages. Greek ideas and reflections are transferred to an Eastern setting or connected with Persian history. Their origin was assuredly Ionian.[2] They betray the naïve interest of the Ionians in their masters, and show the Greek mind projecting its own reflections into a world of which it had only a half-knowledge, with the instinct of making that world more interesting and sympathetic.[3]

But I must return to the scepticism of Herodotus. I have already observed that in the historical post-Homeric period the mythopoeic faculty of the Greeks did not slumber, but myth now took the form of the historical anecdote, or, as the Germans call it, *historische Novelle*. Here they showed consummate felicity in constructing stories with historical background, historical actors, historical motives, and possessing, many of them, a perpetual value because they are seasoned with worldly wisdom and enshrine some criticism of life. These tales differ from the old myths not only in the tendency to point a moral but also in the circumstance that for the most part they do not involve physical impossibilities, though they may imply highly improbable coincidences, or what we may call psychical or political impossibilities. The work of Herodotus is richly furnished with these tales; he had a wonderful flair for a good story; and the gracious garrulity with which he tells historical anecdotes is one of the charms which will secure him readers till the world's end. Gibbon happily observed that Herodotus "sometimes writes for children and sometimes for philosophers"; the anecdotes he relates often appeal to both. He accepts them generally at their face value, and most of them have been taken as more or less literally true till very recent times. The story of the intercourse between Croesus and Solon was rejected as fiction only because it seemed impossible to reconcile it with chro-

---

2. The clear allusion of Otanes, in his defence of democracy, to the Athenian constitution under the lot-system does not necessitate by any means an Athenian origin. It may be conjectured that the peculiar privileged position which Otanes and his descendants were said to have held in the Persian realm suggested the idea of transferring this singularly Hellenic discussion to Susa. Otanes, it is said, was exempted from subjection to the kings because, though he was the leading organizer of the conspiracy, he resigned all claims to the throne which Darius secured. He was thus neither ruler nor subject, an anomalous position which in Greece had a sort of parallel in the membership of a democracy. Hence the suggestion that Otanes believed in democracy, and, when he did not convince his fellow-conspirators, obtained for himself personally and his family the freedom which a democracy bestows.

3. I have been here expressing dissent from the view of some critics that the passages enumerated indicate sophistic influence.

nology. But we are now more sceptical about good stories of this type, and we have come to see how often they are wrought upon, or woven into, some ancient *motif*, which is adapted to a historical setting. The tale of the funeral pyre of Croesus sprang from the burning of the Assyrian god Sandan; it was an up-to-date version of the legend of Sardanapalus. The story of the ring of Polycrates turns on an old motive, the finding of something lost in a fish's belly, but its point in connection with Polycrates has been explained only the other day. The casting of the ring into the sea was symbolic of thalassocracy; it was the same mythical ring as that of Minos, which in the poem of Bacchylides Theseus sought in the halls of Amphitrite; its recovery was fatal to the ruler of the seas.

Herodotus is the Homer of this later form of historical myths, in which the supernatural machinery consisted of oracles or significant dreams or marvellous coincidences. They corresponded to his wavering standard of the credible and probable, which generally excluded what seemed physically impossible. For instance, he positively refuses to believe that statues assumed a sitting posture. He duly records the story that a certain man dived under water a distance of several miles. It was the private opinion of Herodotus that that man arrived in a boat.

Perhaps the story of the miraculous deliverance of Delphi from the Persians may be taken to illustrate the ill-defined limits of his faith. Their oracle declared to the Delphian priests that the god would himself provide for the safety of his sanctuary, and when the Persians came they were repelled, with great havoc, by lightning and by the fall of huge boulders from Parnassus. Herodotus relates this without any hint of scepticism, though he emphasizes the miraculous nature of the events. Now you observe that there is nothing impossible in the alleged physical occurrences; the marvel lies in the opportunity of the coincidence and the fulfilment of the oracular announcement. Against a marvel of this order Herodotus had no prejudice. But another miracle was said to have happened on the same occasion. Certain sacred arms, which were preserved within the shrine and were too sacred to be profaned by human touch, were suddenly discovered lying in a heap in front of the temple. A rationalist—Euripides, for instance—would find no difficulty in such an occurrence, assuming the fact to be certain. Herodotus accepts it as a genuine marvel, without any suggestion that human agency, notwithstanding Delphic asseverations to the contrary, might have been concerned in the matter; and the notable thing is that he considers it less wonderful than the intervention of the physical forces which overwhelmed the Persians. If such a phenomenon as the removal of the arms presented itself to us for criticism—supposing the fact were assured beyond a doubt, and supposing human agency were absolutely excluded by the circumstances—we should regard it as something incomparably more extraordinary than the unquestionably wonderful coincidence of the storm of lightning.[4] Here, in fact, Herodotus has failed to draw the line at what is physically impossible. The truth is that his faith and doubt are alike instinctive; he had never thought the problem out for himself; he had never clearly defined the border between the domains of the credible and the incredible. And so in this episode he has no sooner given us a lesson in faith than he relapses into reserve. For there was yet another marvel to be told. It was said that two armed warriors of superhuman stature pursued the flying Persians and dealt death among their broken ranks. But Herodotus carefully avoids the responsibility of accepting this story. He gives it on the authority of the Persians; he qualifies it by the phrase "as I am informed"; and he adds that the Delphians identified the two warriors with local heroes.

The contrast of the *naïveté* of Herodotus with his scepticism imparts to his epic a very piquant quality. Credulity alternates with a cautious reserve, which is especially noticeable when he is aware of more than one version of an occurrence. He is an expert in the art of not committing himself. He says in one passage, "I am bound to state what is said, but I am not bound to believe." Of the tale that Zalmoxis lived for three years in a subterranean chamber, he professes agnosticism: "I do not disbelieve nor do I absolutely believe it." Occasionally he criticizes and rejects a story, for instance the charge against the Alcmaeonids of treachery at Marathon; but his common practice is to state conflicting accounts and leave the matter there. This method, as it happens, is much more satisfactory to a modern critic than if Herodotus had selected one version, or had attempted to blend different versions together. But it shows him in the light of a collector of historical material, and an accomplished artist in arranging and presenting it, rather than as what we mean by a historian, who considers it his business to sift the evidence, and decide, if possible, between conflicting accounts.

We are often tempted to think of Herodotus as an Ionian, although he was not a native of Ionia. He wrote in Ionic; and he cannot be severed from the school of the Ionian historians, to whom his work owed a great deal more than appears on the surface. But if he had heard himself described as an Ionian writer, he would have been vastly indignant. He

---

4. I do not add the fall of the rocks; for this might have been engineered. The rocks were shown to Herodotus in the temple of Athena Pronaïa (ch. 39); this was just the sort of evidence which would impress him.

is at great pains to dissociate himself from Ionia and Ionian interests. In his account of the Ionian revolt and of the part which the Ionians played in the war with Xerxes, he shows a hardly veiled contempt for a people which, as he says, had been thrice enslaved. He tells us that the name "Ionian was one of no great repute." He is careful to record, without any comment, the Scythian opinion that the Ionians were the most cowardly and unmanly people in the world. He takes frequent opportunities of criticizing adversely the views of Ionian writers. Now I think we may say that this antagonistic attitude was not due entirely or principally to the fact that he belonged by birth to Dorian Halicarnassus. He does indeed insist on the difference of Dorian and Ionian, but the contrast on which his anti-Ionian feeling depended was one within the Ionian race itself— the distinction of the Athenians from the Ionians of Asia. We saw that Herodotus was at Athens before he went to Italy, and his connection with Athens impressed its mark on his political views. He was a warm admirer of the Athenians, and looked with favour and enthusiasm on their empire. He participated in their experiment of colonizing Thurii, became a citizen of their daughter-city. But even if we had not this external proof of his political sympathy, his work testifies to it abundantly. The whole account not only of the Marathonian campaign but of the war with Xerxes is one that redounds to the glory of Athens and flatters Athenian pride. It is, in fact, written mainly from the Athenian point of view, and represents largely, though not exclusively, the Athenian version. The Spartans and the part they took in the war are often handled with irony—for example, they were always arriving too late because they were celebrating a feast. The Corinthians are treated almost with malice. The story would have had a very different complexion if it had been written in the Spartan interest; and even though we have no philo-Spartan historian of the time, a very good case has been made out for the view that Sparta showed as true heroism as Athens. Further, Herodotus takes opportunities to set forth the mythistorical claims of Athens to a hegemony of the Greeks, and represents Athens as asserting those claims at the time of the Persian War. This is an anachronism. At that time Sparta was admittedly the leader and dictator; Athens was a member of the Peloponnesian confederacy, and the strife for supremacy had not begun. Thus the situation is construed in the light of the sequel; history is distorted in the interest of politics; and the grounds of the claim to hegemony which Herodotus ascribes to the Athenians of that time are the stock arguments which we find used in Athenian funeral orations to illustrate and justify the Athenian Empire. In the *Epitaphius* which Pericles pronounced over the citizens killed in the Samian War (439 B.C.) these arguments from myth and history were doubtless marshalled; and that Herodotus was present and listened to it is a conjecture of Eduard Meyer, which has some plausibility, since we find that a famous picturesque phrase used by the orator, likening the dead soldiers to the spring taken out of the year, was adopted by the historian and placed in a new setting.

Admiration for the Athenian Empire in the third quarter of the fifth century meant admiration for Pericles, the chief inspirer of Athenian policy, and the sympathy of Herodotus with Pericles is revealed in the single passage in which he mentions him, where he records the anecdote of his mother's dream that a lion would be born to her. It is revealed, too, in sympathy with the Alcmaeonid family.[5]

His strong phil-Athenian feelings cannot be disconnected from his tone of prejudice and disparagement in treating the Ionians. When the immediate danger of Persian subjection was over, and the Ionian cities which had been leagued with Athens as an equal were brought to submit to her as a mistress, there was little love lost. The Ionian record of the war was one which would have failed to satisfy Athenian patriots as certainly as the Herodotean narrative must have failed to please the Ionians. Herodotus expressly argued that the Athenians were "truly the saviours of Greece"; but he did more: he gave currency and authority to a story which embodied Athenian tradition and justified Athenian Empire, and with such cunning and tact that it has been permanently effective. His admiration for Athens was bound up with his belief in democratic freedom. Until the Peisistratids were overthrown, he says, Athens was an ordinary undistinguished city; but when the Athenians abolished the tyranny and won their freedom, they became by far the first state in Greece.

Herodotus then was a phil-Athenian democrat. If the story is true that the Athenians bestowed on him ten talents (about 12,000 dollars) in recognition of the merits of his work, it was a small remuneration for the service he rendered to the renown of their city. But that he did this service does not degrade his work into anything that could be described as a partisan publication in the offensive sense. It was pragmatical; it reflected the author's political beliefs, and exhibited a strong bias in the preference given to Athenian sources. But it was the work of a historian

---

5. v. 71 rests on the Alcmaeonid tradition. It has been suggested that this sympathy of Herodotus may explain his curious treatment of Themistocles. To this statesman Athens chiefly owed the decisive role she played in the war, and though his good counsels are recognized, he is also treated in an unfriendly spirit of detraction, and represented as an intriguer rather than as a statesman. This looks as if the memory of Themistocles were under a cloud, and this partial obscuration were reflected in Herodotus. Afterwards, Thucydides made a point of doing him justice.

who cannot help being partial; it was not the work of a partisan who becomes a historian for the sake of his cause.

Something more particular must be said about the Herodotean story of the Persian invasion. A self-flattering version of the war had become a tradition at Athens. We have an early sketch of it, in a poetical form, in the *Persae* of Aeschylus (472 B.C.); but Herodotus was probably the first to write it down in a historical form, some twenty years later. Oral traditions (gathered at Athens, Sparta, Delphi, and elsewhere) appear profusely in his work, as every one knows. But he could not have constructed his history of the course of the war from oral traditions alone, or composed such a narrative of events, in which he was too young to take part, thirty years or so afterwards, without the help of some earlier record. We have seen that he depended on Hecataeus for Egypt, though this was just one of the portions of his work where autopsy, and information collected orally, might have sufficed. There is little doubt that Hecataeus was his main guide for early oriental history, and that the same writer was also used for the descriptions of Scythia and Libya, along with other geographical works of the Ionian school. When we come to the invasion of Darius and Xerxes, we find, as we might expect, clear indications that Herodotus here too had a written guide. Throughout the narrative, in the last three books, of the events after Marathon to the end of the second invasion, the historian has naturally to pass backwards and forwards from the Persians to the Greeks. Now there is a remarkable contrast between the character of the narrative when the writer takes us to Susa or to the Persian camp and when he transports us to the cities or tents of the Greeks. In the accounts of what the Greeks did, we are constantly confronted with more than one story, representing various oral traditions which reflect different local interests. But when we follow the movements of the Persians, we have a continuous chronological narrative, by no means always credible, but all of a piece and marked by enumerations and details which point to a more or less contemporary written source, and a source of which Persian, not Greek, history was formally the subject. This source contributes the main thread of the narrative, round which Herodotus has wrought all the additional supplementary and illustrative material he managed to collect. The chronology of Persian events after Marathon is orderly and distinct, contrasting with the uncertainties which beset the digressions on Greek history, such as that on the Spartan kings Cleomenes and Demaratus. Now we know of a history of the Persian War prior to Herodotus, the book of Dionysius of Miletus. I spoke of it in the last lecture, and I also pointed out that the Persian history of Charon of Lampsacus may, not improbably, have come down to the invasion of Xerxes. Either of these books would satisfy the condition that the war was treated as an episode in Persian, not Greek, history, so that it is not unlikely that one of these may have been the source of Herodotus.

Into the warp thus furnished by an older writer is wrought a woof of Athenian tradition, varied here and there by tissue from other sources. And it is noteworthy how in the last three books, comprising the invasion of Xerxes, the imminence of a divine direction of human affairs is strongly accentuated. The sceptical tone is less apparent here than in other parts of the work. From the beginning of the seventh book the dominant note is changed, at least this is the impression I receive; the atmosphere becomes charged with a certain solemnity; it is, I think we might say, rather Athenian than Ionian. Is this difference due to the influence of those Athenian dramas which had glorified the subject, the tragedies of Phrynichus and Aeschylus?

The catastrophe which befalls the Persian expedition is not conceived as the work of jealous gods annoyed by the conspicuous wealth or success of mere mortals. It is rather a divine punishment of the insolence and rashness that are often born of prosperity. This is the Aeschylean doctrine:

> Zeus is a judge who visits heavily
> All whose self-glorious spirit vaults too high.

This Athenian influence in the last books of Herodotus accords with my conjecture that Athens was his headquarters during a part of the ten years or so which elapsed between his banishment and his sailing for Italy.

Herodotus then made a considerable use of older writers [6]—of whom he only names Hecataeus, and usually for the purpose of hinting something uncomplimentary. As the works of these writers have perished, it is very difficult to form a fair estimate of the achievements of Herodotus himself as a historical investigator—apart from his transcendent gifts as an artist

---

6. A complete library of Greek prose works on history would have been very small in 450 B.C., and it would not have been very much larger in 430 B.C. It is difficult to suppose that Herodotus would not have been acquainted with all the historical literature that had been published, or that the works of Dionysius and Charon could have escaped him. Besides Hecataeus the only historian to whom he refers is Scylax (iv. 44), but he mentions him as an explorer and not as an author, though obviously his brief account of the exploration is taken from the report of Scylax. Could he have failed to know the book of this Carian writer on Heraclides of Mylasa? It is remarkable that he ignores the part played by Heraclides of Artemisium. Heraclides is mentioned v. 121. The geographical works of the Ionians are referred to in iv. 36.

and man of letters. His great service consisted probably in the collection of unwritten material concerning modern Greek history; this floating matter he wrought with masterly skill into a framework of facts constructed by predecessors. His maxims of historical criticism may be set down as three: (1) Suspect superhuman and miraculous occurrences, which contradict ordinary experience. But this, in his application of it, leaves a wide room for portents, and it does not cover oracles and dreams. (2) When you are confronted by conflicting evidence or differing versions of the same event, keep an open mind; *audi alteram partem* [I have heard the other side]. But this does not save him from a biased acceptance of Athenian tradition. (3) Autopsy and first-hand oral information are superior to stories at second hand, whether written or oral.[7] This tends to take the naïve form, "I know, for I was there myself," and it placed the historian at the mercy of the vergers and guides in Egyptian temples.

I may illustrate by a couple of examples how Herodotus was sometimes unfortunate in his information gathered on the spot. When he visited Egypt he saw on the Great Pyramid inscriptions which disappeared in the Middle Ages. Probably they were of religious import, appropriate to a royal tomb. But Herodotus tells us that they enumerated the sums of money which were expended on the onions and leeks consumed by the workmen who built the pyramid. This was the interpretation with which the guide satisfied the Greek traveller's curiosity. The other instance I will quote appertains to Babylonian history. Herodotus saw at Babylon the great buildings of a king, with whose name even those of us who have not studied Babylonian annals are probably familiar—King Nebuchadrezzar. He is correctly informed as to the time at which they were built—five generations after the reign of Queen Sammuramat, whom he calls Semiramis. But autopsy did not keep him from falling into a droll error about the potentate who built them. Nebuchadrezzar has had rather bad luck. In the book of Daniel he is metamorphosed into a beast of the field; in Herodotus he is forced to masquerade as a woman. We have to discover his identity under the mask of Queen Nitocris.

We must give full credit to Herodotus for having recognized the principles of criticism which I have indicated, though his application of them is

---

7. Compare, *e.g.*, ii. 99. I have little doubt that Herodotus visited and examined the battle-field of Plataea. Our difficulties in reconstructing the battle (elucidated by Grundy, Woodhouse, and Macan) from his description are not an objection. We may remember that the account of the Battle of Lake Trasimenus by Polybius, who had visited the place and was a master of military science, lends itself to different interpretations. The features of the Pass of Thermopylae as described by Herodotus can be recognized by any traveller to-day; but he can hardly have been there, for he orients it N.S. instead of E.W.

unsatisfactory and sporadic. They are maxims of permanent validity; properly qualified they lie at the basis of the modern developments of what is called historical methodology. But notwithstanding the profession of these axioms of common sense, he was in certain ways so lacking in common sense that parts of his work might seem to have been written by a precocious child. He undertook to write the history of a great war; but he did not possess the most elementary knowledge of the conditions of warfare. His fantastic statement of the impossible numbers of the army of Xerxes exhibits an incompetence which is almost incredible and is alone enough to stamp Herodotus as more of an epic poet than a historian. It matters not whether he worked out the arithmetic for himself or accepted it entirely on authority; this is a case in which to accept is as heinous as to invent. Heinous for a historian; and if we judge Herodotus by the lowest standard as a historian of a war, this case invalidates his claim to competence. But as an epic story-teller he escapes triumphantly. His Catalogue of the Persian host is a counterpart to the Catalogue of the *Iliad:*

mython d' hos hot aoidos epistamenos katelexas.

[as when a bard skillfully recounts a tale.]

His incompetence in military matters is shown, in another way, in his account of the campaign of Thermopylae and Artemisium. The key to their actions lay—and it required no technical training or experience to discern this—in the close connection and interdependence of the Persian land army and the Persian fleet, a fact which governed the Greek measures for defence. Herodotus, though he mentions several things which imply this and enable us more or less to penetrate the strategy of the combatants, fails completely to realize the situation and treats the naval and the land operations as if they were independent.

In his relation of the Persian War, Herodotus does not neglect the chronology, and it is perhaps as satisfactory as we could expect. But it may fairly be questioned whether the credit for this is not to be imputed to an earlier writer—Dionysius or Charon—whom he had the discretion to follow. It is significant that he does not give any formal date which a Greek reader could easily interpret, until he mentions, almost by the way, that the Persian invasion of Attica occurred in the archonship of Calliades.[8]

---

8. He signalizes the years 490–481 by reference to the year of Marathon, but he does not mention the eponymous archon of that year. Even if he had done so a reader would have required a list of Attic archons in order to follow his dates intelligently. Herodotus does not assist his readers by reckoning back from a fixed point which they could realize. Thucydides saw that without such a point dates were entirely in the air, and he dated backward from the first year of the Peloponnesian War.

But while chronology fares pretty well in the last three books, the whole work shows that, while the author copied the dates which his sources supplied, he never attempted to grapple with the chronological difficulties of Greek history, although so many of the episodes which he related raised the problem of synchronizing Hellenic tradition with oriental records. We have no reason to suppose that he avoided the problem because he judged it insoluble; his indifference to it is another manifestation of his epic, quasi-historical mind.

The first phase of Greek historiography culminates and achieves its glory in Herodotus. He reflects its features—its eager research into geography and ethnography (the indispensable groundwork of history), and its predominant interest in the East. He adopts from Hecataeus a critical attitude towards the ancient myths, aided by a rudimentary comparative mythology. But these elements are transfigured by the magic of his epic art and the spell of a higher historical idea. He was the Homer of the Persian War, and that war originally inspired him. His work presents a picture of sixth-century civilization; and it is also a universal history in so far as it gathers the greater part of the known world into a narrative which is concentrated upon a single issue. It is fortunate for literature that he was not too critical; if his criticism had been more penetrating and less naïve, he could not have been a second Homer. He belonged entirely in temper and mentality to the period before the sophistic illumination, which he lived to see but not to understand. . . .

The foregoing consists of Lecture II
from Bury's THE ANCIENT GREEK HISTORIANS.

Lucian

c. 125–190

The Greek satirist Lucian was born at Samosata in northern Syria. The little we know about him comes mostly from his own writings. He tells how he was briefly apprenticed to an uncle, a sculptor, and one day was beaten for breaking a slab of marble. When he returned home he dreamed of two women—one representing Statuary, the other Literature. Each begged him to follow her, and he chose Literature.

After practicing law in Antioch for a time, he journeyed to Macedonia, Greece, Italy, and Gaul, as an itinerant rhetorician and sophist. Back in Athens around 165 A.D., he labored twenty years on his satirical dialogues and composed his best works. Late in his life he accepted a government post in Egypt, a step that took some explaining on his part, for he had previously denounced those who hire out their talents.

Lucian is credited with some eighty works, including dialogues, such as *Sale of Lives* and *Dialogues of the Dead*, and the Olympian fables, which ridicule the pretentions and absurdity of philosophers of the time. In *The True History* he parodies adventure stories. He also wrote romances and autobiographies. Of special interest are his references to the sincerity of the Christians and to that "great man" who was crucified in Palestine.

Some of the writings which go under the name of Lucian are of doubtful authenticity. His dialogues, however, his literary criticism, and such romances as *The True History* are undoubtedly his. They are a model of satirical style and are generally admired. It is easy to see why Gibbon was so fond of them, and how *The True History* could have been the inspiration of Swift's *Gulliver's Travels*.

Lucian has been described as a sophist, a skeptic, and a blasphemer. The Greek sophists were accused of "making the worse appear the better cause." Whether Lucian was a sophist in this sense would depend on your point of view—on which cause you regard as "the better." He certainly attacked cherished popular beliefs and customs relentlessly. His ideal was to show no mercy for shams, and to tell the truth always, and laughingly.

The Way to Write History opens with an account of an imaginary epidemic at Abdera, where the inhabitants had been infected with a melodramatic fever after watching a famous tragic actor. Another absurd epidemic has hit the educated class of his day, Lucian says —the fever to become a historian. These would-be historians have taken it upon themselves to imitate the classic style of Thucydides and Herodotus. They seek in this way to gain some credit for their inaccurate and garbled versions of Roman history. The examples he gives of their fatuous pretentions and stupidity—their bombast and self-seeking flattery—serve as amusing warnings of how history should *not* be written. Some think they have done a good job if they praise the "right" side or the "right" men, but history has no favorites. These writers confuse history with panegyric, Lucian says, and probably he would say the same of some of our present-day historians.

Nothing excuses inaccuracy, Lucian says, neither the pretext of entertaining the reader, nor the desire for poetic beauty. When poetry is confused with history, the result "is nothing but poetry without the wings." Nothing can replace facts, and "facts are not to be collected at haphazard, but with careful, laborious, repeated investigation." On the other hand, the facts are not to be recorded indiscriminately. Too much detail is wearisome and pointless. A selection must be made, but does Lucian give us a principle of selection? How are we to distinguish the essential facts from the incidental?

Lucian seems to say that no one can tell you in advance what facts will be the important ones. What is required is "political insight" and this is "a gift of nature, which can never be learned." You will have to decide for yourself how far this is true. The other main trait required by the historian—a good style—can be acquired, according to Lucian, by a loving study of the classics and diligent practice. Is a lucid, forceful style, then, within reach of everyone? Courage, as would be expected, is a third essential of the historian.

Thucydides is Lucian's ideal historian, and he draws many lessons from *The Peloponnesian War*. It was Thucydides who drew the critical line between the bad and the good historian. Whereas the former makes "a bid for present reputation," the latter seeks to make his work "a possession forever," and to be of service to mankind if history should repeat itself. The issues are clearly drawn, and such questions as these confront us: Are good histories permanent, or do they have to be rewritten by later centuries in the light of new knowledge? And how far does history repeat itself, providing lessons for succeeding generations?

The Way
to Write History

My dear Philo,

There is a story of a curious epidemic at Abdera, just after the accession of King Lysimachus. It began with the whole population's exhibiting feverish symptoms, strongly marked and unintermittent from the very first attack. About the seventh day, the fever was relieved, in some cases by a violent flow of blood from the nose, in others by perspiration not less violent. The mental effects, however, were most ridiculous; they were all stage-struck, mouthing blank verse and ranting at the top of their voices. Their favorite recitation was the *Andromeda* of Euripides; one after another would go through the great speech of Perseus; the whole place was full of pale ghosts, who were our seventh-day tragedians vociferating,

O Love, who lord'st it over Gods and men,

and the rest of it. This continued for some time, till the coming of winter put an end to their madness with a sharp frost. I find the explanation of the form it took in this fact: Archelaus was then the great tragic actor, and in the middle of the summer, during some very hot weather, he had played the *Andromeda* there; most of them took the fever in the theater, and convalescence was followed by a relapse—into tragedy, the *Andromeda* haunting their memories, and Perseus hovering, Gorgon's head in hand, before the mind's eye.

Well, to compare like with like, the majority of our educated class is now suffering from an Abderite epidemic. They are not stage-struck; indeed, that would have been a minor infatuation—to be possessed with other people's verses, not bad ones either. No, but from the beginning of the present excitements—the barbarian war, the Armenian disaster, the succession of victories—you cannot find a man but is writing history; nay, everyone you meet is a Thucydides, a Herodotus, a Xenophon. The old saying must be true, and war be the father of all things, seeing what a litter of historians it has now teemed forth at a birth.

Such sights and sounds, my Philo, brought into my head that old anecdote about the Sinopean. A report that Philip was marching on the town had thrown all Corinth into a bustle; one was furbishing his arms, another wheeling stones, a third patching the wall, a fourth strengthening a battlement, everyone making himself useful somehow or other. Diogenes having nothing to do—of course, no one thought of giving *him* a job—was moved by the sight to gird up his philosopher's cloak and begin rolling his tub dwelling energetically up and down the Craneum; an acquaintance asked, and got, the explanation: "I do not want to be thought the only idler in such a busy multitude; I am rolling my tub to be like the rest."

I too am reluctant to be the only dumb man at so vociferous a season. I do not like walking across the stage, like a "super," in gaping silence; so I decided to roll *my* cask as best I could. I do not intend to write a history, or attempt actual narrative; I am not courageous enough for that; have no apprehensions on my account. I realize the danger of rolling the thing over the rocks, especially if it is only a poor little jar of brittle earthenware like mine; I should very soon knock against some pebble and find myself picking up the pieces. Come, I will tell you my idea for campaigning in safety, and keeping well out of range.

Give a wide berth to all that foam and spray,

and to the anxieties which vex the historian—that I shall be wise enough to do; but I propose to give a little advice, and lay down a few principles for the benefit of those who do venture. I shall have a share in their building, if not in the dedicatory inscription; my finger tips will at least have touched their wet mortar.

However, most of them see no need for advice here: *there might as well be an art of talking, seeing, or eating; history writing is perfectly easy, comes natural, is a universal gift; all that is necessary is the faculty of translating your thoughts into words.* But the truth is—you know it without my telling, old friend—it is *not* a task to be lightly undertaken, or carried through without effort; no, it needs as much care as any sort of composition whatever, if one means to create "a possession for ever," as Thucydides calls it. Well, I know I shall not get a hearing from many of them, and some will be seriously offended—especially any who have finished and produced their work; in cases where its first reception was

favorable, it would be folly to expect the authors to recast or correct. Has
it not the stamp of finality? Is it not almost a state document? Yet even
they may profit by my words; *we* are not likely to be attacked again;
we have disposed of all our enemies; but there might be a Celto-Gothic
or an Indo-Bactrian war; then our friends' composition might be improved by the application of my measuring rod—always supposing that
they recognize its correctness. Failing that, let them do their own mensuration with the old foot rule; the doctor will not particularly mind,
though all Abdera insists on spouting the *Andromeda*.

Advice has two provinces—one of choice, the other of avoidance; let
us first decide what the historian is to avoid—of what faults he must
purge himself—and then proceed to the measures he must take for putting himself on the straight high road. This will include the manner of
his beginning, the order in which he should marshal his facts, the questions of proportion, of discreet silence, of full or cursory narration, of
comment and connection. Of all that, however, later on; for the present
we deal with the vices to which bad writers are liable. As to those faults of
diction, construction, meaning, and general amateurishness, which are
common to every kind of composition, to discuss them is neither compatible with my space nor relevant to my purpose.

But there are mistakes peculiar to history; your own observation will
show you just those which a constant attendance at authors' readings [1]
has impressed on me; you have only to keep your ears open at every opportunity. It will be convenient, however, to refer by the way to a few
illustrations in recent histories. Here is a serious fault to begin with. It is
the fashion to neglect the examination of facts, and give the space
gained to eulogies of generals and commanders; those of their own side
they exalt to the skies, the other side they disparage intemperately.
They forget that between history and panegyric there is a great gulf
fixed, barring communication; in musical phrase, the two things are a
couple of octaves apart. The panegyrist has only one concern—to commend and gratify his living theme some way or other; if misrepresenta-
tion will serve his purpose, he has no objection to that. History, on the
other hand, abhors the intrusion of any least scruple of falsehood; it is
like the windpipe, which the doctors tell us will not tolerate a morsel of
stray food.

---

1. These were very common in Roman Imperial times, for purposes of advertisement,
of eliciting criticism, etc. "The audience at recitations may be compared with the
modern literary reviews, discharging the functions of a preventive and emendatory,
not merely of a correctional, tribunal. Before publication a work might thus be
known to more hearers than it would now find readers." Mayor, *Juvenal*, iii. 9.

Another thing these gentlemen seem not to know is that poetry and history offer different wares, and have their separate rules. Poetry enjoys unrestricted freedom; it has but one law—the poet's fancy. He is inspired and possessed by the Muses; if he chooses to horse his car with winged steeds, or set others agalloping over the sea or standing corn, none challenges his right. His Zeus, with a single cord, may haul up earth and sea, and hold them dangling together—there is no fear the cord may break, the load come tumbling down and be smashed to atoms. In a complimentary picture of Agamemnon, there is nothing against his having Zeus's head and eyes, his brother Poseidon's chest, Ares' belt—in fact, the son of Atreus and Aërope will naturally be an epitome of all divinity; Zeus or Poseidon or Ares could not singly or severally provide the requisite perfections. But, if history adopts such servile arts, it is nothing but poetry without the wings; the exalted tones are missing; and imposition of other kinds without the assistance of meter is only the more easily detected. It is surely a great, a superlative weakness, this inability to distinguish history from poetry. What, bedizen history, like her sister, with tale and eulogy and their attendant exaggerations? As well take some mighty athlete with muscles of steel, rig him up with purple drapery and meretricious ornament, rouge and powder his cheeks; faugh, what an object would one make of him with such defilements!

I would not be understood to exclude eulogy from history altogether; it is to be kept to its place and, used with moderation, is not to tax the reader's patience. I shall presently show, indeed, that in all such matters an eye is to be had to posterity. It is true, there is a school which makes a pretty division of history into the agreeable and the useful, and defends the introduction of panegyric on the ground that it is agreeable, and pleases the general reader. But nothing could be further from the truth. In the first place the division is quite a false one; history has only one concern and aim, and that is the useful; which again has one single source, and that is truth. The agreeable is no doubt an addition, if it is present; so is beauty to an athlete; but a Nicostratus, who is a fine fellow and proves himself a better man than either of his opponents, gets his recognition as a Hercules, however ugly his face may be; and if one opponent is the handsome Alcaeus himself—handsome enough to make Nicostratus in love with him, says the story—that does not affect the issue. History too, if it can deal incidentally in the agreeable, will attract a multitude of lovers; but so long as it does its proper business efficiently—and that is the establishment of truth—it may be indifferent to beauty.

It is further to be remarked that in history sheer extravagance has not even the merit of being agreeable; and the extravagance of eulogy is doubly repulsive, as extravagance and as eulogy; at least it is only welcome to the vulgar majority, not to that critical, that perhaps hypercritical, audience, whom no slip can escape, who are all eyes like Argus but keener than he, who test every word as a money-changer might his coins, rejecting the false on the spot but accepting the good and heavy and true. It is they that we should have in mind as we write history, and never heed the others, though they applaud till they crack their voices. If you neglect the critics, and indulge in the cloying sweetness of tales and eulogies and such baits, you will soon find your history a "Hercules in Lydia." No doubt you have seen some picture of him: he is Omphale's slave, dressed up in an absurd costume, his lion skin and club transferred to her, as though she were the true Hercules, while he, in saffron robe and purple jacket, is combing wool and wincing under Omphale's slipper. A degrading spectacle it is—the dress loose and flapping open, and all that was man in him turned to woman.

The vulgar may very likely extend their favor to this; but the select (whose judgment you disregard) will get a good deal of entertainment out of your heterogeneous, disjointed, fragmentary stuff. There is nothing which has not a beauty of its own; but take it out of its proper sphere, and the misuse turns its beauty to ugliness. Eulogy, I need hardly say, may possibly please one person, the eulogized, but will disgust everyone else; this is particularly so with the monstrous exaggerations which are in fashion; the authors are so intent on the patron hunt that they cannot relinquish it without a full exhibition of servility; they have no idea of finesse, never mask their flattery, but blurt out their unconvincing bald tale anyhow.

The consequence is, they miss even their immediate end; the objects of their praise are more inclined (and quite right too) to dislike and discard them for toadies—if they are men of spirit, at any rate. Aristobulus inserted in his history an account of a single combat between Alexander and Porus, and selected this passage to read aloud to the former; he reckoned that his best chance of pleasing was to invent heroic deeds for the king, and heighten his achievements. Well, they were on board ship in the Hydaspes; Alexander took hold of the book and tossed it overboard; "the author should have been treated the same way, by rights," he added, "for presuming to fight duels for me like that, and shoot down elephants singlehanded." A very natural indignation in Alexander, of a piece with his treatment of the intrusive architect; this person offered to convert the whole of Mount Athos into a colossal statue of the king—who however decided that he was a toady, and actually gave him less employment in ordinary than before.

The fact is, there is nothing agreeable in these things, except to anyone who is fool enough to enjoy commendations which the slightest inquiry will prove to be unfounded; of course there *are* ugly persons—women more especially—who ask artists to paint them as beautiful as they can; they think they will be really better looking if the painter heightens the rose a little and distributes a good deal of the lily. There you have the origin of the present crowd of historians, intent only upon the passing day, the selfish interest, the profit which they reckon to make out of their work; execration is their desert—in the present for their undisguised clumsy flattery, in the future for the stigma which their exaggerations bring upon history in general. If anyone takes some admixture of the agreeable to be an absolute necessity, let him be content with the independent beauties of style; these are agreeable without being false; but they are usually neglected now for the better foisting upon us of irrelevant substitutes.

Passing from that point, I wish to put on record some fresh recollections of Ionian histories—supported, now I think of it, by Greek analogies also of recent date—both concerned with the war already alluded to. You may trust my report, the Graces be my witness; I would take oath to its truth if it were polite to swear on paper. One writer started with invoking the Muses to lend a hand. What a tasteful exordium! How suited to the historic spirit! How appropriate to the style! When he had got a little way on, he compared our ruler to Achilles, and the Parthian king to Thersites; he forgot that Achilles would have done better if he had had Hector instead of Thersites to beat, if there had been a man of might fleeing in front,

> But at his heels a mightier far than he.

He next proceeded to say something handsome about himself, as a fit chronicler of such brilliant deeds. As he got near his point of departure, he threw in a word for his native town of Miletus, adding that he was thus improving on Homer, who never so much as mentioned his birthplace. And he concluded his preface with a plain express promise to advance our cause and personally wage war against the barbarians to the best of his ability. The actual history, and recital of the causes of hostilities, began with these words: "The detestable Vologesus (whom Heaven confound!) commenced war on the following pretext."

Enough of him. Another is a keen emulator of Thucydides, and by way of close approximation to his model starts with his own name—most graceful of beginnings, redolent of Attic thyme! Look at it: "Crepereius Calpurnianus of Pompeiopolis wrote the history of the war between Parthia and Rome, how they warred one upon the other, beginning with the commencement of the war." After that exordium, what need to describe the rest—what harangues he delivers in Armenia, resuscitating our old friend the Corcyrean envoy—what a plague he inflicts on Nisibis (which would not espouse the Roman cause), lifting the whole thing bodily from Thucydides—except the Pelasgicum and the Long Walls, where the victims of the earlier plague found shelter; there the difference ends; like the other, "it began in Ethiopia, whence it descended to Egypt," and to most of the Parthian Empire, where it very discreetly remained. I left him engaged in burying the poor Athenians in Nisibis, and knew quite well how he would continue after my exit. Indeed it is a pretty common belief at present that you are writing like Thucydides if you just use his actual words, *mutatis mutandis* [having made the necessary changes]. Ah, and I almost forgot to mention one thing: this same writer gives many names of weapons and military engines in Latin— *phossa* for trench, *pons* for bridge, and so forth. Just think of the dignity of history, and the Thucydidean style—the Attic embroidered with these Latin words, like a toga relieved and picked out with the purple stripe—so harmonious!

Another puts down a bald list of events, as prosy and commonplace as a private's or a carpenter's or a sutler's diary. However, there is more sense in this poor man's performance; he flies his true colors from the first; he has cleared the ground for some educated person who knows how to deal with history. The only fault I have to find with him is that he inscribes his volumes with a solemnity rather disproportioned to the rank of their contents—"Parthian History, by Callimorphus, Surgeon of the 6th Pikemen, volume so-and-so." Ah, yes, and there is a lamentable preface, which closes with the remark that, since Asclepius is the son of Apollo, and Apollo director of the Muses and patron of all culture, it is very proper for a doctor to write history. Also, he starts in Ionic, but very soon, for no apparent reason, abandons it for everyday Greek, still keeping the Ionic *e*'s and *k*'s and *ou*'s, but otherwise writing like ordinary people— rather too ordinary, indeed.

Perhaps I should balance him with a philosophic historian; this gentleman's name I will conceal, and merely indicate his attitude, as revealed in a recent publication at Corinth. Much had been expected of him, but not enough; starting straight off with the first sentence of the preface, he subjects his readers to a dialectic catechism, his thesis being the highly philosophic one that no one but a philosopher should write history. Very shortly there follows a second logical process, itself followed by a third; in fact the whole preface is one mass of dialectic figures. There is flattery, indeed, *ad nauseam,* eulogy vulgar to the point of farce; but never without the logical trimmings, always that dialectical catechism. I confess it strikes me as a vulgarity also, hardly worthy of a philosopher with so long and white a beard, when he gives it in his preface as our ruler's special good fortune that philosophers should consent to record his actions; he had better have left us to reach that conclusion for ourselves—if at all.

Again, it would be a sinful neglect to omit the man who begins like this: "I devise to tell of Romans and Persians"; then a little later, "For 'twas Heaven's decree that the Persians should suffer evils"; and again, "One Osroes there was, whom Hellenes name Oxyroes"—and much more in that style. He corresponds, you see, to one of my previous examples; only he is a second Herodotus, and the other a second Thucydides.

There is another distinguished artist in words—again rather more Thucydidean than Thucydides—who gives, according to his own idea, the clearest, most convincing descriptions of every town, mountain, plain, or river. I wish my bitterest foe no worse fate than the reading of them. Frigid? Caspian snows, Celtic ice are warm in comparison. A whole book hardly suffices him for the emperor's shield—the Gorgon on its boss, with eyes of blue and white and black, rainbow girdle, and snakes twined and knotted. Why, Vologesus's breeches or his bridle. God bless me, they take up several thousand lines apiece; the same for the look of Osroes' hair as he swims the Tigris—or what the cave was like that sheltered him, ivy and myrtle and bay clustered all together to shut out every ray of light. You observe how indispensable it all is to the history; without the scene, how could we have comprehended the action?

It is helplessness about the real essentials, or ignorance of what should be given, that makes them take refuge in word painting—landscapes, caves, and the like; and when they do come upon a series of important matters, they are just like a slave whose master has left him his money and made him a rich man; he does not know how to put on his clothes or take his food properly: partridges or sweetbreads or hare are served, but he rushes in and fills himself up with pea soup or salt fish till he is fit to burst. Well, the man I spoke of gives the most unconvincing wounds and singular deaths: someone has his big toe injured and dies on the spot; the general Priscus calls out, and seven-and-twenty of the enemy fall dead at the sound. As to the numbers killed, he actually falsifies dispatches; at Europus he slaughters 70,236 of the enemy, while the Romans lose two and have seven wounded! How any man of sense can tolerate such stuff, I do not know.

Here is another point quite worth mention. This writer has such a passion for unadulterated Attic, and for refining speech to the last degree of purity, that he metamorphoses the Latin names and translates them into Greek: Saturninus figures as Cronius, Fronto must be Phrontis, Titianus Titanius, with queerer transmogrifications yet. Further, on the subject of Severian's death, he accuses all other writers of a blunder in putting him to the sword; he is really to have starved himself to death, as the most painless method; the fact, however, is that it was all over in three days, whereas seven days is the regular time for starvation; are we perhaps to conceive an Osroes waiting about for Severian to complete the process, and putting off his assault till after the seventh day?

Then, Philo, how shall we class the historians who indulge in poetical phraseology? "The catapult rocked responsive," they say; "Loud thundered the breach"; or, somewhere else in this delectable history, "Thus Edessa was girdled with clash of arms, and all was din and turmoil," or, "The general pondered in his heart how to attack the wall." Only he fills up the interstices with such wretched common lower-class phrases as "The military prefect wrote His Majesty," "The troops were procuring the needful," "They got a wash [2] and put in an appearance," and so on. It is like an actor with one foot raised on a high buskin, and the other in a slipper.

You will find others writing brilliant high-sounding prefaces of outrageous length, raising great expectations of the wonders to follow—and then comes a poor little appendix of a—history; it is like nothing in the world but a child—say the Eros you must have seen in a picture—playing in an enormous mask of Hercules or a Titan; *parturiunt montes* [the mountains labor (and bring forth mice)], cries the audience, very naturally. That is not the way to do things; the whole should be homogeneous and uniform, and the body in proportion to the head—not a helmet of gold, a ridiculous breastplate patched up out of rags or rotten leather, shield of wicker, and pigskin greaves. You will find plenty of historians prepared to set the Rhodian Colossus' head on the body of a dwarf; others

---

2. It has been suggested that Lucian's criticism is for practical purposes out of date; but Prescott writes: "He was surrounded by a party of friends, who had *dropped in*, it seems, after mass, to inquire after the state of his health, some of whom had remained to partake of his repast."

on the contrary show us headless bodies, and plunge into the facts without exordium. These plead the example of Xenophon, who starts with, "Darius and Parysatis had two children"; if they only knew it, there is such a thing as a *virtual* exordium, not realized as such by everybody; but of that hereafter.

However, any mistake in mere expression or arrangement is excusable; but when you come to fancy geography, differing from the other not by miles or leagues but by whole days' journeys, where is the classical model for that? One writer has taken so little trouble with his facts—never met a Syrian, I suppose, nor listened to the stray information you may pick up at the barber's—that he thus locates Europus: "Europus lies in Mesopotamia, two days' journey from the Euphrates, and is a colony from Edessa." Not content with that, this enterprising person has in the same book taken up my native Samosata and shifted it, citadel, walls, and all, into Mesopotamia, giving it the two rivers for boundaries, and making them shave past it, all but touching the walls on either side. I suspect you would laugh at me, Philo, if I were to set about convincing you that I am neither Parthian nor Mesopotamian, as this whimsical colony planter makes me.

By the way, he has also a very attractive tale of Severian, learned, he assures us on oath, from one of the actual fugitives. According to this, he would not die by the sword, the rope, or poison, but contrived a death which should be tragic and impressive. He was the owner of some large goblets of the most precious glass; having made up his mind to die, he broke the largest of these, and used a splinter of it for the purpose, cutting his throat with the glass. A dagger or a lancet, good enough instruments for a manly and heroic death, he could not come at, forsooth!

Then, as Thucydides composed a funeral oration over the first victims of that old war, our author feels it incumbent on him to do the same for Severian; they all challenge Thucydides, you see, little as he can be held responsible for the Armenian troubles. So he buries Severian, and then solemnly ushers up to the grave, as Pericles' rival, one Afranius Silo, a centurion; the flood of rhetoric which follows is so copious and remarkable that it drew tears from me—ye Graces!—tears of laughter; most of all where the eloquent Afranius, drawing to a close, makes mention, with weeping and distressful moans, of all those costly dinners and toasts. But he is a very Ajax in his conclusion. He draws his sword, gallantly as an Afranius should, and in sight of all cuts his throat over the grave—and God knows it was high time for an execution, if oratory can be felony.

The historian states that all the spectators admired and lauded Afranius; as for me, I was inclined to condemn him on general grounds—he had all but given a catalogue of sauces and dishes, and shed tears over the memory of departed cakes—but his capital offense was that he had not cut the historian-tragedian's throat before he left this life himself.

I assure you, my friend, I could largely increase my list of such offenders; but one or two more will suffice before proceeding to the second part of my undertaking, the suggestions for improvement. There are some, then, who leave alone, or deal very cursorily with, all that is great and memorable; amateurs and not artists, they have no selective faculty, and loiter over copious labored descriptions of the veriest trifles; it is as if a visitor to Olympia, instead of examining, commending or describing to his stay-at-home friends the general greatness and beauty of the Zeus, were to be struck with the exact symmetry and polish of its footstool, or the proportions of its shoe, and give all his attention to these minor points.

For instance, I have known a man get through the Battle of Europus in less than seven whole lines, and then spend twenty mortal hours on a dull and perfectly irrelevant tale about a Moorish trooper. The trooper's name was Mausacas; he wandered up the hills in search of water, and came upon some Syrian yokels getting their lunch; at first they were afraid of him, but when they found he was on the right side, they invited him to share the meal; for one of them had traveled in the Moorish country, having a brother serving in the army. Then come long stories and descriptions of how he hunted there, and saw a great herd of elephants at pasture, and was nearly eaten up by a lion, and what huge fish he had bought at Caesarea. So this quaint historian leaves the terrible carnage to go on at Europus, and lets the pursuit, the forced armistice, the settling of outposts, shift for themselves, while he lingers far into the evening watching Malchion the Syrian cheapen big mackerel at Caesarea; if night had not come all too soon, I dare say he would have dined with him when the fish was cooked. If all this had not been accurately set down in the history, what sad ignorance we should have been left in! The loss to the Romans would have been irreparable if Mausacas the Moor had got nothing to quench his thirst, and come back fasting to camp. Yet I am willfully omitting innumerable details of yet greater importance —the arrival of a flute girl from the next village, the exchange of gifts (Mausacas' was a spear, Malchion's a brooch), and other incidents most essential to the Battle of Europus. It is no exaggeration to say that such writers never give the rose a glance, but devote all their curiosity to the thorns on its stem.

Another entertaining person, who has never set foot outside Corinth, nor traveled as far as its harbor—not to mention seeing Syria or Armenia—starts with words which impressed themselves on my memory: "Seeing is believing: I therefore write what I have seen, not what I have been told." His personal observation has been so close that he describes the Parthian "Dragons" (they use this ensign as a numerical formula—a thousand men to the Dragon, I believe): they are huge live dragons, he says, breeding in Persian territory beyond Iberia; these are first fastened to great poles and hoisted up aloft, striking terror at a distance while the advance is going on; then, when the battle begins, they are released and set on the enemy; numbers of our men, it seems, were actually swallowed by them, and others strangled or crushed in their coils; of all this he was an eyewitness, taking his observations, however, from a safe perch up a tree. Thank goodness he did not come to close quarters with the brutes! We should have lost a very remarkable historian, and one who did doughty deeds in this war with his own right hand; for he had many adventures, and was wounded at Sura (in the course of a stroll from the Craneum to Lerna, apparently). All this he used to read to a Corinthian audience, which was perfectly aware that he had never so much as seen a battle picture. Why, he did not know one weapon or engine from another; the names of maneuvers and formations had no meaning for him; flank or front, line or column, it was all one.

Then there is a splendid fellow who has boiled down into the compass of five hundred lines (or less, to be accurate) the whole business from beginning to end—campaigns in Armenia, in Syria, in Mesopotamia, on the Tigris, and in Media; and having done it, he calls it a history. His title very narrowly misses being longer than his book: "An account of the late campaigns of the Romans in Armenia, Mesopotamia, and Media, by Antiochianus, victor at the festival of Apollo"; he had probably won some junior flat race.

I have known one writer compile a history of the future, including the capture of Vologesus, the execution of Osroes (he is to be thrown to the lions), and, crowning all, our long-deferred triumph. In this prophetic vein, he sweeps hastily on to the end of his work; yet he finds time for the foundation in Mesopotamia of a city, greatest of the great, and fairest of the fair; he is still debating, however, whether the most appropriate name will be Victoria, Concord, or Peacetown; that is yet unsettled; we must leave the fair city unnamed for the present; but it is already thickly populated—with empty dreams and literary drivelings. He has also pledged himself to an account of coming events in India, and a circumnavigation of the Atlantic; nay, the pledge is half redeemed; the preface to the *India* is complete; the third legion, the Celtic contingent, and a small Moorish division have crossed the Indus in full force under Cassius; our most original historian will soon be posting us up in their doings— their method of "receiving elephants," for instance—in letters dated Muziris or Oxydracae.

These people's uneducated antics are infinite; they have no eyes for the noteworthy, nor, if they had eyes, any adequate faculty of expression; invention and fiction provide their matter, and belief in the first word that comes their style; they pride themselves on the number of books they run to, and yet more on their titles; for these again are quite absurd: *So-and-so's so many books of Parthian victories; The Parthis,* book I; *The Parthis,* book II—quite a rival to the *Atthis,* eh? Another does it (I have read the book) still more neatly—*The Parthonicy of Demetrius of Sagalassus.* I do not wish to ridicule or make a jest of these pretty histories; I write for a practical purpose: anyone who avoids these and similar errors is already well on the road to historical success; nay, he is almost there if the logical axiom is correct that, with incompatibles, denial of the one amounts to affirmation of the other.

"Well," I may be told, "you have now a clear field; the thorns and brambles have all been extirpated, the debris of others' buildings has been carted off, the rough places have been made smooth; come, do a little construction yourself, and show that you are not only good at destroying, but capable of yourself planning a model in which criticism itself shall find nothing to criticize."

Well then, my perfect historian must start with two indispensable qualifications: the one is political insight, the other the faculty of expression; the first is a gift of nature, which can never be learned; the second should have been acquired by long practice, unremitting toil, and loving study of the classics. There is nothing technical here, and no room for any advice of mine; this essay does not profess to bestow insight and acumen on those who are not endowed with them by nature; valuable, or invaluable rather, would it have been if it could recast and modify like that, transmute lead into gold, tin into silver, magnify a Conon or Leotrophides into Titormus or Milo.

But what is the function of professional advice? Not the creation of qualities which should be already there, but the indication of their proper use. No trainer, of course—let him be Iccus, Herodicus, Theon, or who he may—will suggest that he can take a Perdiccas and make an Olympic victor of him, fit to face Theagenes of Thasos or Polydamas of Scotussa; what he *will* tell you is that, given a constitution that will stand training, his system will considerably improve it. So with us—we are not to have every failure cast in our teeth if we claim to have invented a system for so great and difficult a subject. We do not offer to take the first comer and make a historian of him—only to point out to anyone who has natural insight and acquired literary skill certain straight roads (they may or may not be so in reality) which will bring him with less waste of time and effort to his goal.

I do not suppose you will object that the man with insight has no need of system and instruction upon the things he is ignorant of; in that case he might have played the harp or flute untaught, and in fact have been omniscient. But, as things are at present, he cannot perform in these ways untaught, though with some assistance he will learn very easily, and soon be able to get along by himself.

You now know what sort of a pupil I (like the trainer) insist upon. He must not be weak either at understanding or at making himself understood, but a man of penetration, a capable administrator—potentially, that is—with a soldierly spirit (which does not however exclude the civil spirit), and some military experience; at the least he must have been in camp, seen troops drilled or maneuvered, know a little about weapons and military engines, the differences between line and column, cavalry and infantry tactics (with the reasons for them), frontal and flank attacks; in a word, none of your armchair strategists relying wholly on hearsay.

But first and foremost, let him be a man of independent spirit, with nothing to fear or hope from anybody; else he will be a corrupt judge open to undue influences. If Philip's eye is knocked out at Olynthus by Aster the Amphipolite archer, it is not his business to exclaim, but just to show him as he is; he is not to think whether Alexander will be annoyed by a circumstantial account of the cruel murder of Clitus at table. If a Cleon has the ear of the assembly, and a monopoly of the tribune, he will not shrink on that account from describing him as a pestilent madman; all Athens will not stop him from dwelling on the Sicilian disaster, the capture of Demosthenes, the death of Nicias, the thirst, the foul water, and the shooting down of the drinkers. He will consider very rightly that no man of sense will blame him for recounting the effects of misfortune or folly in their entirety; he is not the author, but only the reporter of them. If a fleet is destroyed, it is not he who sinks it; if there is a rout, he is not in pursuit—unless perhaps he ought to have prayed for better things, and omitted to do so. Of course, if silence or contradiction would have put matters right, Thucydides might with a stroke of the pen have knocked down the counterwall on Epipolae, sent Hermocrates' trireme to the bottom, let daylight through the accursed Gylippus before he had done blocking the roads with wall and trench, and, finally, have cast the Syracusans into their own quarries and sent the Athenians cruising round Sicily and Italy with Alcibiades' first high hopes still on board. Alas, not Fate itself may undo the work of Fate.

The historian's one task is to tell the thing as it happened. This he cannot do if he is Artaxerxes' physician, trembling before him, or hoping to get a purple cloak, a golden chain, a horse of the Nisaean breed in payment for his laudations. A fair historian, a Xenophon, a Thucydides, will not accept that position. He may nurse some private dislikes, but he will attach far more importance to the public good, and set the truth high above his hate; he may have his favorites, but he will not spare their errors. For history, I say again, has this and this only for its own; if a man will start upon it, he must sacrifice to no god but Truth; he must neglect all else; his sole rule and unerring guide is this—to think not of those who are listening to him now, but of the yet unborn who shall seek his converse.

Anyone who is intent only upon the immediate effect may reasonably be classed among the flatterers; and History has long ago realized that flattery is as little congenial to her as the arts of personal adornment to an athlete's training. An anecdote of Alexander is to the point. "Ah, Onesicritus," said he, "how I should like to come to life again for a little while, and see how your stuff strikes people by that time; at present they have good enough reason to praise and welcome it; that is their way of angling for a share of my favor." On the same principle some people actually accept Homer's history of Achilles, full of exaggerations as it is; the one great guarantee which they recognize of his truth is the fact that his subject was not living; that leaves him no motive for lying.

There stands my model, then: fearless, incorruptible, independent, a believer in frankness and veracity; one that will call a spade a spade, make no concession to likes and dislikes, nor spare any man for pity or respect or propriety; an impartial judge, kind to all, but too kind to none; a literary cosmopolite with neither suzerain nor king, never heeding what this or that man may think, but setting down the thing that befell.

Thucydides is our noble legislator; he marked the admiration that met

Herodotus and gave the Muses' names to his nine books; and thereupon he drew the line which parts a good historian from a bad: our work is to be a possession forever, not a bid for present reputation; we are not to seize upon the sensational, but bequeath the truth to them that come after; he applies the test of use, and defines the end which a wise historian will set before himself: it is that, should history ever repeat itself, the records of the past may give present guidance.

Such are to be my historian's principles. As for diction and style, he is not to set about his work armed to the teeth from the rhetorician's arsenal of impetuosity and incisiveness, rolling periods, close-packed arguments, and the rest; for him a serener mood. His matter should be homogeneous and compact, his vocabulary fit to be understood of the people, for the clearest possible setting forth of his subject.

For to those marks which we set up for the historic spirit—frankness and truth—corresponds one at which the historic style should first of all aim, namely, a lucidity which leaves nothing obscure, impartially avoiding abstruse out-of-the-way expressions, and the illiberal jargon of the market; we wish the vulgar to comprehend, the cultivated to commend us. Ornament should be unobtrusive, and never smack of elaboration, if it is not to remind us of overseasoned dishes.

The historian's spirit should not be without a touch of the poetical; it needs, like poetry, to employ impressive and exalted tones, especially when it finds itself in the midst of battle array and conflicts by land or sea; it is then that the poetic gale must blow to speed the vessel on, and help her ride the waves in majesty. But the diction is to be content with *terra firma*, rising a little to assimilate itself to the beauty and grandeur of the subject, but never startling the hearer, nor forgetting a due restraint; there is great risk at such times of its running wild and falling into poetic frenzy; and then it is that writers should hold themselves in with bit and bridle; with them as with horses an uncontrollable temper means disaster. At these times it is best for the spirit to go ahorseback, and the expression to run beside on foot, holding on to the saddle so as not to be outstripped.

As to the marshaling of your words, a moderate compromise is desirable between the harshness which results from separating what belongs together, and the jingling concatenations—one may almost call them—which are so common; one extreme is a definite vice, and the other repellent.

Facts are not to be collected at haphazard, but with careful, laborious, repeated investigation; when possible, a man should have been present and seen for himself; failing that, he should prefer the disinterested account, selecting the informants least likely to diminish or magnify from partiality. And here comes the occasion for exercising the judgment in weighing probabilities.

The material once complete, or nearly so, an abstract should be made of it, and a rough draft of the whole work put down, not yet distributed into its parts; the detailed arrangement should then be introduced, after which adornment may be added, the diction receive its color, the phrasing and rhythm be perfected.

The historian's position should now be precisely that of Zeus in Homer, surveying now the Mysians', now the Thracian horsemen's land. Even so *he* will survey now his own party (telling us what we looked like to him from his post of vantage), now the Persians, and yet again both at once if they come to blows. And when they are face to face, his eyes are not to be on one division, nor yet on one man, mounted or afoot—unless it be a Brasidas leading the forlorn hope, or a Demosthenes repelling it; his attention should be for the generals first of all; their exhortations should be recorded, the dispositions they make, and the motives and plans that prompted them. When the engagement has begun, he should give us a bird's-eye view of it, show the scales oscillating, and accompany pursuers and pursued alike.

All this, however, with moderation; a subject is not to be ridden to death; no neglect of proportion, no childish engrossment, but easy transitions. He should call a halt here, while he crosses over to another set of operations which demands attention; that settled up, he can return to the first set, now ripe for him; he must pass swiftly to each in turn, keeping his different lines of advance as nearly as possible level, fly from Armenia to Media, thence swoop straight upon Iberia, and then take wing for Italy, everywhere present at the nick of time.

He has to make of his brain a mirror, unclouded, bright, and true of surface; then he will reflect events as they presented themselves to him, neither distorted, discolored, nor variable. Historians are not writing fancy school essays; what they have to say is before them, and will get itself said somehow, being solid fact; their task is to arrange and put it into words; they have not to consider what to say, but how to say it. The historian, we may say, should be like Phidias, Praxiteles, Alcamenes, or any great sculptor. They similarly did not create the gold, silver, ivory, or other material they used; it was ready to their hands, provided by Athens, Elis, or Argos; they only made the model, sawed, polished, cemented, proportioned the ivory, and plated it with gold; that was what their art consisted in—the right arrangement of their material. The historian's business is similar—to superinduce upon events the charm of order, and set them forth in the most lucid fashion he can manage. When subsequently a hearer feels as though he were looking at what is being told him, and expresses his approval, then our historical Phidias' work has reached perfection, and received its appropriate reward.

When all is ready, a writer will sometimes start without formal preface if there is no pressing occasion to clear away preliminaries by that means, though even then his explanation of what he is to say constitutes a virtual preface.

When a formal preface is used, one of the three objects to which a public speaker devotes his exordium may be neglected; the historian, that is, has not to bespeak good will—only attention and an open mind. The way to secure the reader's attention is to show that the affairs to be narrated are great in themselves, throw light on destiny, or come home to his business and bosom; and as to the open mind, the lucidity in the body of the work, which is to secure that, will be facilitated by a preliminary view of the causes in operation and a precise summary of events.

Prefaces of this character have been employed by the best historians—by Herodotus, "to the end that what befell may not grow dim by lapse of time, seeing that it was great and wondrous, and showed forthwith Greeks vanquishing and barbarians vanquished"; and by Thucydides, "believing that that war would be great and memorable beyond any previous one; for indeed great calamities took place during its course."

After the preface, long or short in proportion to the subject, should come an easy natural transition to the narrative; for the body of the history which remains is nothing from beginning to end but a long narrative; it must therefore be graced with the narrative virtues—smooth, level, and consistent progress, neither soaring nor crawling, and the charm of lucidity—which is attained, as I remarked above, partly by the diction, and partly by the treatment of connected events. For, though all parts must be independently perfected, when the first is complete the second will be brought into essential connection with it, and attached like one link of a chain to another; there must be no possibility of separating them; no mere bundle of parallel threads; the first is not simply to be next to the second, but part of it, their extremities intermingling.

Brevity is always desirable, and especially where matter is abundant; and the problem is less a grammatical than a substantial one; the solution, I mean, is to deal summarily with all immaterial details, and give adequate treatment to the principal events; much, indeed, is better omitted altogether. Suppose yourself giving a dinner, and extremely well provided; there is pastry, game, kickshaws without end, wild boar, hare, sweetbreads; well, you will not produce among these a pike or a bowl of pea soup just because they are there in the kitchen; you will dispense with such common things.

Restraint in descriptions of mountains, walls, rivers, and the like is very important; you must not give the impression that you are making a tasteless display of word painting, and expatiating independently while the history takes care of itself. Just a light touch—no more than meets the need of clearness—and you should pass on, evading the snare, and denying yourself all such indulgences. You have the mighty Homer's example in such a case; poet as he is, he yet hurries past Tantalus and Ixion, Tityus and the rest of them. If Parthenius, Euphorion, or Callimachus had been in his place, how many lines do you suppose it would have taken to get the water to Tantalus' lip; how many more to set Ixion spinning? Better still, mark how Thucydides—a very sparing dealer in description—leaves the subject at once, as soon as he has given an idea (very necessary and useful, too) of an engine or a siege operation, of the conformation of Epipolae, or the Syracusan harbor. It may occur to you that his account of the plague is long; but you must allow for the subject; then you will appreciate his brevity; *he* is hastening on; it is only that the weight of matter holds him back in spite of himself.

When it comes in your way to introduce a speech, the first requirement is that it should suit the character both of the speaker and of the occasion; the second is (once more) lucidity; but in these cases you have the counsel's right of showing your eloquence.

Not so with praise or censure; these should be sparing, cautious, avoiding hypercriticism and producing proofs, always brief, and never intrusive; historical characters are not prisoners on trial. Without these precautions you will share the ill name of Theopompus, who delights in flinging accusations broadcast, makes a business of the thing in fact, and of himself rather a public prosecutor than a historian.

It may occasionally happen that some extraordinary story has to be introduced; it should be simply narrated, without guarantee of its truth, thrown down for anyone to make what he can of it; the writer takes no risks and shows no preference.

But the general principle I would have remembered—it will ever be on my lips—is this: do not write merely with an eye to the present, that those now living may commend and honor you; aim at eternity, compose for posterity, and from it ask your reward. And that reward?

That it be said of you, "This was a man indeed, free and free-spoken; flattery and servility were not in him; he was truth all through." It is a name which a man of judgment might well prefer to all the fleeting hopes of the present.

Do you know the story of the great Cnidian architect? He was the builder of that incomparable work, whether for size or beauty, the Pharos tower. Its light was to warn ships far out at sea, and save them from running on the Paraetonia, a spot so fatal to all who get among its reefs that escape is said to be hopeless. When the building was done, he inscribed on the actual masonry his own name, but covered this up with plaster, on which he then added the name of the reigning king. He knew that, as happened later, letters and plaster would fall off together, and reveal the words:

SOSTRATUS SON OF DEXIPHANES OF CNIDUS

ON BEHALF OF ALL MARINERS

TO THE SAVIOUR GODS

He looked not, it appears, to that time, nor to the space of his own little life, but to this time, and to all time, as long as his tower shall stand and his art abide.

So too should the historian write, consorting with Truth and not with flattery, looking to the future hope, not to the gratification of the flattered.

There is your measuring-line for just history. If anyone be found to use it well, I have not written in vain; if none, yet have I rolled my tub on the Craneum.

Great Documents

Great documents do not have "authors"; though individual human beings write the words they contain, they are by definition more than the products of single men. Great documents express the beliefs, ideas, feelings, and knowledge of a great many people. They reflect the age in which they are written.

This is true even when we know, as we do of The Declaration of Independence, for example, that a document was principally the work of one man. The significance of the Declaration does not lie in any originality on Jefferson's part, but in the fact that it was an eloquent and forceful statement of the ideas about law and liberty which prevailed among his countrymen, and which still, we hope, prevail among them today.

In addition to The Declaration of Independence, we include here five documents which are of immense importance in the western tradition of political thought. They range over nearly three hundred years and, when we consider the Charter of the United Nations and the Universal Declaration of Human Rights, over most of the countries of the earth. They incorporate much of the best thinking about the relation of man to the state that has emerged in the modern era.

The first document, The English Bill of Rights, is the most important of the statutes which, taken together with a large body of traditional opinion, make up what we call the British Constitution. It dates back to the seventeenth century and the reign of William and Mary. Parliament had been led by certain extreme acts of their predecessor, James II, to draw up the Declaration of Right, which defined the relation between the king and his subjects. When William and Mary were offered the English crown in 1688, their acceptance depended upon their assent to the Declaration. They assented; and, in 1689, a statute based upon the Declaration—the Bill of Rights— was enacted into law. The spirit, though not always the letter, of this statute has influenced constitutional law in all of the English-speaking countries.

The Virginia Declaration of Rights was drafted by George Mason. It was adopted with revisions by the Virginia Convention on June 12, 1776. It was very influential in America (where it served as the model for the American Bill of Rights) and in France.

The Declaration of the Rights of Man and of the Citizen was drafted by the Marquis de Lafayette. It was adopted by the French Constituent Assembly on August 26, 1789, and was included as a preamble to the Constitution of 1791. It reflects the ideas of Rousseau and the American Declaration of Independence, and it exerted a dynamic influence upon the French Revolution. It has been a source of continuing inspiration to the French, particularly to the liberals who fought against reactionary regimes after the fall of Napoleon.

The Charter of the United Nations was drafted at the Dumbarton Oaks Conference of 1944, by representatives from the United States, the Soviet Union, Great Britain, and China. A fifty-nation conference at San Francisco accepted the draft with only a few minor revisions; it became the UN Charter on June 26, 1945.

The Universal Declaration of Human Rights was drafted by the United Nations Commission on Human Rights, under the chairmanship of Eleanor Roosevelt. It was adopted by the General Assembly on December 10, 1948.

All but one of the documents reprinted here are attempts to define the limits of government and the rights of man—as man and as citizen. Three of these documents speak of "inalienable" rights; one refers to them as "inherent." What is the purpose of such statements of human rights? Why are they necessary? If the rights of man are, indeed, inalienable, how can any government take them away?

We know—from recent as well as ancient history—that such rights are not, in fact, inalienable. Many societies have not recognized them. In other societies, men who once had them have been temporarily—and perhaps permanently—deprived of them.

What then is the role played by declarations of human rights? No simple answer to the question is possible, but perhaps the best brief statement which can be made on the subject is that the rights which these documents call inalienable or inherent are rights of which men *should not* be deprived. They belong to man by reason of his nature as man. They set up a standard by which the justice of a government can be measured. As such, at least in the United States, England, and France, they have served effectively.

The English Bill of Rights
1689

Whereas the Lords Spiritual and Temporal, and Commons, assembled at Westminster, lawfully, fully, and freely representing all the estates of the people of this realm, did, upon the thirteenth day of February, in the year of our Lord one thousand six hundred eighty-eight, present unto their Majesties, then called and known by the names and style of William and Mary, Prince and Princess of Orange, being present in their proper persons, a certain declaration in writing, made by the said Lords and Commons, in the words following, viz.:

Whereas the late King James II, by the assistance of divers evil counsellors, judges, and ministers employed by him, did endeavour to subvert and extirpate the Protestant religion, and the laws and liberties of this kingdom:

1. By assuming and exercising a power of dispensing with and suspending of laws, and the execution of laws, without consent of Parliament.

2. By committing and prosecuting divers worthy prelates for humbly petitioning to be excused from concurring to the same assumed power.

3. By issuing and causing to be executed a commission under the Great Seal for erecting a court, called the Court of Commissioners for Ecclesiastical Causes.

4. By levying money for and to the use of the Crown, by pretence of prerogative, for other time, and in other manner than the same was granted by Parliament.

5. By raising and keeping a standing army within this kingdom in time of peace, without consent of Parliament, and quartering soldiers contrary to law.

6. By causing several good subjects, being Protestants, to be disarmed, at the same time when Papists were both armed and employed contrary to law.

7. By violating the freedom of election of members to serve in Parliament.

8. By prosecutions in the Court of King's Bench, for matters and causes cognizable only in Parliament; and by diverse other arbitrary and illegal courses.

9. And whereas of late years, partial, corrupt, and unqualified persons have been returned and served on juries in trials, and particularly divers jurors in trials for high treason, which were not freeholders.

10. And excessive bail hath been required of persons committed in criminal cases, to elude the benefit of the laws made for the liberty of the subject.

11. And excessive fines have been imposed; and illegal and cruel punishments inflicted.

12. And several grants and promises made of fines and forfeitures, before any conviction of judgment against the persons upon whom the same were to be levied.

All which are utterly and directly contrary to the known laws and statutes, and freedom of this realm.

And whereas the said late King James II, have abdicated the government, and the throne being thereby vacant, his Highness the Prince of Orange (whom it hath pleased Almighty God to make the glorious instrument of delivering this kingdom from popery and arbitrary power) did (by the advice of the Lords Spiritual and Temporal, and divers principal persons of the Commons) cause letters to be written to the Lords Spiritual and Temporal, being Protestants, and other letters to the several counties, cities, universities, boroughs, and Cinque Ports, for the choosing of such persons as represent them, as were of right to be sent to Parliament, to meet and sit at Westminster upon the two-and-twentieth day of January, in this year one thousand six hundred eighty and eight, in order to such an establishment, as that their religion, laws, and liberties might not again be in danger of being subverted; upon which letters, elections have been accordingly made.

And thereupon the said Lords Spiritual and Temporal, and Commons, pursuant to their respective letters and elections, being now assembled in a full and free representation of this nation, taking into their most serious consideration the best means for attaining the ends aforesaid, do in the first place (as their ancestors in like case have usually done), for the vindicating and asserting their ancient rights and liberties, declare:

1. That the pretended power of suspending of laws, or the execution of laws, by regal authority, without consent of parliament, is illegal.

2. That the pretended power of dispensing with laws, or the execution of laws, by regal authority, as it hath been assumed and exercised of late, is illegal.

3. That the commission for erecting the late Court of Commissioners for Ecclesiastical Causes, and all others commissions and courts of like nature, are illegal and pernicious.

4. That levying money for or to the use of the Crown, by pretence of prerogative, without grant of parliament, for longer time or in other manner than the same is or shall be granted, is illegal.

5. That it is the right of the subject to petition the king, and all commandments and prosecutions for such petitioning are illegal.

6. That the raising or keeping a standing army within the kingdom in time of peace, unless it be with consent of parliament, is against law.

7. That the subjects which are Protestants may have arms for their defence suitable to their conditions, and as allowed by law.

8. That election of members of parliament ought to be free.

9. That the freedom of speech, and debates or proceedings in parliament, ought not to be impeached or questioned in any court or place out of parliament.

10. That excessive bail ought not to be required, nor excessive fines imposed; nor cruel and unusual punishment inflicted.

11. That jurors ought to be duly impanelled and returned, and jurors which pass upon men in trials for high treason ought to be freeholders.

12. That all grants and promises of fine and forfeitures of particular persons before conviction are illegal and void.

13. And that for redress of all grievances, and for the amending, strengthening and preserving of the laws, parliaments ought to be held frequently.

And they do claim, demand, and insist upon all and singular the premises, as their undoubted rights and liberties; and that no declarations, judgments, doings or proceedings, to the prejudice of the people in any of the said premises, ought in any wise to be drawn hereafter into consequence or example. . . .

Declaration of the Rights of Man and of the Citizen

1789

T he representatives of the people of France, formed into a National Assembly, considering that ignorance, neglect, or contempt of human rights are the sole causes of public misfortunes and corruptions of government, have resolved to set forth in a solemn declaration these natural, imprescriptible, and inalienable rights, that this declaration being constantly present to the minds of the members of the body social, they may be ever kept attentive to their rights and their duties; that the acts of the legislative and executive powers of government, being capable of being every moment compared with the end of political institutions, may be more respected; and also, that the future claims of the citizens, being directed by simple and incontestable principles, may always tend to the maintenance of the Constitution and the general happiness.

For these reasons the National Assembly doth recognize and declare, in the presence of the Supreme Being, and with the hope of His blessing and favor, the following *sacred* rights of men and of citizens:

I. Men are born, and always continue, free and equal in respect of their rights. Civil distinctions, therefore, can be founded only on public utility.

II. The end of all political associations is the preservation of the natural and imprescriptible rights of man; and these rights are Liberty, Property, Security, and Resistance of Oppression.

III. The nation is essentially the source of all sovereignty; nor can any individual, or any body of men, be entitled to any authority which is not expressly derived from it.

IV. Political liberty consists in the power of doing whatever does not injure another. The exercise of the natural rights of every man has no other limits than those which are necessary to secure to every *other* man the free exercise of the same rights; and these limits are determinable only by the law.

V. The law ought to prohibit only actions hurtful to society. What is not prohibited by the law should not be hindered; nor should anyone be compelled to that which the law does not require.

VI. The law is an expression of the will of the community. All citizens have a right to concur, either personally or by their representatives, in its formation. It should be the same to all, whether it protects or punishes; and all being equal in its sight are equally eligible to all honors, places, and employments, according to their different abilities, without any other distinction than that created by their virtues and talents.

VII. No man should be accused, arrested, or held in confinement, except in cases determined by the law, and according to the forms which it has prescribed. All who promote, solicit, execute, or cause to be executed, arbitrary orders, ought to be punished, and every citizen called upon, or apprehended by virtue of the law, ought immediately to obey, and renders himself culpable by resistance.

VIII. The law ought to impose no other penalties but such as are absolutely and evidently necessary; and no one ought to be punished, but in virtue of a law promulgated before the offense, and legally applied.

IX. Every man being presumed innocent till he has been convicted, whenever his detention becomes indispensable, all rigor to him, more than is necessary to secure his person, ought to be provided against by the law.

X. No man ought to be molested on account of his opinions, not even on account of his religious opinions, provided his avowal of them does not disturb the public order established by the law.

XI. The unrestrained communication of thoughts and opinions being one of the most precious rights of man, every citizen may speak, write, and publish freely, provided he is responsible for the abuse of this liberty, in cases determined by the law.

XII. A public force being necessary to give security to the rights of men and of citizens, that force is instituted for the benefit of the community and not for the particular benefit of the persons with whom it is entrusted.

XIII. A common contribution being necessary for the support of the public force, and for defraying the other expenses of government, it ought to be divided equally among the members of the community, according to their abilities.

xiv. Every citizen has a right, either by himself or his representative, to a free voice in determining the necessity of public contributions, the appropriations of them, and their amount, mode of assessment, and duration.

xv. Every community has a right to demand of all its agents an account of their conduct.

xvi. Every community in which a separation of powers and a security of rights is not provided for wants a constitution.

xvii. The right to property being inviolable and sacred, no one ought to be deprived of it, except in cases of evident public necessity, legally ascertained, and on condition of a previous just indemnity.

The Virginia Declaration of Rights
June 12, 1776

A declaration of rights made by the representatives of the good people of Virginia, assembled in full and free convention; which rights do pertain to them and their posterity, as the basis and foundation of government.

SECTION 1. That all men are by nature equally free and independent and have certain inherent rights, of which, when they enter into a state of society, they cannot, by any compact, deprive or divest their posterity; namely, the enjoyment of life and liberty, with the means of acquiring and possessing property, and pursuing and obtaining happiness and safety.

SECTION 2. That all power is vested in, and consequently derived from, the people; that magistrates are their trustees and servants and at all times amenable to them.

SECTION 3. That government is, or ought to be, instituted for the common benefit, protection, and security of the people, nation, or community; of all the various modes and forms of government, that is best which is capable of producing the greatest degree of happiness and safety and is most effectually secured against the danger of maladministration; and that, when any government shall be found inadequate or contrary to these purposes, a majority of the community hath an indubitable, inalienable, and indefeasible right to reform, alter, or abolish it, in such manner as shall be judged most conducive to the public weal.

SECTION 4. That no man, or set of men, are entitled to exclusive or separate emoluments or privileges from the community, but in consideration of public services; which, not being descendible, neither ought the offices of magistrate, legislator, or judge to be hereditary.

SECTION 5. That the legislative and executive powers of the state should be separate and distinct from the judiciary; and that the members of the two first may be restrained from oppression, by feeling and participating the burdens of the people, they should, at fixed periods, be reduced to a private station, return into that body from which they were originally taken, and the vacancies be supplied by frequent, certain, and regular elections, in which all, or any part, of the former members, to be again eligible, or ineligible, as the laws shall direct.

SECTION 6. That elections of members to serve as representatives of the people, in assembly, ought to be free; and that all men, having sufficient evidence of permanent common interest with, and attachment to, the community, have the right of suffrage and cannot be taxed or deprived of their property for public uses without their own consent, or that of their representatives so elected, nor bound by any law to which they have not, in like manner, assented for the public good.

SECTION 7. That all power of suspending laws, or the execution of laws, by any authority, without consent of the representatives of the people, is injurious to their rights and ought not to be exercised.

SECTION 8. That in all capital or criminal prosecutions a man hath a right to demand the cause and nature of his accusation, to be confronted with the accusers and witnesses, to call for evidence in his favor, and to a speedy trial by an impartial jury of twelve men of his vicinage, without whose unanimous consent he cannot be found guilty; nor can he be compelled to give evidence against himself; that no man be deprived of his liberty, except by the law of the land or the judgment of his peers.

SECTION 9. That excessive bail ought not to be required, nor excessive fines imposed, nor cruel and unusual punishments inflicted.

SECTION 10. That general warrants, whereby an officer or messenger may be commanded to search suspected places without evidence of a fact committed, or to seize any person or persons not named, or whose offense is not particularly described and supported by evidence, are grievous and oppressive and ought not to be granted.

SECTION 11. That in controversies respecting property, and in suits between man and man, the ancient trial by jury is preferable to any other and ought to be held sacred.

SECTION 12. That the freedom of the press is one of the great bulwarks of liberty and can never be restrained but by despotic governments.

SECTION 13. That a well-regulated militia, composed of the body of the people, trained to arms, is the proper, natural, and safe defense of a free state; that standing armies, in time of peace, should be avoided as dangerous to liberty; and that in all cases the military should be under strict subordination to, and governed by, the civil power.

SECTION 14. That the people have a right to uniform government;

and, therefore, that no government separate from or independent of the government of Virginia ought to be erected or established within the limits thereof.

Section 15. That no free government, or the blessings of liberty, can be preserved to any people, but by a firm adherence to justice, moderation, temperance, frugality, and virtue, and by frequent recurrence to fundamental principles.

Section 16. That religion, or the duty which we owe to our Creator, and the manner of discharging it, can be directed only by reason and conviction, not by force or violence; and therefore all men are equally entitled to the free exercise of religion, according to the dictates of conscience; and that it is the mutual duty of all to practice Christian forbearance, love, and charity toward each other.

The Declaration of Independence

A DECLARATION

BY THE REPRESENTATIVES OF THE UNITED STATES OF AMERICA
IN CONGRESS ASSEMBLED, JULY 4, 1776

When, in the course of human events, it becomes necessary for one people to dissolve the political bands which have connected them with another, and to assume among the powers of the earth, the separate and equal station to which the laws of nature and of nature's God entitle them, a decent respect to the opinions of mankind requires that they should declare the causes which impel them to the separation.

We hold these truths to be self-evident, that all men are created equal, that they are endowed by their Creator with certain unalienable rights, that among these are life, liberty and the pursuit of happiness. That to secure these rights, governments are instituted among men, deriving their just powers from the consent of the governed, that whenever any form of government becomes destructive of these ends, it is the right of the people to alter or to abolish it, and to institute new government, laying its foundation on such principles and organizing its powers in such form, as to them shall seem most likely to effect their safety and happiness. Prudence, indeed, will dictate that governments long established should not be changed for light and transient causes; and accordingly all experience hath shown, that mankind are more disposed to suffer, while evils are sufferable, than to right themselves by abolishing the forms to which they are accustomed. But when a long train of abuses and usurpations, pursuing invariably the same object, evinces a design to reduce them under absolute despotism, it is their right, it is their duty, to throw off such government, and to provide new guards for their future security. Such has been the patient sufferance of these colonies; and such is now the necessity which constrains them to alter their former systems of government. The history of the present King of Great Britain is a history of repeated injuries and usurpations, all having in direct object the establishment of an absolute tyranny over these states. To prove this, let facts be submitted to a candid world.

He has refused his assent to laws, the most wholesome and necessary for the public good.

He has forbidden his governors to pass laws of immediate and pressing importance, unless suspended in their operation till his assent should be obtained; and when so suspended, he has utterly neglected to attend to them.

He has refused to pass other laws for the accommodation of large districts of people, unless those people would relinquish the right of representation in the legislature, a right inestimable to them and formidable to tyrants only.

He has called together legislative bodies at places unusual, uncomfortable, and distant from the depository of their public records, for the sole purpose of fatiguing them into compliance with his measures.

He has dissolved representative houses repeatedly, for opposing with manly firmness his invasions on the rights of the people.

He has refused for a long time, after such dissolutions, to cause others to be elected; whereby the legislative powers, incapable of annihilation, have returned to the people at large for their exercise; the state remaining in the meantime exposed to all the dangers of invasion from without, and convulsions within.

He has endeavored to prevent the population of these States; for that purpose obstructing the laws for naturalization of foreigners; refusing to pass others to encourage their migrations hither, and raising the conditions of new appropriations of lands.

He has obstructed the administration of justice, by refusing his assent to laws for establishing judiciary powers.

He has made judges dependent on his will alone, for the tenure of their offices, and the amount and payment of their salaries.

He has erected a multitude of new offices, and sent hither swarms of officers to harass our people, and eat out their substance.

He has kept among us, in times of peace, standing armies without the consent of our legislatures.

He has affected to render the military independent of and superior to the civil power.

He has combined with others to subject us to a jurisdiction foreign to our Constitution, and unacknowledged by our laws; giving his assent to their acts of pretended legislation:

For quartering large bodies of armed troops among us:

For protecting them, by a mock trial, from punishment for any murders which they should commit on the inhabitants of these States:

For cutting off our trade with all parts of the world:

For imposing taxes on us without our consent:

For depriving us, in many cases, of the benefit of trial by jury:

For transporting us beyond seas to be tried for pretended offenses:

For abolishing the free system of English laws in a neighboring province, establishing therein an arbitrary government, and enlarging its boundaries so as to render it at once an example and fit instrument for introducing the same absolute rule into these colonies:

For taking away our charters, abolishing our most valuable laws, and altering fundamentally the forms of our governments:

For suspending our own legislatures, and declaring themselves invested with power to legislate for us in all cases whatsoever.

He has abdicated government here, by declaring us out of his protection and waging war against us.

He has plundered our seas, ravaged our coasts, burnt our towns, and destroyed the lives of our people.

He is at this time transporting large armies of foreign mercenaries to complete the works of death, desolation and tyranny, already begun with circumstances of cruelty and perfidy scarcely paralleled in the most barbarous ages, and totally unworthy the head of a civilized nation.

He has constrained our fellow citizens taken captive on the high seas to bear arms against their country, to become the executioners of their friends and brethren or to fall themselves by their hands.

He has excited domestic insurrections amongst us, and has endeavored to bring on the inhabitants of our frontiers, the merciless Indian savages, whose known rule of warfare is an undistinguished destruction of all ages, sexes and conditions.

In every stage of these oppressions we have petitioned for redress in the most humble terms. Our repeated petitions have been answered only by repeated injury. A prince whose character is thus marked by every act which may define a tyrant is unfit to be the ruler of a free people.

Nor have we been wanting in attentions to our British brethren. We have warned them from time to time of attempts by their legislature to extend an unwarrantable jurisdiction over us. We have reminded them of the circumstances of our emigration and settlement here. We have appealed to their native justice and magnanimity, and we have conjured them by the ties of our common kindred to disavow these usurpations, which would inevitably interrupt our connections and correspondence. They too have been deaf to the voice of justice and of consanguinity. We must, therefore, acquiesce in the necessity which denounces our separation, and hold them, as we hold the rest of mankind, enemies in war, in peace friends.

We, therefore, the representatives of the United States of America, in general Congress, assembled, appealing to the Supreme Judge of the world for the rectitude of our intentions, do, in the name, and by authority of the good people of these colonies, solemnly publish and declare, that these united colonies are, and of right ought to be free and independent states; that they are absolved from all allegiance to the British Crown, and that all political connection between them and the state of Great Britain is and ought to be totally dissolved; and that as free and independent states, they have full power to levy war, conclude peace, contract alliances, establish commerce, and to do all other acts and things which independent states may of right do. And for the support of this declaration, with a firm reliance on the protection of Divine Providence, we mutually pledge to each other our lives, our fortunes and our sacred honor.

Charter of the United Nations

1945

W*e the peoples of the United Nations determined*

to save succeeding generations from the scourge of war, which twice in our lifetime has brought untold sorrow to mankind, and

to reaffirm faith in fundamental human rights, in the dignity and worth of the human person, in the equal rights of men and women and of nations large and small, and

to establish conditions under which justice and respect for the obligations arising from treaties and other sources of international law can be maintained, and

to promote social progress and better standards of life in larger freedom,

and for these ends

to practice tolerance and live together in peace with one another as good neighbors, and

to unite our strength to maintain international peace and security, and

to ensure, by the acceptance of principles and the institution of methods, that armed force shall not be used, save in the common interest, and

to employ international machinery for the promotion of the economic and social advancement of all peoples,

have resolved to combine our efforts to accomplish these aims.

Accordingly, our respective Governments, through representatives assembled in the city of San Francisco, who have exhibited their full powers found to be in good and due form, have agreed to the present Charter of the United Nations and do hereby establish an international organization to be known as the United Nations.

CHAPTER I

PURPOSES AND PRINCIPLES

ARTICLE 1

The Purposes of the United Nations are:

1. To maintain international peace and security, and to that end: to take effective collective measures for the prevention and removal of threats to the peace, and for the suppression of acts of aggression or other breaches of the peace, and to bring about by peaceful means, and in conformity with the principles of justice and international law, adjustment or settlement of international disputes or situations which might lead to a breach of the peace;

2. To develop friendly relations among nations based on respect for the principle of equal rights and self-determination of peoples, and to take other appropriate measures to strengthen universal peace;

3. To achieve international co-operation in solving international problems of an economic, social, cultural, or humanitarian character, and in promoting and encouraging respect for human rights and for fundamental freedoms for all without distinction as to race, sex, language, or religion; and

4. To be a center for harmonizing the actions of nations in the attainment of these common ends.

ARTICLE 2

The Organization and its Members, in pursuit of the Purposes stated in Article 1, shall act in accordance with the following Principles.

1. The Organization is based on the principle of the sovereign equality of all its Members.

2. All Members, in order to ensure to all of them the rights and benefits resulting from membership, shall fulfill in good faith the obligations assumed by them in accordance with the present Charter.

3. All Members shall settle their international disputes by peaceful means in such a manner that international peace and security, and justice, are not endangered.

4. All Members shall refrain in their international relations from the threat or use of force against the territorial integrity or political independence of any state, or in any other manner inconsistent with the Purposes of the United Nations.

5. All Members shall give the United Nations every assistance in any action it takes in accordance with the present Charter, and shall refrain from giving assistance to any state against which the United Nations is taking preventive or enforcement action.

6. The Organization shall ensure that states which are not Members of the United Nations act in accordance with these Principles so far as may be necessary for the maintenance of international peace and security.

7. Nothing contained in the present Charter shall authorize the United Nations to intervene in matters which are essentially within the domestic jurisdiction of any state or shall require the Members to submit such matters to settlement under the present Charter; but this principle shall not prejudice the application of enforcement measures under Chapter VII.

CHAPTER II

MEMBERSHIP

ARTICLE 3

The original Members of the United Nations shall be the states which, having participated in the United Nations Conference on International Organization at San Francisco, or having previously signed the Declaration by United Nations of January 1, 1942, sign the present Charter and ratify it in accordance with Article 110.

ARTICLE 4

1. Membership in the United Nations is open to all other peace-loving states which accept the obligations contained in the present Charter and, in the judgment of the Organization, are able and willing to carry out these obligations.

2. The admission of any such state to membership in the United Nations will be effected by a decision of the General Assembly upon the recommendation of the Security Council.

ARTICLE 5

A Member of the United Nations against which preventive or enforcement action has been taken by the Security Council may be suspended from the exercise of the rights and privileges of membership by the General Assembly upon the recommendation of the Security Council. The exercise of these rights and privileges may be restored by the Security Council.

ARTICLE 6

A Member of the United Nations which has persistently violated the Principles contained in the present Charter may be expelled from the Organization by the General Assembly upon the recommendation of the Security Council.

CHAPTER III

ORGANS

ARTICLE 7

1. There are established as the principal organs of the United Nations: a General Assembly, a Security Council, an Economic and Social Council, a Trusteeship Council, an International Court of Justice, and a Secretariat.

2. Such subsidiary organs as may be found necessary may be established in accordance with the present Charter.

ARTICLE 8

The United Nations shall place no restrictions on the eligibility of men and women to participate in any capacity and under conditions of equality in its principal and subsidiary organs.

CHAPTER IV

THE GENERAL ASSEMBLY

Composition

ARTICLE 9

1. The General Assembly shall consist of all the Members of the United Nations.

2. Each Member shall have not more than five representatives in the General Assembly.

Functions and Powers

ARTICLE 10

The General Assembly may discuss any questions or any matters within the scope of the present Charter or relating to the powers and functions of any organs provided for in the present Charter, and except as provided in Article 12, may make recommendations to the Members of the

United Nations or to the Security Council or to both on any such questions or matters.

1. The General Assembly may consider the general principles of co-operation in the maintenance of international peace and security, including the principles governing disarmament and the regulation of armaments, and may make recommendations with regard to such principles to the Members or to the Security Council or to both.

2. The General Assembly may discuss any questions relating to the maintenance of international peace and security brought before it by any Member of the United Nations, or by the Security Council, or by a state which is not a Member of the United Nations in accordance with Article 35, paragraph 2, and, except as provided in Article 12, may make recommendations with regard to any such questions to the state or states concerned or to the Security Council or to both. Any such question on which action is necessary shall be referred to the Security Council by the General Assembly either before or after discussion.

3. The General Assembly may call the attention of the Security Council to situations which are likely to endanger international peace and security.

4. The powers of the General Assembly set forth in this Article shall not limit the general scope of Article 10.

1. While the Security Council is exercising in respect of any dispute or situation the functions assigned to it in the present Charter, the General Assembly shall not make any recommendation with regard to that dispute or situation unless the Security Council so requests.

2. The Secretary-General, with the consent of the Security Council, shall notify the General Assembly at each session of any matters relative to the maintenance of international peace and security which are being dealt with by the Security Council and shall similarly notify the General Assembly, or the Members of the United Nations if the General Assembly is not in session, immediately the Security Council ceases to deal with such matters.

1. The General Assembly shall initiate studies and make recommendations for the purpose of:

a. promoting international co-operation in the political field and encouraging the progressive development of international law and its codification;

b. promoting international co-operation in the economic, social, cultural, educational, and health fields, and assisting in the realization of human rights and fundamental freedoms for all without distinction as to race, sex, language, or religion.

2. The further responsibilities, functions, and powers of the General Assembly with respect to matters mentioned in paragraph 1 (b) above are set forth in Chapters IX and X.

ARTICLE 14

Subject to the provisions of Article 12, the General Assembly may recommend measures for the peaceful adjustment of any situation, regardless of origin, which it deems likely to impair the general welfare or friendly relations among nations, including situations resulting from a violation of the provisions of the present Charter setting forth the Purposes and Principles of the United Nations.

ARTICLE 15

1. The General Assembly shall receive and consider annual and special reports from the Security Council; these reports shall include an account of the measures that the Security Council has decided upon or taken to maintain international peace and security.

2. The General Assembly shall receive and consider reports from the other organs of the United Nations.

ARTICLE 16

The General Assembly shall perform such functions with respect to the international trusteeship system as are assigned to it under Chapters XII and XIII, including the approval of the trusteeship agreements for areas not designated as strategic.

ARTICLE 17

1. The General Assembly shall consider and approve the budget of the Organization.

2. The expenses of the Organization shall be borne by the Members as apportioned by the General Assembly.

3. The General Assembly shall consider and approve any financial and budgetary arrangements with specialized agencies referred to in Article

57 and shall examine the administrative budgets of such specialized agencies with a view to making recommendations to the agencies concerned.

Voting

ARTICLE 18

1. Each Member of the General Assembly shall have one vote.

2. Decisions of the General Assembly on important questions shall be made by a two-thirds majority of the Members present and voting. These questions shall include: recommendations with respect to the maintenance of international peace and security, the election of the nonpermanent Members of the Security Council, the election of the Members of the Economic and Social Council, the election of Members of the Trusteeship Council in accordance with paragraph 1 (c) of Article 86, the admission of new Members to the United Nations, the suspension of the rights and privileges of membership, the expulsion of Members, questions relating to the operation of the trusteeship system, and budgetary questions.

3. Decisions on other questions, including the determination of additional categories of questions to be decided by a two-thirds majority, shall be made by a majority of the Members present and voting.

ARTICLE 19

A Member of the United Nations which is in arrears in the payment of its financial contributions to the Organization shall have no vote in the General Assembly if the amount of its arrears equals or exceeds the amount of the contributions due from it for the preceding two full years. The General Assembly may, nevertheless, permit such a Member to vote if it is satisfied that the failure to pay is due to conditions beyond the control of the Member.

Procedure

ARTICLE 20

The General Assembly shall meet in regular annual sessions and in such special sessions as occasion may require. Special sessions shall be convoked by the Secretary-General at the request of the Security Council or of a majority of the Members of the United Nations.

ARTICLE 21

The General Assembly shall adopt its own rules of procedure. It shall elect its President for each session.

ARTICLE 22

The General Assembly may establish such subsidiary organs as it deems necessary for the performance of its functions.

CHAPTER V
THE SECURITY COUNCIL

Composition

ARTICLE 23

1. The Security Council shall consist of eleven Members of the United Nations. The Republic of China, France, the Union of Soviet Socialist Republics, the United Kingdom of Great Britain and Northern Ireland, and the United States of America shall be permanent Members of the Security Council. The General Assembly shall elect six other Members of the United Nations to be nonpermanent Members of the Security Council, due regard being specially paid, in the first instance to the contribution of Members of the United Nations to the maintenance of international peace and security and to the other purposes of the Organization, and also to equitable geographical distribution.

2. The nonpermanent Members of the Security Council shall be elected for a term of two years. In the first election of the nonpermanent Members, however, three shall be chosen for a term of one year. A retiring Member shall not be eligible for immediate re-election.

3. Each Member of the Security Council shall have one representative.

Functions and Powers

ARTICLE 24

1. In order to ensure prompt and effective action by the United Nations, its Members confer on the Security Council primary responsibility for the maintenance of international peace and security, and agree that in carrying out its duties under this responsibility the Security Council acts on their behalf.

2. In discharging these duties the Security Council shall act in accordance with the Purposes and Principles of the United Nations. The specific powers granted to the Security Council for the discharge of these duties are laid down in Chapters VI, VII, VIII, and XII.

3. The Security Council shall submit annual and, when necessary, special reports to the General Assembly for its consideration.

ARTICLE 25

The Members of the United Nations agree to accept and carry out the decisions of the Security Council in accordance with the present Charter.

ARTICLE 26

In order to promote the establishment and maintenance of international peace and security with the least diversion for armaments of the world's human and economic resources, the Security Council shall be responsible for formulating, with the assistance of the Military Staff Committee referred to in Article 47, plans to be submitted to the Members of the United Nations for the establishment of a system for the regulation of armaments.

Voting

ARTICLE 27

1. Each Member of the Security Council shall have one vote.

2. Decisions of the Security Council on procedural matters shall be made by an affirmative vote of seven Members.

3. Decisions of the Security Council on all other matters shall be made by an affirmative vote of seven Members including the concurring votes of the permanent Members; provided that, in decisions under Chapter VI, and under paragraph 3 of Article 52, a party to a dispute shall abstain from voting.

Procedure

ARTICLE 28

1. The Security Council shall be so organized as to be able to function continuously. Each Member of the Security Council shall for this purpose be represented at all times at the seat of the Organization.

2. The Security Council shall hold periodic meetings at which each of its Members may, if it so desires, be represented by a member of the government or by some other specially designated representative.

3. The Security Council may hold meetings at such places other than the seat of the Organization as in its judgment will best facilitate its work.

ARTICLE 29

The Security Council may establish such subsidiary organs as it deems necessary for the performance of its functions.

ARTICLE 30

The Security Council shall adopt its own rules of procedure, including the method of selecting its President.

ARTICLE 31

Any Member of the United Nations which is not a Member of the Security Council may participate, without vote, in the discussion of any question brought before the Security Council whenever the latter considers that the interests of that Member are specially affected.

ARTICLE 32

Any Member of the United Nations which is not a Member of the Security Council or any state which is not a Member of the United Nations, if it is a party to a dispute under consideration by the Security Council, shall be invited to participate, without vote, in the discussion relating to the dispute. The Security Council shall lay down such conditions as it deems just for the participation of a state which is not a Member of the United Nations.

CHAPTER VI

PACIFIC SETTLEMENT OF DISPUTES

ARTICLE 33

1. The parties to any dispute, the continuance of which is likely to endanger the maintenance of international peace and security, shall, first of all, seek a solution by negotiation, enquiry, mediation, conciliation, arbitration, judicial settlement, resort to regional agencies or arrangements, or other peaceful means of their own choice.

2. The Security Council shall, when it deems necessary, call upon the parties to settle their dispute by such means.

ARTICLE 34

The Security Council may investigate any dispute, or any situation which might lead to international friction or give rise to a dispute, in order to determine whether the continuance of the dispute or situation is likely to endanger the maintenance of international peace and security.

ARTICLE 35

1. Any Member of the United Nations may bring any dispute, or any situation of the nature referred to in Article 34, to the attention of the Security Council or of the General Assembly.

2. A state which is not a Member of the United Nations may bring to the attention of the Security Council or of the General Assembly any dispute to which it is a party if it accepts in advance, for the purposes of the dispute, the obligations of pacific settlement provided in the present Charter.

3. The proceedings of the General Assembly in respect of matters brought to its attention under this Article will be subject to the provisions of Articles 11 and 12.

ARTICLE 36

1. The Security Council may, at any stage of a dispute of the nature referred to in Article 33 or of a situation of like nature, recommend appropriate procedures or methods of adjustment.

2. The Security Council should take into consideration any procedures for the settlement of the dispute which have already been adopted by the parties.

3. In making recommendations under this Article the Security Council should also take into consideration that legal disputes should as a general rule be referred by the parties to the International Court of Justice in accordance with the provisions of the Statute of the Court.

ARTICLE 37

1. Should the parties to a dispute of the nature referred to in Article 33 fail to settle it by the means indicated in that Article, they shall refer it to the Security Council.

2. If the Security Council deems that the continuance of the dispute is in fact likely to endanger the maintenance of international peace and security, it shall decide whether to take action under Article 36 or to recommend such terms of settlement as it may consider appropriate.

ARTICLE 38

Without prejudice to the provisions of Articles 33 to 37, the Security Council may, if all the parties to any dispute so request, make recommendations to the parties with a view to a pacific settlement of the dispute.

CHAPTER VII

ACTION WITH RESPECT TO THREATS TO THE PEACE, BREACHES OF THE PEACE, AND ACTS OF AGGRESSION

ARTICLE 39

The Security Council shall determine the existence of any threat to the peace, breach of the peace, or act of aggression and shall make recommendations, or decide what measures shall be taken in accordance with Articles 41 and 42, to maintain or restore international peace and security.

ARTICLE 40

In order to prevent an aggravation of the situation, the Security Council may, before making the recommendations or deciding upon the measures provided for in Article 39, call upon the parties concerned to comply with such provisional measures as it deems necessary or desirable. Such provisional measures shall be without prejudice to the rights, claims, or position of the parties concerned. The Security Council shall duly take account of failure to comply with such provisional measures.

ARTICLE 41

The Security Council may decide what measures not involving the use of armed force are to be employed to give effect to its decisions, and it may call upon the Members of the United Nations to apply such measures. These may include complete or partial interruption of economic relations and of rail, sea, air, postal, telegraphic, radio, and other means of communication and the severance of diplomatic relations.

ARTICLE 42

Should the Security Council consider that measures provided for in Article 41 would be inadequate or have proved to be inadequate, it may take such action by air, sea, or land forces as may be necessary to maintain or restore international peace and security. Such action may include demonstrations, blockade, and other operations by air, sea, or land forces of Members of the United Nations.

ARTICLE 43

1. All Members of the United Nations, in order to contribute to the maintenance of international peace and security, undertake to make available to the Security Council, on its call and in accordance with a

special agreement or agreements, armed forces, assistance, and facilities, including rights of passage, necessary for the purpose of maintaining international peace and security.

2. Such agreement or agreements shall govern the numbers and types of forces, their degree of readiness and general location, and the nature of the facilities and assistance to be provided.

3. The agreement or agreements shall be negotiated as soon as possible on the initiative of the Security Council. They shall be concluded between the Security Council and Members or between the Security Council and groups of Members and shall be subject to ratification by the signatory states in accordance with their respective constitutional processes.

ARTICLE 44

When the Security Council has decided to use force it shall, before calling upon a Member not represented on it to provide armed forces in fulfillment of the obligations assumed under Article 43, invite that Member, if the Member so desires, to participate in the decisions of the Security Council concerning the employment of contingents of that Member's armed forces.

ARTICLE 45

In order to enable the United Nations to take urgent military measures, Members shall hold immediately available national air-force contingents for combined international enforcement action. The strength and degree of readiness of these contingents and plans for their combined action shall be determined, within the limits laid down in the special agreement or agreements referred to in Article 43, by the Security Council with the assistance of the Military Staff Committee.

ARTICLE 46

Plans for the application of armed force shall be made by the Security Council with the assistance of the Military Staff Committee.

ARTICLE 47

1. There shall be established a Military Staff Committee to advise and assist the Security Council on all questions relating to the Security Council's military requirements for the maintenance of international peace and security, the employment and command of forces placed at its disposal, the regulation of armaments, and possible disarmament.

2. The Military Staff Committee shall consist of the Chiefs of Staff of the permanent members of the Security Council or their representatives. Any Member of the United Nations not permanently represented on the Committee shall be invited by the Committee to be associated with it when the efficient discharge of the Committee's responsibilities requires the participation of that Member in its work.

3. The Military Staff Committee shall be responsible under the Security Council for the strategic direction of any armed forces placed at the disposal of the Security Council. Questions relating to the command of such forces shall be worked out subsequently.

4. The Military Staff Committee, with the authorization of the Security Council and after consultation with appropriate regional agencies, may establish regional subcommittees.

ARTICLE 48

1. The action required to carry out the decisions of the Security Council for the maintenance of international peace and security shall be taken by all the Members of the United Nations or by some of them, as the Security Council may determine.

2. Such decisions shall be carried out by the Members of the United Nations directly and through their action in the appropriate international agencies of which they are Members.

ARTICLE 49

The Members of the United Nations shall join in affording mutual assistance in carrying out the measures decided upon by the Security Council.

ARTICLE 50

If preventive or enforcement measures against any state are taken by the Security Council, any other state, whether a Member of the United Nations or not, which finds itself confronted with special economic problems arising from the carrying out of those measures shall have the right to consult the Security Council with regard to a solution of those problems.

ARTICLE 51

Nothing in the present Charter shall impair the inherent right of individual or collective self-defense if an armed attack occurs against a Member of the United Nations, until the Security Council has taken the measures necessary to maintain international peace and security. Measures taken by Members in the exercise of this right of self-defense shall be immediately reported to the Security Council and shall not in any way affect the authority and responsibility of the Security Council under the present Charter to take at any time such action as it deems necessary in order to maintain or restore international peace and security.

CHAPTER VIII
REGIONAL ARRANGEMENTS
ARTICLE 52

1. Nothing in the present Charter precludes the existence of regional arrangements or agencies for dealing with such matters relating to the maintenance of international peace and security as are appropriate for regional action, provided that such arrangements or agencies and their activities are consistent with the Purposes and Principles of the United Nations.

2. The Members of the United Nations entering into such arrangements or constituting such agencies shall make every effort to achieve pacific settlement of local disputes through such regional arrangements or by such regional agencies before referring them to the Security Council.

3. The Security Council shall encourage the development of pacific settlement of local disputes through such regional arrangements or by such regional agencies either on the initiative of the states concerned or by reference from the Security Council.

4. This Article in no way impairs the application of Articles 34 and 35.

ARTICLE 53

1. The Security Council shall, where appropriate, utilize such regional arrangements or agencies for enforcement action under its authority. But no enforcement action shall be taken under regional arrangements or by regional agencies without the authorization of the Security Council, with the exception of measures against any enemy state, as defined in paragraph 2 of this Article, provided for pursuant to Article 107 or in regional arrangements directed against renewal of aggressive policy on the part of any such state, until such time as the Organization may, on request of the Governments concerned, be charged with the responsibility for preventing further aggression by such a state.

2. The term enemy state as used in paragraph 1 of this Article applies to any state which during the Second World War has been an enemy of any signatory of the present Charter.

ARTICLE 54

The Security Council shall at all times be kept fully informed of activities undertaken or in contemplation under regional arrangements or by regional agencies for the maintenance of international peace and security.

CHAPTER IX

INTERNATIONAL ECONOMIC AND SOCIAL COOPERATION

ARTICLE 55

With a view to the creation of conditions of stability and well-being which are necessary for peaceful and friendly relations among nations based on respect for the principle of equal rights and self-determination of peoples, the United Nations shall promote:

a. higher standards of living, full employment, and conditions of economic and social progress and development;

b. solutions of international economic, social, health, and related problems; and international cultural and educational co-operation; and

c. universal respect for, and observance of, human rights and fundamental freedoms for all without distinction as to race, sex, language, or religion.

ARTICLE 56

All Members pledge themselves to take joint and separate action in co-operation with the Organization for the achievement of the purposes set forth in Article 55.

ARTICLE 57

1. The various specialized agencies, established by intergovernmental agreement and having wide international responsibilities, as defined in their basic instruments, in economic, social, cultural, educational, health, and related fields, shall be brought into relationship with the United Nations in accordance with the provisions of Article 63.

2. Such agencies thus brought into relationship with the United Nations are hereinafter referred to as specialized agencies.

ARTICLE 58

The Organization shall make recommendations for the co-ordination of the policies and activities of the specialized agencies.

ARTICLE 59

The Organization shall, where appropriate, initiate negotiations among the states concerned for the creation of any new specialized agencies required for the accomplishment of the purposes set forth in Article 55.

ARTICLE 60

Responsibility for the discharge of the functions of the Organization set forth in this Chapter shall be vested in the General Assembly and, under the authority of the General Assembly, in the Economic and Social Council, which shall have for this purpose the powers set forth in Chapter x.

CHAPTER X
THE ECONOMIC AND SOCIAL COUNCIL

Composition

ARTICLE 61

1. The Economic and Social Council shall consist of eighteen Members of the United Nations elected by the General Assembly.

2. Subject to the provisions of paragraph 3, six Members of the Economic and Social Council shall be elected each year for a term of three years. A retiring Member shall be eligible for immediate re-election.

3. At the first election, eighteen Members of the Economic and Social Council shall be chosen. The term of office of six Members so chosen shall expire at the end of one year, and of six other Members at the end of two years, in accordance with arrangements made by the General Assembly.

4. Each Member of the Economic and Social Council shall have one representative.

Functions and Powers

ARTICLE 62

1. The Economic and Social Council may make or initiate studies and reports with respect to international economic, social, cultural, educa-

tional, health and related matters and may make recommendations with respect to any such matters to the General Assembly, to the Members of the United Nations, and to the specialized agencies concerned.

2. It may make recommendations for the purpose of promoting respect for, and observance of, human rights and fundamental freedoms for all.

3. It may prepare draft conventions for submission to the General Assembly, with respect to matters falling within its competence.

4. It may call, in accordance with the rules prescribed by the United Nations, international conferences on matters falling within its competence.

ARTICLE 63

1. The Economic and Social Council may enter into agreements with any of the agencies referred to in Article 57, defining the terms on which the agency concerned shall be brought into relationship with the United Nations. Such agreements shall be subject to approval by the General Assembly.

2. It may co-ordinate the activities of the specialized agencies through consultation with and recommendations to such agencies and through recommendations to the General Assembly and to the Members of the United Nations.

ARTICLE 64

1. The Economic and Social Council may take appropriate steps to obtain regular reports from the specialized agencies. It may make arrangements with the Members of the United Nations and with the specialized agencies to obtain reports on the steps taken to give effect to its own recommendations and to recommendations on matters falling within its competence made by the General Assembly.

2. It may communicate its observations on these reports to the General Assembly.

ARTICLE 65

The Economic and Social Council may furnish information to the Security Council and shall assist the Security Council upon its request.

ARTICLE 66

1. The Economic and Social Council shall perform such functions as fall within its competence in connection with the carrying out of the recommendations of the General Assembly.

2. It may, with the approval of the General Assembly, perform services at the request of Members of the United Nations and at the request of specialized agencies.

3. It shall perform such other functions as are specified elsewhere in the present Charter or as may be assigned to it by the General Assembly.

Voting

ARTICLE 67

1. Each Member of the Economic and Social Council shall have one vote.

2. Decisions of the Economic and Social Council shall be made by a majority of the Members present and voting.

Procedure

ARTICLE 68

The Economic and Social Council shall set up commissions in economic and social fields and for the promotion of human rights, and such other commissions as may be required for the performance of its functions.

ARTICLE 69

The Economic and Social Council shall invite any Member of the United Nations to participate, without vote, in its deliberations on any matter of particular concern to that Member.

ARTICLE 70

The Economic and Social Council may make arrangements for representatives of the specialized agencies to participate, without vote, in its deliberations and in those of the commissions established by it, and for its representatives to participate in the deliberations of the specialized agencies.

ARTICLE 71

The Economic and Social Council may make suitable arrangements for consultation with nongovernmental organizations which are concerned with matters within its competence. Such arrangements may be made with international organizations and, where appropriate, with national organizations after consultation with the Member of the United Nations concerned.

ARTICLE 72

The Economic and Social Council shall adopt its own rules of procedure, including the method of selecting its President.

2. The Economic and Social Council shall meet as required in accordance with its rules, which shall include provision for the convening of meetings on the request of a majority of its Members.

CHAPTER XI

DECLARATION REGARDING NONSELF-GOVERNING TERRITORIES

ARTICLE 73

Members of the United Nations which have or assume responsibilities for the administration of territories whose peoples have not yet attained a full measure of self-government recognize the principle that the interests of the inhabitants of these territories are paramount, and accept as a sacred trust the obligation to promote to the utmost, within the system of international peace and security established by the present Charter, the well-being of the inhabitants of these territories, and, to this end:

a. to ensure, with due respect for the culture of the peoples concerned, their political, economic, social, and educational advancement, their just treatment, and their protection against abuses;

b. to develop self-government, to take due account of the political aspirations of the peoples, and to assist them in the progressive development of their free political institutions, according to the particular circumstances of each territory and its peoples and their varying stages of advancement;

c. to further international peace and security;

d. to promote constructive measures of development, to encourage research, and to co-operate with one another and, when and where appropriate, with specialized international bodies with a view to the practical achievement of the social, economic, and scientific purposes set forth in this Article; and

e. to transmit regularly to the Secretary-General for information purposes, subject to such limitation as security and constitutional considerations may require, statistical and other information of a technical nature relating to economic, social, and educational conditions in the territories for which they are respectively responsible other than those territories to which Chapters xii and xiii apply.

ARTICLE 74

Members of the United Nations also agree that their policy in respect of the territories to which this Chapter applies, no less than in respect to their metropolitan areas, must be based on the general principle of good-neighborliness, due account being taken of the interests and well-being of the rest of the world, in social, economic, and commercial matters.

CHAPTER XII
INTERNATIONAL TRUSTEESHIP SYSTEM

ARTICLE 75

The United Nations shall establish under its authority an international trusteeship system for the administration and supervision of such territories as may be placed thereunder by subsequent individual agreements. These territories are hereinafter referred to as trust territories.

ARTICLE 76

The basic objectives of the trusteeship system, in accordance with the Purposes of the United Nations laid down in Article 1 of the present Charter, shall be:

a. to further international peace and security;

b. to promote the political, economic, social, and educational advancement of the inhabitants of the trust territories, and their progressive development towards self-government or independence as may be appropriate to the particular circumstances of each territory and its peoples and the freely expressed wishes of the peoples concerned, and as may be provided by the terms of each trusteeship agreement;

c. to encourage respect for human rights and for fundamental freedoms for all without distinction as to race, sex, language, or religion, and to encourage recognition of the interdependence of the peoples of the world; and

d. to ensure equal treatment in social, economic, and commercial matters for all Members of the United Nations and their nationals, and also equal treatment for the latter in the administration of justice, without prejudice to the attainment of the foregoing objectives and subject to the provisions of Article 80.

ARTICLE 77

1. The trusteeship system shall apply to such territories in the following categories as may be placed thereunder by means of trusteeship agreements:

a. territories now held under mandate;

b. territories which may be detached from enemy states as a result of the Second World War; and

c. territories voluntarily placed under the system by states responsible for their administration.

2. It will be a matter for subsequent agreement as to which territories in the foregoing categories will be brought under the trusteeship system and upon what terms.

ARTICLE 78

The trusteeship system shall not apply to territories which have become Members of the United Nations, relationship among which shall be based on respect for the principle of sovereign equality.

ARTICLE 79

The terms of trusteeship for each territory to be placed under the trusteeship system, including any alteration or amendment, shall be agreed upon by the states directly concerned, including the mandatory power in the case of territories held under mandate by a Member of the United Nations, and shall be approved as provided for in Articles 83 and 85.

ARTICLE 80

1. Except as may be agreed upon in individual trusteeship agreements, made under Articles 77, 79, and 81, placing each territory under the trusteeship system, and until such agreements have been concluded, nothing in this Chapter shall be construed in or of itself to alter in any manner the rights whatsoever of any states or any peoples or the terms of existing international instruments to which Members of the United Nations may respectively be parties.

2. Paragraph 1 of this Article shall not be interpreted as giving grounds for delay or postponement of the negotiation and conclusion of agreements for placing mandated and other territories under the trusteeship system as provided for in Article 77.

ARTICLE 81

The trusteeship agreement shall in each case include the terms under which the trust territory will be administered and designate the authority which will exercise the administration of the trust territory. Such authority, hereinafter called the administering authority, may be one or more states or the Organization itself.

ARTICLE 82

There may be designated, in any trusteeship agreement, a strategic area or areas which may include part or all of the trust territory to which the agreement applies, without prejudice to any special agreement or agreements made under Article 43.

ARTICLE 83

1. All functions of the United Nations relating to strategic areas, including the approval of the terms of the trusteeship agreements and of their alteration or amendment, shall be exercised by the Security Council.

2. The basic objectives set forth in Article 76 shall be applicable to the people of each strategic area.

3. The Security Council shall, subject to the provisions of the trusteeship agreements and without prejudice to security considerations, avail itself of the assistance of the Trusteeship Council to perform those functions of the United Nations under the trusteeship system relating to political, economic, social, and educational matters in the strategic areas.

ARTICLE 84

It shall be the duty of the administering authority to ensure that the trust territory shall play its part in the maintenance of international peace and security. To this end the administering authority may make use of volunteer forces, facilities, and assistance from the trust territory in carrying out the obligations towards the Security Council undertaken in this regard by the administering authority, as well as for local defense and the maintenance of law and order within the trust territory.

ARTICLE 85

1. The functions of the United Nations with regard to trusteeship agreements for all areas not designated as strategic, including the approval of the terms of the trusteeship agreements and of their alteration or amendment, shall be exercised by the General Assembly.

2. The Trusteeship Council, operating under the authority of the General Assembly, shall assist the General Assembly in carrying out these functions.

CHAPTER XIII

THE TRUSTEESHIP COUNCIL

Composition

ARTICLE 86

1. The Trusteeship Council shall consist of the following Members of the United Nations:

a. those Members administering trust territories;

b. such of those Members mentioned by name in Article 23 as are not administering trust territories; and

c. as many other Members elected for three-year terms by the General Assembly as may be necessary to ensure that the total number of members of the Trusteeship Council is equally divided between those Members of the United Nations which administer trust territories and those which do not.

2. Each Member of the Trusteeship Council shall designate one specially qualified person to represent it therein.

Functions and Powers

ARTICLE 87

The General Assembly and, under its authority, the Trusteeship Council, in carrying out their functions, may:

a. consider reports submitted by the administering authority;

b. accept petitions and examine them in consultation with the administering authority;

c. provide for periodic visits to the respective trust territories at times agreed upon with the administering authority; and

d. take these and other actions in conformity with the terms of the trusteeship agreements.

ARTICLE 88

The Trusteeship Council shall formulate a questionnaire on the political, economic, social, and educational advancement of the inhabitants of each trust territory, and the administering authority for each trust territory within the competence of the General Assembly shall make an annual report to the General Assembly upon the basis of such questionnaire.

Voting

ARTICLE 89

1. Each Member of the Trusteeship Council shall have one vote.

2. Decisions of the Trusteeship Council shall be made by a majority of the Members present and voting.

Procedure

ARTICLE 90

1. The Trusteeship Council shall adopt its own rules of procedure, including the method of selecting its President.

2. The Trusteeship Council shall meet as required in accordance with its rules, which shall include provision for the convening of meetings on the request of a majority of its Members.

ARTICLE 91

The Trusteeship Council shall, when appropriate, avail itself of the assistance of the Economic and Social Council and of the specialized agencies in regard to matters with which they are respectively concerned.

CHAPTER XIV

THE INTERNATIONAL COURT OF JUSTICE

ARTICLE 92

The International Court of Justice shall be the principal judicial organ of the United Nations. It shall function in accordance with the annexed Statute, which is based upon the Statute of the Permanent Court of International Justice and forms an integral part of the present Charter.

ARTICLE 93

1. All Members of the United Nations are *ipso facto* parties to the Statute of the International Court of Justice.

2. A state which is not a Member of the United Nations may become a party to the Statute of the International Court of Justice on conditions to be determined in each case by the General Assembly upon the recommendation of the Security Council.

ARTICLE 94

1. Each Member of the United Nations undertakes to comply with the decision of the International Court of Justice in any case to which it is a party.

2. If any party to a case fails to perform the obligations incumbent upon it under a judgment rendered by the Court, the other party may have recourse to the Security Council, which may, if it deems necessary, make recommendations or decide upon measures to be taken to give effect to the judgment.

ARTICLE 95

Nothing in the present Charter shall prevent Members of the United Nations from entrusting the solution of their differences to other tribunals by virtue of agreements already in existence or which may be concluded in the future.

ARTICLE 96

1. The General Assembly or the Security Council may request the International Court of Justice to give an advisory opinion on any legal question.

2. Other organs of the United Nations and specialized agencies, which may at any time be so authorized by the General Assembly, may also request advisory opinions of the Court on legal questions arising within the scope of their activities.

CHAPTER XV

THE SECRETARIAT

ARTICLE 97

The Secretariat shall comprise a Secretary-General and such staff as the Organization may require. The Secretary-General shall be appointed by the General Assembly upon the recommendation of the Security Council. He shall be the chief administrative officer of the Organization.

ARTICLE 98

The Secretary-General shall act in that capacity in all meetings of the General Assembly, of the Security Council, of the Economic and Social Council, and of the Trusteeship Council, and shall perform such other functions as are entrusted to him by these organs. The Secretary-General shall make an annual report to the General Assembly on the work of the Organization.

The Secretary-General may bring to the attention of the Security Council any matter which in his opinion may threaten the maintenance of international peace and security.

1. In the performance of their duties the Secretary-General and the staff shall not seek or receive instructions from any government or from any other authority external to the Organization. They shall refrain from any action which might reflect on their position as international officials responsible only to the Organization.

2. Each Member of the United Nations undertakes to respect the exclusively international character of the responsibilities of the Secretary-General and the staff and not to seek to influence them in the discharge of their responsibilities.

1. The staff shall be appointed by the Secretary-General under regulations established by the General Assembly.

2. Appropriate staffs shall be permanently assigned to the Economic and Social Council, the Trusteeship Council, and, as required, to other organs of the United Nations. These staffs shall form a part of the Secretariat.

3. The paramount consideration in the employment of the staff and in the determination of the conditions of service shall be the necessity of securing the highest standards of efficiency, competence, and integrity. Due regard shall be paid to the importance of recruiting the staff on as wide a geographical basis as possible.

CHAPTER XVI

MISCELLANEOUS PROVISIONS

1. Every treaty and every international agreement entered into by any Member of the United Nations after the present Charter comes into force

shall as soon as possible be registered with the Secretariat and published by it.

2. No party to any such treaty or international agreement which has not been registered in accordance with the provisions of paragraph 1 of this Article may invoke that treaty or agreement before any organ of the United Nations.

ARTICLE 103

In the event of a conflict between the obligations of the Members of the United Nations under the present Charter and their obligations under any other international agreement, their obligations under the present Charter shall prevail.

ARTICLE 104

The Organization shall enjoy in the territory of each of its Members such legal capacity as may be necessary for the exercise of its functions and the fulfillment of its purposes.

ARTICLE 105

1. The Organization shall enjoy in the territory of each of its Members such privileges and immunities as are necessary for the fulfillment of its purposes.

2. Representatives of the Members of the United Nations and officials of the Organization shall similarly enjoy such privileges and immunities as are necessary for the independent exercise of their functions in connection with the Organization.

3. The General Assembly may make recommendations with a view to determining the details of the application of paragraphs 1 and 2 of this Article or may propose conventions to the Members of the United Nations for this purpose.

CHAPTER XVII
TRANSITIONAL SECURITY ARRANGEMENTS
ARTICLE 106

Pending the coming into force of such special agreements referred to in Article 43 as in the opinion of the Security Council enable it to begin the exercise of its responsibilities under Article 42, the parties to the Four-Nation Declaration, signed at Moscow, October 30, 1943, and

France, shall, in accordance with the provisions of paragraph 5 of that Declaration, consult with one another and as occasion requires with other Members of the United Nations with a view to such joint action on behalf of the Organization as may be necessary for the purpose of maintaining international peace and security.

ARTICLE 107

Nothing in the present Charter shall invalidate or preclude action, in relation to any state which during the Second World War has been an enemy of any signatory to the present Charter, taken or authorized as a result of that war by the Governments having responsibility for such action.

CHAPTER XVIII

AMENDMENTS

ARTICLE 108

Amendments to the present Charter shall come into force for all Members of the United Nations when they have been adopted by a vote of two thirds of the Members of the General Assembly and ratified in accordance with their respective constitutional processes by two thirds of the Members of the United Nations, including all the permanent Members of the Security Council.

ARTICLE 109

1. A General Conference of the Members of the United Nations for the purpose of reviewing the present Charter may be held at a date and place to be fixed by a two-thirds vote of the Members of the General Assembly and by a vote of any seven Members of the Security Council. Each Member of the United Nations shall have one vote in the conference.

2. Any alteration of the present Charter recommended by a two-thirds vote of the conference shall take effect when ratified in accordance with their respective constitutional processes by two thirds of the Members of the United Nations including all the permanent Members of the Security Council.

3. If such a conference has not been held before the tenth annual session of the General Assembly following the coming into force of the present Charter, the proposal to call such a conference shall be placed on the agenda of that session of the General Assembly, and the confer-

ence shall be held if so decided by a majority vote of the Members of the General Assembly and by a vote of any seven Members of the Security Council.

CHAPTER XIX
RATIFICATION AND SIGNATURE

ARTICLE 110

1. The present Charter shall be ratified by the signatory states in accordance with their respective constitutional processes.

2. The ratifications shall be deposited with the Government of the United States of America, which shall notify all the signatory states of each deposit as well as the Secretary-General of the Organization when he has been appointed.

3. The present Charter shall come into force upon the deposit of ratifications by the Republic of China, France, the Union of Soviet Socialist Republics, the United Kingdom of Great Britain and Northern Ireland, and the United States of America, and by a majority of the other signatory states. A protocol of the ratifications deposited shall thereupon be drawn up by the Government of the United States of America which shall communicate copies thereof to all the signatory states.

4. The states signatory to the present Charter which ratify it after it has come into force will become original Members of the United Nations on the date of the deposit of their respective ratifications.

ARTICLE 111

The present Charter, of which the Chinese, French, Russian, English, and Spanish texts are equally authentic, shall remain deposited in the archives of the Government of the United States of America. Duly certified copies thereof shall be transmitted by that Government to the Governments of the other signatory states.

IN FAITH WHEREOF the representatives of the Governments of the United Nations have signed the present Charter.

DONE at the city of San Francisco the twenty-sixth day of June, one thousand nine hundred and forty-five.

Universal Declaration
of Human Rights

1948

PREAMBLE

WHEREAS recognition of the inherent dignity and of the equal and inalienable rights of all members of the human family is the foundation of freedom, justice and peace in the world, and

WHEREAS disregard and contempt for human rights have resulted in barbarous acts which have outraged the conscience of mankind, and the advent of a world in which human beings shall enjoy freedom of speech and belief and freedom from fear and want has been proclaimed as the highest aspiration of the common people, and

WHEREAS it is essential, if man is not to be compelled to have recourse, as a last resort, to rebellion against tyranny and oppression that human rights should be protected by the rule of law, and

WHEREAS it is essential to promote the development of friendly relations between nations, and

WHEREAS the peoples of the United Nations have in the Charter reaffirmed their faith in fundamental human rights, in the dignity and worth of the human person and in the equal rights of men and women, and determined to promote social progress and better standards of life in larger freedom, and

WHEREAS the Member States have pledged themselves to achieve, in co-operation with the United Nations, the promotion of universal respect for and observance of human rights and fundamental freedoms, and

WHEREAS a common understanding of these rights and freedoms is of the greatest importance for the full realization of this pledge,

Now therefore,

THE GENERAL ASSEMBLY

PROCLAIMS this Declaration of Human Rights as a common standard of achievement for all peoples and all nations, to the end that every individual and every organ of society, keeping this declaration constantly in mind, shall strive by teaching and education to promote respect for these rights and freedoms and by progressive measures, national and international, to secure their universal and effective recognition and observance, both among the peoples of member states themselves and among the peoples of territories under their jurisdiction.

ARTICLE 1. All human beings are born free and equal, in dignity and rights. They are endowed with reason and conscience, and should act towards one another in a spirit of brotherhood.

ARTICLE 2. Everyone is entitled to all the rights and freedoms set forth in this declaration, without distinction of any kind, such as race, color, sex, language, religion, political or other opinion, national or social origin, property, birth or other status.

Furthermore, no distinction shall be made on the basis of the political, jurisdictional or international status of the country or territory to which a person belongs, whether it be independent, Trust, Nonself-Governing or under any other limitation of sovereignty.

ARTICLE 3. Everyone has the right to life, liberty and security of person.

ARTICLE 4. No one shall be held in slavery or servitude; slavery and the slave trade shall be prohibited in all their forms.

ARTICLE 5. No one shall be subjected to torture or to cruel, inhuman or degrading treatment or punishment.

ARTICLE 6. Everyone has the right to recognition everywhere as a person before the law.

ARTICLE 7. All are equal before the law and are entitled without any discrimination to equal protection of the law. All are entitled to equal protection against any discrimination in violation of this Declaration and against any incitement to such discrimination.

ARTICLE 8. Everyone has the right to an effective remedy by the competent national tribunals for acts violating the fundamental rights granted him by the Constitution or by law.

ARTICLE 9. No one shall be subjected to arbitrary arrest, detention or exile.

ARTICLE 10. Everyone is entitled in full equality to a fair and public hearing by an independent and impartial tribunal, in the determination of his rights and obligations and of any criminal charge against him.

ARTICLE 11. *1*. Everyone with a penal offense has the right to be presumed innocent until proved guilty according to law in a public trial at which he has had all the guarantees necessary for his defense.

2. No one shall be held guilty of any penal offense on account of any act or omission which did not constitute a penal offense, under national or international law, at the time when it was committed. Nor shall a heavier penalty be imposed than the one that was applicable at the time the penal offense was committed.

ARTICLE 12. No one shall be subjected to arbitrary interference with his privacy, family, home or correspondence, nor to attacks upon his honor and reputation. Everyone has the right to the protection of the law against such interference or attacks.

ARTICLE 13. *1.* Everyone has the right to freedom of movement and residence within the borders of each state.

2. Everyone has the right to leave any country, including his own, and to return to his country.

ARTICLE 14. *1.* Everyone has the right to seek and to enjoy in other countries asylum from persecution.

2. This right may not be invoked in the case of prosecutions genuinely arising from nonpolitical crimes or from acts contrary to the purposes and principles of the United Nations.

ARTICLE 15. *1.* Everyone has the right to a nationality.

2. No one shall be arbitrarily deprived of his nationality nor denied the right to change his nationality.

ARTICLE 16. *1.* Men and women of full age, without any limitation due to race, nationality or religion, have the right to marry and to found a family. They are entitled to equal rights as to marriage, during marriage and at its dissolution.

2. Marriage shall be entered into only with the free and full consent of the intending spouses.

3. The family is the natural and fundamental group unit of society and is entitled to protection by society and the State.

ARTICLE 17. *1.* Everyone has the right to own property alone as well as in association with others.

2. No one shall be arbitrarily deprived of his property.

ARTICLE 18. Everyone has the right to freedom of thought, conscience and religion; this right includes freedom to change his religion or belief, and freedom, either alone or in community with others and in public or private, to manifest his religion or belief in teaching, practice, worship and observance.

ARTICLE 19. Everyone has the right to freedom of opinion and expression; this right includes freedom to hold opinions without interference and to seek, receive and impart information and ideas through any media and regardless of frontiers.

ARTICLE 20. *1.* Everyone has the right to freedom of peaceful assembly and association.

2. No one may be compelled to belong to an association.

ARTICLE 21. *1.* Everyone has the right to take part in the Government of his country, directly or through freely chosen representatives.

2. Everyone has the right of equal access to public service in his country.

3. The will of the people shall be the basis of the authority of government; this will shall be expressed in periodic and genuine elections which shall be by universal and equal suffrage and shall be held by secret vote or by equivalent free voting procedures.

ARTICLE 22. Everyone, as a member of society, has the right to social security and is entitled to the realization, through national effort and international co-operation and in accordance with the organization and resources of each state, of the economic, social and cultural rights indispensable for his dignity and the free development of his personality.

ARTICLE 23. *1.* Everyone has the right to work, to free choice of employment, to just and favorable conditions of work and to protection against unemployment.

2. Everyone, without any discrimination, has the right to equal pay for equal work.

3. Everyone who works has the right to just and favorable remuneration insuring for himself and his family an existence worthy of human dignity, and supplemented, if necessary, by other means of social protection.

4. Everyone has the right to form and to join trade unions for the protection of his interests.

ARTICLE 24. Everyone has the right to rest and leisure, including reasonable limitation of working hours and periodic holidays with pay.

ARTICLE 25. *1.* Everyone has the right to a standard of living adequate for the health and well-being of himself and of his family, including food, clothing, housing and medical care and necessary social services, and the right to security in the event of unemployment, sickness, disability, widowhood, old age or other lack of livelihood in circumstances beyond his control.

2. Motherhood and childhood are entitled to special care and assistance. All children, whether born in or out of wedlock, shall enjoy the same social protection.

ARTICLE 26. *1.* Everyone has the right to education. Education shall be free, at least in the elementary and fundamental stages. Elementary education shall be compulsory. Technical and professional education shall be made generally available, and higher education shall be equally accessible to all on the basis of merit.

2. Education shall be directed to the full development of the human personality and to the strengthening of respect for human rights and fundamental freedoms. It shall promote understanding, tolerance and friendship among all nations, racial or religious groups, and shall further the activities of the United Nations for the maintenance of peace.

3. Parents have a prior right to choose the kind of education that shall be given to their children.

ARTICLE 27. *1.* Everyone has the right freely to participate in the cultural life of the community, to enjoy the arts and to share in scientific advancement and its benefits.

2. Everyone has the right to the protection of the moral and material interests resulting from any scientific, literary or artistic production of which he is the author.

ARTICLE 28. Everyone is entitled to a social and international order in which the rights and freedoms set forth in this declaration can be fully realized.

ARTICLE 29. *1.* Everyone has duties to the community in which alone the free and full development of his personality is possible.

2. In the exercise of his rights and freedoms, everyone shall be subject only to such limitations as are determined by law solely for the purpose of securing due recognition and respect for the rights and freedoms of others and of meeting the just requirements of morality, public order and the general welfare in a democratic society.

3. These rights and freedoms may in no case be exercised contrary to the purposes and principles of the United Nations.

ARTICLE 30. Nothing in this declaration may be interpreted as implying for any state, group or person, any right to engage in any activity or to perform any act aimed at the destruction of any of the rights and freedoms set forth herein.

Thomas Paine

1737–1809

Thomas Paine was born in Norfolk, England, where his father was a Quaker corset maker. Working hard as a sailor, teacher, and exciseman until 1762, and then as a government customs official, he developed a hearty and lasting sympathy with the poor. In 1774 Benjamin Franklin, then in London, persuaded him to migrate to America, and gave him letters of introduction to influential men. On his arrival, he became the editor of the *Pennsylvania Magazine*. In January of 1776, he wrote a pamphlet called *Common Sense,* which, as George Washington said, "worked a powerful change in the minds of many men." By July the ground had been prepared for the signing of The Declaration of Independence.

During the Revolutionary War, Paine was a volunteer aide-de-camp to General Greene, and at this time wrote the first of a series of articles which were later published as *The Crisis.* This, too, had an enormous effect on American opinion. In recognition of his services Paine was granted an estate in New Rochelle, New York, Congress voted him gifts of money, and he was offered various government positions.

In 1787 Paine sailed for England to exhibit one of his inventions— a pierless iron bridge. He soon fell to writing his *The Rights of Man,* which was an answer to Edmund Burke's famous *Reflections on the Revolution in France.* When Paine's book appeared it created so great a stir that the British government did its best to suppress it. In 1792 Paine was indicted for treason, but luckily escaped to France before the trial. He was made a member of the French Revolutionary Convention, but he antagonized Robespierre by opposing the execution of Louis XVI, and was imprisoned. After Robespierre's death, Paine was released and reinstated in the Convention. His *Age of*

Reason, the first part of which appeared in 1794, infuriated conservatives everywhere. But Jefferson took care that it was circulated in the United States and, announcing that its principles were his own, was elected President in 1800. An acrimonious letter to George Washington, however, made Paine many enemies. When he returned to America in 1802 he was coldly received, and lived on his New York estate in obscurity until his death in 1809.

The first issue of *The Crisis* is written with fire and logical precision. "These are the times that try men's souls," Paine begins. "The summer soldier and the sunshine patriot will, in this crisis, shrink from the service of his country." But he who stands firm will deserve the gratitude of all. As he wrote, the seasoned British armies were advancing, and the untrained patriots had suffered cruel reverses. The colonies were not giving united support to the defending troops. Thousands of Tories were lending open or secret aid to the British, and spreading rumors which weakened morale and disrupted military operations.

The time had passed when such men could be blandly tolerated. Every Tory, Paine declared, "is a coward, for a servile, slavish, self-interested fear is the foundation of Toryism." He denounces those who are hostile, fearful, or lukewarm to the American cause, but he never ceases to reason with them. Would they not fight off a robber who broke into their house? Is it any different when a "stupid, stubborn, worthless, brutish" king seeks to bend them to his absolute will? And can they expect mercy from a man who has refused to do justice? Are they not like the Tory innkeeper who prefers to see peace in *his* day, than live to see it in his child's day?

What should we think, Paine asks, of a colony that came to terms with the Indians, and left other colonies exposed to massacre? Is the case any different when the Hessians and British are the invaders? A colony that surrenders to the British will fare worse than the rest.

Notes from the artist: "Paine in his old age, tired and disillusioned, executed in a manner derivative from old woodcuts and steel engravings. Below is Liberty, stepping upon the crown of England to place the wreath of victory upon the head of Washington."

These are the Times that try mens Souls. The Summer Soldier and the Sunshine Patriot will in this Crisis shrink from the Service of his Country; but he that stands it Now deserves the Love and thanks of Man and Woman

MY COUNTRY IS THE WORLD

COMMON SENSE

Thomas Paine

FIRST in WAR
FIRST in PEACE
FIRST in the Hearts
OF HIS COUNTRYMEN.

His arguments multiply. But there is a limit to tolerance. The Tories who will not listen to reason must be driven from the country. And this, as we know, is what happened to many. Far more were persuaded by Paine's appeal to stand by their fighting countrymen.

Paine was universally acclaimed for his wartime pamphlets. His later writings are more controversial, and raised up legions of enemies both in England and in America. Did the fault lie in his character—his truculence? He was clearly not a diplomat like Franklin, nor a conservative like Hamilton. It is hard to see how he could have strenuously campaigned for republicanism, toleration, freedom of speech, and equal rights for all men without incurring the wrath of many important people. Enemies are often proof of a man's sincerity and striking force. The graduated income tax and other tax reforms favoring the poor which Paine advocated, though long since adopted in the United States, were far ahead of his time. Prime Minister Pitt agreed privately that Paine was right, but was quoted as saying: "If I were to encourage Tom Paine's opinions, we should have a bloody revolution." He had Paine indicted for treason.

Paine, like his friend Jefferson, went further than his contemporaries in espousing democracy. Edmund Burke, though he had defended the American Revolution, could not abide the French Revolution. In his *Reflections,* he carried his opposition to the impious doings of the French so far that it became a denial of the democratic principle itself. The people of England, "utterly disclaim the right to choose their own governors," he wrote, and "they will resist the practical assertion of it with their lives and fortunes."

Paine writes in *The Rights of Man*: "That men should take up arms and spend their lives and fortunes, *not* to maintain their rights, but to maintain that they have *not* rights" is, he says, very queer indeed. Perhaps, then, Paine made enemies because he was too advanced and consistent a democrat. Could it be also that he was *needlessly* shocking and provocative; or were the shock and provocation needed?

A Call to Patriots—
December 23, 1776
from *The Crisis*

These are the times that try men's souls. The summer soldier and the sunshine patriot will, in this crisis, shrink from the service of his country; but he that stands it now deserves the love and thanks of man and woman. Tyranny, like hell, is not easily conquered; yet we have this consolation with us, that the harder the conflict, the more glorious the triumph. What we obtain too cheap, we esteem too lightly: 'Tis dearness only that gives everything its value. Heaven knows how to put a proper price upon its goods; and it would be strange, indeed, if so celestial an article as freedom should not be highly rated. Britain, with an army to enforce her tyranny, has declared that she has a right (not only to tax) but "to bind us in all cases whatsoever," and if being bound in that manner is not slavery, then is there not such a thing as slavery upon earth. Even the expression is impious, for so unlimited a power can belong only to God.

Whether the independence of the continent was declared too soon, or delayed too long, I will not now enter into as an argument; my own simple opinion is that had it been eight months earlier it would have been much better. We did not make a proper use of last winter, neither could we while we were in a dependent state. However, the fault, if it were one, was all our own; we have none to blame but ourselves. But no great deal is lost yet; all that Howe has been doing for this month past is rather a ravage than a conquest, which the spirit of the Jerseys a year ago would have quickly repulsed, and which time and a little resolution will soon recover.

I have as little superstition in me as any man living, but my secret opinion has ever been, and still is, that God Almighty will not give up a peo-

461

ple to military destruction, or leave them unsupportedly to perish, who
had so earnestly and so repeatedly sought to avoid the calamities of war
by every decent method which wisdom could invent. Neither have I so
much of the infidel in me as to suppose that He has relinquished the
government of the world, and given us up to the care of devils; and as I
do not, I cannot see on what grounds the king of Britain can look up to
heaven for help against us: A common murderer, a highwayman, or a
housebreaker has as good a pretense as he.

'Tis surprising to see how rapidly a panic will sometimes run through
a country. All nations and ages have been subject to them: Britain has
trembled like an ague at the report of a French fleet of flat-bottomed
boats; and in the fourteenth century the whole English army, after ravag-
ing the kingdom of France, was driven back like men petrified with fear;
and this brave exploit was performed by a few broken forces collected
and headed by a woman, Joan of Arc. Would that heaven might inspire
some Jersey maid to spirit up her countrymen, and save her fair fellow
sufferers from ravage and ravishment! Yet panics, in some cases, have
their uses; they produce as much good as hurt. Their duration is always
short; the mind soon grows through them, and acquires a firmer habit than
before. But their peculiar advantage is that they are the touchstones of
sincerity and hypocrisy, and bring things and men to light which might
otherwise have lain forever undiscovered. In fact, they have the same
effect on secret traitors which an imaginary apparition would have upon
a private murderer. They sift out the hidden thoughts of man, and hold
them up in public to the world. Many a disguised Tory has lately shown
his head, that shall penitentially solemnize with curses the day on which
Howe arrived upon the Delaware.

As I was with the troops at Fort Lee, and marched with them to the
edge of Pennsylvania, I am well acquainted with many circumstances
which those who lived at a distance know but little or nothing of. Our
situation there was exceedingly cramped, the place being on a narrow
neck of land between the North River and the Hackensack. Our force was
inconsiderable, being not one-fourth so great as Howe could bring against
us. We had no army at hand to have relieved the garrison had we shut
ourselves up and stood on the defense. Our ammunition, light artillery,
and the best part of our stores had been removed upon the apprehension
that Howe would endeavor to penetrate the Jerseys, in which case Fort
Lee could be of no use to us; for it must occur to every thinking man,
whether in the army or not, that these kind of field forts are only for
temporary purposes, and last in use no longer than the enemy directs

his force against the particular object, which such forts are raised to defend. Such was our situation and condition at Fort Lee on the morning
of the 20th of November, when an officer arrived with information that
the enemy with 200 boats had landed about seven or eight miles above.
Major General Greene, who commanded the garrison, immediately ordered them under arms, and sent express to his Excellency General
Washington at the town of Hackensack, distant by the way of the ferry
six miles. Our first object was to secure the bridge over the Hackensack,
which laid up the river between the enemy and us, about six miles from
us, and three from them. General Washington arrived in about three-
quarters of an hour, and marched at the head of the troops towards the
bridge, which place I expected we should have a brush for; however they
did not choose to dispute it with us, and the greatest part of our troops
went over the bridge, the rest over the ferry, except some which passed
at a mill on a small creek, between the bridge and the ferry, and made
their way through some marshy grounds up to the town of Hackensack,
and there passed the river. We brought off as much baggage as the wagons could contain; the rest was lost. The simple object was to bring off
the garrison, and to march them on till they could be strengthened by the
Jersey or Pennsylvania militia, so as to be enabled to make a stand. We
stayed four days at Newark, collected in our outposts with some of the
Jersey militia, and marched out twice to meet the enemy on information
of their being advancing, though our numbers were greatly inferior to
theirs. Howe, in my little opinion, committed a great error in generalship
in not throwing a body of forces off from Staten Island through Amboy,
by which means he might have seized all our stores at Brunswick, and
intercepted our march into Pennsylvania: But if we believe the power of
hell to be limited, we must likewise believe that their agents are under
some providential control.

I shall not now attempt to give all the particulars of our retreat to
the Delaware; suffice it for the present to say that both officers and men,
though greatly harassed and fatigued, frequently without rest, covering,
or provision, the inevitable consequences of a long retreat, bore it with a
manly and a martial spirit. All their wishes were one, which was that the
country would turn out and help them to drive the enemy back. Voltaire
has remarked that King William never appeared to full advantage but
in difficulties and in action; the same remark may be made on General
Washington, for the character fits him. There is a natural firmness in some
minds which cannot be unlocked by trifles, but which, when unlocked,
discovers a cabinet of fortitude; and I reckon it among those kind of pub-

lic blessings, which we do not immediately see, that God hath blest him with uninterrupted health, and given him a mind that can even flourish upon care.

I shall conclude this paper with some miscellaneous remarks on the state of our affairs; and shall begin with asking the following question: Why is it that the enemy have left the New England provinces, and made these middle ones the seat of war? The answer is easy: New England is not infested with Tories, and we are. I have been tender in raising the cry against these men, and used numberless arguments to show them their danger, but it will not do to sacrifice a world to either their folly or their baseness. The period is now arrived in which either they or we must change our sentiments, or one or both must fall. And what is a Tory? Good God! what is he? I should not be afraid to go with a hundred Whigs against a thousand Tories were they to attempt to get into arms. Every Tory is a coward, for a servile, slavish, self-interested fear is the foundation of Toryism; and a man under such influence, though he may be cruel, never can be brave.

But, before the line of irrecoverable separation be drawn between us, let us reason the matter together: Your conduct is an invitation to the enemy, yet not one in a thousand of you has heart enough to join him. Howe is as much deceived by you as the American cause is injured by you. He expects you will all take up arms, and flock to his standard with muskets on your shoulders. Your opinions are of no use to him unless you support him personally, for 'tis soldiers, and not Tories, that he wants.

I once felt all that kind of anger which a man ought to feel against the mean principles that are held by the Tories: A noted one, who kept a tavern at Amboy, was standing at his door, with as pretty a child in his hand, about eight or nine years old, as most I ever saw, and after speaking his mind as freely as he thought was prudent, finished with this unfatherly expression, "Well! give me peace in my day." Not a man lives on the continent but fully believes that a separation must some time or other finally take place, and a generous parent should have said, "If there must be trouble, let it be in my day that my child may have peace"; and this single reflection, well applied, is sufficient to awaken every man to duty. Not a place upon earth might be so happy as America. Her situation is remote from all the wrangling world, and she has nothing to do but to trade with them. A man may easily distinguish in himself between temper and principle, and I am as confident as I am that God governs the world that America will never be happy till she gets clear of foreign dominion. Wars, without ceasing, will break out till that period arrives, and the continent must in the end be conqueror; for though the flame of liberty may sometimes cease to shine, the coal never can expire.

America did not, nor does not, want force; but she wanted a proper application of that force. Wisdom is not the purchase of a day, and it is no wonder that we should err at first setting off. From an excess of tenderness, we were unwilling to raise an army, and trusted our cause to the temporary defense of a well-meaning militia. A summer's experience has now taught us better; yet with those troops, while they were collected, we were able to set bounds to the progress of the enemy, and, thank God! they are again assembling. I always considered a militia as the best troops in the world for a sudden exertion, but they will not do for a long campaign. Howe, it is probable, will make an attempt on this city; should he fail on this side the Delaware, he is ruined; if he succeeds, our cause is not ruined. He stakes all on his side against a part on ours; admitting he succeeds, the consequence will be that armies from both ends of the continent will march to assist their suffering friends in the middle states; for he cannot go everywhere, it is impossible. I consider Howe as the greatest enemy the Tories have; he is bringing a war into their country, which, had it not been for him and partly for themselves, they had been clear of. Should he now be expelled, I wish with all the devotion of a Christian that the names of Whig and Tory may never more be mentioned; but should the Tories give him encouragement to come, or assistance if he come, I as sincerely wish that our next year's arms may expel them from the continent, and the Congress appropriate their possessions to the relief of those who have suffered in welldoing. A single successful battle next year will settle the whole. America could carry on a two-years war by the confiscation of the property of disaffected persons, and be made happy by their expulsion. Say not that this is revenge; call it rather the soft resentment of a suffering people who, having no object in view but the good of all, have staked their own all upon a seemingly doubtful event. Yet it is folly to argue against determined hardness; eloquence may strike the ear, and the language of sorrow draw forth the tear of compassion, but nothing can reach the heart that is steeled with prejudice.

Quitting this class of men, I turn with the warm ardor of a friend to those who have nobly stood, and are yet determined to stand, the matter out: I call not upon a few, but upon all; not on this state or that state, but on every state; up and help us; lay your shoulders to the wheel; better have too much force than too little, when so great an object is at stake. Let it be told to the future world that in the depth of winter, when nothing but hope and virtue could survive, that the city and the country, alarmed at one common danger, came forth to meet and to repulse it. Say not that thousands are gone, turn out your tens of thousands; throw not the burden of the day upon Providence but "show your faith by your works" that God may bless you. It matters not where you live, or what rank of life you hold, the evil or the blessing will reach you all. The far and the near, the home counties and the back, the rich and the poor will suffer or rejoice alike. The heart that feels not now is dead. The blood of his children will curse his cowardice who shrinks back at a time when a little might have saved the whole, and made them happy. I love the man that can smile in trouble, that can gather strength from distress, and grow brave by reflection. 'Tis the business of little minds to shrink; but he whose heart is firm, and whose conscience approves his conduct, will pursue his principles unto death. My own line of reasoning is to myself as straight and clear as a ray of light. Not all the treasures of the world, so far as I believe, could have induced me to support an offensive war, for I think it murder; but if a thief break into my house, burn and destroy my property, and kill or threaten to kill me, or those that are in it, and to "bind me in all cases whatsoever" to his absolute will, am I to suffer it? What signifies it to me whether he who does it is a king or a common man; my countryman or not my countryman; whether it is done by an individual villain or an army of them? If we reason to the root of things, we shall find no difference; neither can any just cause be assigned why we should punish in the one case and pardon in the other. Let them call me rebel, and welcome, I feel no concern from it; but I should suffer the misery of devils were I to make a whore of my soul by swearing allegiance to one whose character is that of a sottish, stupid, stubborn, worthless, brutish man. I conceive likewise a horrid idea in receiving mercy from a being who at the last day shall be shrieking to the rocks and mountains to cover him, and fleeing with terror from the orphan, the widow, and the slain of America.

There are cases which cannot be overdone by language, and this is one. There are persons too who see not the full extent of the evil which threatens them; they solace themselves with hopes that the enemy, if they succeed, will be merciful. It is the madness of folly to expect mercy from those who have refused to do justice; and even mercy where conquest is the object is only a trick of war: The cunning of the fox is as murderous as the violence of the wolf; and we ought to guard equally against both. Howe's first object is partly by threats and partly by promise to terrify or seduce the people to deliver up their arms, and receive mercy. The ministry recommended the same plan to Gage, and this is what the Tories call making their peace; "a peace which passeth all understanding" indeed! A peace which would be the immediate forerunner of a worse ruin than any we have yet thought of. Ye men of Pennsylvania, do reason upon these things! Were the back counties to give up their arms, they would fall an easy prey to the Indians, who are all alarmed. This perhaps is what some Tories would not be sorry for. Were the home counties to deliver up their arms, they would be exposed to the resentment of the back counties, who would then have it in their power to chastise their defection at pleasure. And were any one state to give up its arms, that state must be garrisoned by all Howe's army of Britons and Hessians to preserve it from the anger of the rest. Mutual fear is a principal link in the chain of mutual love, and woe be to that state that breaks the compact. Howe is mercifully inviting you to barbarous destruction, and men must be either rogues or fools that will not see it. I dwell not upon the powers of imagination; I bring reason to your ears; and in language as plain as A, B, C, hold up truth to your eyes.

I thank God that I fear not. I see no real cause for fear. I know our situation well, and can see the way out of it. While our army was collected, Howe dared not risk a battle, and it is no credit to him that he decamped from the White Plains, and waited a mean opportunity to ravage the defenseless Jerseys; but it is great credit to us that, with a handful of men, we sustained an orderly retreat for near a hundred miles, brought off our ammunition, all our fieldpieces, the greatest part of our stores, and had four rivers to pass. None can say that our retreat was precipitate, for we were near three weeks in performing it, that the country might have time to come in. Twice we marched back to meet the enemy and remained out till dark. The sign of fear was not seen in our camp, and had not some of the cowardly and disaffected inhabitants spread false alarms through the country, the Jerseys had never been ravaged. Once more we are again collected and collecting; our new army at both ends of the continent is recruiting fast, and we shall be able to open the next campaign with sixty thousand men, well armed and clothed. This is our situation, and who will may know it. By perseverance and fortitude we have the prospect of a glorious issue; by cowardice and submission, the sad choice of a variety of evils—a ravaged country—a depopulated city— habitations without safety, and slavery without hope—our homes turned into barracks and bawdy houses for Hessians, and a future race to provide for whose fathers we shall doubt of. Look on this picture and weep over it! And if there yet remains one thoughtless wretch who believes it not, let him suffer it unlamented.

The foregoing is Number 1
of THE CRISIS PAPERS.

George Washington

1732–1799

George Washington, the undisputed "father of his country," was born on February 22 (New Style; Feb. 11, Old Style), 1732, in Westmoreland County, Virginia. The son of a large Virginia land-owner who died when George was only eleven, he spent most of his youth at the Mount Vernon estate with his beloved half brother Lawrence, who was many years his senior. Although he got little schooling, he taught himself some mathematics, and at the age of fifteen had begun his career as a surveyor. This, of course, was not to be his main profession. Notwithstanding his reported distaste for deception and fighting, he was soon drawn into military operations against the French on the Ohio frontier. In 1755 he was an aid to General Braddock in his disastrous campaign against Fort Duquesne, and was then, at the age of twenty-three, made commander of all the Virginia forces.

At the death of his half brother, Washington inherited the plantation at Mount Vernon. Shortly thereafter he married a wealthy widow, Martha Dandridge Custis, who brought him 15,000 acres and 150 slaves. Washington was now a gentleman farmer and a very wealthy man. He took a great interest in farming and experimental agriculture, and became a member of the Virginia House of Burgesses. As a leader of the opposition to British colonial policy in Virginia, he served as a delegate to the Continental Congress in 1774–75, which was organizing the defense of the colonies. In 1775 he was made Commander in Chief of the Continental Army.

Washington's task was to lead the poorly trained and poorly paid Continental troops to a decisive victory over the seasoned British armies, led by top-notch officers. He himself had no experience in large-scale military operations. Money and supplies of all sorts were grievously short. Most of the thirteen states, newly declared independent, were organizing their governments. There were many conflicts among them and they were weakened within by British sympathizers. The Continental Congress was without force or authority. Yet, as we all know, the war was won after five bitter years. The British surrendered at Yorktown in 1781.

Washington retired in 1783 after dismissing the army, but he was not able to remain a private citizen for long. The thirteen states were torn with dissension, and there was an imperative need for "a more perfect union" if the new nation was to endure and expand westward. Eventually, in 1787, the Constitutional Convention was called. All the great prestige of Washington was necessary to secure the adoption of the new United States Constitution, which greatly restricted the powers of the independent states. There was no question who would be chosen as the first President of the United States, nor could anyone but Washington have done so much, in the first few years, to stabilize the government and unify the country. After eight years in office, he retired gratefully in 1797, and lived his last two years peacefully on his Mount Vernon estate.

First in war, first in peace, and first in the hearts of his countrymen" is almost too good to be true, and yet it is true, in large measure, of Washington. It does not mean that he was always unanimously approved. We remember that in 1777 the war, under his leadership, had gone so disastrously that high officers and members of the Congress tried to have him removed from the command. Sectionalism also played a part in this serious intrigue, which, however, Washington successfully countered. The winter in Valley Forge, however, was one of appalling misery for the battered and freezing army. Washington felt great sympathy for the troops, but he never lost heart; his courage was an example to all. In the spring new strength came, and the war took a brighter turn. It is this unwavering forti-

Notes from the artist: ". . . an equestrian portrait of Washington done in a style to suggest the quaint illustrations of his age. The background is the famous cherry tree, and the quotation is from the Rules of Civility, a set of moral precepts that Washington transcribed in a copybook when he was fourteen years old."

Labour to keep alive in your breast that little spark of celestial fire, called conscience.

G Washington

tude and greatness with which he met every crisis that outweigh his shortcomings, and keep his image enshrined in our memory.

Washington's letter to the governors of all the states in 1783 grappled with the big problems of that time. After the five terrible years of war, there was a natural craving for ease and comfort, and a tendency also to return to the old conflicts that divided sections of the country, states, classes, individuals. Washington pleads for fraternal unity. He argues that "it is indispensable to the happiness of the individual states that there should be lodged somewhere a supreme power to regulate and govern the general concerns of the confederated republic, without which the Union cannot be of long duration."

The obligations contracted during the war must be honorably discharged, and the ignominy of national bankruptcy averted. It would be a shameful thing if the soldiers who have won the war should now, deprived of their promised pay, be obliged to beg for food from door to door. "It therefore is more than a common debt, it is a debt of honor; it can never be considered as a pension or gratuity."

The Farewell Address, thirteen years later, touches on some of the same themes, but also on new ones. Washington has been President now for two terms, and has refused to consider a third. In his first administration he had struck a balance between the conservative Federalists and the liberal Republicans, making Hamilton Secretary of the Treasury and Jefferson Secretary of State. But in his second administration he had swung to the Federalists' side, and had been roundly censured by the Republicans.

Now he appeals again for national unity and solidarity. Bear in mind the common bonds of brotherhood, he counsels. "With slight shades of difference, you have the same religion, manners, habits, and political principles. You have in a common cause fought and triumphed together." Independence and liberty have been won by collective efforts and are collective blessings.

He warns again against the dangers of sectionalism, and insists that strong government, with properly balanced powers, provides the only guarantee, in a large country, of the continued enjoyment of liberty.

What is most novel and controversial in the *Address* is the warning against entangling alliances. Existing treaties should be honored in full, Washington says, but "it is unnecessary and would be unwise to extend them. . . . There can be no greater error than to expect . . . real favors from nation to nation."

Should we take this dictum of Washington's to apply to all nations or only to small or weak ones? The United States of 1796 could not have entered an equal alliance with a strong power. A wide ocean favored its independence on one side, and the vast territory on the other side aroused just fears of foreign penetration. But the strength and circumstances of other countries are very different. Are the nations who choose neutrality today strong or weak? Finally, can a policy which seemed wise in those days be maintained inflexibly in our contemporary world?

Circular Letter
to the Governors of All the States
on Disbanding the Army

The great object, for which I had the honor to hold an appointment in the service of my country, being accomplished, I am now preparing to resign it into the hands of Congress, and to return to that domestic retirement which, it is well known, I left with the greatest reluctance; a retirement for which I have never ceased to sigh, through a long and painful absence, and in which (remote from the noise and trouble of the world) I meditate to pass the remainder of my life, in a state of undisturbed repose. But before I carry this resolution into effect, I think it a duty incumbent on me to make this my last official communication; to congratulate you on the glorious events which Heaven has been pleased to produce in our favor; to offer my sentiments respecting some important subjects which appear to me to be intimately connected with the tranquillity of the United States; to take my leave of your Excellency as a public character; and to give my final blessing to that country in whose service I have spent the prime of my life, for whose sake I have consumed so many anxious days and watchful nights, and whose happiness, being extremely dear to me, will always constitute no inconsiderable part of my own.

Impressed with the liveliest sensibility on this pleasing occasion, I will claim the indulgence of dilating the more copiously on the subjects of our mutual felicitation. When we consider the magnitude of the prize we contended for, the doubtful nature of the contest, and the favorable manner in which it has terminated, we shall find the greatest possible reason for gratitude and rejoicing. This is a theme that will afford infinite delight to every benevolent and liberal mind, whether the event in contemplation be considered as the source of present enjoyment, or the parent of future happiness; and we shall have equal occasion to felicitate ourselves on the lot which Providence has assigned us, whether we view it in a natural, a political, or moral point of light.

The citizens of America, placed in the most enviable condition, as the sole lords and proprietors of a vast tract of continent, comprehending all the various soils and climates of the world, and abounding with all the necessaries and conveniences of life, are now, by the late satisfactory pacification, acknowledged to be possessed of absolute freedom and independency. They are, from this period, to be considered as the actors on a most conspicuous theater, which seems to be peculiarly designated by Providence for the display of human greatness and felicity. Here they are not only surrounded with everything which can contribute to the completion of private and domestic enjoyment, but Heaven has crowned all its other blessings by giving a fairer opportunity for political happiness than any other nation has ever been favored with. Nothing can illustrate these observations more forcibly than a recollection of the happy conjuncture of times and circumstances under which our republic assumed its rank among the nations. The foundation of our empire was not laid in the gloomy age of ignorance and superstition, but at an epoch when the rights of mankind were better understood and more clearly defined than at any former period. The researches of the human mind after social happiness have been carried to a great extent; the treasures of knowledge, acquired by the labors of philosophers, sages, and legislators through a long succession of years, are laid open for our use, and their collected wisdom may be happily applied in the establishment of our forms of government. The free cultivation of letters, the unbounded extension of commerce, the progressive refinement of manners, the growing liberality of sentiment, and, above all, the pure and benign light of revelation have had a meliorating influence on mankind and increased the blessings of society. At this auspicious period, the United States came into existence as a nation; and, if their citizens should not be completely free and happy, the fault will be entirely their own.

Such is our situation, and such are our prospects; but notwithstanding the cup of blessing is thus reached out to us; notwithstanding happiness is ours, if we have a disposition to seize the occasion and make it our own; yet it appears to me there is an option still left to the United States of America, that it is in their choice, and depends upon their conduct, whether they will be respectable and prosperous, or contemptible and miserable, as a nation. This is the time of their political probation; this is the moment when the eyes of the whole world are turned upon them;

this is the moment to establish or ruin their national character forever; this is the favorable moment to give such a tone to our federal government as will enable it to answer the ends of its institution, or this may be the ill-fated moment for relaxing the powers of the Union, annihilating the cement of the confederation, and exposing us to become the sport of European politics, which may play one state against another, to prevent their growing importance, and to serve their own interested purposes. For, according to the system of policy the states shall adopt at this moment, they will stand or fall; and by their confirmation or lapse it is yet to be decided whether the Revolution must ultimately be considered as a blessing or a curse; a blessing or a curse not to the present age alone, for with our fate will the destiny of unborn millions be involved.

With this conviction of the importance of the present crisis, silence in me would be a crime. I will therefore speak to your Excellency the language of freedom and of sincerity without disguise. I am aware, however, that those who differ from me in political sentiment may perhaps remark I am stepping out of the proper line of my duty, and may possibly ascribe to arrogance or ostentation what I know is alone the result of the purest intention. But the rectitude of my own heart, which disdains such unworthy motives; the part I have hitherto acted in life; the determination I have formed of not taking any share in public business hereafter; the ardent desire I feel, and shall continue to manifest, of quietly enjoying in private life, after all the toils of war, the benefits of a wise and liberal government will, I flatter myself, sooner or later convince my countrymen that I could have no sinister views in delivering, with so little reserve, the opinions contained in this address.

There are four things which, I humbly conceive, are essential to the well-being, I may even venture to say to the existence, of the United States as an independent power.

First. An indissoluble union of the states under one federal head.

Secondly. A sacred regard to public justice.

Thirdly. The adoption of a proper peace establishment; and,

Fourthly. The prevalence of that pacific and friendly disposition among the people of the United States which will induce them to forget their local prejudices and policies; to make those mutual concessions which are requisite to the general prosperity; and, in some instances, to sacrifice their individual advantages to the interest of the community.

These are the pillars on which the glorious fabric of our independency and national character must be supported. Liberty is the basis; and whoever would dare to sap the foundation, or overturn the structure, under whatever specious pretext he may attempt it, will merit the bitterest execration, and the severest punishment, which can be inflicted by his injured country.

On the three first articles I will make a few observations, leaving the last to the good sense and serious consideration of those immediately concerned.

Under the first head, although it may not be necessary or proper for me, in this place, to enter into a particular disquisition on the principles of the Union, and to take up the great question which has been frequently agitated, whether it be expedient and requisite for the states to delegate a larger proportion of power to Congress, or not, yet it will be a part of my duty, and that of every true patriot, to assert without reserve, and to insist upon, the following positions: That, unless the states will suffer Congress to exercise those prerogatives they are undoubtedly invested with by the constitution, everything must very rapidly tend to anarchy and confusion. That it is indispensable to the happiness of the individual states that there should be lodged somewhere a supreme power to regulate and govern the general concerns of the confederated republic, without which the Union cannot be of long duration. That there must be a faithful and pointed compliance, on the part of every state, with the late proposals and demands of Congress, or the most fatal consequences will ensue. That whatever measures have a tendency to dissolve the Union, or contribute to violate or lessen the sovereign authority, ought to be considered as hostile to the liberty and independency of America, and the authors of them treated accordingly. And lastly, that unless we can be enabled, by the concurrence of the states, to participate of the fruits of the Revolution, and enjoy the essential benefits of civil society, under a form of government so free and uncorrupted, so happily guarded against the danger of oppression, as has been devised and adopted by the Articles of Confederation, it will be a subject of regret that so much blood and treasure have been lavished for no purpose, that so many sufferings have been encountered without a compensation, and that so many sacrifices have been made in vain.

Many other considerations might here be adduced to prove that, without an entire conformity to the spirit of the Union, we cannot exist as an independent power. It will be sufficient for my purpose to mention but one or two which seem to me of the greatest importance. It is only in our united character, as an empire, that our independence is acknowledged, that our power can be regarded, or our credit supported, among foreign nations. The treaties of the European powers with the United States of America will have no validity on a dissolution of the Union. We shall be left nearly in a state of nature; or we may find, by our own unhappy experience, that there is a natural and necessary progression from the extreme of anarchy to the extreme of tyranny, and that arbitrary power is most easily established on the ruins of liberty abused to licentiousness.

As to the second article, which respects the performance of public justice, Congress have, in their late address to the United States, almost exhausted the subject; they have explained their ideas so fully, and have enforced the obligations the states are under to render complete justice to all the public creditors, with so much dignity and energy that, in my opinion, no real friend to the honor or independency of America can hesitate a single moment, respecting the propriety of complying with the just and honorable measures proposed. If their arguments do not produce conviction, I know of nothing that will have greater influence, especially when we recollect that the system referred to, being the result of the collected wisdom of the continent, must be esteemed, if not perfect, certainly the least objectionable of any that could be devised; and that, if it shall not be carried into immediate execution, a national bankruptcy, with all its deplorable consequences, will take place before any different plan can possibly be proposed and adopted. So pressing are the present circumstances, and such is the alternative now offered to the states.

The ability of the country to discharge the debts which have been incurred in its defense is not to be doubted; an inclination, I flatter myself, will not be wanting. The path of our duty is plain before us; honesty will be found, on every experiment, to be the best and only true policy. Let us then, as a nation, be just; let us fulfill the public contracts, which Congress had undoubtedly a right to make for the purpose of carrying on the war, with the same good faith we suppose ourselves bound to perform our private engagements. In the meantime, let an attention to the cheerful performance of their proper business, as individuals and as members of society, be earnestly inculcated on the citizens of America; then will they strengthen the hands of government, and be happy under its protection; everyone will reap the fruit of his labors, everyone will enjoy his own acquisitions, without molestation and without danger.

In this state of absolute freedom and perfect security, who will grudge to yield a very little of his property to support the common interest of society and ensure the protection of government? Who does not remember the frequent declarations, at the commencement of the war, that we should be completely satisfied if, at the expense of one half, we could defend the remainder of our possessions? Where is the man to be found who wishes to remain indebted for the defense of his own person and property to the exertions, the bravery, and the blood of others without making one generous effort to repay the debt of honor and gratitude? In what part of the continent shall we find any man, or body of men, who would not blush to stand up and propose measures purposely calculated to rob the soldier of his stipend, and the public creditor of his due? And were it possible that such a flagrant instance of injustice could ever happen, would it not excite the general indignation, and tend to bring down upon the authors of such measures the aggravated vengeance of Heaven? If, after all, a spirit of disunion, or a temper of obstinacy and perverseness, should manifest itself in any of the states; if such an ungracious disposition should attempt to frustrate all the happy effects that might be expected to flow from the Union; if there should be a refusal to comply with the requisition for funds to discharge the annual interest of the public debts; and if that refusal should revive again all those jealousies and produce all those evils which are now happily removed, Congress, who have, in all their transactions, shown a great degree of magnanimity and justice, will stand justified in the sight of God and man; and the state alone which puts itself in opposition to the aggregate wisdom of the continent, and follows such mistaken and pernicious counsels, will be responsible for all the consequences.

For my own part, conscious of having acted, while a servant of the public, in the manner I conceived best suited to promote the real interests of my country; having, in consequence of my fixed belief, in some measure pledged myself to the Army that their country would finally do them complete and ample justice; and not wishing to conceal any instance of my official conduct from the eyes of the world, I have thought proper to transmit to your Excellency the enclosed collection of papers, relative to the half pay and commutation granted by Congress to the officers of the Army. From these communications, my decided sentiments will be clearly comprehended, together with the conclusive reasons which induced me, at an early period, to recommend the adoption of this measure, in the most earnest and serious manner. As the proceedings of Congress, the Army, and myself are open to all, and contain, in my opinion, sufficient information to remove the prejudices and errors which may have been entertained by any, I think it unnecessary to say anything more than just to observe that the resolutions of Congress now alluded to are undoubtedly as absolutely binding upon the United States as the most solemn acts of confederation or legislation.

As to the idea, which, I am informed, has in some instances prevailed, that the half pay and commutation are to be regarded merely in the odious light of a pension, it ought to be exploded forever. That provision should be viewed as it really was, a reasonable compensation offered by Congress at a time when they had nothing else to give to the officers of the Army for services then to be performed. It was the only means to prevent a total dereliction of the service. It was a part of their hire. I may be allowed to say, it was the price of their blood, and of your independency; it is therefore more than a common debt, it is a debt of honor; it can never be considered as a pension or gratuity, nor be canceled until it is fairly discharged.

With regard to a distinction between officers and soldiers, it is sufficient that the uniform experience of every nation of the world, combined with our own, proves the utility and propriety of the discrimination. Rewards, in proportion to the aids the public derives from them, are unquestionably due to all its servants. In some lines, the soldiers have perhaps generally had as ample a compensation for their services, by the large bounties which have been paid to them, as their officers will receive in the proposed commutation; in others if, besides the donation of lands, the payment of arrearages of clothing and wages (in which articles all the component parts of the army must be put upon the same footing), we take into the estimate the *douceurs* many of the soldiers have received, and the gratuity of one year's full pay, which is promised to all, possibly their situation (every circumstance being duly considered) will not be deemed less eligible than that of the officers. Should a further reward, however, be judged equitable, I will venture to assert no one will enjoy greater satisfaction than myself on seeing an exemption from taxes for a limited time (which has been petitioned for in some instances) or any other adequate immunity or compensation granted to the brave defenders of their country's cause; but neither the adoption nor rejection of this proposition will in any manner affect, much less militate against, the act of Congress by which they have offered five years' full pay, in lieu of the half pay for life, which had been before promised to the officers of the Army.

Before I conclude the subject of public justice, I cannot omit to mention the obligations this country is under to that meritorious class of veteran noncommissioned officers and privates who have been discharged for inability, in consequence of the resolution of Congress of the 23d of April, 1782, on an annual pension for life. Their peculiar sufferings, their singular merits, and claims to that provision need only be known to interest all the feelings of humanity in their behalf. Nothing but a punctual payment of their annual allowance can rescue them from the most complicated misery; and nothing could be a more melancholy and distressing sight than to behold those who have shed their blood or lost their limbs in the service of their country without a shelter, without a friend, and without the means of obtaining any of the necessaries or comforts of life, compelled to beg their daily bread from door to door. Suffer me to recommend those of this description belonging to your state to the warmest patronage of your Excellency and your legislature.

It is necessary to say but a few words on the third topic which was proposed, and which regards particularly the defense of the Republic, as there can be little doubt but Congress will recommend a proper peace establishment for the United States, in which a due attention will be paid to the importance of placing the militia of the Union upon a regular and respectable footing. If this should be the case, I would beg leave to urge the great advantage of it in the strongest terms. The militia of this country must be considered as the palladium of our security, and the first effectual resort in case of hostility. It is essential, therefore, that the same system should pervade the whole; that the formation and discipline of the militia of the continent should be absolutely uniform; and that the same species of arms, accouterments, and military apparatus should be introduced in every part of the United States. No one, who has not learned it from experience, can conceive the difficulty, expense, and confusion which result from a contrary system, or the vague arrangements which have hitherto prevailed.

If, in treating of political points, a greater latitude than usual has been taken in the course of this address, the importance of the crisis, and the magnitude of the objects in discussion, must be my apology. It is, however, neither my wish nor expectation that the preceding observations should claim any regard, except so far as they shall appear to be dictated by a good intention, consonant to the immutable rules of justice, calculated to produce a liberal system of policy, and founded on whatever experience may have been acquired by a long and close attention to public business. Here I might speak with the more confidence from my actual observations; and if it would not swell this letter (already too prolix) beyond the bounds I had prescribed to myself, I could demonstrate to every mind open to conviction that in less time, and with much less expense than has been incurred, the war might have been brought to the same happy conclusion if the resources of the continent could have been properly drawn forth; that the distresses and disappointments which have very often occurred have, in too many instances, resulted more from a want of energy in the Continental government than a deficiency of means in the particular states; that the inefficacy of measures arising from the want of an adequate authority in the supreme power, from a partial compliance with the requisitions of Congress in some of the states, and from a failure of punctuality in others, while it tended to damp the zeal of those which were more willing to exert themselves, served also to accumulate the expenses of the war, and to frustrate the best concerted plans; and that the discouragement occasioned by the complicated difficulties and embarrassments in which our affairs were by this means involved would have long ago produced the dissolution of any army less patient, less virtuous, and less persevering than that which I have had the honor to command. But, while I mention these things, which are notorious facts, as the defects of our federal constitution, particularly in the prosecution of a war, I beg it may be understood that, as I have ever taken a pleasure in gratefully acknowledging the assistance and support I have derived from every class of citizens, so shall I always be happy to do justice to the unparalleled exertions of the individual states on many interesting occasions.

I have thus freely disclosed what I wished to make known before I surrendered up my public trust to those who committed it to me. The task is now accomplished. I now bid adieu to your Excellency as the chief magistrate of your state, at the same time I bid a last farewell to the cares of office, and all the employments of public life.

It remains, then, to be my final and only request that your Excellency will communicate these sentiments to your legislature at their next meeting, and that they may be considered as the legacy of one who has ardently wished, on all occasions, to be useful to his country, and who, even in the shade of retirement, will not fail to implore the Divine benediction upon it.

I now make it my earnest prayer that God would have you, and the state over which you preside, in His holy protection; that He would incline the hearts of the citizens to cultivate a spirit of subordination and obedience to government; to entertain a brotherly affection and love for one another, for their fellow citizens of the United States at large, and particularly for their brethren who have served in the field; and finally, that He would most graciously be pleased to dispose us all to do justice, to love mercy, and to demean ourselves with that charity, humility, and pacific temper of mind which were the characteristics of the Divine Author of our blessed religion, and without a humble imitation of whose example in these things we can never hope to be a happy nation.

I have the honor to be, with much esteem and respect, Sir, your Excellency's most obedient and most humble servant.

The Farewell Address

Friends and Fellow-Citizens:

The period for a new election of a citizen to administer the executive government of the United States being not far distant, and the time actually arrived when your thoughts must be employed in designating the person who is to be clothed with that important trust, it appears to me proper, especially as it may conduce to a more distinct expression of the public voice, that I should now apprise you of the resolution I have formed to decline being considered among the number of those out of whom a choice is to be made.

I beg you, at the same time, to do me the justice to be assured that this resolution has not been taken without a strict regard to all the considerations appertaining to the relation which binds a dutiful citizen to his country—and that, in withdrawing the tender of service which silence in my situation might imply, I am influenced by no diminution of zeal for your future interest, no deficiency of grateful respect for your past kindness; but am supported by a full conviction that the step is compatible with both.

The acceptance of, and continuance hitherto in, the office to which your suffrages have twice called me have been a uniform sacrifice of inclination to the opinion of duty, and to a deference for what appeared to be your desire. I constantly hoped that it would have been much earlier in my power, consistently with motives which I was not at liberty to disregard, to return to that retirement from which I had been reluctantly drawn. The strength of my inclination to do this, previous to the last election, had even led to the preparation of an address to declare it to you; but mature reflection on the then perplexed and critical posture of our affairs with foreign nations, and the unanimous advice of persons entitled to my confidence, impelled me to abandon the idea.

I rejoice that the state of your concerns, external as well as internal, no longer renders the pursuit of inclination incompatible with the sentiment of duty, or propriety; and am persuaded, whatever partiality may be retained for my services, that in the present circumstances of our country you will not disapprove my determination to retire.

The impressions with which I first undertook the arduous trust were explained on the proper occasion. In the discharge of this trust, I will only say that I have, with good intentions, contributed towards the organization and administration of the government the best exertions of which a very fallible judgment was capable. Not unconscious in the outset of the inferiority of my qualifications, experience in my own eyes, perhaps still more in the eyes of others, has strengthened the motives to diffidence of myself; and every day the increasing weight of years admonishes me more and more that the shade of retirement is as necessary to me as it will be welcome. Satisfied that if any circumstances have given peculiar value to my services, they were temporary, I have the consolation to believe that, while choice and prudence invite me to quit the political scene, patriotism does not forbid it.

In looking forward to the moment which is intended to terminate the career of my public life, my feelings do not permit me to suspend the deep acknowledgment of that debt of gratitude which I owe to my beloved country—for the many honors it has conferred upon me; still more for the steadfast confidence with which it has supported me; and for the opportunities I have thence enjoyed of manifesting my inviolable attachment by services faithful and persevering, though in usefulness unequal to my zeal. If benefits have resulted to our country from these services, let it always be remembered to your praise, and as an instructive example in our annals, that under circumstances in which the passions agitated in every direction were liable to mislead, amidst appearances sometimes dubious—vicissitudes of fortune often discouraging—in situations in which not infrequently want of success has countenanced the spirit of criticism, the constancy of your support was the essential prop of the efforts and a guarantee of the plans by which they were effected. Profoundly penetrated with this idea, I shall carry it with me to the grave, as a strong incitement to unceasing vows that Heaven may continue to you the choicest tokens of its beneficence—that your union and brotherly affection may be perpetual—that the free constitution, which is the work of your hands, may be sacredly maintained—that its administration in every department may be stamped with wisdom and virtue—that, in fine, the happiness of the people of these states, under the auspices of liberty, may be made complete by so careful a preservation and so prudent a use of this blessing as will acquire to them the glory of recommending it to the applause, the affection, and adoption of every nation which is yet a stranger to it.

Here, perhaps, I ought to stop. But a solicitude for your welfare, which cannot end but with my life, and the apprehension of danger, natural to that solicitude, urge me on an occasion like the present to offer to your solemn contemplation, and to recommend to your frequent review, some sentiments which are the result of much reflection, of no inconsiderable observation, and which appear to me all-important to the permanency of your felicity as a people. These will be offered to you with the more freedom as you can only see in them the disinterested warnings of a parting friend who can possibly have no personal motive to bias his counsels. Nor can I forget, as an encouragement to it, your indulgent reception of my sentiments on a former and not dissimilar occasion.

Interwoven as is the love of liberty with every ligament of your hearts, no recommendation of mine is necessary to fortify or confirm the attachment.

The unity of government, which constitutes you one people, is also now dear to you. It is justly so, for it is a main pillar in the edifice of your real independence; the support of your tranquillity at home; your peace abroad; of your safety; of your prosperity; of that very liberty which you so highly prize. But as it is easy to foresee that from different causes, and from different quarters, much pain will be taken, many artifices employed, to weaken in your minds the conviction of this truth; as this is the point in your political fortress against which the batteries of internal and external enemies will be most constantly and actively (though often covertly and insidiously) directed, it is of infinite moment that you should properly estimate the immense value of your national Union to your collective and individual happiness; that you should cherish a cordial, habitual, and immovable attachment to it, accustoming yourselves to think and speak of it as of the palladium of your political safety and prosperity, watching for its preservation with jealous anxiety, discountenancing whatever may suggest even a suspicion that it can in any event be abandoned, and indignantly frowning upon the first dawning of every attempt to alienate any portion of our country from the rest, or to enfeeble the sacred ties which now link together the various parts.

For this you have every inducement of sympathy and interest. Citizens by birth or choice of a common country, that country has a right to concentrate your affections. The name of American, which belongs to you, in your national capacity, must always exalt the just pride of patriotism more than any appellation derived from local discriminations. With slight shades of difference, you have the same religion, manners, habits, and political principles. You have in a common cause fought and triumphed together. The independence and liberty you possess are the work of joint councils and joint efforts of common dangers, sufferings, and successes.

But these considerations, however powerfully they address themselves to your sensibility, are greatly outweighed by those which apply more immediately to your interest. Here every portion of our country finds the most commanding motives for carefully guarding and preserving the Union of the whole.

The North in an unrestrained intercourse with the South, protected by the equal laws of a common government, finds in the productions of the latter great additional resources of maritime and commercial enterprise— and precious materials of manufacturing industry. The South in the same intercourse, benefiting by the agency of the North, sees its agriculture grow and its commerce expand. Turning partly into its own channels the seamen of the North, it finds its particular navigation invigorated; and, while it contributes, in different ways, to nourish and increase the general mass of the national navigation, it looks forward to the protection of a maritime strength to which itself is unequally adapted. The East, in a like intercourse with the West, already finds, and in the progressive improvement of interior communications, by land and water, will more and more find, a valuable vent for the commodities which it brings from abroad, or manufactures at home. The West derives from the East supplies requisite to its growth and comfort—and what is perhaps of still greater consequence, it must of necessity owe the secure enjoyment of indispensable outlets for its own productions to the weight, influence, and the future maritime strength of the Atlantic side of the Union, directed by an indissoluble community of interest, as one nation. Any other tenure by which the West can hold this essential advantage, whether derived from its own separate strength, or from an apostate and unnatural connection with any foreign power, must be intrinsically precarious.

While then every part of our country thus feels an immediate and particular interest in union, all the parts combined cannot fail to find in the united mass of means and efforts, greater strength, greater resource, proportionably greater security from external danger, a less frequent interruption of their peace by foreign nations; and, what is of inestimable value! they must derive from union an exemption from those broils and wars between themselves which so frequently afflict neighboring countries not tied together by the same government, which their own rival-ships alone would be sufficient to produce, but which opposite foreign alliances, attachments, and intrigues would stimulate and embitter. Hence likewise they will avoid the necessity of those overgrown military estab-lishments which under any form of government are inauspicious to lib-erty, and which are to be regarded as particularly hostile to republican liberty: In this sense it is that your Union ought to be considered as a main prop of your liberty, and that the love of the one ought to endear to you the preservation of the other.

These considerations speak a persuasive language to every reflecting and virtuous mind, and exhibit the continuance of the Union as a primary object of patriotic desire. Is there a doubt whether a common govern-ment can embrace so large a sphere? Let experience solve it. To listen to mere speculation in such a case were criminal. We are authorized to hope that a proper organization of the whole, with the auxiliary agency of governments for the respective subdivisions, will afford a happy issue to the experiment. 'Tis well worth a fair and full experiment. With such powerful and obvious motives to union affecting all parts of our coun-try, while experience shall not have demonstrated its impracticability, there will always be reason to distrust the patriotism of those who in any quarter may endeavor to weaken its bands.

In contemplating the causes which may disturb our Union, it occurs as matter of serious concern that any ground should have been furnished for characterizing parties by geographical discriminations—Northern and Southern—Atlantic and Western; whence designing men may endeavor to excite a belief that there is a real difference of local interests and views. One of the expedients of party to acquire influence within particu-lar districts is to misrepresent the opinions and aims of other districts. You cannot shield yourselves too much against the jealousies and heart-burnings which spring from these misrepresentations; they tend to render alien to each other those who ought to be bound together by fraternal affection. The inhabitants of our western country have lately had a useful lesson on this head. They have seen, in the negotiation by the executive, and in the unanimous ratification by the Senate, of the treaty with Spain, and in the universal satisfaction at that event throughout the United States, a decisive proof how unfounded were the suspicions propagated among them of a policy in the general government and in the Atlantic states unfriendly to their interests in regard to the Mississippi. They have been witnesses to the formation of two treaties, that with Great Britain and that with Spain, which secure to them everything they could desire, in respect to our foreign relations, towards confirming their prosperity. Will it not be their wisdom to rely for the preservation of these advantages on the Union by which they were procured? Will they not henceforth be deaf to those advisers, if such there are, who would sever them from their brethren, and connect them with aliens?

To the efficacy and permanency of your Union, a government for the whole is indispensable. No alliances however strict between the parts can be an adequate substitute. They must inevitably experience the infractions and interruptions which all alliances in all times have experienced. Sensible of this momentous truth, you have improved upon your first essay by the adoption of a constitution of government better calculated than your former for an intimate Union, and for the efficacious management of your common concerns. This government, the offspring of our own choice uninfluenced and unawed, adopted upon full investigation and mature deliberation, completely free in its principles, in the distribution of its powers, uniting security with energy, and containing within itself a provision for its own amendment, has a just claim to your confidence and your support. Respect for its authority, compliance with its laws, acquiescence in its measures are duties enjoined by the fundamental maxims of true liberty. The basis of our political systems is the right of the people to make and to alter their constitutions of government. But the constitution which at any time exists, 'till changed by an explicit and authentic act of the whole people, is sacredly obligatory upon all. The very idea of the power and the right of the people to establish government presupposes the duty of every individual to obey the established government.

All obstructions to the execution of the laws, all combinations and associations, under whatever plausible character, with the real design to direct, control, counteract, or awe the regular deliberation and action of the constituted authorities are destructive of this fundamental principle, and of fatal tendency. They serve to organize faction, to give it an artificial and extraordinary force; to put, in the place of the delegated will of the nation, the will of a party, often a small but artful and enterprising minority of the community; and, according to the alternate triumphs of different parties, to make the public administration the mirror of the ill-concerted and incongruous projects of faction rather than the organ of consistent and wholesome plans digested by common councils and modified by mutual interests. However combinations or associations of the above description may now and then answer popular ends, they are likely, in the course of time and things, to become potent engines by which cunning, ambitious, and unprincipled men will be enabled to subvert the power of the people and to usurp for themselves the reins of government, destroying afterwards the very engines which have lifted them to unjust dominion.

Towards the preservation of your government and the permanency of your present happy state, it is requisite not only that you steadily discountenance irregular oppositions to its acknowledged authority but also that you resist with care the spirit of innovation upon its principles, however specious the pretexts. One method of assault may be to effect, in the forms of the Constitution, alterations which will impair the energy of the system, and thus to undermine what cannot be directly overthrown. In all the changes to which you may be invited, remember that time and habit are at least as necessary to fix the true character of governments as of other human institutions—that experience is the surest standard by which to test the real tendency of the existing constitution of a country—that facility in changes upon the credit of mere hypothesis and opinion exposes to perpetual change from the endless variety of hypothesis and opinion—and remember, especially, that for the efficient management of your common interests, in a country so extensive as ours, a government of as much vigor as is consistent with the perfect security of liberty is indispensable. Liberty itself will find in such a government, with powers properly distributed and adjusted, its surest guardian. It is indeed little else than a name where the government is too feeble to withstand the enterprises of faction, to confine each member of the society within the limits prescribed by the laws, and to maintain all in the secure and tranquil enjoyment of the rights of person and property.

I have already intimated to you the danger of parties in the state, with particular reference to the founding of them on geographical discriminations. Let me now take a more comprehensive view, and warn you in the most solemn manner against the baneful effects of the spirit of party generally.

This spirit, unfortunately, is inseparable from our nature, having its root in the strongest passions of the human mind. It exists under different shapes in all governments, more or less stifled, controlled, or repressed; but in those of the popular form, it is seen in its greatest rankness, and is truly their worst enemy.

The alternate domination of one faction over another, sharpened by the spirit of revenge natural to party dissension, which in different ages and countries has perpetrated the most horrid enormities, is itself a frightful despotism. But this leads at length to a more formal and permanent despotism. The disorders and miseries which result gradually incline the minds of men to seek security and repose in the absolute power of an individual: and sooner or later the chief of some prevailing faction, more able or more fortunate than his competitors, turns this disposition to the purposes of his own elevation on the ruins of public liberty.

Without looking forward to an extremity of this kind (which nevertheless ought not to be entirely out of sight), the common and continual mischiefs of the spirit of party are sufficient to make it the interest and duty of a wise people to discourage and restrain it.

It serves always to distract the public councils and enfeeble the public administration. It agitates the community with ill-founded jealousies and false alarms, kindles the animosity of one part against another, foments occasionally riot and insurrection. It opens the doors to foreign influence and corruption, which find a facilitated access to the government itself through the channels of party passions. Thus the policy and the will of one country are subjected to the policy and will of another.

There is an opinion that parties in free countries are useful checks upon the administration of the government, and serve to keep alive the spirit of liberty. This within certain limits is probably true, and, in governments of a monarchical cast, patriotism may look with indulgence, if not with favor, upon the spirit of party. But in those of the popular character, in governments purely elective, it is a spirit not to be encouraged. From their natural tendency, it is certain there will always be enough of that spirit for every salutary purpose, and there being constant danger of excess, the effort ought to be, by force of public opinion, to mitigate and assuage it. A fire not to be quenched, it demands a uniform vigilance to prevent its bursting into a flame, lest, instead of warming, it should consume.

It is important, likewise, that the habits of thinking in a free country should inspire caution in those entrusted with its administration to confine themselves within their respective constitutional spheres, avoiding in the exercise of the powers of one department to encroach upon another. The spirit of encroachment tends to consolidate the powers of all the departments in one, and thus to create, whatever the form of government, a real despotism. A just estimate of that love of power, and proneness to abuse it, which predominates in the human heart is sufficient to satisfy us of the truth of this position. The necessity of reciprocal checks in the exercise of political power, by dividing and distributing it into different depositories, and constituting each the guardian of the public weal against invasions by the others, has been evinced by experiments ancient and modern, some of them in our country and under our own eyes. To preserve them must be as necessary as to institute them. If in the opinion of the people the distribution or modification of the constitutional powers be in any particular wrong, let it be corrected by an amendment in the way which the Constitution designates. But let there be no change by usurpation; for though this, in one instance, may be the instrument of good, it is the customary weapon by which free governments are destroyed. The precedent must always greatly overbalance in permanent evil any partial or transient benefit which the use can at any time yield.

Of all the dispositions and habits which lead to political prosperity, religion and morality are indispensable supports. In vain would that man claim the tribute of patriotism who should labor to subvert these great pillars of human happiness, these firmest props of the duties of men and citizens. The mere politician, equally with the pious man, ought to respect and to cherish them. A volume could not trace all their connections with private and public felicity. Let it simply be asked where is the security for property, for reputation, for life if the sense of religious obligation desert the oaths which are the instruments of investigation in courts of justice? And let us with caution indulge the supposition that morality can be maintained without religion. Whatever may be conceded to the influence of refined education on minds of peculiar structure, reason and experience both forbid us to expect that national morality can prevail in exclusion of religious principle.

'Tis substantially true that virtue or morality is a necessary spring of popular government. The rule indeed extends with more or less force to every species of free government. Who that is a sincere friend to it can look with indifference upon attempts to shake the foundation of the fabric?

Promote, then, as an object of primary importance, institutions for the general diffusion of knowledge. In proportion as the structure of a government gives force to public opinion, it is essential that public opinion should be enlightened.

As a very important source of strength and security, cherish public credit. One method of preserving it is to use it as sparingly as possible: avoiding occasions of expense by cultivating peace, but remembering also that timely disbursements to prepare for danger frequently prevent much greater disbursements to repel it—avoiding likewise the accumulation of debt, not only by shunning occasions of expense but by vigorous exertions in time of peace to discharge the debts which unavoidable wars may have occasioned, not ungenerously throwing upon posterity the burden which we ourselves ought to bear. The execution of these maxims belongs to your representatives, but it is necessary that public opinion should co-operate. To facilitate to them the performance of their duty, it is essential that you should practically bear in mind that towards the payment of debts there must be revenue—that to have revenue there must be taxes—that no taxes can be devised which are not more or less inconvenient and unpleasant—that the intrinsic embarrassment inseparable from the selection of the proper objects (which is always a choice of difficulties) ought to be a decisive motive for a candid construction of the conduct of the government in making it, and for a spirit of acquiescence in the measures for obtaining revenue which the public exigencies may at any time dictate.

Observe good faith and justice towards all nations. Cultivate peace and harmony with all. Religion and morality enjoin this conduct; and can it be that good policy does not equally enjoin it? It will be worthy of a free, enlightened, and, at no distant period, a great nation to give to mankind the magnanimous and too novel example of a people always guided by an exalted justice and benevolence. Who can doubt that in the course of time and things, the fruits of such a plan would richly repay any temporary advantages which might be lost by a steady adherence to it? Can it be that Providence has not connected the permanent felicity of a nation with its virtue? The experiment, at least, is recommended by every sentiment which ennobles human nature. Alas! is it rendered impossible by its vices?

In the execution of such a plan nothing is more essential than that permanent, inveterate antipathies against particular nations and passionate attachments for others should be excluded; and that in place of them just and amicable feelings towards all should be cultivated. The nation which indulges towards another an habitual hatred or an habitual fondness is in some degree a slave. It is a slave to its animosity or to its affection, either of which is sufficient to lead it astray from its duty and its interest. Antipathy in one nation against another disposes each more readily to offer insult and injury, to lay hold of slight causes of umbrage, and to be haughty and intractable, when accidental or trifling occasions of dispute occur. Hence frequent collisions, obstinate, envenomed and bloody contests. The nation promoted by ill will and resentment sometimes impels to war the government, contrary to the best calculations of policy. The government sometimes participates in the national propensity, and adopts through passion what reason would reject; at other times, it makes the animosity of the nation subservient to projects of hostility instigated by pride, ambition, and other sinister and pernicious motives. The peace often, sometimes perhaps the liberty, of nations has been the victim.

So likewise a passionate attachment of one nation for another produces a variety of evils. Sympathy for the favorite nation, facilitating the illusion of an imaginary common interest in cases where no real common interest exists, and infusing into one the enmities of the other, betrays the former into a participation in the quarrels and wars of the latter, without adequate inducement or justification. It leads also to concessions to the favorite nation of privileges denied to others, which is apt doubly to injure the nation making the concessions: by unnecessarily parting with what ought to have been retained, and by exciting jealousy, ill will, and a disposition to retaliate in the parties from whom equal privileges are withheld; and it gives to ambitious, corrupted, or deluded citizens (who devote themselves to the favorite nation) facility to betray or sacrifice the interests of their own country without odium, sometimes even with popularity—gilding with the appearances of a virtuous sense of obligation, a commendable deference for public opinion, or a laudable zeal for public good the base or foolish compliances of ambition, corruption, or infatuation.

As avenues to foreign influence in innumerable ways, such attachments are particularly alarming to the truly enlightened and independent patriot. How many opportunities do they afford to tamper with domestic factions, to practice the arts of seduction, to mislead public opinion, to influence or awe the public councils! Such an attachment of a small or weak towards a great and powerful nation dooms the former to be the satellite of the latter.

Against the insidious wiles of foreign influence, I conjure you to believe me, fellow citizens, the jealousy of a free people ought to be *constantly* awake, since history and experience prove that foreign influence is one of the most baneful foes of republican government. But that jealousy to be useful must be impartial; else it becomes the instrument of the very influence to be avoided, instead of a defense against it. Excessive partiality for one foreign nation and excessive dislike of another cause those whom they actuate to see danger only on one side, and serve to veil and even second the arts of influence on the other. Real patriots, who may resist the intrigues of the favorite, are liable to become suspected and odious; while its tools and dupes usurp the applause and confidence of the people to surrender their interests.

The great rule of conduct for us in regard to foreign nations is, in extending our commercial relations, to have with them as little *political* connection as possible. So far as we have already formed engagements, let them be fulfilled with perfect good faith. Here let us stop.

Europe has a set of primary interests, which to us have none, or a very remote, relation. Hence she must be engaged in frequent controversies, the causes of which are essentially foreign to our concerns. Hence therefore it must be unwise in us to implicate ourselves by artificial ties in the ordinary vicissitudes of her politics, or the ordinary combinations and collisions of her friendships, or enmities.

Our detached and distant situation invites and enables us to pursue a different course. If we remain one people, under an efficient government, the period is not far off when we may defy material injury from external annoyance; when we may take such an attitude as will cause the neutrality we may at any time resolve upon to be scrupulously respected. When belligerent nations, under the impossibility of making acquisitions upon us, will not lightly hazard the giving us provocation; when we may choose peace or war, as our interest guided by our justice shall counsel.

Why forego the advantages of so peculiar a situation? Why quit our own to stand upon foreign ground? Why, by interweaving our destiny with that of any part of Europe, entangle our peace and prosperity in the toils of European ambition, rivalship, interest, humor, or caprice?

'Tis our true policy to steer clear of permanent alliances with any portion of the foreign world; so far, I mean, as we are now at liberty to do it—for let me not be understood as capable of patronizing infidelity to existing engagements (I hold the maxim no less applicable to public than to private affairs that honesty is always the best policy). I repeat it, therefore, let those engagements be observed in their genuine sense. But in my opinion it is unnecessary and would be unwise to extend them.

Taking care always to keep ourselves, by suitable establishments, on a respectably defensive posture, we may safely trust to temporary alliances for extraordinary emergencies.

Harmony, liberal intercourse with all nations are recommended by policy, humanity, and interest. But even our commercial policy should hold an equal and impartial hand: neither seeking nor granting exclusive favors or preferences; consulting the natural course of things; diffusing and diversifying by gentle means the streams of commerce, but forcing nothing; establishing with powers so disposed—in order to give trade a stable course, to define the rights of our merchants, and to enable the government to support them—conventional rules of intercourse, the best that present circumstances and mutual opinion will permit, but temporary, and liable to be from time to time abandoned or varied, as experience and circumstances shall dictate; constantly keeping in view that 'tis folly in one nation to look for disinterested favors from another, that it must pay with a portion of its independence for whatever it may accept under that character, that by such acceptance, it may place itself in the condition of having given equivalents for nominal favors and yet of being reproached with ingratitude for not giving more. There can be no greater error than to expect or calculate upon real favors from nation to nation. 'Tis an illusion which experience must cure, which a just pride ought to discard.

In offering to you, my countrymen, these counsels of an old and affectionate friend, I dare not hope they will make the strong and lasting impression I could wish—that they will control the usual current of the passions, or prevent our nation from running the course which has hitherto marked the destiny of nations. But if I may even flatter myself that they may be productive of some partial benefit; some occasional good; that they may now and then recur to moderate the fury of party spirit, to warn against the mischiefs of foreign intrigue, to guard against the impostures of pretended patriotism, this hope will be a full recompense for the solicitude for your welfare, by which they have been dictated.

How far in the discharge of my official duties, I have been guided by the principles which have been delineated, the public records and other evidences of my conduct must witness to you, and to the world. To myself, the assurance of my own conscience is that I have at least believed myself to be guided by them.

In relation to the still subsisting war in Europe, my proclamation of the 22d of April, 1793, is the index to my plan. Sanctioned by your approving voice and by that of your representatives in both houses of Congress, the spirit of that measure has continually governed me—uninfluenced by any attempts to deter or divert me from it.

After deliberate examination with the aid of the best lights I could obtain, I was well satisfied that our country, under all the circumstances of the case, had a right to take, and was bound in duty and interest, to take a neutral position. Having taken it, I determined, as far as should depend upon me, to maintain it with moderation, perseverance, and firmness.

The considerations which respect the right to hold this conduct, it is not necessary on this occasion to detail. I will only observe that according to my understanding of the matter that right, so far from being denied by any of the belligerent powers, has been virtually admitted by all.

The duty of holding a neutral conduct may be inferred, without anything more, from the obligation which justice and humanity impose on every nation, in cases in which it is free to act, to maintain inviolate the relations of peace and amity towards other nations.

The inducements of interest for observing that conduct will best be referred to your own reflections and experience. With me, a predominant motive has been to endeavor to gain time to our country to settle and mature its yet recent institutions, and to progress without interruption to that degree of strength and consistency which is necessary to give it, humanly speaking, the command of its own fortunes.

Though, in reviewing the incidents of my administration, I am unconscious of intentional error, I am nevertheless too sensible of my defects not to think it probable that I may have committed many errors. Whatever they may be I fervently beseech the Almighty to avert or mitigate the evils to which they may tend. I shall also carry with me the hope that my country will never cease to view them with indulgence; and that after forty-five years of my life dedicated to its service, with an upright zeal, the faults of incompetent abilities will be consigned to oblivion, as myself must soon be to the mansions of rest.

Relying on its kindness in this as in other things, and actuated by that fervent love towards it which is so natural to a man who views in it the native soil of himself and his progenitors for several generations, I anticipate with pleasing expectation that retreat in which I promise myself to realize, without alloy, the sweet enjoyment of partaking, in the midst of my fellow citizens, the benign influence of good laws under a free government—the ever favorite object of my heart, and the happy reward, as I trust, of our mutual cares, labors, and dangers.

Thomas Jefferson

1743–1826

Thomas Jefferson, the son of prosperous landowners, was born in Albemarle County, Virginia, in 1743. After being graduated from the College of William and Mary in Williamsburg, Jefferson took up the study of law. In 1769 he was elected to the Virginia House of Burgesses, and while there he wrote his *Summary View of the Rights of British America* and his *Reply to Lord North*. These exercised such a wide influence that Jefferson was sent to represent Virginia in the Continental Congress.

In 1776, after drafting the Declaration of Independence, Jefferson returned to Virginia as a member of its legislature. Later, as its governor, he was determined to revise its laws. He is responsible for the statute on religious liberty which was adopted in 1786, and for revisions of the inheritance laws which broke up the large estates. Jefferson also tried unsuccessfully to abolish slavery, and, with limited success, to institute free public education.

In 1783 Jefferson was elected to the United States Congress, where he instituted our present decimal system of currency. Two years later he followed Franklin as ambassador to France, returning in 1789 to serve as Secretary of State in the new government under Washington. Jefferson often found himself in conflict with the Federalist group, led by Hamilton, which favored a stronger central govern-

Notes from the artist: "The head of Jefferson is adapted from a contemporary gold-leaf portrait that hung in Monticello during Jefferson's retirement. Above his head is a facsimile of Jefferson's handwritten draft of The Declaration of Independence."

ment, tied to property and financial interests. In 1796 Jefferson became Vice-President under John Adams, and was elected President himself in 1800.

During his two terms in office, Jefferson successfully conducted the Tripoli War against the Barbary pirates, negotiated the purchase of the Louisiana Territory from Napoleon, and launched the Lewis and Clark northwest expedition. At the age of sixty-five, Jefferson retired and returned to his home, Monticello, which he had designed himself. For the next few years he devoted himself to his many interests, including farming, invention, music, and philosophical correspondence. But his greatest preoccupation was the building of the University of Virginia, the basic plan of which was his.

Jefferson died in 1826 on July 4th, fifty years after the publication of The Declaration of Independence. He wrote his own epitaph. It reads: "Here was buried Thomas Jefferson, author of the Declaration of American Independence, of the statute of Virginia for religious freedom, and father of the University of Virginia."

The form of republicanism and democracy which has developed in the United States probably owes more to the ideas of Jefferson than to those of any other man. He had written in The Declaration of Independence "that all men are created equal," and that they have unalienable rights to "life, liberty and the pursuit of happiness." This was "self-evident," and not a matter to be debated pro and con. Every man is as good as another, if not a little better, became the American creed. The French aristocrat Tocqueville, in 1835, was dismayed by the degree to which equalitarianism had pervaded American institutions and manners. Like Plato, he feared the rule of ignorance. In Jefferson's opinion there was absolutely nothing wrong with the people that education would not cure: man is indefinitely perfectible.

Popular rule or democracy had been little tried, and was certainly not proved, in 1781, when Jefferson wrote the following essay. Distrust of the people and a trend back to oligarchy or monarchy were found among the greatest leaders, especially Hamilton and his Federalists. They feared the people; Jefferson feared "the selfishness of the leaders independent of the people." In Virginia they wished to concentrate power in a few hands to meet effectively the British invasion then proceeding; he struggled to preserve the constitution and majority rule, in war as in peace. Otherwise, men who had just escaped from an old tyranny might well be fighting for a new one.

The constitution of the state of Virginia was born of inexperience, Jefferson argued, and was full of faults and hazards. A majority of the citizens who are in the militia and pay taxes have no representation in the legislature, and where there is representation, it is often unequal and unjust. The two houses of legislature are chosen by the same electors and represent the same interests, and the executive and judiciary are dependent on them. Instead of a balance of powers, each checking the presumption of the others, the constitution had resulted in an *"elective despotism."*

Forcefully and wittily, Jefferson argues against the power of the House of Delegates to determine for itself when it has a quorum. Amidst the difficulties occasioned by the invasion, the House might decide to fix the quorum at forty, but if this can be done, it also *could be* reduced to one. A precedent, though well intentioned, may be perilous. What is needed, Jefferson contends, is a convention to correct and clarify the constitution. The people should not be compelled, when their rights are violated, to either rebel or surrender them. These rights must be unmistakably guaranteed in the constitution.

Jefferson's impressions of his colleagues, Washington and Franklin, speak for themselves. In spite of his shortcomings, Washington looms monumental and serene, and we see Franklin's charm and persuasiveness peer through his anecdotes.

The Virginia Constitution
from *Notes on Virginia*

Queen Elizabeth by her letters patent, bearing date March 25, 1584, licensed Sir Walter Raleigh to search for remote heathen lands, not inhabited by Christian people, and granted to him in fee simple all the soil within two hundred leagues of the places where his people should, within six years, make their dwellings or abidings; reserving only to herself and her successors their allegiance and one-fifth part of all the gold and silver ore they should obtain. Sir Walter immediately sent out two ships, which visited Wococon Island in North Carolina, and the next year dispatched seven with one hundred and seven men, who settled in Roanoke Island, about latitude 35° 50'. Here Okisko, king of the Weopomeiocs, in a full council of his people is said to have acknowledged himself the homager of the Queen of England, and, after her, of Sir Walter Raleigh. A supply of fifty men were sent in 1586, and one hundred and fifty in 1587. With these last Sir Walter sent a governor, appointed him twelve assistants, gave them a charter of incorporation, and instructed them to settle on Chesapeake Bay. They landed, however, at Hatorask. In 1588, when a fleet was ready to sail with a new supply of colonists and necessaries, they were detained by the Queen to assist against the Spanish Armada. Sir Walter having now expended £40,000 in these enterprises, obstructed occasionally by the crown without a shilling of aid from it, was under a necessity of engaging others to adventure their money. He, therefore, by deed bearing date the 7th of March, 1589, by the name of Sir Walter Raleigh, Chief Governor of Assamàcòmoc, (probably Acomàc,) alias Wingadacoia, alias Virginia, granted to Thomas Smith and others, in consideration of their adventuring certain sums of money, liberty to trade to this new country free from all customs and taxes for seven years, excepting the fifth part of the gold and silver ore to be obtained; and stipulated with them and the other assistants, then in Virginia, that he would confirm the deed of incorporation which he had given in 1587, with all the prerogatives, jurisdictions, royalties and privileges granted to him by the Queen. Sir Walter, at different times, sent five other adventurers hither, the last of which was in 1602; for in 1603 he was attainted and put into close imprisonment, which put an end to his cares over his infant colony. What was the particular fate of the colonists he had before sent and seated has never been known, whether they were murdered, or incorporated with the savages.

Some gentlemen and merchants, supposing that by the attainder of Sir Walter Raleigh the grant to him was forfeited, not inquiring over-carefully whether the sentence of an English court could affect lands not within the jurisdiction of that court, petitioned King James for a new grant of Virginia to them. He accordingly executed a grant to Sir Thomas Gates and others, bearing date the 9th of March, 1607, under which, in the same year, a settlement was effected at Jamestown, and ever after maintained. Of this grant, however, no particular notice need be taken, as it was superseded by letters patent of the same King, of May 23, 1609, to the Earl of Salisbury and others, incorporating them by the name of "The Treasurer and company of Adventurers and Planters of the City of London for the first colony in Virginia," granting to them and their successors all the lands in Virginia from Point Comfort along the seacoast, to the northward two hundred miles, and from the same point along the seacoast to the southward two hundred miles, and all the space from this precinct on the seacoast up into the land, west and northwest, from sea to sea, and the islands within one hundred miles of it, with all the communities, jurisdictions, royalties, privileges, franchises, and pre-eminencies, within the same, and thereto and thereabouts, by sea and land, appertaining in as ample manner as had before been granted to any adventurer; to be held of the King and his successors, in common socage, yielding one-fifth part of the gold and silver ore to be therein found, for all manner of services; establishing a council in England for the direction of the enterprise, the members of which were to be chosen and displaced by the voice of the majority of the company and adventurers, and were to have the nomination and revocation of governors, officers, and ministers, which by them should be thought needful for the colony, the power of establishing laws and forms of government and magistracy, obligatory not only within the colony, but also on the seas in going and coming to and from it; authorizing them to carry thither any persons who should consent to go, freeing them forever from all taxes and impositions on any goods or merchandise on importations into the colony, or exportation out of it, except the five per cent due for custom on all goods imported into the British dominions, according to the ancient trade of merchants; which five per cent only being paid they might, within thirteen months, re-export the same goods into foreign parts, without any custom, tax, or other duty, to the King or any of his officers, or deputies; with powers of waging war against those who should annoy them; giving to the inhabitants of the colony all the rights of natural subjects, as if born and abiding in England; and declaring that these letters should be construed, in all doubtful parts, in such manner as should be most for the benefit of the grantees.

Afterwards on the 12th of March, 1612, by other letters patent, the King added to his former grants all islands in any part of the ocean between the 30th and 41st degrees of latitude, and within three hundred leagues of any of the parts before granted to the treasurer and company, not being possessed or inhabited by any other Christian prince or state, nor within the limits of the northern colony.

In pursuance of the authorities given to the company by these charters, and more especially of that part in the charter of 1609 which authorized them to establish a form of government, they on the 24th of July, 1621, by charter under their common seal, declared that from thenceforward there should be two supreme councils in Virginia, the one to be called the Council of State, to be placed and displaced by the treasurer, council in England, and company from time to time, whose office was to be that of assisting and advising the governor; the other to be called the General Assembly, to be convened by the governor once yearly or oftener, which was to consist of the Council of State, and two burgesses out of every town, hundred, or plantation, to be respectively chosen by the inhabitants. In this all matters were to be decided by the greater part of the votes present; reserving to the governor a negative voice; and they were to have power to treat, consult, and conclude all emergent occasions concerning the public weal, and to make laws for the behoof and government of the colony, imitating and following the laws and policy of England as nearly as might be; providing that these laws should have no force till ratified in a general court of the company in England, and returned under their common seal; and declaring that, after the government of the colony should be well framed and settled, no orders of the council in England should bind the colony unless ratified in the said General Assembly. The King and company quarreled, and by a mixture of law and force the latter were ousted of all their rights without retribution, after having expended one hundred thousand pounds in establishing the colony, without the smallest aid from government. King James suspended their powers by proclamation of July 15, 1624, and Charles I took the government into his own hands. Both sides had their partisans in the colony, but, in truth, the people of the colony in general thought themselves little concerned in the dispute. There being three parties interested in these several charters, what passed between the first and second it was thought could not affect the third. If the King seized on the powers of the company, they only passed into other hands, without increase or diminution, while the rights of the people remained as they were. But they did not remain so long. The northern parts of their country were granted away to the lords Baltimore and Fairfax; the first of these obtaining also the rights of separate jurisdiction and government. And in 1650 the Parliament, considering itself as standing in the place of their deposed King, and as having succeeded to all his powers, without as well as within the realm, began to assume a right over the colonies, passing an act for inhibiting their trade with foreign nations. This succession to the exercise of kingly authority gave the first color for parliamentary interference with the colonies, and produced that fatal precedent which they continued to follow after they had retired, in other respects, within their proper functions. When this colony, therefore, which still maintained its opposition to Cromwell and the Parliament, was induced in 1651 to lay down their arms, they previously secured their most essential rights by a solemn convention, which, having never seen in print, I will here insert literally from the records.

ARTICLES agreed on and concluded at James Cittie in Virginia for the surrendering and settling of that plantation under the obedience and government of the commonwealth of England by the commissioners of the Councill of State by authoritie of the parliamt of England, and by the Grand assembly of the Governour, Councill, and Burgesses of that countrey.

First it is agreed and consted that the plantation of Virginia, and all the inhabitants thereof, shall be and remain in due obedience and subjection to the Commonwealth of England, according to the laws there established, and that this submission and subscription bee acknowledged a voluntary act not forced nor constrained by a conquest upon the countrey, and that they shall have and enjoy such freedoms and priviledges as belong to the free borne people of England, and that the former government by the Commissions and Instructions be void and null.

2ly. That the Grand assembly as formerly shall convene and transact the affairs of Virginia, wherein nothing is to be acted or done contrairie to the government of the Commonwealth of England and the lawes there established.

3ly. That there shall be a full and totall remission and indempnitie of all acts, words, or writeings done or spoken against the parliament of England in relation to the same.

4ly. That Virginia shall have and enjoy the antient bounds and lymitts granted by the charters of the former kings, and that we shall seek a new charter from the parliament to that purpose against any that have intrencht upon the rights thereof.

5ly. That all the pattents of land granted under the colony seal by any of the precedent governours shall be and remaine in their full force and strength.

6ly. That the priviledge of haveing ffiftie acres of land for every person transported in that collonie shall continue as formerly granted.

7ly. That the people of Virginia have free trade as the people of England do enjoy to all places and with all nations according to the lawes of that commonwealth, and that Virginia shall enjoy all priviledges equall with any English plantations in America.

8ly. That Virginia shall be free from all taxes, customs and impositions whatsoever, and none to be imposed on them without consent of the Grand assembly; and soe that neither fforts nor castle bee erected or garrisons maintained without their consent.

9ly. That noe charge shall be required from this country in respect of this present ffleet.

10ly. That for the future settlement of the countrey in their due obedience, the engagement shall be tendred to all the inhabitants according to act of parliament made to that purpose, that all persons who shall refuse to subscribe the said engagement, shall have a yeare's time if they please to remove themselves and their estates out of Virginia, and in the meantime during the said yeare to have equall justice as formerly.

11ly. That the use of the booke of common prayer shall be permitted for one yeare ensueinge with referrence to the consent of the major part of the parishes, provided that those which relate to kingshipp or that government be not used publiquely, and the continuance of ministers in their places, they not misdemeaning themselves, and the payment of their accustomed dues and agreements made with them respectively shall be left as they now stand dureing this ensueing yeare.

12ly. That no man's cattell shall be questioned as the companies, unless such as have been entrusted with them or have disposed of them without order.

13ly. That all ammunition, powder and armes, other than for private use, shall be delivered up, securitie being given to make satisfaction for it.

14ly. That all goods allreadie brought hither by the Dutch or others which are now on shoar shall be free from surprizall.

15ly. That the quittrents granted unto us by the late kinge for seaven yeares bee confirmed.

16ly. That the commissioners for the parliament subscribeing these articles engage themselves and the honour of parliament for the full performance thereof; and that the present governour, and the councill, and the burgesses do likewise subscribe and engage the whole collony on their parts.

RICHARD BENNETT.—Seale.
WILLIAM CLAIBORNE.—Seale.
EDMOND CURTIS.—Seale.

Theise articles were signed and sealed by the Commissioners of the Councill of state for the Commonwealth of England the twelveth day of March 1651.

The colony supposed that by this solemn convention, entered into with arms in their hands, they had secured the ancient limits of their country, its free trade, its exemption from taxation but by their own Assembly, and exclusion of military force from among them. Yet in every of these points was this convention violated by subsequent Kings and Parliaments, and other infractions of their constitution equally dangerous committed. Their General Assembly, which was composed of the Council of State and Burgesses, sitting together and deciding by plurality of voices, was split into two houses, by which the Council obtained a separate negative on their laws. Appeals from their Supreme Court, which had been fixed by law in their General Assembly, were arbitrarily revoked to England, to be there heard before the King and Council. Instead of four hundred miles on the seacoast, they were reduced, in the space of thirty years, to about one hundred miles. Their trade with foreigners was totally suppressed, and when carried to Great Britain, was there loaded with imposts. It is unnecessary, however, to glean up the several instances of injury, as scattered through American and British history, and the more especially as, by passing on to the accession of the present King, we shall find specimens of them all, aggravated, multiplied and crowded within a small compass of time, so as to evince a fixed design of considering our rights natural, conventional and chartered as mere nullities. The following is an epitome of the first sixteen years of his reign: The colonies were taxed internally and externally; their essential interests sacrificed to individuals in Great Britain; their legislatures suspended; charters annulled; trials by juries taken away; their persons subjected to transportation across the Atlantic, and to trial before foreign judicatories; their supplications for redress thought beneath answer; themselves published as cowards in the councils of their mother country and courts of Europe; armed troops sent among them to enforce submission to these violences; and actual hostilities commenced against them. No alternative was presented but resistance, or unconditional submission. Between these could be no hesitation. They closed in the appeal to arms. They declared themselves independent states. They confederated together into one great republic; thus securing to every state the benefit of a union of their whole force. In each state separately a new form of government was established. Of ours particularly the following are the outlines: The executive powers are lodged in the hands of a governor, chosen annually, and incapable of acting more than three years in seven. He is assisted by a council of eight members. The judiciary powers are divided among several courts, as will be hereafter explained. Legislation is exercised by two houses of Assembly: the one called the House of Delegates, composed of two members from each county, chosen annually by the citizens, possessing an estate for life in one hundred acres of uninhabited land, or twenty-five acres with a house on it, or in a house or lot in some town; the other called the Senate, consisting of twenty-four members, chosen quadrennially by the same electors, who for this purpose are distributed into twenty-four districts. The concurrence of both houses is necessary to the passage of a law. They have the appointment of the governor and council, the judges of the superior courts, auditors, attorney general, treasurer, register of the land office, and delegates to Congress. As the dismemberment of the state had never had its confirmation, but, on the contrary, had always been the subject of protestation and complaint, that it might never be in our own power to raise scruples on that subject, or to disturb the harmony of our new confederacy, the grants to Maryland, Pennsylvania, and the two Carolinas were ratified.

This Constitution was formed when we were new and unexperienced in the science of government. It was the first, too, which was formed in the whole United States. No wonder then that time and trial have discovered very capital defects in it.

1. The majority of the men in the state, who pay and fight for its support, are unrepresented in the legislature, the roll of freeholders entitled to vote not including generally the half of those on the roll of the militia, or of the taxgatherers.

2. Among those who share the representation, the shares are very unequal. Thus the county of Warwick, with only one hundred fighting

men, has an equal representation with the county of Loudon, which has one thousand seven hundred and forty-six. So that every man in Warwick has as much influence in the government as seventeen men in Loudon. But lest it should be thought that an equal interspersion of small among large counties through the whole state may prevent any danger of injury to particular parts of it, we will divide it into districts, and show the proportions of land, of fighting men, and of representation in each. . . .

3. The Senate is, by its constitution, too homogeneous with the House of Delegates. Being chosen by the same electors, at the same time, and out of the same subjects, the choice falls of course on men of the same description. The purpose of establishing different houses of legislation is to introduce the influence of different interests or different principles. Thus in Great Britain it is said their constitution relies on the House of Commons for honesty, and the Lords for wisdom; which would be a rational reliance if honesty were to be bought with money, and if wisdom were hereditary. In some of the American states, the delegates and senators are so chosen as that the first represent the persons, and the second the property of the state. But with us, wealth and wisdom have equal chance for admission into both houses. We do not, therefore, derive from the separation of our legislature into two houses those benefits which a proper complication of principles are capable of producing, and those which alone can compensate the evils which may be produced by their dissensions.

4. All the powers of government, legislative, executive, and judiciary, result to the legislative body. The concentrating these in the same hands is precisely the definition of despotic government. It will be no alleviation that these powers will be exercised by a plurality of hands, and not by a single one. One hundred and seventy-three despots would surely be as oppressive as one. Let those who doubt it turn their eyes on the republic of Venice. As little will it avail us that they are chosen by ourselves. An *elective despotism* was not the government we fought for, but one which should not only be founded on free principles, but in which the powers of government should be so divided and balanced among several bodies of magistracy as that no one could transcend their legal limits without being effectually checked and restrained by the others. For this reason that convention which passed the ordinance of government laid its foundation on this basis, that the legislative, executive, and judiciary departments should be separate and distinct, so that no person should exercise the powers of more than one of them at the same time.

But no barrier was provided between these several powers. The judiciary and executive members were left dependent on the legislative for their subsistence in office, and some of them for their continuance in it. If, therefore, the legislature assumes executive and judiciary powers, no opposition is likely to be made; nor, if made, can it be effectual; because in that case they may put their proceedings into the form of an act of Assembly, which will render them obligatory on the other branches. They have, accordingly, in many instances, decided rights which should have been left to judiciary controversy; and the direction of the executive, during the whole time of their session, is becoming habitual and familiar. And this is done with no ill intention. The views of the present members are perfectly upright. When they are led out of their regular province, it is by art in others, and inadvertence in themselves. And this will probably be the case for some time to come. But it will not be a very long time. Mankind soon learn to make interested uses of every right and power which they possess, or may assume. The public money and public liberty, intended to have been deposited with three branches of magistracy, but found inadvertently to be in the hands of one only, will soon be discovered to be sources of wealth and dominion to those who hold them; distinguished, too, by this tempting circumstance, that they are the instrument as well as the object of acquisition. With money we will get men, said Caesar, and with men we will get money. Nor should our Assembly be deluded by the integrity of their own purposes, and conclude that these unlimited powers will never be abused, because themselves are not disposed to abuse them. They should look forward to a time, and that not a distant one, when a corruption in this, as in the country from which we derive our origin, will have seized the head of government, and be spread by them through the body of the people; when they will purchase the voices of the people, and make them pay the price. Human nature is the same on every side of the Atlantic, and will be alike influenced by the same causes. The time to guard against corruption and tyranny is before they shall have gotten hold of us. It is better to keep the wolf out of the fold than to trust to drawing his teeth and claws after he shall have entered. To render these considerations the more cogent, we must observe in addition:

5. That the ordinary legislature may alter the Constitution itself. On the discontinuance of Assemblies, it became necessary to substitute in their place some other body, competent to the ordinary business of government, and to the calling forth the powers of the state for the maintenance of our opposition to Great Britain. Conventions were therefore

introduced, consisting of two delegates from each county, meeting together and forming one house, on the plan of the former House of Burgesses, to whose places they succeeded. These were at first chosen anew for every particular session. But in March, 1775, they recommended to the people to choose a convention which should continue in office a year. This was done, accordingly, in April, 1775, and in the July following that convention passed an ordinance for the election of delegates in the month of April annually. It is well known that in July, 1775, a separation from Great Britain and establishment of republican government had never yet entered into any person's mind. A convention, therefore, chosen under that ordinance cannot be said to have been chosen for the purposes which certainly did not exist in the minds of those who passed it. Under this ordinance, at the annual election in April, 1776, a convention for the year was chosen. Independence and the establishment of a new form of government were not even yet the objects of the people at large. One extract from the pamphlet called Common Sense had appeared in the Virginia papers in February, and copies of the pamphlet itself had got in a few hands. But the idea had not been opened to the mass of the people in April, much less can it be said that they had made up their minds in its favor.

So that the electors of April, 1776, no more than the legislators of July, 1775, not thinking of independence and a permanent republic, could not mean to vest in these delegates powers of establishing them, or any authorities other than those of the ordinary legislature. So far as a temporary organization of government was necessary to render our opposition energetic, so far their organization was valid. But they received in their creation no powers but what were given to every legislature before and since. They could not, therefore, pass an act transcendent to the powers of other legislatures. If the present Assembly pass an act, and declare it shall be irrevocable by subsequent Assemblies, the declaration is merely void, and the act repealable, as other acts are. So far, and no farther authorized, they organized the government by the ordinance entitled a constitution or form of government. It pretends to no higher authority than the other ordinances of the same session; it does not say that it shall be perpetual; that it shall be unalterable by other legislatures; that it shall be transcendent above the powers of those who they knew would have equal power with themselves. Not only the silence of the instrument is a proof they thought it would be alterable, but their own practice also; for this very convention, meeting as a House of Delegates in General Assembly with the Senate in the autumn of that year, passed acts of assembly in

contradiction to their ordinance of government; and every Assembly from
that time to this has done the same. I am safe, therefore, in the position
that the Constitution itself is alterable by the ordinary legislature. Though
this opinion seems founded on the first elements of common sense, yet is
the contrary maintained by some persons. (1) Because, say they, the
conventions were vested with every power necessary to make effectual
opposition to Great Britain. But to complete this argument, they must
go on, and say further that effectual opposition could not be made to
Great Britain without establishing a form of government perpetual and
unalterable by the legislature; which is not true. An opposition which at
some time or other was to come to an end could not need a perpetual
institution to carry it on; and a government amendable as its defects
should be discovered was as likely to make effectual resistance as one
that should be unalterably wrong. Besides, the Assemblies were as much
vested with all powers requisite for resistance as the conventions were.
If, therefore, these powers included that of modeling the form of government in the one case, they did so in the other. The Assemblies then as
well as the conventions may model the government; that is, they may
alter the ordinance of the government. (2) They urge that if the convention had meant that this instrument should be alterable, as their
other ordinances were, they would have called it an ordinance; but
they have called it a *constitution*, which, *ex vi termini*, means "an act
above the power of the ordinary legislature." I answer that *constitutio*,
constitutium, statutum, lex, are convertible terms. . . . Thus in the
statute 25 Hen. VIII. c. 19, § 1, "*Constitutions* and *ordinances*" are used
as synonymous. The term *constitution* has many other significations in
physics and politics; but in jurisprudence, whenever it is applied to any
act of the legislature, it invariably means a statute, law, or ordinance,
which is the present case. No inference then of a different meaning can
be drawn from the adoption of this title; on the contrary, we might conclude that, by their affixing to it a term synonymous with ordinance or
statute. But of what consequence is their meaning, where their power is
denied? If they meant to do more than they had power to do, did this
give them power? It is not the name, but the authority that renders an
act obligatory. . . . To get rid of the magic supposed to be in the word
constitution, let us translate it into its definition as given by those who
think it above the power of the law; and let us suppose the convention,
instead of saying, "We the ordinary legislature establish a *constitution*,"
had said, "We the ordinary legislature establish an act *above the power
of the ordinary legislature*." Does not this expose the absurdity of the at-

tempt? (3) But, say they, the people have acquiesced, and this has given it an authority superior to the laws. It is true that the people did not rebel against it; and was that a time for the people to rise in rebellion? Should a prudent acquiescence, at a critical time, be construed into a confirmation of every illegal thing done during that period? Besides, why should they rebel? At an annual election they had chosen delegates for the year to exercise the ordinary powers of legislation, and to manage the great contest in which they were engaged. These delegates thought the contest would be best managed by an organized government. They therefore, among others, passed an ordinance of government. They did not presume to call it perpetual and unalterable. They well knew they had no power to make it so; that our choice of them had been for no such purpose, and at a time when we could have no such purpose in contemplation. Had an unalterable form of government been meditated, perhaps we should have chosen a different set of people. There was no cause then for the people to rise in rebellion. But to what dangerous lengths will this argument lead? Did the acquiescence of the colonies under the various acts of power exercised by Great Britain in our infant state confirm these acts, and so far invest them with the authority of the people as to render them unalterable, and our present resistance wrong? On every unauthoritative exercise of power by the legislature must the people rise in rebellion, or their silence be construed into a surrender of that power to them? If so, how many rebellions should we have had already? One certainly for every session of Assembly. The other states in the Union have been of opinion that to render a form of government unalterable by ordinary acts of Assembly, the people must delegate persons with special powers. They have accordingly chosen special conventions to form and fix their governments. The individuals then who maintain the contrary opinion in this country should have the modesty to suppose it possible that they may be wrong, and the rest of America right. But if there be only a possibility of their being wrong, if only a plausible doubt remains of the validity of the ordinance of government, is it not better to remove that doubt by placing it on a bottom which none will dispute? If they be right we shall only have the unnecessary trouble of meeting once in convention. If they be wrong, they expose us to the hazard of having no fundamental rights at all. True it is, this is no time for deliberating on forms of government. While an enemy is within our bowels, the first object is to expel him. But when this shall be done, when peace shall be established, and leisure given us for intrenching within good forms the rights for which we have bled, let no man be found indolent

enough to decline a little more trouble for placing them beyond the reach
of question. If anything more be requisite to produce a conviction of the
expediency of calling a convention at a proper season to fix our form of
government, let it be the reflection:

6. That the Assembly exercises a power of determining the quorum of
their own body which may legislate for us. After the establishment of the
new form they adhered to the *Lex majoris partis,* founded in common
law as well as common right. It is the natural law of every Assembly of
men whose numbers are not fixed by any other law. They continued for
some time to require the presence of a majority of their whole number
to pass an act. But the British Parliament fixes its own quorum; our
former Assemblies fixed their own quorum; and one precedent in favor
of power is stronger than a hundred against it. The House of Delegates,
therefore, have lately voted that, during the present dangerous invasion,
forty members shall be a house to proceed to business. They have been
moved to this by the fear of not being able to collect a house. But this
danger could not authorize them to call that a house which was none;
and if they may fix it at one number, they may at another, till it loses
its fundamental character of being a representative body. As this vote
expires with the present invasion, it is probable the former rule will be
permitted to revive; because at present no ill is meant. The power, however, of fixing their own quorum has been avowed, and a precedent set.
From forty it may be reduced to four, and from four to one; from a house
to a committee, from a committee to a chairman or speaker, and thus an
oligarchy or monarchy be substituted under forms supposed to be regular. "All bad precedents arise out of good; but where power comes into
the hands of the ignorant or the indifferent, that new precedent proceeds
from the worthy and the fit to the unworthy and the unfit."

When, therefore, it is considered that there is no legal obstacle to the
assumption by the Assembly of all the powers legislative, executive, and
judiciary, and that these may come to the hands of the smallest rag of
delegation, surely the people will say, and their representatives, while
yet they have honest representatives, will advise them to say, that they
will not acknowledge as laws any acts not considered and assented to
by the major part of their delegates.

In enumerating the defects of the Constitution, it would be wrong to
count among them what is only the error of particular persons. In December, 1776, our circumstances being much distressed, it was proposed
in the House of Delegates to create a *dictator,* invested with every power
legislative, executive, and judiciary, civil and military, of life and of

death, over our persons and over our properties; and in June, 1781, again under calamity, the same proposition was repeated, and wanted a few votes only of being passed. One who entered into this contest from a pure love of liberty, and a sense of injured rights, who determined to make every sacrifice, and to meet every danger, for the re-establishment of those rights on a firm basis, who did not mean to expend his blood and substance for the wretched purpose of changing this matter for that, but to place the powers of governing him in a plurality of hands of his own choice, so that the corrupt will of no one man might in future oppress him, must stand confounded and dismayed when he is told that a considerable portion of that plurality had mediated the surrender of them into a single hand, and, in lieu of a limited monarchy, to deliver him over to a despotic one! How must we find his efforts and sacrifices abused and baffled, if he may still, by a single vote, be laid prostrate at the feet of one man! In God's name, from whence have they derived this power? Is it from our ancient laws? None such can be produced. Is it from any principle in our new Constitution expressed or implied? Every lineament expressed or implied is in full opposition to it. Its fundamental principle is that the state shall be governed as a commonwealth. It provides a republican organization, proscribes under the name of *prerogative* the exercise of all powers undefined by the laws; places on this basis the whole system of our laws; and by consolidating them together chooses that they should be left to stand or fall together, never providing for any circumstances, nor admitting that such could arise, wherein either should be suspended; no, not for a moment. Our ancient laws expressly declare that those who are but delegates themselves shall not delegate to others powers which require judgment and integrity in their exercise. Or was this proposition moved on a supposed right in the movers of abandoning their posts in a moment of distress? The same laws forbid the abandonment of that post, even on ordinary occasions; and much more a transfer of their powers into other hands and other forms without consulting the people. They never admit the idea that these, like sheep or cattle, may be given from hand to hand without an appeal to their own will. Was it from the necessity of the case? Necessities which dissolve a government do not convey its authority to an oligarchy or a monarchy. They throw back into the hands of the people the powers they had delegated, and leave them as individuals to shift for themselves. A leader may offer but not impose himself, nor be imposed on them. Much less can their necks be submitted to his sword, their breath to be held at his will or caprice. The necessity which should operate these tremendous effects should at least be palpable and irresistible. Yet in both instances, where it was feared, or pretended with us, it was belied by the event. It was belied, too, by the preceding experience of our sister states, several of whom had grappled through greater difficulties without abandoning their forms of government. When the proposition was first made, Massachusetts had found even the government of committees sufficient to carry them through an invasion. But we at the time of that proposition were under no invasion. When the second was made, there had been added to this example those of Rhode Island, New York, New Jersey, and Pennsylvania, in all of which the republican form had been found equal to the task of carrying them through the severest trials. In this state alone did there exist so little virtue that fear was to be fixed in the hearts of the people, and to become the motive of their exertions and principle of their government? The very thought alone was treason against the people; was treason against mankind in general, as riveting forever the chains which bow down their necks, by giving to their oppressors a proof, which they would have trumpeted through the universe, of the imbecility of republican government, in times of pressing danger, to shield them from harm. Those who assume the right of giving away the reins of government in any case must be sure that the herd, whom they hand on to the rods and hatchet of the dictator, will lay their necks on the block when they shall nod to them. But if our assemblies supposed such a recognition in the people, I hope they mistook their character. I am of opinion that the government, instead of being braced and invigorated for greater exertions under their difficulties, would have been thrown back upon the bungling machinery of county committees for administration, till a convention could have been called, and its wheels again set into regular motion. What a cruel moment was this for creating such an embarrassment, for putting to the proof the attachment of our countrymen to republican government! Those who meant well, of the advocates of this measure (and most of them meant well, for I know them personally, had been their fellow laborer in the common cause, and had often proved the purity of their principles), had been seduced in their judgment by the example of an ancient republic, whose constitution and circumstances were fundamentally different. They had sought this precedent in the history of Rome, where alone it was to be found, and where at length, too, it had proved fatal. They had taken it from a republic rent by the most bitter factions and tumults, where the government was of a heavy-handed unfeeling aristocracy, over a people ferocious, and rendered desperate by poverty and wretchedness; tumults which could not be allayed under the most trying circumstances, but by the omnipotent hand of a single despot. Their constitution, therefore, allowed a temporary tyrant to be erected, under the name of a dictator; and that temporary tyrant, after a few examples, became perpetual. They misapplied this precedent to a people mild in their dispositions, patient under their trial, united for the public liberty, and affectionate to their leaders. But if from the constitution of the Roman government there resulted to their Senate a power of submitting all their rights to the will of one man, does it follow that the Assembly of Virginia have the same authority? What clause in our constitution has substituted that of Rome, by way of residuary provision, for all cases not otherwise provided for? Or if they may step *ad libitum* into any other form of government for precedents to rule us by, for what oppression may not a precedent be found in this world of the *bellum omnium in omnia* [war of all against all]? Searching for the foundations of this proposition, I can find none which may pretend a color of right or reason, but the defect before developed, that there being no barrier between the legislative, executive, and judiciary departments, the legislature may seize the whole; that having seized it, and possessing a right to fix their own quorum, they may reduce that quorum to one, whom they may call a chairman, speaker, dictator, or by any other name they please. Our situation is indeed perilous, and I hope my countrymen will be sensible of it, and will apply, at a proper season, the proper remedy; which is a convention to fix the Constitution, to amend its defects, to bind up the several branches of government by certain laws, which, when they transgress, their acts shall become nullities; to render unnecessary an appeal to the people, or in other words a rebellion, on every infraction of their rights, on the peril that their acquiescence shall be construed into an intention to surrender those rights.

---

*The foregoing is taken
from Thomas Jefferson's* NOTES ON VIRGINIA.

First Inaugural Address

C Friends and Fellow Citizens:

alled upon to undertake the duties of the first executive office
of our country, I avail myself of the presence of that portion of my fellow
citizens which is here assembled, to express my grateful thanks for the
favor with which they have been pleased to look toward me, to declare
a sincere consciousness that the task is above my talents, and that I approach it with those anxious and awful presentiments which the greatness of the charge and the weakness of my powers so justly inspire. A
rising nation, spread over a wise and fruitful land, traversing all the
seas with the rich productions of their industry, engaged in commerce
with nations who feel power and forget right, advancing rapidly to destinies beyond the reach of mortal eye—when I contemplate these transcendent objects, and see the honor, the happiness, and the hopes of this
beloved country committed to the issue and the auspices of this day, I
shrink from the contemplation, and humble myself before the magnitude of the undertaking. Utterly, indeed, should I despair did not the
presence of many whom I here see remind me that, in the other high authorities provided by our constitution, I shall find resources of wisdom,
of virtue, and of zeal on which to rely under all difficulties. To you, then,
gentlemen, who are charged with the sovereign functions of legislation,
and to those associated with you, I look with encouragement for that
guidance and support which may enable us to steer with safety the vessel
in which we are all embarked amid the conflicting elements of a troubled
world.

During the contest of opinion through which we have passed, the animation of discussion and of exertions has sometimes worn an aspect
which might impose on strangers unused to think freely and to speak and
to write what they think; but this being now decided by the voice of the
nation, announced according to the rules of the constitution, all will, of
course, arrange themselves under the will of the law, and unite in com-

mon efforts for the common good. All, too, will bear in mind this sacred principle, that though the will of the majority is in all cases to prevail, that will, to be rightful, must be reasonable; that the minority possess their equal rights, which equal laws must protect, and to violate which would be oppression. Let us, then, fellow citizens, unite with one heart and one mind. Let us restore to social intercourse that harmony and affection without which liberty and even life itself are but dreary things. And let us reflect that having banished from our land that religious intolerance under which mankind so long bled and suffered, we have yet gained little if we countenance a political intolerance as despotic, as wicked, and capable of as bitter and bloody persecutions. During the throes and convulsions of the ancient world, during the agonizing spasms of infuriated man, seeking through blood and slaughter his long-lost liberty, it was not wonderful that the agitations of the billows should reach even this distant and peaceful shore; that this should be more felt and feared by some and less by others; that this should divide opinions as to measures of safety. But every difference of opinion is not a difference of principle. We have called by different names brethren of the same principle. We are all republicans—we are federalists. If there be any among us who would wish to dissolve this Union or to change its republican form, let them stand undisturbed as monuments of the safety with which error of opinion may be tolerated where reason is left free to combat it. I know, indeed, that some honest men fear that a republican government cannot be strong; that this government is not strong enough. But would the honest patriot, in the full tide of successful experiment, abandon a government which has so far kept us free and firm, on the theoretic and visionary fear that this government, the world's best hope, may by possibility want energy to preserve itself? I trust not. I believe this, on the contrary, the strongest government on earth. I believe it is the only one where every man, at the call of the laws, would fly to the standard of the law, and would meet invasions of the public order as his own personal concern. Sometimes it is said that man cannot be trusted with the government of himself. Can he, then, be trusted with the government of others? Or have we found angels in the forms of kings to govern him? Let history answer this question.

Let us, then, with courage and confidence pursue our own federal and republican principles, our attachment to our union and representative government. Kindly separated by nature and a wide ocean from the exterminating havoc of one quarter of the globe; too high-minded to endure the degradations of the others; possessing a chosen country, with room

enough for our descendants to the hundredth and thousandth generation; entertaining a due sense of our equal right to the use of our own
faculties, to the acquisitions of our industry, to honor and confidence
from our fellow citizens, resulting not from birth but from our actions
and their sense of them; enlightened by a benign religion, professed, indeed, and practiced in various forms, yet all of them including honesty,
truth, temperance, gratitude, and the love of man; acknowledging and
adoring an overruling Providence, which by all its dispensations proves
that it delights in the happiness of man here and his greater happiness
hereafter; with all these blessings, what more is necessary to make us a
happy and prosperous people? Still one thing more, fellow citizens—a
wise and frugal government, which shall restrain men from injuring one
another, which shall leave them otherwise free to regulate their own pursuits of industry and improvement, and shall not take from the mouth of
labor the bread it has earned. This is the sum of good government, and
this is necessary to close the circle of our felicities.

About to enter, fellow citizens, on the exercise of duties which comprehend everything dear and valuable to you, it is proper that you should
understand what I deem the essential principles of our government, and
consequently those which ought to shape its administration. I will com-
press them within the narrowest compass they will bear, stating the general principle, but not all its limitations. Equal and exact justice to all
men, of whatever state or persuasion, religious or political; peace, commerce, and honest friendship with all nations—entangling alliances with
none; the support of the state governments in all their rights, as the most
competent administrations for our domestic concerns and the surest
bulwarks against antirepublican tendencies; the preservation of the general government in its whole constitutional vigor, as the sheet anchor of
our peace at home and safety abroad; a jealous care of the right of election by the people—a mild and safe corrective of abuses which are lopped
by the sword of the revolution where peaceable remedies are unpro-
vided; absolute acquiescence in the decisions of the majority—the vital
principle of republics, from which there is no appeal but to force, the
vital principle and immediate parent of despotism; a well-disciplined
militia—our best reliance in peace and for the first moments of war, till
regulars may relieve them; the supremacy of the civil over the military
authority; economy in the public expense, that labor may be lightly bur-
dened; the honest payment of our debts and sacred preservation of the
public faith; encouragement of agriculture, and of commerce as its hand-
maid; the diffusion of information and the arraignment of all abuses at

the bar of public reason, freedom of religion; freedom of the press; freedom of person under the protection of the habeas corpus; and trial by juries impartially selected—these principles form the bright constellation which has gone before us, and guided our steps through an age of revolution and reformation. The wisdom of our sages and the blood of our heroes have been devoted to their attainment. They should be the creed of our political faith—the text of civil instruction—the touchstone by which to try the services of those we trust; and should we wander from them in moments of error or alarm, let us hasten to retrace our steps and to regain the road which alone leads to peace, liberty, and safety.

I repair, then, fellow citizens, to the post you have assigned me. With experience enough in subordinate offices to have seen the difficulties of this, the greatest of all, I have learned to expect that it will rarely fall to the lot of imperfect man to retire from this station with the reputation and the favor which bring him into it. Without pretensions to that high confidence reposed in our first and great revolutionary character, whose pre-eminent services had entitled him to the first place in his country's love, and destined for him the fairest page in the volume of faithful history, I ask so much confidence only as may give firmness and effect to the legal administration of your affairs. I shall often go wrong through defect of judgment. When right, I shall often be thought wrong by those whose positions will not command a view of the whole ground. I ask your indulgence for my own errors, which will never be intentional; and your support against the errors of others, who may condemn what they would not if seen in all its parts. The approbation implied by your suffrage is a consolation to me for the past; and my future solicitude will be to retain the good opinion of those who have bestowed it in advance, to conciliate that of others by doing them all the good in my power, and to be instrumental to the happiness and freedom of all.

Relying, then, on the patronage of your good will, I advance with obedience to the work, ready to retire from it whenever you become sensible how much better choice it is in your power to make. And may that Infinite Power which rules the destinies of the universe lead our councils to what is best, and give them a favorable issue for your peace and prosperity

Biographical Sketches

THE CHARACTER OF GEORGE WASHINGTON

I think I knew General Washington intimately and thoroughly; and were I called on to delineate his character, it should be in terms like these.

His mind was great and powerful, without being of the very first order; his penetration strong, though not so acute as that of a Newton, Bacon, or Locke; and as far as he saw, no judgment was ever sounder. It was slow in operation, being little aided by invention or imagination, but sure in conclusion. Hence the common remark of his officers, of the advantage he derived from councils of war, where hearing all suggestions, he selected whatever was best; and certainly no general ever planned his battles more judiciously. But if deranged during the course of the action, if any member of his plan was dislocated by sudden circumstances, he was slow in re-adjustment. The consequence was that he often failed in the field, and rarely against an enemy in station, as at Boston and York. He was incapable of fear, meeting personal dangers with the calmest unconcern. Perhaps the strongest feature in his character was prudence, never acting until every circumstance, every consideration, was maturely weighed; refraining if he saw a doubt, but, when once decided, going through with his purpose, whatever obstacles opposed. His integrity was most pure, his justice the most inflexible I have ever known, no motives of interest or consanguinity, of friendship or hatred, being able to bias his decision. He was, indeed, in every sense of the words, a wise, a good, and a great man. His temper was naturally irritable and high toned; but reflection and resolution had obtained a firm and habitual ascendency over it. If ever, however, it broke its bonds, he was most tremendous in his wrath. In his expenses he was honorable, but exact; liberal in contributions to whatever promised utility; but frowning and unyielding on all visionary projects, and all unworthy calls on his charity. His heart was not warm in its affections; but he exactly calculated every man's value, and gave him a solid esteem proportioned to it. His person, you know, was fine, his stature exactly what one would wish, his deportment easy, erect and noble; the best horseman of his age, and the most graceful figure that could be seen on horseback. Although in the circle of his friends, where he might be unreserved with safety, he took a free share in conversation, his colloquial talents were not above mediocrity, possessing neither copiousness of ideas, nor fluency of words. In public, when called on for a sudden opinion, he was unready, short and embarrassed. Yet he wrote readily, rather diffusely, in an easy and correct style. This he had acquired by conversation with the world, for his education was merely reading, writing and common arithmetic, to which he added surveying at a later day. His time was employed in action chiefly, reading little, and that only in agriculture and English history. His correspondence became necessarily extensive, and, with journalizing his agricultural proceedings, occupied most of his leisure hours within doors. On the whole, his character was, in its mass, perfect, in nothing bad, in few points indifferent; and it may truly be said that never did nature and fortune combine more perfectly to make a man great, and to place him in the same constellation with whatever worthies have merited from man an everlasting remembrance. For his was the singular destiny and merit, of leading the armies of his country successfully through an arduous war, for the establishment of its independence; of conducting its councils through the birth of a government, new in its forms and principles, until it had settled down into a quiet and orderly train; and of scrupulously obeying the laws through the whole of his career, civil and military, of which the history of the world furnishes no other example.

. . . I am satisfied the great body of republicans think of him as I do. We were, indeed, dissatisfied with him on his ratification of the British treaty. But this was short lived. We knew his honesty, the wiles with which he was encompassed, and that age had already begun to relax the firmness of his purposes; and I am convinced he is more deeply seated in the love and gratitude of the republicans than in the Pharisaical homage of the federal monarchists. For he was no monarchist from preference of his judgment. The soundness of that gave him correct views of the rights of man, and his severe justice devoted him to them. He has often declared to me that he considered our new Constitution as an experiment on the practicability of republican government, and with what dose of liberty man could be trusted for his own good; that he was determined the experiment should have a fair trial, and would lose the last drop of his blood in support of it. And these declarations he repeated to me the oftener and more pointedly because he knew my suspicions of Colonel Hamilton's views, and probably had heard from him the same declarations which I had, to wit, "that the British constitution, with its unequal representation, corruption and other existing abuses, was the most perfect government which had ever been established on earth, and that a reformation of those abuses would make it an impracticable government." I do believe that General Washington had not a firm confidence in the durability of our government. He was naturally distrustful of men, and inclined to gloomy apprehensions; and I was ever persuaded that a belief that we must at length end in something like a British constitution had some weight in his adoption of the ceremonies of levees, birthdays, pompous meetings with Congress, and other forms of the same character, calculated to prepare us gradually for a change which he believed possible, and to let it come on with as little shock as might be to the public mind.

These are my opinions of General Washington, which I would vouch at the judgment seat of God, having been formed on an acquaintance of thirty years. I served with him in the Virginia legislature from 1769 to the Revolutionary War, and again, a short time in Congress, until he left us to take command of the army. During the war and after it we corresponded occasionally, and in the four years of my continuance in the office of Secretary of State, our intercourse was daily, confidential and cordial. After I retired from that office, great and malignant pains were taken by our federal monarchists, and not entirely without effect, to make him view me as a theorist, holding French principles of government, which would lead infallibly to licentiousness and anarchy. And to this he listened the more easily, from my known disapprobation of the British treaty. I never saw him afterwards, or these malignant insinuations should have been dissipated before his just judgment, as mists before the sun. I felt on his death, with my countrymen, that "verily a great man hath fallen this day in Israel."

ANECDOTES OF BENJAMIN FRANKLIN

Our revolutionary process, as is well known, commenced by petitions, memorials, remonstrances, etc., from the old Congress. These were followed by a non-importation agreement, as a pacific instrument of coercion. While that was before us, and sundry exceptions, as of arms, ammunition, etc., were moved from different quarters of the house, I was sitting by Dr. Franklin and observed to him that I thought we should except books; that we ought not to exclude science, even coming from an enemy. He thought so too, and I proposed the exception, which was agreed to. Soon after it occurred that medicine should be excepted, and I suggested that also to the Doctor. "As to that," said he, "I will tell you a story. When I was in London, in such a year, there was a weekly club of physicians, of which Sir John Pringle was president, and I was invited by my friend Dr. Fothergill to attend when convenient. Their rule was to propose a thesis one week and discuss it the next. I happened there when the question to be considered was whether physicians had, on the whole, done most good or harm? The young members, particularly, having discussed it very learnedly and eloquently till the subject was exhausted, one of them observed to Sir John Pringle, that although it was not usual for the President to take part in a debate, yet they were desirous to know his opinion on the question. He said they must first tell him whether, under the appellation of physicians, they meant to include *old women;* if they did he thought they had done more good than harm, otherwise more harm than good."

The Confederation of the States, while on the carpet before the old Congress, was strenuously opposed by the smaller States, under apprehensions that they would be swallowed up by the larger ones. We were long engaged in the discussion; it produced great heats, much ill humor, and intemperate declarations from some members. Dr. Franklin at length brought the debate to a close with one of his little apologues. He observed that "at the time of the union of England and Scotland, the Duke of Argyle was most violently opposed to that measure, and among other things predicted that, as the whale had swallowed Jonah, so Scotland would be swallowed by England. However," said the Doctor, "when Lord Bute came into the government, he soon brought into its administration so many of his countrymen, that it was found in event that Jonah swallowed the whale." This little story produced a *general* laugh, and restored good humor, and the article of difficulty was passed.

When Dr. Franklin went to France, on his revolutionary mission, his eminence as a philosopher, his venerable appearance, and the cause on which he was sent, rendered him extremely popular. For all ranks and conditions of men there entered warmly into the American interest. He was, therefore, feasted and invited into all the court parties. At these he sometimes met the old Duchess of Bourbon, who, being a chess player of about his force, they very generally played together. Happening once to put her king into prize, the Doctor took it. "Ah," said she, "we do not take kings so." "We do in America," said the Doctor.

At one of these parties the Emperor Joseph III, then at Paris incognito, under the title of Count Falkenstein, was overlooking the game in silence, while the company was engaged in animated conversations on the American question. "How happens it M. le Comte," said the Duchess, "that while we all feel so much interest in the cause of the Americans, you say nothing for them?" "I am a king by trade," said he.

When the Declaration of Independence was under the consideration of Congress, there were two or three unlucky expressions in it which gave offense to some members. The words "Scotch and other foreign auxiliaries" excited the ire of a gentleman or two of that country. Severe strictures on the conduct of the British king, in negotiating our repeated repeals of the law which permitted the importation of slaves, were disapproved by some Southern gentlemen, whose reflections were not yet matured to the full abhorrence of that traffic. Although the offensive expressions were immediately yielded these gentlemen continued their depredations on other parts of the instrument. I was sitting by Dr. Franklin, who perceived that I was not insensible to these mutilations. "I have made it a rule," said he, "whenever in my power, to avoid becoming the draughtsmen of papers to be reviewed by a public body. I took my lesson from an incident which I will relate to you. When I was a journeyman printer, one of my companions, an apprentice hatter, having served out his time, was about to open shop for himself. His first concern was to have a handsome signboard, with a proper inscription. He composed it in these words, 'John Thompson, *Hatter, makes* and *sells hats* for ready money,' with a figure of a hat subjoined; but he thought he would submit it to his friends for their amendments. The first he showed it to thought the word '*Hatter*' tautologous, because followed by the words 'makes hats,' which show he was a hatter. It was struck out. The next observed that the word '*makes*' might as well be omitted, because his customers would not care who made the hats. If good and to their mind, they would buy, by whomsoever made. He struck it out. A third said he thought the words '*for ready money*' were useless, as it was not the custom of the place to sell on credit. Everyone who purchased expected to pay. They were parted with, and the inscription now stood, 'John Thompson sells hats.' '*Sells hats!*' says his next friend. Why nobody will expect you to give them away, what then is the use of that word? It was stricken out, and '*hats*' followed it, the rather as there was one painted on the board.

So the inscription was reduced ultimately to 'John Thompson' with the figure of a hat subjoined."

The Doctor told me at Paris the two following anecdotes of the Abbé Raynal. He had a party to dine with him one day at Passy, of whom one half were Americans, the other half French, and among the last was the Abbé. During the dinner he got on his favorite theory of the degeneracy of animals, and even of man, in America, and urged it with his usual eloquence. The Doctor at length noticing the accidental stature and position of his guests, at table, "Come," says he, "M. l'Abbé, let us try this question by the fact before us. We are here one half Americans, and one half French, and it happens that the Americans have placed themselves on one side of the table, and our French friends are on the other. Let both parties rise, and we will see on which side nature has degenerated." It happened that his American guests were Carmichael, Harmer, Humphreys, and others of the finest stature and form; while those of the other side were remarkably diminutive, and the Abbé himself particularly was a mere shrimp. He parried the appeal, however, by a complimentary admission of exceptions, among which the Doctor himself was a conspicuous one.

The Doctor and Silas Deane were in conversation one day at Passy, on the numerous errors in the Abbé's *Histoire des deux Indes,* when he happened to step in. After the usual salutations, Silas Deane said to him, "The Doctor and myself, Abbé, were just speaking of the errors of fact into which you have been led in your history." "Oh, no Sir," said the Abbé, "that is impossible. I took the greatest care not to insert a single fact for which I had not the most unquestionable authority." "Why," says Deane, "there is the story of Polly Baker, and the eloquent apology you have put into her mouth, when brought before a court of Massachusetts to suffer punishment under a law which you cite, for having had a bastard. I know there never was such a law in Massachusetts." "Be assured," said the Abbé, "you are mistaken, and that that is a true story. I do not immediately recollect indeed the particular information on which I quote it; but I am certain that I had for it unquestionable authority." Doctor Franklin, who had been for some time shaking with unrestrained laughter at the Abbé's confidence in his authority for that tale, said, "I will tell you, Abbé, the origin of that story. When I was a printer and editor of a newspaper, we were sometimes slack of news, and to amuse our customers, I used to fill up our vacant columns with anecdotes and fables, and fancies of my own, and this of Polly Baker is a story of my making, on one of these occasions." The Abbé, without the least disconcert, exclaimed with a laugh, "Oh, very well, Doctor, I had rather relate your stories than other men's truths."

---

*"The Character of George Washington" is taken
from Jefferson's letter to Dr. Walter Jones, written January 2, 1814;
the "Anecdotes of Benjamin Franklin" are taken
from a letter to Robert Walsh, written December 4, 1818.*

Benjamin Franklin

1706–1790

Benjamin Franklin—workman, printer, inventor, scientist, philosopher, and statesman—was the fifteenth child of a New England soap- and candlemaker. He was born in Boston in 1706, and attended school there till the age of ten. In Philadelphia, at seventeen, he had learned the printer's trade, and had started his career as an author in the *New England Courant*. With a promise of help from Governor Keith of Pennsylvania, he sailed for England in 1724, to get equipment to set up a printing firm of his own. The promise proved hollow, however, and he returned to Philadelphia two years later a wiser man.

Then the remarkable success story began. In 1730 Franklin was owner of his own printing shop and publisher of the *Pennsylvania Gazette*, and had become an author. In *Poor Richard's Almanack*, which he published from the early 1730's through 1757, he drew an unforgettable picture of Yankee commonsense, shrewdness, thrift, and enterprise. His pithy sayings epitomized, and helped to shape, the new American. So successful were Franklin's printing operations that he was able to retire from business at forty-two, and to devote himself to science.

Although engrossed in many enterprises, Franklin had somehow found time to study literature, history, technological problems, science, and foreign languages. His self-taught genius was eventually acknowledged by scholars and scientists in many countries. His most spectacular achievement was his demonstration—by way of a kite sailed in a thunderstorm—that lightning is electricity. His most lasting achievement may have been the founding of the American Philosophical Society in 1743, and the Academy of Philadelphia in 1751.

Franklin also found time to hold various public offices. He was

post-master general for the northern colonies (1753–74), a delegate
to the Albany Congress (1754), and twenty years later he was made
president of the Pennsylvania Executive Council. On several important diplomatic missions to England and to France, his shrewdness, wit, amiability, and scientific reputation made a strong impression, and difficult negotiations prospered.

He had sought a compromise with England, but when he saw this
was impossible, he threw all his weight behind the Revolution. He
died at the age of eighty-four, full of honor—a highly original
American, but also a very typical one.

In 1743 Franklin proposed the establishment of a Philosophical
Society. He had observed the lack of communication in what he
called "a long tract of continent." Reading newspapers from other
colonies, he became aware of intellectual interests scattered over a
wide area. It was obvious that some regular means of exchanging
ideas was needed. The model for the proposed Philosophical Society
was The Royal Society of London, which had been founded in 1660.
Franklin knew what a great part The Royal Society had played in
advancing science in England, and hoped for similar developments,
though on a smaller scale, in the New World.

Like The Royal Society, Franklin's Philosophical Society was to
combine technology with pure science, was to promote shipping,
industry, and agriculture, as well as mathematics, physics, chemistry,
and the biological sciences. He believed that science and technology
were interdependent, and that the one would fructify the other. As
science advanced, the colonies would be strengthened economically.
Life would be made far easier and richer by laborsaving machinery
and improvements in agriculture. Men might be transported from
place to place with great rapidity, he said—sustained in the air. In
short, Franklin had great hopes for technology, and they have been
fully confirmed.

*Notes from the artist: "The seated portrait of Franklin is based
upon a rare, contemporary water color. In the background are suggestions
of Franklin's private career as a printer and his public career
as a diplomat and patriot. The segmented snake, representing the colonies,
was designed by Franklin more than twenty years before the American
Revolution. The quotation is from a letter to Josiah Quincy."*

As early as 1743, Franklin proposed the founding of an educational institution—an Academy—in Philadelphia, and he projected it in a pamphlet which he himself printed in 1749. The school opened under his sponsorship in 1751.

It is well to remember that Pennsylvania had few schools at the time of Franklin; the teachers were poorly prepared and even more poorly paid. A few children of the wealthy were educated by tutors, but the rest had few opportunities. It was typical of Franklin's practical turn of mind and also of his sincerity that he not only *proposed* the establishment of the Academy but also took a keen interest in the financial arrangements which would alone make it possible. Separating well-to-do citizens from their money for educational purposes was something new and painful. Yet Franklin's efforts were successful. The school weathered financial drought and eventually became the University of Pennsylvania.

Franklin's ideas on education were a combination of old and new, and forecast the kind of education which was to prevail in the United States. He proposed that the students learn "those things that are likely to be most useful and most ornamental." The emphasis on the useful was new, and so was the provision for exercise and sports to promote health. The recommendation that the masters "look on the students as in some sort their children" and "treat them with familiarity and affection" was novel and humane.

Franklin's central idea was that learning and learning alone confers "benignity of mind" and "an ability to serve mankind, one's country, friends, and family." This ideal is worth comparing with the aims of education as expressed by other writers included in this set—Swift, Bacon, Schopenhauer, Dewey, and Faraday.

A Proposal for Promoting Useful Knowledge among the British Plantations in America

The English are possessed of a long tract of continent, from Nova Scotia to Georgia, extending north and south through different climates, having different soils, producing different plants, mines, and minerals, and capable of different improvements, manufactures, etc.

The first drudgery of settling new colonies, which confines the attention of people to mere necessaries, is now pretty well over; and there are many in every province in circumstances that set them at ease, and afford leisure to cultivate the finer arts and improve the common stock of knowledge. To such of these who are men of speculation, many hints must from time to time arise, many observations occur, which if well examined, pursued, and improved might produce discoveries to the advantage of some or all of the British plantations, or to the benefit of mankind in general.

But as from the extent of the country such persons as widely separated, and seldom can see and converse or be acquainted with each other, so that many useful particulars remain uncommunicated, die with the discoverers, and are lost to mankind; it is, to remedy this inconvenience for the future, proposed:

That one society be formed of *virtuosi* or ingenious men, residing in the several colonies, to be called The American Philosophical Society, who are to maintain a constant correspondence.

That Philadelphia, being the city nearest the center of the continent colonies, communicating with all of them northward and southward by post, and with all the islands by sea, and having the advantage of a good growing library, be the center of the Society.

That at Philadelphia there be always at least seven members, viz., a physician, a botanist, a mathematician, a chemist, a mechanician, a

533

geographer, and a general natural philosopher, besides a president, treasurer, and secretary.

That these members meet once a month, or oftener, at their own expense, to communicate to each other their observations and experiments; to receive, read, and consider such letters, communications, or queries as shall be sent from distant members; to direct the dispersing of copies of such communications as are valuable, to other distant members, in order to procure their sentiments thereupon.

That the subjects of the correspondence be: all new-discovered plants, herbs, trees, roots, their virtues, uses, etc.; methods of propagating them, and making such as are useful, but particular to some plantations, more general; improvements of vegetable juices, as ciders, wines, etc.; new methods of curing or preventing diseases; all new-discovered fossils in different countries, as mines, minerals, and quarries; new and useful improvements in any branch of mathematics; new discoveries in chemistry, such as improvements in distillation, brewing, and assaying of ores; new mechanical inventions for saving labor, as mills and carriages, and for raising and conveying of water, draining of meadows, etc.; all new arts, trades, and manufactures that may be proposed or thought of; surveys, maps, and charts of particular parts of the seacoasts or inland countries; course and junction of rivers and great roads, situation of lakes and mountains, nature of the soil and productions; new methods of improving the breed of useful animals; introducing other sorts from foreign countries; new improvements in planting, gardening, and clearing land; and all philosophical experiments that let light into the nature of things, tend to increase the power of man over matter, and multiply the conveniences or pleasures of life.

That a correspondence, already begun by some intended members, shall be kept up by this Society with the Royal Society of London, and with the Dublin Society.

That every member shall have abstracts sent him quarterly, of everything valuable communicated to the Society's Secretary at Philadelphia; free of all charge except the yearly payment hereafter mentioned.

That, by permission of the postmaster-general, such communications pass between the Secretary of the Society and the members, postage free.

That, for defraying the expense of such experiments as the Society shall judge proper to cause to be made, and other contingent charges for the common good, every member sent a piece of eight per annum to the treasurer, at Philadelphia, to form a common stock, to be disbursed by order of the President with the consent of the majority of the members that can conveniently be consulted thereupon, to such persons and places where and by whom the experiments are to be made, and otherwise as there shall be occasion; of which disbursements an exact account shall be kept, and communicated yearly to every member.

That, at the first meetings of the members at Philadelphia, such rules be formed for regulating their meetings and transactions for the general benefit as shall be convenient and necessary; to be afterwards changed and improved as there shall be occasion, wherein due regard is to be had to the advice of distant members.

That, at the end of every year, collections be made and printed of such experiments, discoveries, and improvements as may be thought of public advantage; and that every member have a copy sent him.

That the business and duty of the Secretary be to receive all letters intended for the Society, and lay them before the President and members at their meetings; to abstract, correct, and methodize such papers as require it, and as he shall be directed to do by the President, after they have been considered, debated, and digested in the Society; to enter copies thereof in the Society's books, and make out copies for distant members; to answer their letters by direction of the President, and keep records of all material transactions of the Society.

Benjamin Franklin, the writer of this Proposal, offers himself to serve the Society as their secretary till they shall be provided with one more capable.

Proposals Relating
to the Education of Youth
in Pennsylvania

ADVERTISEMENT TO THE READER

It has long been regretted as a misfortune to the youth of this province that we have no academy in which they might receive the accomplishments of a regular education. The following paper of hints towards forming a plan for that purpose is so far approved by some public-spirited gentlemen, to whom it has been privately communicated, that they have directed a number of copies to be made by the press, and properly distributed, in order to obtain the sentiments and advice of men of learning, understanding, and experience in these matters; and have determined to use their interest and best endeavours to have the scheme, when completed, carried gradually into execution; in which they have reason to believe they shall have the hearty concurrence and assistance of many who are well-wishers to their country. Those who incline to favor the design with their advice, either as to the parts of learning to be taught, the order of study, the method of teaching, the economy of the school, or any other matter of importance to the success of the undertaking are desired to communicate their sentiments as soon as may be, by letter directed to B. FRANKLIN, *Printer*, in Philadelphia.

PROPOSALS

The good education of youth has been esteemed by wise men in all ages as the surest foundation of the happiness both of private families and of commonwealths. Almost all governments have therefore made it a principal object of their attention to establish and endow with proper revenues such seminaries of learning as might supply the succeeding age with men qualified to serve the public with honor to themselves, and to their country.

Many of the first settlers of these provinces were men who had received a good education in Europe, and to their wisdom and good management we owe much of our present prosperity. But their hands were full, and they could not do all things. The present race are not thought to be generally of equal ability: for though the American youth are allowed not to want capacity, yet the best capacities require cultivation, it being truly with them as with the best ground, which unless well tilled and sowed with profitable seed produces only ranker weeds.

That we may obtain the advantages arising from an increase in knowledge, and prevent as much as may be the mischievous consequences that would attend a general ignorance among us, the following hints are offered towards forming a plan for the education of the youth of Pennsylvania, viz.

It is proposed:

That some persons of leisure and public spirit apply for a charter by which they may be incorporated, with power to erect an academy for the education of youth, to govern the same, provide masters, make rules, receive donations, purchase lands, etc., and to add to their number, from time to time, such other persons as they shall judge suitable.

That the members of the corporation make it their pleasure, and in some degree their business, to visit the Academy often, encourage and countenance the youth, countenance and assist the masters, and by all means in their power advance the usefulness and reputation of the design; that they look on the students as in some sort their children, treat them with familiarity and affection, and, when they have behaved well, and gone through their studies, and are to enter the world, zealously unite, and make all the interest that can be made to establish them, whether in business, offices, marriages, or any other thing for their advantage, preferably to all other persons whatsoever even of equal merit.

And if men may, and frequently do, catch such a taste for cultivating flowers, for planting, grafting, inoculating [grafting], and the like, as to despise all other amusements for their sake, why may not we expect they should acquire a relish for that more useful culture of young minds? Thompson says,

> 'Tis joy to see the human blossoms blow,
> When infant reason grows apace, and calls
> For the kind hand of an assiduous care.
> Delightful task! to rear the tender thought,

> To teach the young idea how to shoot;
> To pour the fresh instruction o'er the mind,
> To breathe th' enliv'ning spirit, and to fix
> The generous purpose in the glowing breast.

That a house be provided for the Academy, if not in the town, not many miles from it; the situation high and dry, and if it may be, not far from a river, having a garden, orchard, meadow, and a field or two.

That the house be furnished with a library (if in the country; if in the town, the town libraries may serve) with maps of all countries, globes, some mathematical instruments, and apparatus for experiments in natural philosophy, and for mechanics; prints of all kinds, prospects, buildings, machines, etc.

That the rector be a man of good understanding, good morals, diligent and patient, learned in the languages and sciences, and a correct pure speaker and writer of the English tongue; to have such tutors under him as shall be necessary.

That the boarding scholars diet together, plainly, temperately, and frugally.

That, to keep them in health, and to strengthen and render active their bodies, they be frequently exercised in running, leaping, wrestling, and swimming, etc.

That they have peculiar habits to distinguish them from other youth, if the Academy be in or near the town; for this, among other reasons, that their behavior may be the better observed.

As to their studies, it would be well if they could be taught everything that is useful, and everything that is ornamental: but art is long, and their time is short. It is therefore proposed that they learn those things that are likely to be most useful and most ornamental. Regard being had to the several professions for which they are intended.

All should be taught to write a fair hand, and swift, as that is useful for all. And with it may be learned something of drawing, by imitation of prints, and some of the first principles of perspective.

Arithmetic, accounts, and some of the first principles of geometry and astronomy.

The English language might be taught by grammar; in which some of our best writers, as Tillotson, Addison, Pope, Algernon Sidney, Cato's Letters, etc., should be classics: the styles principally to be cultivated being the clear and the concise. Reading should also be taught, and pronouncing, properly, distinctly, emphatically; not with an even tone, which underdoes, nor a theatrical, which overdoes nature.

To form their style they should be put on writing letters to each other, making abstracts of what they read; or writing the same things in their own words; telling or writing stories lately read, in their own expressions. All to be revised and corrected by the tutor, who should give his reasons, and explain the force and import of words, etc.

To form their pronunciation they may be put on making declamations, repeating speeches, delivering orations, etc.; the tutor assisting at the rehearsals, teaching, advising, correcting their accent, etc.

But if history be made a constant part of their reading, such as the translations of the Greek and Roman historians, and the modern histories of ancient Greece and Rome, etc., may not almost all kinds of useful knowledge be that way introduced to advantage, and with pleasure to the student? As

Geography, by reading with maps, and being required to point out the places where the greatest actions were done, to give their old and new names, with the bounds, situation, extent of the countries concerned, etc.

Chronology, by the help of Helvicus or some other writer of the kind, who will enable them to tell when those events happened, what princes were contemporaries, what states or famous men flourished about that time, etc. The several principal epochs to be first well fixed in their memories.

Ancient customs, religious and civil, being frequently mentioned in history, will give occasion for explaining them; in which the prints of medals, basso-relievos, and ancient monuments will greatly assist.

Morality, by descanting and making continual observations on the causes of the rise or fall of any man's character, fortune, power, etc. mentioned in history; the advantages of temperance, order, frugality, industry, perseverance, etc. Indeed, the general natural tendency of reading good history must be to fix in the minds of youth deep impressions of the beauty and usefulness of virtue of all kinds, public spirit, fortitude, etc.

History will show the wonderful effects of oratory in governing, turning, and leading great bodies of mankind, armies, cities, nations. When the minds of youth are struck with admiration at this, then is the time to give them the principles of that art which they will study with taste and application. Then they may be made acquainted with the best models among the ancients, their beauties being particularly pointed out to them. Modern political oratory being chiefly performed by the pen and press, its advantages over the ancient in some respects are to be shown; as that its effects are more extensive, more lasting, etc.

History will also afford frequent opportunities of showing the necessity of a public religion, from its usefulness to the public; the advantage of a religious character among private persons; the mischiefs of superstition, etc.; and the excellency of the Christian religion above all others ancient or modern.

History will also give occasion to expatiate on the advantage of civil orders and constitutions; how men and their properties are protected by joining in societies and establishing government; their industry encouraged and rewarded, arts invented, and life made more comfortable: the advantages of liberty, mischiefs of licentiousness, benefits arising from good laws and a due execution of justice, etc. Thus may the first principles of sound politics be fixed in the minds of youth.

On historical occasions, questions of right and wrong, justice and injustice will naturally arise, and may be put to youth, which they may debate in conversation and in writing. When they ardently desire victory, for the sake of the praise attending it, they will begin to feel the want, and be sensible of the use of logic, or the art of reasoning to discover truth, and of arguing to defend it, and convince adversaries. This would be the time to acquaint them with the principles of that art. Grotius, Pufendorf, and some other writers of the same kind may be used on these occasions to decide their disputes. Public disputes warm the imagination, whet the industry, and strengthen the natural abilities.

When youth are told that the great men whose lives and actions they read in history spoke two of the best languages that ever were, the most expressive, copious, beautiful; and that the finest writings, the most correct compositions, the most perfect productions of human wit and wisdom are in those languages, which have endured ages, and will endure while there are men; that no translation can do them justice, or give the pleasure found in reading the originals; that those languages contain all science; that one of them is become almost universal, being the language of learned men in all countries; that to understand them is a distinguishing ornament, etc., they may be thereby made desirous of learning those languages, and their industry sharpened in the acquisition of them. All intended for divinity should be taught the Latin and Greek; for physics, the Latin, Greek, and French; for law, the Latin and French; merchants, the French, German, and Spanish: And though all should not be compelled to learn Latin, Greek, or the modern foreign languages, yet none that have an ardent desire to learn them should be refused; their English, arithmetic, and other studies absolutely necessary being at the same time not neglected.

If the new Universal History were also read, it would give a connected idea of human affairs, so far as it goes, which should be followed by the best modern histories, particularly of our mother country; then of these colonies, which should be accompanied with observations on their rise, increase, use to Great Britain, encouragements, discouragements, etc., the means to make them flourish, secure their liberties, etc.

With the history of men, times, and nations should be read at proper hours or days some of the best histories of nature, which would not only be delightful to youth, and furnish them with matter for their letters, etc., as well as other history, but afterwards of great use to them, whether they are merchants, handicraftsmen, or divines; enabling the first the better to understand many commodities, drugs, etc.; the second to improve his trade or handicraft by new mixtures, materials, etc.; and the last to adorn his discourses by beautiful comparisons, and strengthen them by new proofs of divine providence. The conversation of all will be improved by it, as occasions frequently occur of making natural observations, which are instructive, agreeable, and entertaining in almost all companies. Natural history will also afford opportunities of introducing many observations relating to the preservation of health which may be afterwards of great use. Arbuthnot on air and aliment, Sanctorius on perspiration, Lémery on foods, and some others may now be read, and a very little explanation will make them sufficiently intelligible to youth.

While they are reading natural history, might not a little gardening, planting, grafting, inoculating, etc., be taught and practiced; and now and then excursions made to the neighboring plantations of the best farmers, their methods observed and reasoned upon for the information of youth? The improvement of agriculture being useful to all, and skill in it no disparagement to any.

The history of commerce, of the invention of arts, rise of manufactures, progress of trade, change of its seats, with the reasons, causes, etc., may also be made entertaining to youth, and will be useful to all. And this, with the accounts in other history of the prodigious force and effect of engines and machines used in war, will naturally introduce a desire to be instructed in mechanics, and to be informed of the principles of that art by which weak men perform such wonders, labor is saved, manufactures expedited, etc. This will be the time to show them prints of ancient and modern machines, to explain them, to let them be copied, and to give lectures in mechanical philosophy.

With the whole should be constantly inculcated and cultivated that benignity of mind which shows itself in searching for and seizing every opportunity to serve and to oblige; and is the foundation of what is called good breeding, highly useful to the possessor, and most agreeable to all.

The idea of what is true merit should also be often presented to youth, explained and impressed on their minds, as consisting in an inclination joined with an ability to serve mankind, one's country, friends and family; which ability is (with the blessing of God) to be acquired or greatly increased by true learning, and should indeed be the great aim and end of all learning.

Jean de Crèvecoeur

1735–1813

Born at Caen, Normandy, January 31, 1735, Michel Guillaume Jean de Crèvecoeur (the name in French means "heartbreak") got his later schooling in England and served four years as an officer and map maker under General Montcalm in Canada. Soon after 1759, when Wolfe broke the French power at Quebec, Crèvecoeur seems to have moved down into the American colonies. He changed his name to J. Hector St. John, became a citizen, and married Mehitable Tippet of Yonkers, New York.

They settled on a large farm in Orange County, New York, and had three children. There Crèvecoeur must have written his *Letters from an American Farmer*. The Revolution brought a day-and-night terror of Indian raids and made enemies of friends and neighbors (the farmer in the book actually decides to take his family and live with friendly Indians). Crèvecoeur was apparently called back to France by his father. He took his eldest son along. They were imprisoned by the British in New York. When they finally sailed, their ship was wrecked off the Irish coast.

In London, Crèvecoeur sold his book for thirty guineas (about $153). Quickly it went through eight editions in five countries. It was published in Philadelphia in 1793. He became a celebrated man, admired by Hazlitt, Lamb, and Coleridge, the friend of Franklin, Buffon, and Mme D'Houdetot. Crèvecoeur translated and enlarged his book in French. Back in America as consul to three of the new states in 1784, he found his wife dead and his younger children in the care of Boston friends.

He brought the children together in New York, set up a packet-ship service between France and America, and went back to studying botany. Later he fattened the French *Letters* into a three-volume

543

work. He was recalled to France in 1790. There he wrote a second three-volume book, this one about his travels in Pennsylvania and New York. Crèvecoeur died in 1813. In the 1920's, a batch of his unpublished English essays came to light in a French attic. The publication of these, coupled with D. H. Lawrence's praise of him, revived his reputation.

H e seems so familiar, such a cheerful, everyday friend, that we can hardly believe he was alive when the United States was born. He reminds us of Jefferson and of Rousseau. They share the tone of the Age of Reason. In this tone, we feel the classical idealism of Greece and Rome, strained through Plutarch. Like Virgil and Horace, Crèvecoeur lived in a time of wars and civil wars. The farm in Orange County, like Horace's farm in the Sabine Hills, was his moment of paradise. But already there was a strain of the new Romantic century in him. It came out strongly in his views of nature. He was an amateur in that great company of early American naturalists—Audubon, John and William Bartram, Alexander Wilson, Rafinesque—who discovered an earthly heaven in their new country. Thoreau would come after them.

As a man of the Age of Reason, Crèvecoeur was also a man of ideas. These come to a kind of focus in his essay "The Making of Americans," in *Letters from an American Farmer*. Perhaps he was not the first to ask that question, but he seems to have been the first to make a real try at answering it. He brings an imaginary Englishman to look at us and thereby displays the already broad difference between Englishman and American. We are blended together, Crèvecoeur writes, out of all kinds of Europeans. This is the first we hear of the melting pot. He thinks—and here, perhaps, he was largely mistaken—that religions will combine as nationalities do.

"Some few towns excepted," he says, "we are all tillers of the earth. . . ." So he thinks of Americans, by and large, as farmers, and of labor as a good. He speaks of a man's liberty and happiness on his own acres; of his love for wife and children, and the domestic virtue that springs from this; of the mild laws and encouraging government that make it possible; of the equality each man feels in rejecting the aristocracy of Europe. He sees the hideous evil and the still unjust gentleness of slavery. He observes the one and the many, and shows us half a dozen typical immigrants. Tocqueville,[1] who visited the United States a generation later, in the 1830's, gives us a wider and more thoughtful view of democracy's workings and shows us the American types already in being.

What would Crèvecoeur think of us now, in the second half of the twentieth century? We are largely gathered in cities. He felt that our hope lay in freedom on the land. Like so many other eighteenth- and nineteenth-century Americans, he thought of country living as more favorable to virtue. Was he right, then or now? Would he consider our tract houses in the suburbs much the same thing as farmers living on their own land? Would he feel that we have abolished the whole injustice of slavery, or that there is more yet to be done? Would he find reasons for the bigness of our government, the complexity of our techniques, our ambitions on the moon? How would he feel the first time he encountered a parking meter or took off in a jet airplane? Read him, this eighteenth-century American who had such high hopes for us, and see if you can guess whether we would please him or disappoint him.

---

[1] See "Observations on American Life and Government" in Vol. 6, pp. 564–690, in this set.

The Making of Americans

from *Letters from an American Farmer*

I wish I could be acquainted with the feelings and thoughts which must agitate the heart and present themselves to the mind of an enlightened Englishman when he first lands on this continent. He must greatly rejoice that he lived at a time to see this fair country discovered and settled; he must necessarily feel a share of national pride when he views the chain of settlements which embellishes these extended shores. When he says to himself, this is the work of my countrymen, who, when convulsed by factions, afflicted by a variety of miseries and wants, restless and impatient, took refuge here. They brought along with them their national genius, to which they principally owe what liberty they enjoy, and what substance they possess. Here he sees the industry of his native country displayed in a new manner, and traces in their works the embryos of all the arts, sciences, and ingenuity which flourish in Europe. Here he beholds fair cities, substantial villages, extensive fields, an immense country filled with decent houses, good roads, orchards, meadows, and bridges, where a hundred years ago all was wild, woody, and uncultivated! What a train of pleasing ideas this fair spectacle must suggest; it is a prospect which must inspire a good citizen with the most heartfelt pleasure. The difficulty consists in the manner of viewing so extensive a scene. He is arrived on a new continent; a modern society offers itself to his contemplation, different from what he had hitherto seen. It is not composed, as in Europe, of great lords who possess everything, and of a herd of people who have nothing. Here are no aristocratical families, no courts, no kings, no bishops, no ecclesiastical dominion, no invisible power giving to a few a very visible one; no great manufacturers employing thousands, no great refinements of luxury. The rich and the poor are not so far removed from each other as they are in Europe. Some few towns excepted, we are all tillers of the earth, from Nova Scotia to West Florida. We are a people of cultivators, scattered over an immense territory, communicating with each other by means of good roads and navigable rivers, united by the silken bands of mild government, all respecting the laws without dreading their power, because they are equitable. We are all animated with the spirit of an industry which is unfettered and unrestrained, because each person works for himself. If he travels through our rural districts he views not the hostile castle and the haughty mansion, contrasted with the clay-built hut and miserable cabin, where cattle and men help to keep each other warm, and dwell in meanness, smoke, and indigence. A pleasing uniformity of decent competence appears throughout our habitations. The meanest of our log houses is a dry and comfortable habitation. Lawyer or merchant are the fairest titles our towns afford; that of a farmer is the only appellation of the rural inhabitants of our country. It must take some time ere he can reconcile himself to our dictionary, which is but short in words of dignity and names of honor. There, on a Sunday, he sees a congregation of respectable farmers and their wives, all clad in neat homespun, well mounted or riding in their own humble wagons. There is not among them an esquire, saving the unlettered magistrate. There he sees a parson as simple as his flock, a farmer who does not riot on the labor of others. We have no princes for whom we toil, starve, and bleed: we are the most perfect society now existing in the world. Here man is free as he ought to be; nor is this pleasing equality so transitory as many others are. Many ages will not see the shores of our great lakes replenished with inland nations, nor the unknown bounds of North America entirely peopled. Who can tell how far it extends? Who can tell the millions of men whom it will feed and contain? for no European foot has as yet traveled half the extent of this mighty continent!

The next wish of this traveler will be to know whence came all these people? They are a mixture of English, Scotch, Irish, French, Dutch, Germans, and Swedes. From this promiscuous breed, that race now called Americans has arisen. The eastern provinces must indeed be excepted, as being the unmixed descendants of Englishmen. I have heard many wish that they had been more intermixed also: for my part, I am no wisher, and think it much better as it has happened. They exhibit a most conspicuous figure in this great and variegated picture; they too enter for a great share in the pleasing perspective displayed in these thirteen provinces. I know it is fashionable to reflect on them, but I respect them for what they have done; for the accuracy and wisdom with which they have settled their territory; for the decency of their manners; for their early love of letters; their ancient college, the first in this hemisphere; for their industry, which to me who am but a farmer is the criterion of everything. There never was a people, situated as they are, who with so ungrateful a soil have done more in so short a time. Do you think that the monarchical ingredients which are more prevalent in other governments have purged them from all foul stains? Their histories assert the contrary.

In this great American asylum, the poor of Europe have by some means met together, and in consequence of various causes; to what purpose should they ask one another what countrymen they are? Alas, two-thirds of them had no country. Can a wretch who wanders about, who works and starves, whose life is a continual scene of sore affliction or pinching penury; can that man call England or any other kingdom his country? A country that had no bread for him, whose fields procured him no harvest, who met with nothing but the frowns of the rich, the severity of the laws, with jails and punishments; who owned not a single foot of the extensive surface of this planet? No! urged by a variety of motives, here they came. Everything has tended to regenerate them; new laws, a new mode of living, a new social system; here they are become men: in Europe they were as so many useless plants, wanting vegetative mold and refreshing showers; they withered, and were mowed down by want, hunger, and war; but now by the power of transplantation, like all other plants they have taken root and flourished! Formerly they were not numbered in any civil lists of their country, except in those of the poor; here they rank as citizens. By what invisible power has this surprising metamorphosis been performed? By that of the laws and that of their industry. The laws, the indulgent laws, protect them as they arrive, stamping on them the symbol of adoption; they receive ample rewards for their labors; these accumulated rewards procure them lands; those lands confer on them the title of freemen, and to that title every benefit is affixed which men can possibly require. This is the great operation daily performed by our laws. From whence proceed these laws? From our government. Whence the government? It is derived from the original genius and strong desire of the people ratified and confirmed by the crown. This is the great chain which links us all, this is the picture which every province exhibits, Nova Scotia excepted. There the crown has done all; either there were no people who had genius, or it was not much attended to: the consequence is that the province is very thinly inhabited indeed; the power of the crown in conjunction with the mosquitoes has prevented men from settling there. Yet some parts of it flourished once, and it contained a mild, harmless set of people. But for the fault of a few leaders, the whole were banished. The greatest political error the crown ever committed in America was to cut off men from a country which wanted nothing but men!

What attachment can a poor European emigrant have for a country where he had nothing? The knowledge of the language, the love of a few kindred as poor as himself were the only cords that tied him: his country is now that which gives him land, bread, protection, and consequence: *Ubi panis ibi patria* ["Where there is bread, there is my country"] is the motto of all emigrants. What then is the American, this new man? He is either a European or the descendant of a European, hence that strange mixture of blood, which you will find in no other country. I could point out to you a family whose grandfather was an Englishman, whose wife was Dutch, whose son married a French woman, and whose present four sons have now four wives of different nations. He is an American who, leaving behind him all his ancient prejudices and manners, receives new ones from the new mode of life he has embraced, the new government he obeys, and the new rank he holds. He becomes an American by being received in the broad lap of our great Alma Mater. Here individuals of all nations are melted into a new race of men, whose labors and posterity will one day cause great changes in the world. Americans are the western pilgrims, who are carrying along with them that great mass of arts, sciences, vigor, and industry which began long since in the east; they will finish the great circle. The Americans were once scattered all over Europe; here they are incorporated into one of the finest systems of population which has ever appeared, and which will hereafter become distinct by the power of the different climates they inhabit. The American ought therefore to love this country much better than that wherein either he or his forefathers were born. Here the rewards of his industry follow with equal steps the progress of his labor; his labor is founded on the basis of nature, self-interest; can it want a stronger allurement? Wives and children, who before in vain demanded of him a morsel of bread, now, fat and frolicsome, gladly help their father to clear those fields whence exuberant crops are to arise to feed and to clothe them all; without any part being claimed, either by a despotic prince, a rich abbot, or a mighty lord. Here religion demands but little of him; a small voluntary salary to the minister, and gratitude to God; can he refuse these? The American is a new man, who acts upon new principles; he must therefore entertain new ideas, and form new opinions. From involuntary idleness, servile dependence, penury, and useless labor, he has passed to toils of a very different nature, rewarded by ample subsistence. This is an American.

British America is divided into many provinces, forming a large association scattered along a coast 1500 miles extent and about 200 wide. This society I would fain examine, at least such as it appears in the middle provinces; if it does not afford that variety of tinges and gradations which may be observed in Europe, we have colors peculiar to ourselves. For instance, it is natural to conceive that those who live near the sea must be very different from those who live in the woods; the intermediate space will afford a separate and distinct class.

Men are like plants; the goodness and flavor of the fruit proceeds from the peculiar soil and exposition in which they grow. We are nothing but what we derive from the air we breathe, the climate we inhabit, the government we obey, the system of religion we profess, and the nature of our employment. Here you will find but few crimes; these have acquired as yet no root among us. I wish I were able to trace all my ideas; if my ignorance prevents me from describing them properly, I hope I shall be able to delineate a few of the outlines, which are all I propose.

Those who live near the sea feed more on fish than on flesh, and often encounter that boisterous element. This renders them more bold and enterprising; this leads them to neglect the confined occupations of the land. They see and converse with a variety of people; their intercourse with mankind becomes extensive. The sea inspires them with a love of traffic, a desire of transporting produce from one place to another; and leads them to a variety of resources which supply the place of labor. Those who inhabit the middle settlements, by far the most numerous, must be very different; the simple cultivation of the earth purifies them, but the indulgences of the government, the soft remonstrances of religion, the rank of independent freeholders must necessarily inspire them with sentiments very little known in Europe among people of the same class. What do I say? Europe has no such class of men; the early knowledge they acquire, the early bargains they make, give them a great degree of sagacity. As freemen they will be litigious; pride and obstinacy are often the cause of lawsuits; the nature of our laws and governments may be another. As citizens it is easy to imagine that they will carefully read the newspapers, enter into every political disquisition, freely blame or censure governors and others. As farmers they will be careful and anxious to get as much as they can, because what they get is their own. As northern men they will love the cheerful cup. As Christians, religion curbs them not in their opinions; the general indulgence leaves every one to think for himself in spiritual matters; the laws inspect our actions, our thoughts are left to God. Industry, good living, selfishness, litigiousness, country politics, the pride of freemen, religious indifference are their characteristics. If you recede still farther from the sea, you will come into more modern settlements; they exhibit the same strong lineaments in a ruder appearance. Religion seems to have still less influence, and their manners are less improved.

Now we arrive near the great woods, near the last inhabited districts; there men seem to be placed still farther beyond the reach of government, which in some measure leaves them to themselves. How can it pervade every corner; as they were driven there by misfortunes, necessity of beginnings, desire of acquiring large tracts of land, idleness, frequent want of economy, ancient debts, the reunion of such people does not afford a very pleasing spectacle. When discord, want of unity and friendship, when either drunkenness or idleness prevail in such remote districts, contention, inactivity, and wretchedness must ensue. There are not the same remedies to these evils as in a long-established community. The few magistrates they have are in general little better than the rest; they are often in a perfect state of war; that of man against man, sometimes decided by blows, sometimes by means of the law; that of man against every wild inhabitant of these venerable woods, of which they are come to dispossess them. There men appear to be no better than carnivorous animals of a superior rank, living on the flesh of wild animals when they can catch them, and when they are not able, they subsist on grain. He who would wish to see America in its proper light, and have a true idea of its feeble beginnings and barbarous rudiments, must visit our extended line of frontiers where the last settlers dwell, and where he may see the first labors of settlement, the mode of clearing the earth, in all their different appearances; where men are left wholly dependent on their native tempers, and on the spur of uncertain industry, which often fails when not sanctified by the efficacy of a few moral rules. There, remote from the power of example, and check of shame, many families exhibit the most hideous parts of our society. They are a kind of forlorn hope, preceding by ten or twelve years the most respectable army of veterans which come after them. In that space, prosperity will polish some, vice and the law will drive off the rest, who, uniting again with others like themselves, will recede still farther, making room for more industrious people, who will finish their improvements, convert the log house into a convenient habitation, and rejoicing that the first heavy labors are finished, will change in a few years that hitherto barbarous country into a fine, fertile, well-regulated district. Such is our progress, such is the march of the Europeans toward the interior parts of this continent. In all societies there are offcasts; this impure part serves as our precursors or pioneers; my father himself was one of that class, but he came upon honest principles, and was therefore one of the few who held fast; by good conduct and temperance, he transmitted to me his fair inheritance, when not above one in fourteen of his contemporaries had the same good fortune.

Forty years ago this smiling country was thus inhabited; it is now purged, a general decency of manners prevails throughout, and such has been the fate of our best countries.

Exclusive of those general characteristics, each province has its own, founded on the government, climate, mode of husbandry, customs, and peculiarity of circumstances. Europeans submit insensibly to these great powers, and become, in the course of a few generations, not only Americans in general, but either Pennsylvanians, Virginians, or provincials under some other name. Whoever traverses the continent must easily observe those strong differences, which will grow more evident in time. The inhabitants of Canada, Massachusetts, the middle provinces, the southern ones will be as different as their climates; their only points of unity will be those of religion and language.

As I have endeavored to show you how Europeans become Americans, it may not be disagreeable to show you likewise how the various Christian sects introduced wear out, and how religious indifference becomes prevalent. When any considerable number of a particular sect happen to dwell contiguous to each other, they immediately erect a temple, and there worship the Divinity agreeably to their own peculiar ideas. Nobody disturbs them. If any new sect springs up in Europe, it may happen that many of its professors will come and settle in America. As they bring their zeal with them, they are at liberty to make proselytes if they can, and to build a meeting and to follow the dictates of their consciences; for neither the government nor any other power interferes. If they are peaceable subjects, and are industrious, what is it to their neighbors how and in what manner they think fit to address their prayers to the Supreme Being? But if the sectaries are not settled close together, if they are mixed with other denominations, their zeal will cool for want of fuel, and will be extinguished in a little time. Then the Americans become as to religion, what they are as to country, allied to all. In them the name of Englishman, Frenchman, and European is lost, and in like manner, the strict modes of Christianity as practised in Europe are lost also. This effect will extend itself still farther hereafter, and though this may appear to you as a strange idea, yet it is a very true one. I shall be able perhaps hereafter to explain myself better, in the meanwhile, let the following example serve as my first justification.

Let us suppose you and I to be traveling; we observe that in this house, to the right, lives a Catholic, who prays to God as he has been taught, and believes in transubstantiation; he works and raises wheat, he has a large family of children, all hale and robust; his belief, his prayers offend nobody. About one mile farther on the same road, his next neighbor may be a good honest plodding German Lutheran, who addresses himself to the same God, the God of all, agreeably to the modes he has been educated in, and believes in consubstantiation; by so doing he scandalizes nobody; he also works in his fields, embellishes the earth, clears swamps, etc. What has the world to do with his Lutheran principles? He persecutes nobody, and nobody persecutes him; he visits his neighbors, and his neighbors visit him. Next to him lives a seceder, the most enthusiastic of all sectaries; his zeal is hot and fiery, but separated as he is from others of the same complexion, he has no congregation of his own to resort to, where he might cabal and mingle religious pride with worldly obstinacy. He likewise raises good crops, his house is handsomely painted, his orchard is one of the fairest in the neighborhood. How does it concern the welfare of the country, or of the province at large, what this man's religious sentiments are, or really whether he has any at all? He is a good farmer; he is a sober, peaceable, good citizen: William Penn himself would not wish for more. This is the visible character, the invisible one is only guessed at, and is nobody's business. Next again lives a Low Dutchman, who implicitly believes the rules laid down by the synod of Dort. He conceives no other idea of a clergyman than that of an hired man; if he does his work well he will pay him the stipulated sum; if not he will dismiss him, and do without his sermons, and let his church be shut up for years. But notwithstanding this coarse idea, you will find his house and farm to be the neatest in all the country; and you will judge by his wagon and fat horses that he thinks more of the affairs of this world than of those of the next. He is sober and laborious; therefore he is all he ought to be as to the affairs of this life; as for those of the next, he must trust to the great Creator. Each of these people instruct their children as well as they can, but these instructions are feeble compared to those which are given to the youth of the poorest class in Europe. Their children will therefore grow up less zealous and more indifferent in matters of religion than their parents. The foolish vanity, or rather the fury of making proselytes, is unknown here; they have no time, the seasons call for all their attention, and thus in a few years, this mixed neighborhood will exhibit a strange religious medley that will be neither pure Catholicism nor pure Calvinism. A very perceptible indifference even in the first generation will become apparent; and it may happen that the daughter of the Catholic will marry the son of the seceder, and settle by themselves at a distance from their parents. What religious education will they give their children? A very imperfect one. If there happens to be in the neighborhood any place of worship, we will suppose a Quakers' meeting; rather than not show their fine clothes, they will go to it, and some of them may perhaps attach themselves to that society. Others will remain in a perfect state of indifference; the children of these zealous parents will not be able to tell what their religious principles are, and their grandchildren still less. The neighborhood of a place of worship generally leads them to it, and the action of going thither is the strongest evidence they can give of their attachment to any sect. The Quakers are the only people who retain a fondness for their own mode of worship; for be they ever so far separated from each other, they hold a sort of communion with the society, and seldom depart from its rules, at least in this country. Thus all sects are mixed as well as all nations; thus religious indifference is imperceptibly disseminated from one end of the continent to the other; which is at present one of the strongest characteristics of the Americans. Where this will reach no one can tell; perhaps it may leave a vacuum fit to receive other systems. Persecution, religious pride, the love of contradiction are the food of what the world commonly calls religion. These motives have ceased here: zeal in Europe is confined, here it evaporates in the great distance it has to travel; there it is a grain of powder enclosed, here it burns away in the open air, and consumes without effect.

But to return to our backsettlers. I must tell you that there is something in the proximity of the woods which is very singular. It is with men as it is with the plants and animals that grow and live in the forests; they are entirely different from those that live in the plains. I will candidly tell you all my thoughts, but you are not to expect that I shall advance any reasons. By living in or near the woods, their actions are regulated by the wildness of the neighborhood. The deer often come to eat their grain, the wolves to destroy their sheep, the bears to kill their hogs, the foxes to catch their poultry. This surrounding hostility immediately puts the gun into their hands; they watch these animals, they kill some; and thus by defending their property, they soon become professed hunters; this is the progress; once hunters, farewell to the plow. The chase renders them ferocious, gloomy, and unsociable: a hunter wants no neighbor; he rather hates them, because he dreads the competition. In a little time their success in the woods makes them neglect their tillage. They trust to the natural fecundity of the earth, and therefore do little; carelessness in fencing often exposes what little they sow to destruction; they are not at home to watch; in order therefore to make up the deficiency, they go oftener to the woods. That new mode of life brings along with it a new set of manners, which I cannot easily describe. These new manners, being grafted on the old stock, produce a strange sort of lawless profligacy, the impressions of which are indelible. The manners of the Indian natives are respectable, compared with this European medley. Their wives and children live in sloth and inactivity; and having no proper pursuits, you may judge what education the latter receive. Their tender minds have nothing else to contemplate but the example of their parents; like them they grow up a mongrel breed, half civilized, half savage, except nature stamps on them some constitutional propensities. That rich, that voluptuous sentiment is gone that struck them so forcibly; the possession of their freeholds no longer conveys to their minds the same pleasure and pride. To all these reasons you must add their lonely situation, and you cannot imagine what an effect on manners the great distances they live from each other has! Consider one of the last settlements in its first view: of what is it composed? Europeans who have not that sufficient share of knowledge they ought to have in order to prosper; people who have suddenly passed from oppression, dread of government, and fear of laws into the unlimited freedom of the woods. This sudden change must have a very great effect on most men, and on that class particularly. Eating of wild meat, whatever you may think, tends to alter their temper, though all the proof I can adduce is that I have seen it; and having no place of worship to resort to, what little society this might afford is denied them. The Sunday meetings, exclusive of religious benefits, were the only social bonds that might have inspired them with some degree of emulation in neatness. Is it then surprising to see men thus situated, immersed in great and heavy labors, degenerate a little? It is rather a wonder the effect is not more diffusive. The Moravians and the Quakers are the only instances in exception to what I have advanced. The first never settle singly, it is a colony of the society which emigrates; they carry with them their forms, worship, rules, and decency: the others never begin so hard, they are always able to buy improvements, in which there is a great advantage, for by that time the country is recovered from its first barbarity. Thus our bad people are those who are half cultivators and half hunters; and the worst of them are those who have degenerated altogether into the hunting state. As old plowmen and new men of the woods, as Europeans and new made Indians, they contract the vices of both; they adopt the moroseness and ferocity of a native, without his mildness, or even his industry at home. If manners are not refined, at least they are rendered simple and inoffensive by tilling the earth; all our wants are supplied by it, our time is divided between labor and rest, and leaves none for the commission of great misdeeds. As hunters it is divided between the toil of the chase, the idleness of repose, or the indulgence of inebriation. Hunting is but a licentious idle life, and if it does not always pervert good dispositions, yet, when it is united with bad luck, it leads to want: want stimulates that propensity to rapacity and injustice, too natural to needy men, which is the fatal gradation. After this explanation of the effects which follow by living in the woods, shall we yet vainly flatter ourselves with the hope of converting the Indians? We should rather begin with converting our backsettlers; and now if I dare mention the name of religion, its sweet accents would be lost in the immensity of these woods. Men thus placed are not fit either to receive or remember its mild instructions; they want temples and ministers, but as soon as men cease to remain at home, and begin to lead an erratic life, let them be either tawny or white, they cease to be its disciples.

Thus have I faintly and imperfectly endeavored to trace our society from the sea to our woods! Yet you must not imagine that every person who moves back acts upon the same principles, or falls into the same degeneracy. Many families carry with them all their decency of conduct, purity of morals, and respect of religion; but these are scarce, the power of example is sometimes irresistible. Even among these backsettlers, their depravity is greater or less, according to what nation or province they belong. Were I to adduce proofs of this, I might be accused of partiality. If there happen to be some rich intervals, some fertile bottoms, in those remote districts, the people will there prefer tilling the land to hunting, and will attach themselves to it; but even on these fertile spots you may plainly perceive the inhabitants to acquire a great degree of rusticity and selfishness.

It is in consequence of this straggling situation, and the astonishing power it has on manners, that the backsettlers of both the Carolinas, Virginia, and many other parts have been long a set of lawless people; it has been even dangerous to travel among them. Government can do nothing in so extensive a country; better it should wink at these irregularities than that it should use means inconsistent with its usual mildness. Time will efface those stains: in proportion as the great body of population approaches them they will reform, and become polished and subordinate. Whatever has been said of the four New England provinces, no such degeneracy of manners has ever tarnished their annals; their backsettlers have been kept within the bounds of decency, and government, by means of wise laws, and by the influence of religion. What a detestable idea such people must have given to the natives of the Europeans! They trade with them, the worst of people are permitted to do that which none but persons of the best characters should be employed in. They get drunk with them, and often defraud the Indians. Their avarice, removed from the eyes of their superiors, knows no bounds; and aided by a little superiority of knowledge, these traders deceive them, and even sometimes shed blood. Hence those shocking violations, those sudden devastations which have so often stained our frontiers, when hundreds of innocent people have been sacrificed for the crimes of a few. It was in consequence of such behavior that the Indians took the hatchet against the Virginians in 1774. Thus are our first steps trod, thus are our first trees felled, in general, by the most vicious of our people; and thus the path is opened for the arrival of a second and better class, the true American freeholders; the most respectable set of people in this part of the world: respectable for their industry, their happy independence, the great share of freedom they possess, the good regulation of their families, and for extending the trade and the dominion of our mother country.

Europe contains hardly any other distinctions but lords and tenants; this fair country alone is settled by freeholders, the possessors of the soil they cultivate, members of the government they obey, and the framers of their own laws by means of their representatives. This is a thought which you have taught me to cherish; our difference from Europe, far from diminishing, rather adds to our usefulness and consequence as men and subjects. Had our forefathers remained there, they would only have crowded it, and perhaps prolonged those convulsions which had shook it so long. Every industrious European who transports himself here may be compared to a sprout growing at the foot of a great tree; it enjoys and draws but a little portion of sap; wrench it from the parent roots, transplant it, and it will become a tree bearing fruit also. Colonists are therefore entitled to the consideration due to the most useful subjects; a hundred families barely existing in some parts of Scotland, will here in six years, cause an annual exportation of 10,000 bushels of wheat: 100 bushels being but a common quantity for an industrious family to sell if they cultivate good land. It is here then that the idle may be employed, the useless become useful, and the poor become rich; but by riches I do not mean gold and silver, we have but little of those metals; I mean a better sort of wealth, cleared lands, cattle, good houses, good clothes, and an increase of people to enjoy them.

There is no wonder that this country has so many charms, and presents to Europeans so many temptations to remain in it. A traveler in Europe becomes a stranger as soon as he quits his own kingdom; but it is otherwise here. We know, properly speaking, no strangers; this is every person's country; the variety of our soils, situations, climates, governments, and produce, hath something which must please everybody. No sooner does a European arrive, no matter of what condition, than his eyes are opened upon the fair prospect; he hears his language spoken, he retraces many of his own country manners, he perpetually hears the names of families and towns with which he is acquainted; he sees happiness and prosperity in all places disseminated; he meets with hospitality, kindness, and plenty everywhere; he beholds hardly any poor, he seldom hears of punishments and executions; and he wonders at the elegance of our towns, those miracles of industry and freedom. He cannot admire enough our rural districts, our convenient roads, good taverns, and our many accommodations; he involuntarily loves a country where everything is so lovely. When in England, he was a mere Englishman; here he stands on a larger portion of the globe, not less than its fourth part, and may see the productions of the north, in iron and naval stores; the provisions of Ireland, the grain of Egypt, the indigo, the rice of China. He does not find, as in Europe, a crowded society, where every place is overstocked; he does not feel that perpetual collision of parties, that difficulty of beginning, that contention which oversets so many. There is room for everybody in America; has he any particular talent, or industry? he exerts it in order to procure a livelihood, and it succeeds. Is he a merchant? the avenues of trade are infinite; is he eminent in any respect? he will be employed and respected. Does he love a country life? pleasant farms present themselves; he may purchase what he wants, and thereby become an American farmer. Is he a laborer, sober and industrious? he need not go many miles, nor receive many informations before he will be hired, well fed at the table of his employer, and paid four or five times more than he can get in Europe. Does he want uncultivated lands? thousands of acres present themselves, which he may purchase cheap. Whatever be his talents or inclinations, if they are moderate, he may satisfy them. I do not mean that everyone who comes will grow rich in a little time; no, but he may procure an easy, decent maintenance, by his industry. Instead of starving he will be fed, instead of being idle he will have employment; and these are riches enough for such men as come over here. The rich stay in Europe, it is only the middling and the poor that emigrate. Would you wish to travel in independent idleness, from north to south, you will find easy access, and the most cheerful reception at every house; society without ostentation, good cheer without pride, and every decent diversion which the country affords, with little expense. It is no wonder that the European who has lived here a few years is desirous to remain; Europe with all its pomp is not to be compared to this continent for men of middle stations or laborers.

A European, when he first arrives, seems limited in his intentions, as well as in his views; but he very suddenly alters his scale; two hundred miles formerly appeared a very great distance, it is now but a trifle; he no sooner breathes our air than he forms schemes, and embarks in designs he never would have thought of in his own country. There the plenitude of society confines many useful ideas, and often extinguishes the most laudable schemes which here ripen into maturity. Thus Europeans become Americans.

"The Making of Americans"
consists of the first part of Letter III
in LETTERS FROM AN AMERICAN FARMER.

Alexis de Tocqueville

1805–1859

Undoubtedly the most illustrious of all political analysts since Aristotle and Machiavelli." This is the way Wilhelm Dilthey, the famous German philosopher, describes Alexis de Tocqueville. It is an estimate with which many philosophers and political scientists would agree.

Alexis Charles Henri Maurice Clérel de Tocqueville was born in Verneuil on July 29, 1805. His family had been part of the French nobility prior to the Revolution of 1789, and he grew up in an atmosphere where the aristocratic values had been preserved. He received much of his early education at home, and at eighteen took up the study of law. When he was twenty-one, he became a magistrate at Versailles under the government of Charles X.

Charles's government was toppled by the Revolution of 1830, and Tocqueville sought some way to dissociate himself from the new government without appearing disloyal. Along with his close friend Gustave de Beaumont, he petitioned the government for a commission to survey the penal institutions in America. The prison survey was only a pretext. His primary aim was to view at first hand the democratic system as it operated in the United States. The commission was granted, and he and Beaumont sailed for America, arriving in New York City in May, 1831. From there they began a tour that

---

Notes from the artist: "Head study of Tocqueville beneath a quotation from Democracy in America. *At right is Gustave de Beaumont, whose sketch of Tocqueville entitled 'Ready for the Wilderness' was the basis for the equestrian portrait."*

It is true that around every man a fatal circle is traced beyond which he cannot pass; but within the wide verge of that circle he is powerful and free; as it is with man, so with communities.

Alexis De Tocqueville

took them as far north as Canada and as far south as New Orleans. They traveled more than seven thousand miles by steamer, stagecoach, and horseback before returning to France the following February.

Once the report on American prisons was completed, Tocqueville turned to the work that was the real purpose of his travels—*Democracy in America*. The first part appeared in 1835. It was received with great enthusiasm and soon was translated into several languages. The second part appeared in 1840. It was also well received, but it did not generate as much excitement as its predecessor. In commenting on the complete work, John Stuart Mill said that it constituted "the beginning of a new era in the science of politics."

The success of *Democracy in America* advanced Tocqueville to the front rank of French political thinkers. He was honored widely and eventually was persuaded to return to politics. He was elected to the Chamber of Deputies in 1839, where he remained until 1851. Then, withdrawing from public life, he began preparing the work that many consider his masterpiece, *L'Ancien Régime et la Révolution*. Its first volume, published in 1856, was even more successful than *Democracy in America*. Unfortunately, ill-health prevented him from completing the other volumes. He died in Cannes at the age of fifty-three.

Democracy in America is one of the most remarkable books ever written. Based upon observations made by a twenty-six-year-old man during a period of only nine months, it has never been surpassed as an analysis of American society. Even today, more than one hundred and thirty years after Tocqueville visited the United States, it is still one of the best commentaries available on American institutions, practices, beliefs, and attitudes.

One of the reasons why *Democracy in America* has been of such lasting value is that Tocqueville was not so much interested in America as in democracy. Of all the nations that were then being transformed into democracies, the United States was the one in which the development of democracy had been "most peaceful and most complete." By comparing what he knew of other societies with what he observed in America, Tocqueville could see the effects of democracy upon social institutions and upon the lives and characters of men. He took great pains to distinguish between the effects that seemed to be characteristic of democracy in general and those that were peculiar to American democracy. As a result, he was able to see below the surface of American society to its underlying principles and tendencies.

Tocqueville's great interest in democratic societies stemmed from his conviction that democracy was the wave of the future; the movement towards it was "universal" and "irresistible." The democratic revolution was already under way in Europe, and its outcome was anticipated with fear by some, with hope by others. These hopes and fears were, in almost every instance, based upon ignorance. Tocqueville's aim was to provide his countrymen (and other Europeans) with the truth about democracy, its "evils and the advantages." He elaborated upon his purpose in a letter to a friend: "I wished to show what a democratic people really was in our day. . . . To those who have fancied an ideal democracy, a brilliant and easily realized dream, I endeavored to show that they had clothed the picture in false colors. . . . To those for whom the word *democracy* is synonymous with destruction, anarchy, spoliation, and murder, I have tried to show that under a democratic government the fortunes and rights of society may be respected, liberty preserved, and religion honored."

Because of space limitations, only part of *Democracy in America* is reprinted here. The complete work covers almost every important aspect of American life, and the high level of observation and analysis is sustained throughout.

Observations on American Life and Government

from *Democracy in America*

INTRODUCTION

Among the novel objects that attracted my attention during my stay in the United States, nothing struck me more forcibly than the general equality of conditions. I readily discovered the prodigious influence which this primary fact exercises on the whole course of society, by giving a certain direction to public opinion, and a certain tenor to the laws; by imparting new maxims to the governing powers, and peculiar habits to the governed.

I speedily perceived that the influence of this fact extends far beyond the political character and the laws of the country, and that it has no less empire over civil society than over the government; it creates opinions, engenders sentiments, suggests the ordinary practices of life, and modifies whatever it does not produce.

The more I advanced in the study of American society, the more I perceived that the equality of conditions is the fundamental fact from which all others seem to be derived, and the central point at which all my observations constantly terminated.

I then turned my thoughts to our own hemisphere, where I imagined that I discerned something analogous to the spectacle which the New World presented to me. I observed that the equality of conditions is daily progressing towards those extreme limits which it seems to have reached in the United States; and that the democracy which governs the American communities appears to be rapidly rising into power in Europe.

I hence conceived the idea of the book which is now before the reader.

It is evident to all alike that a great democratic revolution is going on among us; but there are two opinions as to its nature and consequences. To some it appears to be a novel accident, which as such may still be checked; to others it seems irresistible because it is the most uniform, the most ancient, and the most permanent tendency which is to be found in history.

Let us recollect the situation of France seven hundred years ago, when the territory was divided among a small number of families who were the owners of the soil and the rulers of the inhabitants; the right of governing descended with the family inheritance from generation to generation; force was the only means by which man could act on man; and landed property was the sole source of power.

Soon, however, the political power of the clergy was founded, and began to exert itself: the clergy opened its ranks to all classes, to the poor and the rich, the villain and the lord; equality penetrated into the government through the church, and the being who as a serf must have vegetated in perpetual bondage took his place as a priest in the midst of nobles, and not unfrequently above the heads of kings.

The different relations of men became more complicated and more numerous as society gradually became more stable and more civilized. Thence the want of civil laws was felt; and the order of legal functionaries soon rose from the obscurity of the tribunals and their dusty chambers to appear at the court of the monarch, by the side of the feudal barons in their ermine and their mail.

While the kings were ruining themselves by their great enterprises, and the nobles exhausting their resources by private wars, the lower orders were enriching themselves by commerce. The influence of money began to be perceptible in state affairs. The transactions of business opened a new road to power, and the financier rose to a station of political influence in which he was at once flattered and despised.

Gradually the spread of mental acquirements, and the increasing taste for literature and art, opened chances of success to talent; science became a means of government, intelligence led to social power, and the man of letters took a part in the affairs of the state.

The value attached to the privileges of birth decreased in the exact proportion in which new paths were struck out to advancement. In the eleventh century nobility was beyond all price; in the thirteenth it might be purchased; it was conferred for the first time in 1270; and equality was thus introduced into the government by the aristocracy itself.

In the course of these seven hundred years, it sometimes happened that in order to resist the authority of the crown, or to diminish the power of their rivals, the nobles granted a certain share of political rights to the people. Or, more frequently, the king permitted the lower orders to enjoy a degree of power, with the intention of repressing the aristocracy.

In France the kings have always been the most active and the most constant of levelers. When they were strong and ambitious, they spared no pains to raise the people to the level of the nobles; when they were temperate or weak, they allowed the people to rise above themselves. Some assisted the democracy by their talents, others by their vices. Louis XI and Louis XIV reduced every rank beneath the throne to the same subjection; Louis XV descended, himself and all his court, into the dust.

As soon as land was held on any other than a feudal tenure, and personal property began in its turn to confer influence and power, every improvement which was introduced in commerce or manufacture was a fresh element of the equality of conditions. Henceforward every new discovery, every new want which it engendered, and every new desire which craved satisfaction, was a step towards the universal level. The taste for luxury, the love of war, the sway of fashion, and the most superficial as well as the deepest passions of the human heart, co-operated to enrich the poor and to impoverish the rich.

From the time when the exercise of the intellect became the source of strength and of wealth, it is impossible not to consider every addition to science, every fresh truth, and every new idea as a germ of power placed within the reach of the people. Poetry, eloquence, and memory, the grace of wit, the glow of imagination, the depth of thought, and all the gifts which are bestowed by Providence with an equal hand turned to the advantage of the democracy; and even when they were in the possession of its adversaries, they still served its cause by throwing into relief the natural greatness of man; its conquests spread, therefore, with those of civilization and knowledge; and literature became an arsenal, where the poorest and the weakest could always find weapons to their hand.

In perusing the pages of our history, we shall scarcely meet with a single great event, in the lapse of seven hundred years, which has not turned to the advantage of equality.

The Crusades and the wars of the English decimated the nobles and divided their possessions: the erection of communities introduced an element of democratic liberty into the bosom of feudal monarchy; the invention of firearms equalized the villain and the noble on the field of battle; printing opened the same resources to the minds of all classes;

the post was organized so as to bring the same information to the door of the poor man's cottage, and to the gate of the palace; and Protestantism proclaimed that all men are alike able to find the road to heaven. The discovery of America offered a thousand new paths to fortune and placed riches and power within the reach of the adventurous and the obscure.

If we examine what has happened in France at intervals of fifty years, beginning with the eleventh century, we shall invariably perceive that a twofold revolution has taken place in the state of society. The noble has gone down on the social ladder, and the *roturier* has gone up; the one descends as the other rises. Every half-century brings them nearer to each other, and they will very shortly meet.

Nor is this phenomenon at all peculiar to France. Whithersoever we turn our eyes we shall witness the same continual revolution throughout the whole of Christendom.

The various occurrences of national existence have everywhere turned to the advantage of democracy; all men have aided it by their exertions: those who have intentionally labored in its cause, and those who have served it unwittingly; those who have fought for it and those who have declared themselves its opponents have all been driven along in the same track, have all labored to one end, some ignorantly and some unwillingly; all have been blind instruments in the hands of God.

The gradual development of the equality of conditions is therefore a providential fact, and it possesses all the characteristics of a divine decree: it is universal, it is durable, it constantly eludes all human interference, and all events as well as all men contribute to its progress.

Would it, then, be wise to imagine that a social impulse which dates from so far back can be checked by the efforts of a generation? Is it credible that the democracy which has annihilated the feudal system, and vanquished kings, will respect the citizen and the capitalist? Will it stop now that it is grown so strong, and its adversaries so weak?

None can say which way we are going, for all terms of comparison are wanting: the equality of conditions is more complete in the Christian countries of the present day than it has been at any time, or in any part of the world, so that the extent of what already exists prevents us from foreseeing what may be yet to come.

The whole book which is here offered to the public has been written under the impression of a kind of religious dread produced in the author's mind by the contemplation of so irresistible a revolution, which has advanced for centuries in spite of such amazing obstacles, and which is still proceeding in the midst of the ruins it has made.

It is not necessary that God himself should speak in order to disclose to us the unquestionable signs of His will; we can discern them in the habitual course of nature, and in the invariable tendency of events: I know, without a special revelation, that the planets move in the orbits traced by the Creator's finger.

If the men of our time were led by attentive observation, and by sincere reflection, to acknowledge that the gradual and progressive development of social equality is at once the past and future of their history, this solitary truth would confer the sacred character of a divine decree upon the change. To attempt to check democracy would be in that case to resist the will of God; and the nations would then be constrained to make the best of the social lot awarded to them by Providence.

The Christian nations of our age seem to me to present a most alarming spectacle; the impulse which is bearing them along is so strong that it cannot be stopped, but it is not yet so rapid that it cannot be guided: their fate is in their hands; yet a little while and it may be so no longer.

The first duty which is at this time imposed upon those who direct our affairs is to educate the democracy; to warm its faith, if that be possible; to purify its morals; to direct its energies; to substitute a knowledge of business for its inexperience, and an acquaintance with its true interests for its blind propensities; to adapt its government to time and place, and to modify it in compliance with the occurrences and the actors of the age.

A new science of politics is indispensable to a new world.

This, however, is what we think of least; launched in the middle of a rapid stream, we obstinately fix our eyes on the ruins which may still be descried upon the shore we have left, while the current sweeps us along, and drives us backwards toward the gulf.

In no country in Europe has the great social revolution which I have been describing made such rapid progress as in France; but it has always been borne on by chance. The heads of the state have never had any forethought for its exigencies, and its victories have been obtained without their consent or without their knowledge. The most powerful, the most intelligent, and the most moral classes of the nation have never attempted to connect themselves with it in order to guide it. The people has consequently been abandoned to its wild propensities, and it has grown up like those outcasts who receive their education in the public streets, and who are unacquainted with aught but the vices and wretchedness of society. The existence of a democracy was seemingly unknown, when on a sudden it took possession of the supreme power. Everything was then submitted to its caprices; it was worshiped as the idol of strength; until, when it was enfeebled by its own excesses, the legislator conceived the rash project of annihilating its power, instead of instructing it and correcting its vices; no attempt was made to fit it to govern, but all were bent on excluding it from the government.

The consequence of this has been that the democratic revolution has been effected only in the material parts of society, without that concomitant change in laws, ideas, customs and manners which was necessary to render such a revolution beneficial. We have gotten a democracy, but without the conditions which lessen its vices and render its natural advantages more prominent; and although we already perceive the evils it brings, we are ignorant of the benefits it may confer.

While the power of the crown, supported by the aristocracy, peaceably governed the nations of Europe, society possessed, in the midst of its wretchedness, several different advantages which can now scarcely be appreciated or conceived.

The power of a part of his subjects was an insurmountable barrier to the tyranny of the prince; and the monarch, who felt the almost divine character which he enjoyed in the eyes of the multitude, derived a motive for the just use of his power from the respect which he inspired.

High as they were placed above the people, the nobles could not but take that calm and benevolent interest in its fate which the shepherd feels towards his flock; and without acknowledging the poor as their equals, they watched over the destiny of those whose welfare Providence had entrusted to their care.

The people never having conceived the idea of a social condition different from its own, and entertaining no expectation of ever ranking with its chiefs, received benefits from them without discussing their rights. It grew attached to them when they were clement and just, and it submitted without resistance or servility to their exactions, as to the inevitable visitations of the arm of God. Custom, and the manners of the time, had moreover created a species of law in the midst of violence, and established certain limits to oppression.

As the noble never suspected that anyone would attempt to deprive him of the privileges which he believed to be legitimate, and as the serf looked upon his own inferiority as a consequence of the immutable order of nature, it is easy to imagine that a mutual exchange of good will took place between two classes so differently gifted by fate. Inequality and wretchedness were then to be found in society; but the souls of neither rank of men were degraded.

Men are not corrupted by the exercise of power or debased by the habit of obedience; but by the exercise of a power which they believe to be illegal and by obedience to a rule which they consider to be usurped and oppressive.

On one side was wealth, strength, and leisure, accompanied by the refinements of luxury, the elegance of taste, the pleasures of wit, and the religion of art. On the other was labor, and a rude ignorance; but in the midst of this coarse and ignorant multitude, it was not uncommon to meet with energetic passions, generous sentiments, profound religious convictions, and independent virtues.

The body of a state thus organized might boast of its stability, its power, and, above all, of its glory.

But the scene is now changed; and gradually the two ranks mingle; the divisions which once severed mankind are lowered; property is divided, power is held in common, the light of intelligence spreads, and the capacities of all classes are equally cultivated; the state becomes democratic, and the empire of democracy is slowly and peaceably introduced into the institutions and the manners of the nation.

I can conceive a society in which all men would profess an equal attachment and respect for the laws of which they are the common authors; in which the authority of the state would be respected as necessary, though not as divine; and the loyalty of the subject to the chief magistrate would not be a passion, but a quiet and rational persuasion. Every individual being in the possession of rights which he is sure to retain, a kind of manly reliance and reciprocal courtesy would arise between all classes, alike removed from pride and meanness.

The people, well acquainted with its true interests, would allow that, in order to profit by the advantages of society, it is necessary to satisfy its demands. In this state of things, the voluntary association of the citizens might supply the individual exertions of the nobles, and the community would be alike protected from anarchy and from oppression.

I admit that in a democratic state thus constituted society will not be stationary, but the impulses of the social body may be regulated and directed forwards; if there be less splendor than in the halls of an aristocracy, the contrast of misery will be less frequent also; the pleasures of enjoyment may be less excessive, but those of comfort will be more general; the sciences may be less perfectly cultivated, but ignorance will be less common; the impetuosity of the feelings will be repressed, and the habits of the nation softened; there will be more vices and fewer crimes.

In the absence of enthusiasm and of an ardent faith, great sacrifices may be obtained from the members of a commonwealth by an appeal to their understandings and their experience; each individual will feel the same necessity for uniting with his fellow citizens to protect his own weakness; and as he knows that if they are to assist he must co-operate, he will readily perceive that his personal interest is identified with the interest of the community.

The nation, taken as a whole, will be less brilliant, less glorious, and perhaps less strong; but the majority of the citizens will enjoy a greater degree of prosperity, and the people will remain quiet, not because it despairs of amelioration, but because it is conscious of the advantages of its condition.

If all the consequences of this state of things were not good or useful, society would at least have appropriated all such as were useful and good; and having once and forever renounced the social advantages of aristocracy, mankind would enter into possession of all the benefits which democracy can afford.

But here it may be asked what we have adopted in the place of those institutions, those ideas, and those customs of our forefathers which we have abandoned.

The spell of royalty is broken, but it has not been succeeded by the majesty of the laws; the people has learned to despise all authority, but fear now extorts a larger tribute of obedience than that which was formerly paid by reverence and by love.

I perceive that we have destroyed those independent beings which were able to cope with tyranny singlehanded; but it is the government that has inherited the privileges of which families, corporations, and individuals have been deprived; the weakness of the whole community has therefore succeeded that influence of a small body of citizens, which, if it was sometimes oppressive, was often conservative.

The division of property has lessened the distance which separated the rich from the poor; but it would seem that the nearer they draw to each other, the greater is their mutual hatred, and the more vehement the envy and the dread with which they resist each other's claims to power; the notion of right is alike insensible to both classes, and force affords to both the only argument for the present, and the only guarantee for the future.

The poor man retains the prejudices of his forefathers without their faith, and their ignorance without their virtues; he has adopted the doctrine of self-interest as the rule of his actions, without understanding the science which controls it, and his egotism is no less blind than his devotedness was formerly.

If society is tranquil, it is not because it relies upon its strength and its well-being, but because it knows its weakness and its infirmities; a single effort may cost it its life; everybody feels the evil, but no one has courage or energy enough to seek the cure; the desires, the regret, the sorrows, and the joys of the time produce nothing that is visible or permanent, like the passions of old men which terminate in impotence.

We have, then, abandoned whatever advantages the old state of things afforded, without receiving any compensation from our present condition; we have destroyed an aristocracy, and we seem inclined to survey its ruins with complacency, and to fix our abode in the midst of them.

The phenomena which the intellectual world presents are not less deplorable. The democracy of France, checked in its course or abandoned to its lawless passions, has overthrown whatever crossed its path, and has shaken all that it has not destroyed. Its empire on society has not been gradually introduced, or peaceably established, but it has constantly advanced in the midst of disorder and the agitation of a conflict. In the heat of the struggle each partisan is hurried beyond the limits of his opinions by the opinions and the excesses of his opponents, until he loses sight of the end of his exertions, and holds a language which disguises his real sentiments or secret instincts. Hence arises the strange confusion which we are witnessing.

I cannot recall to my mind a passage in history more worthy of sorrow and of pity than the scenes which are happening under our eyes; it is as if the natural bond which unites the opinions of man to his tastes, and his actions to his principles, was now broken; the sympathy which has always been acknowledged between the feelings and the ideas of mankind appears to be dissolved, and all the laws of moral analogy to be abolished.

Zealous Christians may be found among us whose minds are nurtured in the love and knowledge of a future life, and who readily espouse the cause of human liberty as the source of all moral greatness. Christianity, which has declared that all men are equal in the sight of God, will not refuse to acknowledge that all citizens are equal in the eye of the law. But, by a singular concourse of events, religion is entangled in those institutions which democracy assails, and it is not unfrequently brought to reject the equality it loves, and to curse that cause of liberty as a foe, which it might hallow by its alliance.

By the side of these religious men I discern others whose looks are turned to the earth more than to heaven; they are the partisans of liberty, not only as the source of the noblest virtues, but more especially as the root of all solid advantages; and they sincerely desire to extend its sway, and to impart its blessings to mankind. It is natural that they should hasten to invoke the assistance of religion, for they must know that liberty cannot be established without morality, nor morality without faith; but they have seen religion in the ranks of their adversaries, and they inquire no further; some of them attack it openly, and the remainder are afraid to defend it.

In former ages slavery has been advocated by the venal and slavish-minded, while the independent and the warmhearted were struggling without hope to save the liberties of mankind. But men of high and generous characters are now to be met with whose opinions are at variance with their inclinations, and who praise that servility which they have themselves never known. Others, on the contrary, speak in the name of liberty, as if they were able to feel its sanctity and its majesty, and loudly claim for humanity those rights which they have always disowned.

There are virtuous and peaceful individuals whose pure morality, quiet habits, affluence, and talents fit them to be the leaders of the surrounding population; their love of their country is sincere, and they are prepared to make the greatest sacrifices to its welfare, but they confound the abuses of civilization with its benefits, and the idea of evil is inseparable in their minds from that of novelty.

Not far from this class is another party, whose object is to materialize mankind, to hit upon what is expedient without heeding what is just, to acquire knowledge without faith, and prosperity apart from virtue; assuming the title of the champions of modern civilization, and placing themselves in a station which they usurp with insolence, and from which they are driven by their own unworthiness.

Where are we then?

The religionists are the enemies of liberty, and the friends of liberty attack religion; the high-minded and the noble advocate subjection, and the meanest and most servile minds preach independence; honest and enlightened citizens are opposed to all progress, while men without patriotism and without principles are the apostles of civilization and of intelligence.

Has such been the fate of the centuries which have preceded our own? and has man always inhabited a world, like the present, where nothing is linked together, where virtue is without genius, and genius without honor; where the love of order is confounded with a taste for oppression, and the holy rites of freedom with a contempt of law; where the light thrown by conscience on human actions is dim, and where nothing seems to be any longer forbidden or allowed, honorable or shameful, false or true?

I cannot, however, believe that the Creator made man to leave him in an endless struggle with the intellectual miseries which surround us: God destines a calmer and a more certain future to the communities of Europe; I am unacquainted with His designs, but I shall not cease to believe in them because I cannot fathom them, and I had rather mistrust my own capacity than His justice.

There is a country in the world where the great revolution which I am speaking of seems nearly to have reached its natural limits; it has been effected with ease and simplicity—say rather that this country has attained the consequences of the democratic revolution which we are undergoing without having experienced the revolution itself.

The emigrants who fixed themselves on the shores of America in the beginning of the seventeenth century severed the democratic principle from all the principles which repressed it in the old communities of Europe, and transplanted it unalloyed to the New World. It has there been allowed to spread in perfect freedom, and to put forth its consequences in the laws by influencing the manners of the country.

It appears to me beyond a doubt that sooner or later we shall arrive, like the Americans, at an almost complete equality of conditions. But I do not conclude from this that we shall ever be necessarily led to draw the same political consequences which the Americans have derived from a similar social organization. I am far from supposing that they have chosen the only form of government which a democracy may adopt; but the identity of the efficient cause of laws and manners in the two countries is sufficient to account for the immense interest we have in becoming acquainted with its effects in each of them.

It is not, then, merely to satisfy a legitimate curiosity that I have examined America: my wish has been to find instruction by which we may ourselves profit. Whoever should imagine that I have intended to write a panegyric would be strangely mistaken, and on reading this book he will perceive that such was not my design; nor has it been my object to advocate any form of government in particular, for I am of opinion that absolute excellence is rarely to be found in any legislation. I have not even affected to discuss whether the social revolution, which I believe to be irresistible, is advantageous or prejudicial to mankind. I have acknowledged this revolution as a fact already accomplished or on the eve of its accomplishment; and I have selected the nation, from among those which have undergone it, in which its development has been the most peaceful and the most complete, in order to discern its natural consequences, and, if it be possible, to distinguish the means by which it may be rendered profitable. I confess that in America I saw more than America; I sought the image of democracy itself, with its inclinations, its character, its prejudices, and its passions, in order to learn what we have to fear or to hope from its progress.

In the first part of this work I have attempted to show the tendency given to the laws by the democracy of America, which is abandoned almost without restraint to its instinctive propensities, and to exhibit the course it prescribes to the government and the influence it exercises on affairs. I have sought to discover the evils and the advantages which it produces. I have examined the precautions used by the Americans to direct it, as well as those which they have not adopted, and I have undertaken to point out the causes which enable it to govern society. I do not know whether I have succeeded in making known what I saw in America, but I am certain that such has been my sincere desire, and that I have never, knowingly, molded facts to ideas, instead of ideas to facts.

Whenever a point could be established by the aid of written documents, I have had recourse to the original text, and to the most authentic and approved works. I have cited my authorities in the notes, and anyone may refer to them. Whenever an opinion, a political custom, or a remark on the manners of the country was concerned, I endeavored to consult the most enlightened men I met with. If the point in question was important or doubtful, I was not satisfied with one testimony, but I formed my opinion on the evidence of several witnesses. Here the reader must necessarily believe me upon my word. I could frequently have quoted names which are either known to him, or which deserve to be so, in proof of what I advance; but I have carefully abstained from this practice. A stranger frequently hears important truths at the fireside of his host, which the latter would perhaps conceal from the ear of friendship; he consoles himself with his guest for the silence to which he is restricted, and the shortness of the traveler's stay takes away all fear of his indiscretion. I carefully noted every conversation of this nature as soon as it occurred, but these notes will never leave my writing case; I had rather injure the success of my statements than add my name to the list of those strangers who repay the generous hospitality they have received by subsequent chagrin and annoyance.

I am aware that, notwithstanding my care, nothing will be easier than to criticize this book, if anyone ever chooses to criticize it.

Those readers who may examine it closely will discover the fundamental idea which connects the several parts together. But the diversity of the subjects I have had to treat is exceedingly great, and it will not be difficult to oppose an isolated fact to the body of facts which I quote, or an isolated idea to the body of ideas I put forth. I hope to be read in the spirit which has guided my labors, and that my book may be judged by the general impression it leaves, as I have formed my own judgment not on any single reason, but upon the mass of evidence.

It must not be forgotten that the author who wishes to be understood is obliged to push all his ideas to their utmost theoretical consequences, and often to the verge of what is false or impracticable; for if it be necessary sometimes to quit the rules of logic in active life, such is not the case in discourse, and a man finds that almost as many difficulties spring from inconsistency of language as usually arise from consistency of conduct.

I conclude by pointing out myself what many readers will consider the principal defect of the work. This book is written to favor no particular views, and in composing it I have entertained no design of serving or attacking any party. I have undertaken not to see differently, but to look further than parties, and while they are busied for the morrow, I have turned my thoughts to the future. . . .

Social Condition of the Anglo-Americans

A social condition is commonly the result of circumstances, sometimes of laws, oftener still of these two causes united; but wherever it exists, it may justly be considered as the source of almost all the laws, the usages, and the ideas which regulate the conduct of nations: whatever it does not produce it modifies.

It is therefore necessary, if we would become acquainted with the legislation and the manners of a nation, to begin by the study of its social condition.

THE STRIKING CHARACTERISTIC OF THE SOCIAL CONDITION OF THE ANGLO-AMERICANS IS ITS ESSENTIAL DEMOCRACY

Many important observations suggest themselves upon the social condition of the Anglo-Americans; but there is one which takes precedence of all the rest. The social condition of the Americans is eminently democratic; this was its character at the foundation of the Colonies, and is still more strongly marked at the present day.

I have stated in the preceding chapter that great equality existed among the emigrants who settled on the shores of New England. The germ of aristocracy was never planted in that part of the Union. The only influence which obtained there was that of intellect; the people were used to reverence certain names as the emblems of knowledge and virtue. Some of their fellow citizens acquired a power over the rest which might truly have been called aristocratic, if it had been capable of transmission from father to son.

This was the state of things to the east of the Hudson: to the southwest of that river, and in the direction of the Floridas, the case was different. In most of the states situated to the southwest of the Hudson, some great English proprietors had settled, who had imported with them aristocratic principles and the English law of descent. I have explained the reasons why it was impossible ever to establish a powerful aristocracy in America; these reasons existed with less force to the southwest of the Hudson. In the South, one man, aided by slaves, could cultivate a great extent of country; it was therefore common to see rich landed proprietors. But their influence was not altogether aristocratic as that term is understood in Europe, since they possessed no privileges; and the cultivation of their estates being carried on by slaves, they had no tenants depending on them, and consequently no patronage. Still, the great proprietors south of the Hudson constituted a superior class, having ideas and tastes of its own, and forming the center of political action. This kind of aristocracy sympathized with the body of the people, whose passions and interests it easily embraced; but it was too weak and too short-lived to excite either love or hatred for itself. This was the class which headed the insurrection in the South, and furnished the best leaders of the American Revolution.

At the period of which we are now speaking society was shaken to its center: the people, in whose name the struggle had taken place, conceived the desire of exercising the authority which it had acquired; its democratic tendencies were awakened; and having thrown off the yoke of the mother country, it aspired to independence of every kind. The influence of individuals gradually ceased to be felt, and custom and law united together to produce the same result.

But the law of descent was the last step to equality. I am surprised that ancient and modern jurists have not attributed to this law a greater influence on human affairs.[1] It is true that these laws belong to civil affairs; but they ought nevertheless to be placed at the head of all political institutions; for, while political laws are only the symbol of a nation's condition, they exercise an incredible influence upon its social state. They have, moreover, a sure and uniform manner of operating upon society, affecting, as it were, generations yet unborn.

Through their means man acquires a kind of preternatural power over the future lot of his fellow creatures. When the legislator has regulated the law of inheritance, he may rest from his labor. The machine once put in motion will go on for ages, and advance, as if self-guided, towards a given point. When framed in a particular manner, this law unites, draws together, and vests property and power in a few hands: its tendency is clearly aristocratic. On opposite principles its action is still more rapid; it divides, distributes, and disperses both property and power. Alarmed by the rapidity of its progress, those who despair of arresting its motion endeavor to obstruct it by difficulties and impediments; they vainly seek to counteract its effect by contrary efforts: but it gradually reduces or destroys every obstacle, until by its incessant activity the bulwarks of the influence of wealth are ground down to the fine and shifting sand which is the basis of democracy. When the law of inheritance permits, still more when it decrees, the equal division of a father's property among all his children, its effects are of two kinds: it is important to distinguish them from each other, although they tend to the same end.

In virtue of the law of partible inheritance, the death of every proprietor brings about a kind of revolution in property: not only do his possessions change hands, but their very nature is altered, since they are parceled into shares which become smaller and smaller at each division. This is the direct and, as it were, the physical effect of the law. It follows, then, that in countries where equality of inheritance is established by law, property, and especially landed property, must have a tendency to perpetual diminution. The effects, however, of such legislation would only be perceptible after a lapse of time if the law was abandoned to its own working, for supposing the family to consist of two children (and in a country peopled as France is the average number is not above

1. I understand by the law of descent all those laws whose principal object is to regulate the distribution of property after the death of its owner. The law of entail is of this number: it certainly prevents the owner from disposing of his possessions before his death; but this is solely with the view of preserving them entire for the heir. The principal object, therefore, of the law of entail is to regulate the descent of property after the death of its owner: its other provisions are merely means to this end.

three), these children, sharing among them the fortune of both parents, would not be poorer than their father or mother.

But the law of equal division exercises its influence not merely upon the property itself, but it affects the minds of the heirs and brings their passions into play. These indirect consequences tend powerfully to the destruction of large fortunes, and especially of large domains.

Among nations whose law of descent is founded upon the right of primogeniture, landed estates often pass from generation to generation without undergoing division. The consequence of which is that family feeling is to a certain degree incorporated with the estate. The family represents the estate, the estate the family; whose name, together with its origin, its glory, its power, and its virtues, is thus perpetuated in an imperishable memorial of the past, and a sure pledge of the future.

When the equal partition of property is established by law, the intimate connection is destroyed between family feeling and the preservation of the paternal estate: the property ceases to represent the family, for as it must inevitably be divided after one or two generations, it has evidently a constant tendency to diminish, and must in the end be completely dispersed. The sons of the great landed proprietor, if they are few in number, or if fortune befriends them, may indeed entertain the hope of being as wealthy as their father, but not that of possessing the same property as he did; their riches must necessarily be composed of elements different from his.

Now, from the moment that you divest the landowner of that interest in the preservation of his estate which he derives from association, from tradition, and from family pride, you may be certain that sooner or later he will dispose of it; for there is a strong pecuniary interest in favor of selling, as floating capital produces higher interest than real property, and is more readily available to gratify the passions of the moment.

Great landed estates which have once been divided never come together again; for the small proprietor draws from his land a better revenue, in proportion, than the large owner does from his; and of course he sells it at a higher rate.[2] The calculations of gain, therefore, which decide the rich man to sell his domain will still more powerfully influence him against buying small estates to unite them into a large one.

What is called family pride is often founded upon an illusion of self-

---

2. I do not mean to say that the small proprietor cultivates his land better, but he cultivates it with more ardor and care, so that he makes up by his labor for his want of skill.

love. A man wishes to perpetuate and immortalize himself, as it were, in his great-grandchildren. Where the *esprit de famille* ceases to act, individual selfishness comes into play. When the idea of family becomes vague, indeterminate, and uncertain, a man thinks of his present convenience; he provides for the establishment of his succeeding generation and no more.

Either a man gives up the idea of perpetuating his family, or at any rate he seeks to accomplish it by other means than that of a landed estate.

Thus not only does the law of partible inheritance render it difficult for families to preserve their ancestral domains entire, but it deprives them of the inclination to attempt it, and compels them in some measure to co-operate with the law in their own extinction.

The law of equal distribution proceeds by two methods: by acting upon things, it acts upon persons; by influencing persons, it affects things. By these means the law succeeds in striking at the root of landed property, and dispersing rapidly both families and fortunes.[3]

Most certainly it is not for us Frenchmen of the nineteenth century, who daily witness the political and social changes which the law of partition is bringing to pass, to question its influence. It is perpetually conspicuous in our country, overthrowing the walls of our dwellings and removing the landmarks of our fields. But although it has produced great effects in France, much still remains for it to do. Our recollections, opinions, and habits present powerful obstacles to its progress.

In the United States it has nearly completed its work of destruction, and there we can best study its results. The English laws concerning the transmission of property were abolished in almost all the states at the time of the Revolution. The law of entail was so modified as not to interrupt the free circulation of property. The first generation having passed away, estates began to be parceled out; and the change became more

---

3. Land being the most stable kind of property, we find, from time to time, rich individuals who are disposed to make great sacrifices in order to obtain it, and who willingly forfeit a considerable part of their income to make sure of the rest. But these are accidental cases. The preference for landed property is no longer found habitually in any class but among the poor. The small landowner, who has less information, less imagination, and fewer passions than the great one, is generally occupied with the desire of increasing his estate: and it often happens that by inheritance, by marriage, or by the chances of trade, he is gradually furnished with the means. Thus, to balance the tendency which leads men to divide their estates, there exists another, which incites them to add to them. This tendency, which is sufficient to prevent estates from being divided ad infinitum, is not strong enough to create great territorial possessions, certainly not to keep them up in the same family.

and more rapid with the progress of time. At this moment, after a lapse of a little more than sixty years, the aspect of society is totally altered; the families of the great landed proprietors are almost all commingled with the general mass. In the state of New York, which formerly contained many of these, there are but two who still keep their heads above the stream; and they must shortly disappear. The sons of these opulent citizens are become merchants, lawyers, or physicians. Most of them have lapsed into obscurity. The last trace of hereditary ranks and distinctions is destroyed—the law of partition has reduced all to one level.

I do not mean that there is any deficiency of wealthy individuals in the United States; I know of no country, indeed, where the love of money has taken stronger hold on the affections of men, and where a profounder contempt is expressed for the theory of the permanent equality of property. But wealth circulates with inconceivable rapidity, and experience shows that it is rare to find two succeeding generations in the full enjoyment of it.

This picture, which may perhaps be thought to be overcharged, still gives a very imperfect idea of what is taking place in the new states of the West and Southwest. At the end of the last century a few bold adventurers began to penetrate into the valleys of the Mississippi, and the mass of the population very soon began to move in that direction: communities unheard of till then were seen to emerge from the wilds; states whose names were not in existence a few years before claimed their place in the American Union; and in the western settlements we may behold democracy arrived at its utmost extreme. In these states, founded offhand, and, as it were, by chance, the inhabitants are but of yesterday. Scarcely known to one another, the nearest neighbors are ignorant of each other's history. In this part of the American continent, therefore, the population has not experienced the influence of great names and great wealth, nor even that of the natural aristocracy of knowledge and virtue. None are there to wield that respectable power which men willingly grant to the remembrance of a life spent in doing good before their eyes. The new states of the West are already inhabited; but society has no existence among them.

It is not only the fortunes of men which are equal in America; even their acquirements partake in some degree of the same uniformity. I do not believe that there is a country in the world where, in proportion to the population, there are so few uninstructed, and at the same time so few learned, individuals. Primary instruction is within the reach of everybody; superior instruction is scarcely to be obtained by any. This is not surprising; it is in fact the necessary consequence of what we have advanced above. Almost all the Americans are in easy circumstances, and can therefore obtain the first elements of human knowledge.

In America there are comparatively few who are rich enough to live without a profession. Every profession requires an apprenticeship, which limits the time of instruction to the early years of life. At fifteen they enter upon their calling, and thus their education ends at the age when ours begins. Whatever is done afterwards is with a view to some special and lucrative object: a science is taken up as a matter of business, and the only branch of it which is attended to is such as admits of an immediate practical application.

In America most of the rich men were formerly poor; most of those who now enjoy leisure were absorbed in business during their youth; the consequence of which is that when they might have had a taste for study, they had no time for it, and when the time is at their disposal they have no longer the inclination.

There is no class, then, in America, in which the taste for intellectual pleasures is transmitted with hereditary fortune and leisure, and by which the labors of the intellect are held in honor. Accordingly there is an equal want of the desire and the power of application to these objects.

A middling standard is fixed in America for human knowledge. All approach as near to it as they can: some as they rise, others as they descend. Of course, an immense multitude of persons are to be found who entertain the same number of ideas on religion, history, science, political economy, legislation, and government. The gifts of intellect proceed directly from God, and man cannot prevent their unequal distribution. But in consequence of the state of things which we have here represented, it happens that although the capacities of men are widely different, as the Creator has doubtless intended they should be, they are submitted to the same method of treatment.

In America the aristocratic element has always been feeble from its birth; and if at the present day it is not actually destroyed, it is at any rate so completely disabled that we can scarcely assign to it any degree of influence in the course of affairs.

The democratic principle, on the contrary, has gained so much strength by time, by events, and by legislation as to have become not only predominant but all-powerful. There is no family or corporate authority, and it is rare to find even the influence of individual character enjoy any durability.

America, then, exhibits in her social state a most extraordinary phenomenon. Men are there seen on a greater equality in point of fortune and intellect, or, in other words, more equal in their strength, than in any other country of the world, or in any age of which history has preserved the remembrance.

POLITICAL CONSEQUENCES OF THE SOCIAL CONDITION OF THE ANGLO-AMERICANS

The political consequences of such a social condition as this are easily deducible.

It is impossible to believe that equality will not eventually find its way into the political world as it does everywhere else. To conceive of men remaining forever unequal upon one single point, yet equal on all others, is impossible; they must come in the end to be equal upon all.

Now I know of only two methods of establishing equality in the political world; every citizen must be put in possession of his rights, or rights must be granted to no one. For nations which are arrived at the same stage of social existence as the Anglo-Americans, it is therefore very difficult to discover a medium between the sovereignty of all and the absolute power of one man: and it would be vain to deny that the social condition which I have been describing is equally liable to each of these consequences.

There is, in fact, a manly and lawful passion for equality which excites men to wish all to be powerful and honored. This passion tends to elevate the humble to the rank of the great; but there exists also in the human heart a depraved taste for equality, which impels the weak to attempt to lower the powerful to their own level, and reduces men to prefer equality in slavery to inequality with freedom. Not that those nations whose social condition is democratic naturally despise liberty; on the contrary, they have an instinctive love of it. But liberty is not the chief and constant object of their desires; equality is their idol: they make rapid and sudden efforts to obtain liberty; and if they miss their aim, resign themselves to their disappointment; but nothing can satisfy them except equality, and rather than lose it they resolve to perish.

On the other hand, in a state where the citizens are nearly on an equality, it becomes difficult for them to preserve their independence against the aggressions of power. No one among them being strong enough to engage in the struggle with advantage, nothing but a general combination can protect their liberty. And such a union is not always to be found.

From the same social position, then, nations may derive one or the other of two great political results; these results are extremely different from each other, but they may both proceed from the same cause.

The Anglo-Americans are the first nations who, having been exposed to this formidable alternative, have been happy enough to escape the dominion of absolute power. They have been allowed by their circumstances, their origin, their intelligence, and especially by their moral feeling, to establish and maintain the sovereignty of the people.

The Principle of the Sovereignty of the People in America

Whenever the political laws of the United States are to be discussed, it is with the doctrine of the sovereignty of the people that we must begin.

The principle of the sovereignty of the people, which is to be found, more or less, at the bottom of almost all human institutions, generally remains concealed from view. It is obeyed without being recognized, or if for a moment it be brought to light, it is hastily cast back into the gloom of the sanctuary.

"The will of the nation" is one of those expressions which have been most profusely abused by the wily and the despotic of every age. To the eyes of some it has been represented by the venal suffrages of a few of the satellites of power; to others, by the votes of a timid or an interested minority; and some have even discovered it in the silence of a people, on the supposition that the fact of submission established the right of command.

In America, the principle of the sovereignty of the people is not either barren or concealed, as it is with some other nations; it is recognized by the customs and proclaimed by the laws; it spreads freely, and arrives without impediment at its most remote consequences. If there be a country in the world where the doctrine of the sovereignty of the people can be fairly appreciated, where it can be studied in its application to the affairs of society, and where its dangers and its advantages may be foreseen, that country is assuredly America.

I have already observed that, from their origin, the sovereignty of the people was the fundamental principle of the greater number of British colonies in America. It was far, however, from then exercising as much influence on the government of society as it now does. Two obstacles, the one external, the other internal, checked its invasive progress.

It could not ostensibly disclose itself in the laws of colonies which were still constrained to obey the mother country: it was therefore obliged to spread secretly, and to gain ground in the provincial assemblies, and especially in the townships.

American society was not yet prepared to adopt it with all its consequences. The intelligence of New England, and the wealth of the country to the south of the Hudson, (as I have shown in the preceding chapter,) long exercised a sort of aristocratic influence which tended to retain the exercise of social authority in the hands of a few. The public functionaries were not universally elected, and the citizens were not all of them electors. The electoral franchise was everywhere placed within certain limits, and made dependent on a certain qualification, which was exceedingly low in the North, and more considerable in the South.

The American Revolution broke out, and the doctrine of the sovereignty of the people, which had been nurtured in the townships and municipalities, took possession of the state. Every class was enlisted in its cause; battles were fought, and victories obtained for it, until it became the law of laws.

A no less rapid change was effected in the interior of society, where the law of descent completed the abolition of local influences.

At the very time when this consequence of the laws and of the revolution was apparent to every eye, victory was irrevocably pronounced in favor of the democratic cause. All power was, in fact, in its hands, and resistance was no longer possible. The higher orders submitted without a murmur and without a struggle to an evil which was thenceforth inevitable. The ordinary fate of falling powers awaited them; each of their several members followed his own interest; and as it was impossible to wring the power from the hands of a people which they did not detest sufficiently to brave, their only aim was to secure its good will at any price. The most democratic laws were consequently voted by the very men whose interests they impaired: and thus, although the higher classes did not excite the passions of the people against their order, they accelerated the triumph of the new state of things; so that, by a singular change, the democratic impulse was found to be most irresistible in the very states where the aristocracy had the firmest hold.

The state of Maryland, which had been founded by men of rank, was the first to proclaim universal suffrage, and to introduce the most democratic forms into the conduct of its government.

When a nation modifies the elective qualification, it may easily be foreseen that sooner or later that qualification will be entirely abolished.

There is no more invariable rule in the history of society: the further electoral rights are extended, the greater is the need of extending them; for after each concession the strength of the democracy increases, and its demands increase with its strength. The ambition of those who are below the appointed rate is irritated in exact proportion to the great number of those who are above it. The exception at last becomes the rule, concession follows concession, and no stop can be made short of universal suffrage.

At the present day the principle of the sovereignty of the people has acquired, in the United States, all the practical development which the imagination can conceive. It is unencumbered by those fictions which have been thrown over it in other countries, and it appears in every possible form according to the exigency of the occasion. Sometimes the laws are made by the people in a body, as at Athens; and sometimes its representatives, chosen by universal suffrage, transact business in its name, and almost under its immediate control.

In some countries a power exists which, though it is in a degree foreign to the social body, directs it, and forces it to pursue a certain track. In others the ruling force is divided, being partly within and partly without the ranks of the people. But nothing of the kind is to be seen in the United States; there society governs itself for itself. All power centers in its bosom; and scarcely an individual is to be met with who would venture to conceive, or, still less, to express, the idea of seeking it elsewhere. The nation participates in the making of its laws by the choice of its legislators, and in the execution of them by the choice of the agents of the executive government; it may almost be said to govern itself, so feeble and so restricted is the share left to the administration, so little do the authorities forget their popular origin and the power from which they emanate. . . .

Liberty of the Press in the United States

The influence of the liberty of the press does not affect political opinions alone, but it extends to all the opinions of men, and it modifies customs as well as laws. In another part of this work I shall attempt to determine the degree of influence which the liberty of the press has exercised upon civil society in the United States, and to point out the direction which it has given to the ideas, as well as the tone which it has imparted to the character and the feelings, of the Anglo-Americans, but at present I purpose simply to examine the effects produced by the liberty of the press in the political world.

I confess that I do not entertain that firm and complete attachment to the liberty of the press which things that are supremely good in their very nature are wont to excite in the mind; and I approve of it more from a recollection of the evils it prevents than from a consideration of the advantages it ensures.

If anyone could point out an intermediate, and yet a tenable, position between the complete independence and the entire subjection of the public expression of opinion, I should perhaps be inclined to adopt it; but the difficulty is to discover this position. If it is your intention to correct the abuses of unlicensed printing and to restore the use of orderly language, you may in the first instance try the offender by a jury; but if the jury acquits him, the opinion which was that of a single individual becomes the opinion of the country at large. Too much and too little has therefore hitherto been done: if you proceed, you must bring the delinquent before permanent magistrates; but even here the cause must be heard before it can be decided; and the very principles which no book would have ventured to avow are blazoned forth in the pleadings, and what was obscurely hinted at in a single composition is then repeated in a multitude of other publications. The language in which a thought is embodied is the mere carcass of the thought, and not the idea itself; tribunals may condemn the form, but the sense and spirit of the work is too subtle for their authority: too much has still been done to recede, too little to attain your end; you must therefore proceed. If you establish a censorship of the press, the tongue of the public speaker will still make itself heard, and you have only increased the mischief. The powers of thought do not rely, like the powers of physical strength, upon the number of their mechanical agents, nor can a host of authors be reckoned like the troops which compose an army; on the contrary, the authority of a principle is often increased by the smallness of the number of men by whom it is expressed. The words of a strong-minded man, which penetrate amidst the passions of a listening assembly, have more power than the vociferations of a thousand orators; and if it be allowed to speak freely in any public place, the consequence is the same as if free speaking was allowed in every village. The liberty of discourse must therefore be destroyed as well as the liberty of the press; this is the necessary term of your efforts; but if your object was to repress the abuses of liberty, they have brought you to the feet of a despot. You have been led from the extreme of independence to the extreme of subjection, without meeting with a single tenable position for shelter or repose.

There are certain nations which have peculiar reasons for cherishing the liberty of the press, independently of the general motives which I have just pointed out. For in certain countries which profess to enjoy the privileges of freedom, every individual agent of the government may violate the laws with impunity, since those whom he oppresses cannot prosecute him before the courts of justice. In this case the liberty of the press is not merely a guarantee, but it is the only guarantee of their liberty and their security which the citizens possess. If the rulers of these nations proposed to abolish the independence of the press, the people would be justified in saying: "Give us the right of prosecuting your offenses before the ordinary tribunals, and perhaps we may then waive our right of appeal to the tribunal of public opinion."

But in the countries in which the doctrine of the sovereignty of the people ostensibly prevails, the censorship of the press is not only dangerous, but it is absurd. When the right of every citizen to co-operate in the government of society is acknowledged, every citizen must be presumed to possess the power of discriminating between the different opinions of his contemporaries, and of appreciating the different facts from which inferences may be drawn. The sovereignty of the people and the liberty of the press may therefore be looked upon as correlative institutions; just as the censorship of the press and universal suffrage are two things which are irreconcilably opposed, and which cannot long be retained among the institutions of the same people. Not a single individual of the twelve millions who inhabit the territory of the United States has as yet dared to propose any restrictions to the liberty of the press. The first newspaper over which I cast my eyes, upon my arrival in America, contained the following article:

In all this affair, the language of Jackson has been that of a heartless despot, solely occupied with the preservation of his own authority. Ambition is his crime, and it will be his punishment too: intrigue is his native element, and intrigue will confound his tricks, and will deprive him of his power: he governs by means of corruption, and his immoral practices will redound to his shame and confusion. His conduct in the political arena has been that of a shameless and lawless gamester. He succeeded at the time, but the hour of retribution approaches, and he will be obliged to disgorge his winnings, to throw aside his false dice, and to end his days in some retirement, where he may curse his madness at his leisure; for repentance is a virtue with which his heart is likely to remain for ever unacquainted.

It is not uncommonly imagined in France that the virulence of the press originates in the uncertain social condition, in the political excitement, and the general sense of consequent evil which prevail in that country; and it is therefore supposed that as soon as society has resumed a certain degree of composure, the press will abandon its present vehemence. I am inclined to think that the above causes explain the reason of the extraordinary ascendency it has acquired over the nation, but that they do not exercise much influence upon the tone of its language. The periodical press appears to me to be actuated by passions and propensities independent of the circumstances in which it is placed; and the present position of America corroborates this opinion.

America is perhaps, at this moment, the country of the whole world which contains the fewest germs of revolution; but the press is not less destructive in its principles than in France, and it displays the same violence without the same reasons for indignation. In America, as in France, it constitutes a singular power, so strangely composed of mingled good and evil that it is at the same time indispensable to the existence of freedom, and nearly incompatible with the maintenance of public order. Its power is certainly much greater in France than in the United States, though nothing is more rare in the latter country than to hear of a prosecution having been instituted against it. The reason of this is perfectly simple: the Americans having once admitted the doctrine of the sovereignty of the people, apply it with perfect consistency. It was never their intention to found a permanent state of things with elements which undergo daily modifications; and there is consequently nothing criminal in an attack upon the existing laws, provided it be not attended with a violent infraction of them. They are moreover of opinion that courts of justice are unable to check the abuses of the press; and that as the subtlety of human language perpetually eludes the severity of judicial analysis, offenses of this nature are apt to escape the hand which attempts to apprehend them. They hold that to act with efficacy upon the press, it would be necessary to find a tribunal not only devoted to the existing order of things but capable of surmounting the influence of public opinion, a tribunal which should conduct its proceedings without publicity, which should pronounce its decrees without assigning its motives, and punish the intentions even more than the language of an author. Whosoever should have the power of creating and maintaining a tribunal of this kind would waste his time in prosecuting the liberty of the press; for he would be the supreme master of the whole community, and he would be as free to rid himself of the authors as of their writings. In this question, therefore, there is no medium between servitude and extreme license; in order to enjoy the inestimable benefits which the liberty of the press ensures, it is necessary to submit to the inevitable evils which it engenders. To expect to acquire the former and to escape the latter is to cherish one of those illusions which commonly mislead nations in their times of sickness, when, tired with faction and exhausted by effort, they attempt to combine hostile opinions and contrary principles upon the same soil.

The small influence of the American journals is attributable to several reasons, among which are the following:

The liberty of writing, like all other liberty, is most formidable when it is a novelty; for a people which has never been accustomed to co-operate in the conduct of state affairs places implicit confidence in the first tribune who arouses its attention. The Anglo-Americans have enjoyed this liberty ever since the foundation of the settlements; moreover, the press cannot create human passions by its own power, however skillfully it may kindle them where they exist. In America politics are discussed with animation and a varied activity, but they rarely touch those deep passions which are excited whenever the positive interest of a part of the community is impaired; but in the United States the interests of the community are in a most prosperous condition. A single glance upon a French and an American newspaper is sufficient to show the difference which exists between the two nations on this head. In France the space allotted to commercial advertisements is very limited, and the intelligence is not considerable, but the most essential part of the journal is that which contains the discussion of the politics of the day. In America three quarters of the enormous sheet which is set before the reader are filled with advertisements, and the remainder is frequently occupied by political intelligence or trivial anecdotes. It is only from time to time that one finds a corner devoted to passionate discussions like those with which the journalists of France are wont to indulge their readers.

It has been demonstrated by observation, and discovered by the innate sagacity of the pettiest as well as the greatest of despots, that the influence of a power is increased in proportion as its direction is rendered more central. In France the press combines a twofold centralization; almost all its power is centered in the same spot, and vested in the same hands, for its organs are far from numerous. The influence of a public press thus constituted upon a skeptical nation must be unbounded. It is an enemy with which a government may sign an occasional truce, but which it is difficult to resist for any length of time.

Neither of these kinds of centralization exists in America. The United States have no metropolis; the intelligence as well as the power of the country are dispersed abroad, and instead of radiating from a point, they cross each other in every direction: the Americans have established no central control over the expression of opinion, any more than over the conduct of business. These are circumstances which do not depend on human foresight; but it is owing to the laws of the Union that there are no licenses to be granted to printers, no securities demanded from editors as in France, and no stamp duty as in France and England. The consequence of this is that nothing is easier than to set up a newspaper, and a small number of readers suffices to defray the expenses of the editor.

The number of periodical and occasional publications which appears in the United States actually surpasses belief. The most enlightened Americans attribute the subordinate influence of the press to this excessive dissemination; and it is adopted as an axiom of political science in that country that the only way to neutralize the effect of public journals is to multiply them indefinitely. I cannot conceive that a truth which is so self-evident should not already have been more generally admitted in Europe; it is comprehensible that the persons who hope to bring about revolutions by means of the press should be desirous of confining its action to a few powerful organs, but it is perfectly incredible that the partisans of the existing state of things, and the natural supporters of the laws, should attempt to diminish the influence of the press by concentrating its authority. The governments of Europe seem to treat the press with the courtesy of the knights of old; they are anxious to furnish it with the same central power which they have found to be so trusty a weapon, in order to enhance the glory of their resistance to its attacks.

In America there is scarcely a hamlet which has not its own newspaper. It may readily be imagined that neither discipline nor unity of design can be communicated to so multifarious a host, and each one is consequently led to fight under his own standard. All the political journals of the United States are indeed arrayed on the side of the administration or against it; but they attack and defend it in a thousand different ways. They cannot succeed in forming those great currents of opinion which overwhelm the most solid obstacles. This division of the influence of the press produces a variety of other consequences which are scarcely less remarkable. The facility with which journals can be established induces a multitude of individuals to take a part in them; but as the extent of competition precludes the possibility of considerable profit, the most distinguished classes of society are rarely led to engage in these undertakings. But such is the number of the public prints that even if they were a source of wealth writers of ability could not be found to direct them all. The journalists of the United States are usually placed in a very humble position, with a scanty education and a vulgar turn of mind. The will of the majority is the most general of laws, and it establishes certain habits which form the characteristics of each peculiar class of society; thus it dictates the etiquette practiced at courts and the etiquette of the bar. The characteristics of the French journalist consist in a violent, but frequently an eloquent and lofty, manner of discussing the politics of the day; and the exceptions to this habitual practice are only occasional. The characteristics of the American journalist consist in an open and coarse appeal to the passions of the populace; and he habitually abandons the principles of political science to assail the characters of individuals, to track them into private life, and disclose all their weaknesses and errors.

Nothing can be more deplorable than this abuse of the powers of thought; I shall have occasion to point out hereafter the influence of the newspapers upon the taste and the morality of the American people, but my present subject exclusively concerns the political world. It cannot be denied that the effects of this extreme license of the press tend indirectly to the maintenance of public order. The individuals who are already in the possession of a high station in the esteem of their fellow citizens are afraid to write in the newspapers, and they are thus deprived of the most powerful instrument which they can use to excite the passions of the multitude to their own advantage.[4]

The personal opinions of the editors have no kind of weight in the eyes of the public; the only use of a journal is that it imparts the knowledge of certain facts, and it is only by altering or distorting those facts that a journalist can contribute to the support of his own views.

But although the press is limited to these resources, its influence in America is immense. It is the power which impels the circulation of political life through all the districts of that vast territory. Its eye is constantly open to detect the secret springs of political designs, and to summon the leaders of all parties to the bar of public opinion. It rallies the interests of the community round certain principles, and it draws up the creed which factions adopt; for it affords a means of intercourse between

---

4. They only write in the papers when they choose to address the people in their own name; as, for instance, when they are called upon to repel calumnious imputations, and to correct a misstatement of facts.

parties which hear and which address each other without ever having been in immediate contact. When a great number of the organs of the press adopt the same line of conduct, their influence becomes irresistible; and public opinion, when it is perpetually assailed from the same side, eventually yields to the attack. In the United States each separate journal exercises but little authority; but the power of the periodical press is only second to that of the people.

In the United States the democracy perpetually raises fresh individuals to the conduct of public affairs; and the measures of the administration are consequently seldom regulated by the strict rules of consistency or of order. But the general principles of the government are more stable, and the opinions most prevalent in society are generally more durable than in many other countries. When once the Americans have taken up an idea, whether it be well or ill founded, nothing is more difficult than to eradicate it from their minds. The same tenacity of opinion has been observed in England, where, for the last century, greater freedom of conscience and more invincible prejudices have existed than in all the other countries of Europe. I attribute this consequence to a cause which may at first sight appear to have a very opposite tendency, namely, to the liberty of the press. The nations among which this liberty exists are as apt to cling to their opinions from pride as from conviction. They cherish them because they hold them to be just, and because they exercised their own free will in choosing them; and they maintain them, not only because they are true, but because they are their own. Several other reasons conduce to the same end.

It was remarked by a man of genius that "ignorance lies at the two ends of knowledge." Perhaps it would have been more correct to have said that absolute convictions are to be met with at the two extremities, and that doubt lies in the middle; for the human intellect may be considered in three distinct states, which frequently succeed one another.

A man believes implicitly because he adopts a proposition without inquiry. He doubts as soon as he is assailed by the objections which his inquiries may have aroused. But he frequently succeeds in satisfying these doubts, and then he begins to believe afresh. He no longer lays hold on a truth in its most shadowy and uncertain form, but he sees it clearly before him, and he advances onwards by the light it gives him.[5]

---

5. It may, however, be doubted whether this rational and self-guiding conviction arouses as much fervor or enthusiastic devotedness in men as their first dogmatical belief.

When the liberty of the press acts upon men who are in the first of these three states, it does not immediately disturb their habit of believing implicitly without investigation, but it constantly modifies the objects of their intuitive convictions. The human mind continues to discern but one point upon the whole intellectual horizon, and that point is in continual motion. Such are the symptoms of sudden revolutions, and of the misfortunes which are sure to befall those generations which abruptly adopt the unconditional freedom of the press.

The circle of novel ideas is, however, soon terminated; the touch of experience is upon them, and the doubt and mistrust which their uncertainty produces become universal. We may rest assured that the majority of mankind will either believe they know not wherefore or will not know what to believe. Few are the beings who can ever hope to attain to that state of rational and independent conviction which true knowledge can beget, in defiance of the attacks of doubt.

It has been remarked that in times of great religious fervor men sometimes change their religious opinions; whereas in times of general skepticism everyone clings to his own persuasion. The same thing takes place in politics under the liberty of the press. In countries where all the theories of social science have been contested in their turn, the citizens who have adopted one of them stick to it, not so much because they are assured of its excellence as because they are not convinced of the superiority of any other. In the present age, men are not very ready to die in defense of their opinions, but they are rarely inclined to change them; and there are fewer martyrs as well as fewer apostates.

Another still more valid reason may yet be adduced: when no abstract opinions are looked upon as certain, men cling to the mere propensities and external interests of their position, which are naturally more tangible and more permanent than any opinions in the world.

It is not a question of easy solution whether the aristocracy or the democracy is most fit to govern a country. But it is certain that democracy annoys one part of the community, and that aristocracy oppresses another part. When the question is reduced to the simple expression of the struggle between poverty and wealth, the tendency of each side of the dispute becomes perfectly evident without further controversy.

Political Associations in the United States

In no country in the world has the principle of association been more successfully used, or more unsparingly applied to a multitude of different objects, than in America. Besides the permanent associations which are established by law under the names of townships, cities, and counties, a vast number of others are formed and maintained by the agency of private individuals.

The citizen of the United States is taught from his earliest infancy to rely upon his own exertions in order to resist the evils and the difficulties of life. He looks upon the social authority with an eye of mistrust and anxiety, and he only claims its assistance when he is quite unable to shift without it. This habit may even be traced in the schools of the rising generation, where the children in their games are wont to submit to rules which they have themselves established, and to punish misdemeanors which they have themselves defined. The same spirit pervades every act of social life. If a stoppage occurs in a thoroughfare, and the circulation of the public is hindered, the neighbors immediately constitute a deliberative body; and this extemporaneous assembly gives rise to an executive power which remedies the inconvenience before anybody has thought of recurring to an authority superior to that of the persons immediately concerned. If the public pleasures are concerned, an association is formed to provide for the splendor and the regularity of the entertainment. Societies are formed to resist enemies which are exclusively of a moral nature, and to diminish the vice of intemperance. In the United States associations are established to promote public order, commerce, industry, morality, and religion; for there is no end which the human will, seconded by the collective exertions of individuals, despairs of attaining.

I shall hereafter have occasion to show the effects of association upon the course of society, and I must confine myself for the present to the political world. When once the right of association is recognized, the citizens may employ it in several different ways.

An association consists simply in the public assent which a number of individuals give to certain doctrines; and in the engagement which they contract to promote the spread of those doctrines by their exertions. The right of associating with these views is very analogous to the liberty of unlicensed writing; but societies thus formed possess more authority than the press. When an opinion is represented by a society, it necessarily assumes a more exact and explicit form. It numbers its partisans, and compromises their welfare in its cause; they, on the other hand, become acquainted with each other, and their zeal is increased by their number. An association unites the efforts of minds which have a tendency to diverge, in one single channel, and urges them vigorously towards one single end which it points out.

The second degree in the right of association is the power of meeting.

When an association is allowed to establish centers of action at certain important points in the country, its activity is increased, and its influence extended. Men have the opportunity of seeing each other; means of execution are more readily combined; and opinions are maintained with a degree of warmth and energy which written language cannot approach.

Lastly, in the exercise of the right of political association, there is a third degree: the partisans of an opinion may unite in electoral bodies, and choose delegates to represent them in a central assembly. This is, properly speaking, the application of the representative system to a party.

Thus, in the first instance, a society is formed between individuals professing the same opinion, and the tie which keeps it together is of a purely intellectual nature: in the second case, small assemblies are formed which only represent a faction of the party. Lastly, in the third case, they constitute a separate nation in the midst of the nation, a government within the government. Their delegates, like the real delegates of the majority, represent the entire collective force of their party; and they enjoy a certain degree of that national dignity and great influence which belong to the chosen representatives of the people. It is true that they have not the right of making the laws; but they have the power of attacking those which are in being, and of drawing up beforehand those which they may afterwards cause to be adopted.

If, in a people which is imperfectly accustomed to the exercise of freedom, or which is exposed to violent political passions, a deliberating minority, which confines itself to the contemplation of future laws, be placed in juxtaposition to the legislative majority, I cannot but believe that public tranquillity incurs very great risks in that nation. There is doubtless a very wide difference between proving that one law is in itself better than another, and proving that the former ought to be substituted for the latter. But the imagination of the populace is very apt to overlook this difference, which is so apparent to the minds of thinking men. It sometimes happens that a nation is divided into two nearly equal parties, each of which affects to represent the majority. If, in immediate contiguity to the directing power, another power be established which exercises almost as much moral authority as the former, it is not to be believed that it will long be content to speak without acting, or that it will always be restrained by the abstract consideration of the nature of associations, which are meant to direct but not to enforce opinions, to suggest but not to make the laws.

The more we consider the independence of the press in its principal consequences, the more are we convinced that it is the chief, and, so to speak, the constitutive element of freedom in the modern world. A nation which is determined to remain free is therefore right in demanding the unrestrained exercise of this independence. But the *unrestrained* liberty of political association cannot be entirely assimilated to the liberty of the press. The one is at the same time less necessary and more dangerous than the other. A nation may confine it within certain limits without forfeiting any part of its self-control; and it may sometimes be obliged to do so in order to maintain its own authority.

In America the liberty of association for political purposes is unbounded. An example will show in the clearest light to what an extent this privilege is tolerated.

The question of the tariff, or of free trade, produced a great manifestation of party feeling in America: the tariff was not only a subject of debate as a matter of opinion, but it exercised a favorable or a prejudicial influence upon several very powerful interests of the states. The North attributed a great portion of its prosperity, and the South all its sufferings, to this system; insomuch that for a long time the tariff was the sole source of the political animosities which agitated the Union.

In 1831, when the dispute was raging with the utmost virulence, a private citizen of Massachusetts proposed to all the enemies of the tariff, by means of the public prints, to send delegates to Philadelphia in order to consult together upon the means which were most fitted to promote freedom of trade. This proposal circulated in a few days from Maine to New Orleans by the power of the printing press; the opponents of the tariff adopted it with enthusiasm, meetings were formed on all sides, and delegates were named. The majority of these individuals were well known, and some of them had earned a considerable degree of celebrity. South Carolina alone, which afterwards took up arms in the same cause, sent sixty-three delegates. On the 1st October, 1831, this assembly, which according to the American custom had taken the name of a convention, met at Philadelphia; it consisted of more than two hundred members. Its debates were public, and they at once assumed a legislative character; the extent of the powers of Congress, the theories of free trade, and the different clauses of the tariff were discussed in turn. At the end of ten days' deliberation the convention broke up, after having published an address to the American people, in which it declared:

i. That Congress had not the right of making a tariff, and that the existing tariff was unconstitutional;

ii. That the prohibition of free trade was prejudicial to the interests of all nations, and to that of the American people in particular.

It must be acknowledged that the unrestrained liberty of political association has not hitherto produced in the United States those fatal consequences which might perhaps be expected from it elsewhere. The right of association was imported from England, and it has always existed in America, so that the exercise of this privilege is now amalgamated with the manners and customs of the people. At the present time, the liberty of association has become a necessary guarantee against the tyranny of the majority. In the United States, as soon as a party has become preponderant, all the public authority passes under its control. Its private supporters occupy all the places, and have all the force of the administration at their disposal. As the most distinguished partisans of the other side of the question are unable to surmount the obstacles which exclude them from power, they require some means of establishing themselves upon their own basis, and of opposing the moral authority of the minority to the physical power which domineers over it. Thus a dangerous expedient is used to obviate a still more formidable danger.

The omnipotence of the majority appears to me to present such extreme perils to the American republics that the dangerous measure which is used to repress it seems to be more advantageous than prejudicial. And here I am about to advance a proposition which may remind the reader of what I said before in speaking of municipal freedom: There are no countries in which associations are more needed to prevent the despotism of faction or the arbitrary power of a prince than those which are democratically constituted. In aristocratic nations, the body of the nobles and the more opulent part of the community are in themselves natural associations, which act as checks upon the abuses of power. In countries in which these associations do not exist, if private individuals are unable to create an artificial and a temporary substitute for them, I can imagine no permanent protection against the most galling tyranny; and a great people may be oppressed by a small faction, or by a single individual, with impunity.

The meeting of a great political convention (for there are conventions of all kinds), which may frequently become a necessary measure, is always a serious occurrence, even in America, and one which is never looked forward to, by the judicious friends of the country, without alarm.

This was very perceptible in the Convention of 1831, at which the exertions of all the most distinguished members of the assembly tended to moderate its language, and to restrain the subjects which it treated within certain limits. It is probable, in fact, that the Convention of 1831 exercised a very great influence upon the minds of the malcontents, and prepared them for the open revolt against the commercial laws of the Union which took place in 1832.

It cannot be denied that the unrestrained liberty of association for political purposes is the privilege which a people is longest in learning how to exercise. If it does not throw the nation into anarchy, it perpetually augments the chances of that calamity. On one point, however, this perilous liberty offers a security against dangers of another kind; in countries where associations are free, secret societies are unknown. In America there are numerous factions, but no conspiracies.

The most natural privilege of man, next to the right of acting for himself, is that of combining his exertions with those of his fellow creatures, and of acting in common with them. I am therefore led to conclude that the right of association is almost as inalienable as the right of personal liberty. No legislator can attack it without impairing the very foundations of society. Nevertheless, if the liberty of association is a fruitful source of advantages and prosperity to some nations, it may be perverted or carried to excess by others, and the element of life may be changed into an element of destruction. A comparison of the different methods which associations pursue, in those countries in which they are managed with discretion, as well as in those where liberty degenerates into license, may perhaps be thought useful both to governments and to parties.

The greater part of Europeans look upon an association as a weapon which is to be hastily fashioned, and immediately tried in the conflict. A society is formed for discussion, but the idea of impending action prevails in the minds of those who constitute it: it is, in fact, an army; and the time given to parley serves to reckon up the strength and to animate the courage of the host, after which they direct their march against the enemy. Resources which lie within the bounds of the law may suggest themselves, to the persons who compose it, as means, but never as the only means, of success.

Such, however, is not the manner in which the right of association is understood in the United States. In America the citizens who form the minority associate, in order, in the first place, to show their numerical strength, and so to diminish the moral authority of the majority; and, in the second place, to stimulate competition, and to discover those arguments which are most fitted to act upon the majority: for they always entertain hopes of drawing over their opponents to their own side, and of afterwards disposing of the supreme power in their name. Political associations in the United States are therefore peaceable in their intentions, and strictly legal in the means which they employ; and they assert with perfect truth that they only aim at success by lawful expedients.

The difference which exists between the Americans and ourselves depends on several causes. In Europe there are numerous parties so diametrically opposed to the majority that they can never hope to acquire its support, and at the same time they think that they are sufficiently strong in themselves to struggle and to defend their cause. When a party of this kind forms an association, its object is not to conquer but to fight. In America, the individuals who hold opinions very much opposed to those of the majority are no sort of impediment to its power; and all other parties hope to win it over to their own principles in the end. The exercise of the right of association becomes dangerous in proportion to the impossibility which excludes great parties from acquiring the majority. In a country like the United States, in which the differences of opinion are mere differences of hue, the right of association may remain unrestrained without evil consequences. The inexperience of many of the European nations in the enjoyment of liberty leads them only to look upon the liberty of association as a right of attacking the government. The first notion which presents itself to a party, as well as to an individual, when it has acquired a consciousness of its own strength, is that of violence: the notion of persuasion arises at a later period, and is only derived from experience. The English, who are divided into parties which differ most essentially from each other, rarely abuse the right of association, because they have long been accustomed to exercise it. In France, the passion for war is so intense that there is no undertaking so mad, or so injurious to the welfare of the state, that a man does not consider himself honored in defending it, at the risk of his life.

But perhaps the most powerful of the causes which tend to mitigate the excesses of political association in the United States is universal suffrage. In countries in which universal suffrage exists, the majority is never doubtful, because neither party can pretend to represent that portion of the community which has not voted. The associations which are formed are aware, as well as the nation at large, that they do not represent the majority: this is, indeed, a condition inseparable from their existence; for if they did represent the preponderating power, they would change the law instead of soliciting its reform. The consequence of this is that the moral influence of the government which they attack is very much increased, and their own power is very much enfeebled.

In Europe there are few associations which do not affect to represent the majority, or which do not believe that they represent it. This conviction or this pretension tends to augment their force amazingly, and contributes no less to legalize their measures. Violence may seem to be excusable in defense of the cause of oppressed right. Thus it is, in the vast labyrinth of human laws, that extreme liberty sometimes corrects the abuses of license, and that extreme democracy obviates the dangers of democratic government. In Europe, associations consider themselves, in some degree, as the legislative and executive councils of the people, which is unable to speak for itself. In America, where they only represent a minority of the nation, they argue and they petition.

The means which the associations of Europe employ are in accordance with the end which they propose to obtain. As the principal aim of these bodies is to act and not to debate, to fight rather than to persuade, they are naturally led to adopt a form of organization which differs from the ordinary customs of civil bodies, and which assumes the habits and the maxims of military life. They centralize the direction of their resources as much as possible, and they entrust the power of the whole party to a very small number of leaders.

The members of these associations reply to a watchword, like soldiers on duty; they profess the doctrine of passive obedience; say, rather, that in uniting together they at once abjure the exercise of their own judgment and free will: and the tyrannical control which these societies exercise is often far more insupportable than the authority possessed over society by the government which they attack. Their moral force is much diminished by these excesses, and they lose the powerful interest which is always excited by a struggle between oppressors and the oppressed. The man who in given cases consents to obey his fellows with servility, and who submits his activity, and even his opinions, to their control, can have no claim to rank as a free citizen.

The Americans have also established certain forms of government which are applied to their associations, but these are invariably borrowed from the forms of the civil administration. The independence of each individual is formally recognized; the tendency of the members of the association points, as it does in the body of the community, towards the same end, but they are not obliged to follow the same track. No one abjures the exercise of his reason and his free will; but everyone exerts that reason and that will for the benefit of a common undertaking.

Government of the Democracy in America

I am well aware of the difficulties which attend this part of my subject, but although every expression which I am about to make use of may clash, upon some one point, with the feelings of the different parties which divide my country, I shall speak my opinion with the most perfect openness.

In Europe we are at a loss how to judge the true character and the more permanent propensities of democracy, because in Europe two conflicting principles exist, and we do not know what to attribute to the principles themselves, and what to refer to the passions which they bring into collision. Such, however, is not the case in America; there the people reigns without any obstacle, and it has no perils to dread, and no injuries to avenge. In America, democracy is swayed by its own free propensities: its course is natural, and its activity is unrestrained; the United States consequently afford the most favorable opportunity of studying its real character. And to no people can this inquiry be more vitally interesting than to the French nation, which is blindly driven onwards by a daily and irresistible impulse, towards a state of things which may prove either despotic or republican, but which will assuredly be democratic.

UNIVERSAL SUFFRAGE

I have ready observed that universal suffrage has been adopted in all the states of the Union: it consequently occurs among different populations which occupy very different positions in the scale of society. I have had opportunities of observing its effects in different localities, and among races of men who are nearly strangers to each other by their language, their religion, and their manner of life; in Louisiana as well as in New England, in Georgia and in Canada. I have remarked that universal suffrage is far from producing in America either all the good or all the evil consequences which are assigned to it in Europe, and that its effects differ very widely from those which are usually attributed to it.

CHOICE OF THE PEOPLE AND INSTINCTIVE PREFERENCES
OF THE AMERICAN DEMOCRACY

Many people in Europe are apt to believe without saying it, or to say without believing it, that one of the great advantages of universal suffrage is that it entrusts the direction of public affairs to men who are worthy of the public confidence. They admit that the people is unable to govern for itself, but they aver that it is always sincerely disposed to promote the welfare of the state, and that it instinctively designates those persons who are animated by the same good wishes, and who are the most fit to wield the supreme authority. I confess that the observations I made in America by no means coincide with these opinions. On my arrival in the United States, I was surprised to find so much distinguished talent among the subjects, and so little among the heads of the government. It is a well-authenticated fact that at the present day the most able men in the United States are very rarely placed at the head of affairs; and it must be acknowledged that such has been the result in proportion as democracy has outstepped all its former limits. The race of American statesmen has evidently dwindled most remarkably in the course of the last fifty years.

Several causes may be assigned to this phenomenon. It is impossible, notwithstanding the most strenuous exertions, to raise the intelligence of the people above a certain level. Whatever may be the facilities of acquiring information, whatever may be the profusion of easy methods and of cheap science, the human mind can never be instructed and educated without devoting a considerable space of time to those objects.

The greater or the lesser possibility of subsisting without labor is therefore the necessary boundary of intellectual improvement. This boundary is more remote in some countries, and more restricted in others; but it must exist somewhere as long as the people is constrained to work in order to procure the means of physical subsistence, that is to say, as long as it retains its popular character. It is therefore quite as difficult to imagine a state in which all the citizens should be very well informed as a state in which they should all be wealthy: these two difficulties may be looked upon as correlative. It may very readily be admitted that the mass of the citizens are sincerely disposed to promote the welfare of their country; nay more, it may even be allowed that the lower classes are less apt to be swayed by considerations of personal interest than the higher orders; but it is always more or less impossible for them to discern the best means of attaining the end which they desire with sincerity. Long and patient observation, joined to a multitude of different notions, is required to form a just estimate of the character of a single individual; and can it be supposed that the vulgar have the power of succeeding in an inquiry which misleads the penetration of genius itself? The people has neither the time nor the means which are essential to the prosecution of an investigation of this kind: its conclusions are hastily formed from a superficial inspection of the more prominent features of a question. Hence it often assents to the clamor of a mountebank who knows the secret of stimulating its tastes, while its truest friends frequently fail in their exertions.

Moreover, the democracy is not only deficient in that soundness of judgment which is necessary to select men really deserving of its confidence, but it has neither the desire nor the inclination to find them out. It cannot be denied that democratic institutions have a very strong tendency to promote the feeling of envy in the human heart, not so much because they afford to everyone the means of rising to the level of any of his fellow citizens as because those means perpetually disappoint the persons who employ them. Democratic institutions awaken and foster a passion for equality which they can never entirely satisfy. This complete equality eludes the grasp of the people at the very moment at which it thinks to hold it fast, and "flies," as Pascal says, "with eternal flight"; the people is excited in the pursuit of an advantage which is more precious because it is not sufficiently remote to be unknown, or sufficiently near to be enjoyed. The lower orders are agitated by the chance of success, they are irritated by its uncertainty; and they pass from the enthusiasm of pursuit to the exhaustion of ill success, and lastly to the acrimony of disappointment. Whatever transcends their own limits appears to be an obstacle to their desires, and there is no kind of superiority, however legitimate it may be, which is not irksome in their sight.

It has been supposed that the secret instinct which leads the lower orders to remove their superiors as much as possible from the direction of public affairs is peculiar to France. This, however, is an error; the propensity to which I allude is not inherent in any particular nation, but in democratic institutions in general; and although it may have been heightened by peculiar political circumstances, it owes its origin to a higher cause.

In the United States, the people is not disposed to hate the superior classes of society; but it is not very favorably inclined towards them, and it carefully excludes them from the exercise of authority. It does not entertain any dread of distinguished talents, but it is rarely captivated by them; and it awards its approbation very sparingly to such as have risen without the popular support.

While the natural propensities of democracy induce the people to reject the most distinguished citizens as its rulers, these individuals are no less apt to retire from a political career, in which it is almost impossible to retain their independence or to advance without degrading themselves. This opinion has been very candidly set forth by Chancellor Kent, who says, in speaking with great eulogiums of that part of the Constitution which empowers the executive to nominate the judges: "It is indeed probable that the men who are best fitted to discharge the duties of this high office would have too much reserve in their manners, and too much austerity in their principles, for them to be returned by the majority at an election where universal suffrage is adopted." Such were the opinions which were printed without contradiction in America in the year 1830!

I hold it to be sufficiently demonstrated that universal suffrage is by no means a guarantee of the wisdom of the popular choice; and that whatever its advantages may be, this is not one of them.

CAUSES WHICH MAY PARTLY CORRECT THESE TENDENCIES OF THE DEMOCRACY

When a state is threatened by serious dangers, the people frequently succeeds in selecting the citizens who are the most able to save it. It has been observed that man rarely retains his customary level in presence of very critical circumstances; he rises above, or he sinks below his usual condition, and the same thing occurs in nations at large. Extreme perils sometimes quench the energy of a people instead of stimulating it; they excite, without directing its passions; and instead of clearing, they confuse its powers of perception. The Jews deluged the smoking ruins of their temple with the carnage of the remnant of their host. But it is more common, both in the case of nations and in that of individuals, to find extraordinary virtues arising from the very imminence of the danger. Great characters are then thrown into relief, as the edifices which are concealed by the gloom of night are illuminated by the glare of a conflagration. At those dangerous times genius no longer abstains from presenting itself in the arena; and the people, alarmed by the perils of its situation, buries its envious passions in a short oblivion. Great names may then be drawn from the urn of election.

I have already observed that the American statesmen of the present day are very inferior to those who stood at the head of affairs fifty years ago. This is as much a consequence of the circumstances as of the laws of the country. When America was struggling in the high cause of independence to throw off the yoke of another country, and when it was about to usher a new nation into the world, the spirits of its inhabitants were roused to the height which their great efforts required. In this general excitement, the most distinguished men were ready to forestall the wants of the community, and the people clung to them for support and placed them at its head. But events of this magnitude are rare; and it is from an inspection of the ordinary course of affairs that our judgment must be formed.

If passing occurrences sometimes act as checks upon the passions of democracy, the intelligence and the manners of the community exercise an influence which is not less powerful, and far more permanent. This is extremely perceptible in the United States.

In New England the education and the liberties of the communities were engendered by the moral and religious principles of their founders. Where society has acquired a sufficient degree of stability to enable it to hold certain maxims and to retain fixed habits, the lower orders are accustomed to respect intellectual superiority, and to submit to it without complaint, although they set at nought all those privileges which wealth and birth have introduced among mankind. The democracy in New England consequently makes a more judicious choice than it does elsewhere.

But as we descend towards the South, to those states in which the constitution of society is more modern and less strong, where instruction is less general, and where the principles of morality, of religion, and of liberty are less happily combined, we perceive that the talents and the virtues of those who are in authority become more and more rare.

Lastly, when we arrive at the new southwestern states, in which the constitution of society dates but from yesterday, and presents an agglomeration of adventurers and speculators, we are amazed at the persons who are invested with public authority, and we are led to ask by what force, independent of the legislation and of the men who direct it, the state can be protected, and society be made to flourish.

There are certain laws of a democratic nature which contribute, nevertheless, to correct, in some measure, the dangerous tendencies of democracy. On entering the House of Representatives of Washington, one is struck by the vulgar demeanor of that great assembly. The eye frequently does not discover a man of celebrity within its walls. Its members are almost all obscure individuals whose names present no associations to the mind: they are mostly village lawyers, men in trade, or even persons belonging to the lower classes of society. In a country in which education is very general, it is said that the representatives of the people do not always know how to write correctly.

At a few yards' distance from this spot is the door of the Senate, which contains within a small space a large proportion of the celebrated men of America. Scarcely an individual is to be perceived in it who does not recall the idea of an active and illustrious career: the Senate is composed of eloquent advocates, distinguished generals, wise magistrates, and statesmen of note, whose language would at all times do honor to the most remarkable parliamentary debates of Europe.

What then is the cause of this strange contrast, and why are the most able citizens to be found in one assembly rather than in the other? Why is the former body remarkable for its vulgarity and its poverty of talent, while the latter seems to enjoy a monopoly of intelligence and of sound judgment? Both of these assemblies emanate from the people; both of them are chosen by universal suffrage; and no voice has hitherto been heard to assert, in America, that the Senate is hostile to the interests of the people. From what cause, then, does so startling a difference arise? The only reason which appears to me adequately to account for it is that the House of Representatives is elected by the populace directly, and that the Senate is elected by elected bodies. The whole body of the citizens names the legislature of each state, and the federal Constitution converts these legislatures into so many electoral bodies, which return the members of the Senate. The senators are elected by an indirect application of universal suffrage: for the legislatures which name them are not aristocratic or privileged bodies which exercise the electoral franchise in their own right; but they are chosen by the totality of the citizens; they are generally elected every year, and new members may constantly be chosen who will employ their electoral rights in conformity with the wishes of the public. But this transmission of the popular authority through an assembly of chosen men operates an important change in it, by refining its discretion and improving the forms which it adopts. Men who are chosen in this manner accurately represent the majority of the nation which governs them; but they represent the elevated thoughts which are current in the community, the generous propensities which prompt its nobler actions, rather than the petty passions which disturb, or the vices which disgrace it.

The time may be already anticipated at which the American republics will be obliged to introduce the plan of election by an elected body more frequently into their system of representation, or they will incur no small risk of perishing miserably among the shoals of democracy.

And here I have no scruple in confessing that I look upon this peculiar system of election as the only means of bringing the exercise of political power to the level of all classes of the people. Those thinkers who regard this institution as the exclusive weapon of a party, and those who fear, on the other hand, to make use of it, seem to me to fall into as great an error in the one case as in the other.

INFLUENCE WHICH THE AMERICAN DEMOCRACY HAS EXERCISED ON THE LAWS RELATING TO ELECTIONS

When elections recur at long intervals, the state is exposed to violent agitation every time they take place. Parties exert themselves to the utmost in order to gain a prize which is so rarely within their reach; and as the evil is almost irremediable for the candidates who fail, the consequences of their disappointed ambition may prove most disastrous. If, on the other hand, the legal struggle can be repeated within a short space of time, the defeated parties take patience.

When elections occur frequently, their recurrence keeps society in a perpetual state of feverish excitement, and imparts a continual instability to public affairs.

Thus, on the one hand the state is exposed to the perils of a revolution, on the other to perpetual mutability; the former system threatens the very existence of the government, the latter is an obstacle to all steady and consistent policy. The Americans have preferred the second of these evils to the first; but they were led to this conclusion by their instinct much more than by their reason; for a taste for variety is one of the characteristic passions of democracy. An extraordinary mutability has, by this means, been introduced into their legislation.

Many of the Americans consider the instability of their laws as a necessary consequence of a system whose general results are beneficial. But no one in the United States affects to deny the fact of this instability, or to contend that it is not a great evil.

Hamilton, after having demonstrated the utility of a power which might prevent, or which might at least impede, the promulgation of bad laws, adds, "It may perhaps be said that the power of preventing bad laws includes that of preventing good ones; and may be used to the one purpose as well as to the other. But this objection will have little weight with those who can properly estimate the mischiefs of that inconstancy and mutability in the laws which form the greatest blemish in the character and genius of our governments." [6]

And again in No. 62 of the same work, he observes: ". . . The facility and excess of law-making seem to be the diseases to which our govern-

6. *The Federalist*, No. 73, *Great Books of the Western World*, Vol. 43, p. 220 [Ed.].

ments are most liable. . . . [To trace the mischievous effects of] the mutability in the public councils arising from a rapid succession of new members [would fill a volume]. Every new election in the States is found to change one half of the representatives. From this change of men must proceed a change of opinions [and of] measures, . . . [which] forfeits the respect and confidence of other nations, . . . poisons the blessing of liberty itself . . . [and diminishes] the attachment and reverence . . . of the people towards a political system which betrays so many marks of infirmity. . . ." [7]

Jefferson himself, the greatest democrat whom the democracy of America has as yet produced, pointed out the same evils.

"The instability of our laws," said he in a letter to Madison, "is really a very serious inconvenience. I think that we ought to have obviated it by deciding that a whole year should always be allowed to elapse between the bringing in of a bill and the final passing of it. It should afterwards be discussed and put to the vote without the possibility of making any alteration in it; and if the circumstances of the case required a more speedy decision, the question should not be decided by a simple majority, but by a majority of at least two-thirds of both houses."

PUBLIC OFFICERS UNDER THE CONTROL OF THE DEMOCRACY IN AMERICA

Public officers in the United States are commingled with the crowd of citizens; they have neither palaces, nor guards, nor ceremonial costumes. This simple exterior of the persons in authority is connected, not only with the peculiarities of the American character, but with the fundamental principles of that society. In the estimation of the democracy, a government is not a benefit, but a necessary evil. A certain degree of power must be granted to public officers, for they would be of no use without it. But the ostensible semblance of authority is by no means indispensable to the conduct of affairs; and it is needlessly offensive to the susceptibility of the public. The public officers themselves are well aware that they only enjoy the superiority over their fellow citizens which they derive from their authority, upon condition of putting themselves on a level with the whole community by their manners. A public officer in the United States is uniformly civil, accessible to all the world, attentive to all requests, and obliging in his replies. I was pleased by

7. *The Federalist*, No. 62, *Great Books of the Western World*, Vol. 43, pp. 189–191 [Ed.].

these characteristics of a democratic government; and I was struck by the manly independence of the citizens, who respect the office more than the officer, and who are less attached to the emblems of authority than to the man who bears them.

I am inclined to believe that the influence which costumes really exercise, in an age like that in which we live, has been a good deal exaggerated. I never perceived that a public officer in America was the less respected while he was in the discharge of his duties because his own merit was set off by no adventitious signs. On the other hand, it is very doubtful whether a peculiar dress contributes to the respect which public characters ought to have for their own position, at least when they are not otherwise inclined to respect it. When a magistrate (and in France such instances are not rare) indulges his trivial wit at the expense of the prisoner, or derides the predicament in which a culprit is placed, it would be well to deprive him of his robes of office, to see whether he would recall some portion of the natural dignity of mankind when he is reduced to the apparel of a private citizen.

A democracy may, however, allow a certain show of magisterial pomp, and clothe its officers in silks and gold, without seriously compromising its principles. Privileges of this kind are transitory: they belong to the place, and are distinct from the individual; but if public officers are not uniformly remunerated by the state, the public charges must be entrusted to men of opulence and independence, who constitute the basis of an aristocracy; and if the people still retains its right of election, that election can only be made from a certain class of citizens.

When a democratic republic renders offices which had formerly been remunerated gratuitous, it may safely be believed that that state is advancing to monarchical institutions; and when a monarchy begins to remunerate such officers as had hitherto been unpaid, it is a sure sign that it is approaching towards a despotic or a republican form of government. The substitution of paid for unpaid functionaries is of itself, in my opinion, sufficient to constitute a serious revolution.

I look upon the entire absence of gratuitous functionaries in America as one of the most prominent signs of the absolute dominion which democracy exercises in that country. All public services, of whatsoever nature they may be, are paid; so that everyone has not merely a right, but also the means of performing them. Although, in democratic states, all the citizens are qualified to occupy stations in the government, all are not tempted to try for them. The number and the capacities of the candidates are more apt to restrict the choice of electors than the conditions of the candidateship.

In nations in which the principle of election extends to every place in the state, no political career can, properly speaking, be said to exist. Men are promoted as if by chance to the rank which they enjoy, and they are by no means sure of retaining it. The consequence is that in tranquil times public functions offer but few lures to ambition. In the United States the persons who engage in the perplexities of political life are individuals of very moderate pretensions. The pursuit of wealth generally diverts men of great talents and of great passions from the pursuit of power: and it very frequently happens that a man does not undertake to direct the fortune of the state until he has discovered his incompetence to conduct his own affairs. The vast number of very ordinary men who occupy public stations is quite as attributable to these causes as to the bad choice of the democracy. In the United States, I am not sure that the people would return the men of superior abilities who might solicit its support, but it is certain that men of this description do not come forward.

ARBITRARY POWER OF MAGISTRATES[8] UNDER THE RULE OF THE AMERICAN DEMOCRACY

In two different kinds of government the magistrates exercise a considerable degree of arbitrary power; namely, under the absolute government of a single individual, and under that of a democracy.

This identical result proceeds from causes which are nearly analogous.

In despotic states the fortune of no citizen is secure; and public officers are not more safe than private individuals. The sovereign, who has under his control the lives, the property, and sometimes the honor of the men whom he employs, does not scruple to allow them a great latitude of action because he is convinced that they will not use it to his prejudice. In despotic states the sovereign is so attached to the exercise of his power that he dislikes the constraint even of his own regulations; and he is well pleased that his agents should follow a somewhat fortuitous line of conduct, provided he be certain that their actions will never counteract his desires.

In democracies, as the majority has every year the right of depriving

---

8. I here use the word magistrates in the widest sense in which it can be taken; I apply it to all the officers to whom the execution of the laws is entrusted.

the officers whom it has appointed of their power, it has no reason to fear any abuse of their authority. As the people is always able to signify its wishes to those who conduct the government, it prefers leaving them to make their own exertions, to prescribing an invariable rule of conduct which would at once fetter their activity and the popular authority.

It may even be observed, on attentive consideration, that under the rule of a democracy the arbitrary power of the magistrate must be still greater than in despotic states. In the latter, the sovereign has the power of punishing all the faults with which he becomes acquainted, but it would be vain for him to hope to become acquainted with all those which are committed. In the former the sovereign power is not only supreme, but it is universally present. The American functionaries are, in point of fact, much more independent in the sphere of action which the law traces out for them than any public officer in Europe. Very frequently the object which they are to accomplish is simply pointed out to them, and the choice of the means is left to their own discretion.

In New England, for instance, the selectmen of each township are bound to draw up the list of persons who are to serve on the jury; the only rule which is laid down to guide them in their choice is that they are to select citizens possessing the elective franchise and enjoying a fair reputation.[9] In France the lives and liberties of the subjects would be thought to be in danger if a public officer of any kind was entrusted with so formidable a right. In New England the same magistrates are empowered to post the names of habitual drunkards in public houses, and to prohibit the inhabitants of a town from supplying them with liquor.[10] A censorial power of this excessive kind would be revolting to the population of the most absolute monarchies; here, however, it is submitted to without difficulty.

Nowhere has so much been left by the law to the arbitrary determination of the magistrate as in democratic republics, because this arbitrary power is unattended by any alarming consequences. It may even be asserted that the freedom of the magistrate increases as the elective franchise is extended, and as the duration of the time of office is shortened. Hence arises the great difficulty which attends the conversion of a democratic republic into a monarchy. The magistrate ceases to be elective,

---

9. See the Act of 27th February, 1813. General Collection of the Laws of Massachusetts, vol. ii., p. 331. It should be added that the jurors are afterwards drawn from these lists by lot.

10. See Act of 28th February, 1787. General Collection of the Laws of Massachusetts, vol. i., p. 302.

but he retains the rights and the habits of an elected officer, which lead directly to despotism.

It is only in limited monarchies that the law, which prescribes the sphere in which public officers are to act, superintends all their measures. The cause of this may be easily detected. In limited monarchies the power is divided between the king and the people, both of whom are interested in the stability of the magistrate. The king does not venture to place the public officers under the control of the people, lest they should be tempted to betray his interests; on the other hand, the people fears lest the magistrates should serve to oppress the liberties of the country if they were entirely dependent upon the crown: they cannot therefore be said to depend on either the one or the other. The same cause which induces the king and the people to render public officers independent suggests the necessity of such securities as may prevent their independence from encroaching upon the authority of the former and the liberties of the latter. They consequently agree as to the necessity of restricting the functionary to a line of conduct laid down beforehand, and they are interested in confining him by certain regulations which he cannot evade.

INSTABILITY OF THE ADMINISTRATION
IN THE UNITED STATES

The authority which public men possess in America is so brief, and they are so soon commingled with the ever-changing population of the country, that the acts of a community frequently leave fewer traces than the occurrences of a private family. The public administration is, so to speak, oral and traditionary. But little is committed to writing, and that little is wafted away forever, like the leaves of the sibyl, by the smallest breeze.

The only historical remains in the United States are the newspapers; but if a number be wanting, the chain of time is broken, and the present is severed from the past. I am convinced that in fifty years it will be more difficult to collect authentic documents concerning the social condition of the Americans at the present day, than it is to find remains of the administration of France during the Middle Ages; and if the United States were ever invaded by barbarians, it would be necessary to have recourse to the history of other nations, in order to learn anything of the people which now inhabits them.

The instability of the administration has penetrated into the habits of the people: it even appears to suit the general taste, and no one cares for what occurred before his time. No methodical system is pursued; no archives are formed; and no documents are brought together when it would be very easy to do so. Where they exist little store is set upon them; and I have among my papers several original public documents which were given to me in answer to some of my inquiries. In America society seems to live from hand to mouth, like an army in the field. Nevertheless, the art of administration may undoubtedly be ranked as a science, and no sciences can be improved if the discoveries and observations of successive generations are not connected together in the order in which they occur. One man, in the short space of his life, remarks a fact; another conceives an idea; the former invents a means of execution, the latter reduces a truth to a fixed proposition; and mankind gathers the fruits of individual experience upon its way, and gradually forms the sciences. But the persons who conduct the administration in America can seldom afford any instruction to each other; and when they assume the direction of society, they simply possess those attainments which are most widely disseminated in the community, and no experience peculiar to themselves. Democracy, carried to its furthest limits, is therefore prejudicial to the art of government; and for this reason, it is better adapted to a people already versed in the conduct of an administration than to a nation which is uninitiated in public affairs.

This remark, indeed, is not exclusively applicable to the science of administration. Although a democratic government is founded upon a very simple and natural principle, it always presupposes the existence of a high degree of culture and enlightenment in society.[11] At the first glance it may be imagined to belong to the earliest ages of the world; but maturer observation will convince us that it could only come last in the succession of human history.

CHARGES LEVIED BY THE STATE UNDER THE RULE OF THE AMERICAN DEMOCRACY

Before we can affirm whether a democratic form of government is economical or not, we must establish a suitable standard of comparison. The question would be one of easy solution, if we were to attempt to draw a parallel between a democratic republic and an absolute monarchy. The

11. It is needless to observe that I speak here of the democratic form of government as applied to a people, not merely to a tribe.

public expenditure would be found to be more considerable under the former than under the latter; such is the case with all free states compared to those which are not so. It is certain that despotism ruins individuals by preventing them from producing wealth, much more than by depriving them of the wealth they have produced: it dries up the source of riches, while it usually respects acquired property. Freedom, on the contrary, engenders far more benefits than it destroys; and the nations which are favored by free institutions invariably find that their resources increase even more rapidly than their taxes.

My present object is to compare free nations to each other and to point out the influence of democracy upon the finances of a state.

Communities, as well as organic bodies, are subject to certain fixed rules in their formation which they cannot evade. They are composed of certain elements which are common to them at all times and under all circumstances. The people may always be mentally divided into three distinct classes. The first of these classes consists of the wealthy; the second, of those who are in easy circumstances; and the third is composed of those who have little or no property, and who subsist more especially by the work which they perform for the two superior orders. The proportion of the individuals who are included in these three divisions may vary according to the condition of society; but the divisions themselves can never be obliterated.

It is evident that each of these classes will exercise an influence, peculiar to its own propensities, upon the administration of the finances of the state. If the first of the three exclusively possesses the legislative power, it is probable that it will not be sparing of the public funds, because the taxes which are levied on a large fortune only tend to diminish the sum of superfluous enjoyment, and are, in point of fact, but little felt. If the second class has the power of making the laws, it will certainly not be lavish of taxes, because nothing is so onerous as a large impost which is levied upon a small income. The government of the middle classes appears to me to be the most economical, though perhaps not the most enlightened, and certainly not the most generous, of free governments.

But let us now suppose that the legislative authority is vested in the lowest orders: there are two striking reasons which show that the tendency of the expenditure will be to increase, not to diminish.

As the great majority of those who create the laws are possessed of no property upon which taxes can be imposed, all the money which is spent for the community appears to be spent to their advantage, at no cost of their own; and those who are possessed of some little property readily find means of regulating the taxes so that they are burdensome to the wealthy and profitable to the poor, although the rich are unable to take the same advantage when they are in possession of the government.

In countries in which the poor [12] should be exclusively invested with the power of making the laws, no great economy of public expenditure ought to be expected: that expenditure will always be considerable, either because the taxes do not weigh upon those who levy them or because they are levied in such a manner as not to weigh upon those classes. In other words, the government of the democracy is the only one under which the power which lays on taxes escapes the payment of them.

It may be objected (but the argument has no real weight) that the true interest of the people is indissolubly connected with that of the wealthier portion of the community, since it cannot but suffer by the severe measures to which it resorts. But is it not the true interest of kings to render their subjects happy; and the true interest of nobles to admit recruits into their order on suitable grounds? If remote advantages had power to prevail over the passions and the exigencies of the moment, no such thing as a tyrannical sovereign or an exclusive aristocracy could ever exist.

Again, it may be objected that the poor are never invested with the sole power of making the laws; but I reply that wherever universal suffrage has been established, the majority of the community unquestionably exercises the legislative authority; and if it be proved that the poor always constitute the majority, it may be added, with perfect truth, that in the countries in which they possess the elective franchise, they possess the sole power of making laws. But it is certain that in all the nations of the world the greater number has always consisted of those persons who hold no property, or of those whose property is insufficient to exempt them from the necessity of working in order to procure an easy subsistence. Universal suffrage does therefore in point of fact invest the poor with the government of society.

The disastrous influence which popular authority may sometimes exercise upon the finances of a state was very clearly seen in some of the democratic republics of antiquity, in which the public treasure was exhausted in order to relieve indigent citizens, or to supply the games and

---

12. The word *poor* is used here, and throughout the remainder of this chapter, in a relative, not in an absolute, sense. Poor men in America would often appear rich in comparison with the poor of Europe; but they may with propriety be styled poor in comparison with their more affluent countrymen.

theatrical amusements of the populace. It is true that the representative system was then very imperfectly known, and that, at the present time, the influence of popular passions is less felt in the conduct of public affairs; but it may be believed that the delegate will in the end conform to the principles of his constituents, and favor their propensities as much as their interests.

The extravagance of democracy is, however, less to be dreaded in proportion as the people acquires a share of property, because on the one hand the contributions of the rich are then less needed, and on the other, it is more difficult to lay on taxes which do not affect the interests of the lower classes. On this account universal suffrage would be less dangerous in France than in England, because in the latter country the property on which taxes may be levied is vested in fewer hands. America, where the great majority of the citizens is possessed of some fortune, is in a still more favorable position than France.

There are still further causes which may increase the sum of public expenditure in democratic countries. When the aristocracy governs, the individuals who conduct the affairs of state are exempted, by their own station in society, from every kind of privation; they are contented with their position; power and renown are the objects for which they strive; and, as they are placed far above the obscurer throng of citizens, they do not always distinctly perceive how the well-being of the mass of the people ought to redound to their own honor. They are not indeed callous to the sufferings of the poor, but they cannot feel those miseries as acutely as if they were themselves partakers of them. Provided that the people appear to submit to its lot, the rulers are satisfied, and they demand nothing further from the government. An aristocracy is more intent upon the means of maintaining its influence than upon the means of improving its condition.

When, on the contrary, the people is invested with the supreme authority, the perpetual sense of their own miseries impels the rulers of society to seek for perpetual ameliorations. A thousand different objects are subjected to improvement; the most trivial details are sought out as susceptible of amendment; and those changes which are accompanied with considerable expense are more especially advocated, since the object is to render the condition of the poor more tolerable, who cannot pay for themselves.

Moreover, all democratic communities are agitated by an ill-defined excitement, and by a kind of feverish impatience, that engenders a multitude of innovations, almost all of which are attended with expense.

In monarchies and aristocracies the natural taste which the rulers have for power and for renown is stimulated by the promptings of ambition, and they are frequently incited by these temptations to very costly undertakings. In democracies, where the rulers labor under privations, they can only be courted by such means as improve their well-being, and these improvements cannot take place without a sacrifice of money. When a people begins to reflect upon its situation, it discovers a multitude of wants to which it had not before been subject, and to satisfy these exigencies recourse must be had to the coffers of the state. Hence it arises that the public charges increase in proportion as civilization spreads, and that imposts are augmented as knowledge pervades the community.

The last cause which frequently renders a democratic government dearer than any other is that a democracy does not always succeed in moderating its expenditure, because it does not understand the art of being economical. As the designs which it entertains are frequently changed, and the agents of those designs are still more frequently removed, its undertakings are often ill conducted or left unfinished: in the former case the state spends sums out of all proportion to the end which it proposes to accomplish; in the second, the expense itself is unprofitable.

TENDENCIES OF THE AMERICAN DEMOCRACY AS REGARDS THE SALARIES OF PUBLIC OFFICERS

There is a powerful reason which usually induces democracies to economize upon the salaries of public officers. As the number of citizens who dispense the remuneration is extremely large in democratic countries, so the number of persons who can hope to be benefited by the receipt of it is comparatively small. In aristocratic countries, on the contrary, the individuals who appoint high salaries have almost always a vague hope of profiting by them. These appointments may be looked upon as a capital which they create for their own use, or at least as a resource for their children.

It must however be allowed that a democratic state is most parsimonious towards its principal agents. In America the secondary officers are much better paid, and the dignitaries of the administration much worse, than they are elsewhere.

These opposite effects result from the same cause: the people fixes the salaries of the public officers in both cases; and the scale of remuneration is determined by the consideration of its own wants. It is held to be fair that the servants of the public should be placed in the same easy circumstances as the public itself;[13] but when the question turns upon the salaries of the great officers of state, this rule fails, and chance alone can guide the popular decision. The poor have no adequate conception of the wants which the higher classes of society may feel. The sum which is scanty to the rich appears enormous to the poor man whose wants do not extend beyond the necessaries of life; and in his estimation the governor of a state with his two or three hundred a year is a very fortunate and enviable being.[14] If you undertake to convince him that the representative of a great people ought to be able to maintain some show of splendor in the eyes of foreign nations, he will perhaps assent to your meaning; but when he reflects on his own humble dwelling, and on the hard-earned produce of his wearisome toil, he remembers all that he could do with a salary which you say is insufficient, and he is startled or almost frightened at the sight of such uncommon wealth. Besides, the secondary public officer is almost on a level with the people, while the others are raised above it. The former may therefore excite his interest, but the latter begins to arouse his envy.

This is very clearly seen in the United States, where the salaries seem to decrease as the authority of those who receive them augments.[15]

---

13. The easy circumstances in which secondary functionaries are placed in the United States result also from another cause, which is independent of the general tendencies of democracy: every kind of private business is very lucrative, and the state would not be served at all if it did not pay its servants. The country is in the position of a commercial undertaking, which is obliged to sustain an expensive competition, notwithstanding its tastes for economy.

14. The state of Ohio, which contains a million of inhabitants, gives its governor a salary of only 1,200 dollars (£260) a year.

15. To render this assertion perfectly evident, it will suffice to examine the scale of salaries of the agents of the federal government. I have added the salaries attached to the corresponding officers in France under the constitutional monarchy, to complete the comparison.

UNITED STATES	FRANCE
Treasury Department	*Ministère de Finances*
Messenger .... 700$. (150l.)	Huissier .... 1500 fr. (60l.)
Clerk with lowest	Clerk with lowest
salary .... 1000$. (217l.)	salary .. 1000 to 1800 fr. (40l. to 72l.)
Clerk with highest	Clerk with highest
salary .... 1600$. (347l.)	salary 3200 to 3600 fr. (128l. to 144l.)
Chief Clerk ...... 2000$. (434l.)	Secrétaire-général ... 20,000 fr. (800l.)
Secretary of State . 6000$. (1,300l.)	The Minister ...... 80,000 fr. (3,200l.)
The President ... 25,000$. (5,400l.)	The King ... 12,000,000 fr. (480,000l.)

I have perhaps done wrong in selecting France as my standard of comparison. In France the democratic tendencies of the nation exercise an ever increasing influence upon the government, and the Chambers show a disposition to raise the low salaries and to lower the principal ones. Thus, the Minister of Finance, who

Under the rule of an aristocracy it frequently happens, on the contrary, that while the high officers are receiving munificent salaries, the inferior ones have not more than enough to procure the necessaries of life. The reason of this fact is easily discoverable from causes very analogous to those to which I have just alluded. If a democracy is unable to conceive the pleasures of the rich, or to witness them without envy, an aristocracy is slow to understand, or, to speak more correctly, is unacquainted with the privations of the poor. The poor man is not (if we use the term aright) the fellow of the rich one; but he is a being of another species. An aristocracy is therefore apt to care but little for the fate of its subordinate agents; and their salaries are only raised when they refuse to perform their service for too scanty a remuneration.

It is the parsimonious conduct of democracy towards its principal officers which has countenanced a supposition of far more economical propensities than any which it really possesses It is true that it scarcely allows the means of honorable subsistence to the individuals who conduct its affairs; but enormous sums are lavished to meet the exigencies or to facilitate the enjoyments of the people.[16] The money raised by taxation may be better employed, but it is not saved. In general, democracy gives largely to the community, and very sparingly to those who govern it. The reverse is the case in aristocratic countries, where the money of the state is expended to the profit of the persons who are at the head of affairs.

DIFFICULTY OF DISTINGUISHING THE CAUSES
WHICH CONTRIBUTE TO THF ECONOMY
OF THE AMERICAN GOVERNMENT

We are liable to frequent errors in the research of those facts which exercise a serious influence upon the fate of mankind, since nothing is more difficult than to appreciate their real value. One people is naturally inconsistent and enthusiastic, another is sober and calculating, and these

---

received 160,000 fr under the empire, receives 80,000 fr. in 1835; the Directeurs-Généraux of Finance, who then received 50,000 fr., now receive only 20,000 fr. [If the author could have foreseen the possibility of the restoration of the Empire in France, he would have anticipated the revival of the Imperial rate of public salaries, which has since taken place.—1861.]

16. See the American budgets for the cost of indigent citizens and gratuitous instruction. In 1831, £50,000 were spent in the state of New York for the maintenance of the poor: and at least £200,000 were devoted to gratuitous instruction (William's New York Annual Register, 1832, pp. 205 and 243). The state of New York contained only 1,900,000 inhabitants in the year 1830; which is not more than double the amount of population in the Départment du Nord in France.

characteristics originate in their physical constitution, or in remote causes with which we are unacquainted.

There are nations which are fond of parade and the bustle of festivity, and which do not regret the costly gaieties of an hour. Others, on the contrary, are attached to more retiring pleasures, and seem almost ashamed of appearing to be pleased. In some countries the highest value is set upon the beauty of public edifices; in others the productions of art are treated with indifference, and everything which is unproductive is looked down upon with contempt. In some renown, in others money, is the ruling passion.

Independently of the laws, all these causes concur to exercise a very powerful influence upon the conduct of the finances of the state. If the Americans never spend the money of the people in galas, it is not only because the imposition of taxes is under the control of the people, but because the people takes no delight in public rejoicings. If they repudiate all ornament from their architecture, and set no store on any but the more practical and homely advantages, it is not only because they live under democratic institutions, but because they are a commercial nation. The habits of private life are continued in public; and we ought carefully to distinguish that economy which depends upon their institutions from that which is the natural result of their manners and customs.

WHETHER THE EXPENDITURE OF THE UNITED STATES CAN BE COMPARED TO THAT OF FRANCE

Many attempts have recently been made in France to compare the public expenditure of that country with the expenditure of the United States; all these attempts have, however, been unattended by success; and a few words will suffice to show that they could not have had a satisfactory result.

In order to estimate the amount of the public charges of a people, two preliminaries are indispensable: it is necessary, in the first place, to know the wealth of that people; and in the second, to learn what portion of that wealth is devoted to the expenditure of the state. To show the amount of taxation without showing the resources which are destined to meet the demand is to undertake a futile labor; for it is not the expenditure but the relation of the expenditure to the revenue which it is desirable to know.

The same rate of taxation which may easily be supported by a wealthy contributor will reduce a poor one to extreme misery. The wealth of nations is composed of several distinct elements, of which population is the first, real property the second, and personal property the third. The first of these three elements may be discovered without difficulty. Among civilized nations it is easy to obtain an accurate census of the inhabitants; but the two others cannot be determined with so much facility. It is difficult to take an exact account of all the lands in a country which are under cultivation, with their natural or their acquired value; and it is still more impossible to estimate the entire personal property which is at the disposal of a nation, and which eludes the strictest analysis by the diversity and the number of shapes under which it may occur. And, indeed, we find that the most ancient civilized nations of Europe, including even those in which the administration is most central, have not succeeded, as yet, in determining the exact condition of their wealth.

In America the attempt has never been made; for how would such an investigation be possible in a country where society has not yet settled into habits of regularity and tranquillity; where the national government is not assisted by a multitude of agents whose exertions it can command, and direct to one sole end; and where statistics are not studied because no one is able to collect the necessary documents, or to find time to peruse them? Thus the primary elements of the calculations which have been made in France cannot be obtained in the Union; the relative wealth of the two countries is unknown: the property of the former is not accurately determined, and no means exist of computing that of the latter.

I consent therefore, for the sake of the discussion, to abandon this necessary term of the comparison, and I confine myself to a computation of the actual amount of taxation, without investigating the relation which subsists between the taxation and the revenue. But the reader will perceive that my task has not been facilitated by the limits which I here lay down for my researches.

It cannot be doubted that the central administration of France, assisted by all the public officers who are at its disposal, might determine with exactitude the amount of the direct and indirect taxes levied upon the citizens. But this investigation, which no private individual can undertake, has not hitherto been completed by the French government, or, at least, its results have not been made public. We are acquainted with the sum total of the charges of the state; we know the amount of the departmental expenditure; but the expenses of the communal divisions have not been computed, and the amount of the public expenses of France is consequently unknown.

If we now turn to America, we shall perceive that the difficulties are multiplied and enhanced. The Union publishes an exact return of the amount of its expenditure; the budgets of the four and twenty states furnish similar returns of their revenues; but the expenses incident to the affairs of the counties and the townships are unknown.[17]

The authority of the federal government cannot oblige the provincial governments to throw any light upon this point; and even if these governments were inclined to afford their simultaneous co-operation, it may be doubted whether they possess the means of procuring a satisfactory answer. Independently of the natural difficulties of the task, the political organization of the country would act as a hindrance to the success of their efforts. The county and town magistrates are not appointed by the authorities of the state, and they are not subjected to their control. It is therefore very allowable to suppose that if the state were desirous of obtaining the returns which we require, its design would be counteracted by the neglect of those subordinate officers whom it would be obliged to employ.[18] It is in point of fact useless to inquire what the Americans

---

17. The Americans, as we have seen, have four separate budgets, the Union, the states, the counties, and the townships having each severally their own. During my stay in America I made every endeavor to discover the amount of the public expenditure in the townships and counties of the principal states of the Union, and I readily obtained the budget of the larger townships, but I found it quite impossible to procure that of the smaller ones. I possess, however, some documents relating to county expenses which, although incomplete, are still curious. I have to thank Mr. Richards, Mayor of Philadelphia, for the budgets of thirteen of the counties of Pennsylvania, viz. Lebanon, Centre, Franklin, Fayette, Montgomery, Luzerne, Dauphin, Butler, Alleghany, Columbia, Northampton, Northumberland, and Philadelphia, for the year 1830. Their population at that time consisted of 495,207 inhabitants. On looking at the map of Pennsylvania, it will be seen that these thirteen counties are scattered in every direction, and so generally affected by the causes which usually influence the condition of a country that they may easily be supposed to furnish a correct average of the financial state of the counties of Pennsylvania in general: and thus upon reckoning that the expenses of these counties amounted in the year 1830 to about £72,330, or nearly 3s. for each inhabitant, and calculating that each of them contributed in the same year about 10s. 2d. towards the Union, and about 3s. to the state of Pennsylvania, it appears that they each contributed as their share of all the public expenses (except those of the townships) the sum of 16s. 2d. This calculation is doubly incomplete, as it applies only to a single year and to one part of the public charges; but it has at least the merit of not being conjectural.

18. Those who have attempted to draw a comparison between the expenses of France and America have at once perceived that no such comparison could be drawn between the total expenditure of the two countries; but they have endeavored to contrast detached portions of this expenditure. It may readily be shown that this second system is not at all less defective than the first.

If I attempt to compare the French budget with the budget of the Union, it must be remembered that the latter embraces much fewer objects than the central government of the former country, and that the expenditure must consequently

might do to forward this inquiry, since it is certain that they have hitherto done nothing at all. There does not exist a single individual at the present day, in America or in Europe, who can inform us what each citizen of the Union annually contributes to the public charges of the nation.[19]

Hence we must conclude that it is no less difficult to compare the social expenditure than it is to estimate the relative wealth of France and America. I will even add that it would be dangerous to attempt this comparison; for when statistics are not based upon computations which are strictly accurate, they mislead instead of guiding aright. The mind is

be much smaller. If I contrast the budgets of the departments to those of the states which constitute the Union, it must be observed that as the power and control exercised by the states is much greater than that which is exercised by the departments, their expenditure is also more considerable. As for the budgets of the counties, nothing of the kind occurs in the French system of finances; and it is, again, doubtful whether the corresponding expenses should be referred to the budget of the state or to those of the municipal divisions.

Municipal expenses exist in both countries, but they are not always analogous. In America the townships discharge a variety of offices which are reserved in France to the departments or to the state. It may, moreover, be asked what is to be understood by the municipal expenses of America. The organization of the municipal bodies or townships differs in the several states. Are we to be guided by what occurs in New England or in Georgia, in Pennsylvania or in the state of Illinois?

A kind of analogy may very readily be perceived between certain budgets in the two countries; but as the elements of which they are composed always differ more or less, no fair comparison can be instituted between them.

19. Even if we knew the exact pecuniary contributions of every French and American citizen to the coffers of the state, we should only come at a portion of the truth. Governments do not only demand supplies of money, but they call for personal services, which may be looked upon as equivalent to a given sum. When a state raises an army, besides the pay of the troops which is furnished by the entire nation, each soldier must give up his time, the value of which depends on the use he might make of it if he were not in the service. The same remark applies to the militia: the citizen who is in the militia devotes a certain portion of valuable time to the maintenance of the public peace, and he does in reality surrender to the state those earnings which he is prevented from gaining. Many other instances might be cited in addition to these. The governments of France and of America both levy taxes of this kind, which weigh upon the citizens; but who can estimate with accuracy their relative amount in the two countries?

This, however, is not the last of the difficulties which prevent us from comparing the expenditure of the Union with that of France. The French government contracts certain obligations which do not exist in America, and vice versa. The French government pays the clergy; in America the voluntary principle prevails. In America there is a legal provision for the poor; in France they are abandoned to the charity of the public. The French public officers are paid by a fixed salary, in America they are allowed certain perquisites. In France contributions in kind take place on very few roads; in America upon almost all the thoroughfares: in the former country the roads are free to all travelers; in the latter turnpikes abound. All these differences in the manner in which contributions are levied in the two countries enhance the difficulty of comparing their expenditure; for there are certain expenses which the citizens would not be subject to, or which would at any rate be much less considerable, if the state did not take upon itself to act in the name of the public.

easily imposed upon by the false affectation of exactitude, which prevails even in the misstatements of the science, and it adopts with confidence the errors which are apparelled in the forms of mathematical truth.

We abandon, therefore, our numerical investigation, with the hope of meeting with data of another kind. In the absence of positive documents, we may form an opinion as to the proportion which the taxation of a people bears to its real prosperity, by observing whether its external appearance is flourishing; whether, after having discharged the calls of the state, the poor man retains the means of subsistence, and the rich the means of enjoyment; and whether both classes are contented with their position, seeking, however, to ameliorate it by perpetual exertions, so that industry is never in want of capital, nor capital unemployed by industry. The observer who draws his inferences from these signs will, undoubtedly, be led to the conclusion that the American of the United States contributes a much smaller portion of his income to the state than the citizen of France. Nor, indeed, can the result be otherwise.

A portion of the French debt is the consequence of two successive invasions; and the Union has no similar calamity to fear. A nation placed upon the continent of Europe is obliged to maintain a large standing army; the isolated position of the Union enables it to have only 6,000 soldiers. The French have a fleet of 300 sail; the Americans have 52 vessels. How, then, can the inhabitant of the Union be called upon to contribute as largely as the inhabitant of France? No parallel can be drawn between the finances of two countries so differently situated.

It is by examining what actually takes place in the Union, and not by comparing the Union with France, that we may discover whether the American government is really economical. On casting my eyes over the different republics which form the confederation, I perceive that their governments lack perseverance in their undertakings, and that they exercise no steady control over the men whom they employ. Whence I naturally infer that they must often spend the money of the people to no purpose, or consume more of it than is really necessary to their undertakings. Great efforts are made, in accordance with the democratic origin of society, to satisfy the exigencies of the lower orders, to open the career of power to their endeavors, and to diffuse knowledge and comfort among them. The poor are maintained, immense sums are annually devoted to public instruction, all services whatsoever are remunerated, and the most subordinate agents are liberally paid. If this kind of government appears to me to be useful and rational, I am nevertheless constrained to admit that it is expensive.

Wherever the poor direct public affairs and dispose of the national resources, it appears certain that as they profit by the expenditure of the state, they are apt to augment that expenditure.

I conclude therefore, without having recourse to inaccurate computations, and without hazarding a comparison which might prove incorrect, that the democratic government of the Americans is not a cheap government, as is sometimes asserted; and I have no hesitation in predicting that if the people of the United States is ever involved in serious difficulties, its taxation will speedily be increased to the rate of that which prevails in the greater part of the aristocracies and the monarchies of Europe.

CORRUPTION AND VICES OF THE RULERS IN A DEMOCRACY, AND CONSEQUENT EFFECTS UPON PUBLIC MORALITY

A distinction must be made when the aristocratic and the democratic principles mutually inveigh against each other as tending to facilitate corruption. In aristocratic governments the individuals who are placed at the head of affairs are rich men, who are solely desirous of power. In democracies statesmen are poor, and they have their fortunes to make. The consequence is that in aristocratic states the rulers are rarely accessible to corruption, and have very little craving for money; while the reverse is the case in democratic nations.

But in aristocracies, as those who are desirous of arriving at the head of affairs are possessed of considerable wealth, and as the number of persons by whose assistance they may rise is comparatively small, the government is, if I may use the expression, put up to a sort of auction. In democracies, on the contrary, those who are covetous of power are very seldom wealthy, and the number of citizens who confer that power is extremely great. Perhaps in democracies the number of men who might be bought is by no means smaller, but buyers are rarely to be met with; and, besides, it would be necessary to buy so many persons at once that the attempt is rendered nugatory.

Many of the men who have been in the administration in France during the last forty years have been accused of making their fortunes at the expense of the state or of its allies, a reproach which was rarely addressed to the public characters of the ancient monarchy. But in France the practice of bribing electors is almost unknown, while it is notoriously and publicly carried on in England. In the United States I never heard a man accused of spending his wealth in corrupting the populace; but I have often heard the probity of public officers questioned; still more frequently have I heard their success attributed to low intrigues and immoral practices.

If, then, the men who conduct the government of an aristocracy sometimes endeavor to corrupt the people, the heads of a democracy are themselves corrupt. In the former case the morality of the people is directly assailed; in the latter, an indirect influence is exercised upon the people which is still more to be dreaded.

As the rulers of democratic nations are almost always exposed to the suspicion of dishonorable conduct, they in some measure lend the authority of the government to the base practices of which they are accused. They thus afford an example which must prove discouraging to the struggles of virtuous independence, and must foster the secret calculations of a vicious ambition. If it be asserted that evil passions are displayed in all ranks of society; that they ascend the throne by hereditary right; and that despicable characters are to be met with at the head of aristocratic nations as well as in the sphere of a democracy, this objection has but little weight in my estimation. The corruption of men who have casually risen to power has a coarse and vulgar infection in it, which renders it contagious to the multitude. On the contrary, there is a kind of aristocratic refinement and an air of grandeur in the depravity of the great, which frequently prevents it from spreading abroad.

The people can never penetrate into the perplexing labyrinth of court intrigue, and it will always have difficulty in detecting the turpitude which lurks under elegant manners, refined tastes, and graceful language. But to pillage the public purse and to vend the favors of the state are arts which the meanest villain may comprehend, and hope to practice in his turn.

In reality it is far less prejudicial to witness the immorality of the great than to witness that immorality which leads to greatness. In a democracy, private citizens see a man of their own rank in life who rises from that obscure position, and who becomes possessed of riches and of power in a few years. The spectacle excites their surprise and their envy, and they are led to inquire how the person who was yesterday their equal is today their ruler. To attribute his rise to his talents or his virtues is unpleasant, for it is tacitly to acknowledge that they are themselves less virtuous and less talented than he was. They are therefore led (and not unfrequently their conjecture is a correct one) to impute his success mainly to some one of his defects; and an odious mixture is thus formed of the ideas of turpitude and power, unworthiness and success, utility and dishonor.

EFFORTS OF WHICH A DEMOCRACY IS CAPABLE

I here warn the reader that I speak of a government which implicitly follows the real desires of the people, and not of a government which simply commands in its name. Nothing is so irresistible as a tyrannical power commanding in the name of the people, because, while it exercises that moral influence which belongs to the decision of the majority, it acts at the same time with the promptitude and the tenacity of a single man.

It is difficult to say what degree of exertion a democratic government may be capable of making at a crisis in the history of the nation. But no great democratic republic has hitherto existed in the world. To style the oligarchy which ruled over France in 1793 by that name would be to offer an insult to the republican form of government. The United States afford the first example of the kind.

The American Union has now subsisted for half a century, in the course of which time its existence has only once been attacked, namely, during the War of Independence. At the commencement of that long war, various occurrences took place which betokened an extraordinary zeal for the service of the country.[20] But as the contest was prolonged, symptoms of private egotism began to show themselves. No money was poured into the public treasury; few recruits could be raised to join the army; the people wished to acquire independence, but was very ill disposed to undergo the privations by which alone it could be obtained. "Tax laws," says Hamilton in the Federalist, "have in vain been multiplied; new methods to enforce the collection have in vain been tried; the public expectation has been uniformly disappointed, and the treasuries of the States have remained empty. The popular system of administration inherent in the nature of popular government, coinciding with the real scarcity of money incident to a languid and mutilated state of trade, has hitherto defeated every experiment for extensive collections, and has at length taught the different legislatures the folly of attempting them."[21]

The United States have not had any serious war to carry on ever since that period. In order, therefore, to appreciate the sacrifices which democratic nations may impose upon themselves, we must wait until the

---

20. One of the most singular of these occurrences was the resolution which the Americans took of temporarily abandoning the use of tea. Those who know that men usually cling more to their habits than to their life will doubtless admire this great though obscure sacrifice which was made by a whole people.
21. *The Federalist*, No. 12, *Great Books of the Western World*, Vol. 43, p. 57 [Ed.].

American people is obliged to put half its entire income at the disposal of the government, as was done by the English; or until it sends forth a twentieth part of its population to the field of battle, as was done by France.

In America the use of conscription is unknown, and men are induced to enlist by bounties. The notions and habits of the people of the United States are so opposed to compulsory enlistment, that I do not imagine it can ever be sanctioned by the laws. What is termed the conscription in France is assuredly the heaviest tax upon the population of that country; yet how could a great continental war be carried on without it? The Americans have not adopted the British impressment of seamen, and they have nothing which corresponds to the French system of maritime conscription; the navy, as well as the merchant service, is supplied by voluntary service. But it is not easy to conceive how a people can sustain a great maritime war without having recourse to one or the other of these two systems. Indeed, the Union, which has fought with some honor upon the seas, has never possessed a very numerous fleet, and the equipment of the small number of American vessels has always been excessively expensive.

I have heard American statesmen confess that the Union will have great difficulty in maintaining its rank on the seas without adopting the system of impressment or of maritime conscription; but the difficulty is to induce the people, which exercises the supreme authority, to submit to impressment or any compulsory system.

It is incontestable that in times of danger a free people displays far more energy than one which is not so. But I incline to believe that this is more especially the case in those free nations in which the democratic element preponderates. Democracy appears to me to be much better adapted for the peaceful conduct of society, or for an occasional effort of remarkable vigor, than for the hardy and prolonged endurance of the storms which beset the political existence of nations. The reason is very evident: it is enthusiasm which prompts men to expose themselves to dangers and privations; but they will not support them long without reflection. There is more calculation, even in the impulses of bravery, than is generally attributed to them; and although the first efforts are suggested by passion, perseverance is maintained by a distinct regard of the purpose in view. A portion of what we value is exposed in order to save the remainder.

But it is this distinct perception of the future, founded upon a sound judgment and an enlightened experience, which is most frequently wanting in democracies. The populace is more apt to feel than to reason; and if its present sufferings are great, it is to be feared that the still greater sufferings attendant upon defeat will be forgotten.

Another cause tends to render the efforts of a democratic government less persevering than those of an aristocracy. Not only are the lower classes less awakened than the higher orders to the good or evil chances of the future, but they are liable to suffer far more acutely from present privations. The noble exposes his life, indeed, but the chance of glory is equal to the chance of harm. If he sacrifices a large portion of his income to the state, he deprives himself for a time of the pleasures of affluence; but to the poor man death is embellished by no pomp or renown, and the imposts which are irksome to the rich are fatal to him.

This relative impotence of democratic republics is, perhaps, the greatest obstacle to the foundation of a republic of this kind in Europe. In order that such a state should subsist in one country of the Old World, it would be necessary that similar institutions should be introduced into all the other nations.

I am of opinion that a democratic government tends in the end to increase the real strength of society; but it can never combine, upon a single point and at a given time, so much power as an aristocracy or a monarchy. If a democratic country remained during a whole century subject to a republican government, it would probably at the end of that period be more populous and more prosperous than the neighboring despotic states. But it would have incurred the risk of being conquered much oftener than they would in that lapse of years.

SELF-CONTROL OF THE AMERICAN DEMOCRACY

The difficulty which a democracy has in conquering the passions, and subduing the exigencies of the moment, with a view to the future, is conspicuous in the most trivial occurrences of the United States. The people which is surrounded by flatterers has great difficulty in surmounting its inclinations; and whenever it is solicited to undergo a privation or any kind of inconvenience, even to attain and end which is sanctioned by its own rational conviction, it almost always refuses to comply at first. The deference of the Americans to the laws has been very justly applauded; but it must be added that in America the legislation is made by the people and for the people. Consequently, in the United States the law favors those classes which are most interested in evading it elsewhere. It may therefore be supposed that an offensive law, which should not be acknowledged to be one of immediate utility, would either not be enacted or would not be obeyed.

In America there is no law against fraudulent bankruptcies, not because they are few but because there are a great number of bankruptcies. The dread of being prosecuted as a bankrupt acts with more intensity upon the mind of the majority of the people than the fear of being involved in losses or ruin by the failure of other parties; and a sort of guilty tolerance is extended by the public conscience to an offense which everyone condemns in his individual capacity. In the new states of the Southwest, the citizens generally take justice into their own hands, and murders are of very frequent occurrence. This arises from the rude manners and the ignorance of the inhabitants of those deserts, who do not perceive the utility of investing the law with adequate force, and who prefer duels to prosecutions.

Someone observed to me one day, in Philadelphia, that almost all crimes in America are caused by the abuse of intoxicating liquors, which the lower classes can procure in great abundance from their excessive cheapness. "How comes it," said I, "that you do not put a duty upon brandy?" "Our legislators," rejoined my informant, "have frequently thought of this expedient; but the task of putting it in operation is a difficult one: a revolt might be apprehended; and the members who should vote for a law of this kind would be sure of losing their seats." "Whence I am to infer," replied I, "that the drinking population constitutes the majority in your country, and that temperance is somewhat unpopular."

When these things are pointed out to the American statesmen, they content themselves with assuring you that time will operate the necessary change, and that the experience of evil will teach the people its true interests. This is frequently true: although a democracy is more liable to error than a monarch or a body of nobles, the chances of its regaining the right path, when once it has acknowledged its mistake, are greater also, because it is rarely embarrassed by internal interests which conflict with those of the majority and resist the authority of reason. But a democracy can only obtain truth as the result of experience, and many nations may forfeit their existence while they are awaiting the consequences of their errors.

The great privilege of the Americans does not simply consist in their being more enlightened than other nations but in their being able to repair the faults they may commit. To which it must be added that a democracy cannot derive substantial benefit from past experience unless it be arrived at a certain pitch of knowledge and civilization. There are tribes and peoples whose education has been so vicious, and whose character presents so strange a mixture of passion, of ignorance, and of erroneous notions upon all subjects, that they are unable to discern the causes of their own wretchedness, and they fall a sacrifice to ills with which they are unacquainted.

I have crossed vast tracts of country that were formerly inhabited by powerful Indian nations which are now extinct; I have myself passed some time in the midst of mutilated tribes, which witness the daily decline of their numerical strength and of the glory of their independence; and I have heard these Indians themselves anticipate the impending doom of their race. Every European can perceive means which would rescue these unfortunate beings from inevitable destruction. They alone are insensible to the expedient; they feel the woe which year after year heaps upon their heads, but they will perish to a man without accepting the remedy. It would be necessary to employ force to induce them to submit to the protection and the constraint of civilization.

The incessant revolutions which have convulsed the South American provinces for the last quarter of a century have frequently been adverted to with astonishment, and expectations have been expressed that those nations would speedily return to their *natural state*. But can it be affirmed that the turmoil of revolution is not actually the most natural state of the South American Spaniards at the present time? In that country society is plunged into difficulties from which all its efforts are insufficient to rescue it. The inhabitants of that fair portion of the Western Hemisphere seem obstinately bent on pursuing the work of inward havoc. If they fall into a momentary repose from the effects of exhaustion, that repose prepares them for a fresh state of frenzy. When I consider their condition, which alternates between misery and crime, I should be inclined to believe that despotism itself would be a benefit to them if it were possible that the words despotism and benefit could ever be united in my mind.

CONDUCT OF FOREIGN AFFAIRS
BY THE AMERICAN DEMOCRACY

We have seen that the federal Constitution entrusts the permanent direction of the external interests of the nation to the President and the

Senate,[22] which tends in some degree to detach the general foreign policy of the Union from the control of the people. It cannot therefore be asserted, with truth, that the external affairs of state are conducted by the democracy.

The policy of America owes its rise to Washington, and after him to Jefferson, who established those principles which it observes at the present day. Washington said in the admirable letter which he addressed to his fellow citizens, and which may be looked upon as his political bequest to the country:

> The great rule of conduct for us in regard to foreign nations is, in extending our commercial relations, to have with them as little *political* connection as possible. So far as we have already formed engagements, let them be fulfilled with perfect good faith. Here let us stop.
>
> Europe has a set of primary interests, which to us have none, or a very remote relation. Hence, she must be engaged in frequent controversies, the causes of which are essentially foreign to our concerns. Hence, therefore, it must be unwise in us to implicate ourselves, by artificial ties, in the ordinary vicissitudes of her politics, or the ordinary combinations and collisions of her friendships or enmities.
>
> Our detached and distant situation invites and enables us to pursue a different course. If we remain one people, under an efficient government, the period is not far off when we may defy material injury from external annoyance; when we may take such an attitude as will cause the neutrality we may at any time resolve upon to be scrupulously respected; when belligerent nations, under the impossibility of making acquisitions upon us, will not lightly hazard the giving us provocation; when we may choose peace or war, as our interest, guided by justice, shall counsel.
>
> Why forgo the advantages of so peculiar a situation? Why quit our own to stand upon foreign ground? Why, by interweaving our destiny with that of any part of Europe, entangle our peace and prosperity in the toils of European ambition, rivalship, interest, humour, or caprice?
>
> It is our true policy to steer clear of permanent alliances with any portion of the foreign world; so far, I mean, as we are now at liberty to do it; for let me not be understood as capable of patronizing infidelity to existing engagements. I hold the maxim no less applicable to public than to private affairs, that honesty is always the best policy. I repeat it, there-

---

22. "The President," says the Constitution, Art. II., sect. 2, § 2, "shall have power, by and with the advice and consent of the Senate, to make treaties, provided two-thirds of the senators present concur." The reader is reminded that the senators are returned for a term of six years, and that they are chosen by the legislature of each state.

fore, let those engagements be observed in their genuine sense; but in my opinion it is unnecessary, and would be unwise, to extend them.

Taking care always to keep ourselves, by suitable establishments, in a respectable defensive posture, we may safely trust to temporary alliances for extraordinary emergencies.

In a previous part of the same letter, Washington makes the following admirable and just remark: "The nation which indulges towards another an habitual hatred, or an habitual fondness, is in some degree a slave. It is a slave to its animosity or to its affection, either of which is sufficient to lead it astray from its duty and its interest."

The political conduct of Washington was always guided by these maxims. He succeeded in maintaining his country in a state of peace, while all the other nations of the globe were at war; and he laid it down as a fundamental doctrine that the true interest of the Americans consisted in a perfect neutrality with regard to the internal dissensions of the European powers.

Jefferson went still further, and he introduced a maxim into the policy of the Union which afirms that "the Americans ought never to solicit any privileges from foreign nations, in order not to be obliged to grant similar privileges themselves."

These two principles, which were so plain and so just as to be adapted to the capacity of the populace, have greatly simplified the foreign policy of the United States. As the Union takes no part in the affairs of Europe, it has, properly speaking, no foreign interests to discuss, since it has at present no powerful neighbors on the American continent. The country is as much removed from the passions of the Old World by its position as by the line of policy which it has chosen; and it is neither called upon to repudiate nor to espouse the conflicting interests of Europe; while the dissensions of the New World are still concealed within the bosom of the future.

The Union is free from all pre-existing obligations; and it is consequently enabled to profit by the experience of the old nations of Europe without being obliged, as they are, to make the best of the past and to adapt it to their present circumstances, or to accept that immense inheritance which they derive from their forefathers—an inheritance of glory mingled with calamities, and of alliances conflicting with national antipathies. The foreign policy of the United States is reduced by its very nature to await the chances of the future history of the nation; and for the present it consists more in abstaining from interference than in exerting its activity.

It is therefore very difficult to ascertain, at present, what degree of sagacity the American democracy will display in the conduct of the foreign policy of the country; and upon this point its adversaries, as well as its advocates, must suspend their judgment. As for myself, I have no hesitation in avowing my conviction that it is most especially in the conduct of foreign relations that democratic governments appear to me to be decidedly inferior to governments carried on upon different principles. Experience, instruction, and habit may almost always succeed in creating a species of practical discretion in democracies, and that science of the daily occurrences of life which is called good sense. Good sense may suffice to direct the ordinary course of society; and among a people whose education has been provided for, the advantages of democratic liberty in the internal affairs of the country may more than compensate for the evils inherent in a democratic government. But such is not always the case in the mutual relations of foreign nations.

Foreign politics demand scarcely any of those qualities which a democracy possesses; and they require, on the contrary, the perfect use of almost all those faculties in which it is deficient. Democracy is favorable to the increase of the internal resources of a state; it tends to diffuse a moderate independence; it promotes the growth of public spirit, and fortifies the respect which is entertained for law in all classes of society: and these are advantages which only exercise an indirect influence over the relations which one people bears to another. But a democracy is unable to regulate the details of an important undertaking, to persevere in a design, and to work out its execution in the presence of serious obstacles. It cannot combine its measures with secrecy, and it will not await their consequences with patience. These are qualities which more especially belong to an individual or to an aristocracy; and they are precisely the means by which an individual people attains to a predominant position.

If, on the contrary, we observe the natural defects of aristocracy, we shall find that their influence is comparatively innoxious in the direction of the external affairs of a state. The capital fault of which aristocratic bodies may be accused is that they are more apt to contrive their own advantage than that of the mass of the people. In foreign politics it is rare for the interest of the aristocracy to be in any way distinct from that of the people.

The propensity which democracies have to obey the impulse of passion rather than the suggestions of prudence, and to abandon a mature design for the gratification of a momentary caprice, was very clearly seen in

America on the breaking out of the French Revolution. It was then as evident to the simplest capacity as it is at the present time, that the interest of the Americans forbade them to take any part in the contest which was about to deluge Europe with blood, but which could by no means injure the welfare of their own country. Nevertheless the sympathies of the people declared themselves with so much violence in behalf of France, that nothing but the inflexible character of Washington, and the immense popularity which he enjoyed, could have prevented the Americans from declaring war against England. And even then, the exertions which the austere reason of that great man made to repress the generous but imprudent passions of his fellow citizens very nearly deprived him of the sole recompense which he had ever claimed—that of his country's love. The majority then reprobated the line of policy which he adopted, and which has since been unanimously approved by the nation.[23]

If the Constitution and the favor of the public had not entrusted the direction of the foreign affairs of the country to Washington, it is certain that the American nation would at that time have taken the very measures which it now condemns.

Almost all the nations which have ever exercised a powerful influence upon the destinies of the world, by conceiving, following up, and executing vast designs—from the Romans to the English—have been governed by aristocratic institutions. Nor will this be a subject of wonder when we recollect that nothing in the world has so absolute a fixity of purpose as an aristocracy. The mass of the people may be led astray by ignorance or passion; the mind of a king may be biased, and his perseverance in his designs may be shaken—besides which a king is not immortal—but an aristocratic body is too numerous to be led astray by the blandishments of intrigue; and yet not numerous enough to yield readily

---

23. See the fifth volume of Marshall's *Life of Washington.* "In a government constituted like that of the United States," he says, "it is impossible for the chief magistrate, however firm he may be, to oppose for any length of time the torrent of popular opinion; and the prevalent opinion of that day seemed to incline to war. In fact, in the session of Congress held at the time, it was frequently seen that Washington had lost the majority in the House of Representatives." The violence of the language used against him in public was extreme, and in a political meeting they did not scruple to compare him indirectly to the treacherous Arnold. "By the opposition," says Marshall, "the friends of the administration were declared to be an aristocratic and corrupt faction, who, from a desire to introduce monarchy, were hostile to France and under the influence of Britain; that they were a paper nobility, whose extreme sensibility at every measure which threatened the funds, induced a tame submission to injuries and insults, which the interests and honour of the nation required them to resist."

to the intoxicating influence of unreflecting passion: it has the energy of a firm and enlightened individual added to the power which it derives from its perpetuity.

What the Real Advantages Are Which American Society Derives from the Government of the Democracy

Before I enter upon the subject of the present chapter, I am induced to remind the reader of what I have more than once adverted to in the course of this book. The political institutions of the United States appear to me to be one of the forms of government which a democracy may adopt; but I do not regard the American Constitution as the best, or as the only one which a democratic people may establish. In showing the advantages which the Americans derive from the government of democracy, I am therefore very far from meaning, or from believing, that similar advantages can only be obtained from the same laws.

GENERAL TENDENCY OF THE LAWS UNDER THE RULE OF THE AMERICAN DEMOCRACY AND HABITS OF THOSE WHO APPLY THEM

The defects and the weaknesses of a democratic government may very readily be discovered; they are demonstrated by the most flagrant instances, while its beneficial influence is less perceptibly exercised. A single glance suffices to detect its evil consequences, but its good qualities can only be discerned by long observation. The laws of the American democracy are frequently defective or incomplete. They sometimes attack vested rights, or give a sanction to others which are dangerous to the community; but even if they were good, the frequent changes which they undergo would be an evil. How comes it, then, that the American republics prosper, and maintain their position?

In the consideration of laws, a distinction must be carefully observed between the end at which they aim, and the means by which they are directed to that end; between their absolute, and their relative excellence. If it be the intention of the legislator to favor the interests of the minority at the expense of the majority, and if the measures he takes to accomplish the object he has in view with the least possible expense of time and exertion, the law may be well drawn up, although its purpose be bad; and the more efficacious it is, the greater is the mischief which it causes.

Democratic laws generally tend to promote the welfare of the greatest possible number; for they emanate from the majority of the citizens, who are subject to error, but who cannot have an interest opposed to their own advantage. The laws of an aristocracy tend, on the contrary, to concentrate wealth and power in the hands of the minority, because an aristocracy, by its very nature, constitutes a minority. It may therefore be asserted, as a general proposition, that the purpose of a democracy in the conduct of its legislation is useful to a greater number of citizens than that of an aristocracy. This is, however, the sum total of its advantages.

Aristocracies are infinitely more expert in the science of legislation than democracies ever can be. They are possessed of a self-control which protects them from the errors of temporary excitement; and they form lasting designs which they mature with the assistance of favorable opportunities. Aristocratic government proceeds with the dexterity of art; it understands how to make the collective force of all its laws converge at the same time to a given point. Such is not the case with democracies, whose laws are almost always ineffective or inopportune. The means of democracy are therefore more imperfect than those of aristocracy, and the measures which it unwittingly adopts are frequently opposed to its own cause; but the object it has in view is more useful.

Let us now imagine a community so organized by nature, or by its constitution, that it can support the transitory action of bad laws, and that it can await, without destruction, the general tendency of the legislation: we shall then be able to conceive that a democratic government, notwithstanding its defects, will be most fitted to conduce to the prosperity of this community. This is precisely what has occurred in the United States; and I repeat what I have before remarked, that the great advantage of the Americans consists in their being able to commit faults which they may afterwards repair.

An analogous observation may be made respecting public officers. It is easy to perceive that the American democracy frequently errs in the choice of the individuals to whom it entrusts the power of the administration; but it is more difficult to say why the state prospers under their rule. In the first place it is to be remarked that if in a democratic state the governors have less honesty and less capacity than elsewhere, the governed on the other hand are more enlightened and more attentive to their interests. As the people in democracies is more incessantly vigilant in its affairs, and more jealous of its rights, it prevents its representatives from abandoning that general line of conduct which its own interest prescribes. In the second place it must be remembered that if the democratic magistrate is more apt to misuse his power, he possesses it for a shorter period of time. But there is yet another reason which is still more general and conclusive. It is no doubt of importance to the welfare of nations that they should be governed by men of talents and virtue; but it is perhaps still more important that the interests of those men should not differ from the interests of the community at large; for if such were the case, virtues of a high order might become useless, and talents might be turned to a bad account. I say that it is important that the interests of the persons in authority should not conflict with or oppose the interests of the community at large; but I do not insist upon their having the same interests as the *whole* population, because I am not aware that such a state of things ever existed in any country.

No political form has hitherto been discovered which is equally favorable to the prosperity and the development of all the classes into which society is divided. These classes continue to form, as it were, a certain number of distinct nations in the same nation; and experience has shown that it is no less dangerous to place the fate of these classes exclusively in the hands of any one of them, than it is to make one people the arbiter of the destiny of another. When the rich alone govern, the interest of the poor is always endangered; and when the poor make the laws, that of the rich incurs very serious risks. The advantage of democracy does not consist, therefore, as has sometimes been asserted, in favoring the prosperity of all, but simply in contributing to the well-being of the greatest possible number.

The men who are entrusted with the direction of public affairs in the United States are frequently inferior, both in point of capacity and of morality, to those whom aristocratic institutions would raise to power. But their interest is identified and confounded with that of the majority of their fellow citizens. They may frequently be faithless, and frequently mistaken; but they will never systematically adopt a line of conduct opposed to the will of the majority; and it is impossible that they should give a dangerous or an exclusive tendency to the government.

The maladministration of a democratic magistrate is a mere isolated fact, which only occurs during the short period for which he is elected. Corruption and incapacity do not act as common interests which may connect men permanently with one another. A corrupt or an incapable magistrate will not concert his measures with another magistrate, simply because that individual is as corrupt and as incapable as himself; and these two men will never unite their endeavors to promote the corruption and inaptitude of their remote posterity. The ambition and the maneuvers of the one will serve, on the contrary, to unmask the other. The vices of a magistrate, in democratic states, are usually peculiar to his own person.

But under aristocratic governments public men are swayed by the interest of their order, which, if it is sometimes confounded with the interests of the majority, is very frequently distinct from them. This interest is the common and lasting bond which unites them together: it induces them to coalesce, and to combine their efforts in order to attain an end which does not always ensure the greatest happiness of the greatest number; and it serves not only to connect the persons in authority but to unite them to a considerable portion of the community, since a numerous body of citizens belongs to the aristocracy without being invested with official functions. The aristocratic magistrate is therefore constantly supported by a portion of the community, as well as by the government of which he is a member.

The common purpose which connects the interest of the magistrates in aristocracies with that of a portion of their contemporaries identifies it with that of future generations; their influence belongs to the future as much as to the present. The aristocratic magistrate is urged at the same time towards the same point by the passions of the community, by his own, and I may almost add by those of his posterity. Is it, then, wonderful that he does not resist such repeated impulses? And indeed aristocracies are often carried away by the spirit of their order without being corrupted by it; and they unconsciously fashion society to their own ends, and prepare it for their own descendants.

The English aristocracy is perhaps the most liberal which ever existed, and no body of men has ever, uninterruptedly, furnished so many honorable and enlightened individuals to the government of a country. It cannot, however, escape observation that in the legislation of England the good of the poor has been sacrificed to the advantage of the rich, and the rights of the majority to the privileges of the few. The consequence is that England, at the present day, combines the extremes of fortune in the bosom of her society; and her perils and calamities are almost equal to her power and her renown.

In the United States, where the public officers have no interests to promote connected with their caste, the general and constant influence of the government is beneficial, although the individuals who conduct it are frequently unskillful and sometimes contemptible. There is indeed a secret tendency in democratic institutions to render the exertions of the citizens subservient to the prosperity of the community, notwithstanding their private vices and mistakes; while in aristocratic institutions there is a secret propensity which, notwithstanding the talents and the virtues of those who conduct the government, leads them to contribute to the evils which oppress their fellow creatures. In aristocratic governments public men may frequently do injuries which they do not intend; and in democratic states they produce advantages which they never thought of.

PUBLIC SPIRIT IN THE UNITED STATES

There is one sort of patriotic attachment which principally arises from that instinctive, disinterested and undefinable feeling which connects the affections of man with his birthplace. This natural fondness is united to a taste for ancient customs, and to a reverence for ancestral traditions of the past; those who cherish it love their country as they love the mansion of their fathers. They enjoy the tranquillity which it affords them; they cling to the peaceful habits which they have contracted within its bosom; they are attached to the reminiscences which it awakens, and they are even pleased by the state of obedience in which they are placed. This patriotism is sometimes stimulated by religious enthusiasm, and then it is capable of making the most prodigious efforts. It is in itself a kind of religion: it does not reason, but it acts from the impulse of faith and of sentiment. By some nations the monarch has been regarded as a personification of the country; and the fervor of patriotism being converted into the fervor of loyalty, they took a sympathetic pride in his conquests, and gloried in his power. At one time, under the ancient monarchy, the French felt a sort of satisfaction in the sense of their dependence upon the arbitrary pleasure of their king, and they were wont to say with pride, "We are the subjects of the most powerful king in the world."

But, like all instinctive passions, this kind of patriotism is more apt to prompt transient exertion than to supply the motives of continuous endeavor. It may save the state in critical circumstances, but it will not unfrequently allow the nation to decline in the midst of peace. While the manners of a people are simple, and its faith unshaken; while society is steadily based upon traditional institutions, whose legitimacy has never been contested, this instinctive patriotism is wont to endure.

But there is another species of attachment to a country which is more rational than the one we have been describing. It is perhaps less generous and less ardent, but it is more fruitful and more lasting; it is coeval with the spread of knowledge, it is nurtured by the laws, it grows by the exercise of civil rights, and, in the end, it is confounded with the personal interest of the citizen. A man comprehends the influence which the prosperity of his country has upon his own welfare; he is aware that the laws authorize him to contribute his assistance to that prosperity, and he labors to promote it as a portion of his interest in the first place, and as a portion of his right in the second.

But epochs sometimes occur, in the course of the existence of a nation, at which the ancient customs of a people are changed, public morality destroyed, religious belief disturbed, and the spell of tradition broken, while the diffusion of knowledge is yet imperfect, and the civil rights of the community are ill secured, or confined within very narrow limits. The country then assumes a dim and dubious shape in the eyes of the citizens; they no longer behold it in the soil which they inhabit, for that soil is to them a dull inanimate clod; nor in the usages of their forefathers, which they have been taught to look upon as a debasing yoke; nor in religion, for that they doubt; nor in the laws, which do not originate in their own authority; nor in the legislator, whom they fear and despise. The country is lost to their senses, they can neither discover it under its own nor under borrowed features, and they entrench themselves within the dull precincts of a narrow egotism. They are emancipated from prejudice without having acknowledged the empire of reason; they are neither animated by the instinctive patriotism of monarchical subjects nor by the thinking patriotism of republican citizens; but they have stopped halfway between the two, in the midst of confusion and of distress.

In this predicament, to retreat is impossible, for a people cannot restore the vivacity of its earlier times any more than a man can return to the innocence and the bloom of childhood; such things may be regretted, but they cannot be renewed. The only thing, then, which remains to be done is to proceed, and to accelerate the union of private with public interests, since the period of disinterested patriotism is gone by forever.

I am certainly very far from averring that, in order to obtain this result, the exercise of political rights should be immediately granted to all the members of the community. But I maintain that the most powerful and perhaps the only means of interesting men in the welfare of their country which we still possess is to make them partakers in the government. At the present time civic zeal seems to me to be inseparable from the exercise of political rights; and I hold that the number of citizens will be found to augment or to decrease in Europe in proportion as those rights are extended.

In the United States, the inhabitants were thrown but as yesterday upon the soil which they now occupy, and they brought neither customs nor traditions with them there; they meet each other for the first time with no previous acquaintance; in short, the instinctive love of their country can scarcely exist in their minds; but everyone takes as zealous an interest in the affairs of his township, his county, and of the whole state as if they were his own, because everyone, in his sphere, takes an active part in the government of society.

The lower orders in the United States are alive to the perception of the influence exercised by the general prosperity upon their own welfare; and simple as this observation is, it is one which is but too rarely made by the people. But in America the people regards this prosperity as the result of its own exertions; the citizen looks upon the fortune of the public as his private interest, and he co-operates in its success, not so much from a sense of pride or of duty, as from what I shall venture to term cupidity.

It is unnecessary to study the institutions and the history of the Americans in order to discover the truth of this remark, for their manners render it sufficiently evident. As the American participates in all that is done in his country, he thinks himself obliged to defend whatever may be censured; for it is not only his country which is attacked upon these occasions, but it is himself. The consequence is that his national pride resorts to a thousand artifices, and to all the petty tricks of individual vanity.

Nothing is more embarrassing in the ordinary intercourse of life than this irritable patriotism of the Americans. A stranger may be very well inclined to praise many of the institutions of their country, but he begs permission to blame some of the peculiarities which he observes—a permission which is however inexorably refused. America is therefore a free country, in which, lest anybody should be hurt by your remarks, you are not allowed to speak freely of private individuals or of the state; of the citizens or of the authorities; of public or of private undertakings; or, in short, of anything at all, except it be of the climate and the soil; and even then Americans will be found ready to defend either the one or the other as if they had been contrived by the inhabitants of the country.

In our times, option must be made between the patriotism of all and the government of a few, for the force and activity which the first confers are irreconcilable with the guarantees of tranquillity which the second furnishes.

NOTION OF RIGHTS IN THE UNITED STATES

After the idea of virtue, I know no higher principle than that of right; or to speak more accurately, these two ideas are commingled in one. The idea of right is simply that of virtue introduced into the political world. It is the idea of right which enabled men to define anarchy and tyranny; and which taught them to remain independent without arrogance, as well as to obey without servility. The man who submits to violence is debased by his compliance; but when he obeys the mandate of one who possesses that right of authority which he acknowledges in a fellow creature, he rises in some measure above the person who delivers the command. There are no great men without virtue, and there are no great nations—it may almost be added that there would be no society—without the notion of rights; for what is the condition of a mass of rational and intelligent beings who are only united together by the bond of force?

I am persuaded that the only means which we possess at the present time of inculcating the notion of rights, and of rendering it, as it were, palpable to the senses, is to invest all the members of the community with the peaceful exercise of certain rights: this is very clearly seen in children, who are men without the strength and the experience of manhood. When a child begins to move in the midst of the objects which surround him, he is instinctively led to turn everything which he can lay his hands upon to his own purposes; he has no notion of the property of others; but as he gradually learns the value of things, and begins to perceive that he may in his turn be deprived of his possessions, he becomes more circumspect, and he observes those rights in others which he wishes to have respected in himself. The principle which the child derives from the possession of his toys is taught to the man by the objects which he may call his own. In America those complaints against property in general, which are so frequent in Europe, are never heard, because in America there are no paupers; and as everyone has property of his own to defend, everyone recognizes the principle upon which he holds it.

The same thing occurs in the political world. In America the lowest classes have conceived a very high notion of political rights, because they exercise those rights; and they refrain from attacking those of other people in order to ensure their own from attack. While in Europe the same classes sometimes recalcitrate even against the supreme power, the American submits without a murmur to the authority of the pettiest magistrate.

This truth is exemplified by the most trivial details of national peculiarities. In France very few pleasures are exclusively reserved for the higher classes; the poor are admitted wherever the rich are received; and they consequently behave with propriety, and respect whatever contributes to the enjoyments in which they themselves participate. In England, where wealth has a monopoly of amusement as well as of power, complaints are made that whenever the poor happen to steal into the enclosures which are reserved for the pleasures of the rich, they commit acts of wanton mischief: can this be wondered at, since care has been taken that they should have nothing to lose?

The government of the democracy brings the notion of political rights to the level of the humblest citizens, just as the dissemination of wealth brings the notion of property within the reach of all the members of the community; and I confess that, to my mind, this is one of its greatest advantages. I do not assert that it is easy to teach men to exercise political rights; but I maintain that when it is possible, the effects which result from it are highly important: and I add that if there ever was a time at which such an attempt ought to be made, that time is our own. It is clear that the influence of religious belief is shaken, and that the notion of divine rights is declining; it is evident that public morality is vitiated, and the notion of moral rights is also disappearing: these are general symptoms of the substitution of argument for faith, and of calculation for the impulses of sentiment. If, in the midst of this general disruption, you do not succeed in connecting the notion of rights with that of personal interest, which is the only immutable point in the human heart, what means will you have of governing the world except by fear? When I am told that since the laws are weak and the populace is wild, since passions are excited and the authority of virtue is paralyzed no measures must be taken to increase the rights of the democracy, I reply that it is for these very reasons that some measures of the kind must be taken; and I am persuaded that governments are still more interested in taking them than society at large, because governments are liable to be destroyed, and society cannot perish.

I am not, however, inclined to exaggerate the example which America furnishes. In those states the people are invested with political rights at a time when they could scarcely be abused, for the citizens were few in number and simple in their manners. As they have increased, the Americans have not augmented the power of the democracy, but they have, if I may use the expression, extended its dominions.

It cannot be doubted that the moment at which political rights are granted to a people that had before been without them, is a very critical, though it be a necessary one. A child may kill before he is aware of the value of life; and he may deprive another person of his property before he is aware that his own may be taken away from him. The lower orders, when first they are invested with political rights, stand, in relation to those rights, in the same position as the child does to the whole of nature, and the celebrated adage may then be applied to them, *Homo puer robustus* [A man is a robust child]. This truth may even be perceived in America. The states in which the citizens have enjoyed their rights longest are those in which they make the best use of them.

It cannot be repeated too often that nothing is more fertile in prodigies than the art of being free; but there is nothing more arduous than the apprenticeship of liberty. Such is not the case with despotic institutions; despotism often promises to make amends for a thousand previous ills; it supports the right, it protects the oppressed, and it maintains public order. The nation is lulled by the temporary prosperity which accrues to it, until it is roused to a sense of its own misery. Liberty, on the contrary, is generally established in the midst of agitation, it is perfected by civil discord, and its benefits cannot be appreciated until it is already old.

RESPECT FOR THE LAW IN THE UNITED STATES

It is not always feasible to consult the whole people, either directly or indirectly, in the formation of the law; but it cannot be denied that when such a measure is possible, the authority of the law is very much augmented. This popular origin, which impairs the excellence and the wisdom of legislation, contributes prodigiously to increase its power. There is an amazing strength in the expression of the determination of a whole people; and when it declares itself, the imagination of those who are most inclined to contest it is overawed by its authority. The truth of this fact is very well known by parties; and they consequently strive to make out a majority whenever they can. If they have not the greater numbers of voters on their side, they assert that the true majority abstained from voting; and if they are foiled even there, they have recourse to the body of those persons who had no votes to give.

In the United States, except slaves, servants, and paupers in the receipt of relief from the townships, there is no class of persons who do not exercise the elective franchise, and who do not indirectly contribute to make the laws. Those who design to attack the laws must consequently either modify the opinion of the nation or trample upon its decision.

A second reason, which is still more weighty, may be further adduced; in the United States everyone is personally interested in enforcing the obedience of the whole community to the law; for as the minority may shortly rally the majority to its principles, it is interested in professing that respect for the decrees of the legislator which it may soon have occasion to claim for its own. However irksome an enactment may be, the citizen of the United States complies with it, not only because it is the work of the majority, but because it originates in his own authority; and he regards it as a contract to which he is himself a party.

In the United States, then, that numerous and turbulent multitude does not exist which always looks upon the law as its natural enemy, and accordingly surveys it with fear and with distrust. It is impossible, on the other hand, not to perceive that all classes display the utmost reliance upon the legislation of their country, and that they are attached to it by a kind of parental affection.

I am wrong, however, in saying all classes; for as in America the European scale of authority is inverted, the wealthy are there placed in a position analogous to that of the poor in the Old World, and it is the opulent classes which frequently look upon the law with suspicion. I have already observed that the advantage of democracy is not, as has been sometimes asserted, that it protects the interests of the whole community, but simply that it protects those of the majority. In the United States, where the poor rule, the rich have always some reason to dread the abuses of their power. This natural anxiety of the rich may produce a sullen dissatisfaction, but society is not disturbed by it; for the same reason which induces the rich to withhold their confidence in the legislative authority makes them obey its mandates: their wealth, which prevents them from making the law, prevents them from withstanding it. Among civilized nations revolts are rarely excited except by such persons as have nothing to lose by them; and if the laws of a democracy are not always worthy of respect, at least they always obtain it, for those who usually infringe the laws have no excuse for not complying with the enactments they have themselves made, and by which they are themselves benefited, while the citizens whose interests might be promoted by the infraction of them are induced, by their character and their station, to submit to the decisions of the legislature, whatever they may be. Besides which, the people in America obeys the law not only because it emanates from the popular authority, but because that authority may modify it in any points which may prove vexatory; a law is observed because it is a self-imposed evil in the first place, and an evil of transient duration in the second.

ACTIVITY WHICH PERVADES ALL THE BRANCHES OF THE BODY POLITIC IN THE UNITED STATES; INFLUENCE WHICH IT EXERCISES UPON SOCIETY

On passing from a country in which free institutions are established to one where they do not exist, the traveler is struck by the change: in the former all is bustle and activity; in the latter everything is calm and motionless. In the one, amelioration and progress are the general topics of inquiry; in the other, it seems as if the community only aspired to repose in the enjoyment of the advantages which it has acquired. Nevertheless, the country which exerts itself so strenuously to promote its welfare is generally more wealthy and more prosperous than that which appears to be so contented with its lot; and when we compare them together, we can scarcely conceive how so many new wants are daily felt in the former, while so few seem to occur in the latter.

If this remark is applicable to those free countries in which monarchical and aristocratic institutions subsist, it is still more striking with regard to democratic republics. In these states it is not only a portion of the people which is busied with the amelioration of its social condition, but the whole community is engaged in the task; and it is not the exigencies and the convenience of a single class for which a provision is to be made, but the exigencies and the convenience of all ranks of life.

It is not impossible to conceive the surpassing liberty which the Americans enjoy; some idea may likewise be formed of the extreme equality which subsists among them, but the political activity which pervades the United States must be seen in order to be understood. No sooner do you set foot upon the American soil than you are stunned by a kind of tumult; a confused clamor is heard on every side; and a thousand simultaneous voices demand the immediate satisfaction of their social wants. Everything is in motion around you; here, the people of one quarter of a town are met to decide upon the building of a church; there, the election of a representative is going on; a little further, the delegates of a district are posting to the town in order to consult upon some local improvements; or in another place the laborers of a village quit their plows to deliberate upon the project of a road or a public school. Meetings are called for the sole purpose of declaring their disapprobation of the line of conduct pursued by the government; while in other assemblies the citizens salute the authorities of the day as the fathers of their country. Societies are formed which regard drunkenness as the principal cause of the evils under which the state labors, and which solemnly bind themselves to give a constant example of temperance.[24]

The great political agitation of the American legislative bodies, which is the only kind of excitement that attracts the attention of foreign countries, is a mere episode or a sort of continuation of that universal movement which originates in the lowest classes of the people and extends successively to all the ranks of society. It is impossible to spend more efforts in the pursuit of enjoyment.

The cares of political life engross a most prominent place in the occupation of a citizen in the United States; and almost the only pleasure of which an American has any idea is to take a part in the government, and to discuss the part he has taken. This feeling pervades the most trifling habits of life; even the women frequently attend public meetings, and listen to political harangues as a recreation after their household labors. Debating clubs are to a certain extent a substitute for theatrical entertainments: an American cannot converse, but he can discuss; and when he attempts to talk he falls into a dissertation. He speaks to you as if he was addressing a meeting; and if he should chance to warm in the course of the discussion, he will infallibly say "Gentlemen," to the person with whom he is conversing.

In some countries the inhabitants display a certain repugnance to avail themselves of the political privileges with which the law invests them; it would seem that they set too high a value upon their time to spend it on the interests of the community; and they prefer to withdraw within the exact limits of a wholesome egotism, marked out by four sunk fences and a quickset hedge. But if an American were condemned to confine his activity to his own affairs, he would be robbed of one half of his existence; he would feel an immense void in the life which he is accustomed to lead, and his wretchedness would be unbearable.[25] I am persuaded that if ever a despotic government is established in America, it will find

---

24. At the time of my stay in the United States the temperance societies already consisted of more than 270,000 members; and their effect had been to diminish the consumption of fermented liquors by 500,000 gallons per annum in the state of Pennsylvania alone.

25. The same remark was made at Rome under the first Caesars. Montesquieu somewhere alludes to the excessive despondency of certain Roman citizens who, after the excitement of political life, were all at once flung back into the stagnation of private life.

it more difficult to surmount the habits which free institutions have engendered, than to conquer the attachment of the citizens to freedom.

This ceaseless agitation which democratic government has introduced into the political world influences all social intercourse. I am not sure that upon the whole this is not the greatest advantage of democracy; and I am much less inclined to applaud it for what it does than for what it causes to be done.

It is incontestable that the people frequently conducts public business very ill; but it is impossible that the lower orders should take a part in public business without extending the circle of their ideas, and without quitting the ordinary routine of their mental acquirements. The humblest individual who is called upon to co-operate in the government of society acquires a certain degree of self-respect; and as he possesses authority, he can command the services of minds much more enlightened than his own. He is canvassed by a multitude of applicants who seek to deceive him in a thousand different ways, but who instruct him by their deceit. He takes a part in political undertakings which did not originate in his own conception, but which give him a taste for undertakings of the kind. New ameliorations are daily pointed out in the property which he holds in common with others, and this gives him the desire of improving that property which is more peculiarly his own. He is perhaps neither happier nor better than those who came before him, but he is better informed and more active. I have no doubt that the democratic institutions of the United States, joined to the physical constitution of the country, are the cause (not the direct, as is so often asserted, but the indirect cause) of the prodigious commercial activity of the inhabitants. It is not engendered by the laws, but the people learns how to promote it by the experience derived from legislation.

When the opponents of democracy assert that a single individual performs the duties which he undertakes much better than the government of the community, it appears to me that they are perfectly right. The government of an individual, supposing an equality of instruction on either side, is more consistent, more persevering, and more accurate than that of a multitude, and it is much better qualified judiciously to discriminate the characters of the men it employs. If any deny what I advance, they have certainly never seen a democratic government, or have formed their opinion upon very partial evidence. It is true that even when local circumstances and the disposition of the people allow democratic institutions to subsist, they never display a regular and methodical system of government. Democratic liberty is far from accomplishing all the projects it undertakes, with the skill of an adroit despotism. It frequently abandons them before they have borne their fruits, or risks them when the consequences may prove dangerous; but in the end it produces more than any absolute government, and if it do fewer things well, it does a greater number of things. Under its sway, the transactions of the public administration are not nearly so important as what is done by private exertion. Democracy does not confer the most skillful kind of government upon the people, but it produces that which the most skillful governments are frequently unable to awaken, namely, an all-pervading and restless activity, a superabundant force, and an energy which is inseparable from it, and which may, under favorable circumstances, beget the most amazing benefits. These are the true advantages of democracy.

In the present age, when the destinies of Christendom seem to be in suspense, some hasten to assail democracy as its foe while it is yet in its early growth; and others are ready with their vows of adoration for this new deity which is springing forth from chaos: but both parties are very imperfectly acquainted with the object of their hatred or of their desires; they strike in the dark, and distribute their blows by mere chance.

We must first understand what the purport of society and the aim of government is held to be. If it be your intention to confer a certain elevation upon the human mind, and to teach it to regard the things of this world with generous feelings, to inspire men with a scorn of mere temporal advantage, to give birth to living convictions, and to keep alive the spirit of honorable devotedness; if you hold it to be a good thing to refine the habits, to embellish the manners, to cultivate the arts of a nation, and to promote the love of poetry, of beauty, and of renown; if you would constitute a people not unfitted to act with power upon all other nations, nor unprepared for those high enterprises which, whatever be the result of its efforts, will leave a name forever famous in time—if you believe such to be the principal object of society, you must avoid the government of democracy, which would be a very uncertain guide to the end you have in view.

But if you hold it to be expedient to divert the moral and intellectual activity of man to the production of comfort, and to the acquirement of the necessaries of life; if a clear understanding be more profitable to man than genius; if your object be not to stimulate the virtues of heroism, but to create habits of peace; if you had rather witness vices than crimes, and are content to meet with fewer noble deeds, provided offenses be diminished in the same proportion; if, instead of living in the midst of a brilliant state of society, you are contented to have prosperity around you; if, in short, you are of opinion that the principal object of a government is not to confer the greatest possible share of power and of glory upon the body of the nation, but to ensure the greatest degree of enjoyment, and the least degree of misery to each of the individuals who compose it—if such be your desires, you can have no surer means of satisfying them than by equalizing the conditions of men and establishing democratic institutions.

But if the time be past at which such a choice was possible, and if some superhuman power impel us towards one or the other of these two governments without consulting our wishes, let us at least endeavor to make the best of that which is allotted to us; and let us so inquire into its good and its evil propensities as to be able to foster the former, and repress the latter to the utmost. . . .

CONCLUSION

I have now nearly reached the close of my inquiry; hitherto, in speaking of the future destiny of the United States, I have endeavored to divide my subject into distinct portions in order to study each of them with more attention. My present object is to embrace the whole from one single point; the remarks I shall make will be less detailed, but they will be more sure. I shall perceive each object less distinctly, but I shall descry the principal facts with more certainty. A traveler who has just left the walls of an immense city climbs the neighboring hill; as he goes further off he loses sight of the men whom he has so recently quitted; their dwellings are confused in a dense mass; he can no longer distinguish the public squares, and he can scarcely trace out the great thoroughfares; but his eye has less difficulty in following the boundaries of the city, and for the first time he sees the shape of the vast whole. Such is the future destiny of the British race in North America to my eye; the details of the stupendous picture are overhung with shade, but I conceive a clear idea of the entire subject.

The territory now occupied or possessed by the United States of America forms about one-twentieth part of the habitable earth. But extensive as these confines are, it must not be supposed that the Anglo-American race will always remain within them; indeed, it has already far overstepped them.

There was once a time at which we also might have created a great French nation in the American wilds, to counterbalance the influence of the English upon the destinies of the New World. France formerly possessed a territory in North America scarcely less extensive than the whole of Europe. The three greatest rivers of that continent then flowed within her dominions. The Indian tribes which dwelt between the mouth of the St. Lawrence and the delta of the Mississippi were unaccustomed to any other tongue but ours; and all the European settlements scattered over that immense region recalled the traditions of our country. Louisbourg, Montmorency, Duquesne, Saint-Louis, Vincennes, New Orleans (for such were the names they bore) are words dear to France and familiar to our ears.

But a concourse of circumstances, which it would be tedious to enumerate,[26] have deprived us of this magnificent inheritance. Wherever the French settlers were numerically weak and partially established they have disappeared; those who remain are collected on a small extent of country, and are now subject to other laws. The 400,000 French inhabitants of Lower Canada constitute, at the present time, the remnant of an old nation lost in the midst of a new people. A foreign population is increasing around them unceasingly and on all sides which already penetrates among the ancient masters of the country, predominates in their cities, and corrupts their language. This population is identical with that of the United States; it is therefore with truth that I asserted that the British race is not confined within the frontiers of the Union, since it already extends to the northeast.

To the northwest nothing is to be met with but a few insignificant Russian settlements; but to the southwest, Mexico presents a barrier to the Anglo-Americans. Thus, the Spaniards and the Anglo-Americans are, properly speaking, the only two races which divide the possession of the New World. The limits of separation between them have been settled by a treaty; but although the conditions of that treaty are exceedingly favorable to the Anglo-Americans, I do not doubt that they will shortly infringe this arrangement. Vast provinces, extending beyond the frontiers of the Union towards Mexico, are still destitute of inhabitants. The natives of the United States will forestall the rightful occupants of these solitary regions. They will take possession of the soil, and establish social institutions, so that when the legal owner arrives at length, he will find the wilderness under cultivation, and strangers quietly settled in the midst of his inheritance.

The lands of the New World belong to the first occupant, and they are the natural reward of the swiftest pioneer. Even the countries which are

---

26. The foremost of these circumstances is that nations which are accustomed to free institutions and municipal government are better able than any others to found prosperous colonies. The habit of thinking and governing for oneself is indispensable in a new country, where success necessarily depends, in a great measure, upon the individual exertions of the settlers.

already peopled will have some difficulty in securing themselves from this invasion. I have already alluded to what is taking place in the province of Texas. The inhabitants of the United States are perpetually migrating to Texas, where they purchase land; and although they conform to the laws of the country, they are gradually founding the empire of their own language and their own manners. The province of Texas is still part of the Mexican dominions, but it will soon contain no Mexicans; the same thing has occurred whenever the Anglo-Americans have come into contact with populations of a different origin.

It cannot be denied that the British race has acquired an amazing preponderance over all the other European races in the New World; and that it is very superior to them in civilization, in industry, and in power. As long as it is only surrounded by desert or thinly-peopled countries, as long as it encounters no dense populations upon its route, through which it cannot work its way, it will assuredly continue to spread. The lines marked out by treaties will not stop it; but it will everywhere transgress these imaginary barriers.

The geographical position of the British race in the New World is peculiarly favorable to its rapid increase. Above its northern frontiers the icy regions of the Pole extend; and a few degrees below its southern confines lies the burning climate of the Equator. The Anglo-Americans are therefore placed in the most temperate and habitable zone of the continent.

It is generally supposed that the prodigious increase of population in the United States is posterior to their Declaration of Independence. But this is an error: the population increased as rapidly under the colonial system as it does at the present day; that is to say, it doubled in about twenty-two years. But this proportion, which is now applied to millions, was then applied to thousands of inhabitants; and the same fact which was scarcely noticeable a century ago is now evident to every observer.

The British subjects in Canada, who are dependent on a king, augment and spread almost as rapidly as the British settlers of the United States, who live under a republican government. During the War of Independence, which lasted eight years, the population continued to increase without intermission in the same ratio. Although powerful Indian nations allied with the English existed, at that time, upon the western frontiers, the emigration westward was never checked. While the enemy laid waste the shores of the Atlantic, Kentucky, the western parts of Pennsylvania, and the states of Vermont and of Maine were filling with inhabitants. Nor did the unsettled state of the Constitution, which succeeded the war, prevent the increase of the population, or stop its progress across the wilds. Thus, the difference of laws, the various conditions of peace and war, of order and of anarchy, have exercised no perceptible influence upon the gradual development of the Anglo-Americans. This may be readily understood; for the fact is that no causes are sufficiently general to exercise a simultaneous influence over the whole of so extensive a territory. One portion of the country always offers a sure retreat from the calamities which afflict another part; and however great may be the evil, the remedy which is at hand is greater still.

It must not, then, be imagined that the impulse of the British race in the New World can be arrested. The dismemberment of the Union, and the hostilities which might ensue, the abolition of republican institutions, and the tyrannical government which might succeed it may retard this impulse, but they cannot prevent it from ultimately fulfilling the destinies to which that race is reserved. No power upon earth can close upon the emigrants that fertile wilderness which offers resources to all industry and a refuge from all want. Future events, of whatever nature they may be, will not deprive the Americans of their climate or of their inland seas, of their great rivers or of their exuberant soil. Nor will bad laws, revolutions, and anarchy, be able to obliterate that love of prosperity and that spirit of enterprise which seem to be the distinctive characteristics of their race, or to extinguish that knowledge which guides them on their way.

Thus, in the midst of the uncertain future, one event at least is sure. At a period which may be said to be near (for we are speaking of the life of a nation), the Anglo-Americans will alone cover the immense space contained between the polar regions and the tropics, extending from the coasts of the Atlantic to the shores of the Pacific Ocean. The territory which will probably be occupied by the Anglo-Americans at some future time may be computed to equal three-quarters of Europe in extent.[27] The climate of the Union is upon the whole preferable to that of Europe, and its natural advantages are not less great; it is therefore evident that its population will at some future time be proportionate to our own. Europe, divided as it is between so many different nations, and torn as it has been by incessant wars and the barbarous manners of the Middle Ages, has notwithstanding attained a population of 410 inhabitants to the square league. What cause can prevent the United States from having as numerous a population in time?

Many ages must elapse before the divers offsets of the British race in

_____

27. The United States already extend over a territory equal to one-half of Europe. The area of Europe is 500,000 square leagues, and its population 205,000,000 of inhabitants.

America cease to present the same homogeneous characteristics: and the time cannot be foreseen at which a permanent inequality of conditions will be established in the New World. Whatever differences may arise, from peace or from war, from freedom or oppression, from prosperity or want, between the destinies of the different descendants of the great Anglo-American family, they will at least preserve an analogous social condition, and they will hold in common the customs and the opinions to which that social condition has given birth.

In the Middle Ages, the tie of religion was sufficiently powerful to imbue all the different populations of Europe with the same civilization. The British of the New World have a thousand other reciprocal ties; and they live at a time when the tendency to equality is general among mankind. The Middle Ages were a period when everything was broken up; when each people, each province, each city, and each family, had a strong tendency to maintain its distinct individuality. At the present time an opposite tendency seems to prevail, and the nations seem to be advancing to unity. Our means of intellectual intercourse unite the most remote parts of the earth; and it is impossible for men to remain strangers to each other, or to be ignorant of the events which are taking place in any corner of the globe. The consequence is that there is less difference, at the present day, between the Europeans and their descendants in the New World than there was between certain towns in the thirteenth century which were only separated by a river. If this tendency to assimilation brings foreign nations closer to each other, it must a fortiori prevent the descendants of the same people from becoming aliens to each other.

The time will therefore come when one hundred and fifty millions of men will be living in North America,[28] equal in condition, the progeny of one race, owing their origin to the same cause, and preserving the same civilization, the same language, the same religion, the same habits, the same manners, and imbued with the same opinions, propagated under the same forms. The rest is uncertain, but this is certain; and it is a fact new to the world—a fact fraught with such portentous consequences as to baffle the efforts even of the imagination.

There are, at the present time, two great nations in the world which seem to tend towards the same end, although they started from different points: I allude to the Russians and the Americans. Both of them have grown up unnoticed; and while the attention of mankind was directed

---

28. This would be a population proportionate to that of Europe, taken at a mean rate of 410 inhabitants to the square league.

elsewhere, they have suddenly assumed a most prominent place among the nations; and the world learned their existence and their greatness at almost the same time.

All other nations seem to have nearly reached their natural limits, and only to be charged with the maintenance of their power; but these are still in the act of growth: [29] all the others are stopped, or continue to advance with extreme difficulty; these are proceeding with ease and with celerity along a path to which the human eye can assign no term. The American struggles against the natural obstacles which oppose him; the adversaries of the Russian are men: the former combats the wilderness and savage life; the latter, civilization with all its weapons and its arts: the conquests of the one are therefore gained by the plowshare; those of the other, by the sword. The Anglo-American relies upon personal interest to accomplish his ends, and gives free scope to the unguided exertions and common sense of the citizens; the Russian centers all the authority of society in a single arm: the principal instrument of the former is freedom; of the latter, servitude. Their starting point is different, and their courses are not the same; yet each of them seems to be marked out by the will of Heaven to sway the destinies of half the globe.

---

29. Russia is the country in the Old World in which population increases most rapidly in proportion.

The foregoing consists of the Introduction, Chapters III, IV, XI–XIV, and the Conclusion of Volume I of de Tocqueville's DEMOCRACY IN AMERICA, *translated by Henry Reeve.*

Why Democratic Nations
Show a More Ardent and Enduring Love
of Equality than of Liberty

The first and most intense passion which is engendered by the equality of conditions is, I need hardly say, the love of that same equality. My readers will therefore not be surprised that I speak of it before all others.

Everybody has remarked that in our time, and especially in France, this passion for equality is every day gaining ground in the human heart. It has been said a hundred times that our contemporaries are far more ardently and tenaciously attached to equality than to freedom; but, as I do not find that the causes of the fact have been sufficiently analyzed, I shall endeavor to point them out.

It is possible to imagine an extreme point at which freedom and equality would meet and be confounded together. Let us suppose that all the members of the community take a part in the government, and that each one of them has an equal right to take a part in it. As none is different from his fellows, none can exercise a tyrannical power: men will be perfectly free, because they will all be entirely equal; and they will all be perfectly equal, because they will be entirely free. To this ideal state democratic nations tend. Such is the completest form that equality can assume upon earth; but there are a thousand others which, without being equally perfect, are not less cherished by those nations.

The principle of equality may be established in civil society, without prevailing in the political world. Equal rights may exist of indulging in the same pleasures, of entering the same professions, of frequenting the same places—in a word, of living in the same manner and seeking wealth by the same means, although all men do not take an equal share in the government.

A kind of equality may even be established in the political world, though there should be no political freedom there. A man may be the equal of all his countrymen save one, who is the master of all without distinction, and who selects equally from among them all the agents of his power.

Several other combinations might be easily imagined by which very great equality would be united to institutions more or less free, or even to institutions wholly without freedom.

Although men cannot become absolutely equal unless they be entirely free, and consequently equality, pushed to its furthest extent, may be confounded with freedom, yet there is good reason for distinguishing the one from the other. The taste which men have for liberty and that which they feel for equality are, in fact, two different things; and I am not afraid to add that, among democratic nations, they are two unequal things.

Upon close inspection, it will be seen that there is in every age some peculiar and preponderating fact with which all others are connected; this fact almost always gives birth to some pregnant idea or some ruling passion, which attracts to itself, and bears away in its course, all the feelings and opinions of the time: it is like a great stream, towards which each of the surrounding rivulets seem to flow.

Freedom has appeared in the world at different times and under various forms; it has not been exclusively bound to any social condition, and it is not confined to democracies. Freedom cannot, therefore, form the distinguishing characteristic of democratic ages. The peculiar and preponderating fact which marks those ages as its own is the equality of conditions; the ruling passion of men in those periods is the love of this equality. Ask not what singular charm the men of democratic ages find in being equal, or what special reasons they may have for clinging so tenaciously to equality rather than to the other advantages which society holds out to them: equality is the distinguishing characteristic of the age they live in; that, of itself, is enough to explain that they prefer it to all the rest.

But independently of this reason there are several others which will at all times habitually lead men to prefer equality to freedom.

If a people could ever succeed in destroying, or even in diminishing, the equality which prevails in its own body, this could only be accomplished by long and laborious efforts. Its social condition must be modified, its laws abolished, its opinions superseded, its habits changed, its manners corrupted. But political liberty is more easily lost; to neglect to hold it fast is to allow it to escape.

Men therefore not only cling to equality because it is dear to them; they also adhere to it because they think it will last forever.

That political freedom may compromise in its excesses the tranquillity, the property, the lives of individuals, is obvious to the narrowest and most unthinking minds. But, on the contrary, none but attentive and clear-sighted men perceive the perils with which equality threatens us, and they commonly avoid pointing them out. They know that the calamities they apprehend are remote, and flatter themselves that they will only fall upon future generations, for which the present generation takes but little thought. The evils which freedom sometimes brings with it are immediate; they are apparent to all, and all are more or less affected by them. The evils which extreme equality may produce are slowly disclosed; they creep gradually into the social frame; they are only seen at intervals, and at the moment at which they become most violent, habit already causes them to be no longer felt.

The advantages which freedom brings are only shown by length of time; and it is always easy to mistake the cause in which they originate. The advantages of equality are instantaneous, and they may constantly be traced from their source.

Political liberty bestows exalted pleasures, from time to time, upon a certain number of citizens. Equality every day confers a number of small enjoyments on every man. The charms of equality are every instant felt, and are within the reach of all; the noblest hearts are not insensible to them, and the most vulgar souls exult in them. The passion which equality engenders must therefore be at once strong and general. Men cannot enjoy political liberty unpurchased by some sacrifices, and they never obtain it without great exertions. But the pleasures of equality are self-proffered: each of the petty incidents of life seems to occasion them, and in order to taste them nothing is required but to live.

Democratic nations are at all times fond of equality, but there are certain epochs at which the passion they entertain for it swells to the height of fury. This occurs at the moment when the old social system, long menaced, completes its own destruction after a last intestine struggle, and when the barriers of rank are at length thrown down. At such times men pounce upon equality as their booty, and they cling to it as to some precious treasure which they fear to lose. The passion for equality penetrates on every side into men's hearts, expands there, and fills them entirely. Tell them not that by this blind surrender of themselves to an exclusive passion they risk their dearest interests: they are deaf. Show them not freedom escaping from their grasp, while they are looking another way: they are blind—or rather, they can discern but one sole object to be desired in the universe.

What I have said is applicable to all democratic nations: what I am about to say concerns the French alone. Among most modern nations, and especially among all those of the continent of Europe, the taste and the idea of freedom only began to exist and to extend itself at the time when social conditions were tending to equality, and as a consequence of that very equality. Absolute kings were the most efficient levelers of ranks among their subjects. Among these nations equality preceded freedom; equality was therefore a fact of some standing when freedom was still a novelty: the one had already created customs, opinions, and laws belonging to it, when the other, alone and for the first time, came into actual existence. Thus the latter was still only an affair of opinion and of taste, while the former had already crept into the habits of the people, possessed itself of their manners, and given a particular turn to the smallest actions in their lives. Can it be wondered that the men of our own time prefer the one to the other?

I think that democratic communities have a natural taste for freedom: left to themselves, they will seek it, cherish it, and view any privation of it with regret. But for equality, their passion is ardent, insatiable, incessant, invincible: they call for equality in freedom; and if they cannot obtain that, they still call for equality in slavery. They will endure poverty, servitude, barbarism—but they will not endure aristocracy.

This is true at all times, and especially true in our own. All men and all powers seeking to cope with this irresistible passion will be overthrown and destroyed by it. In our age, freedom cannot be established without it, and despotism itself cannot reign without its support.

Of Individualism in Democratic Countries

I have shown how it is that in ages of equality every man seeks for his opinions within himself: I am now about to show how it is that, in the same ages, all his feelings are turned towards himself alone. *Individualism* is a novel expression, to which a novel idea has given birth. Our fathers were only acquainted with egotism. Egotism is a passionate and exaggerated love of self which leads a man to connect everything with his own person and to prefer himself to everything in the world. Individualism is a mature and calm feeling which disposes each member of the community to sever himself from the mass of his fellow creatures, and to draw apart with his family and his friends; so that, after he has thus formed a little circle of his own, he willingly leaves society at large to itself. Egotism originates in blind instinct: individualism proceeds from erroneous judgment more than from depraved feelings; it originates as much in the deficiencies of the mind as in the perversity of the heart.

Egotism blights the germ of all virtue: individualism, at first, only saps the virtues of public life; but, in the long run, it attacks and destroys all others, and is at length absorbed in downright egotism. Egotism is a vice as old as the world, which does not belong to one form of society more than to another; individualism is of democratic origin, and it threatens to spread in the same ratio as the equality of conditions.

Among aristocratic nations, as families remain for centuries in the same condition, often on the same spot, all generations become as it were contemporaneous. A man almost always knows his forefathers, and respects them: he thinks he already sees his remote descendants, and he loves them. He willingly imposes duties on himself towards the former and the latter; and he will frequently sacrifice his personal gratifications to those who went before and to those who will come after him.

Aristocratic institutions have, moreover, the effect of closely binding every man to several of his fellow citizens. As the classes of an aristocratic people are strongly marked and permanent, each of them is regarded by its own members as a sort of lesser country, more tangible and more cherished than the country at large. As in aristocratic communities all the citizens occupy fixed positions, one above the other, the result is that each of them always sees a man above himself whose patronage is necessary to him, and below himself another man whose co-operation he may claim.

Men living in aristocratic ages are therefore almost always closely attached to something placed out of their own sphere, and they are often disposed to forget themselves. It is true that in those ages the notion of human fellowship is faint, and that men seldom think of sacrificing themselves for mankind; but they often sacrifice themselves for other men. In democratic ages, on the contrary, when the duties of each individual to the race are much more clear, devoted service to any one man becomes more rare; the bond of human affection is extended, but it is relaxed.

Among democratic nations new families are constantly springing up, others are constantly falling away, and all that remain change their condition; the woof of time is every instant broken, and the track of generations effaced. Those who went before are soon forgotten; of those who will come after no one has any idea: the interest of man is confined to those in close propinquity to himself.

As each class approximates to other classes, and intermingles with them, its members become indifferent and as strangers to one another. Aristocracy had made a chain of all the members of the community, from the peasant to the king: democracy breaks that chain, and severs every link of it.

As social conditions become more equal, the number of persons increases who, although they are neither rich enough nor powerful enough to exercise any great influence over their fellow creatures, have nevertheless acquired or retained sufficient education and fortune to satisfy their own wants. They owe nothing to any man, they expect nothing from any man; they acquire the habit of always considering themselves as standing alone, and they are apt to imagine that their whole destiny is in their own hands.

Thus not only does democracy make every man forget his ancestors, but it hides his descendants, and separates his contemporaries from him; it throws him back forever upon himself alone, and threatens in the end to confine him entirely within the solitude of his own heart.

Individualism Stronger at the Close of a Democratic Revolution than at Other Periods

The period when the construction of democratic society upon the ruins of an aristocracy has just been completed is especially that at which this separation of men from one another, and the egotism resulting from it, most forcibly strike the observation. Democratic communities not only contain a large number of independent citizens, but they are constantly filled with men who, having entered but yesterday upon their independent condition, are intoxicated with their new power. They entertain a presumptuous confidence in their strength, and as they do not suppose that they can henceforward ever have occasion to claim the assistance of their fellow creatures, they do not scruple to show that they care for nobody but themselves.

An aristocracy seldom yields without a protracted struggle, in the course of which implacable animosities are kindled between the different classes of society. These passions survive the victory, and traces of them may be observed in the midst of the democratic confusion which ensues.

Those members of the community who were at the top of the late gradations of rank cannot immediately forget their former greatness; they will long regard themselves as aliens in the midst of the newly composed society. They look upon all those whom this state of society has made their equals as oppressors, whose destiny can excite no sympathy; they have lost sight of their former equals, and feel no longer bound by a common interest to their fate: each of them, standing aloof, thinks that he is reduced to care for himself alone. Those, on the contrary, who were formerly at the foot of the social scale, and who have been brought up to the common level by a sudden revolution, cannot enjoy their newly acquired independence without secret uneasiness; and if they meet with some of their former superiors on the same footing as themselves, they stand aloof from them with an expression of triumph and of fear.

It is, then, commonly at the outset of democratic society that citizens are most disposed to live apart. Democracy leads men not to draw near to their fellow creatures; but democratic revolutions lead them to shun each other, and perpetuate in a state of equality the animosities which the state of inequality engendered.

The great advantage of the Americans is that they have arrived at a state of democracy without having to endure a democratic revolution, and that they are born equal instead of becoming so.

That the Americans Combat the Effects of Individualism by Free Institutions

Despotism, which is of a very timorous nature, is never more secure of continuance than when it can keep men asunder; and all its influence is commonly exerted for that purpose. No vice of the human heart is so acceptable to it as egotism: a despot easily forgives his subjects for not loving him, provided they do not love each other. He does not ask them to assist him in governing the state; it is enough that they do not aspire to govern it themselves. He stigmatizes as turbulent and unruly spirits those who would combine their exertions to promote the prosperity of the community; and, perverting the natural meaning of words, he applauds as good citizens those who have no sympathy for any but themselves.

Thus the vices which despotism engenders are precisely those which equality fosters. These two things mutually and perniciously complete and assist each other. Equality places men side by side, unconnected by any common tie; despotism raises barriers to keep them asunder: the former predisposes them not to consider their fellow creatures; the latter makes general indifference a sort of public virtue.

Despotism then, which is at all times dangerous, is more particularly to be feared in democratic ages. It is easy to see that in those same ages men stand most in need of freedom. When the members of a community are forced to attend to public affairs, they are necessarily drawn from the circle of their own interests, and snatched at times from self-observation. As soon as a man begins to treat of public affairs in public, he begins to perceive that he is not so independent of his fellow men as he had at first imagined, and that, in order to obtain their support, he must often lend them his co-operation.

When the public is supreme, there is no man who does not feel the value of public good will, or who does not endeavor to court it by drawing to himself the esteem and affection of those among whom he is to live. Many of the passions which congeal and keep asunder human hearts are then obliged to retire and hide below the surface. Pride must be dissembled; disdain dares not break out; egotism fears its own self. Under a free government, as most public offices are elective, the men whose elevated minds or aspiring hopes are too closely circumscribed in private life constantly feel that they cannot do without the population which surrounds them. Men learn at such times to think of their fellow men from ambitious motives; and they frequently find it, in a manner, their interest to forget themselves.

I may here be met by an objection derived from electioneering intrigues, the meannesses of candidates, and the calumnies of their opponents. These are opportunities for animosity which occur the oftener the more frequent elections become. Such evils are doubtless great, but they are transient; whereas the benefits which attend them remain. The desire of being elected may lead some men for a time to violent hostility; but this same desire leads all men in the long run mutually to support each other; and, if it happens that an election accidentally severs two friends, the electoral system brings a multitude of citizens permanently together, who would always have remained unknown to each other. Freedom engenders private animosities, but despotism gives birth to general indifference.

The Americans have combated by free institutions the tendency of equality to keep men asunder, and they have subdued it. The legislators of America did not suppose that a general representation of the whole nation would suffice to ward off a disorder at once so natural to the frame of democratic society, and so fatal; they also thought that it would be well to infuse political life into each portion of the territory, in order to multiply to an infinite extent opportunities of acting in concert for all the members of the community, and to make them constantly feel their mutual dependence on each other. The plan was a wise one. The general affairs of a country only engage the attention of leading politicians, who assemble from time to time in the same places; and as they often lose sight of each other afterwards, no lasting ties are established between them. But if the object be to have the local affairs of a district conducted by the men who reside there, the same persons are always in contact, and they are, in a manner, forced to be acquainted, and to adapt themselves to one another.

It is difficult to draw a man out of his own circle to interest him in the destiny of the state, because he does not clearly understand what influence the destiny of the state can have upon his own lot. But if it be proposed to make a road cross the end of his estate, he will see at a glance that there is a connection between this small public affair and his greatest private affairs; and he will discover, without its being shown to him, the close tie which unites private to general interest. Thus, far more may be done by entrusting to the citizens the administration of minor affairs than by surrendering to them the control of important ones, towards interesting them in the public welfare and convincing them that they constantly stand in need one of the other in order to provide for it. A brilliant achievement may win for you the favor of a people at one stroke; but to earn the love and respect of the population which surrounds you, a long succession of little services rendered and of obscure good deeds—a constant habit of kindness, and an established reputation for disinterestedness—will be required. Local freedom, then, which leads a great number of citizens to value the affection of their neighbors and of their kindred, perpetually brings men together and forces them to help one another, in spite of the propensities which sever them.

In the United States the more opulent citizens take great care not to stand aloof from the people; on the contrary, they constantly keep on easy terms with the lower classes: they listen to them, they speak to them every day. They know that the rich in democracies always stand in need of the poor; and that in democratic ages you attach a poor man to you more by your manner than by benefits conferred. The magnitude of such benefits, which sets off the difference of conditions, causes a secret irritation to those who reap advantage from them; but the charm of simplicity of manners is almost irresistible: their affability carries men away, and even their want of polish is not always displeasing. This truth does not take root at once in the minds of the rich. They generally resist it as long as the democratic revolution lasts, and they do not acknowledge it immediately after that revolution is accomplished. They are very ready to do good to the people, but they still choose to keep them at arm's length; they think that is sufficient, but they are mistaken. They might spend fortunes thus without warming the hearts of the population around them; that population does not ask them for the sacrifice of their money, but of their pride.

It would seem as if every imagination in the United States were upon the stretch to invent means of increasing the wealth and satisfying the wants of the public. The best-informed inhabitants of each district constantly use their information to discover new truths which may augment the general prosperity; and, if they have made any such discoveries, they eagerly surrender them to the mass of the people.

When the vices and weaknesses frequently exhibited by those who govern in America are closely examined, the prosperity of the people occasions—but improperly occasions—surprise. Elected magistrates do not make the American democracy flourish; it flourishes because the magistrates are elective.

It would be unjust to suppose that the patriotism and the zeal which every American displays for the welfare of his fellow citizens are wholly insincere. Although private interest directs the greater part of human actions in the United States, as well as elsewhere, it does not regulate them all. I must say that I have often seen Americans make great and real sacrifices to the public welfare; and I have remarked a hundred instances in which they hardly ever failed to lend faithful support to each other. The free institutions which the inhabitants of the United States possess, and the political rights of which they make so much use, remind every citizen, and in a thousand ways, that he lives in society. They every instant impress upon his mind the notion that it is the duty as well as the interest of men to make themselves useful to their fellow creatures; and as he sees no particular ground of animosity to them, since he is never either their master or their slave, his heart readily leans to the side of kindness. Men attend to the interests of the public, first by necessity, afterwards by choice: what was intentional becomes an instinct; and by dint of working for the good of one's fellow citizens, the habit and the taste for serving them is at length acquired.

Many people in France consider equality of conditions as one evil, and political freedom as a second. When they are obliged to yield to the former, they strive at least to escape from the latter. But I contend that in order to combat the evils which equality may produce there is only one effectual remedy—namely, political freedom.

Of the Use Which the Americans Make of Public Associations in Civil Life

I do not propose to speak of those political associations by the aid of which men endeavor to defend themselves against the despotic influence of a majority, or against the aggressions of regal power. That subject I have already treated.[1] If each citizen did not learn, in proportion as he

---

1. See p. 596, *supra*.

individually becomes more feeble and consequently more incapable of preserving his freedom singlehanded, to combine with his fellow citizens for the purpose of defending it, it is clear that tyranny would unavoidably increase together with equality.

Those associations only which are formed in civil life, without reference to political objects, are here adverted to. The political associations which exist in the United States are only a single feature in the midst of the immense assemblage of associations in that country. Americans of all ages, all conditions, and all dispositions, constantly form associations. They have not only commercial and manufacturing companies, in which all take part, but associations of a thousand other kinds—religious, moral, serious, futile, extensive or restricted, enormous or diminutive. The Americans make associations to give entertainments, to found establishments for education, to build inns, to construct churches, to diffuse books, to send missionaries to the antipodes; and in this manner they found hospitals, prisons, and schools. If it be proposed to advance some truth, or to foster some feeling by the encouragement of a great example, they form a society. Wherever, at the head of some new undertaking, you see the government in France, or a man of rank in England, in the United States you will be sure to find an association.

I met with several kinds of associations in America, of which I confess I had no previous notion; and I have often admired the extreme skill with which the inhabitants of the United States succeed in proposing a common object to the exertions of a great many men, and in getting them voluntarily to pursue it.

I have since traveled over England, whence the Americans have taken some of their laws and many of their customs; and it seemed to me that the principle of association was by no means so constantly or so adroitly used in that country. The English often perform great things singly; whereas the Americans form associations for the smallest undertakings. It is evident that the former people consider association as a powerful means of action, but the latter seem to regard it as the only means they have of acting.

Thus the most democratic country on the face of the earth is that in which men have in our time carried to the highest perfection the art of pursuing in common the object of their common desires, and have applied this new science to the greatest number of purposes. Is this the result of accident? or is there in reality any necessary connection between the principle of association and that of equality?

Aristocratic communities always contain, among a multitude of persons who by themselves are powerless, a small number of powerful and wealthy citizens, each of whom can achieve great undertakings single-handed. In aristocratic societies men do not need to combine in order to act, because they are strongly held together. Every wealthy and power-ful citizen constitutes the head of a permanent and compulsory associa-tion, composed of all those who are dependent upon him, or whom he makes subservient to the execution of his designs.

Among democratic nations, on the contrary, all the citizens are inde-pendent and feeble; they can do hardly anything by themselves, and none of them can oblige his fellow men to lend him their assistance. They all, therefore, fall into a state of incapacity, if they do not learn voluntarily to help each other. If men living in democratic countries had no right and no inclination to associate for political purposes, their independence would be in great jeopardy; but they might long preserve their wealth and their cultivation: whereas if they never acquired the habit of form-ing associations in ordinary life, civilization itself would be endangered. A people among which individuals should lose the power of achieving great things singlehanded, without acquiring the means of producing them by united exertions, would soon relapse into barbarism.

Unhappily, the same social condition which renders associations so necessary to democratic nations renders their formation more difficult among those nations than among all others. When several members of an aristocracy agree to combine, they easily succeed in doing so: as each of them brings great strength to the partnership, the number of its mem-bers may be very limited; and when the members of an association are limited in number, they may easily become mutually acquainted, under-stand each other, and establish fixed regulations. The same opportunities do not occur among democratic nations, where the associated members must always be very numerous for their association to have any power.

I am aware that many of my countrymen are not in the least embar-rassed by this difficulty. They contend that the more enfeebled and in-competent the citizens become, the more able and active the government ought to be rendered, in order that society at large may execute what individuals can no longer accomplish. They believe this answers the whole difficulty, but I think they are mistaken.

A government might perform the part of some of the largest American companies; and several states, members of the Union, have already at-tempted it; but what political power could ever carry on the vast multi-tude of lesser undertakings which the American citizens perform every day with the assistance of the principle of association? It is easy to foresee that the time is drawing near when man will be less and less able to produce, of himself alone, the commonest necessaries of life. The task of the governing power will therefore perpetually increase, and its very efforts will extend it every day. The more it stands in the place of associations, the more will individuals, losing the notion of combining together, require its assistance: these are causes and effects which unceasingly engender each other. Will the administration of the country ultimately assume the management of all the manufactures which no single citizen is able to carry on? And if a time at length arrives, when, in consequence of the extreme subdivision of landed property, the soil is split into an infinite number of parcels, so that it can only be cultivated by companies of husbandmen, will it be necessary that the head of the government should leave the helm of state to follow the plow? The morals and the intelligence of a democratic people would be as much endangered as its business and manufactures if the government ever wholly usurped the place of private companies.

Feelings and opinions are recruited, the heart is enlarged, and the human mind is developed by no other means than by the reciprocal influence of men upon each other. I have shown that these influences are almost null in democratic countries; they must therefore be artificially created, and this can only be accomplished by associations.

When the members of an aristocratic community adopt a new opinion, or conceive a new sentiment, they give it a station, as it were, beside themselves, upon the lofty platform where they stand; and opinions or sentiments so conspicuous to the eyes of the multitude are easily introduced into the minds or hearts of all around. In democratic countries the governing power alone is naturally in a condition to act in this manner; but it is easy to see that its action is always inadequate, and often dangerous. A government can no more be competent to keep alive and to renew the circulation of opinions and feelings among a great people, than to manage all the speculations of productive industry. No sooner does a government attempt to go beyond its political sphere and to enter upon this new track than it exercises, even unintentionally, an insupportable tyranny; for a government can only dictate strict rules, the opinions which it favors are rigidly enforced, and it is never easy to discriminate between its advice and its commands. Worse still will be the case if the government really believes itself interested in preventing all circulation of ideas; it will then stand motionless and oppressed by the heaviness of voluntary torpor. Governments therefore should not be the only active powers: associations ought, in democratic nations, to stand in lieu of those powerful private individuals whom the equality of conditions has swept away.

As soon as several of the inhabitants of the United States have taken up an opinion or a feeling which they wish to promote in the world, they look out for mutual assistance; and as soon as they have found each other out, they combine. From that moment they are no longer isolated men, but a power seen from afar, whose actions serve for an example, and whose language is listened to. The first time I heard in the United States that a hundred thousand men had bound themselves publicly to abstain from spirituous liquors, it appeared to me more like a joke than a serious engagement; and I did not at once perceive why these temperate citizens could not content themselves with drinking water by their own firesides. I at last understood that these hundred thousand Americans, alarmed by the progress of drunkenness around them, had made up their minds to patronize temperance. They acted just in the same way as a man of high rank who should dress very plainly, in order to inspire the humbler orders with a contempt of luxury. It is probable that if these hundred thousand men had lived in France, each of them would singly have memorialized the government to watch the public houses all over the kingdom.

Nothing, in my opinion, is more deserving of our attention than the intellectual and moral associations of America. The political and industrial associations of that country strike us forcibly; but the others elude our observation, or if we discover them, we understand them imperfectly, because we have hardly ever seen anything of the kind. It must, however, be acknowledged that they are as necessary to the American people as the former, and perhaps more so.

In democratic countries the science of association is the mother of science; the progress of all the rest depends upon the progress it has made.

Among the laws which rule human societies there is one which seems to be more precise and clear than all others. If men are to remain civilized, or to become so, the art of associating together must grow and improve, in the same ratio in which the equality of conditions is increased. . . .

Influence of Democracy on Kindred

I have just examined the changes which the equality of conditions produces in the mutual relations of the several members of the community among democratic nations, and among the Americans in particular. I would now go deeper, and inquire into the closer ties of kindred. My object here is not to seek for new truths, but to show in what manner facts already known are connected with my subject.

It has been universally remarked that in our time the several members of a family stand upon an entirely new footing towards each other; that the distance which formerly separated a father from his sons has been lessened; and that paternal authority, if not destroyed, is at least impaired.

Something analogous to this, but even more striking, may be observed in the United States. In America the family, in the Roman and aristocratic signification of the word, does not exist. All that remains of it are a few vestiges in the first years of childhood, when the father exercises, without opposition, that absolute domestic authority which the feebleness of his children renders necessary, and which their interest, as well as his own incontestable superiority, warrants. But as soon as the young American approaches manhood, the ties of filial obedience are relaxed day by day: master of his thoughts, he is soon master of his conduct. In America there is, strictly speaking, no adolescence: at the close of boyhood the man appears, and begins to trace out his own path.

It would be an error to suppose that this is preceded by a domestic struggle, in which the son has obtained by a sort of moral violence the liberty that his father refused him. The same habits, the same principles which impel the one to assert his independence, predispose the other to consider the use of that independence as an incontestable right. The former does not exhibit any of those rancorous or irregular passions which disturb men long after they have shaken off an established authority; the latter feels none of that bitter and angry regret which is apt to survive a bygone power. The father foresees the limits of his authority long beforehand, and when the time arrives he surrenders it without a struggle. The son looks forward to the exact period at which he will be his own master; and he enters upon his freedom without precipitation and without effort, as a possession which is his own and which no one seeks to wrest from him.[2]

---

2. The Americans however have not yet thought fit to strip the parent, as has been done in France, of one of the chief elements of parental authority, by depriving him of the power of disposing of his property at his death. In the United States there are no restrictions on the powers of a testator.

In this respect, as in almost all others, it is easy to perceive that if the political legislation of the Americans is much more democratic than that of the French, the civil legislation of the latter is infinitely more democratic than that of the former. This may easily be accounted for. The civil legislation of France was the

It may perhaps not be without utility to show how these changes which take place in family relations are closely connected with the social and political revolution which is approaching its consummation under our own observation.

There are certain great social principles, which a people either introduces everywhere, or tolerates nowhere. In countries which are aristocratically constituted with all the gradations of rank, the government never makes a direct appeal to the mass of the governed: as men are united together, it is enough to lead the foremost—the rest will follow. This is equally applicable to the family, as to all aristocracies which have a head.

Among aristocratic nations, social institutions recognize, in truth, no one in the family but the father; children are received by society at his hands; society governs him, he governs them. Thus the parent has not only a natural right, but he acquires a political right, to command them. He is the author and the support of his family, but he is also its constituted ruler.

In democracies, where the government picks out every individual singly from the mass, to make him subservient to the general laws of the community, no such intermediate person is required: a father is there, in the eye of the law, only a member of the community, older and richer than his sons.

When most of the conditions of life are extremely unequal, and the inequality of these conditions is permanent, the notion of a superior grows upon the imaginations of men: if the law invested him with no privileges, custom and public opinion would concede them. When, on the contrary, men differ but little from each other, and do not always remain in dissimilar conditions of life, the general notion of a superior becomes weaker and less distinct: it is vain for legislation to strive to place him who obeys very much beneath him who commands; the manners of the time bring the two men nearer to one another, and draw them daily towards the same level.

---

work of a man who saw that it was his interest to satisfy the democratic passions of his contemporaries in all that was not directly and immediately hostile to his own power. He was willing to allow some popular principles to regulate the distribution of property and the government of families, provided they were not to be introduced into the administration of public affairs. While the torrent of democracy overwhelmed the civil laws of the country, he hoped to find an easy shelter behind its political institutions. This policy was at once both adroit and selfish: but a compromise of this kind could not last; for in the end political institutions never fail to become the image and expression of civil society; and in this sense it may be said that nothing is more political in a nation than its civil legislation.

Although the legislation of an aristocratic people should grant no peculiar privileges to the heads of families, I shall not be the less convinced that their power is more respected and more extensive than in a democracy; for I know that, whatsoever the laws may be, superiors always appear higher and inferiors lower in aristocracies than among democratic nations.

When men live more for the remembrance of what has been than for the care of what is, and when they are more given to attend to what their ancestors thought than to think themselves, the father is the natural and necessary tie between the past and the present—the link by which the ends of these two chains are connected. In aristocracies, then, the father is not only the civil head of the family, but the oracle of its traditions, the expounder of its customs, the arbiter of its manners. He is listened to with deference, he is addressed with respect, and the love which is felt for him is always tempered with fear.

When the condition of society becomes democratic and men adopt as their general principle that it is good and lawful to judge of all things for oneself, using former points of belief not as a rule of faith but simply as a means of information, the power which the opinions of a father exercise over those of his sons diminishes as well as his legal power.

Perhaps the subdivision of estates which democracy brings with it contributes more than anything else to change the relations existing between a father and his children. When the property of the father of a family is scanty, his son and himself constantly live in the same place, and share the same occupations: habit and necessity bring them together, and force them to hold constant communication; the inevitable consequence is a sort of familiar intimacy, which renders authority less absolute and which can ill be reconciled with the external forms of respect.

Now in democratic countries the class of those who are possessed of small fortunes is precisely that which gives strength to the notions, and a particular direction to the manners, of the community. That class makes its opinions preponderate as universally as its will, and even those who are most inclined to resist its commands are carried away in the end by its example. I have known eager opponents of democracy who allowed their children to address them with perfect colloquial equality.

Thus, at the same time that the power of aristocracy is declining, the austere, the conventional, and the legal part of parental authority vanishes, and a species of equality prevails around the domestic hearth. I know not, upon the whole, whether society loses by the change, but I am inclined to believe that man individually is a gainer by it. I think that, in proportion as manners and laws become more democratic, the relation of father and son becomes more intimate and more affectionate; rules and authority are less talked of; confidence and tenderness are oftentimes increased, and it would seem that the natural bond is drawn closer in proportion as the social bond is loosened.

In a democratic family the father exercises no other power than that with which men love to invest the affection and the experience of age; his orders would perhaps be disobeyed, but his advice is for the most part authoritative. Though he be not hedged in with ceremonial respect, his sons at least accost him with confidence; no settled form of speech is appropriated to the mode of addressing him, but they speak to him constantly, and are ready to consult him day by day: the master and the constituted ruler have vanished—the father remains.

Nothing more is needed, in order to judge of the difference between the two states of society in this respect, than to peruse the family correspondence of aristocratic ages. The style is always correct, ceremonious, stiff, and so cold that the natural warmth of the heart can hardly be felt in the language. The language, on the contrary, addressed by a son to his father in democratic countries is always marked by mingled freedom, familiarity and affection, which at once show that new relations have sprung up in the bosom of the family.

A similar revolution takes place in the mutual relations of children. In aristocratic families, as well as in aristocratic society, every place is marked out beforehand. Not only does the father occupy a separate rank, in which he enjoys extensive privileges, but even the children are not equal among themselves. The age and sex of each irrevocably determine his rank, and secure to him certain privileges: most of these distinctions are abolished or diminished by democracy.

In aristocratic families the eldest son, inheriting the greater part of the property and almost all the rights of the family, becomes the chief, and to a certain extent, the master, of his brothers. Greatness and power are for him—for them, mediocrity and dependence. Nevertheless it would be wrong to suppose that, among aristocratic nations, the privileges of the eldest son are advantageous to himself alone, or that they excite nothing but envy and hatred in those around him. The eldest son commonly endeavors to procure wealth and power for his brothers, because the general splendor of the house is reflected back on him who represents it; the younger sons seek to back the elder brother in all his undertakings, because the greatness and power of the head of the family better enable him to provide for all its branches. The different members of an aristocratic family are therefore very closely bound together; their interests are connected, their minds agree, but their hearts are seldom in harmony.

Democracy also binds brothers to each other, but by very different means. Under democratic laws all the children are perfectly equal, and consequently independent: nothing brings them forcibly together, but nothing keeps them apart; and as they have the same origin, as they are trained under the same roof, as they are treated with the same care, and as no peculiar privilege distinguishes or divides them, the affectionate and youthful intimacy of early years easily springs up between them. Scarcely any opportunities occur to break the tie thus formed at the outset of life; for their brotherhood brings them daily together without embarrassing them. It is not then by interest, but by common associations and by the free sympathy of opinion and of taste, that democracy unites brothers to each other. It divides their inheritance, but it allows their hearts and minds to mingle together.

Such is the charm of these democratic manners, that even the partisans of aristocracy are caught by it; and after having experienced it for some time, they are by no means tempted to revert to the respectful and frigid observances of aristocratic families. They would be glad to retain the domestic habits of democracy, if they might throw off its social conditions and its laws; but these elements are indissolubly united, and it is impossible to enjoy the former without enduring the latter.

The remarks I have made on filial love and fraternal affection are applicable to all the passions which emanate spontaneously from human nature itself.

If a certain mode of thought or feeling is the result of some peculiar condition of life, when that condition is altered nothing whatever remains of the thought or feeling. Thus a law may bind two members of the community very closely to one another; but that law being abolished, they stand asunder. Nothing was more strict than the tie which united the vassal to the lord under the feudal system: at the present day the two men know not each other: the fear, the gratitude, and the affection which formerly connected them have vanished, and not a vestige of the tie remains.

Such, however, is not the case with those feelings which are natural to mankind. Whenever a law attempts to tutor these feelings in any particular manner, it seldom fails to weaken them; by attempting to add to their intensity, it robs them of some of their elements, for they are never stronger than when left to themselves.

Democracy, which destroys or obscures almost all the old conventional rules of society, and which prevents men from readily assenting to new ones, entirely effaces most of the feelings to which these conventional rules have given rise; but it only modifies some others, and frequently imparts to them a degree of energy and sweetness unknown before.

Perhaps it is not impossible to condense into a single proposition the whole meaning of this chapter, and of several others that preceded it. Democracy loosens social ties, but it draws the ties of nature more tight; it brings kindred more closely together, while it places the various members of the community more widely apart.

Education of Young Women
in the United States

No free communities ever existed without morals; and, as I observed in the former part of this work, morals are the work of woman. Consequently, whatever affects the condition of women, their habits, and their opinions has great political importance in my eyes.

Among almost all Protestant nations young women are far more the mistresses of their own actions than they are in Catholic countries. This independence is still greater in Protestant countries like England, which have retained or acquired the right of self-government; the spirit of freedom is then infused into the domestic circle by political habits and by religious opinions. In the United States the doctrines of Protestantism are combined with great political freedom and a most democratic state of society; and nowhere are young women surrendered so early or so completely to their own guidance.

Long before an American girl arrives at the age of marriage, her emancipation from maternal control begins. She has scarcely ceased to be a child, when she already thinks for herself, speaks with freedom, and acts on her own impulse. The great scene of the world is constantly open to her view. Far from seeking concealment, it is every day disclosed to her more completely, and she is taught to survey it with a firm and calm gaze. Thus the vices and dangers of society are early revealed to her; as she sees them clearly, she views them without illusions, and braves them without fear; for she is full of reliance on her own strength, and her reliance seems to be shared by all who are about her.

An American girl scarcely ever displays that virginal bloom in the midst of young desires, or that innocent and ingenuous grace which usually attend the European woman in the transition from girlhood to youth. It is rarely that an American woman at any age displays childish timidity or ignorance. Like the young women of Europe, she seeks to please, but she knows precisely the cost of pleasing. If she does not abandon herself to evil, at least she knows that it exists; and she is remarkable rather for purity of manners than for chastity of mind.

I have been frequently surprised, and almost frightened, at the singular address and happy boldness with which young women in America contrive to manage their thoughts and their language, amidst all the difficulties of stimulating conversation; a philosopher would have stumbled at every step along the narrow path which they trod without accidents and without effort. It is easy indeed to perceive that, even amidst the independence of early youth, an American woman is always mistress of herself: she indulges in all permitted pleasures, without yielding herself up to any of them; and her reason never allows the reins of self-guidance to drop, though it often seems to hold them loosely.

In France, where remnants of every age are still so strangely mingled in the opinions and tastes of the people, women commonly receive a reserved, retired, and almost conventual education, as they did in aristocratic times; and then they are suddenly abandoned, without a guide and without assistance, in the midst of all the irregularities inseparable from democratic society.

The Americans are more consistent. They have found out that in a democracy the independence of individuals cannot fail to be very great, youth premature, tastes ill restrained, customs fleeting, public opinion often unsettled and powerless, paternal authority weak, and marital authority contested. Under these circumstances, believing that they had little chance of repressing in woman the most vehement passions of the human heart, they held that the surer way was to teach her the art of combating those passions for herself. As they could not prevent her virtue from being exposed to frequent danger, they determined that she should know how best to defend it; and more reliance was placed on the free vigor of her will than on safeguards which have been shaken or overthrown. Instead then of inculcating mistrust of herself, they constantly seek to enhance her confidence in her own strength of character. As it is neither possible nor desirable to keep a young woman in perpetual and complete ignorance, they hasten to give her a precocious knowledge on all subjects. Far from hiding the corruptions of the world from her, they prefer that she should see them at once and train herself to shun them;

and they hold it of more importance to protect her conduct than to be overscrupulous of her innocence.

Although the Americans are a very religious people, they do not rely on religion alone to defend the virtue of woman; they seek to arm her reason also. In this they have followed the same method as in several other respects: they first make the most vigorous efforts to bring individual independence to exercise a proper control over itself, and they do not call in the aid of religion until they have reached the utmost limits of human strength.

I am aware that an education of this kind is not without danger; I am sensible that it tends to invigorate the judgment at the expense of the imagination, and to make cold and virtuous women instead of affectionate wives and agreeable companions to man. Society may be more tranquil and better regulated, but domestic life has often fewer charms. These however are secondary evils, which may be braved for the sake of higher interests. At the stage at which we are now arrived the time for choosing is no longer within our control; a democratic education is indispensable to protect women from the dangers with which democratic institutions and manners surround them.

The Young Woman
in the Character of a Wife

In America the independence of woman is irrecoverably lost in the bonds of matrimony: if an unmarried woman is less constrained there than elsewhere, a wife is subjected to stricter obligations. The former makes her father's house an abode of freedom and of pleasure; the latter lives in the home of her husband as if it were a cloister. Yet these two different conditions of life are perhaps not so contrary as may be supposed, and it is natural that the American women should pass through the one to arrive at the other.

Religious peoples and trading nations entertain peculiarly serious notions of marriage: the former consider the regularity of woman's life as the best pledge and most certain sign of the purity of her morals; the latter regard it as the highest security for the order and prosperity of the household. The Americans are at the same time a puritanical people and a commercial nation. Their religious opinions, as well as their trading habits, consequently lead them to require much abnegation on the part of women, and a constant sacrifice of her pleasures to her duties which is seldom demanded of her in Europe. Thus in the United States the inexorable opinion of the public carefully circumscribes woman within the narrow circle of domestic interests and duties, and forbids her to step beyond it.

Upon her entrance into the world a young American woman finds these notions firmly established; she sees the rules which are derived from them; she is not slow to perceive that she cannot depart for an instant from the established usages of her contemporaries, without putting in jeopardy her peace of mind, her honor, nay even her social existence; and she finds the energy required for such an act of submission in the firmness of her understanding and in the virile habits which her education has given her. It may be said that she has learned by the use of her independence to surrender it without a struggle and without a murmur when the time comes for making the sacrifice.

But no American woman falls into the toils of matrimony as into a snare held out to her simplicity and ignorance. She has been taught beforehand what is expected of her, and voluntarily and freely does she enter upon this engagement. She supports her new condition with courage, because she chose it. As in America paternal discipline is very relaxed and the conjugal tie very strict, a young woman does not contract the latter without considerable circumspection and apprehension. Precocious marriages are rare. Thus American women do not marry until their understandings are exercised and ripened; whereas in other countries most women generally only begin to exercise and to ripen their understandings after marriage.

I by no means suppose, however, that the great change which takes place in all the habits of women in the United States as soon as they are married ought solely to be attributed to the constraint of public opinion; it is frequently imposed upon themselves by the sole effort of their own will. When the time for choosing a husband is arrived, that cold and stern reasoning power which has been educated and invigorated by the free observation of the world teaches an American woman that a spirit of levity and independence in the bonds of marriage is a constant subject of annoyance, not of pleasure; it tells her that the amusements of the girl cannot become the recreations of the wife, and that the sources of a married woman's happiness are in the home of her husband. As she clearly discerns beforehand the only road which can lead to domestic happiness, she enters upon it at once, and follows it to the end without seeking to turn back.

The same strength of purpose which the young wives of America display, in bending themselves at once and without repining to the austere duties of their new condition, is no less manifest in all the great trials of their lives. In no country in the world are private fortunes more precarious than in the United States. It is not uncommon for the same man, in the course of his life, to rise and sink again through all the grades which lead from opulence to poverty. American women support these vicissitudes with calm and unquenchable energy: it would seem that their desires contract, as easily as they expand, with their fortunes.

The greater part of the adventurers who migrate every year to people the western wilds, belong, as I observed in the former part of this work, to the old Anglo-American race of the northern states. Many of these men, who rush so boldly onwards in pursuit of wealth, were already in the enjoyment of a competency in their own part of the country. They take their wives along with them, and make them share the countless perils and privations which always attend the commencement of these expeditions. I have often met, even on the verge of the wilderness, with young women who, after having been brought up amidst all the comforts of the large towns of New England had passed, almost without any intermediate stage, from the wealthy abode of their parents to a comfortless hovel in a forest. Fever, solitude, and a tedious life had not broken the springs of their courage. Their features were impaired and faded, but their looks were firm: they appeared to be at once sad and resolute. I do not doubt that these young American women had amassed, in the education of their early years, that inward strength which they displayed under these circumstances. The early culture of the girl may still therefore be traced, in the United States, under the aspect of marriage: her part is changed, her habits are different, but her character is the same.

That the Equality of Conditions Contributes to the Maintenance of Good Morals in America

Some philosophers and historians have said, or have hinted, that the strictness of female morality was increased or diminished simply by the distance of a country from the equator. This solution of the difficulty was an easy one; and nothing was required but a globe and a pair of compasses to settle in an instant one of the most difficult problems in the condition of mankind. But I am not aware that this principle of the materialists is supported by facts. The same nations have been chaste or dissolute, at different periods of their history; the strictness or the laxity of their morals depended therefore on some variable cause, not only on the natural qualities of their country, which were invariable. I do not deny that in certain climates the passions which are occasioned by the mutual attraction of the sexes are peculiarly intense; but I am of opinion that this natural intensity may always be excited or restrained by the condition of society and by political institutions.

Although the travelers who have visited North America differ on a great number of points, they all agree in remarking that morals are far more strict there than elsewhere. It is evident that on this point the Americans are very superior to their progenitors, the English. A superficial glance at the two nations will establish the fact.

In England, as in all other countries of Europe, public malice is constantly attacking the frailties of women. Philosophers and statesmen are heard to deplore that morals are not sufficiently strict, and the literary productions of the country constantly lead one to suppose so. In America all books, novels not excepted, suppose women to be chaste, and no one thinks of relating affairs of gallantry.

No doubt this great regularity of American morals originates partly in the country, in the race of the people, and in their religion: but all these causes, which operate elsewhere, do not suffice to account for it; recourse must be had to some special reason.

This reason appears to me to be the principle of equality and the institutions derived from it. Equality of conditions does not of itself engender regularity of morals, but it unquestionably facilitates and increases it.

Among aristocratic nations birth and fortune frequently make two such different beings of man and woman that they can never be united to each other. Their passions draw them together, but the condition of society, and the notions suggested by it, prevent them from contracting a permanent and ostensible tie. The necessary consequence is a great number of transient and clandestine connections. Nature secretly avenges herself for the constraint imposed upon her by the laws of man.

This is not so much the case when the equality of conditions has swept away all the imaginary, or the real, barriers which separated man from woman. No girl then believes that she cannot become the wife of the man who loves her; and this renders all breaches of morality before marriage very uncommon: for, whatever be the credulity of the passions, a woman will hardly be able to persuade herself that she is beloved, when her lover is perfectly free to marry her and does not.

The same cause operates, though more indirectly, on married life. Nothing better serves to justify an illicit passion, either to the minds of those who have conceived it or to the world which looks on, than compulsory or accidental marriages.[3]

In a country in which a woman is always free to exercise her power of choosing, and in which education has prepared her to choose rightly, public opinion is inexorable to her faults. The rigor of the Americans arises in part from this cause. They consider marriages as a covenant which is often onerous, but every condition of which the parties are strictly bound to fulfill, because they knew all those conditions beforehand and were perfectly free not to have contracted them.

The very circumstances which render matrimonial fidelity more obligatory also render it more easy.

In aristocratic countries the object of marriage is rather to unite property than persons; hence the husband is sometimes at school and the wife at nurse when they are betrothed. It cannot be wondered at if the conjugal tie which holds the fortunes of the pair united allows their hearts to rove; this is the natural result of the nature of the contract. When, on the contrary, a man always chooses a wife for himself, without any external coercion or even guidance, it is generally a conformity of tastes and opinions which brings a man and a woman together, and this same conformity keeps and fixes them in close habits of intimacy.

Our forefathers had conceived a very strange notion on the subject of marriage: as they had remarked that the small number of love matches which occurred in their time almost always turned out ill, they resolutely inferred that it was exceedingly dangerous to listen to the dictates of the heart on the subject. Accident appeared to them to be a better guide than choice.

Yet it was not very difficult to perceive that the examples which they witnessed did in fact prove nothing at all. For in the first place, if demo-

---

3. The literature of Europe sufficiently corroborates this remark. When a European author wishes to depict in a work of imagination any of those great catastrophes in matrimony which so frequently occur among us, he takes care to bespeak the compassion of the reader by bringing before him ill-assorted or compulsory marriages. Although habitual tolerance has long since relaxed our morals, an author could hardly succeed in interesting us in the misfortunes of his characters, if he did not first palliate their faults. This artifice seldom fails: the daily scenes we witness prepare us long beforehand to be indulgent. But American writers could never render these palliations probable to their readers; their customs and laws are opposed to it; and as they despair of rendering levity of conduct pleasing, they cease to depict it. This is one of the causes to which must be attributed the small number of novels published in the United States.

cratic nations leave a woman at liberty to choose her husband, they take care to give her mind sufficient knowledge, and her will sufficient strength, to make so important a choice: whereas the young women who, among aristocratic nations, furtively elope from the authority of their parents to throw themselves of their own accord into the arms of men whom they have had neither time to know, nor ability to judge of, are totally without those securities. It is not surprising that they make a bad use of their freedom of action the first time they avail themselves of it; nor that they fall into such cruel mistakes, when, not having received a democratic education, they choose to marry in conformity to democratic customs. But this is not all. When a man and woman are bent upon marriage in spite of the differences of an aristocratic state of society, the difficulties to be overcome are enormous. Having broken or relaxed the bonds of filial obedience, they have then to emancipate themselves by a final effort from the sway of custom and the tyranny of opinion; and when at length they have succeeded in this arduous task, they stand estranged from their natural friends and kinsmen: the prejudice they have crossed separates them from all and places them in a situation which soon breaks their courage and sours their hearts.

If, then, a couple married in this manner are first unhappy and afterwards criminal, it ought not to be attributed to the freedom of their choice, but rather to their living in a community in which this freedom of choice is not admitted.

Moreover it should not be forgotten that the same effort which makes a man violently shake off a prevailing error commonly impels him beyond the bounds of reason; that, to dare to declare war, in however just a cause, against the opinion of one's age and country, a violent and adventurous spirit is required, and that men of this character seldom arrive at happiness or virtue, whatever be the path they follow. And this, it may be observed by the way, is the reason why in the most necessary and righteous revolutions it is so rare to meet with virtuous or moderate revolutionary characters. There is then no just ground for surprise if a man, who in an age of aristocracy chooses to consult nothing but his own opinion and his own taste in the choice of a wife, soon finds that infractions of morality and domestic wretchedness invade his household; but when this same line of action is in the natural and ordinary course of things, when it is sanctioned by parental authority and backed by public opinion, it cannot be doubted that the internal peace of families will be increased by it, and conjugal fidelity more rigidly observed.

Almost all men in democracies are engaged in public or professional life; and on the other hand the limited extent of common incomes obliges a wife to confine herself to the house, in order to watch in person and very closely over the details of domestic economy. All these distinct and compulsory occupations are so many natural barriers which, by keeping the two sexes asunder, render the solicitations of the one less frequent and less ardent—the resistance of the other more easy.

Not indeed that the equality of conditions can ever succeed in making men chaste, but it may impart a less dangerous character to their breaches of morality. As no one has then either sufficient time or opportunity to assail a virtue armed in self-defense, there will be at the same time a great number of courtesans and a great number of virtuous women. This state of things causes lamentable cases of individual hardship, but it does not prevent the body of society from being strong and alert: it does not destroy family ties, or enervate the morals of the nation. Society is endangered not by the great profligacy of a few, but by laxity of morals among all. In the eyes of a legislator, prostitution is less to be dreaded than intrigue.

The tumultuous and constantly harassed life which equality makes men lead, not only distracts them from the passion of love, by denying them time to indulge in it, but it diverts them from it by another more secret but more certain road. All men who live in democratic ages more or less contract the ways of thinking of the manufacturing and trading classes; their minds take a serious, deliberate, and positive turn; they are apt to relinquish the ideal, in order to pursue some visible and proximate object, which appears to be the natural and necessary aim of their desires. Thus the principle of equality does not destroy the imagination, but lowers its flight to the level of the earth.

No men are less addicted to reverie than the citizens of a democracy; and few of them are ever known to give way to those idle and solitary meditations which commonly precede and produce the great emotions of the heart. It is true they attach great importance to procuring for themselves that sort of deep, regular, and quiet affection which constitutes the charm and safeguard of life, but they are not apt to run after those violent and capricious sources of excitement which disturb and abridge it.

I am aware that all this is only applicable in its full extent to America, and cannot at present be extended to Europe. In the course of the last half century, while laws and customs have impelled several European nations with unexampled force towards democracy, we have not had occasion to observe that the relations of man and woman have become more orderly or more chaste. In some places the very reverse may be detected:

some classes are more strict—the general morality of the people appears to be more lax. I do not hesitate to make the remark, for I am as little disposed to flatter my contemporaries as to malign them.

This fact must distress, but it ought not to surprise us. The propitious influence which a democratic state of society may exercise upon orderly habits is one of those tendencies which can only de discovered after a time. If the equality of conditions is favorable to purity of morals, the social commotion by which conditions are rendered equal is adverse to it. In the last fifty years, during which France has been undergoing this transformation, that country has rarely had freedom, always disturbance. Amidst this universal confusion of notions and this general stir of opinions—amidst this incoherent mixture of the just and the unjust, of truth and falsehood, of right and might—public virtue has become doubtful, and private morality wavering. But all revolutions, whatever may have been their object or their agents, have at first produced similar consequences; even those which have in the end drawn the bonds of morality more tightly began by loosening them. The violations of morality which the French frequently witness do not appear to me to have a permanent character; and this is already betokened by some curious signs of the times.

Nothing is more wretchedly corrupt than an aristocracy which retains its wealth when it has lost its power, and which still enjoys a vast deal of leisure after it is reduced to mere vulgar pastimes. The energetic passions and great conceptions which animated it heretofore leave it then; and nothing remains to it but a host of petty consuming vices, which cling about it like worms upon a carcass.

No one denies that the French aristocracy of the last century was extremely dissolute; whereas established habits and ancient belief still preserved some respect for morality among the other classes of society. Nor will it be contested that at the present day the remnants of that same aristocracy exhibit a certain severity of morals; while laxity of morals appears to have spread among the middle and lower ranks. So that the same families which were most profligate fifty years ago are nowadays the most exemplary, and democracy seems only to have strengthened the morality of the aristocratic classes. The French Revolution, by dividing the fortunes of the nobility, by forcing them to attend assiduously to their affairs and to their families, by making them live under the same roof with their children, and in short by giving a more rational and serious turn to their minds, has imparted to them, almost without their being aware of it, a reverence for religious belief, a love of order, of tranquil pleasures, of domestic endearments, and of comfort; whereas the rest of the nation, which had naturally these same tastes, was carried away into excesses by the effort which was required to overthrow the laws and political habits of the country.

The old French aristocracy has undergone the consequences of the Revolution, but it neither felt the revolutionary passions, nor shared in the anarchical excitement which produces that crisis; it may easily be conceived that this aristocracy feels the salutary influence of the revolution in its manners before those who achieve it. It may therefore be said, though at first it seems paradoxical, that, at the present day, the most antidemocratic classes of the nation principally exhibit the kind of morality which may reasonably be anticipated from democracy. I cannot but think that when we shall have obtained all the effects of this democratic revolution, after having got rid of the tumult it has caused, the observations which are now only applicable to the few will gradually become true of the whole community.

How the Americans Understand the Equality of the Sexes

I have shown how democracy destroys or modifies the different inequalities which originate in society: but is this all? or does it not ultimately affect that great inequality of man and woman which has seemed, up to the present day, to be eternally based in human nature? I believe that the social changes which bring nearer to the same level the father and son, the master and servant, and superiors and inferiors generally speaking, will raise woman and make her more and more the equal of man. But here, more than ever, I feel the necessity of making myself clearly understood; for there is no subject on which the coarse and lawless fancies of our age have taken a freer range.

There are people in Europe who, confounding together the different characteristics of the sexes, would make of man and woman beings not only equal but alike. They would give to both the same functions, impose on both the same duties, and grant to both the same rights; they would mix them in all things—their occupations, their pleasures, their business. It may readily be conceived that by thus attempting to make one sex equal to the other both are degraded; and from so preposterous a medley of the works of nature, nothing could ever result but weak men and disorderly women.

It is not thus that the Americans understand that species of democratic equality which may be established between the sexes. They admit that as nature has appointed such wide differences between the physical and moral constitution of man and woman, her manifest design was to give a distinct employment to their various faculties; and they hold that improvement does not consist in making beings so dissimilar do pretty nearly the same things, but in getting each of them to fulfill their respective tasks in the best possible manner. The Americans have applied to the sexes the great principle of political economy which governs the manufactures of our age, by carefully dividing the duties of man from those of woman, in order that the great work of society may be the better carried on.

In no country has such constant care been taken as in America to trace two clearly distinct lines of action for the two sexes, and to make them keep pace one with the other, but in two pathways which are always different. American women never manage the outward concerns of the family, or conduct a business, or take a part in political life; nor are they, on the other hand, ever compelled to perform the rough labor of the fields, or to make any of those laborious exertions which demand the exertion of physical strength. No families are so poor as to form an exception to this rule. If on the one hand an American woman cannot escape from the quiet circle of domestic employments, on the other hand she is never forced to go beyond it. Hence it is that the women of America, who often exhibit a masculine strength of understanding and a manly energy, generally preserve great delicacy of personal appearance and always retain the manners of women, although they sometimes show that they have the hearts and minds of men.

Nor have the Americans ever supposed that one consequence of democratic principles is the subversion of marital power, or the confusion of the natural authorities in families. They hold that every association must have a head in order to accomplish its object, and that the natural head of the conjugal association is man. They do not therefore deny him the right of directing his partner; and they maintain that in the smaller association of husband and wife, as well as in the great social community, the object of democracy is to regulate and legalize the powers which are necessary, not to subvert all power.

This opinion is not peculiar to one sex, and contested by the other: I never observed that the women of America consider conjugal authority as a fortunate usurpation of their rights, nor that they thought themselves degraded by submitting to it. It appeared to me, on the contrary, that they attach a sort of pride to the voluntary surrender of their own will, and make it their boast to bend themselves to the yoke, not to shake it off. Such at least is the feeling expressed by the most virtuous of their sex; the others are silent; and in the United States it is not the practice for a guilty wife to clamor for the rights of women while she is trampling on her holiest duties.

It has often been remarked that in Europe a certain degree of contempt lurks even in the flattery which men lavish upon women: although a European frequently affects to be the slave of woman, it may be seen that he never sincerely thinks her his equal. In the United States men seldom compliment women, but they daily show how much they esteem them. They constantly display an entire confidence in the understanding of a wife, and a profound respect for her freedom; they have decided that her mind is just as fitted as that of a man to discover the plain truth, and her heart as firm to embrace it; and they have never sought to place her virtue, any more than his, under the shelter of prejudice, ignorance, and fear.

It would seem that in Europe, where man so easily submits to the despotic sway of women, they are nevertheless curtailed of some of the greatest qualities of the human species, and considered as seductive but imperfect beings; and (what may well provoke astonishment) women ultimately look upon themselves in the same light, and almost consider it as a privilege that they are entitled to show themselves futile, feeble, and timid. The women of America claim no such privileges.

Again it may be said that in our morals we have reserved strange immunities to man; so that there is, as it were, one virtue for his use, and another for the guidance of his partner; and that, according to the opinion of the public, the very same act may be punished alternately as a crime, or only as a fault. The Americans know not this iniquitous division of duties and rights; among them the seducer is as much dishonored as his victim.

It is true that the Americans rarely lavish upon women those eager attentions which are commonly paid them in Europe; but their conduct to women always implies that they suppose them to be virtuous and refined; and such is the respect entertained for the moral freedom of the sex, that in the presence of a woman the most guarded language is used, lest her ear should be offended by an expression. In America a young unmarried woman may, alone and without fear, undertake a long journey.

The legislators of the United States, who have mitigated almost all the penalties of criminal law, still make rape a capital offense, and no crime is visited with more inexorable severity by public opinion. This may be accounted for; as the Americans can conceive nothing more precious than a woman's honor, and nothing which ought so much to be respected as her independence, they hold that no punishment is too severe for the man who deprives her of them against her will. In France, where the same offense is visited with far milder penalties, it is frequently difficult to get a verdict from a jury against the prisoner. Is this a consequence of contempt of decency or contempt of women? I cannot but believe that it is a contempt of one and of the other.

Thus the Americans do not think that man and woman have either the duty or the right to perform the same offices, but they show an equal regard for both their respective parts; and though their lot is different, they consider both of them as beings of equal value. They do not give to the courage of woman the same form or the same direction as to that of man; but they never doubt her courage: and if they hold that man and his partner ought not always to exercise their intellect and understanding in the same manner, they at least believe the understanding of the one to be as sound as that of the other, and her intellect to be as clear. Thus, then, while they have allowed the social inferiority of woman to subsist, they have done all they could to raise her morally and intellectually to the level of man; and in this respect they appear to me to have excellently understood the true principle of democratic improvement.

As for myself, I do not hesitate to avow that, although the women of the United States are confined within the narrow circle of domestic life, and their situation is in some respects one of extreme dependence, I have nowhere seen woman occupying a loftier position; and if I were asked, now that I am drawing to the close of this work, in which I have spoken of so many important things done by the Americans, to what the singular prosperity and growing strength of that people ought mainly to be attributed, I should reply—to the superiority of their women.

The foregoing consists of Book II, Chapters I–V,
and Book III, Chapters VIII–XII,
of Volume II of de Tocqueville's DEMOCRACY IN AMERICA,
translated by Henry Reeve.

Henry David Thoreau

1817–1862

Henry David Thoreau, the famous poet-naturalist and philosopher, is remembered as much for his life as for his writings. He is the outstanding American example of the individual who is determined to live according to his own lights, no matter how unconventional his life may be. He has become a symbol of rebellion and nonconformity.

Thoreau was born in Concord, Massachusetts, on July 12, 1817. As a boy he spent much of his time roaming the outdoors, but there was little else in his early life to suggest his later eccentricity. His career at Harvard College (1833–1837) was an unexceptional one. It was while at Harvard that he first came under the spell of Ralph Waldo Emerson. He was deeply stirred by a reading of Emerson's *Nature*,[1] and for many years Emerson was to be the most important intellectual influence in his life.

After graduating from college, Thoreau taught school briefly. Then, with his brother, John, he made a boat trip that became the subject of one of his major works, *A Week on the Concord and Merrimack Rivers*. From 1841 to 1843 he lived with the Emerson family, working as a handy man. It was shortly after leaving the Emerson household that he decided to move to Walden Pond, at that time part of the uninhabited wilds of Massachusetts.

Thoreau had several reasons for moving to Walden Pond, but probably of greatest importance was his desire to live as simply as possible. He was convinced that most of the trappings of civilization were unnecessary for human happiness. He thought it was a great mistake for men to spend so much of their time working to obtain

---

[1] See Vol. 10, pp. 512–524, in this set.

things they did not really need. The result was, he said, that "the mass of men lead lives of quiet desperation." He wanted to prove— to himself and to others—that life could be simpler and more joyful.

Thoreau lived at Walden Pond for two years, renouncing everything he considered inessential. ("Few lives contain so many renunciations," said Emerson.) His shelter was a cabin measuring ten feet by fifteen feet that he had built with his own hands. His diet consisted mainly of rice, bread made from rye and Indian meal, potatoes, and wild fruit. Occasionally he ate fish or some salt pork. During the first eight months of his stay, his expenses (including the cost of his cabin) amounted to sixty-two dollars. His account of his experiences at Walden Pond, entitled *Walden,* is one of the classics of American literature.

After the Walden experiment, Thoreau engaged in a variety of activities. He worked as a surveyor, gave lectures, made excursions to Cape Cod and the Maine woods, and wrote essays for periodicals. He also became involved in the abolitionist movement and, during the last years of his life, was greatly distressed by the failure of the United States government to do anything about freeing the slaves. He died early in May, 1862, of tuberculosis.

When obedience to the laws of the state requires an individual to act against his conscience, which should he obey—the law or his conscience? One traditional answer to this question is that given by Socrates in the *Crito.* Socrates says that the individual "must do what his city and country order him; or he must change their view of what is just." [2] In other words, the individual has the right to persuade the state to *change* the law, but so long as the law remains unchanged, he must obey it.

In *Civil Disobedience,* Thoreau gives the opposite answer. For

---

[2] See Great Books of the Western World, Vol. 7, p. 217.

Notes from the artist: "Head study of Thoreau. At right are a bird on a bough of a tree, suggesting Walden, *and also a quotation from that most famous of Thoreau's works. At left is the figure of Mohandas Gandhi, who acknowledged Thoreau's influence upon his own thought and philosophy."*

Simplify,
Simplify

Henry D. Thoreau

him, loyalty of conscience takes precedence over loyalty to the state. If a man's conscience tells him that a law is unjust, he must oppose the law. But it is not enough merely to express disapproval, or to promise to vote against the law at the next election. The individual should take action to hinder the law's enforcement. He should refuse to do what the law orders, even if it means imprisonment. Thoreau was convinced that a dedicated minority—even a minority of one—could exert great political influence. "A minority is powerless when it conforms to the majority," he said, "but it is irresistible when it clogs by its whole weight."

Civil Disobedience is the most widely read and influential of Thoreau's political essays. Mohandas Gandhi, the great Indian leader, acknowledged his indebtedness to it for many of his ideas concerning nonviolent resistance. It has also played an important role in the attack upon racial segregation in the United States.

A Plea for Captain John Brown is, in many respects, a perfect companion piece to *Civil Disobedience*. Opinions about John Brown vary widely, but for Thoreau he was an extraordinary example of the man of conscience who has devoted his life to the cause of justice—the type of man he had called for in *Civil Disobedience*. Thoreau had been impressed with John Brown ever since their first meeting in 1857, and his *Plea* was inspired by Brown's arrest at Harpers Ferry, Virginia, in 1859.

The Harpers Ferry incident was only one part of John Brown's lifelong fight against slavery. He and his five sons had been active in the struggle to determine whether Kansas would be a free state or a slave state. He had personally ordered the murder of five proslavery settlers in retaliation for the killing of five free-state settlers. He remained in Kansas until 1859, when he began working on a scheme to establish a refuge for fugitive slaves in the mountains of Virginia. The attack upon Harpers Ferry was part of this scheme. The attack failed, and Brown and his associates were captured, convicted of treason, and hanged. In the eyes of the abolitionists (including Thoreau) Brown was a martyr; southerners thought him a madman and a scoundrel. The full truth about John Brown will probably never be known, but Thoreau's *Plea* is a moving testament to the force of his personality.

Civil Disobedience

I heartily accept the motto, "That government is best which governs least"; and I should like to see it acted up to more rapidly and systematically. Carried out, it finally amounts to this, which also I believe, "That government is best which governs not at all"; and when men are prepared for it, that will be the kind of government which they will have. Government is at best but an expedient; but most governments are usually, and all governments are sometimes, inexpedient. The objections which have been brought against a standing army, and they are many and weighty, and deserve to prevail, may also at last be brought against a standing government. The standing army is only an arm of the standing government. The government itself, which is only the mode which the people have chosen to execute their will, is equally liable to be abused and perverted before the people can act through it. Witness the present Mexican War, the work of comparatively a few individuals using the standing government as their tool; for, in the outset, the people would not have consented to this measure.

This American government—what is it but a tradition, though a recent one, endeavoring to transmit itself unimpaired to posterity, but each instant losing some of its integrity? It has not the vitality and force of a single living man; for a single man can bend it to his will. It is a sort of wooden gun to the people themselves. But it is not the less necessary for this; for the people must have some complicated machinery or other, and hear its din, to satisfy that idea of government which they have. Governments show thus how successfully men can be imposed on, even impose on themselves, for their own advantage. It is excellent, we must all allow. Yet this government never of itself furthered any enterprise, but by the alacrity with which it got out of its way. *It* does not keep the country free. *It* does not settle the West. *It* does not educate. The character inherent in the American people has done all that has been accomplished; and it would have done somewhat more, if the government had not sometimes got in its way. For government is an expedient by which men would fain succeed in letting one another alone; and, as has been said, when it is most expedient, the governed are most let alone by it. Trade and commerce, if they were not made of India rubber, would never manage to bounce over the obstacles which legislators are continually putting in their way; and, if one were to judge these men wholly by the effects of their actions and not partly by their intentions, they would deserve to be classed and punished with those mischievous persons who put obstructions on the railroads.

But, to speak practically and as a citizen, unlike those who call themselves no-government men, I ask for, not at once no government, but *at once* a better government. Let every man make known what kind of government would command his respect, and that will be one step toward obtaining it.

After all, the practical reason why, when the power is once in the hands of the people, a majority are permitted, and for a long period continue, to rule is not because they are most likely to be in the right, nor because this seems fairest to the minority, but because they are physically the strongest. But a government in which the majority rule in all cases cannot be based on justice, even as far as men understand it. Can there not be a government in which majorities do not virtually decide right and wrong, but conscience?—in which majorities decide only those questions to which the rule of expediency is applicable? Must the citizen ever for a moment, or in the least degree, resign his conscience to the legislator? Why has every man a conscience, then? I think that we should be men first, and subjects afterward. It is not desirable to cultivate a respect for the law, so much as for the right. The only obligation which I have a right to assume is to do at any time what I think right. It is truly enough said, that a corporation has no conscience; but a corporation of conscientious men is a corporation *with* a conscience. Law never made men a whit more just; and, by means of their respect for it, even the well-disposed are daily made the agents of injustice. A common and natural result of an undue respect for law is that you may see a file of soldiers, colonel, captain, corporal, privates, powder monkeys, and all, marching in admirable order over hill and dale to the wars, against their wills, ay, against their common sense and consciences, which makes it very steep marching indeed, and produces a palpitation of the heart. They have no doubt that it is a damnable business in which they are concerned; they are all peaceably inclined. Now, what are they? Men at all? or small movable forts and magazines, at the service of some unscrupulous man in power? Visit the navy yard, and behold a marine, such a man as an American government can make, or such as it can make a man with its black arts—a mere shadow and reminiscence of humanity, a man laid out alive and standing, and already, as one may say, buried under arms with funeral accompaniments, though it may be,

> Not a drum was heard, not a funeral note,
> As his corse to the rampart we hurried;
> Not a soldier discharged his farewell shot
> O'er the grave where our hero we buried.

The mass of men serve the state thus, not as men mainly, but as machines, with their bodies. They are the standing army, and the militia, jailers, constables, *posse comitatus,* etc. In most cases there is no free exercise whatever of the judgment or of the moral sense; but they put themselves on a level with wood and earth and stones; and wooden men can perhaps be manufactured that will serve the purpose as well. Such command no more respect than men of straw or a lump of dirt. They have the same sort of worth only as horses and dogs. Yet such as these even are commonly esteemed good citizens. Others—as most legislators, politicians, lawyers, ministers, and officeholders—serve the state chiefly with their heads; and, as they rarely make any moral distinctions, they are as likely to serve the Devil, without *intending* it, as God. A very few, as heroes, patriots, martyrs, reformers in the great sense, and *men,* serve the state with their consciences also, and so necessarily resist it for the most part; and they are commonly treated as enemies by it. A wise man will only be useful as a man, and will not submit to be "clay," and "stop a hole to keep the wind away," but leave that office to his dust at least:

> I am too highborn to be propertied,
> To be a secondary at control,
> Or useful serving man and instrument
> To any sovereign state throughout the world.

He who gives himself entirely to his fellow men appears to them useless and selfish; but he who gives himself partially to them is pronounced a benefactor and philanthropist.

How does it become a man to behave toward this American government today? I answer that he cannot without disgrace be associated with it. I cannot for an instant recognize that political organization as *my* government which is the *slave's* government also.

All men recognize the right of revolution; that is, the right to refuse allegiance to, and to resist, the government, when its tyranny or its inefficiency are great and unendurable. But almost all say that such is not the case now. But such was the case, they think, in the Revolution of '75. If one were to tell me that this was a bad government because it taxed certain foreign commodities brought to its ports, it is most probable that I should not make an ado about it, for I can do without them. All machines have their friction; and possibly this does enough good to counterbalance the evil. At any rate, it is a great evil to make a stir about it. But when the friction comes to have its machine, and oppression and robbery are organized, I say, let us not have such a machine any longer. In other words, when a sixth of the population of a nation which has undertaken to be the refuge of liberty are slaves, and a whole country is unjustly overrun and conquered by a foreign army, and subjected to military law, I think that it is not too soon for honest men to rebel and revolutionize. What makes this duty the more urgent is the fact that the country so overrun is not our own, but ours is the invading army.

Paley, a common authority with many on moral questions, in his chapter on the "Duty of Submission to Civil Government," resolves all civil obligation into expediency; and he proceeds to say, "that so long as the interest of the whole society requires it, that is, so long as the established government cannot be resisted or changed without public inconveniency, it is the will of God that the established government be obeyed, and no longer. . . . This principle being admitted, the justice of every particular case of resistance is reduced to a computation of the quantity of the danger and grievance on the one side, and of the probability and expense of redressing it on the other." Of this, he says, every man shall judge for himself. But Paley appears never to have contemplated those cases to which the rule of expediency does not apply, in which a people, as well as an individual, must do justice, cost what it may. If I have unjustly wrested a plank from a drowning man, I must restore it to him though I drown myself. This, according to Paley, would be inconvenient. But he that would save his life, in such a case, shall lose it. This people must cease to hold slaves, and to make war on Mexico, though it cost them their existence as a people.

In their practice, nations agree with Paley; but does any one think that Massachusetts does exactly what is right at the present crisis?

> A drab of state, a cloth-o'-silver slut,
> To have her train borne up, and her soul trail in the dirt.

Practically speaking, the opponents to a reform in Massachusetts are not a hundred thousand politicians at the South, but a hundred thousand merchants and farmers here, who are more interested in commerce and agriculture than they are in humanity, and are not prepared to do justice to the slave and to Mexico, *cost what it may*. I quarrel not with far-off foes, but with those who, near at home, co-operate with, and do the bidding of, those far away, and without whom the latter would be harmless. We are accustomed to say that the mass of men are unprepared; but improvement is slow, because the few are not materially wiser or better than the many. It is not so important that many should be as good as you, as that there be some absolute goodness somewhere; for that will leaven the whole lump. There are thousands who are *in opinion* opposed to slavery and to the war, who yet in effect do nothing to put an end to them; who, esteeming themselves children of Washington and Franklin, sit down with their hands in their pockets, and say that they know not what to do, and do nothing; who even postpone the question of freedom to the question of free trade, and quietly read the prices current along with the latest advices from Mexico after dinner, and, it may be, fall asleep over them both. What is the price current of an honest man and patriot today? They hesitate, and they regret, and sometimes they petition; but they do nothing in earnest and with effect. They will wait, well disposed, for others to remedy the evil, that they may no longer have it to regret. At most, they give only a cheap vote, and a feeble countenance and Godspeed, to the right, as it goes by them. There are nine hundred and ninety-nine patrons of virtue to one virtuous man. But it is easier to deal with the real possessor of a thing than with the temporary guardian of it.

All voting is a sort of gaming, like checkers or backgammon, with a slight moral tinge to it, a playing with right and wrong, with moral questions; and betting naturally accompanies it. The character of the voters is not staked. I cast my vote, perchance, as I think right; but I am not vitally concerned that that right should prevail. I am willing to leave it to the majority. Its obligation, therefore, never exceeds that of expediency. Even voting *for the right* is *doing* nothing for it. It is only expressing to men feebly your desire that it should prevail. A wise man will not leave the right to the mercy of chance, nor wish it to prevail through the power of the majority. There is but little virtue in the action of masses of men. When the majority shall at length vote for the abolition of slavery, it will be because they are indifferent to slavery, or because there is but little slavery left to be abolished by their vote. *They* will then be the only slaves. Only *his* vote can hasten the abolition of slavery who asserts his own freedom by his vote.

I hear of a convention to be held at Baltimore, or elsewhere, for the selection of a candidate for the Presidency, made up chiefly of editors, and men who are politicians by profession; but I think, what is it to any independent, intelligent, and respectable man what decision they may come to? Shall we not have the advantage of his wisdom and honesty, nevertheless? Can we not count upon some independent votes? Are there not many individuals in the country who do not attend conventions? But no: I find that the respectable man, so called, has immediately drifted from his position, and despairs of his country, when his country has more reason to despair of him. He forthwith adopts one of the candidates thus selected as the only *available* one, thus proving that he is himself *available* for any purposes of the demagogue. His vote is of no more worth than that of any unprincipled foreigner or hireling native, who may have been bought. O for a man who is a *man*, and, as my neighbor says, has a bone in his back which you cannot pass your hand through! Our statistics are at fault: the population has been returned too large. How many *men* are there to a square thousand miles in this country? Hardly one. Does not America offer any inducement for men to settle here? The American has dwindled into an Odd Fellow, one who may be known by the development of his organ of gregariousness, and a manifest lack of intellect and cheerful self-reliance; whose first and chief concern, on coming into the world, is to see that the almshouses are in good repair; and, before yet he has lawfully donned the virile garb, to collect a fund for the support of the widows and orphans that may be; who, in short, ventures to live only by the aid of the mutual insurance company, which has promised to bury him decently.

It is not a man's duty, as a matter of course, to devote himself to the eradication of any, even the most enormous wrong; he may still properly have other concerns to engage him; but it is his duty, at least, to wash his hands of it, and, if he gives it no thought longer, not to give it practically his support. If I devote myself to other pursuits and contemplations, I must first see, at least, that I do not pursue them sitting upon another man's shoulders. I must get off him first, that he may pursue his contemplations too. See what gross inconsistency is tolerated. I have heard some of my townsmen say, "I should like to have them order me out to help put down an insurrection of the slaves, or to march to Mexico—see if I would go"; and yet these very men have each, directly by their allegiance, and so indirectly, at least, by their money, furnished a substitute. The soldier is applauded who refuses to serve in an unjust war by those who do not refuse to sustain the unjust government which makes the war; is applauded by those whose own act and authority he disregards and sets at naught; as if the state were penitent to that degree that it hired one to scourge it while it sinned, but not to that degree that it left off sinning for a moment. Thus, under the name of Order and Civil Government, we are all made at last to pay homage to and support our own meanness. After the first blush of sin comes its indifference; and from immoral it becomes, as it were, *un*moral, and not quite unnecessary to that life which we have made.

The broadest and most prevalent error requires the most disinterested virtue to sustain it. The slight reproach to which the virtue of patriotism is commonly liable, the noble are most likely to incur. Those who, while they disapprove of the character and measures of a government, yield to it their allegiance and support are undoubtedly its most conscientious supporters, and so frequently the most serious obstacles to reform. Some are petitioning the state to dissolve the Union, to disregard the requisitions of the President. Why do they not dissolve it themselves—the union between themselves and the state—and refuse to pay their quota into its treasury? Do not they stand in the same relation to the state that the state does to the Union? And have not the same reasons prevented the state from resisting the Union which have prevented them from resisting the state?

How can a man be satisfied to entertain an opinion merely, and enjoy *it*? Is there any enjoyment in it, if his opinion is that he is aggrieved? If you are cheated out of a single dollar by your neighbor, you do not rest satisfied with knowing that you are cheated, or with saying that you are cheated, or even with petitioning him to pay you your due; but you take effectual steps at once to obtain the full amount, and see that you are never cheated again. Action from principle, the perception and the performance of right, changes things and relations; it is essentially revolutionary, and does not consist wholly with anything which was. It not only divides states and churches, it divides families; ay, it divides the *individual*, separating the diabolical in him from the divine.

Unjust laws exist: shall we be content to obey them, or shall we endeavor to amend them, and obey them until we have succeeded, or shall we transgress them at once? Men generally, under such a government as this, think that they ought to wait until they have persuaded the majority to alter them. They think that, if they should resist, the remedy would be worse than the evil. But it is the fault of the government itself that the

remedy *is* worse than the evil. *It* makes it worse. Why is it not more apt
to anticipate and provide for reform? Why does it not cherish its wise
minority? Why does it cry and resist before it is hurt? Why does it not
encourage its citizens to be on the alert to point out its faults, and *do*
better than it would have them? Why does it always crucify Christ, and
excommunicate Copernicus and Luther, and pronounce Washington and
Franklin rebels?

One would think that a deliberate and practical denial of its authority
was the only offense never contemplated by government; else why has it
not assigned its definite, its suitable and proportionate penalty? If a man
who has no property refuses but once to earn nine shillings for the state,
he is put in prison for a period unlimited by any law that I know, and
determined only by the discretion of those who placed him there; but if
he should steal ninety times nine shillings from the state, he is soon permitted to go at large again.

If the injustice is part of the necessary friction of the machine of government, let it go, let it go: perchance it will wear smooth—certainly
the machine will wear out. If the injustice has a spring, or a pulley, or a
rope, or a crank, exclusively for itself, then perhaps you may consider
whether the remedy will not be worse than the evil; but if it is of such
a nature that it requires you to be the agent of injustice to another, then,
I say, break the law. Let your life be a counterfriction to stop the machine. What I have to do is to see, at any rate, that I do not lend myself
to the wrong which I condemn.

As for adopting the ways which the state has provided for remedying
the evil, I know not of such ways. They take too much time, and a man's
life will be gone. I have other affairs to attend to. I came into this world,
not chiefly to make this a good place to live in, but to live in it, be it
good or bad. A man has not everything to do, but something; and because he cannot do *everything*, it is not necessary that he should do
something wrong. It is not my business to be petitioning the governor or
the legislature any more than it is theirs to petition me; and if they should
not hear my petition, what should I do then? But in this case the state
has provided no way: its very Constitution is the evil. This may seem to
be harsh and stubborn and unconciliatory; but it is to treat with the utmost kindness and consideration the only spirit that can appreciate or
deserves it. So is all change for the better, like birth and death, which
convulse the body.

I do not hesitate to say that those who call themselves Abolitionists
should at once effectually withdraw their support, both in person and

property, from the government of Massachusetts and not wait till they constitute a majority of one before they suffer the right to prevail through them. I think that it is enough if they have God on their side, without waiting for that other one. Moreover, any man more right than his neighbors constitutes a majority of one already.

I meet this American government, or its representative, the state government, directly, and face to face, once a year—no more—in the person of its taxgatherer; this is the only mode in which a man situated as I am necessarily meets it; and it then says distinctly, Recognize me; and the simplest, most effectual and, in the present posture of affairs, the indispensablest mode of treating with it on this head, of expressing your little satisfaction with and love for it, is to deny it then. My civil neighbor, the taxgatherer, is the very man I have to deal with—for it is, after all, with men and not with parchment that I quarrel—and he has voluntarily chosen to be an agent of the government. How shall he ever know well what he is and does as an officer of the government, or as a man, until he is obliged to consider whether he shall treat me, his neighbor, for whom he has respect, as a neighbor and well-disposed man, or as a maniac and disturber of the peace, and see if he can get over this obstruction to his neighborliness without a ruder and more impetuous thought or speech corresponding with his action. I know this well, that if one thousand, if one hundred, if ten men whom I could name—if ten *honest* men only—ay, if *one* HONEST man, in this state of Massachusetts, *ceasing to hold slaves*, were actually to withdraw from this copartnership, and be locked up in the county jail therefor, it would be the abolition of slavery in America. For it matters not how small the beginning may seem to be: what is once well done is done forever. But we love better to talk about it: that we say is our mission. Reform keeps many scores of newspapers in its service, but not one man. If my esteemed neighbor, the state's ambassador, who will devote his days to the settlement of the question of human rights in the council chamber, instead of being threatened with the prisons of Carolina, were to sit down the prisoner of Massachusetts, that state which is so anxious to foist the sin of slavery upon her sister—though at present she can discover only an act of inhospitality to be the ground of a quarrel with her—the legislature would not wholly waive the subject the following winter.

Under a government which imprisons any unjustly, the true place for a just man is also a prison. The proper place today, the only place which Massachusetts has provided for her freer and less desponding spirits, is in her prisons, to be put out and locked out of the state by her own act,

as they have already put themselves out by their principles. It is there
that the fugitive slave, and the Mexican prisoner on parole, and the
Indian come to plead the wrongs of his race should find them; on that
separate but more free and honorable ground, where the state places
those who are not *with* her but *against* her, the only house in a slave
state in which a free man can abide with honor. If any think that their
influence would be lost there, and their voices no longer afflict the ear of
the state, that they would not be as an enemy within its walls, they do
not know by how much truth is stronger than error, nor how much more
eloquently and effectively he can combat injustice who has experienced
a little in his own person. Cast your whole vote, not a strip of paper
merely, but your whole influence. A minority is powerless while it conforms to the majority; it is not even a minority then; but it is irresistible
when it clogs by its whole weight. If the alternative is to keep all just
men in prison, or give up war and slavery, the state will not hesitate
which to choose. If a thousand men were not to pay their tax bills this
year, that would not be a violent and bloody measure, as it would be to
pay them, and enable the state to commit violence and shed innocent
blood. This is, in fact, the definition of a peaceable revolution, if any such
is possible. If the taxgatherer, or any other public officer, asks me, as one
has done, "But what shall I do?" my answer is, "If you really wish to do
anything, resign your office." When the subject has refused allegiance,
and the officer has resigned his office, then the revolution is accomplished.
But even suppose blood should flow. Is there not a sort of blood shed
when the conscience is wounded? Through this wound a man's real manhood and immortality flow out, and he bleeds to an everlasting death. I
see this blood flowing now.

I have contemplated the imprisonment of the offender, rather than
the seizure of his goods—though both will serve the same purpose—
because they who assert the purest right, and consequently are most
dangerous to a corrupt state, commonly have not spent much time in
accumulating property. To such the state renders comparatively small
service, and a slight tax is wont to appear exorbitant, particularly if they
are obliged to earn it by special labor with their hands. If there were one
who lived wholly without the use of money, the state itself would hesitate
to demand it of him. But the rich man—not to make any invidious comparison—is always sold to the institution which makes him rich. Absolutely speaking, the more money, the less virtue; for money comes
between a man and his objects, and obtains them for him; and it was
certainly no great virtue to obtain it. It puts to rest many questions which

he would otherwise be taxed to answer; while the only new question which it puts is the hard but superfluous one, how to spend it. Thus his moral ground is taken from under his feet. The opportunities of living are diminished in proportion as what are called the "means" are increased. The best thing a man can do for his culture when he is rich is to endeavor to carry out those schemes which he entertained when he was poor. Christ answered the Herodians according to their condition. "Show me the tribute money," said he—and one took a penny out of his pocket; if you use money which has the image of Caesar on it and which he has made current and valuable, that is, *if you are men of the state,* and gladly enjoy the advantages of Caesar's government, then pay him back some of his own when he demands it. "Render therefore to Caesar that which is Caesar's, and to God those things which are God's," leaving them no wiser than before as to which was which; for they did not wish to know.

When I converse with the freest of my neighbors, I perceive that, whatever they may say about the magnitude and seriousness of the question, and their regard for the public tranquillity, the long and the short of the matter is that they cannot spare the protection of the existing government, and they dread the consequences to their property and families of disobedience to it. For my own part, I should not like to think that I ever rely on the protection of the state. But, if I deny the authority of the state when it presents its tax bill, it will soon take and waste all my property, and so harass me and my children without end. This is hard. This makes it impossible for a man to live honestly, and at the same time comfortably, in outward respects. It will not be worth the while to accumulate property; that would be sure to go again. You must hire or squat somewhere, and raise but a small crop, and eat that soon. You must live within yourself, and depend upon yourself always tucked up and ready for a start, and not have many affairs. A man may grow rich in Turkey even, if he will be in all respects a good subject of the Turkish government. Confucius said: "If a state is governed by the principles of reason, poverty and misery are subjects of shame; if a state is not governed by the principles of reason, riches and honors are the subjects of shame." No: until I want the protection of Massachusetts to be extended to me in some distant southern port, where my liberty is endangered, or until I am bent solely on building up an estate at home by peaceful enterprise, I can afford to refuse allegiance to Massachusetts, and her right to my property and life. It costs me less in every sense to incur the penalty of disobedience to the state than it would to obey. I should feel as if I were worth less in that case.

Some years ago, the state met me in behalf of the church, and commanded me to pay a certain sum toward the support of a clergyman whose preaching my father attended, but never I myself. "Pay," it said, "or be locked up in the jail." I declined to pay, But, unfortunately, another man saw fit to pay it. I did not see why the schoolmaster should be taxed to support the priest, and not the priest the schoolmaster; for I was not the state's schoolmaster, but I supported myself by voluntary subscription. I did not see why the lyceum should not present its tax bill, and have the state to back its demand, as well as the church. However, at the request of the selectmen, I condescended to make some such statement as this in writing: "Know all men by these presents, that I, Henry Thoreau, do not wish to be regarded as a member of any incorporated society which I have not joined." This I gave to the town clerk; and he has it. The state, having thus learned that I did not wish to be regarded as a member of that church, has never made a like demand on me since; though it said that it must adhere to its original presumption that time. If I had known how to name them, I should then have signed off in detail from all the societies which I never signed on to; but I did not know where to find a complete list.

I have paid no poll tax for six years. I was put into a jail once on this account, for one night; and, as I stood considering the walls of solid stone, two or three feet thick, the door of wood and iron, a foot thick, and the iron grating which strained the light, I could not help being struck with the foolishness of that institution which treated me as if I were mere flesh and blood and bones, to be locked up. I wondered that it should have concluded at length that this was the best use it could put me to, and had never thought to avail itself of my services in some way. I saw that, if there was a wall of stone between me and my townsmen, there was a still more difficult one to climb or break through before they could get to be as free as I was. I did not for a moment feel confined, and the walls seemed a great waste of stone and mortar. I felt as if I alone of all my townsmen had paid my tax. They plainly did not know how to treat me, but behaved like persons who are underbred. In every threat and in every compliment there was a blunder; for they thought that my chief desire was to stand the other side of that stone wall. I could not but smile to see how industriously they locked the door on my meditations, which followed them out again without let or hindrance, and *they* were really all that was dangerous. As they could not reach me, they had resolved to punish my body; just as boys, if they cannot come at some person against whom they have a spite, will abuse his dog. I saw that the state was half-witted, that it was timid as a lone woman with her silver spoons, and that it did not know its friends from its foes, and I lost all my remaining respect for it, and pitied it.

Thus the state never intentionally confronts a man's sense, intellectual or moral, but only his body, his senses. It is not armed with superior wit or honesty, but with superior physical strength. I was not born to be forced. I will breathe after my own fashion. Let us see who is the strongest. What force has a multitude? They only can force me who obey a higher law than I. They force me to become like themselves. I do not hear of *men* being *forced* to live this way or that by masses of men. What sort of life were that to live? When I meet a government which says to me, "Your money or your life," why should I be in haste to give it my money? It may be in a great strait, and not know what to do: I cannot help that. It must help itself; do as I do. It is not worth the while to snivel about it. I am not responsible for the successful working of the machinery of society. I am not the son of the engineer. I perceive that, when an acorn and a chestnut fall side by side, the one does not remain inert to make way for the other, but both obey their own laws, and spring and grow and flourish as best they can, till one, perchance, overshadows and destroys the other. If a plant cannot live according to its nature, it dies; and so a man.

The night in prison was novel and interesting enough. The prisoners in their shirt sleeves were enjoying a chat and the evening air in the doorway when I entered. But the jailer said, "Come, boys, it is time to lock up"; and so they dispersed, and I heard the sound of their steps returning into the hollow apartments. My roommate was introduced to me by the jailer as "a first-rate fellow and a clever man." When the door was locked, he showed me where to hang my hat, and how he managed matters there. The rooms were whitewashed once a month; and this one, at least, was the whitest, most simply furnished, and probably the neatest apartment in the town. He naturally wanted to know where I came from, and what brought me there; and, when I had told him, I asked him in my turn how he came there, presuming him to be an honest man, of course; and, as the world goes, I believe he was. "Why," said he, "they accuse me of burning a barn; but I never did it." As near as I could discover, he had probably gone to bed in a barn when drunk, and smoked his pipe there; and so a barn was burnt. He had the reputation of being a clever man, had been there some three months waiting for his trial to come on, and would have to wait as much longer; but he was quite domesticated and contented, since he got his board for nothing, and thought that he was well treated.

He occupied one window, and I the other; and I saw that if one stayed there long, his principal business would be to look out the window. I had soon read all the tracts that were left there, and examined where former prisoners had broken out, and where a grate had been sawed off, and heard the history of the various occupants of that room; for I found that even here there was a history and a gossip which never circulated beyond the walls of the jail. Probably this is the only house in the town where verses are composed which are afterward printed in a circular form, but not published. I was shown quite a long list of verses which were composed by some young men who had been detected in an attempt to escape, who avenged themselves by singing them.

I pumped my fellow prisoner as dry as I could, for fear I should never see him again; but at length he showed me which was my bed, and left me to blow out the lamp.

It was like traveling into a far country, such as I had never expected to behold, to lie there for one night. It seemed to me that I never had heard the town clock strike before, nor the evening sounds of the village; for we slept with the windows open, which were inside the grating. It was to see my native village in the light of the Middle Ages, and our Concord was turned into a Rhine stream, and visions of knights and castles passed before me. They were the voices of old burghers that I heard in the streets. I was an involuntary spectator and auditor of whatever was done and said in the kitchen of the adjacent village inn—a wholly new and rare experience to me. It was a closer view of my native town. I was fairly inside of it. I never had seen its institutions before. This is one of its peculiar institutions; for it is a shire town. I began to comprehend what its inhabitants were about.

In the morning, our breakfasts were put through the hole in the door, in small oblong-square tin pans made to fit, and holding a pint of chocolate with brown bread, and an iron spoon. When they called for the vessels again, I was green enough to return what bread I had left; but my comrade seized it, and said that I should lay that up for lunch or dinner. Soon after he was let out to work at haying in a neighboring field, whither he went every day, and would not be back till noon; so he bade me good day, saying that he doubted if he should see me again.

When I came out of prison—for someone interfered, and paid that tax —I did not perceive that great changes had taken place on the common, such as he observed who went in a youth and emerged a tottering and gray-headed man; and yet a change had to my eyes come over the scene —the town, and state, and country—greater than any that mere time could effect. I saw yet more distinctly the state in which I lived. I saw to what extent the people among whom I lived could be trusted as good neighbors and friends; that their friendship was for summer weather only; that they did not greatly propose to do right; that they were a distinct race from me by their prejudices and superstitions, as the Chinamen and Malays are; that in their sacrifices to humanity they ran no risks, not even to their property; that after all they were not so noble but they treated the thief as he had treated them, and hoped, by a certain outward observance and a few prayers, and by walking in a particular straight though useless path from time to time, to save their souls. This may be to judge my neighbors harshly; for I believe that many of them are not aware that they have such an institution as the jail in their village.

It was formerly the custom in our village when a poor debtor came out of jail for his acquaintances to salute him, looking through their fingers, which were crossed to represent the grating of a jail window, "How do ye do?" My neighbors did not thus salute me, but first looked at me, and then at one another, as if I had returned from a long journey. I was put into jail as I was going to the shoemaker's to get a shoe which was mended. When I was let out the next morning, I proceeded to finish my errand, and, having put on my mended shoe, joined a huckleberry party, who were impatient to put themselves under my conduct; and in half an hour—for the horse was soon tackled—was in the midst of a huckleberry field, on one of our highest hills, two miles off, and then the state was nowhere to be seen.

This is the whole history of "My Prisons."

I have never declined paying the highway tax, because I am as desirous of being a good neighbor as I am of being a bad subject; and as for supporting schools, I am doing my part to educate my fellow countrymen now. It is for no particular item in the tax bill that I refuse to pay it. I simply wish to refuse allegiance to the state, to withdraw and stand aloof from it effectually. I do not care to trace the course of my dollar, if I could, till it buys a man or a musket to shoot with—the dollar is innocent—but I am concerned to trace the effects of my allegiance. In fact, I quietly declare war with the state, after my fashion, though I will still make what use and get what advantage of her I can, as is usual in such cases.

If others pay the tax which is demanded of me, from a sympathy with the state, they do but what they have already done in their own case, or rather they abet injustice to a greater extent than the state requires. If they pay the tax from a mistaken interest in the individual taxed, to save his property, or prevent his going to jail, it is because they have not considered wisely how far they let their private feelings interfere with the public good.

This, then, is my position at present. But one cannot be too much on his guard in such a case, lest his action be biased by obstinacy or an undue regard for the opinions of men. Let him see that he does only what belongs to himself and to the hour.

I think sometimes, Why, this people mean well, they are only ignorant; they would do better if they knew how: why give your neighbors this pain to treat you as they are not inclined to? But I think again, This is no reason why I should do as they do, or permit others to suffer much greater pain of a different kind. Again, I sometimes say to myself, When many millions of men, without heat, without ill will, without personal feeling of any kind, demand of you a few shillings only, without the possibility, such is their constitution, of retracting or altering their present demand, and without the possibility, on your side, of appeal to any other millions, why expose yourself to this overwhelming brute force? You do not resist cold and hunger, the winds and the waves, thus obstinately; you quietly submit to a thousand similar necessities. You do not put your head into the fire. But just in proportion as I regard this as not wholly a brute force, but partly a human force, and consider that I have relations to those millions as to so many millions of men, and not of mere brute or inanimate things, I see that appeal is possible, first and instantaneously, from them to the Maker of them, and, secondly, from them to themselves. But if I put my head deliberately into the fire, there is no appeal to fire or to the Maker of fire, and I have only myself to blame. If I could convince myself that I have any right to be satisfied with men as they are, and to treat them accordingly, and not according, in some respects, to my requisitions and expectations of what they and I ought to be, then, like a good Mussulman and fatalist, I should endeavor to be satisfied with things as they are, and say it is the will of God. And, above all, there is this difference between resisting this and a purely brute or natural force, that I can resist this with some effect; but I cannot expect, like Orpheus, to change the nature of the rocks and trees and beasts.

I do not wish to quarrel with any man or nation. I do not wish to split hairs, to make fine distinctions, or set myself up as better than my neighbors. I seek rather, I may say, even an excuse for conforming to the laws of the land. I am but too ready to conform to them. Indeed, I have reason to suspect myself on this head; and each year, as the taxgatherer comes round, I find myself disposed to review the acts and position of the general and state governments, and the spirit of the people, to discover a pretext for conformity.

> We must affect our country as our parents,
> And if at any time we alienate
> Our love or industry from doing it honor,
> We must respect effects and teach the soul
> Matter of conscience and religion,
> And not desire of rule or benefit.

I believe that the state will soon be able to take all my work of this sort out of my hands, and then I shall be no better a patriot than my fellow countrymen. Seen from a lower point of view, the Constitution, with all its faults, is very good; the law and the courts are very respectable; even this state and this American government are, in many respects, very admirable, and rare things, to be thankful for, such as a great many have described them; but seen from a point of view a little higher, they are what I have described them; seen from a higher still, and the highest, who shall say what they are, or that they are worth looking at or thinking of at all?

However, the government does not concern me much, and I shall bestow the fewest possible thoughts on it. It is not many moments that I live under a government, even in this world. If a man is thought-free, fancy-free, imagination-free, that which *is not* never for a long time appearing *to be* to him, unwise rulers or reformers cannot fatally interrupt him.

I know that most men think differently from myself; but those whose lives are by profession devoted to the study of these or kindred subjects content me as little as any. Statesmen and legislators, standing so completely within the institution, never distinctly and nakedly behold it. They speak of moving society, but have no resting place without it. They may be men of a certain experience and discrimination, and have no doubt invented ingenious and even useful systems, for which we sincerely thank them; but all their wit and usefulness lie within certain not very wide limits. They are wont to forget that the world is not governed by policy and expediency. Webster never goes behind government, and so cannot speak with authority about it. His words are wisdom to those legislators who contemplate no essential reform in the existing government; but for thinkers, and those who legislate for all time, he never once glances at the subject. I know of those whose serene and wise speculations on this theme would soon reveal the limits of his mind's range and hospitality. Yet, compared with the cheap professions of most reformers, and the still cheaper wisdom and eloquence of politicians in general, his are almost the only sensible and valuable words, and we thank Heaven for him. Comparatively, he is always strong, original, and, above all, practical. Still, his quality is not wisdom, but prudence. The lawyer's truth is not Truth, but consistency or a consistent expediency. Truth is always in harmony with herself, and is not concerned chiefly to reveal the justice that may consist with wrongdoing. He well deserves to be called, as he has been called, the Defender of the Constitution. There are really no blows to be given by him but defensive ones. He is not a leader, but a follower. His leaders are the men of '87. "I have never made an effort," he says, "and never propose to make an effort; I have never countenanced an effort, and never mean to countenance an effort, to disturb the arrangement as originally made, by which the various States came into the Union." Still thinking of the sanction which the Constitution gives to slavery, he says, "Because it was a part of the original compact, let it stand." Notwithstanding his special acuteness and ability, he is unable to take a fact out of its merely political relations, and behold it as it lies absolutely to be disposed of by the intellect—what, for instance, it behooves a man to do here in America today with regard to slavery—but ventures, or is driven, to make some such desperate answer as the following, while professing to speak absolutely, and as a private man—from which what new and singular code of social duties might be inferred? "The manner," says he, "in which the governments of those States where slavery exists are to regulate it is for their own consideration, under their responsibility to their constituents, to the general laws of propriety, humanity, and justice, and to God. Associations formed elsewhere, springing from a feeling of humanity, or other cause, have nothing whatever to do with it. They have never received any encouragement from me, and they never will."

They who know of no purer sources of truth, who have traced up its stream no higher, stand, and wisely stand, by the Bible and the Constitution, and drink at it there with reverence and humility; but they who behold where it comes trickling into this lake or that pool, gird up their loins once more, and continue their pilgrimage toward its fountainhead.

No man with a genius for legislation has appeared in America. They are rare in the history of the world. There are orators, politicians, and eloquent men by the thousand; but the speaker has not yet opened his mouth to speak who is capable of settling the much-vexed questions of the day. We love eloquence for its own sake, and not for any truth which it may utter, or any heroism it may inspire. Our legislators have not yet learned the comparative value of free trade and of freedom, of union, and of rectitude to a nation. They have no genius or talent for comparatively humble questions of taxation and finance, commerce and manufactures and agriculture. If we were left solely to the wordy wit of legislators in Congress for our guidance, uncorrected by the seasonable experience and the effectual complaints of the people, America would not long retain her rank among the nations. For eighteen hundred years, though perchance I have no right to say it, the New Testament has been written; yet where is the legislator who has wisdom and practical talent enough to avail himself of the light which it sheds on the science of legislation?

The authority of government, even such as I am willing to submit to —for I will cheerfully obey those who know and can do better than I, and in many things even those who neither know nor can do so well—is still an impure one: to be strictly just, it must have the sanction and consent of the governed. It can have no pure right over my person and property but what I concede to it. The progress from an absolute to a limited monarchy, from a limited monarchy to a democracy, is a progress toward a true respect for the individual. Even the Chinese philosopher was wise enough to regard the individual as the basis of the empire. Is a democracy, such as we know it, the last improvement possible in government? Is it not possible to take a step further toward recognizing and organizing the rights of man? There will never be a really free and enlightened state until the state comes to recognize the individual as a higher and independent power, from which all its own power and authority are derived, and treats him accordingly. I please myself with imagining a state at last which can afford to be just to all men, and to treat the individual with respect as a neighbor; which even would not think it inconsistent with its own repose if a few were to live aloof from it, not meddling with it, nor embraced by it, who fulfilled all the duties of neighbors and fellow men. A state which bore this kind of fruit, and suffered it to drop off as fast as it ripened, would prepare the way for a still more perfect and glorious state, which also I have imagined, but not yet anywhere seen.

A Plea
for Captain John Brown

I trust that you will pardon me for being here. I do not wish to force my thoughts upon you, but I feel forced myself. Little as I know of Captain Brown, I would fain do my part to correct the tone and statements of the newspapers, and of my countrymen generally, respecting his character and actions. It costs us nothing to be just. We can at least express our sympathy with, and admiration of, him and his companions, and that is what I now propose to do.

First, as to his history. I will endeavor to omit, as much as possible, what you have already read. I need not describe his person to you, for probably most of you have seen and will not soon forget him. I am told that his grandfather, John Brown, was an officer in the Revolution; that he himself was born in Connecticut about the beginning of this century, but early went with his father to Ohio. I heard him say that his father was a contractor who furnished beef to the army there, in the War of 1812; that he accompanied him to the camp, and assisted him in that employment, seeing a good deal of military life—more, perhaps, than if he had been a soldier; for he was often present at the councils of the officers. Especially, he learned by experience how armies are supplied and maintained in the field—a work which, he observed, requires at least as much experience and skill as to lead them in battle. He said that few persons had any conception of the cost, even the pecuniary cost, of firing a single bullet in war. He saw enough, at any rate, to disgust him with a military life; indeed, to excite in him a great abhorrence of it; so much so, that though he was tempted by the offer of some petty office in the army, when he was about eighteen, he not only declined that, but he also refused to train when warned, and was fined for it. He then resolved that he would never have anything to do with any war, unless it were a war for liberty.

When the troubles in Kansas began, he sent several of his sons thither to strengthen the party of the Free State men, fitting them out with such weapons as he had; telling them that if the troubles should increase, and there should be need of him, he would follow, to assist them with his hand and counsel. This, as you all know, he soon after did; and it was through his agency, far more than any other's, that Kansas was made free.

For a part of his life he was a surveyor, and at one time he was engaged in woolgrowing, and he went to Europe as an agent about that business. There, as everywhere, he had his eyes about him, and made many original observations. He said, for instance, that he saw why the soil of England was so rich, and that of Germany (I think it was) so poor, and he thought of writing to some of the crowned heads about it. It was because in England the peasantry live on the soil which they cultivate, but in Germany they are gathered into villages at night. It is a pity that he did not make a book of his observations.

I should say that he was an old-fashioned man in his respect for the Constitution, and his faith in the permanence of this Union. Slavery he deemed to be wholly opposed to these, and he was its determined foe.

He was by descent and birth a New England farmer, a man of great common sense, deliberate and practical as that class is, and tenfold more so. He was like the best of those who stood at Concord Bridge once, on Lexington Common, and on Bunker Hill, only he was firmer and higher principled than any that I have chanced to hear of as there. It was no abolition lecturer that converted him. Ethan Allen and Stark, with whom he may in some respects be compared, were rangers in a lower and less important field. They could bravely face their country's foes, but he had the courage to face his country herself when she was in the wrong. A western writer says, to account for his escape from so many perils, that he was concealed under a "rural exterior"; as if, in that prairie land, a hero should, by good rights, wear a citizen's dress only.

He did not go to the college called Harvard, good old Alma Mater as she is. He was not fed on the pap that is there furnished. As he phrased it, "I know no more of grammar than one of your calves." But he went to the great university of the West, where he sedulously pursued the study of Liberty, for which he had early betrayed a fondness, and having taken many degrees, he finally commenced the public practice of Humanity in Kansas, as you all know. Such were *his humanities*, and not any study of grammar. He would have left a Greek accent slanting the wrong way, and righted up a falling man.

He was one of that class of whom we hear a great deal, but, for the most part, see nothing at all—the Puritans. It would be in vain to kill him. He died lately in the time of Cromwell, but he reappeared here. Why should he not? Some of the Puritan stock are said to have come over and settled in New England. They were a class that did something else than celebrate their forefathers' day, and eat parched corn in remembrance of that time. They were neither Democrats nor Republicans, but men of simple habits, straightforward, prayerful; not thinking much of rulers who did not fear God, not making many compromises, nor seeking after available candidates.

"In his camp," as one has recently written, and as I have myself heard him state, "he permitted no profanity; no man of loose morals was suffered to remain there, unless, indeed, as a prisoner of war. 'I would rather,' said he, 'have the smallpox, yellow fever, and cholera, all together in my camp, than a man without principle. . . . It is a mistake, sir, that our people make, when they think that bullies are the best fighters, or that they are the fit men to oppose these southerners. Give me men of good principles, God-fearing men, men who respect themselves, and with a dozen of them I will oppose any hundred such men as these Buford ruffians.' " He said that if one offered himself to be a soldier under him, who was forward to tell what he could or would do if he could only get sight of the enemy, he had but little confidence in him.

He was never able to find more than a score or so of recruits whom he would accept, and only about a dozen, among them his sons, in whom he had perfect faith. When he was here some years ago, he showed to a few a little manuscript book—his "orderly book" I think he called it— containing the names of his company in Kansas, and the rules by which they bound themselves; and he stated that several of them had already sealed the contract with their blood. When someone remarked that, with the addition of a chaplain, it would have been a perfect Cromwellian troop, he observed that he would have been glad to add a chaplain to the list, if he could have found one who could fill that office worthily. It is easy enough to find one for the United States Army. I believe that he had prayers in his camp morning and evening, nevertheless.

He was a man of Spartan habits, and at sixty was scrupulous about his diet at your table, excusing himself by saying that he must eat sparingly and fare hard, as became a soldier, or one who was fitting himself for difficult enterprises, a life of exposure.

A man of rare common sense and directness of speech, as of action; a transcendentalist above all, a man of ideas and principles—that was what distinguished him. Not yielding to a whim or transient impulse, but carrying out the purpose of a life. I noticed that he did not overstate anything, but spoke within bounds. I remember, particularly, how, in his speech here, he referred to what his family had suffered in Kansas, without ever giving the least vent to his pent-up fire. It was a volcano with an ordinary chimney flue. Also referring to the deeds of certain Border Ruffians, he said, rapidly paring away his speech, like an experienced soldier, keeping a reserve of force and meaning, "They had a perfect right to be hung." He was not in the least a rhetorician, was not talking to Buncombe or his constituents anywhere, had no need to invent anything but to tell the simple truth, and communicate his own resolution; therefore he appeared incomparably strong, and eloquence in Congress and elsewhere seemed to me at a discount. It was like the speeches of Cromwell compared with those of an ordinary king.

As for his tact and prudence, I will merely say, that at a time when scarcely a man from the Free States was able to reach Kansas by any direct route, at least without having his arms taken from him, he, carrying what imperfect guns and other weapons he could collect, openly and slowly drove an oxcart through Missouri, apparently in the capacity of a surveyor, with his surveying compass exposed in it, and so passed unsuspected, and had ample opportunity to learn the designs of the enemy. For some time after his arrival he still followed the same profession. When, for instance, he saw a knot of the ruffians on the prairie, discussing, of course, the single topic which then occupied their minds, he would, perhaps, take his compass and one of his sons, and proceed to run an imaginary line right through the very spot on which that conclave had assembled, and when he came up to them, he would naturally pause and have some talk with them, learning their news, and, at last, all their plans perfectly; and having thus completed his real survey he would resume his imaginary one, and run on his line till he was out of sight.

When I expressed surprise that he could live in Kansas at all, with a price set upon his head, and so large a number, including the authorities, exasperated against him, he accounted for it by saying, "It is perfectly well understood that I will not be taken." Much of the time for some years he has had to skulk in swamps, suffering from poverty and from sickness, which was the consequence of exposure, befriended only by Indians and a few whites. But though it might be known that he was lurking in a particular swamp, his foes commonly did not care to go in after him. He could even come out into a town where there were more Border Ruffians than Free State men, and transact some business, without delaying long, and yet not be molested; for, said he, "no little handful of men were willing to undertake it, and a large body could not be got together in season."

As for his recent failure, we do not know the facts about it. It was evidently far from being a wild and desperate attempt. His enemy, Mr. Vallandigham, is compelled to say that "it was among the best planned and executed conspiracies that ever failed."

Not to mention his other successes, was it a failure, or did it show a want of good management, to deliver from bondage a dozen human beings, and walk off with them by broad daylight, for weeks if not months, at a leisurely pace, through one state after another, for half the length of the North, conspicuous to all parties, with a price set upon his head, going into a courtroom on his way and telling what he had done, thus convincing Missouri that it was not profitable to try to hold slaves in his neighborhood?—and this, not because the government menials were lenient, but because they were afraid of him.

Yet he did not attribute his success, foolishly, to "his star," or to any magic. He said, truly, that the reason why such greatly superior numbers quailed before him was, as one of his prisoners confessed, because they *lacked a cause*—a kind of armor which he and his party never lacked. When the time came, few men were found willing to lay down their lives in defense of what they knew to be wrong; they did not like that this should be their last act in this world.

But to make haste to *his* last act, and its effects.

The newspapers seem to ignore, or perhaps are really ignorant of the fact that there are at least as many as two or three individuals to a town throughout the North who think much as the present speaker does about him and his enterprise. I do not hesitate to say that they are an important and growing party. We aspire to be something more than stupid and timid chattels, pretending to read history and our Bibles, but desecrating every house and every day we breathe in. Perhaps anxious politicians may prove that only seventeen white men and five Negroes were concerned in the late enterprise; but their very anxiety to prove this might suggest to themselves that all is not told. Why do they still dodge the truth? They are so anxious because of a dim consciousness of the fact, which they do not distinctly face, that at least a million of the free inhabitants of the United States would have rejoiced if it had succeeded. They at most only criticize the tactics. Though we wear no crape, the thought of that man's position and probable fate is spoiling many a man's day here at the North for other thinking. If anyone who has seen him here can pursue successfully any other train of thought, I do not know what he is made of. If there is any such who gets his usual allowance of sleep, I will warrant him to fatten easily under any circumstances which do not touch his body or purse. I put a piece of paper and a pencil under my pillow, and when I could not sleep I wrote in the dark.

On the whole, my respect for my fellow men, except as one may outweigh a million, is not being increased these days. I have noticed the cold-blooded way in which newspaper writers and men generally speak of this event, as if an ordinary malefactor, though one of unusual "pluck" —as the Governor of Virginia is reported to have said, using the language of the cockpit, "the gamest man he ever saw"—had been caught, and were about to be hung. He was not dreaming of his foes when the governor thought he looked so brave. It turns what sweetness I have to gall, to hear, or hear of, the remarks of some of my neighbors. When we heard at first that he was dead, one of my townsmen observed that "he died as the fool dieth"; which, pardon me, for an instant suggested a likeness in him dying to my neighbor living. Others, craven hearted, said disparagingly that "he threw his life away," because he resisted the government. Which way have they thrown *their* lives, pray?—such as would praise a man for attacking singly an ordinary band of thieves or murderers. I hear another ask, Yankee-like, "What will he gain by it?" as if he expected to fill his pockets by this enterprise. Such a one has no idea of gain but in this worldly sense. If it does not lead to a "surprise" party, if he does not get a new pair of boots, or a vote of thanks, it must be a failure. "But he won't gain anything by it." Well, no, I don't suppose he could get four-and-sixpence a day for being hung, take the year round; but then he stands a chance to save a considerable part of his soul—and *such* a soul!—when *you* do not. No doubt you can get more in your market for a quart of milk than for a quart of blood, but that is not the market that heroes carry their blood to.

Such do not know that like the seed is the fruit, and that, in the moral world, when good seed is planted, good fruit is inevitable, and does not depend on our watering and cultivating; that when you plant, or bury, a hero in his field, a crop of heroes is sure to spring up. This is a seed of such force and vitality that it does not ask our leave to germinate.

The momentary charge at Balaklava, in obedience to a blundering command, proving what a perfect machine the soldier is, has, properly enough, been celebrated by a poet laureate; but the steady, and for the most part successful, charge of this man, for some years, against the legions of slavery, in obedience to an infinitely higher command, is as much more memorable than that as an intelligent and conscientious man is superior to a machine. Do you think that that will go unsung?

"Served him right," "A dangerous man," "He is undoubtedly insane." So they proceed to live their sane, and wise, and altogether admirable lives, reading their Plutarch a little, but chiefly pausing at that feat of Putnam, who was let down into a wolf's den; and in this wise they nourish themselves for brave and patriotic deeds sometime or other. The Tract Society could afford to print that story of Putnam. You might open the district schools with the reading of it, for there is nothing about slavery or the church in it; unless it occurs to the reader that some pastors are *wolves* in sheep's clothing. "The American Board of Commissioners for Foreign Missions," even, might dare to protest against *that* wolf. I have heard of boards, and of American boards, but it chances that I never heard of this particular lumber till lately. And yet I hear of northern men, and women, and children, by families, buying a "life membership" in such societies as these. A life membership in the grave! You can get buried cheaper than that.

Our foes are in our midst and all about us. There is hardly a house but is divided against itself, for our foe is the all but universal woodenness of both head and heart, the want of vitality in man, which is the effect of our vice; and hence are begotten fear, superstition, bigotry, persecution, and slavery of all kinds. We are mere figureheads upon a hulk, with livers in the place of hearts. The curse is the worship of idols, which at length changes the worshipper into a stone image himself; and the New Englander is just as much an idolater as the Hindu. This man was an exception, for he did not set up even a political graven image between him and his God.

A church that can never have done with excommunicating Christ while it exists! Away with your broad and flat churches, and your narrow and tall churches! Take a step forward, and invent a new style of outhouses. Invent a salt that will save you, and defend our nostrils.

The modern Christian is a man who has consented to say all the prayers in the liturgy, provided you will let him go straight to bed and sleep quietly afterward. All his prayers begin with "Now I lay me down to sleep," and he is forever looking forward to the time when he shall go to his "*long* rest." He has consented to perform certain old-established charities, too, after a fashion, but he does not wish to hear of any new-fangled ones; he doesn't wish to have any supplementary articles added to the contract, to fit it to the present time. He shows the whites of his eyes on the Sabbath, and the blacks all the rest of the week. The evil is not merely a stagnation of blood, but a stagnation of spirit. Many, no doubt, are well disposed, but sluggish by constitution and by habit, and they cannot conceive of a man who is actuated by higher motives than they are. Accordingly they pronounce this man insane, for they know that *they* could never act as he does, as long as they are themselves.

We dream of foreign countries, of other times and races of men, placing them at a distance in history or space; but let some significant event like the present occur in our midst, and we discover, often, this distance and this strangeness between us and our nearest neighbors. *They* are our Austrias, and Chinas, and South Sea Islands. Our crowded society becomes well spaced all at once, clean and handsome to the eye, a city of magnificent distances. We discover why it was that we never got beyond compliments and surfaces with them before; we become aware of as many versts between us and them as there are between a wandering Tartar and a Chinese town. The thoughtful man becomes a hermit in the thoroughfares of the market place. Impassable seas suddenly find their level between us, or dumb steppes stretch themselves out there. It is the difference of constitution, of intelligence, and faith, and not streams and mountains, that make the true and impassable boundaries between individuals and between states. None but the like-minded can come plenipotentiary to our court.

I read all the newspapers I could get within a week after this event, and I do not remember in them a single expression of sympathy for these men. I have since seen one noble statement, in a Boston paper, not editorial. Some voluminous sheets decided not to print the full report of Brown's words to the exclusion of other matter. It was as if a publisher should reject the manuscript of the New Testament, and print Wilson's last speech. The same journal which contained this pregnant news was chiefly filled, in parallel columns, with the reports of the political conventions that were being held. But the descent to them was too steep. They should have been spared this contrast—been printed in an extra, at least. To turn from the voices and deeds of earnest men to the *cackling* of political conventions! Office seekers and speechmakers, who do not so much as lay an honest egg, but wear their breasts bare upon an egg of chalk! Their great game is the game of straws, or rather that universal aboriginal game of the platter, at which the Indians cried *hub, bub!* Exclude the reports of religious and political conventions, and publish the words of a living man.

But I object not so much to what they have omitted as to what they have inserted. Even the *Liberator* called it "a misguided, wild, and apparently insane—effort." As for the herd of newspapers and magazines, I do not chance to know an editor in the country who will deliberately print anything which he knows will ultimately and permanently reduce the number of his subscribers. They do not believe that it would be expedient. How then can they print truth? If we do not say pleasant things, they argue, nobody will attend to us. And so they do like some traveling auctioneers, who sing an obscene song, in order to draw a crowd around them. Republican editors, obliged to get their sentences ready for the morning edition, and accustomed to look at everything by the twilight of politics, express no admiration, nor true sorrow even, but call these men "deluded fanatics," "mistaken men," "insane," or "crazed." It suggests what a *sane* set of editors we are blessed with, *not* "mistaken men"; who know very well on which side their bread is buttered, at least.

A man does a brave and humane deed, and at once, on all sides, we hear people and parties declaring, "I didn't do it, nor countenance *him* to do it, in any conceivable way. It can't be fairly inferred from my past career." I, for one, am not interested to hear you define your position. I don't know that I ever was or ever shall be. I think it is mere egotism, or impertinent at this time. Ye needn't take so much pains to wash your skirts of him. No intelligent man will ever be convinced that he was any creature of yours. He went and came, as he himself informs us, "under the auspices of John Brown and nobody else." The Republican party does not perceive how many his *failure* will make to vote more correctly than they would have them. They have counted the votes of Pennsylvania & Co., but they have not correctly counted Captain Brown's vote. He has taken the wind out of their sails—the little wind they had—and they may as well lie to and repair.

What though he did not belong to your clique! Though you may not approve of his method or his principles, recognize his magnanimity. Would you not like to claim kindredship with him in that, though in no other thing he is like, or likely, to you? Do you think that you would lose your reputation so? What you lost at the spile, you would gain at the bung.

If they do not mean all this, then they do not speak the truth, and say what they mean. They are simply at their old tricks still.

"It was always conceded to him," *says one who calls him crazy,* "that he was a conscientious man, very modest in his demeanor, apparently inoffensive, until the subject of slavery was introduced, when he would exhibit a feeling of indignation unparalleled."

The slave ship is on her way, crowded with its dying victims; new cargoes are being added in mid-ocean; a small crew of slaveholders, countenanced by a large body of passengers, is smothering four millions under the hatches, and yet the politician asserts that the only proper way by which deliverance is to be obtained is by "the quiet diffusion of the sentiments of humanity," without any "outbreak." As if the sentiments of humanity were ever found unaccompanied by its deeds, and you could disperse them, all finished to order, the pure article, as easily as water with a watering pot, and so lay the dust. What is that that I hear cast overboard? The bodies of the dead that have found deliverance. That is the way we are "diffusing" humanity, and its sentiments with it.

Prominent and influential editors, accustomed to deal with politicians, men of an infinitely lower grade, say, in their ignorance, that he acted "on the principle of revenge." They do not know the man. They must enlarge themselves to conceive of him. I have no doubt that the time will come when they will begin to see him as he was. They have got to conceive of a man of faith and of religious principle, and not a politician or an Indian; of a man who did not wait till he was personally interfered with or thwarted in some harmless business before he gave his life to the cause of the oppressed.

If Walker may be considered the representative of the South, I wish I could say that Brown was the representative of the North. He was a superior man. He did not value his bodily life in comparison with ideal things. He did not recognize unjust human laws, but resisted them as he was bid. For once we are lifted out of the trivialness and dust of politics into the region of truth and manhood. No man in America has ever stood up so persistently and effectively for the dignity of human nature, knowing himself for a man, and the equal of any and all governments. In that sense he was the most American of us all. He needed no babbling lawyer, making false issues, to defend him. He was more than a match for all the judges that American voters, or officeholders of whatever grade, can create. He could not have been tried by a jury of his peers, because his peers did not exist. When a man stands up serenely against the condemnation and vengeance of mankind, rising above them literally *by a whole body*—even though he were of late the vilest murderer, who has settled that matter with himself—the spectacle is a sublime one—didn't ye know it, ye *Liberators*, ye *Tribunes*, ye *Republicans?*—and we become criminal in comparison. Do yourselves the honor to recognize him. He needs none of your respect.

As for the Democratic journals, they are not human enough to affect me at all. I do not feel indignation at anything they may say.

I am aware that I anticipate a little, that he was still, at the last accounts, alive in the hands of his foes; but that being the case, I have all along found myself thinking and speaking of him as physically dead.

I do not believe in erecting statues to those who still live in our hearts, whose bones have not yet crumbled in the earth around us, but I would rather see the statue of Captain Brown in the Massachusetts Statehouse yard than that of any other man whom I know. I rejoice that I live in this age, that I am his contemporary.

What a contrast, when we turn to that political party which is so anxiously shuffling him and his plot out of its way, and looking around for some available slaveholder, perhaps, to be its candidate, at least for one who will execute the Fugitive Slave Law, and all those other unjust laws which he took up arms to annul!

Insane! A father and six sons, and one son-in-law, and several more men besides—as many at least as twelve disciples—all struck with insanity at once; while the sane tyrant holds with a firmer gripe than ever his four millions of slaves, and a thousand sane editors, his abettors, are saving their country and their bacon! Just as insane were his efforts in Kansas. Ask the tyrant who is his most dangerous foe, the sane man or the insane? Do the thousands who know him best, who have rejoiced at his deeds in Kansas, and have afforded him material aid there, think him insane? Such a use of this word is a mere trope with most who persist in using it, and I have no doubt that many of the rest have already in silence retracted their words.

Read his admirable answers to Mason and others. How they are dwarfed and defeated by the contrast! On the one side, half-brutish, half-timid questioning; on the other, truth, clear as lightning, crashing into their obscene temples. They are made to stand with Pilate, and Gessler, and the Inquisition. How ineffectual their speech and action! and what a void their silence! They are but helpless tools in this great work. It was no human power that gathered them about this preacher.

What have Massachusetts and the North sent a few *sane* representatives to Congress for, of late years?—to declare with effect what kind of sentiments? All their speeches put together and boiled down—and probably they themselves will confess it—do not match for manly directness and force, and for simple truth, the few casual remarks of crazy John Brown on the floor of the Harpers Ferry enginehouse—that man whom you are about to hang, to send to the other world, though not to represent *you* there. No, he was not our representative in any sense. He was too fair a specimen of a man to represent the like of us. Who, then, *were* his constituents? If you read his words understandingly you will find out. In his case there is no idle eloquence, no made, nor maiden speech, no compliments to the oppressor. Truth is his inspirer, and earnestness the polisher of his sentences. He could afford to lose his Sharps rifles, while he retained his faculty of speech—a Sharps rifle of infinitely surer and longer range.

And the *New York Herald* reports the conversation *verbatim!* It does not know of what undying words it is made the vehicle.

I have no respect for the penetration of any man who can read the report of that conversation and still call the principle in it insane. It has the ring of a saner sanity than an ordinary discipline and habits of life, than an ordinary organization, secure. Take any sentence of it—"Any questions that I can honorably answer, I will; not otherwise. So far as I am myself concerned, I have told everything truthfully. I value my word, sir." The few who talk about his vindictive spirit, while they really admire his heroism, have no test by which to detect a noble man, no amalgam to combine with his pure gold. They mix their own dross with it.

It is a relief to turn from these slanders to the testimony of his more truthful, but frightened jailers and hangmen. Governor Wise speaks far more justly and appreciatingly of him than any northern editor, or politician, or public personage, that I chance to have heard from. I know that you can afford to hear him again on this subject. He says: "They are themselves mistaken who take him to be a madman. . . . He is cool, collected, and indomitable, and it is but just to him to say that he was humane to his prisoners. . . . And he inspired me with great trust in his integrity as a man of truth. He is a fanatic, vain and garrulous" (I leave that part to Mr. Wise), "but firm, truthful, and intelligent. His men, too, who survive, are like him. . . . Colonel Washington says that he was the coolest and firmest man he ever saw in defying danger and death. With one son dead by his side, and another shot through, he felt the pulse of his dying son with one hand, and held his rifle with the other, and commanded his men with the utmost composure, encouraging them to be firm, and to sell their lives as dear as they could. Of the three white prisoners, Brown, Stevens, and Coppoc, it was hard to say which was most firm."

Almost the first northern men whom the slaveholder has learned to respect!

The testimony of Mr. Vallandigham, though less valuable, is of the same purport, that "it is vain to underrate either the man or his conspiracy. . . . He is the farthest possible removed from the ordinary ruffian, fanatic, or madman."

"All is quiet at Harpers Ferry," say the journals. What is the character of that calm which follows when the law and the slaveholder prevail? I regard this event as a touchstone designed to bring out, with glaring distinctness, the character of this government. We needed to be thus assisted to see it by the light of history. It needed to see itself. When a government puts forth its strength on the side of injustice, as ours to maintain slavery and kill the liberators of the slave, it reveals itself a merely brute force, or worse, a demoniacal force. It is the head of the plug-uglies. It is more manifest than ever that tyranny rules. I see this government to be effectually allied with France and Austria in oppressing mankind. There sits a tyrant holding fettered four millions of slaves; here comes their heroic liberator. This most hypocritical and diabolical government looks up from its seat on the gasping four millions, and inquires with an assumption of innocence: "What do you assault me for? Am I not an honest man? Cease agitation on this subject, or I will make a slave of you, too, or else hang you."

We talk about a *representative* government; but what a monster of a government is that where the noblest faculties of the mind, and the *whole* heart, are not *represented*. A semihuman tiger or ox, stalking over the earth, with its heart taken out and the top of its brain shot away. Heroes have fought well on their stumps when their legs were shot off, but I never heard of any good done by such a government as that.

The only government that I recognize—and it matters not how few are at the head of it, or how small its army—is that power that establishes justice in the land, never that which establishes injustice. What shall we think of a government to which all the truly brave and just men in the land are enemies, standing between it and those whom it oppresses? A government that pretends to be Christian and crucifies a million Christs every day!

Treason! Where does such treason take its rise? I cannot help thinking of you as you deserve, ye governments. Can you dry up the fountains of thought? High treason, when it is resistance to tyranny here below, has its origin in, and is first committed by, the power that makes and forever recreates man. When you have caught and hung all these human rebels, you have accomplished nothing but your own guilt, for you have not struck at the fountainhead. You presume to contend with a foe against whom West Point cadets and rifled cannon *point* not. Can all the art of the cannon founder tempt matter to turn against its maker? Is the form in which the founder thinks he casts it more essential than the constitution of it and of himself?

The United States have a coffle of four millions of slaves. They are determined to keep them in this condition; and Massachusetts is one of the confederated overseers to prevent their escape. Such are not all the inhabitants of Massachusetts, but such are they who rule and are obeyed here. It was Massachusetts, as well as Virginia, that put down this insurrection at Harpers Ferry. She sent the marines there, and she will have *to pay the penalty of her sin.*

Suppose that there is a society in this state that out of its own purse and magnanimity saves all the fugitive slaves that run to us, and protects our colored fellow citizens, and leaves the other work to the government, so called. Is not that government fast losing its occupation, and becoming contemptible to mankind? If private men are obliged to perform the offices of government, to protect the weak and dispense justice, then the government becomes only a hired man, or clerk, to perform menial or indifferent services. Of course, that is but the shadow of a government whose existence necessitates a Vigilant Committee. What should we think of the Oriental Cadi even, behind whom worked in secret a Vigilant Committee? But such is the character of our Northern states generally; each has its Vigilant Committee. And, to a certain extent, these crazy governments recognize and accept this relation. They say, virtually, "We'll be glad to work for you on these terms, only don't make a noise about it." And thus the government, its salary being insured, withdraws into the back shop, taking the Constitution with it, and bestows most of its labor on repairing that. When I hear it at work sometimes, as I go by, it reminds me, at best, of those farmers who in winter contrive to turn a penny by following the coopering business. And what kind of spirit is their barrel made to hold? They speculate in stocks, and bore holes in mountains, but they are not competent to lay out even a decent highway. The only *free* road, the Underground Railroad, is owned and managed by the Vigilant Committee. *They* have tunneled under the whole breadth of the land. Such a government is losing its power and respectability as surely as water runs out of a leaky vessel, and is held by one that can contain it.

I hear many condemn these men because they were so few. When were the good and the brave ever in a majority? Would you have had him wait till that time came?—till you and I came over to him? The very fact that he had no rabble or troop of hirelings about him would alone distinguish him from ordinary heroes. His company was small indeed, because few could be found worthy to pass muster. Each one who there laid down his life for the poor and oppressed was a picked man, culled out of many thousands, if not millions; apparently a man of principle, of rare courage, and devoted humanity; ready to sacrifice his life at any moment for the benefit of his fellow man. It may be doubted if there were as many more their equals in these respects in all the country—I speak of his followers only—for their leader, no doubt, scoured the land far and wide, seeking to swell his troop. These alone were ready to step between the oppressor and the oppressed. Surely they were the very best men you could select to be hung. That was the greatest compliment which this country could pay them. They were ripe for her gallows. She has tried a long time, she has hung a good many, but never found the right one before.

When I think of him, and his six sons, and his son-in-law, not to enumerate the others, enlisted for this fight, proceeding coolly, reverently, humanely to work, for months if not years, sleeping and waking upon it, summering and wintering the thought, without expecting any reward but a good conscience, while almost all America stood ranked on the other side—I say again that it affects me as a sublime spectacle. If he had had any journal advocating *"his cause,"* any organ, as the phrase is, monotonously and wearisomely playing the same old tune, and then passing round the hat, it would have been fatal to his efficiency. If he had acted in any way so as to be let alone by the government, he might have been suspected. It was the fact that the tyrant must give place to him, or he to the tyrant, that distinguished him from all the reformers of the day that I know.

It was his peculiar doctrine that a man has a perfect right to interfere by force with the slaveholder, in order to rescue the slave. I agree with him. They who are continually shocked by slavery have some right to be shocked by the violent death of the slaveholder, but no others. Such will be more shocked by his life than by his death. I shall not be forward to think him mistaken in his method who quickest succeeds to liberate the slave. I speak for the slave when I say that I prefer the philanthropy of Captain Brown to that philanthropy which neither shoots me nor liberates me. At any rate, I do not think it is quite sane for one to spend his whole life in talking or writing about this matter, unless he is continuously inspired, and I have not done so. A man may have other affairs to attend to. I do not wish to kill nor to be killed, but I can foresee circumstances in which both these things would be by me unavoidable. We preserve the so-called peace of our community by deeds of petty violence every day. Look at the policeman's billy and handcuffs! Look at the jail! Look at the gallows! Look at the chaplain of the regiment! We are hoping only to live safely on the outskirts of *this* provisional army. So we defend ourselves and our henroosts, and maintain slavery. I know that the mass of my countrymen think that the only righteous use that can be made of Sharps rifles and revolvers is to fight duels with them, when we are insulted by other nations, or to hunt Indians, or shoot fugitive slaves with them, or the like. I think that for once the Sharps rifles and the revolvers were employed in a righteous cause. The tools were in the hands of one who could use them.

The same indignation that is said to have cleared the temple once will clear it again. The question is not about the weapon, but the spirit in which you use it. No man has appeared in America, as yet, who loved his fellow man so well, and treated him so tenderly. He lived for him. He took up his life and he laid it down for him. What sort of violence is that which is encouraged, not by soldiers, but by peaceable citizens, not so much by laymen as by ministers of the Gospel, not so much by the fighting sects as by the Quakers, and not so much by Quaker men as by Quaker women?

This event advertises me that there is such a fact as death—the possibility of a man's dying. It seems as if no man had ever died in America before; for in order to die you must first have lived. I don't believe in the hearses, and palls, and funerals that they have had. There was no death in the case, because there had been no life; they merely rotted or sloughed off, pretty much as they had rotted or sloughed along. No temple's veil was rent, only a hole dug somewhere. Let the dead bury their dead. The best of them fairly ran down like a clock. Franklin, Washington—they were let off without dying; they were merely missing one day. I hear a good many pretend that they are going to die; or that they have died, for aught that I know. Nonsense! I'll defy them to do it. They haven't got life enough in them. They'll deliquesce like fungi, and keep a hundred eulogists mopping the spot where they left off. Only half a dozen or so have died since the world began. Do you think that you are going to die, Sir? No! There's no hope of you. You haven't got your lesson yet. You've got to stay after school. We make a needless ado about capital punishment—taking lives, when there is no life to take. *Memento mori!* We don't understand that sublime sentence which some worthy got sculptured on his gravestone once. We've interpreted it in a groveling and sniveling sense; we've wholly forgotten how to die.

But be sure you do die nevertheless. Do your work, and finish it. If you know how to begin, you will know when to end.

These men, in teaching us how to die, have at the same time taught us how to live. If this man's acts and words do not create a revival, it will be the severest possible satire on the acts and words that do. It is the best news that America has ever heard. It has already quickened the feeble pulse of the North, and infused more and more generous blood into her veins and heart than any number of years of what is called commercial and political prosperity could. How many a man who was lately contemplating suicide has now something to live for!

One writer says that Brown's peculiar monomania made him to be "dreaded by the Missourians as a supernatural being." Sure enough, a hero in the midst of us cowards is always so dreaded. He is just that thing. He shows himself superior to nature. He has a spark of divinity in him.

> Unless above himself he can
> Erect himself, how poor a thing is man!

Newspaper editors argue also that it is a proof of his *insanity* that he thought he was appointed to do this work which he did—that he did not suspect himself for a moment! They talk as if it were impossible that a man could be "divinely appointed" in these days to do any work whatever; as if vows and religion were out of date as connected with any man's daily work; as if the agent to abolish slavery could only be somebody appointed by the President, or by some political party. They talk as if a man's death were a failure, and his continued life, be it of whatever character, were a success.

When I reflect to what a cause this man devoted himself, and how religiously, and then reflect to what cause his judges and all who condemn him so angrily and fluently devote themselves, I see that they are as far apart as the heavens and earth are asunder.

The amount of it is, our *"leading men"* are a harmless kind of folk, and they know *well enough* that *they* were not divinely appointed, but elected by the votes of their party.

Who is it whose safety requires that Captain Brown be hung? Is it indispensable to any northern man? Is there no resource but to cast this man also to the Minotaur? If you do not wish it, say so distinctly. While these things are being done, beauty stands veiled and music is a screeching lie. Think of him—of his rare qualities!—such a man as it takes ages to make, and ages to understand; no mock hero, nor the representative of any party. A man such as the sun may not rise upon again in this benighted land. To whose making went the costliest material, the finest adamant; sent to be the redeemer of those in captivity; and the only use to which you can put him is to hang him at the end of a rope! You who pretend to care for Christ crucified, consider what you are about to do to him who offered himself to be the savior of four millions of men.

Any man knows when he is justified, and all the wits in the world cannot enlighten him on that point. The murderer always knows that he is justly punished; but when a government takes the life of a man without the consent of his conscience, it is an audacious government, and is taking a step towards its own dissolution. Is it not possible that an individual may be right and a government wrong? Are laws to be enforced simply because they were made? or declared by any number of men to be good, if they are *not* good? Is there any necessity for a man's being a tool to perform a deed of which his better nature disapproves? Is it the intention of lawmakers that *good* men shall be hung ever? Are judges to interpret the law according to the letter, and not the spirit? What right have *you* to enter into a compact with yourself that you *will* do thus or so, against the light within you? Is it for *you* to *make up* your mind, to form any resolution whatever, and not accept the convictions that are forced upon you, and which ever pass your understanding? I do not believe in lawyers, in that mode of attacking or defending a man, because you descend to meet the judge on his own ground, and, in cases of the highest importance, it is of no consequence whether a man breaks a human law or not. Let lawyers decide trivial cases. Businessmen may arrange that among themselves. If they were the interpreters of the everlasting laws which rightfully bind man, that would be another thing. A counterfeiting law-factory, standing half in a slave land and half in a free! What kind of laws for free men can you expect from that?

I am here to plead his cause with you. I plead not for his life, but for his character—his immortal life; and so it becomes your cause wholly, and is not his in the least. Some eighteen hundred years ago Christ was crucified; this morning, perchance, Captain Brown was hung. These are the two ends of a chain which is not without its links. He is not Old Brown any longer; he is an angel of light.

I see now that it was necessary that the bravest and humanest man in all the country should be hung. Perhaps he saw it himself. I *almost fear* that I may yet hear of his deliverance, doubting if a prolonged life, if *any* life, can do as much good as his death.

"Misguided!" "Garrulous!" "Insane!" "Vindictive!" So ye write in your easy chairs, and thus he wounded responds from the floor of the armory, clear as a cloudless sky, true as the voice of nature is: "No man sent me here; it was my own prompting and that of my Maker. I acknowledge no master in human form."

And in what a sweet and noble strain he proceeds, addressing his captors, who stand over him: "I think, my friends, you are guilty of a great wrong against God and humanity, and it would be perfectly right for anyone to interfere with you so far as to free those you willfully and wickedly hold in bondage."

And, referring to his movement: "It is, in my opinion, the greatest service a man can render to God."

"I pity the poor in bondage that have none to help them; that is why I am here; not to gratify any personal animosity, revenge, or vindictive spirit. It is my sympathy with the oppressed and the wronged, that are as good as you, and as precious in the sight of God."

You don't know your testament when you see it.

"I want you to understand that I respect the rights of the poorest and weakest of colored people, oppressed by the slave power, just as much as I do those of the most wealthy and powerful."

"I wish to say, furthermore, that you had better, all you people at the South, prepare yourselves for a settlement of that question, that must come up for settlement sooner than you are prepared for it. The sooner you are prepared the better. You may dispose of me very easily. I am nearly disposed of now; but this question is still to be settled—this Negro question, I mean; the end of that is not yet."

I foresee the time when the painter will paint that scene, no longer going to Rome for a subject; the poet will sing it; the historian record it; and, with the Landing of the Pilgrims and the Declaration of Independence, it will be the ornament of some future national gallery, when at least the present form of slavery shall be no more here. We shall then be at liberty to weep for Captain Brown. Then, and not till then, we will take our revenge.

Abraham Lincoln

1809–1865

Nothing in Abraham Lincoln's early life was designed to make him the great figure that he became. His father, Thomas, was a wandering homesteader, and Lincoln's family roved through three states in his early years, from Kentucky, where Lincoln was born on February 12, 1809, to Indiana and to Illinois. During those years Lincoln farmed, chopped trees, operated a flatboat on the Ohio River, and worked as a clerk in a store at New Salem, Illinois. In 1832, during the Black Hawk War against the Indians, Lincoln signed up in the local militia and was elected captain by the men of his company. At twenty-three he was already recognized as a natural leader.

During his early political career Lincoln was encouraged to study for the law. He did so on his own, as he said, never "in a college or an academy as a student." In 1836 he received a license to practice and soon established his office in Springfield, Illinois, where he met and married Mary Todd, the future mother of his four sons.

Lincoln first won national prominence when he campaigned against Stephen A. Douglas for the United States Senate. A series of debates with Douglas did not win him the election but brought him to the attention of the country. In the 1860 Republican National Convention Lincoln was nominated for President and won the national election. By the time Lincoln was inaugurated some southern states had already seceded from the Union. The country was soon plunged into civil war, and Lincoln was faced with the exhausting duties of a wartime President. He was re-elected in 1864, when the end of the war was in view and the task of reconstruction loomed ahead. Unfortunately, Lincoln never lived to see the country through that difficult period. He was shot by the actor John Wilkes Booth on April 14, 1865, only five days after the end of the war, and died on the following morning. As the funeral train carried his body back to Springfield, thousands mourned the man who had served them through their great crisis.

Abraham Lincoln's speeches and writings were designed to clarify and direct the events of his period. Some of his speeches, such as the Gettysburg Address, are unexcelled in precision and power. It is more than likely that he could have been a great creative writer. He had no formal education, but the books he read as a boy had the happiest of influences upon him—such books as the *Bible, Pilgrim's Progress, Robinson Crusoe,* and Aesop's *Fables.* His later readings in history and law, and his study of Euclid's *Elements* and of English grammar served to point and polish his prose style. His writings have the pungency of the fables, the precision of mathematics, and the splendid resonance of the Bible.

With one exception all of the selections here are addressed to the public. The exception is a brief note found in his papers—the "Meditation on the Divine Will." It is interesting because in this private speculation Lincoln echoes a note which runs through many of his important speeches. It is the thought that God must have willed this contest where each side believed itself to be in the right. He adds despairingly: "Yet the contest proceeds."

Lincoln's first speech in the East was made on February 27 at Cooper Institute in New York, shortly before he was nominated for the Presidency. Here he is the sharp-witted, hard-hitting lawyer, flaying the Democrats and defending the Republican policy of restricting the institution of slavery. Ridiculing the stand taken by pro-slavery Democrats, he says that they are "for the 'gur-reat pur-rinciple' that 'if one man would enslave another, no third man should object,' fantastically called 'Popular Sovereignty.'" He points out that the United States Constitution, which southerners invoke, gives

---

Notes from the artist: ". . . a double portrait of Lincoln in a semisurrealistic style was used to suggest the two sides of his career, statesman and humanitarian. At left is an interpretation of an old slave sale poster, while at the right are facsimiles of two of Lincoln's notes."

them no right to take slaves to free territories, and he shows that Jefferson regarded slavery as an evil, to be eventually eradicated. "Let us have faith that right makes might," he says in closing, "and . . . dare to do our duty."

On March 4, 1861, when Lincoln took the oath of office, southern states were already seceding from the Union. In his *First Inaugural Address*, Lincoln takes a humane and conciliatory point of view, argues the irrationality of war, and pleads for "a patient confidence in the ultimate justice of the people." This is more than the lawyer speaking; this is the man who has just taken on an appalling responsibility and is making a last effort to stave off the impending disaster.

In the deceptively simple *Gettysburg Address* of November 19, 1863, Lincoln states the ideal of government to which he rededicates the forces of the Union—so "that these dead shall not have died in vain." The re-establishment of the Union and the restoration of peace was always foremost in his mind. In his *Second Inaugural Address*, of March 4, 1865, even before the end of the war, he urged the people, while prosecuting the war to its end, to have "malice toward none," and "charity for all."

The letter to Horace Greeley of August 22, 1862, shows Lincoln in the unenviable role of conciliating the radical and the moderate elements of his government. In his last, prophetic address, which urged an understanding of the defeated South, he shows the strain of his prolonged debate with those who might still destroy the Union. Here the man who was nicknamed "Father Abraham" pleads for his recalcitrant children: "Finding themselves safely at home," he says, "it would be utterly immaterial whether they had ever been abroad."

It is little wonder that the admiration of Lincoln has become a cement binding all sections of the Union, which he did so much to preserve.

Address at Cooper Institute[1]

February 27, 1860

ut enough! Let all who believe that "our fathers, who framed
the government under which we live, understood this question just as
well, and even better, than we do now," speak as they spoke, and act
as they acted upon it. This is all Republicans ask—all Republicans desire—in relation to slavery. As those fathers marked it, so let it be again
marked, as an evil not to be extended, but to be tolerated and protected
only because of and so far as its actual presence among us makes that
toleration and protection a necessity. Let all the guaranties those fathers
gave it be, not grudgingly, but fully and fairly maintained. For this Republicans contend, and with this, so far as I know or believe, they will
be content.

And now, if they would listen—as I suppose they will not—I would
address a few words to the Southern people.

I would say to them: You consider yourselves a reasonable and a just
people; and I consider that in the general qualities of reason and justice
you are not inferior to any other people. Still, when you speak of us Republicans, you do so only to denounce us as reptiles, or, at the best, as
no better than outlaws. You will grant a hearing to pirates or murderers,
but nothing like it to "Black Republicans." In all your contentions with
one another, each of you deems an unconditional condemnation of "Black
Republicanism" as the first thing to be attended to. Indeed, such condemnation of us seems to be an indispensable prerequisite—license, so
to speak—among you to be admitted or permitted to speak at all. Now,
can you, or not, be prevailed upon to pause and to consider whether
this is quite just to us, or even to yourselves? Bring forward your charges
and specifications, and then be patient long enough to hear us deny or
justify.

You say we are sectional. We deny it. That makes an issue; and the
burden of proof is upon you. You produce your proof; and what is it?

---

1. This selection excludes Lincoln's opening statements on the founding fathers' attitude toward slavery.

Why, that our party has no existence in your section—gets no votes in your section. The fact is substantially true; but does it prove the issue? If it does, then in case we should, without change of principle, begin to get votes in your section, we should thereby cease to be sectional. You cannot escape this conclusion; and yet, are you willing to abide by it: If you are, you will probably soon find that we have ceased to be sectional, for we shall get votes in your section this very year. You will then begin to discover, as the truth plainly is, that your proof does not touch the issue. The fact that we get no votes in your section is a fact of your making, and not of ours. And if there be fault in that fact, that fault is primarily yours, and remains so until you show that we repel you by some wrong principle or practice. If we do repel you by any wrong principle or practice, the fault is ours; but this brings you to where you ought to have started—to a discussion of the right or wrong of our principle. If our principle, put in practice, would wrong your section for the benefit of ours, or for any other object, then our principle, and we with it, are sectional, and are justly opposed and denounced as such. Meet us, then, on the question of whether our principle, put in practice, would wrong your section; and so meet us as if it were possible that something may be said on our side. Do you accept the challenge? No! Then you really believe that the principle which "our fathers who framed the government under which we live" thought so clearly right as to adopt it, and endorse it again and again, upon their official oaths, is in fact so clearly wrong as to demand your condemnation without a moment's consideration.

Some of you delight to flaunt in our faces the warning against sectional parties given by Washington in his Farewell Address. Less than eight years before Washington gave that warning, he had, as President of the United States, approved and signed an act of Congress, enforcing the prohibition of slavery in the Northwestern Territory, which act embodied the policy of the government upon that subject up to and at the very moment he penned that warning; and about one year after he penned it, he wrote Lafayette that he considered that prohibition a wise measure, expressing in the same connection his hope that we should at some time have a confederacy of free states.

Bearing this in mind, and seeing that sectionalism has since arisen upon this same subject, is that warning a weapon in your hands against us, or in our hands against you? Could Washington himself speak, would he cast the blame of that sectionalism upon us, who sustain his policy, or upon you who repudiate it? We respect that warning of Washington, and we commend it to you, together with his example pointing to the right application of it.

But you say you are conservative—eminently conservative—while we are revolutionary, destructive, or something of the sort. What is conservatism? Is it not adherence to the old and tried, against the new and untried? We stick to, contend for, the identical old policy on the point in controversy which was adopted by "our fathers who framed the government under which we live"; while you with one accord reject, and scout, and spit upon that old policy, and insist upon substituting something new. True, you disagree among yourselves as to what that substitute shall be. You are divided on new propositions and plans, but you are unanimous in rejecting and denouncing the old policy of the fathers. Some of you are for reviving the foreign slave trade; some for a Congressional slave code for the territories; some for Congress forbidding the territories to prohibit slavery within their limits; some for maintaining slavery in the territories through the judiciary; some for the "gur-reat pur-rinciple" that "if one man would enslave another, no third man should object," fantastically called "Popular Sovereignty"; but never a man among you in favor of federal prohibition of slavery in federal territories, according to the practice of "Our fathers who framed the government under which we live." Not one of all your various plans can show a precedent or an advocate in the century within which our government originated. Consider, then, whether your claim of conservatism for yourselves, and your charge of destructiveness against us, are based on the most clear and stable foundations.

Again, you say we have made the slavery question more prominent than it formerly was. We deny it. We admit that it is more prominent, but we deny that we made it so. It was not we, but you, who discarded the old policy of the fathers. We resisted, and still resist, your innovation; and thence comes the greater prominence of the question. Would you have that question reduced to its former proportions? Go back to that old policy. What has been will be again, under the same conditions. If you would have the peace of the old times, readopt the precepts and policy of the old times.

You charge that we stir up insurrections among your slaves. We deny it; and what is your proof? Harper's Ferry! John Brown!! [2] John Brown

---

2. John Brown, an abolitionist, had attempted in 1859 to incite a slave rebellion by seizing the federal arsenal at Harper's Ferry, Virginia. He was captured and executed by Virginia. Lincoln was here carefully dissociating the Republican party from the extreme elements represented by Brown.

was no Republican; and you have failed to implicate a single Republican in his Harper's Ferry enterprise. If any member of our party is guilty in that matter, you know it or you do not know it. If you do know it, you are inexcusable for not designating the man and proving the fact. If you do not know it, you are inexcusable for asserting it, and especially for persisting in the assertion after you have tried and failed to make the proof. You need not be told that persisting in a charge which one does not know to be true is simply malicious slander.

Some of you admit that no Republican designedly aided or encouraged the Harper's Ferry affair; but still insist that our doctrines and declarations necessarily lead to such results. We do not believe it. We know we hold to no doctrine, and make no declaration, which were not held to and made by "our fathers who framed the government under which we live." You never dealt fairly by us in relation to this affair. When it occurred, some important state elections were near at hand, and you were in evident glee with the belief that, by charging the blame upon us, you could get an advantage of us in those elections. The elections came, and your expectations were not quite fulfilled. Every Republican man knew that, as to himself at least, your charge was a slander, and he was not much inclined by it to cast his vote in your favor. Republican doctrines and declarations are accompanied with a continual protest against any interference whatever with your slaves, or with you about your slaves. Surely, this does not encourage them to revolt. True, we do, in common with "our fathers, who framed the government under which we live," declare our belief that slavery is wrong; but the slaves do not hear us declare even this. For anything we say or do, the slaves would scarcely know there is a Republican party. I believe they would not, in fact, generally know it but for your misrepresentations of us, in their hearing. In your political contests among yourselves, each faction charges the other with sympathy with Black Republicanism; and then, to give point to the charge, defines Black Republicanism to simply be insurrection, blood and thunder among the slaves.

Slave insurrections are no more common now than they were before the Republican party was organized. What induced the Southampton insurrection,[3] twenty-eight years ago, in which, at least, three times as many lives were lost as at Harper's Ferry? You can scarcely stretch your very elastic fancy to the conclusion that Southampton was "got up by Black Republicanism." In the present state of things in the United States,

---

3. A slave uprising in Virginia in 1831.

I do not think a general, or even a very extensive, slave insurrection is possible. The indispensable concert of action cannot be attained. The slaves have no means of rapid communication; nor can incendiary freemen, black or white, supply it. The explosive materials are everywhere in parcels; but there neither are, nor can be supplied, the indispensable connecting trains.

Much is said by Southern people about the affection of slaves for their masters and mistresses; and a part of it, at least, is true. A plot for an uprising could scarcely be devised and communicated to twenty individuals before some one of them, to save the life of a favorite master or mistress, would divulge it. This is the rule; and the slave revolution in Haiti [4] was not an exception to it, but a case occurring under peculiar circumstances. The gunpowder plot of British history, though not connected with slaves, was more in point. In that case, only about twenty were admitted to the secret; and yet one of them, in his anxiety to save a friend, betrayed the plot to that friend, and, by consequence, averted the calamity. Occasional poisonings from the kitchen, and open or stealthy assassinations in the field, and local revolts extending to a score or so, will continue to occur as the natural results of slavery; but no general insurrection of slaves, as I think, can happen in this country for a long time. Whoever much fears, or much hopes for such an event, will be alike disappointed.

In the language of Mr. Jefferson, uttered many years ago, "It is still in our power to direct the process of emancipation, and deportation, peaceably, and in such slow degrees, as that the evil will wear off insensibly; and their places be, *pari passu*, filled up by free white laborers. If, on the contrary, it is left to force itself on, human nature must shudder at the prospect held up."

Mr. Jefferson did not mean to say, nor do I, that the power of emancipation is in the federal government. He spoke of Virginia; and, as to the power of emancipation, I speak of the slaveholding states only. The federal government, however, as we insist, has the power of restraining the extension of the institution—the power to insure that a slave insurrection shall never occur on any American soil which is now free from slavery.

John Brown's effort was peculiar. It was not a slave insurrection. It was an attempt by white men to get up a revolt among slaves, in which the slaves refused to participate. In fact, it was so absurd that the slaves, with all their ignorance, saw plainly enough it could not succeed. That

---

4. A revolution in 1791.

affair, in its philosophy, corresponds with the many attempts, related in history, at the assassination of kings and emperors. An enthusiast broods over the oppression of a people till he fancies himself commissioned by Heaven to liberate them. He ventures the attempt, which ends in little else than his own execution. Orsini's [5] attempt on Louis Napoleon, and John Brown's attempt at Harper's Ferry, were, in their philosophy, precisely the same. The eagerness to cast blame on old England in the one case, and on New England in the other, does not disprove the sameness of the two things.

And how much would it avail you, if you could, by the use of John Brown, Helper's book,[6] and the like, break up the Republican organization? Human action can be modified to some extent, but human nature cannot be changed. There is a judgment and a feeling against slavery in this nation, which cast at least a million and a half of votes. You cannot destroy that judgment and feeling—that sentiment—by breaking up the political organization which rallies around it. You can scarcely scatter and disperse an army which has been formed into order in the face of your heaviest fire; but if you could, how much would you gain by forcing the sentiment which created it out of the peaceful channel of the ballot box, into some other channel? What would that other channel probably be? Would the number of John Browns be lessened or enlarged by the operation?

But you will break up the Union rather than submit to a denial of your constitutional rights.

That has a somewhat reckless sound; but it would be palliated, if not fully justified, were we proposing, by the mere force of numbers, to deprive you of some right, plainly written down in the Constitution. But we are proposing no such thing.

When you make these declarations you have a specific and well-understood allusion to an assumed constitutional right of yours, to take slaves into the federal territories, and to hold them there as property. But no such right is specifically written in the Constitution. That instrument is literally silent about any such right. We, on the contrary, deny that such a right has any existence in the Constitution, even by implication.

Your purpose, then, plainly stated, is that you will destroy the government, unless you be allowed to construe and enforce the Constitution as

5. Felice Orsini, an Italian who attempted to assassinate Louis Napoleon in 1858.
6. Hinton R. Helper, author of *The Impending Crisis of the South,* an attack upon slavery by a former North Carolinian which infuriated the South.

you please, on all points in dispute between you and us. You will rule or ruin in all events.

This, plainly stated, is your language. Perhaps you will say the Supreme Court has decided the disputed constitutional question in your favor. Not quite so. But waiving the lawyer's distinction between dictum and decision, the Court have decided the question for you in a sort of way. The Court have substantially said, it is your constitutional right to take slaves into the federal territories, and to hold them there as property. When I say the decision was made in a sort of way, I mean it was made in a divided court, by a bare majority of the judges, and they not quite agreeing with one another in the reasons for making it; that it is so made as that its avowed supporters disagree with one another about its meaning, and that it was mainly based upon a mistaken statement of fact—the statement in the opinion that "the right of property in a slave is distinctly and expressly affirmed in the Constitution."

An inspection of the Constitution will show that the right of property in a slave is not "*distinctly* and *expressly* affirmed" in it. Bear in mind, the judges do not pledge their judicial opinion that such right is *impliedly* affirmed in the Constitution; but they pledge their veracity that it is "*distinctly* and *expressly*" affirmed there—"distinctly," that is, not mingled with anything else—"expressly," that is, in words meaning just that, without the aid of an inference, and susceptible of no other meaning.

If they had only pledged their judicial opinion that such right is affirmed in the instrument by implication, it would be open to others to show that neither the word "slave" nor "slavery" is to be found in the Constitution, nor the word "property" even, in any connection with language alluding to the things slave, or slavery, and that wherever in that instrument the slave is alluded to, he is called a "person"; and wherever his master's legal right in relation to him is alluded to, it is spoken of as "service or labor which may be due"—as a debt payable in service or labor. Also, it would be open to show, by contemporaneous history, that this mode of alluding to slaves and slavery, instead of speaking of them, was employed on purpose to exclude from the Constitution the idea that there could be property in man.

To show all this is easy and certain.

When this obvious mistake of the judges shall be brought to their notice, is it not reasonable to expect that they will withdraw the mistaken statement, and reconsider the conclusion based upon it?

And then it is to be remembered that "our fathers, who framed the government under which we live"—the men who made the Constitution —decided this same constitutional question in our favor, long ago—decided it without division among themselves, when making the decision; without division among themselves about the meaning of it after it was made, and, so far as any evidence is left, without basing it upon any mistaken statement of fact.

Under all these circumstances, do you really feel yourselves justified to break up this government, unless such a court decision as yours is shall be at once submitted to as a conclusive and final rule of political action? But you will not abide the election of a Republican president! In that supposed event, you say, you will destroy the Union; and then, you say, the great crime of having destroyed it will be upon us! That is cool. A highwayman holds a pistol to my ear, and mutters through his teeth, "Stand and deliver, or I shall kill you, and then you will be a murderer!"

To be sure, what the robber demanded of me—my money—was my own; and I had a clear right to keep it; but it was no more my own than my vote is my own; and the threat of death to me, to extort my money, and the threat of destruction to the Union, to extort my vote, can scarcely be distinguished in principle.

A few words now to Republicans. It is exceedingly desirable that all parts of this great confederacy shall be at peace, and in harmony, one with another. Let us Republicans do our part to have it so. Even though much provoked, let us do nothing through passion and ill temper. Even though the Southern people will not so much as listen to us, let us calmly consider their demands, and yield to them if, in our deliberate view of our duty, we possibly can. Judging by all they say and do, and by the subject and nature of their controversy with us, let us determine, if we can, what will satisfy them.

Will they be satisfied if the territories be unconditionally surrendered to them? We know they will not. In all their present complaints against us, the territories are scarcely mentioned. Invasions and insurrections are the rage now. Will it satisfy them, if, in the future, we have nothing to do with invasions and insurrections? We know it will not. We so know, because we know we never had anything to do with invasions and insurrections; and yet this total abstaining does not exempt us from the charge and the denunciation.

The question recurs, what will satisfy them? Simply this: We must not only let them alone, but we must, somehow, convince them that we do let them alone. This, we know by experience, is no easy task. We have been so trying to convince them from the very beginning of our organization, but with no success. In all our platforms and speeches we have constantly protested our purpose to let them alone; but this has had no tendency to convince them. Alike unavailing to convince them is the fact that they have never detected a man of us in any attempt to disturb them.

These natural, and apparently adequate means all failing, what will convince them? This, and this only: cease to call slavery *wrong*, and join them in calling it *right*. And this must be done thoroughly—done in *acts* as well as in *words*. Silence will not be tolerated—we must place ourselves avowedly with them. Senator Douglas' new sedition law must be enacted and enforced, suppressing all declarations that slavery is wrong, whether made in politics, in presses, in pulpits, or in private. We must arrest and return their fugitive slaves with greedy pleasure. We must pull down our free state constitutions. The whole atmosphere must be disinfected from all taint of opposition to slavery, before they will cease to believe that all their troubles proceed from us.

I am quite aware they do not state their case precisely in this way. Most of them would probably say to us, "Let us alone, *do* nothing to us, and *say* what you please about slavery." But we do let them alone—have never disturbed them—so that, after all, it is what we say which dissatisfies them. They will continue to accuse us of doing, until we cease saying.

I am also aware they have not, as yet, in terms, demanded the overthrow of our free-state constitutions. Yet those constitutions declare the wrong of slavery, with more solemn emphasis, than do all other sayings against it; and when all these other sayings shall have been silenced, the overthrow of these constitutions will be demanded, and nothing be left to resist the demand. It is nothing to the contrary that they do not demand the whole of this just now. Demanding what they do, and for the reason they do, they can voluntarily stop nowhere short of this consummation. Holding, as they do, that slavery is morally right, and socially elevating, they cannot cease to demand a full national recognition of it, as a legal right, and a social blessing.

Nor can we justifiably withhold this, on any ground save our conviction that slavery is wrong. If slavery is right, all words, acts, laws, and constitutions against it are themselves wrong, and should be silenced, and swept away. If it is right, we cannot justly object to its nationality—its universality; if it is wrong, they cannot justly insist upon its extension—its enlargement. All they ask, we could readily grant, if we thought slavery right; all we ask, they could as readily grant, if they thought it wrong. Their thinking it right, and our thinking it wrong, is the precise fact upon which depends the whole controversy. Thinking it right, as they do, they are not to blame for desiring its full recognition, as being right; but, thinking it wrong, as we do, can we yield to them? Can we cast our votes with their view, and against our own? In view of our moral, social, and political responsibilities, can we do this?

Wrong as we think slavery is, we can yet afford to let it alone where it is, because that much is due to the necessity arising from its actual presence in the nation; but can we, while our votes will prevent it, allow it to spread into the national territories, and to overrun us here in these free states? If our sense of duty forbids this, then let us stand by our duty, fearlessly and effectively. Let us be diverted by none of those sophistical contrivances wherewith we are so industriously plied and belabored—contrivances such as groping for some middle ground between the right and the wrong, vain as the search for a man who should be neither a living man nor a dead man—such as a policy of "don't care" on a question about which all true men do care—such as Union appeals beseeching true Union men to yield to Disunionists, reversing the divine rule, and calling, not the sinners, but the righteous to repentance—such as invocations to Washington, imploring men to unsay what Washington said, and undo what Washington did.

Neither let us be slandered from our duty by false accusations against us, nor frightened from it by menaces of destruction to the government nor of dungeons to ourselves. LET US HAVE FAITH THAT RIGHT MAKES MIGHT, AND IN THAT FAITH, LET US, TO THE END, DARE TO DO OUR DUTY AS WE UNDERSTAND IT.

First Inaugural Address

March 4, 1861

Fellow citizens of the United States:

In compliance with a custom as old as the government itself, I appear before you to address you briefly, and to take, in your presence, the oath prescribed by the Constitution of the United States, to be taken by the President "before he enters on the execution of his office."

I do not consider it necessary, at present, for me to discuss those matters of administration about which there is no special anxiety, or excitement.

Apprehension seems to exist among the people of the Southern states that by the accession of a Republican administration their property, and their peace, and personal security are to be endangered. There has never been any reasonable cause for such apprehension. Indeed, the most ample evidence to the contrary has all the while existed, and been open to their inspection. It is found in nearly all the published speeches of him who now addresses you. I do but quote from one of those speeches when I declare that "I have no purpose, directly or indirectly, to interfere with the institution of slavery in the states where it exists. I believe I have no lawful right to do so, and I have no inclination to do so." Those who nominated and elected me did so with full knowledge that I had made this and many similar declarations, and had never recanted them. And more than this, they placed in the platform, for my acceptance, and as a law to themselves, and to me, the clear and emphatic resolution which I now read:

"*Resolved,* That the maintenance inviolate of the rights of the states, and especially the right of each state to order and control its own domestic institutions according to its own judgment exclusively, is essential to that balance of power on which the perfection and endurance of our political fabric depend; and we denounce the lawless invasion by armed

747

force of the soil of any state or territory, no matter under what pretext, as among the gravest of crimes."

I now reiterate these sentiments: and in doing so, I only press upon the public attention the most conclusive evidence of which the case is susceptible, that the property, peace and security of no section are to be in anywise endangered by the now incoming administration. I add too that all the protection which, consistently with the Constitution and the laws, can be given will be cheerfully given to all the states when lawfully demanded, for whatever cause—as cheerfully to one section as to another.

There is much controversy about the delivering up of fugitives from service or labor. The clause I now read is as plainly written in the Constitution as any other of its provisions:

"No person held to service or labor in one state, under the law thereof, escaping into another, shall, in consequence of any law or regulation therein, be discharged from such service or labor, but shall be delivered up on claim of the party to whom such service or labor may be due."

It is scarcely questioned that this provision was intended by those who made it for the reclaiming of what we call fugitive slaves; and the intention of the lawgiver is the law. All members of Congress swear their support to the whole Constitution—to this provision as much as to any other. To the proposition, then, that slaves whose cases come within the terms of this clause "shall be delivered up," their oaths are unanimous. Now, if they would make the effort in good temper, could they not, with nearly equal unanimity, frame and pass a law by means of which to keep good that unanimous oath?

There is some difference of opinion whether this clause should be enforced by national or by state authority; but surely that difference is not a very material one. If the slave is to be surrendered, it can be of but little consequence to him, or to others, by which authority it is done. And should anyone, in any case, be content that his oath shall go unkept, on a merely unsubstantial controversy as to *how* it shall be kept?

Again, in any law upon this subject, ought not all the safeguards of liberty known in civilized and humane jurisprudence to be introduced, so that a free man be not, in any case, surrendered as a slave? And might it not be well, at the same time, to provide by law for the enforcement of that clause in the Constitution which guarantees that "The citizen of each state shall be entitled to all privileges and immunities of citizens in the several states?"

I take the official oath today, with no mental reservations, and with no purpose to construe the Constitution or laws by any hypercritical rules. And while I do not choose now to specify particular acts of Congress as proper to be enforced, I do suggest that it will be much safer for all, both in official and private stations, to conform to, and abide by, all those acts which stand unrepealed, than to violate any of them, trusting to find impunity in having them held to be unconstitutional.

It is seventy-two years since the first inauguration of a President under our national Constitution. During that period fifteen different and greatly distinguished citizens have, in succession, administered the executive branch of the government. They have conducted it through many perils; and, generally, with great success. Yet, with all this scope for precedent, I now enter upon the same task for the brief constitutional term of four years, under great and peculiar difficulty. A disruption of the federal Union heretofore only menaced is now formidably attempted.

I hold, that in contemplation of universal law, and of the Constitution, the Union of these states is perpetual. Perpetuity is implied, if not expressed, in the fundamental law of all national governments. It is safe to assert that no government proper ever had a provision in its organic law for its own termination. Continue to execute all the express provisions of our national Constitution, and the Union will endure forever—it being impossible to destroy it, except by some action not provided for in the instrument itself.

Again, if the United States be not a government proper, but an association of states in the nature of contract merely, can it, as a contract, be peaceably unmade by less than all the parties who made it? One party to a contract may violate it—break it so to speak; but does it not require all to lawfully rescind it?

Descending from these general principles, we find the proposition that, in legal contemplation, the Union is perpetual, confirmed by the history of the Union itself. The Union is much older than the Constitution. It was formed in fact by the Articles of Association in 1774. It was matured and continued by the Declaration of Independence in 1776. It was further matured and the faith of all the then thirteen states expressedly plighted and engaged that it should be perpetual, by the Articles of Confederation in 1778. And finally, in 1787, one of the declared objects for ordaining and establishing the Constitution was *"to form a more perfect union."*

But if destruction of the Union, by one, or by a part only, of the states, be lawfully possible, the Union is *less* perfect than before the Constitution, having lost the vital element of perpetuity.

It follows from these views that no state, upon its own mere motion, can lawfully get out of the Union—that *resolves* and *ordinances* to that effect are legally void; and that acts of violence, within any state or states, against the authority of the United States are insurrectionary or revolutionary, according to circumstances.

I therefore consider that, in view of the Constitution and the laws, the Union is unbroken; and, to the extent of my ability, I shall take care, as the Constitution itself expressly enjoins upon me, that the laws of the Union be faithfully executed in all the states. Doing this I deem to be only a simple duty on my part; and I shall perform it, so far as practicable, unless my rightful masters, the American people, shall withhold the requisite means, or, in some authoritative manner, direct the contrary. I trust this will not be regarded as a menace, but only as the declared purpose of the Union that it *will* constitutionally defend, and maintain, itself.

In doing this there needs to be no bloodshed or violence; and there shall be none, unless it be forced upon the national authority. The power confided to me will be used to hold, occupy, and possess the property and places belonging to the government, and to collect the duties and imposts; but beyond what may be necessary for these objects, there will be no invasion—no using of force against or among the people anywhere. Where hostility to the United States, in any interior locality, shall be so great and so universal as to prevent competent resident citizens from holding the federal offices, there will be no attempt to force obnoxious strangers among the people for that object. While the strict legal right may exist in the government to enforce the exercise of these offices, the attempt to do so would be so irritating, and so nearly impracticable with all, that I deem it better to forego, for the time, the uses of such offices.

The mails, unless repelled, will continue to be furnished in all parts of the Union. So far as possible, the people everywhere shall have that sense of perfect security which is most favorable to calm thought and reflection. The course here indicated will be followed, unless current events, and experience, shall show a modification, or change, to be proper; and in every case and exigency, my best discretion will be exercised, according to circumstances actually existing, and with a view and a hope of a peaceful solution of the national troubles, and the restoration of fraternal sympathies and affections.

That there are persons in one section or another who seek to destroy the Union at all events, and are glad of any pretext to do it, I will neither affirm or deny; but if there be such, I need address no word to them. To those, however, who really love the Union, may I not speak?

Before entering upon so grave a matter as the destruction of our national fabric, with all its benefits, its memories, and its hopes, would it not be wise to ascertain precisely why we do it? Will you hazard so desperate a step, while there is any possibility that any portion of the ills you fly from have no real existence? Will you, while the certain ills you fly to are greater than all the real ones you fly from? Will you risk the commission of so fearful a mistake?

All profess to be content in the Union, if all constitutional rights can be maintained. Is it true, then, that any right, plainly written in the Constitution, has been denied? I think not. Happily the human mind is so constituted that no party can reach to the audacity of doing this. Think, if you can, of a single instance in which a plainly written provision of the Constitution has ever been denied. If, by the mere force of numbers, a majority should deprive a minority of any clearly written constitutional right, it might, in a moral point of view, justify revolution —certainly would if such right were a vital one. But such is not our case. All the vital rights of minorities, and of individuals, are so plainly assured to them, by affirmations and negations, guarantees and prohibitions, in the Constitution that controversies never arise concerning them. But no organic law can ever be framed with a provision specifically applicable to every question which may occur in practical administration. No foresight can anticipate, nor any document of reasonable length contain express provisions for, all possible questions. Shall fugitives from labor be surrendered by national or by state authority? The Constitution does not expressly say. *May* Congress prohibit slavery in the territories? The Constitution does not expressly say. *Must* Congress protect slavery in the territories? The Constitution does not expressly say.

From questions of this class spring all our constitutional controversies, and we divide upon them into majorities and minorities. If the minority will not acquiesce, the majority must, or the government must cease. There is no other alternative; for continuing the government is acquiescence on one side or the other. If a minority, in such case, will secede rather than acquiesce, they make a precedent which, in turn, will divide and ruin them; for a minority of their own will secede from them whenever a majority refuses to be controlled by such minority. For instance, why may not any portion of a new confederacy, a year or two hence, arbitrarily secede again, precisely as portions of the present Union now claim to secede from it. All who cherish disunion sentiments are now being educated to the exact temper of doing this. Is there such perfect identity of interests among the states to compose a new Union as to produce harmony only, and prevent renewed secession?

Plainly, the central idea of secession is the essence of anarchy. A majority, held in restraint by constitutional checks, and limitations, and always changing easily with deliberate changes of popular opinions and sentiments, is the only true sovereign of a free people. Whoever rejects it does, of necessity, fly to anarchy or to despotism. Unanimity is impossible; the rule of a minority, as a permanent arrangement, is wholly inadmissible; so that, rejecting the majority principle, anarchy, or despotism in some form, is all that is left.

I do not forget the position assumed by some, that constitutional questions are to be decided by the Supreme Court; nor do I deny that such decisions must be binding in any case upon the parties to a suit, as to the object of that suit, while they are also entitled to very high respect and consideration, in all parallel cases, by all other departments of the government. And while it is obviously possible that such decision may be erroneous in any given case, still the evil effect following it, being limited to that particular case, with the chance that it may be overruled and never become a precedent for other cases, can better be borne than could the evils of a different practice. At the same time the candid citizen must confess that if the policy of the government, upon vital questions affecting the whole people, is to be irrevocably fixed by decisions of the Supreme Court, the instant they are made, in ordinary litigation between parties, in personal actions, the people will have ceased to be their own rulers, having, to that extent, practically resigned their government into the hands of that eminent tribunal. Nor is there, in this view, any assault upon the court, or the judges. It is a duty, from which they may not shrink, to decide cases properly brought before them; and it is no fault of theirs, if others seek to turn their decisions to political purposes.

One section of our country believes slavery is *right,* and ought to be extended, while the other believes it is *wrong,* and ought not to be extended. This is the only substantial dispute. The fugitive slave clause of the Constitution, and the law for the suppression of the foreign slave trade, are each as well enforced, perhaps, as any law can ever be in a community where the moral sense of the people imperfectly supports the law itself. The great body of the people abide by the dry legal obligation in both cases, and a few break over in each. This, I think, cannot be perfectly cured; and it would be worse in both cases *after* the separation of the sections than before. The foreign slave trade, now imperfectly suppressed, would be ultimately revived without restriction in one section; while fugitive slaves, now only partially surrendered, would not be surrendered at all by the other.

Physically speaking, we cannot separate. We cannot remove our respective sections from each other, nor build an impassable wall between them. A husband and wife may be divorced, and go out of the presence, and beyond the reach, of each other; but the different parts of our country cannot do this. They cannot but remain face to face; and intercourse, either amicable or hostile, must continue between them. Is it possible then to make that intercourse more advantageous, or more satisfactory, *after* separation than *before?* Can aliens make treaties easier than friends can make laws? Can treaties be more faithfully enforced between aliens than laws can among friends? Suppose you go to war, you cannot fight always; and when, after much loss on both sides, and no gain on either, you cease fighting, the identical old questions, as to terms of intercourse, are again upon you.

This country, with its institutions, belongs to the people who inhabit it. Whenever they shall grow weary of the existing government, they can exercise their *constitutional* right of amending it, or their *revolutionary* right to dismember or overthrow it. I cannot be ignorant of the fact that many worthy and patriotic citizens are desirous of having the national Constitution amended. While I make no recommendation of amendments, I fully recognize the rightful authority of the people over the whole subject, to be exercised in either of the modes prescribed in the instrument itself; and I should, under existing circumstances, favor, rather than oppose, a fair opportunity being afforded the people to act upon it.

I will venture to add that, to me, the convention mode seems preferable, in that it allows amendments to originate with the people themselves, instead of only permitting them to take or reject propositions originated by others, not especially chosen for the purpose, and which might not be precisely such as they would wish to either accept or refuse. I understand a proposed amendment to the Constitution—which amendment, however, I have not seen—has passed Congress, to the effect that the federal government shall never interfere with the domestic institutions of the states, including that of persons held to service. To avoid misconstruction of what I have said, I depart from my purpose not to

speak of particular amendments, so far as to say that, holding such a provision to now be implied constitutional law, I have no objection to its
being made express, and irrevocable.

The chief magistrate derives all his authority from the people, and
they have conferred none upon him to fix terms for the separation of the
states. The people themselves can do this also if they choose; but the
executive, as such, has nothing to do with it. His duty is to administer
the present government, as it came to his hands, and to transmit it, unimpaired by him, to his successor.

Why should there not be a patient confidence in the ultimate justice
of the people? Is there any better, or equal, hope in the world? In our
present differences, is either party without faith of being in the right? If
the Almighty Ruler of nations, with his eternal truth and justice, be on
your side of the North, or on yours of the South, that truth, and that
justice, will surely prevail, by the judgment of this great tribunal, the
American people.

By the frame of the government under which we live, this same people
have wisely given their public servants but little power for mischief; and
have, with equal wisdom, provided for the return of that little to their
own hands at very short intervals.

While the people retain their virtue, and vigilance, no administration,
by any extreme of wickedness or folly, can very seriously injure the
government, in the short space of four years.

My countrymen, one and all, think calmly and well upon this whole
subject. Nothing valuable can be lost by taking time. If there be an object to *hurry* any of you, in hot haste, to a step which you would never
take deliberately, that object will be frustrated by taking time; but no
good object can be frustrated by it. Such of you as are now dissatisfied
still have the old Constitution unimpaired, and, on the sensitive point,
the laws of your own framing under it; while the new administration will
have no immediate power, if it would, to change either. If it were admitted that you who are dissatisfied hold the right side in the dispute,
there still is no single good reason for precipitate action. Intelligence,
patriotism, Christianity, and a firm reliance on Him, who has never yet
forsaken this favored land, are still competent to adjust, in the best way,
all our present difficulty.

In *your* hands, my dissatisfied fellow countrymen, and not in *mine,* is
the momentous issue of civil war. The government will not assail *you.*
You can have no conflict, without being yourselves the aggressors. *You*
have no oath registered in Heaven to destroy the government, while *I*

shall have the most solemn one to "preserve, protect and defend" it.

I am loath to close. We are not enemies, but friends. We must not be enemies. Though passion may have strained, it must not break our bonds of affection. The mystic chords of memory, stretching from every battle-field and patriot grave to every living heart and hearthstone all over this broad land, will yet swell the chorus of the Union, when again touched, as surely they will be, by the better angels of our nature.

Letter to Horace Greeley

EXECUTIVE MANSION,
Washington, August 22, 1862

Hon. Horace Greeley:
Dear Sir:

I have just read yours of the 19th addressed to myself through the New York *Tribune*. If there be in it any statements, or assumptions of fact, which I may know to be erroneous, I do not now and here controvert them. If there be in it any inferences which I may believe to be falsely drawn, I do not now and here, argue against them. If there be perceptible in it an impatient and dictatorial tone, I waive it in deference to an old friend, whose heart I have always supposed to be right.

As to the policy I "seem to be pursuing," as you say, I have not meant to leave anyone in doubt.

I would save the Union. I would save it the shortest way under the Constitution. The sooner the national authority can be restored, the nearer the Union will be "the Union as it was." If there be those who would not save the Union unless they could at the same time *save* slavery, I do not agree with them. If there be those who would not save the Union unless they could at the same time *destroy* slavery, I do not agree with them. My paramount object in this struggle *is* to save the Union, and is *not* either to save or to destroy slavery. If I could save the Union without freeing *any* slave, I would do it; and if I could save it by freeing *all* the slaves, I would do it; and if I could save it by freeing some and leaving others alone, I would also do that. What I do about slavery, and the colored race, I do because I believe it helps to save the Union; and what I forbear, I forbear because I do *not* believe it would help to save the Union. I shall do *less* whenever I shall believe what I am doing hurts the cause, and I shall do *more* whenever I shall believe doing more will help the cause. I shall try to correct errors when shown to be errors; and I shall adopt new views so fast as they shall appear to be true views.

I have here stated my purpose according to my view of *official* duty; and I intend no modification of my oft-expressed *personal* wish that all men everywhere could be free.   Yours,

A. Lincoln

Meditation
on the Divine Will

[September 2, 1862?]

The will of God prevails. In great contests each party claims to act in accordance with the will of God. Both *may* be, and one *must* be, wrong. God can not be *for* and *against* the same thing at the same time. In the present civil war it is quite possible that God's purpose is something different from the purpose of either party—and yet the human instrumentalities, working just as they do, are of the best adaptation to effect His purpose. I am almost ready to say this is probably true—that God wills this contest, and wills that it shall not end yet. By His mere quiet power, on the minds of the now contestants, He could have either *saved* or *destroyed* the Union without a human contest. Yet the contest began. And having begun He could give the final victory to either side any day. Yet the contest proceeds.

The Gettysburg Address

November 19, 1863

Fourscore and seven years ago our fathers brought forth on this continent a new nation conceived in liberty and dedicated to the proposition that all men are created equal. Now we are engaged in a great civil war testing whether that nation, or any nation so conceived and so dedicated, can long endure. We are met on a great battlefield of that war. We have come to dedicate a portion of that field as a final resting place for those who here gave their lives that that nation might live. It is altogether fitting and proper that we should do this. But, in a larger sense, we cannot dedicate, we cannot consecrate, we cannot hallow this ground. The brave men, living and dead, who struggled here have consecrated it far above our poor power to add or detract. The world will little note nor long remember what we say here, but it can never forget what they did here. It is for us the living rather to be dedicated here to the unfinished work which they who fought here have thus far so nobly advanced. It is rather for us to be here dedicated to the great task remaining before us—that from these honored dead we take increased devotion to that cause for which they gave the last full measure of devotion—that we here highly resolve that these dead shall not have died in vain, that this nation under God shall have a new birth of freedom, and that government of the people, by the people, for the people, shall not perish from the earth.

Second Inaugural Address

March 4, 1865

At this second appearing to take the oath of the presidential office, there is less occasion for an extended address than there was at the first. Then a statement, somewhat in detail, of a course to be pursued seemed fitting and proper. Now, at the expiration of four years, during which public declarations have been constantly called forth on every point and phase of the great contest which still absorbs the attention and engrosses the energies of the nation, little that is new could be presented. The progress of our arms, upon which all else chiefly depends, is as well known to the public as to myself; and it is, I trust, reasonably satisfactory and encouraging to all. With high hope for the future, no prediction in regard to it is ventured.

On the occasion corresponding to this four years ago, all thoughts were anxiously directed to an impending civil war. All dreaded it—all sought to avert it. While the inaugural address was being delivered from this place, devoted altogether to *saving* the Union without war, insurgent agents were in the city seeking to *destroy* it without war—seeking to dissolve the Union, and divide effects, by negotiation. Both parties deprecated war; but one of them would *make* war rather than let the nation survive; and the other would *accept* war rather than let it perish. And the war came.

One-eighth of the whole population were colored slaves, not distributed generally over the Union, but localized in the Southern part of it. These slaves constituted a peculiar and powerful interest. All knew that this interest was, somehow, the cause of the war. To strengthen, perpetuate, and extend this interest was the object for which the insurgents would rend the Union, even by war; while the government claimed no right to do more than to restrict the territorial enlargement of it. Neither party expected for the war the magnitude, or the duration, which it has already attained. Neither anticipated that the *cause* of the conflict might cease with, or even before, the conflict itself should cease. Each looked for an easier triumph, and a result less fundamental and astounding. Both read the same Bible, and pray to the same God; and each invokes His aid against the other. It may seem strange that any men should dare to ask a just God's assistance in wringing their bread from the sweat of other men's faces; but let us judge not that we be not judged. The prayers of both could not be answered; that of neither has been answered fully. The Almighty has His own purposes. "Woe unto the world because of offenses! for it must needs be that offenses come; but woe to that man by whom the offense cometh!" If we shall suppose that American slavery is one of those offenses which, in the providence of God, must needs come, but which, having continued through His appointed time, He now wills to remove, and that He gives to both North and South this terrible war as the woe due to those by whom the offense came, shall we discern therein any departure from those divine attributes which the believers in a living God always ascribe to Him? Fondly do we hope—fervently do we pray—that this mighty scourge of war may speedily pass away. Yet, if God wills that it continue, until all the wealth piled by the bondman's two hundred and fifty years of unrequited toil shall be sunk, and until every drop of blood drawn with the lash shall be paid by another drawn with the sword, as was said three thousand years ago, so still it must be said "the judgments of the Lord are true and righteous altogether."

With malice toward none; with charity for all; with firmness in the right as God gives us to see the right, let us strive on to finish the work we are in; to bind up the nation's wounds; to care for him who shall have borne the battle, and for his widow, and his orphan—to do all which may achieve and cherish a just and a lasting peace, among ourselves and with all nations.

Last Public Address

W

 April 11, 1865

e meet this evening, not in sorrow, but in gladness of heart. The evacuation of Petersburg and Richmond and the surrender of the principal insurgent army give hope of a righteous and speedy peace whose joyous expression cannot be restrained. In the midst of this, however, He from Whom all blessings flow must not be forgotten. A call for a national thanksgiving is being prepared, and will be duly promulgated. Nor must those whose harder part gives us the cause of rejoicing be overlooked. Their honors must not be parceled out with others. I myself was near the front, and had the high pleasure of transmitting much of the good news to you; but no part of the honor, for plan or execution, is mine. To General Grant, his skillful officers, and brave men, all belongs. The gallant navy stood ready, but was not in reach to take active part.

By these recent successes the reinauguration of the national authority —reconstruction—which has had a large share of thought from the first, is pressed much more closely upon our attention. It is fraught with great difficulty. Unlike the case of a war between independent nations, there is no authorized organ for us to treat with. No one man has authority to give up the rebellion for any other man. We simply must begin with, and mould from, disorganized and discordant elements. Nor is it a small additional embarrassment that we, the loyal people, differ among ourselves as to the mode, manner, and means of reconstruction.

As a general rule, I abstain from reading the reports of attacks upon myself, wishing not to be provoked by that to which I cannot properly offer an answer. In spite of this precaution, however, it comes to my knowledge that I am much censured for some supposed agency in setting up, and seeking to sustain, the new state government of Louisiana. In this I have done just so much as, and no more than, the public knows. In the annual message of December, 1863, and the accompanying proclamation, I presented *a* plan of reconstruction (as the phrase goes)

762

which, I promised, if adopted by any state, would be acceptable to, and sustained by, the executive government of the nation. I distinctly stated that this was not the only plan which might possibly be acceptable; and I also distinctly protested that the executive claimed no right to say when or whether members should be admitted to seats in Congress from such states. This plan was, in advance, submitted to the then Cabinet, and distinctly approved by every member of it. One of them suggested that I should then, and in that connection, apply the Emancipation Proclamation to the theretofore excepted parts of Virginia and Louisiana; that I should drop the suggestion about apprenticeship for freed people, and that I should omit the protest against my own power in regard to the admission of members to Congress; but even he approved every part and parcel of the plan which has since been employed or touched by the action of Louisiana.

The new constitution of Louisiana, declaring emancipation for the whole state, practically applies the proclamation to the part previously excepted. It does not adopt apprenticeship for freed people; and it is silent, as it could not well be otherwise, about the admission of members to Congress. So that, as it applies to Louisiana, every member of the Cabinet fully approved the plan. The message went to Congress, and I received many commendations of the plan, written and verbal; and not a single objection to it, from any professed emancipationist, came to my knowledge until after the news reached Washington that the people of Louisiana had begun to move in accordance with it. From about July, 1862, I had corresponded with different persons supposed to be interested in seeking a reconstruction of a state government for Louisiana. When the message of 1863, with the plan before mentioned, reached New Orleans, General Banks wrote me that he was confident the people, with his military co-operation, would reconstruct substantially on that plan. I wrote to him and some of them to try it; they tried it, and the result is known. Such has been my only agency in getting up the Louisiana government. As to sustaining it, my promise is out, as before stated. But, as bad promises are better broken than kept, I shall treat this as a bad promise and break it, whenever I shall be convinced that keeping it is adverse to the public interest. But I have not yet been so convinced.

I have been shown a letter on this subject, supposed to be an able one, in which the writer expresses regret that my mind has not seemed to be definitely fixed on the question whether the seceded states, so called, are in the Union or out of it. It would perhaps add astonishment to his regret were he to learn that since I have found professed Union men endeavoring to make that question, I have purposely forborne any public expression upon it. As appears to me that question has not been, nor yet is, a practically material one, and that any discussion of it, while it thus remains practically immaterial, could have no effect other than the mischievous one of dividing our friends. As yet, whatever it may become, that question is bad as the basis of a controversy, and good for nothing at all—a merely pernicious abstraction.

We all agree that the seceded states, so called, are out of their proper practical relation with the Union; and that the sole object of the government, civil and military, in regard to those states is to again get them into their proper practical relation. I believe that it is not only possible, but in fact easier, to do this without deciding, or even considering, whether these states have ever been out of the Union, than with it. Finding themselves safely at home, it would be utterly immaterial whether they had ever been abroad. Let us all join in doing the acts necessary to restoring the proper practical relations between these states and the Union; and each forever after innocently indulge his own opinion whether, in doing the act, he brought the states from without into the Union, or only gave them proper assistance, they never having been out of it.

The amount of constituency, so to speak, on which the new Louisiana government rests would be more satisfactory to all if it contained fifty, thirty, or even twenty thousand, instead of only about twelve thousand, as it does. It is also unsatisfactory to some that the elective franchise is not given to the colored man. I would myself prefer that it were now conferred on the very intelligent, and on those who serve our cause as soldiers. Still the question is not whether the Louisiana government, as it stands, is quite all that is desirable. The question is "Will it be wiser to take it as it is, and help to improve it; or to reject and disperse it?" "Can Louisiana be brought into proper practical relation with the Union sooner by sustaining or by discarding her new state government?"

Some twelve thousand voters in the heretofore slave state of Louisiana have sworn allegiance to the Union, assumed to be the rightful political power of the state, held elections, organized a state government, adopted a free-state constitution, giving the benefit of public schools equally to black and white, and empowering the legislature to confer the elective franchise upon the colored man. Their legislature has already voted to ratify the constitutional amendment recently passed by Congress, abolishing slavery throughout the nation. These twelve thousand persons are thus fully committed to the Union, and to perpetual freedom in the state —committed to the very things, and nearly all things, the nation wants— and they ask the nation's recognition, and its assistance to make good their committal. Now, if we reject and spurn them, we do our utmost to disorganize and disperse them. We in effect say to the white men, "You are worthless or worse; we will neither help you nor be helped by you." To the blacks we say, "This cup of liberty which these, your old masters, hold to your lips we will dash from you, and leave you to the chances of gathering the spilled and scattered contents in some vague and undefined when, where, and how." If this course, discouraging and paralyzing both white and black, has any tendency to bring Louisiana into proper practical relations with the Union, I have so far been unable to perceive it. If, on the contrary, we recognize and sustain the new government of Louisiana, the converse of all this is made true. We encourage the hearts and nerve the arms of the twelve thousand to adhere to their work, and argue for it, and proselyte for it, and fight for it, and feed it, and grow it, and ripen it to a complete success. The colored man, too, in seeing all united for him, is inspired with vigilance, and energy, and daring, to the same end. Grant that he desires the elective franchise, will he not attain it sooner by saving the already advanced steps toward it, than by running backward over them? Concede that the new government of Louisiana is only to what it should be as the egg is to the fowl, we shall sooner have the fowl by hatching the egg than by smashing it. Again, if we reject Louisiana, we also reject one vote in favor of the proposed amendment to the national constitution. To meet this proposition, it has been argued that no more than three-fourths of those states which have not attempted secession are necessary to validly ratify the amendment. I do not commit myself against this, further than to say that such a ratification would be questionable, and sure to be persistently questioned; while a ratification by three-fourths of all the states would be unquestioned and unquestionable.

I repeat the question. Can Louisiana be brought into proper practical relation with the Union sooner by sustaining or by discarding her new state government?

What has been said of Louisiana will apply generally to other states. And yet so great peculiarities pertain to each state; and such important and sudden changes occur in the same state; and, withal, so new and unprecedented is the whole case that no exclusive and inflexible plan can safely be prescribed as to details and collaterals. Such exclusive and inflexible plan would surely become a new entanglement. Important principles may, and must, be inflexible.

In the present "situation," as the phrase goes, it may be my duty to make some new announcement to the people of the South. I am considering, and shall not fail to act, when satisfied that action will be proper.

GATEWAY TO THE GREAT BOOKS

VOLUME 7	VOLUME 8
BACON	BACON
SWIFT	TYNDALL
HUME	EVE CURIE
PLUTARCH	DARWIN
STEVENSON	FABRE
RUSKIN	EISELEY
WILLIAM JAMES	RACHEL CARSON
SCHOPENHAUER	HALDANE
FARADAY	HUXLEY
BURKE	GALTON
CALHOUN	BERNARD
MACAULAY	PAVLOV
VOLTAIRE	WÖHLER
DANTE	LYELL
ROUSSEAU	GALILEO
KANT	CAMPANELLA
CLAUSEWITZ	FARADAY
MALTHUS	MENDELEEV
	HELMHOLTZ